Kawasaki ZR550 & 750 Zephyr Fours

Service and Repair Manual

Matthew Coombs

(3382-264-2Z1)

Models covered

ZR550 B Zephyr. 553cc. UK 1991 to 1997
ZR550 B Zephyr. 553cc. US 1990 to 1993
ZR750 C Zephyr. 738cc. UK 1991 to 1996
ZR750 C Zephyr. 738cc. US 1991 to 1993
ZR750 D Zephyr. 738cc. UK 1996 to 1997

© Haynes Publishing 2000

ABCDE
FGHIJ
KLMNO
PQRS

A book in the **Haynes Service and Repair Manual Series**

ISBN **1 85960 382 3**

Library of Congress Catalog Card Number 97-61067

British Library Cataloguing in Publication Data
A catalogue record for this book is available from the British Library.

Printed by **J H Haynes & Co Ltd, Sparkford, Nr Yeovil,
Somerset BA22 7JJ, England**

Haynes Publishing
Sparkford, Nr Yeovil, Somerset BA22 7JJ, England

Haynes North America, Inc
861 Lawrence Drive, Newbury Park, California 91320, USA

Editions Haynes
Tour Aurore – IBC, 18 Place des Reflets
92975 Paris La Defense 2 Cedex, France

Haynes Publishing Nordiska AB
Box 1504, 751 45 UPPSALA, Sweden

Contents

LIVING WITH YOUR KAWASAKI ZEPHYR

Introduction

Daily (pre-ride) checks

MAINTENANCE

Routine maintenance and servicing

Contents

REPAIRS AND OVERHAUL

Engine, transmission and associated systems

Chassis components

Electrical system

Wiring diagrams

REFERENCE

Index

Kawasaki The Green Meanies

by Julian Ryder

Kawasaki Heavy Industries

Kawasaki is a company of contradictions. It is the smallest of the big four Japanese manufacturers but the biggest company, it was the last of the four to make and market motorcycles yet it owns the oldest name in the Japanese industry, and it was the first to set up a factory in the USA. Kawasaki Heavy Industries, of which the motorcycle operation is but a small component, is a massive company with its heritage firmly in the old heavy industries like shipbuilding and railways; nowadays it is as much involved in aerospace as in motorcycles.

In fact it may be because of this that Kawasaki's motorcycles have always been quirky, you get the impression that they are designed by a small group of enthusiasts who are given an admirably free hand. More realistically, it may be that Kawasaki's designers have experience with techniques and materials from other engineering disciplines. Either way, Kawasaki have managed to be the factory who surprise us more than the rest. Quite often, they do this by totally ignoring a market segment the others are scrabbling over, but more often they hit us with pure, undiluted performance.

The origins of the company, and its name, go back to 1878 when Shozo Kawasaki set up a dockyard in Tokyo. By the late 1930s, the company was making its own steel in massive steelworks and manufacturing railway locos and rolling stock. In the run up to war, the Kawasaki Aircraft Company was set up in 1937 and it was this arm of the now giant operation that would look to motorcycle engine manufacture in post-war Japan.

They bought their high-technology experience to bear first on engines which were sold on to a number of manufacturers as original equipment. Both two- and four-stroke units were made, a 58 cc and 148 cc OHC unit. One of the customer companies was Meihatsu Heavy Industries, another company within the Kawasaki group, which in 1961 was shaken up and renamed Kawasaki Auto Sales. At the same time, the Akashi factory which was to be Kawasaki's main production facility until the Kobe earthquake of 1995, was opened. Shortly afterwards, Kawasaki took over the ailing Meguro company, Japan's oldest motorcycle maker, thus instantly obtaining a range of bigger bikes which were marketed as Kawasaki-Meguros. The following year, the first bike to be made and sold as a Kawasaki was produced, a 125 cc single called the B8 and in 1963 a motocross version, the B8M appeared.

The three cylinder two-stroke 750

Model development

Kawasaki's first appearance on a road-race circuit came in 1965 with a batch of disc-valve 125 twins. They were no match for the opposition from Japan in the shape of Suzuki and Yamaha or for the fading force of the factory MZs from East Germany. Only after the other Japanese factories had pulled out of the class did Kawasaki win, with British rider Dave Simmonds becoming World 125 GP Champion in 1969 on a bike that looked astonishingly similar to the original racer. That same year Kawasaki reorganised once again, this time merging three companies to form Kawasaki Heavy Industries. One of the new organisation's objectives was to take motorcycle production forward and exploit markets outside Japan.

KHI achieved that target immediately and set out their stall for the future with the astonishing and frightening H1. This three-cylinder air-cooled 500 cc two-stroke was arguably the first modern pure performance bike to hit the market. It hypnotised a whole generation of motorcyclists who'd never before encountered such a ferocious, wheelie inducing power band or such shattering straight-line speed allied to questionable handling. And as for the 750 cc version ...

The triples perfectly suited the late '60s, fitting in well with the student demonstrations of 1968 and the anti-establishment ethos of the Summer of Love. Unfortunately, the oil crisis would put an end to the thirsty strokers but Kawasaki had another high-performance ace up their corporate sleeve. Or rather they thought they did.

The 1968 Tokyo Show saw probably the single most significant new motorcycle ever made unveiled: the Honda CB750. At Kawasaki it caused a major shock, for they also had a 750 cc four, code-named New York Steak, almost ready to roll and it was a double, rather than single, overhead cam motor. Bravely, they took the decision to go ahead - but with the motor taken out to 900 cc. The result was the Z1, unveiled at the 1972 Cologne Show. It was a bike straight out of the same mould as the H1, scare stories spread about unmanageable power, dubious straight-line stability and frightening handling, none of which stopped the sales graph rocketing upwards and led to the coining of the term 'superbike'. While rising fuel prices cut short development of the big two-strokes, the Z1 went on to found a dynasty, indeed its genes can still be detected in Kawasaki's latest products like the ZZ-R1100 (Ninja ZX-11).

This is another characteristic of the way Kawasaki operates. Models quite often have very long lives, or gradually evolve. There is no major difference between that first Z1 and the air-cooled GPz range. Add water-cooling and you have the GPZ900, which in turn metamorphosed into the GPZ1000RX and then the ZX-10 and the ZZ-R1100. Indeed, the

The first Superbike, Kawasaki's 900 cc Z1

One of the two-stroke engined KH and KE range - the KE100B

The GT750 - a favourite hack for despatch riders

last three models share the same 58 mm stroke. The bikes are obviously very different but it's difficult to put your finger on exactly why.

Other models have remained effectively untouched for over a decade: the KH and KE single-cylinder air-cooled two-stroke learner bikes, the GT550 and 750 shaft-drive hacks favoured by big city despatch riders and the GPz305 being prime examples. It's only when they step outside the performance field that Kawasakis seems less sure. Their first factory

The high-performance ZXR750

customs were dire, you simply got the impression that the team that designed them didn't have their heart in the job. Only when the Classic range appeared in 1995 did they get it right.

Racing success

Kawasaki also have a more focused approach to racing than the other factories. The policy has always been to race the road bikes and with just a couple of exceptions that's what they've done. Even Simmonds' championship winner bore a strong resemblance to the twins they were selling in the late '60s and racing versions of the 500 and 750 cc triples were also sold as over-the-counter racers, the H1R and H2R. The 500 was in the forefront of the two-stroke assault on MV Agusta but wasn't a Grand Prix winner. It was the 750 that made the impact and carried the factory's image in F750 racing against the Suzuki triples and Yamaha fours.

The factory's decision to use green, usually regarded as an unlucky colour in sport, meant its bikes and personnel stood out and the phrase 'Green Meanies' fitted them perfectly. The Z1 motor soon became a full 1000 cc and powered Kawasaki's assault in F1 racing, notably in endurance which Kawasaki saw as being most closely related to its road bikes.

That didn't stop them dominating 250 and 350 cc GPs with a tandem twin two-stroke in the late '70s and early '80s, but their path-breaking monocoque 500 while a race winner never won a world title. When Superbike arrived, Kawasaki's road 750s weren't as track-friendly as the opposition's out-and-out race replicas. This makes Scott Russell's World title on the ZXR750 in 1993 even more praiseworthy, for the homologation bike, the ZXR750RR, was much heavier and much more of a road bike than the Italian and Japanese competition.

The company's Supersport 600 contenders have similarly been more sports-tourers than race-replicas, yet they too have been competitive on the track. Indeed, the flagship bike, the ZZ-R1100, is most definitely a sports tourer capable of carrying two people and their luggage at high speed in comfort all day and then doing it again the next day. Try that on one of the race replicas and you'll be in need of a course of treatment from a chiropractor.

Through doing it their way Kawasaki developed a brand loyalty for their performance bikes that kept the Z1's derivatives in production until the mid-'80s and turned the bike into a classic in its model life. You could even argue that the Z1 lives on in the shape of the 1100 Zephyr's GPz1100-derived motor. And that's another Kawasaki invention, the retro bike. But when you look at what many commentators refer to as the retro boom, especially in Japan, you find that it is no such thing. It is the Zephyr boom. Just another example of Japan's most surprising motorcycle manufacturer getting it right again.

The 550 and 750 Zephyrs

The alleged retro boom that swept all before it on the motorcycling scene of the early 1990s didn't really happen. What boom there was in back-to-basics bikes was limited to one family of bikes from one maker: Kawasaki's Zephyrs. In fact the boom really only happened in Japan where the first Zephyr, the 400 cc version, was a major sales success in that very fashion conscious market where a major attraction was the catalogue of after-market parts that could be used personalise a bike.

Kawasaki took the risk of exporting the retro concept for the 1991 model year with a family of three Zephyrs, the closely related ZR550 and 750 and the ZR1100. The idea was to hark back to the glory days of Kawasaki's double-overhead-cam air-cooled fours, the Z650, the GPz750 and of course the mighty Z1000.

The 550 was in fact an overbored version of the Japan-only 400 while the 750 shared the 66 x 54 mm bore and stroke of the old GPz750 and the other three-quarter litre air-cooled Kawasakis. Both were delivered in a cleverly designed package that looked very reminiscent of the old bikes but incorporated the benefits of progress in bike design in the intervening ten years.

The first 550, the B1, got that favourite '80s accessory the four-into-one exhaust as standard along with digital ignition, oil cooler, alloy swinging-arm, piggyback shocks, five-spoke alloy wheels and three disc brakes. Bolting that lot onto a standard Z1 would have cost you a lot of money back in 1980. The 750 got the same goodies but was recognisable by its three-spoke wheels.

The arrival of the Zephyrs coincided with a new type of motorcycle buyer in many countries, the rider returning to bikes after a long absence. These so-called 'born-again bikers' could relate immediately to the Zephyrs and, crucially, found them unthreatening in the way full-on sportsters were not. Other manufacturers scrabbled to

Kawasaki ZR750 D Zephyr

bring out their own retro bikes but Kawasaki had the crucial advantage of being there first and reaped the rewards. No other retro came anywhere near either the 550 or 750 in the sales charts.

The 550 felt comparatively small and was popular with newly qualified riders whereas the 750 came to transcend its image and be regarded as a good basic bike, not just a cute retro. Meanwhile, back in Japan, they'd started racing them in a new class known as Naked Bike.

The formula was basically right first time and the two smaller Zephyrs have remained almost totally unchanged from their launch in 1991 with the 550B1 and 750C1 until the 1996 model year. Even then the 550 escaped and went on to the become the B6 while the 750 got its first important modifications and became the 750D1. Even then the changes were mainly cosmetic. The modern, racy

three-spoked alloy wheels were swapped for a totally retro set of spoked wheels and to emphasise the Z1 heritage there was a paint option of the very same brown and orange two-tone scheme that graced Kawasaki's very first DOHC four, although they called it 'luminous chestnut brown and luminous tangerine orange'. Quite.

No other bike took part in the early '90s retro boom although later models like the Suzuki Bandits and Triumph Speed Triples did re-popularise the idea of an unfaired bike. They are not the same thing. The Zephyr can trace its ancestry directly back to the machines it takes its styling cues and its riding position from, it runs twin shocks, a tubular steel frame and an air-cooled motor. There are one or two other bikes that could truthfully be labelled as retros but the Zephyrs aren't just the only successful retros, they're the most honest retros.

Acknowledgements

Our thanks are due to Paul Branson Motorcycles of Yeovil who supplied the ZR550 and Bridge Motorcycle World of Exeter who supplied the ZR750 featured in the photographs throughout this manual. Thanks are also due to Kawasaki Motors (UK) Ltd for the supply of technical information and permission to use some of the line drawings featured. We would also like to thank the Avon Rubber Company, who kindly supplied information and technical assistance on tyre fitting, and NGK Spark plugs (UK) Ltd for information on spark plug maintenance and electrode conditions.

Thanks are also due to the Kawasaki Information Service and Kel Edge for supplying colour transparencies, and to Phil Flowers for carrying out the cover photography. The introduction, "Kawasaki - The Green Meanies" was written by Julian Ryder.

About this Manual

The aim of this manual is to help you get the best value from your motorcycle. It can do so in several ways. It can help you decide what work must be done, even if you choose to have it done by a dealer; it provides information and procedures for routine maintenance and servicing; and it offers diagnostic and repair procedures to follow when trouble occurs.

We hope you use the manual to tackle the work yourself. For many simpler jobs, doing it yourself may be quicker than arranging an appointment to get the motorcycle into a dealer and making the trips to leave it and

pick it up. More importantly, a lot of money can be saved by avoiding the expense the shop must pass on to you to cover its labour and overhead costs. An added benefit is the sense of satisfaction and accomplishment that you feel after doing the job yourself.

References to the left or right side of the motorcycle assume you are sitting on the seat, facing forward.

We take great pride in the accuracy of information given in this manual, but motorcycle manufacturers make alterations and design changes during the production run of a particular motorcycle of which they do not inform us. No liability can be accepted by the authors or publishers for loss, damage or injury caused by any errors in, or omissions from, the information given.

Professional mechanics are trained in safe working procedures. However enthusiastic you may be about getting on with the job at hand, take the time to ensure that your safety is not put at risk. A moment's lack of attention can result in an accident, as can failure to observe simple precautions.

There will always be new ways of having accidents, and the following is not a comprehensive list of all dangers; it is intended rather to make you aware of the risks and to encourage a safe approach to all work you carry out on your bike.

Asbestos

● Certain friction, insulating, sealing and other products - such as brake pads, clutch linings, gaskets, etc. - contain asbestos. Extreme care must be taken to avoid inhalation of dust from such products since it is hazardous to health. If in doubt, assume that they do contain asbestos.

Fire

● Remember at all times that petrol is highly flammable. Never smoke or have any kind of naked flame around, when working on the vehicle. But the risk does not end there - a spark caused by an electrical short-circuit, by two metal surfaces contacting each other, by careless use of tools, or even by static electricity built up in your body under certain conditions, can ignite petrol vapour, which in a confined space is highly explosive. Never use petrol as a cleaning solvent. Use an approved safety solvent.

● Always disconnect the battery earth terminal before working on any part of the fuel or electrical system, and never risk spilling fuel on to a hot engine or exhaust.

● It is recommended that a fire extinguisher of a type suitable for fuel and electrical fires is kept handy in the garage or workplace at all times. Never try to extinguish a fuel or electrical fire with water.

Fumes

● Certain fumes are highly toxic and can quickly cause unconsciousness and even death if inhaled to any extent. Petrol vapour comes into this category, as do the vapours from certain solvents such as trichloro-ethylene. Any draining or pouring of such volatile fluids should be done in a well ventilated area.

● When using cleaning fluids and solvents, read the instructions carefully. Never use materials from unmarked containers - they may give off poisonous vapours.

● Never run the engine of a motor vehicle in an enclosed space such as a garage. Exhaust fumes contain carbon monoxide which is extremely poisonous; if you need to run the engine, always do so in the open air or at least have the rear of the vehicle outside the workplace.

The battery

● Never cause a spark, or allow a naked light near the vehicle's battery. It will normally be giving off a certain amount of hydrogen gas, which is highly explosive.

● Always disconnect the battery ground (earth) terminal before working on the fuel or electrical systems (except where noted).

● If possible, loosen the filler plugs or cover when charging the battery from an external source. Do not charge at an excessive rate or the battery may burst.

● Take care when topping up, cleaning or carrying the battery. The acid electrolyte, evenwhen diluted, is very corrosive and should not be allowed to contact the eyes or skin. Always wear rubber gloves and goggles or a face shield. If you ever need to prepare electrolyte yourself, always add the acid slowly to the water; never add the water to the acid.

Electricity

● When using an electric power tool, inspection light etc., always ensure that the appliance is correctly connected to its plug and that, where necessary, it is properly grounded (earthed). Do not use such appliances in damp conditions and, again, beware of creating a spark or applying excessive heat in the vicinity of fuel or fuel vapour. Also ensure that the appliances meet national safety standards.

● A severe electric shock can result from touching certain parts of the electrical system, such as the spark plug wires (HT leads), when the engine is running or being cranked, particularly if components are damp or the insulation is defective. Where an electronic ignition system is used, the secondary (HT) voltage is much higher and could prove fatal.

Remember...

✘ **Don't** start the engine without first ascertaining that the transmission is in neutral.

✘ **Don't** suddenly remove the pressure cap from a hot cooling system - cover it with a cloth and release the pressure gradually first, or you may get scalded by escaping coolant.

✘ **Don't** attempt to drain oil until you are sure it has cooled sufficiently to avoid scalding you.

✘ **Don't** grasp any part of the engine or exhaust system without first ascertaining that it is cool enough not to burn you.

✘ **Don't** allow brake fluid or antifreeze to contact the machine's paintwork or plastic components.

✘ **Don't** siphon toxic liquids such as fuel, hydraulic fluid or antifreeze by mouth, or allow them to remain on your skin.

✘ **Don't** inhale dust - it may be injurious to health (see Asbestos heading).

✘ **Don't** allow any spilled oil or grease to remain on the floor - wipe it up right away, before someone slips on it.

✘ **Don't** use ill-fitting spanners or other tools which may slip and cause injury.

✘ **Don't** lift a heavy component which may be beyond your capability - get assistance.

✘ **Don't** rush to finish a job or take unverified short cuts.

✘ **Don't** allow children or animals in or around an unattended vehicle.

✘ **Don't** inflate a tyre above the recommended pressure. Apart from overstressing the carcass, in extreme cases the tyre may blow off forcibly.

✔ **Do** ensure that the machine is supported securely at all times. This is especially important when the machine is blocked up to aid wheel or fork removal.

✔ **Do** take care when attempting to loosen a stubborn nut or bolt. It is generally better to pull on a spanner, rather than push, so that if you slip, you fall away from the machine rather than onto it.

✔ **Do** wear eye protection when using power tools such as drill, sander, bench grinder etc.

✔ **Do** use a barrier cream on your hands prior to undertaking dirty jobs - it will protect your skin from infection as well as making the dirt easier to remove afterwards; but make sure your hands aren't left slippery. Note that long-term contact with used engine oil can be a health hazard.

✔ **Do** keep loose clothing (cuffs, ties etc. and long hair) well out of the way of moving mechanical parts.

✔ **Do** remove rings, wristwatch etc., before working on the vehicle - especially the electrical system.

✔ **Do** keep your work area tidy - it is only too easy to fall over articles left lying around.

✔ **Do** exercise caution when compressing springs for removal or installation. Ensure that the tension is applied and released in a controlled manner, using suitable tools which preclude the possibility of the spring escaping violently.

✔ **Do** ensure that any lifting tackle used has a safe working load rating adequate for the job.

✔ **Do** get someone to check periodically that all is well, when working alone on the vehicle.

✔ **Do** carry out work in a logical sequence and check that everything is correctly assembled and tightened afterwards.

✔ **Do** remember that your vehicle's safety affects that of yourself and others. If in doubt on any point, get professional advice.

● If in spite of following these precautions, you are unfortunate enough to injure yourself, seek medical attention as soon as possible.

Frame and engine numbers

The frame serial number is stamped into the right-hand side of the steering head. The engine number is stamped into the top of the right-hand side of the crankcase, behind the cylinder block. Both of these numbers should be recorded and kept in a safe place so they can be furnished to law enforcement officials in the event of a theft. There is also a carburettor identification number on the side of each carburettor body.

The frame serial number, engine serial number and carburettor identification number should also be kept in a handy place (such as with your driver's licence) so they are always available when purchasing or ordering parts for your machine.

The procedures in this manual identify the bikes by model code. To determine the model code, refer to the frame numbers given in the accompanying table. Note that the production year may not necessarily coincide with the date of registration. Engine numbers for all 550 models commence KZ550DE060001 and for all 750 models KZ750EE150001.

UK Models	Year	Frame no.
ZR550 B2	1991	ZR550B-004001 to 012000
ZR550 B3	1992	ZR550B-012001 to 022000
ZR550 B4	1993	ZR550B-022001 to 030000
ZR550 B5	1994	ZR550B-030001 to 036000
ZR550 B6	1995/6/7	ZR550B-036001 on
ZR750 C1	1991	ZR750C-000001 to 018500
ZR750 C2	1992	ZR750C-018501 to 035000
ZR750 C3	1993	ZR750C-035001 to 040000
ZR750 C4	1994/5	ZR750C-040001 on
ZR750 C5	1995/6	ZR750C-050001 on
ZR750 D1	1996/7	ZR750D-000001 on

US models	Year	Frame no.
ZR550 B1	1990	JKAZRFB1*LA000001 to 004000
ZR550 B2	1991	JKAZRFB1*MA004001 on
ZR550 B3†	1992	JKAZRFB1*NA012001 to 022000
ZR550 B4†	1993	JKAZRFB1*PA022001 on
ZR750 C1	1991	JKAZRDC1*MA00001 to 018500
ZR750 C2	1992	JKAZRDC1*NA018501 on
ZR750 C3†	1993	JKAZRDC1*PA035001 on

†*Canada only*

The frame number is stamped on the steering head

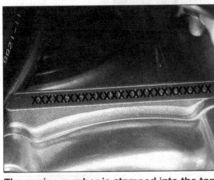

The engine number is stamped into the top of the crankcase behind the cylinder block

Buying spare parts

Once you have found all the identification numbers, record them for reference when buying parts. Since the manufacturers change specifications, parts and vendors (companies that manufacture various components on the machine), providing the ID numbers is the only way to be reasonably sure that you are buying the correct parts.

Whenever possible, take the worn part to the dealer so direct comparison with the new component can be made. Along the trail from the manufacturer to the parts shelf, there are numerous places that the part can end up with the wrong number or be listed incorrectly.

The two places to purchase new parts for your motorcycle - the accessory store and the franchised dealer - differ in the type of parts they carry. While dealers can obtain virtually every part for your motorcycle, the accessory dealer is usually limited to normal high wear items such as shock absorbers, tune-up parts, various engine gaskets, cables, chains, brake parts, etc. Rarely will an accessory outlet have major suspension components, cylinders, transmission gears, or cases.

Used parts can be obtained for roughly half the price of new ones, but you can't always be sure of what you're getting. Once again, take your worn part to the breaker (wrecking yard) for direct comparison.

Whether buying new, used or rebuilt parts, the best course is to deal with someone who specialises in parts for your particular make.

1 Engine/transmission oil level

Before you start:

✔ Take the motorcycle on a short run to allow it to reach normal operating temperature.

Caution: Do not run the engine in an enclosed space such as a garage or shop.

✔ Stop the engine and support the motorcycle in an upright position on level ground, using an auxiliary stand or an assistant if required. Allow it to stand for a few minutes to allow the oil level to stabilise.

✔ The oil level is viewed through the window in the clutch cover on the right-hand side of the engine. Wipe the glass clean before inspection to make the check easier.

Bike care:

● If you have to add oil frequently, you should check whether you have any oil leaks. If there is no sign of oil leakage from the joints and gaskets the engine could be burning oil (see *Fault Finding*).

The correct oil

● Modern, high-revving engines place great demands on their oil. It is very important that the correct oil for your bike is used.
● Always top up with a good quality oil of the specified type and viscosity and do not overfill the engine.

Oil type	API grade SE, SF or SG
Oil viscosity	SAE 10W/40, 10W/50, 20W/40 or 20W/50

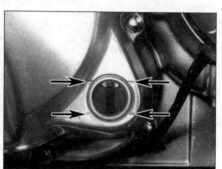

1 Wipe the oil level window in the clutch cover so that it is clean.

2 On 550 models, with the motorcycle held vertical, the oil level should lie between the upper and lower level lines marked on the clutch cover (arrowed).

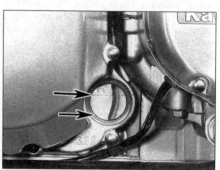

3 On 750 models, with the motorcycle held vertical, the oil level should lie between the H and L lines marked on the plate behind the window (arrowed).

4 If the level is below the lower line, remove the filler cap from the top of the clutch cover.

5 Top the engine up with the recommended grade and type of oil, to bring the level up to the upper line (550 models) or the H line (750 models) on the window.

2 Suspension, steering and drive chain

Suspension and steering:

● Check that the front and rear suspension operates smoothly without binding.
● Check that the suspension is adjusted as required.
● Check that the steering moves smoothly from lock-to-lock.
● Check that all nuts and bolts, including axles and controls, are properly tightened.

Drive chain:

● Check that the drive chain slack isn't excessive, and adjust if necessary (see Chapter 1).
● If the chain looks dry, lubricate it (see Chapter 1).

3 Brake fluid levels

Bike care:

● The fluid in the front and rear brake master cylinder reservoirs will drop slightly as the brake pads wear down.

● If either fluid reservoir requires repeated topping-up this is an indication of an hydraulic leak somewhere in the system, which should be investigated immediately.

Before you start:

✔ Position the motorcycle on its stand, and turn the handlebars until the top of the master cylinder is as level as possible. If necessary, tilt the motorcycle to make it level. Remove the seat (see Chapter 7) for access to the rear brake fluid reservoir.

✔ Make sure you have the correct hydraulic fluid - DOT 4 is recommended. Wrap a rag around the reservoir being worked on to ensure that any spillage does not come into contact with painted surfaces.

● Check for signs of fluid leakage from the hydraulic hoses and components - if found, rectify immediately.

● Check the operation of both brakes before taking the machine on the road; if there is evidence of air in the system (spongy feel to lever or pedal), it must be bled as described in Chapter 6.

Warning: Brake and clutch hydraulic fluid can harm your eyes and damage painted surfaces, so use extreme caution when handling and pouring it and cover surrounding surfaces with rag. Do not use fluid that has been standing open for some time, as it absorbs moisture from the air which can cause a dangerous loss of braking effectiveness.

1 The front brake fluid level is checked via the sightglass in the reservoir - it must be above the low level mark (arrowed).

2 If the level is below the mark, remove the two screws (arrowed) to free the brake fluid reservoir cover, and remove the cover, diaphragm plate and diaphragm.

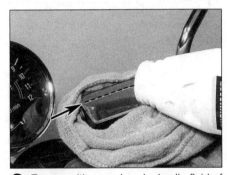

3 Top up with new clean hydraulic fluid of the recommended type until the level is up to the high level mark on the inside of the reservoir (arrowed). Take care to avoid spills (see **Warning** above).

4 Ensure that the diaphragm is correctly seated before installing the plate and cover.

5 The rear brake fluid level can be seen through the translucent body of the reservoir which is located under the seat. Remove the seat for access (see Chapter 7). The fluid must lie between the UPPER and LOWER level marks (arrowed). To top up, unscrew the cap, then remove the plate and diaphragm.

4 Legal and safety checks

Lighting and signalling:

● Take a minute to check that the headlight, taillight, brake light, instrument lights and turn signals all work correctly.

● Check that the horn sounds when the switch is operated.

● A working speedometer is a statutory requirement in the UK.

Safety:

● Check that the throttle grip rotates smoothly and snaps shut when released,

and that it does so in all steering positions. Also check for the correct amount of freeplay (see Chapter 1).

● Check that the clutch lever operates smoothly and with the correct amount of freeplay (see Chapter 1).

● Check that the brake pads have not worn down to or beyond their wear limit - there must be at least 1 mm of lining left on each brake pad (see Chapter 1).

● Check that the engine shuts off when the kill switch is operated.

● Check that sidestand return spring holds the stand securely up when retracted. The same applies to the centre stand (where fitted).

Fuel:

● This may seem obvious, but check that you have enough fuel to complete your journey. If you notice signs of fuel leakage - rectify the cause immediately.

● Ensure you use the correct grade unleaded fuel - see Chapter 3 Specifications.

5 Tyres

Tyre care:

● Check the tyres carefully for cuts, tears, embedded nails or other sharp objects and excessive wear. Operation of the motorcycle with excessively worn tyres is extremely hazardous, as traction and handling are directly affected.
● Check the condition of the tyre valve and ensure the dust cap is in place.
● Pick out any stones or nails which may have become embedded in the tyre tread. If left, they will eventually penetrate through the casing and cause a puncture.
● If tyre damage is apparent, or unexplained loss of pressure is experienced, seek the advice of a tyre fitting specialist without delay.

Tyre tread depth:

● At the time of writing UK law requires that tread depth must be at least 1 mm over 3/4 of the tread breadth all the way around the tyre, with no bald patches. Many riders, however, consider 2 mm tread depth minimum to be a safer limit. Kawasaki recommend the following minimum tread depths.

Front	.1 mm
Rear - below 80 mph (130 km/h)	.2 mm
Rear - above 80 mph (130 km/h)	.3 mm

● Many tyres now incorporate wear indicators in the tread. Find the wear indicator pointer on the tyre sidewall (this will vary according to the tyre fitted) to locate the indicator bar; replace the tyre if the tread has worn down to the bar.

1 Check the tyre pressures when the tyres are **cold** and keep them properly inflated.

2 Measure tread depth at the centre of the tyre using a tread depth gauge.

3 Tyre tread wear indicator bar location marking (arrowed) - usually either an arrow, a triangle or the letters TWI on the sidewall.

The correct pressures:

● The tyres must be checked when **cold**, not immediately after riding. Note that low tyre pressures may cause the tyre to slip on the rim or come off. High tyre pressures will cause abnormal tread wear and unsafe handling.

● Use an accurate pressure gauge.
● Proper air pressure will increase tyre life and provide maximum stability and ride comfort.

Front	.28 psi (2.0 Bar)
Rear	.32 psi (2.2 Bar)

Chapter 1
Routine maintenance and servicing

Contents

Degrees of difficulty

Easy, suitable for novice with little experience	**Fairly easy,** suitable for beginner with some experience	**Fairly difficult,** suitable for competent DIY mechanic

Difficult, suitable for experienced DIY mechanic	**Very difficult,** suitable for expert DIY or professional

Engine

Spark plugs

ZR550

B1 and B2 US models	NGK D9EA or Nippondenso X27ES-U
All other models	NGK DR9EA or Nippondenso X27ESR-U
Electrode gap	0.6 to 0.7 mm

ZR750

UK C1, C2, C3 and C4 models	NGK DR8ES or Nippondenso X27ESR-U
US C1, C2, C3 and C4 models	NGK D9EA or Nippondenso X27ES-U
All other models	NGK DR9EA or Nippondenso X27ESR-U
Electrode gap	0.6 to 0.7 mm

Engine idle speed

ZR550

UK models	1300 ± 50 rpm
US models	1200 ± 50 rpm
ZR750	1100 ± 50 rpm
Carburettor synchronisation - max difference between carburettors ..	2 cm Hg
Cylinder identification	from left to right, numbered 1, 2, 3 and 4

Valve clearances (COLD engine)

ZR550

Intake valves	0.10 to 0.20 mm
Exhaust valves	0.15 to 0.25 mm
ZR750 - intake and exhaust	0.08 to 0.18 mm

Cylinder compression

ZR550	128 to 198 psi (9 to 14 Bar)
ZR750	109 to 170 psi (7.7 to 12 Bar)

Oil pressure (with engine warm - oil at 90°C)

ZR550	31 to 36 psi (2.2 to 2.5 Bar) at 4000 rpm
ZR750	28 to 36 psi (2.0 to 2.5 Bar) at 4000 rpm

Miscellaneous

Drive chain

Freeplay	35 to 40 mm
Stretch limit (21 pin length - see text)	323 mm
Brake pad friction material minimum thickness	1 mm

Freeplay adjustments

Clutch lever	2.0 to 3.0 mm
Throttle grip	2.0 to 3.0 mm (see text)
Choke lever	2.0 to 3.0 mm

Brake pedal - distance below top of footrest

ZR550	35 mm
ZR750	40 mm

Tyre pressures (cold)

Front	28 psi (2.0 Bar)
Rear	32 psi (2.25 Bar)
Tyre tread depth	see *Daily (pre-ride) checks*

Recommended lubricants and fluids

Drive chain lubricant	Heavy motor oil (SAE 90), or aerosol chain lube suitable for O-ring chains
Engine/transmission oil type	API grade SE, SF or SG motor oil
Engine/transmission oil viscosity	SAE 10W40, 10W50, 20W40 or 20W50

Engine/transmission oil capacity

ZR550

Oil change	2.6 litres
Oil and filter change	2.7 litres
Following engine overhaul - dry engine, new filter	3.0 litres

ZR750

Oil change	3.0 litres
Oil and filter change	3.5 litres
Following engine overhaul - dry engine, new filter	3.6 litres
Brake fluid	DOT 4

Recommended lubricants and fluids (continued)

Fork oil type	SAE 10W20 fork oil
Fork oil capacity	
ZR550	
Oil change	350 cc
Following fork overhaul (completely dry)	408 to 416 cc
ZR750	
C1 and C2 models	
Oil change	400 cc
Following fork overhaul (completely dry)	466 to 474 cc
C3, C4 and C5 models	
Oil change	417 cc
Following fork overhaul (completely dry)	490 cc
D1 model	
Oil change	400 cc
Following fork overhaul (completely dry)	463 to 471 cc
Fork oil level*	
ZR550	96 to 100 mm*
ZR750	
C1 and C2 models	108 to 112 mm*
C3, C4 and C5 models	88 to 92 mm*
D1 model	111 to 115 mm*

*Oil level is measured from the top of the tube with the fork spring removed and the leg fully compressed.

Miscellaneous

Wheel bearings	Multi-purpose grease
Swingarm bearings	Multi-purpose grease
Steering head bearings	Multi-purpose grease
Inner cables	Cable lubricant
Cable ends	Multi-purpose grease
Lever and stand pivot points	Motor oil
Throttle grip	Multi-purpose grease or dry film lubricant

Torque settings

Chain adjuster clamp bolts	39 Nm
Torque arm nuts	
ZR550	32 Nm
ZR750	34 Nm
Spark plugs	14 Nm
Cylinder head nuts and bolts	
ZR550	
Cylinder head 8 mm nuts	25 Nm
Cylinder head 6 mm bolts	12 Nm
Cylinder head 6 mm nuts	9.8 Nm
ZR750	
Cylinder head bolts	29 Nm
Cylinder head nuts	39 Nm
Oil drain plug	29 Nm
Oil filter bolt	20 Nm
Steering stem bolt	39 Nm
Pulse generator assembly cover bolts	10 Nm
Fork oil drain screw	1.5 Nm
Fork top bolt	23 Nm
Fork clamp bolts	
ZR550	21 Nm
ZR750	20 Nm
Shock absorber lower mounting nuts	39 Nm
Swingarm pivot nut	
ZR550	93 Nm
ZR750	109 Nm
Oil gallery plug	15 Nm

1

Maintenance schedule - ZR550 B & ZR750 C models

Note: *The daily (pre-ride) checks at the beginning of the manual cover those items which should be inspected on a daily basis. Always perform the pre-ride inspection at every maintenance interval (in addition to the procedures listed). The intervals listed below are the intervals recommended by the manufacturer for the models covered in this manual. Your owner's handbook may have different intervals if your model is not specifically covered by this manual. If in doubt, check with a Kawasaki dealer.*

Daily (pre-ride)

☐ See *'Daily (pre-ride) checks'* at the beginning of this manual.

After the initial 500 miles (800 km)

Note: *This check is usually performed by a Kawasaki dealer after the first 500 miles (800 km) from new. Thereafter, maintenance is carried out according to the following intervals of the schedule.*

Every 200 miles (300 km)

Carry out all the items under the Daily (pre-ride) checks, plus the following

☐ Clean and lubricate the drive chain (Section 1).

Every 500 miles (800 km)

Carry out all the items under the Daily (pre-ride) checks, plus the following

☐ Check and adjust drive chain freeplay (Section 2).

Every 3000 miles (5000 km) or six months

Carry out all the items under the Daily (pre-ride) checks and the 200 mile (300 km) and 500 mile (800 km) check, plus the following

☐ Clean and check the spark plugs (Section 3).
☐ Check the air suction valve (US models only) (Section 4).
☐ Check and adjust the engine idle speed (Section 5).
☐ Check carburettor synchronisation (Section 6).
☐ Check the evaporative emission control (EVAP) system (California models only) (Section 7).
☐ Check and empty the air filter drain reservoir (750 models only) (Section 8).
☐ Change the engine oil (Section 9).
☐ Check the operation of the clutch (Section 10).
☐ Check for drive chain wear and stretch (Section 11).
☐ Check the brake pads for wear (Section 12).
☐ Check the operation of the brakes, and for fluid leakage (Section 13).
☐ Check the steering head bearing freeplay (Section 14).
☐ Check the tyre and wheel condition, and the tyre tread depth (Section 15).
☐ Check and lubricate the stands, lever pivots and cables (Section 16).
☐ Check the battery electrolyte level (ZR550 B1, B2, B3 and B4 models only) (Section 17).

Every 6000 miles (10 000 km) or twelve months

Carry out all the items under the 3000 mile (5000 km) check, plus the following:

☐ Check the valve clearances (Section 18).
☐ Clean the air filter element (Section 21).
☐ Check throttle/choke cable operation and freeplay (Section 22).
☐ Change the engine oil and replace the oil filter (Section 23).
☐ Check the fuel hoses and system components (Section 24).
☐ Tighten the cylinder head nuts (Section 25).
☐ Check the front and rear suspension (Section 26).
☐ Re-grease the swingarm pivot and bearings (Section 27).
☐ Check the tightness of all nuts and bolts (Section 28).

Every 12 000 miles (20 000 km) or two years

Carry out all the items under the 6000 mile (10 000 km) check, plus the following:

☐ Replace the air filter (Section 29).
☐ Change the brake fluid (Section 30).
☐ Re-grease the steering head bearings (Section 31).

Every 18 000 miles (30 000 km) or two years

Carry out all the items under the 6000 mile (10 000 km) check, plus the following:

☐ Change the front fork oil (Section 33).

Every two years

☐ Replace the brake master cylinder and caliper seals (Section 34).

Every four years

☐ Replace the brake hoses (Section 35).
☐ Replace the fuel hoses (Section 36).

Non-scheduled maintenance

☐ Check the headlight aim (Section 37).
☐ Check the wheel bearings (Section 38).
☐ Check the cylinder compression (Section 39).
☐ Check the engine oil pressure (Section 40). ·

Maintenance schedule - ZR750 D model

Note: *The daily (pre-ride) checks at the beginning of the manual cover those items which should be inspected on a daily basis. Always perform the pre-ride inspection at every maintenance interval (in addition to the procedures listed). The intervals listed below are the intervals recommended by the manufacturer for the models covered in this manual. Your owner's handbook may have different intervals if your model is not specifically covered by this manual. If in doubt, check with a Kawasaki dealer.*

Daily (pre-ride)
☐ See *'Daily (pre-ride) checks'* at the beginning of this manual.

After the initial 600 miles (1000 km)
Note: *This check is usually performed by a Kawasaki dealer after the first 600 miles (1000 km) from new. Thereafter, maintenance is carried out according to the following intervals of the schedule.*

Every 400 miles (600 km)
Carry out all the items under the Daily (pre-ride) checks, plus the following
☐ Clean and lubricate the drive chain (Section 1).

Every 600 miles (1000 km)
Carry out all the items under the Daily (pre-ride) checks, plus the following
☐ Check and adjust drive chain freeplay (Section 2).

Every 4000 miles (6000 km) or six months
Carry out all the items under the Daily (pre-ride) checks and the 400 mile (600 km) and 600 mile (1000 km) check, plus the following
☐ Clean and check the spark plugs (Section 3).
☐ Check the air suction valve (US models only) (Section 4).
☐ Check the evaporative emission control (EVAP) system (California models only) (Section 7).
☐ Check and empty the air filter drain reservoir (Section 8).
☐ Change the engine oil (Section 9).
☐ Check the operation of the clutch (Section 10).
☐ Check for drive chain wear and stretch (Section 11).
☐ Check the brake pads for wear (Section 12).
☐ Check the operation of the brakes, and for fluid leakage (Section 13).
☐ Check the steering head bearing freeplay (Section 14).
☐ Check the tyre and wheel condition, and the tyre tread depth (Section 15).
☐ Check and lubricate the stands, lever pivots and cables (Section 16).

Every 7500 miles (12 000 km) or twelve months
Carry out all the items under the 4000 mile (6000 km) check, plus the following:
☐ Check and adjust the engine idle speed (Section 19).
☐ Check carburettor synchronisation (Section 20).
☐ Check the valve clearances (Section 18).
☐ Clean the air filter element (Section 21).
☐ Check throttle/choke cable operation and freeplay (Section 22).
☐ Change the engine oil and replace the oil filter (Section 23).
☐ Check the fuel hoses and system components (Section 24).
☐ Check the front and rear suspension (Section 26).
☐ Re-grease the swingarm pivot and bearings (Section 27).
☐ Check the tightness of all nuts and bolts (Section 28).

Every 15 000 miles (24 000 km) or two years
Carry out all the items under the 7500 mile (12 000 km) check, plus the following:
☐ Replace the air filter (Section 29).
☐ Change the brake fluid (Section 30).
☐ Re-grease the steering head bearings (Section 31).
☐ Change the front fork oil (Section 32).

Every four years
☐ Replace the brake master cylinder and caliper seals (Section 34).
☐ Replace the brake hoses (Section 35).
☐ Replace the fuel hoses (Section 36).

Non-scheduled maintenance
☐ Check the headlight aim (Section 37).
☐ Check the wheel bearings (Section 38).
☐ Check the cylinder compression (Section 39).
☐ Check the engine oil pressure (Section 40).

1

Component locations on right-hand side

1 Rear brake fluid reservoir
2 Battery
3 Front brake fluid reservoir
4 Throttle cable upper adjuster

5 Front fork seals
6 Brake pads
7 Engine oil gallery plug
8 Engine oil level window

9 Engine oil filler cap
10 Clutch cable lower adjuster
11 Air filter drain reservoir
   (750 models)

12 Rear brake light switch and
   pedal height adjuster

Component locations on left-hand side

1 Clutch cable upper adjuster
2 Steering head bearings
3 Spark plugs and valves

4 Fuel tap filter
5 Throttle stop screw (idle speed)
6 Air filter

7 Drive chain adjusters
8 Drive chain
9 Swingarm pivot bearings

10 Engine oil filter
11 Engine oil drain plug
12 Front brake pads

Introduction

1 This Chapter is designed to help the home mechanic maintain his/her motorcycle for safety, economy, long life and peak performance.
2 Deciding where to start or plug into the routine maintenance schedule depends on several factors. If the warranty period on your motorcycle has just expired, and if it has been maintained according to the warranty standards, you may want to pick up routine maintenance as it coincides with the next mileage or calendar interval. If you have owned the machine for some time but

have never performed any maintenance on it, then you may want to start at the nearest interval and include some additional procedures to ensure that nothing important is overlooked. If you have just had a major engine overhaul, then you may want to start the maintenance routine from the beginning. If you have a used machine and have no knowledge of its history or maintenance record, you may desire to combine all the checks into one large service initially and then settle into the maintenance schedule prescribed.

3 Before beginning any maintenance or repair, the machine should be cleaned thoroughly, especially around the oil filter, spark plugs, valve cover, side panels, carburettors, etc. Cleaning will help ensure that dirt does not contaminate the engine and will allow you to detect wear and damage that could otherwise easily go unnoticed.
4 Certain maintenance information is sometimes printed on decals attached to the motorcycle. If the information on the decals differs from that included here, use the information on the decal.

Every 200 miles (300 km) - ZR550 B & ZR750 C
Every 400 miles (600 km) - ZR750 D

1 **Drive chain -**
cleaning and lubrication

1 Place the machine on its centre stand (where fitted), or support the machine on an auxiliary stand so that the rear wheel is off the ground. Rotate the back wheel whilst cleaning and lubricating the chain to access all the links.
2 Wash the chain in paraffin (kerosene), then wipe it off and allow it to dry, using compressed air if available. If the chain is excessively dirty it should be removed from the machine and allowed to soak in the paraffin (see Chapter 5).
Caution: Don't use petrol (gasoline), solvent or other cleaning fluids which

might damage the internal sealing properties of the chain. Don't use high-pressure water. The entire process shouldn't take longer than ten minutes - if it does, the O-rings in the chain rollers could be damaged.
3 The best time to lubricate the chain is after the motorcycle has been ridden, as when the chain is warm the lubricant penetrates the joints between the side plates better than when cold.
4 Apply the specified lubricant (see Specifications at the beginning of the Chapter) to the area where the side plates overlap - not to the middle of the rollers **(see illustration)**. After applying the lubricant, let it soak in for a few minutes before wiping off any excess.
Caution: If you use an aerosol drive chain lubricant, make sure it is marked as being

suitable for O-ring chains, otherwise the O-rings could be damaged by the lubricant solvents and additives.

1.4 Apply the specified lubricant to the overlap between the sideplates

Every 500 miles (800 km) - ZR550 B & ZR750 C
Every 600 miles (1000 km) - ZR750 D

2 **Drive chain -** freeplay check
and adjustment

Check

1 A neglected drive chain won't last long and can quickly damage the sprockets. Routine chain adjustment will ensure maximum chain and sprocket life.
2 To check the chain, shift the transmission into neutral and make sure the ignition switch is OFF. Rotate the rear wheel until the chain is positioned with the tightest point at the centre of its bottom run, then place the machine on its sidestand. Make sure that the adjuster is in

the same position on each side relative to the cut-out in the swingarm.
3 Measure the amount of freeplay on the chain's bottom run, at a point midway between the two sprockets, then compare your measurement to the value listed in this Chapter's Specifications **(see illustration)**. Since the chain will rarely wear evenly, rotate the rear wheel so that another section of chain can be checked; do this several times to check the entire length of chain. In some cases where lubrication has been neglected, corrosion and galling may cause the links to bind and kink, which effectively shortens the chain's length. If the chain is tight between the sprockets, rusty or kinked, or if any of the pins are loose or the rollers damaged, it's time to

replace it with a new one. If you find a tight area, mark it with felt pen or paint, and repeat the measurement after the bike has been

2.3 Measuring drive chain freeplay

1

2.5a Slacken the chain adjuster clamp bolt (arrowed) on each end of the swingarm . . .

2.5b . . . and the brake torque arm nuts (arrowed)

2.6a Turn the adjuster using a 12 mm Allen key

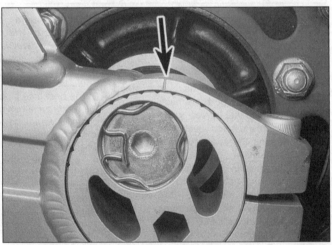

2.6b Make sure the notches on each adjuster are in the same position relative to the cut-out in the swingarm (arrowed)

ridden. If the chain is still tight in the same area, it may be damaged or worn. Because a tight or kinked chain can damage the transmission output shaft bearing, it's a good idea to replace it.

Adjustment

4 Rotate the rear wheel until the chain is positioned with the tightest point at the centre of its bottom run, then place the machine on its sidestand.

5 Slacken the chain adjuster clamp bolt on each end of the swingarm, and the nuts securing the brake torque arm to the swingarm and the rear brake caliper bracket **(see illustrations)**.

6 Using a 12 mm Allen key (one is supplied in the motorcycle's tool kit which is stored under the seat), rotate the chain adjuster on each side of the swingarm evenly until the amount of freeplay specified at the beginning of the Chapter is obtained at the centre of the bottom run of the chain **(see illustration)**. You will probably find that as you turn one adjuster

the other adjuster turns as well. Following chain adjustment, make sure that each adjuster is in the same position relative to the cut-out in each side of the swingarm **(see illustration)**. It is important that the same notch on each adjuster aligns with the swingarm cut-out; if not, the rear wheel will be out of alignment with the front.

7 If there is a discrepancy in the chain adjuster positions, adjust one of the chain adjusters so that its position is exactly the same as the other. Check the chain freeplay as described above and readjust if necessary.

8 Tighten the adjuster clamp bolts and the torque arm nuts to the specified torque setting **(see illustrations)**.

2.8a Tighten the adjuster clamp bolts . . .

2.8b . . . and the torque arm nuts to the specified torque setting

Every 3000 miles (5000 km) - ZR550 B & ZR750 C
Every 4000 miles (6000 km) - ZR750 D

3 Spark plugs - gap check and adjustment

1 Make sure your spark plug socket is the correct size before attempting to remove the plugs - a suitable one is supplied in the motorcycle's tool kit which is stored under the seat.

2 Remove the seat (see Chapter 7) and disconnect the battery negative (–) lead.

3 Clean the area around the plug caps to prevent any dirt falling into the spark plug channels.

4 Check that the cylinder location is marked on each plug lead, then pull the spark plug cap off each spark plug **(see illustration)**. Using either the plug removing tool supplied in the bike's toolkit or a socket type wrench,

unscrew the plugs from the cylinder head **(see illustration)**. Lay each plug out in relation to its cylinder; if either plug shows up a problem it will then be easy to identify the troublesome cylinder.

5 Inspect the electrodes for wear. Both the centre and side electrodes should have square edges and the side electrode should be of uniform thickness. Look for excessive deposits and evidence of a cracked or chipped insulator around the centre electrode. Compare your spark plugs to the colour spark plug reading chart on the inside rear cover. Check the threads, the washer and the ceramic insulator body for cracks and other damage.

6 If the electrodes are not excessively worn, and if the deposits can be easily removed with a wire brush, the plugs can be re-gapped and re-used (if no cracks or chips are visible in the

insulator). If in doubt concerning the condition of the plugs, replace them with new ones, as the expense is minimal.

7 Cleaning spark plugs by sandblasting is permitted, provided you clean the plugs with a high flash-point solvent afterwards.

8 Before installing the plugs, make sure they are the correct type and heat range and check the gap between the electrodes (they are not pre-set on new plugs). For best results, use a wire-type gauge rather than a flat (feeler) gauge to check the gap **(see illustrations)**. Compare the gap to that specified and adjust as necessary. If the gap must be adjusted, bend the side electrode only and be very careful not to chip or crack the insulator nose **(see illustration)**. Make sure the washer is in place before installing each plug.

9 Since the cylinder head is made of aluminium, which is soft and easily damaged,

3.4a Pull off the spark plug cap . . .

3.4b . . . then unscrew the spark plug

1

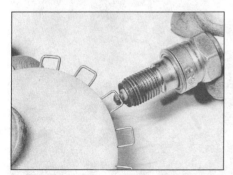

3.8a A wire type gauge is recommended to measure the spark plug electrode gap

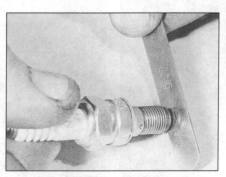

3.8b A blade type feeler gauge can also be used

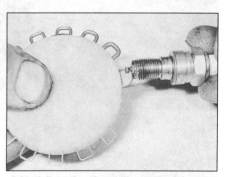

3.8c Adjust the electrode gap by bending the side electrode only

3.9 Thread the plug in as far as possible by hand

thread the plugs into the heads by hand **(see illustration)**. Once the plugs are finger-tight, the job can be finished with the tool supplied or a socket. Tighten the spark plugs to the specified torque setting; do not over-tighten them.

Stripped plug threads in the cylinder head can be repaired with a Heli-coil insert - see "Tools and workshop tips" in the Reference section.

10 Reconnect the spark plug caps, making sure they are securely connected to the correct cylinder. Connect the battery negative (–) lead and install the seat.

4 Air suction valves - check (US models)

1 Remove the fuel tank (see Chapter 3).
2 Unscrew the four bolts securing each suction valve cover to the valve cover, then lift the covers off and remove the reed valve assemblies, noting which way up they fit.
3 Check the reeds for cracks, warpage and any other damage or deterioration. Also check the contact areas between the reeds and the

reed holders, and the holders themselves, for any signs of damage or deterioration. Any carbon deposits or other foreign particles can be cleaned off using a high flash-point solvent. Replace the reed valve assemblies if there is any doubt about their condition. On 550 models, also check the condition of the upper and lower gaskets and replace them if necessary.
4 Install the valve assemblies with their gaskets (550 models), making sure the projection on each valve holder faces up, then install the covers and tighten the bolts securely.

5 Idle speed - check and adjustment (ZR550 B and ZR750 C)

1 The idle speed should be checked and adjusted before and after the carburettors are synchronised (balanced) and when it is obviously too high or too low. Before adjusting the idle speed, make sure the valve clearances and spark plug gaps are correct. Also, turn the handlebars back-and-forth and see if the idle speed changes as this is done. If it does, the throttle cable may not be adjusted correctly, or may be worn out. This is a dangerous condition that can cause loss of control of the bike. Be sure to correct this problem before proceeding.
2 The engine should be at normal operating temperature, which is usually reached after 10 to 15 minutes of stop and go riding. Place the motorcycle on its centre stand (where fitted), or support it upright using an auxiliary stand, and make sure the transmission is in neutral.
3 With the engine idling, adjust the idle speed by turning the throttle stop screw in or out until the idle speed listed in this Chapter's Specifications is obtained. The throttle stop screw is located on the left-hand end of the carburettors on 550 models, and under the carburettors in the middle on 750 models **(see illustrations)**.

4 Snap the throttle open and shut a few times, then recheck the idle speed. If necessary, repeat the adjustment procedure.
5 If a smooth, steady idle can't be achieved, the fuel/air mixture may be incorrect (see Chapter 3) or the carburettors may need synchronising (see Section 6). On US models, check the air suction valves (see Section 4).

6 Carburettors - synchronisation (ZR550 B and ZR750 C)

⚠ *Warning: Petrol (gasoline) is extremely flammable, so take extra precautions when you work on any part of the fuel system. Don't smoke or allow open flames or bare light bulbs near the work area, and don't work in a garage where a natural gas-type appliance is present. If you spill any fuel on your skin, rinse it off immediately with soap and water. When you perform any kind of work on the fuel system, wear safety glasses and have a fire extinguisher suitable for a Class B type fire (flammable liquids) on hand.*

⚠ *Warning: Take great care not to burn your hand on the hot engine unit when accessing the gauge take-off points on the intake manifolds. Do not allow exhaust gases to build up in the work area; either perform the check outside or use an exhaust gas extraction system.*

1 Carburettor synchronisation is simply the process of adjusting the carburettors so they pass the same amount of fuel/air mixture to each cylinder. This is done by measuring the vacuum produced in each cylinder. Carburettors that are out of synchronisation will result in decreased fuel mileage, increased engine temperature, less than ideal throttle response and higher vibration levels. Before synchronising the carburettors, make sure the valve clearances are properly set.

5.3a Throttle stop screw - 550 models

5.3b Throttle stop screw (arrowed) - 750 models

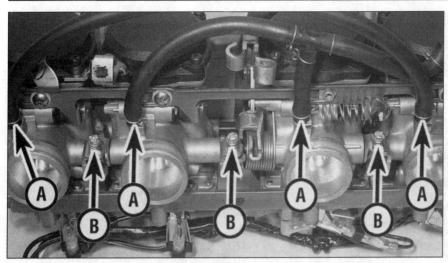

**6.5 Pull the hoses or caps off the vacuum take-off stubs (A).
The synchronisation screws (B) are in between each pair of carburettors**

2 To properly synchronise the carburettors, you will need some sort of vacuum gauge set-up with a gauge for each cylinder, or a manometer, which is a calibrated tube arrangement that utilises columns of mercury or steel rods to indicate engine vacuum. **Note:** *Due to the nature of the synchronisation procedure and the need for special instruments, most owners leave the task to a Kawasaki dealer.*

3 Start the engine and let it run until it reaches normal operating temperature, then shut it off.

4 Remove the fuel tank (see Chapter 3).

5 Disconnect the fuel tap vacuum hose and remove the blanking caps or hoses (UK models), or EVAP and suction valve hoses or blanking caps as appropriate (US and California models) from the take-off stubs on the carburettors **(see illustration)**. Make a note of which hoses fit where.

6 Connect the gauge hoses to the take-off adapters. Make sure there are no air leaks as false readings will result.

7 Arrange a temporary fuel supply, either by using a small temporary tank or by using extra long fuel pipes to the now remote fuel tank. Alternatively, position the tank on a suitable base on the motorcycle, taking care not to scratch any paintwork, and making sure that the tank is safely and securely supported.

8 Start the engine and let it idle. If the gauges are fitted with damping adjustment, set this so that the needle flutter is just eliminated but so that they can still respond to small changes in pressure.

9 The vacuum readings for all of the cylinders should be the same. If the vacuum readings vary, proceed as follows.

10 The carburettors are adjusted by turning the synchronising screws situated in-between each carburettor, in the throttle linkage **(see illustration 6.5)**. **Note:** *Do not press down on the screws whilst adjusting them, otherwise a false reading will be obtained.* First synchronise the outer left carburettor (no. 1) to the inner left carburettor (no. 2) until the readings are the same. Then synchronise the outer right carburettor (no. 4) to the inner right carburettor (no. 3). Finally synchronise the left-hand carburettors (nos. 1 and 2) to the right-hand carburettors (nos. 3 and 4) using the centre synchronising screw. When all the carburettors are synchronised, open and close the throttle quickly to settle the linkage, and recheck the gauge readings, readjusting if necessary.

11 When the adjustment is complete, recheck the vacuum readings, then adjust the idle speed by turning the throttle stop screw until the idle speed listed in this Chapter's Specifications is obtained. Remove the gauge hoses, then install the fuel tap vacuum hose and the take-off blanking caps or hoses, or EVAP and suction valve hoses onto the carburettors.

12 Detach the temporary fuel supply and install the fuel tank (see Chapter 3).

7 Evaporative emission control (EVAP) system - check (California models)

1 Visually inspect all the EVAP system hoses for kinks and splits and any other damage or deterioration. Make sure that the hoses are securely connected with a clamp on each end. Replace any hoses that are damaged or deteriorated. See Chapter 3 for further information and a diagram of the EVAP system.

8 Air filter reservoir - draining (750 models)

1 The drain hose from the bottom of the air filter housing has a reservoir to store any oil that drains from the housing. The reservoir is located at the back of the clutch cover on the right-hand side of the engine.

2 Lift the rubber boot and check for any oil in the reservoir **(see illustration)**. If any oil is present, remove the drain plug from the bottom of the reservoir hose and allow the oil to drain into a suitable container **(see illustration)**. Make sure the drain plug is securely installed on completion.

1

8.2a Check for any oil in the reservoir (arrowed)

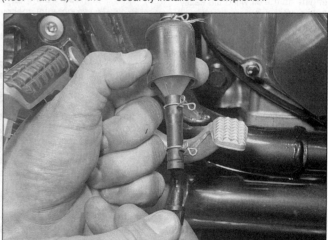

8.2b Remove the plug and allow any oil to drain out

9.3 Remove the oil filler cap to vent the crankcase (arrowed)

9.4 Remove the drain plug and allow the oil to drain completely

9 Engine - oil change

 Warning: Be careful when draining the oil, as the exhaust pipes, the engine, and the oil itself can cause severe burns.

1 Consistent routine oil changes are the single most important maintenance procedure you can perform on a motorcycle. The oil not only lubricates the internal parts of the engine, transmission and clutch, but it also acts as a coolant, a cleaner, a sealant, and a protectant. Because of these demands, the oil takes a terrific amount of abuse and should be replaced often with new oil of the recommended grade and type. Saving a little money on the difference in cost between a good oil and a cheap oil won't pay off if the engine is damaged. **Note:** *The oil filter should be changed with every second oil change.*

2 Before changing the oil, warm up the engine so the oil will drain easily.

3 Put the motorcycle on its centre stand (where fitted), or support it upright using an auxiliary stand, and position a clean drain tray below the engine. Unscrew the oil filler cap on the clutch cover to vent the crankcase and to act as a reminder that there is no oil in the engine **(see illustration)**.

4 Next, unscrew the oil drain plug from the bottom of the engine and allow the oil to flow into the drain tray **(see illustration)**. Discard the sealing washer on the drain plug as it should be replaced whenever the plug is removed.

5 When the oil has completely drained, fit a new sealing washer over the drain plug. Fit the plug to the sump and tighten it to the torque setting specified at the beginning of the Chapter **(see illustration)**. Avoid overtightening, as damage to the sump will result.

6 Refill the crankcase to the proper level using the recommended type and amount of oil (see *Daily (pre-ride) checks*). With the motorcycle held vertical, the oil level should lie between the high and low level lines on the inspection window in the clutch cover (see *Daily (pre-ride) checks*). Install the filler cap. Start the engine and let it run for two or three minutes (make sure that the oil pressure light extinguishes after a few seconds). Shut it off, wait a few minutes, then check the oil level. If necessary, add more oil to bring the level up to the high level line on the inspection window. Check that there are no leaks from around the drain plug.

 Saving a little money on the difference between good and cheap oils won't pay off if the engine suffers damage.

7 The old oil drained from the engine cannot be re-used and should be disposed of properly. Check with your local refuse disposal company, disposal facility or environmental agency to see whether they will accept the used oil for recycling. Don't pour used oil into drains or onto the ground.

9.5 Fit a new sealing washer onto the drain plug and tighten it to the specified torque setting

HAYNES HiNT *Check the old oil carefully - if it is very metallic coloured, then the engine is experiencing wear from break-in (new engine) or from insufficient lubrication. If there are flakes or chips of metal in the oil, then something is drastically wrong internally and the engine will have to be disassembled for inspection and repair. If there are pieces of fibre-like material in the oil, the clutch is experiencing excessive wear and should be checked.*

10 Clutch - check

1 Periodic adjustment of the clutch cable is necessary to compensate for wear in the clutch plates and stretch of the cable. Pull in the clutch lever gently until the cable slack is taken up, then measure the gap between the lever and bracket comparing it with freeplay specification at the beginning of the Chapter **(see illustration)**. If adjustment is required, it

10.1 Measuring clutch lever freeplay

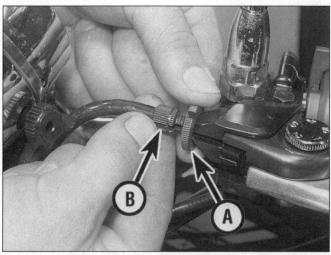

10.2 Lockring (A), adjuster (B) (lever end)

10.4 Slacken the locknuts (arrowed) and move the adjuster as required

can be made at either the lever end of the cable or at the clutch end.

2 To adjust the freeplay at the lever, loosen the locking ring and turn the adjuster in or out until the required amount of freeplay is obtained **(see illustration)**. To increase freeplay, turn the adjuster clockwise. To reduce freeplay, turn the adjuster anti-clockwise. Tighten the locking ring securely.

3 If all the adjustment has been taken up at the lever, reset the adjuster to give the maximum amount of freeplay, then set the correct amount of freeplay using the adjuster at the clutch end of the cable. Subsequent adjustments can then be made using the lever adjuster only.

4 To adjust the freeplay at the clutch, loosen the locknuts and move the adjuster until the required amount of freeplay is obtained, then tighten the locknuts against the bracket **(see illustration)**. To increase freeplay, move the

adjuster down in the bracket. To reduce freeplay, pull the adjuster up in the bracket.

5 The clutch lever has a span adjuster which alters the distance of the lever from the handlebar **(see illustration)**. Pull the lever away from the handlebar and turn the adjuster dial until the setting which best suits the rider is obtained. There are five positions. Align the number for the setting required with the triangular mark on the lever bracket.

11 Drive chain - wear and stretch check

1 Check the entire length of the chain for damaged rollers, loose links and pins and replace the chain if damage is found. If the chain has reached the end of its adjustment, it must be replaced.

2 The amount of chain stretch can be

measured and compared to the stretch limit specified at the beginning of the Chapter. Place the machine on its sidestand and remove the chain guard (see Chapter 7), then hang a 10 kg (22 lb) weight from the bottom run of the chain. Measure along the top run the length of 21 pins (from the centre of the 1st pin to the centre of the 21st pin) and compare the result with the service limit specified at the beginning of the Chapter **(see illustration)**. Rotate the rear wheel so that several sections of the chain are measured. If any measurement exceeds the service limit the chain must be replaced (see Chapter 5). **Note:** *It is good practice to replace the chain and sprockets as a set.*

3 Check the teeth on the engine sprocket and rear wheel sprocket for wear (see Chapter 5).

4 Inspect the drive chain slider on the swingarm for excessive wear and replace it if necessary (see Chapter 5).

1

10.5 Set the lever span adjuster as required

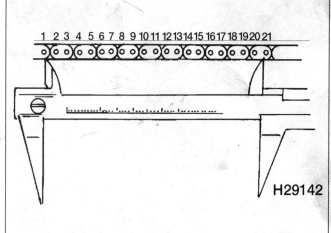

11.2 Measure the distance between the 1st and 21st pins to determine chain stretch

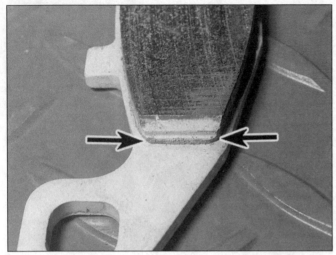

12.1a Brake pad wear indicator step - all pad types except 550 B3, B4 and B5 rear, and 750 D front

12.1b Brake pad wear indicator cut-outs - 550 B3, B4 and B5 rear

12 Brake pads - wear check

1 Each brake pad has wear indicator steps, cut-outs or grooves that can be viewed without removing the pads from the caliper **(see illustrations)**. If the pads are worn to or beyond the wear limit, they must be replaced. If the pads are dirty or if you are in doubt as to the amount of friction material remaining, remove them for inspection (see Chapter 6) and measure the thickness of the material. If the thickness of the material remaining is 1 mm or less, the pads must be replaced. **Note:** *Some after-market pads may use different indicators to those on the original equipment pads shown.*

2 Refer to Chapter 6 for details of pad replacement.

13 Brake system - check

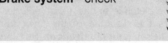

1 A routine general check of the brake system will ensure that any problems are discovered and remedied before the rider's safety is jeopardised.

General checks

2 Check the brake lever and pedal for loose connections, improper or rough action, excessive play, bends, and other damage. Replace any damaged parts with new ones (see Chapter 6).

3 Make sure all brake fasteners are tight. Check the brake pads for wear (see Section 12) and make sure the fluid level in the reservoirs is correct (see *Daily (pre-ride) checks*). Look for leaks at the hose connections and check for

cracks in the hoses **(see illustration)**. If the lever or pedal is spongy, bleed the brakes (see Chapter 6).

4 The front brake lever has a span adjuster which alters the distance of the lever from the handlebar **(see illustration)**. Pull the lever away from the handlebar and turn the adjuster dial until the setting which best suits the rider is obtained. There are four positions. Align the number for the setting required with the triangular mark on the lever bracket.

Brake light

5 Make sure the brake light operates when the front brake lever is depressed. The front brake light switch is not adjustable. If it fails to operate properly, check it (see Chapter 8).

6 Make sure the brake light is activated after about 10 mm of brake pedal travel or just before the rear brake takes effect. If adjustment is necessary, hold the switch and turn the adjusting nut on the switch body until

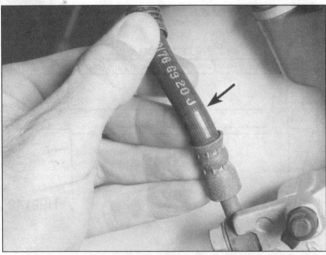

13.3 Flex the brake hoses and check for cracks, bulges and leaking fluid

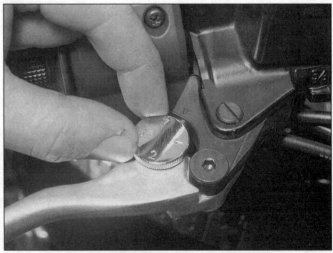

13.4 Adjusting the front brake lever span

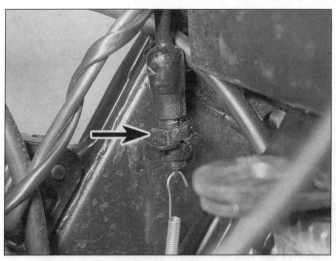

13.6 Rear brake light switch adjuster nut (arrowed)

13.7a Measuring rear brake pedal height

the brake light is activated when required (see illustration). If the switch doesn't operate the brake light, check it (see Chapter 8).

Brake pedal height

7 Check the position of the brake pedal. The distance from the top of the brake pedal tip to the top of the rider's footrest should be as specified at the beginning of the Chapter (see illustration). If the pedal height is incorrect, slacken the locknut on the master cylinder pushrod, then turn the pushrod using a spanner on the hex at the top of the rod until the pedal is at the correct height (see illustration).

8 If access to the pushrod is too restricted, remove the footrest bracket mounting bolts and detach the brake light switch spring from the pedal, then draw the bracket away from the frame, taking care not to twist or strain the master cylinder hoses. On completion tighten

the locknut securely. Adjust the rear brake light switch after adjusting the pedal height (see Step 6).

14 Steering head bearings - freeplay check and adjustment

1 This motorcycle is equipped with tapered-roller type steering head bearings which can become dented, rough or loose during normal use of the machine. In extreme cases, worn or loose steering head bearings can cause steering wobble - a condition that is potentially dangerous.

Check

2 Place the motorcycle on its centre stand. Raise the front wheel off the ground either by having an assistant push down on the rear or by placing a support under the engine.

3 Point the front wheel straight-ahead and slowly move the handlebars from side-to-side. Any dents or roughness in the bearing races will be felt and the bars will not move smoothly and freely.

4 Next, grasp the fork sliders and try to move them forward and backward (see illustration). Any looseness in the steering head bearings will be felt as front-to-rear movement of the forks. If play is felt in the bearings, adjust the steering head as follows.

> **HAYNES HINT** *Freeplay in the fork due to worn fork bushes can be misinterpreted for steering head bearing play - do not confuse the two.*

Adjustment

5 Remove the fuel tank to avoid the possibility of damage should a tool slip while

1

13.7b Master cylinder pushrod locknut (A) and adjuster hex (B)

14.4 Checking for play in the steering head bearings

14.5a Slacken the steering stem bolt (arrowed) . . .

14.5b . . . and the bottom yoke clamp bolts for each fork (arrowed)

adjustment is being made (see Chapter 3). Slacken the steering stem bolt, then slacken the fork clamp bolts in the bottom yoke **(see illustrations)**. **Note:** *Depending on the tools available, it may be necessary to displace the handlebars in order to provide enough clearance for access to the steering stem bolt (see Chapter 5).* Also slacken the bolt securing the headlight support frame to the bottom yoke, located behind the brake hose union.

6 Using a suitable C-spanner or drift located in one of the notches in the adjuster ring locknut, slacken the locknut slightly **(see illustration)**. Now initially slacken, then tighten or slacken further the adjuster ring as required until all freeplay in the forks is removed, yet the steering is able to move freely from side to side. The object is to set the adjuster ring so that the bearings are under a very light loading, just enough to remove any freeplay. Tighten the locknut against the adjuster ring finger-tight only.
Caution: Take great care not to apply excessive pressure because this will cause premature failure of the bearings.
7 If the bearings cannot be set up properly, or if there is any binding, roughness or

14.6 Using a drift located into one of the notches, slacken the locknut, then adjust the bearings via the adjuster nut below it

notchiness, they will have to be removed for inspection or replacement (see Chapter 5).
8 With the bearings correctly adjusted, tighten the steering stem bolt and the fork clamp bolts to the torque settings specified at the beginning of the Chapter. **Note:** *Depending on the tools available, it may be necessary to displace the handlebars in order to provide enough clearance for a socket and torque wrench on the steering stem bolt (see Chapter 5).*
9 Check the bearing adjustment as described above and re-adjust if necessary.

15 Wheels and tyres - check

Tyres

1 Check the tyre condition and tread depth thoroughly - see *Daily (pre-ride) checks*.

Wheels

2 The cast wheels used on all except ZR750 D models are virtually maintenance free, but they should be kept clean and checked periodically for cracks and other damage. Also check the wheel runout and alignment (see Chapter 6). Never attempt to repair damaged cast wheels; they must be replaced with new ones. Check the valve rubber for signs of damage or deterioration and have it replaced if necessary. Also, make sure the valve stem cap is in place and tight.
3 On ZR750 D models, visually check the spokes for damage, breakage or corrosion. A broken or bent spoke must be renewed immediately because the load taken by it will be transferred to adjacent spokes which may in turn fail.
4 If you suspect that any of the spokes are incorrectly tensioned, tap each one lightly

with a screwdriver and note the sound produced. Properly tensioned spokes will make a sharp pinging sound, loose ones will produce a lower pitch and overtightened ones will be higher pitched. Unevenly tensioned spokes will promote rim misalignment - seek the help of a wheel building expert if this is suspected.

16 Stands, lever pivots and cables - lubrication

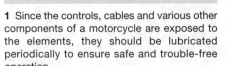

1 Since the controls, cables and various other components of a motorcycle are exposed to the elements, they should be lubricated periodically to ensure safe and trouble-free operation.
2 The footrests, clutch and brake levers, brake pedal, gearshift lever linkage and stand pivots should be lubricated frequently. In order for the lubricant to be applied where it will do the most good, the component should be disassembled. However, if chain and cable lubricant is being used, it can be applied to the pivot joint gaps and will usually work its way into the areas where friction occurs. If motor oil or light grease is being used, apply it sparingly as it may attract dirt (which could cause the controls to bind or wear at an accelerated rate). **Note:** *One of the best lubricants for the control lever pivots is a dry-film lubricant (available from many sources by different names).*
3 To lubricate the cables, disconnect the relevant cable at its upper end, then lubricate the cable with a pressure adapter, or if one is not available, using the set-up shown **(see illustrations)**. See Chapter 3 for the choke and throttle cable removal procedures, and Chapter 2 for the clutch cable.
4 The speedometer cable should be removed (see Chapter 8) and the inner cable withdrawn

from the outer cable and lubricated with motor oil or cable lubricant. Do not lubricate the upper few inches of the cable as the lubricant may travel up into the instrument head.

17 Battery - electrolyte level check (ZR550 B1, B2, B3 and B4 models only)

Caution: Be extremely careful when handling or working around the battery. The electrolyte is very caustic and an explosive gas (hydrogen) is given off when the battery is charging.

1 Remove the seat (see Chapter 7).

2 The electrolyte level is visible through the translucent battery case - it should be between the UPPER and LOWER level marks.

3 If the electrolyte is low, remove the battery (see Chapter 8), then remove the cell caps and fill each cell to the upper level mark with distilled water. Do not use tap water (except in

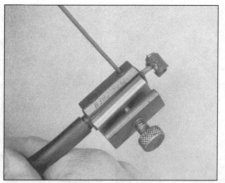

16.3a Lubricating a cable with a pressure lubricator. Make sure the tool seals around the inner cable

an emergency), and do not overfill. The cell holes are quite small, so it may help to use a clean plastic squeeze bottle with a small spout to add the water. Install the battery cell caps, tightening them securely, then install the battery.

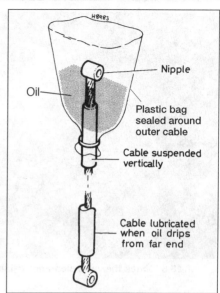

16.3b Lubricating a cable with a makeshift funnel and motor oil

Every 6000 miles (10 000 km) or 12 months - ZR550 B & ZR750 C

Every 7500 miles (12 000 km) or 12 months - ZR750 D

18 Valve clearances - check and adjustment

1 The engine must be completely cool for this maintenance procedure, so let the machine sit overnight before beginning.

2 Remove the valve cover (see Chapter 2). Unscrew the spark plugs to allow the engine to be turned over easier (see Section 3).

3 Make a chart or sketch of all four valve positions so that a note of each clearance can be made against the relevant valve.

4 Unscrew the bolts securing the pulse generator coil cover to the right-hand side crankcase cover **(see illustration)**. The

engine can be rotated using a 17 mm socket on the timing rotor hex and turning it in a clockwise direction only. Alternatively, place the motorcycle on its centre stand, select a high gear and rotate the rear wheel by hand in its normal direction of rotation.

Caution: DO NOT use the timing rotor bolt to turn the crankshaft - it may snap or strip out. Also be sure to turn the engine in its normal direction of rotation.

5 Rotate the engine until the T mark on the rotor aligns with the static timing mark on the crankcase **(see illustrations)**. At this point either no. 1 cylinder or no. 4 cylinder will be at top dead centre (TDC) on the compression stroke. Check the position of the cam lobes on no. 1 cylinder. If they are facing away from

each other, no. 1 cylinder is at TDC on the compression stroke. If the cam lobes are facing each other, the lobes on no. 4 cylinder will be facing away from each other and no. 4 is at TDC on the compression stroke.

6 With no. 1 cylinder at TDC on the compression stroke, the following valves can be checked:

a) No. 1, intake and exhaust
b) No. 2, exhaust
c) No. 3, intake

7 With no. 4 cylinder at TDC on the compression stroke, the following valves can be checked:

a) No. 2, intake
b) No. 3, exhaust
c) No. 4, intake and exhaust

1

18.4 The pulse generator assembly cover is secured by two bolts (arrowed)

18.5a Rotate the engine using a 17 mm socket on the timing rotor hex . . .

18.5b . . . so that the T mark on the rotor aligns with the static timing mark on the crankcase (arrowed)

18.8 Check the valve clearance using a feeler gauge

18.12a Lift the follower off its valve . . .

8 Insert a feeler gauge of the same thickness as the correct valve clearance (see Specifications) between the cam base and follower of each valve and check that it is a firm sliding fit - you should feel a slight drag when you pull the gauge out **(see illustration)**. If not , use the feeler gauges to obtain the exact clearance. Record the measured clearance on the chart.

9 Rotate the engine so that the timing rotor turns through 360° and the T mark is once again correctly aligned, then measure the valve clearance of the remaining valves using the method described in Step 8.

10 When all clearances have been measured and charted, identify whether the clearance on any valve falls outside that specified. If it does, the shim between the follower and the valve must be replaced with one of a thickness which will restore the correct clearance.

11 Shim replacement requires removal of the camshafts (see Chapter 2). There is no need to remove both camshafts if shims from only one side of the engine need replacing.

12 With the camshaft removed, remove the cam follower of the valve in question, then prise the shim out of the top of the valve using a small screwdriver and remove it using a pair of pliers **(see illustrations)**.

13 The shim size should be stamped on its face. A shim size of 250 denotes a thickness of 2.50 mm, 245 is 2.45 mm. It is recommended that the shim is measured to check that it has not worn **(see illustration)**. Shims are available in 0.05 mm increments from 2.00 mm to 3.20 mm.

14 Using the appropriate shim selection chart, find where the measured valve clearance and existing shim thickness values intersect and read off the shim size required **(see illustrations)**. Obtain and install the replacement shim, noting that its size marking should be installed downwards and that the shim should be lubricated with molybdenum disulphide grease - this will also hold it in

18.12b . . . then remove the shim

18.13 Measure the shim using a micrometer to confirm its size

	PRESENT SHIM Example ↓																								
PART No. (92025-)	1090	1091	1082	1093	1094	1085	1096	1087	1098	1099	1100	1101	1102	1103	1104	1105	1106	1107	1108	1109	1110	1111	1112	1113	1114
MARK	200	205	210	215	220	225	230	235	240	248	250	255	260	265	270	275	280	285	290	295	300	305	310	315	320
THICKNESS (mm)	2.00	2.05	2.10	2.15	2.20	2.25	2.30	2.35	2.40	2.45	2.50	2.55	2.60	2.65	2.70	2.75	2.80	2.85	2.90	2.95	3.00	3.05	3.10	3.15	3.20
0.00 ~ 0.03				2.00	2.00	2.05	2.10	2.15	2.20	2.25	2.30	2.35	2.40	2.45	2.50	2.55	2.60	2.65	2.70	2.75	2.80	2.85	2.90	2.95	3.00 3.05
0.04 ~ 0.07			2.00	2.00	2.05	2.10	2.15	2.20	2.25	2.30	2.35	2.40	2.45	2.50	2.55	2.60	2.65	2.70	2.75	2.80	2.85	2.90	2.95	3.00	3.05 3.10
0.08 ~ 0.18	SPECIFIED CLEARANCE / NO CHANGE REQUIRED																								
0.19 ~ 0.22	2.05	2.10	2.15	2.20	2.25	2.30	2.35	2.40	2.45	2.50	2.55	2.60	2.65	2.70	2.75	2.80	2.85	2.90	2.95	3.00	3.05	3.10	3.15	3.20	
0.23 ~ 0.27	2.10	2.15	2.20	2.25	2.30	2.35	2.40	2.45	2.50	2.55	2.60	2.65	2.70	2.75	2.80	2.85	2.90	2.95	3.00	3.05	3.10	3.15	3.20		
0.28 ~ 0.32	2.15	2.20	2.25	2.30	2.35	2.40	2.45	2.50	2.55	2.60	2.65	2.70	2.75	2.80	2.85	2.90	2.95	3.00	3.05	3.10	3.15	3.20			
0.33 ~ 0.37	2.20	2.25	2.30	2.35	2.40	2.45	2.50	2.55	2.60	2.65	2.70	2.75	2.80	2.85	2.90	2.95	3.00	3.05	3.10	3.15	3.20				
0.38 ~ 0.42	2.25	2.30	2.35	2.40	2.45	2.50	2.55	2.60	2.65	2.70	2.75	2.80	2.85	2.90	2.95	3.00	3.05	3.10	3.15	3.20					
0.43 ~ 0.47	2.30	2.35	2.40	2.45	2.50	2.55	2.60	2.65	2.70	2.75	2.80	2.85	2.90	2.95	3.00	3.05	3.10	3.15	3.20						
0.48 ~ 0.52	2.35	2.40	2.45	2.50	2.55	2.60	2.65	2.70	2.75	2.80	2.85	2.90	2.95	3.00	3.05	3.10	3.15	3.20							
0.53 ~ 0.57	2.40	2.45	2.50	2.55	2.60	2.65	2.70	2.75	2.80	2.85	2.90	2.95	3.00	3.05	3.10	3.15	3.20								
0.58 ~ 0.62	2.45	2.50	2.55	2.60	2.65	2.70	2.75	2.80	2.85	2.90	2.95	3.00	3.05	3.10	3.15	3.20									
0.63 ~ 0.67	2.50	2.55	2.60	2.65	2.70	2.75	2.80	2.85	2.90	2.95	3.00	3.05	3.10	3.15	3.20										
0.68 ~ 0.72	2.55	2.60	2.65	2.70	2.75	2.80	2.85	2.90	2.95	3.00	3.05	3.10	3.15	3.20											
0.73 ~ 0.77	2.60	2.65	2.70	2.75	2.80	2.85	2.90	2.95	3.00	3.05	3.10	3.15	3.20												
0.78 ~ 0.82	2.65	2.70	2.75	2.80	2.85	2.90	2.95	3.00	3.05	3.10	3.15	3.20													
0.83 ~ 0.87	2.70	2.75	2.80	2.85	2.90	2.95	3.00	3.05	3.10	3.15	3.20														
0.88 ~ 0.92	2.75	2.80	2.85	2.90	2.95	3.00	3.05	3.10	3.15	3.20															
0.93 ~ 0.97	2.80	2.85	2.90	2.95	3.00	3.05	3.10	3.15	3.20																
0.98 ~ 1.02	2.85	2.90	2.95	3.00	3.05	3.10	3.15	3.20																	
1.03 ~ 1.07	2.90	2.95	3.00	3.05	3.10	3.15	3.20																		
1.08 ~ 1.12	2.95	3.00	3.05	3.10	3.15	3.20																			
1.13 ~ 1.17	3.00	3.05	3.10	3.15	3.20																				
1.18 ~ 1.22	3.05	3.10	3.15	3.20																					
1.23 ~ 1.27	3.10	3.15	3.20																						
1.28 ~ 1.32	3.15	3.20																							
1.33 ~ 1.38	3.20																								

(left axis: VALVE CLEARANCE MEASUREMENT; Example →)

INSTALL THE SHIM OF THIS THICKNESS (mm)

18.14a Shim selection chart - ZR750 - intake and exhaust valves

18.14b Shim selection chart - ZR550 - intake valves

VALVE CLEARANCE (mm)	2.00	2.05	2.10	2.15	2.20	2.25	2.30	2.35	2.40	2.45	2.50	2.55	2.60	2.65	2.70	2.75	2.80	2.85	2.90	2.95	3.00	3.05	3.10	3.15	3.20
PART No. (92025-)	1090	1091	1092	1093	1094	1095	1096	1097	1098	1099	1100	1101	1102	1103	1104	1105	1106	1107	1108	1109	1110	1111	1112	1113	1114
MARK	200	205	210	215	220	225	230	235	240	245	250	255	260	265	270	275	280	285	290	295	300	305	310	315	320
0.00 ~ 0.02			2.00	2.05	2.10	2.15	2.20	2.25	2.30	2.35	2.40	2.45	2.50	2.55	2.60	2.65	2.70	2.75	2.80	2.85	2.90	2.95	3.00	3.05	
0.03 ~ 0.07		2.00	2.05	2.10	2.15	2.20	2.25	2.30	2.35	2.40	2.45	2.50	2.55	2.60	2.65	2.70	2.75	2.80	2.85	2.90	2.95	3.00	3.05	3.10	
0.08 ~ 0.09	2.00	2.05	2.10	2.15	2.20	2.25	2.30	2.35	2.40	2.45	2.50	2.55	2.60	2.65	2.70	2.75	2.80	2.85	2.90	2.95	3.00	3.05	3.10	3.15	
0.10 ~ 0.20	SPECIFIED CLEARANCE / NO CHANGE REQUIRED																								
0.21 ~ 0.22	2.05	2.10	2.15	2.20	2.25	2.30	2.35	2.40	2.45	2.50	2.55	2.60	2.65	2.70	2.75	2.80	2.85	2.90	2.95	3.00	3.05	3.10	3.15	3.20	
0.23 ~ 0.27	2.10	2.15	2.20	2.25	2.30	2.35	2.40	2.45	2.50	2.55	2.60	2.65	2.70	2.75	2.80	2.85	2.90	2.95	3.00	3.05	3.10	3.15	3.20		
0.28 ~ 0.32	2.15	2.20	2.25	2.30	2.35	2.40	2.45	2.50	2.55	2.60	2.65	2.70	2.75	2.80	2.85	2.90	2.95	3.00	3.05	3.10	3.15	3.20			
0.33 ~ 0.37	2.20	2.25	2.30	2.35	2.40	2.45	2.50	2.55	2.60	2.65	2.70	2.75	2.80	2.85	2.90	2.95	3.00	3.05	3.10	3.15	3.20				
0.38 ~ 0.42	2.25	2.30	2.35	2.40	2.45	2.50	2.55	2.60	2.65	2.70	2.75	2.80	2.85	2.90	2.95	3.00	3.05	3.10	3.15	3.20					
0.43 ~ 0.47	2.30	2.35	2.40	2.45	2.50	2.55	2.60	2.65	2.70	2.75	2.80	2.85	2.90	2.95	3.00	3.05	3.10	3.15	3.20						
0.48 ~ 0.52	2.35	2.40	2.45	2.50	2.55	2.60	2.65	2.70	2.75	2.80	2.85	2.90	2.95	3.00	3.05	3.10	3.15	3.20							
0.53 ~ 0.57	2.40	2.45	2.50	2.55	2.60	2.65	2.70	2.75	2.80	2.85	2.90	2.95	3.00	3.05	3.10	3.15	3.20								
0.58 ~ 0.62	2.45	2.50	2.55	2.60	2.65	2.70	2.75	2.80	2.85	2.90	2.95	3.00	3.05	3.10	3.15	3.20									
0.63 ~ 0.67	2.50	2.55	2.60	2.65	2.70	2.75	2.80	2.85	2.90	2.95	3.00	3.05	3.10	3.15	3.20										
0.68 ~ 0.72	2.55	2.60	2.65	2.70	2.75	2.80	2.85	2.90	2.95	3.00	3.05	3.10	3.15	3.20											
0.73 ~ 0.77	2.60	2.65	2.70	2.75	2.80	2.85	2.90	2.95	3.00	3.05	3.10	3.15	3.20												
0.78 ~ 0.82	2.65	2.70	2.75	2.80	2.85	2.90	2.95	3.00	3.05	3.10	3.15	3.20													
0.83 ~ 0.87	2.70	2.75	2.80	2.85	2.90	2.95	3.00	3.05	3.10	3.15	3.20														
0.88 ~ 0.92	2.75	2.80	2.85	2.90	2.95	3.00	3.05	3.10	3.15	3.20															
0.93 ~ 0.97	2.80	2.85	2.90	2.95	3.00	3.05	3.10	3.15	3.20																
0.98 ~ 1.02	2.85	2.90	2.95	3.00	3.05	3.10	3.15	3.20																	
1.03 ~ 1.07	2.90	2.95	3.00	3.05	3.10	3.15	3.20																		
1.08 ~ 1.12	2.95	3.00	3.05	3.10	3.15	3.20																			
1.13 ~ 1.17	3.00	3.05	3.10	3.15	3.20																				
1.18 ~ 1.22	3.05	3.10	3.15	3.20																					
1.23 ~ 1.27	3.10	3.15	3.20																						
1.28 ~ 1.32	3.15	3.20																							
1.33 ~ 1.37	3.20																								

INSTALL THE SHIM OF THIS THICKNESS (mm)

18.14c Shim selection chart - ZR550 - exhaust valves

VALVE CLEARANCE (mm)	2.00	2.05	2.10	2.15	2.20	2.25	2.30	2.35	2.40	2.45	2.50	2.55	2.60	2.65	2.70	2.75	2.80	2.85	2.90	2.95	3.00	3.05	3.10	3.15	3.20
PART No. (92025-)	1090	1091	1092	1093	1094	1095	1096	1097	1098	1099	1100	1101	1102	1103	1104	1105	1106	1107	1108	1109	1110	1111	1112	1113	1114
MARK	200	205	210	215	220	225	230	235	240	245	250	255	260	265	270	275	280	285	290	295	300	305	310	315	320
0.00 ~ 0.02				2.00	2.05	2.10	2.15	2.20	2.25	2.30	2.35	2.40	2.45	2.50	2.55	2.60	2.65	2.70	2.75	2.80	2.85	2.90	2.95	3.00	
0.03 ~ 0.07			2.00	2.05	2.10	2.15	2.20	2.25	2.30	2.35	2.40	2.45	2.50	2.55	2.60	2.65	2.70	2.75	2.80	2.85	2.90	2.95	3.00	3.05	
0.08 ~ 0.12		2.00	2.05	2.10	2.15	2.20	2.25	2.30	2.35	2.40	2.45	2.50	2.55	2.60	2.65	2.70	2.75	2.80	2.85	2.90	2.95	3.00	3.05	3.10	
0.13 ~ 0.14	2.00	2.05	2.10	2.15	2.20	2.25	2.30	2.35	2.40	2.45	2.50	2.55	2.60	2.65	2.70	2.75	2.80	2.85	2.90	2.95	3.00	3.05	3.10	3.15	
0.15 ~ 0.25	SPECIFIED CLEARANCE / NO CHANGE REQUIRED																								
0.26 ~ 0.27	2.05	2.10	2.15	2.20	2.25	2.30	2.35	2.40	2.45	2.50	2.55	2.60	2.65	2.70	2.75	2.80	2.85	2.90	2.95	3.00	3.05	3.10	3.15	3.20	
0.28 ~ 0.32	2.10	2.15	2.20	2.25	2.30	2.35	2.40	2.45	2.50	2.55	2.60	2.65	2.70	2.75	2.80	2.85	2.90	2.95	3.00	3.05	3.10	3.15	3.20		
0.33 ~ 0.37	2.15	2.20	2.25	2.30	2.35	2.40	2.45	2.50	2.55	2.60	2.65	2.70	2.75	2.80	2.85	2.90	2.95	3.00	3.05	3.10	3.15	3.20			
0.38 ~ 0.42	2.20	2.25	2.30	2.35	2.40	2.45	2.50	2.55	2.60	2.65	2.70	2.75	2.80	2.85	2.90	2.95	3.00	3.05	3.10	3.15	3.20				
0.43 ~ 0.47	2.25	2.30	2.35	2.40	2.45	2.50	2.55	2.60	2.65	2.70	2.75	2.80	2.85	2.90	2.95	3.00	3.05	3.10	3.15	3.20					
0.48 ~ 0.52	2.30	2.35	2.40	2.45	2.50	2.55	2.60	2.65	2.70	2.75	2.80	2.85	2.90	2.95	3.00	3.05	3.10	3.15	3.20						
0.53 ~ 0.57	2.35	2.40	2.45	2.50	2.55	2.60	2.65	2.70	2.75	2.80	2.85	2.90	2.95	3.00	3.05	3.10	3.15	3.20							
0.58 ~ 0.62	2.40	2.45	2.50	2.55	2.60	2.65	2.70	2.75	2.80	2.85	2.90	2.95	3.00	3.05	3.10	3.15	3.20								
0.63 ~ 0.67	2.45	2.50	2.55	2.60	2.65	2.70	2.75	2.80	2.85	2.90	2.95	3.00	3.05	3.10	3.15	3.20									
0.68 ~ 0.72	2.50	2.55	2.60	2.65	2.70	2.75	2.80	2.85	2.90	2.95	3.00	3.05	3.10	3.15	3.20										
0.73 ~ 0.77	2.55	2.60	2.65	2.70	2.75	2.80	2.85	2.90	2.95	3.00	3.05	3.10	3.15	3.20											
0.78 ~ 0.82	2.60	2.65	2.70	2.75	2.80	2.85	2.90	2.95	3.00	3.05	3.10	3.15	3.20												
0.83 ~ 0.87	2.65	2.70	2.75	2.80	2.85	2.90	2.95	3.00	3.05	3.10	3.15	3.20													
0.88 ~ 0.92	2.70	2.75	2.80	2.85	2.90	2.95	3.00	3.05	3.10	3.15	3.20														
0.93 ~ 0.97	2.75	2.80	2.85	2.90	2.95	3.00	3.05	3.10	3.15	3.20															
0.98 ~ 1.02	2.80	2.85	2.90	2.95	3.00	3.05	3.10	3.15	3.20																
1.03 ~ 1.07	2.85	2.90	2.95	3.00	3.05	3.10	3.15	3.20																	
1.08 ~ 1.12	2.90	2.95	3.00	3.05	3.10	3.15	3.20																		
1.13 ~ 1.17	2.95	3.00	3.05	3.10	3.15	3.20																			
1.18 ~ 1.22	3.00	3.05	3.10	3.15	3.20																				
1.23 ~ 1.27	3.05	3.10	3.15	3.20																					
1.28 ~ 1.32	3.10	3.15	3.20																						
1.33 ~ 1.37	3.15	3.20																							
1.38 ~ 1.45	3.20																								

INSTALL THE SHIM OF THIS THICKNESS (mm)

position on the valve while the follower and camshaft are installed.

15 Lubricate the follower with molybdenum disulphide grease and install it onto the valve. Repeat the process for any other valves which required attention, then install the camshafts (see Chapter 2).

16 Rotate the crankshaft several turns to seat the new shim(s), then re-check the clearances.

17 Install all disturbed components following the reverse of the removal sequence. Apply a smear of sealant to the crankcase joints on the pulse generator assembly cover mating surface **(see illustration)**. Install the pulse generator assembly cover using a new gasket and tighten its bolts to the torque setting specified at the beginning of this Chapter **(see illustration)**.

19 Idle speed - check and adjustment (ZR750 D)

1 The procedure for checking and adjusting the idle speed is the same as for the other models (see Section 5).

20 Carburettors - synchronisation (ZR750 D)

1 The procedure for synchronising the carburettors is the same as for the other models (see Section 6).

21 Air filter - cleaning

1 Remove the fuel tank and the tank bracket (see Chapter 3).

2 Unscrew the two screws securing the air filter cover to the filter housing **(see illustration)**. Remove the cover and withdraw the filter from the housing **(see illustrations)**.

3 Tap the filter on a hard surface to dislodge any dirt. Soak the element in a high flash-point solvent until it is clean, then if compressed air is available, use it to dry the element, directing the air from the inside out **(see illustration)**. Otherwise dry it by shaking it or leaving it in the open air for a while.

18.17a Apply a smear of sealant to the areas shown (arrowed) . . .

18.17b . . . then install the cover using a new gasket

1

21.2a Remove the two screws (arrowed) securing the cover to the air filter housing (550 model shown)

21.2b Remove the cover . . .

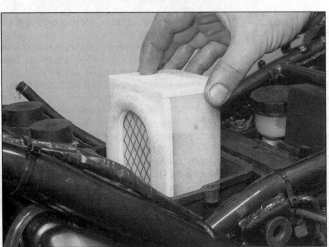

21.2c . . . and withdraw the filter

21.3 Dry the element using compressed air directed from the inside outwards

4 Check the element and its cage for signs of damage. If the element is torn or cannot be cleaned, replace it with a new one.

5 Soak the element in SE or SF grade SAE 30 oil, then wrap it in a clean rag and squeeze it as dry as possible **(see illustration)**. Install the filter by reversing the removal procedure. Press the front of the element against the housing as you fit the cover to ensure it seats correctly.

Caution: If the machine is continually ridden in dusty conditions, the filter should be cleaned more frequently.

22 Throttle and choke cable - check

Throttle cables

1 Make sure the throttle grip rotates easily from fully closed to fully open with the front wheel turned at various angles. The grip should return automatically from fully open to fully closed when released.

2 If the throttle sticks, this is probably due to a cable fault. Remove the cables (refer to Chapter 3) and lubricate them (Section 16). Install the cables, making sure they are correctly routed. If this fails to improve the operation of the throttle, the cables must be replaced. Note that in very rare cases the fault could lie in the carburettors rather than the cables, necessitating the removal of the carburettors and inspection of the throttle linkage (see Chapter 3).

3 With the throttle operating smoothly, check the freeplay in the twistgrip and compare with the amount specified **(see illustration)**. If the

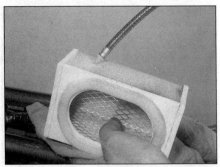

21.5 Apply oil to the element, then squeeze it out

22.3 Throttle cable freeplay is measured in terms of twistgrip rotation

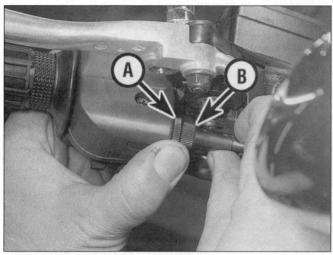

22.4 Throttle accelerator cable adjuster locknut (A), adjuster (B)

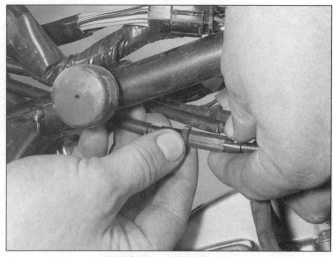

22.8 Choke cable adjuster

amount of freeplay is incorrect, adjust the cables to correct it.

4 Freeplay adjustments can be made at the throttle end of the cables. Loosen the locknut on the accelerator cable where it leaves the handlebar **(see illustration)**. Turn the adjuster until the specified amount of freeplay is obtained (see this Chapter's Specifications), then retighten the locknut.

5 If the cable can't be adjusted to within specifications, screw the adjuster all the way in, then remove the fuel tank for access to the cable lower adjusters at the carburettor end. Adjust the in-line adjusters in the accelerator and decelerator cables using the same procedure. If the cables still can't be adjusted to within specifications, replace them (see Chapter 3).

 Warning: Turn the handlebars all the way through their travel with the engine idling. Idle speed should not change. If it does, the cable may be routed incorrectly. Correct this condition before riding the bike.

6 Check that the throttle twistgrip operates smoothly and snaps shut quickly when released.

Choke cable

7 If the choke does not operate smoothly this is probably due to a cable fault. Remove the cable (see Chapter 3) and lubricate it (see Section 16). Install the cable, routing it so it takes the smoothest route possible.

8 Check for a small amount of freeplay (see Specifications) in the cable before the plungers in the carburettors move. If adjustment is necessary, remove the fuel tank, then use the adjuster in the middle of the cable, using the method described in Step 4 above for the throttle cables **(see illustration)**. If this fails to improve the operation of the choke, the cable must be replaced. Note that in very rare cases the fault could lie in the carburettors rather than the cable,

necessitating the removal of the carburettors and inspection of the choke plungers (see Chapter 3).

23 Engine - oil and oil filter change

 Warning: Be careful when draining the oil, as the exhaust pipes, the engine, and the oil itself can cause severe burns.

1 Consistent routine oil and filter changes are the single most important maintenance procedure you can perform on a motorcycle. The oil not only lubricates the internal parts of the engine, transmission and clutch, but it also acts as a coolant, a cleaner, a sealant, and a protectant. Because of these demands, the oil takes a terrific amount of abuse and should be replaced often with new oil of the recommended grade and type. Saving a little money on the difference in cost between a good oil and a cheap oil won't pay off if the engine is damaged. The oil filter should be changed with every second oil change.

2 Before changing the oil, warm up the engine so the oil will drain easily.

3 Put the motorcycle on its centre stand (where fitted), or support it upright using an auxiliary stand, and position a clean drain tray below the engine. Unscrew the oil filler cap on the clutch cover to vent the crankcase and to act as a reminder that there is no oil in the engine **(see illustration 9.3)**.

4 Next, unscrew the oil drain plug from the bottom of the engine and allow the oil to flow into the drain tray **(see illustration 9.4)**. Discard the sealing washer on the drain plug as it should be replaced whenever the plug is removed.

5 When the oil has completely drained, fit a new sealing washer over the drain plug. Fit the plug to the sump and tighten it to the torque setting specified at the beginning of the Chapter **(see illustration 9.5)** - avoid overtightening, as damage to the sump will result.

6 Now place the drain tray below the oil filter. Unscrew the oil filter cover bolt and drop the filter assembly out of the engine **(see illustrations)**. Twist the filter out of its seat and off its bolt, then remove the washer and spring **(see illustration)**. If the washer is not on top of the spring, it will be stuck to the underside of the filter. Make sure you retrieve it before discarding the filter. Withdraw the

1

23.6a Unscrew the oil filter cover bolt (arrowed) . . .

23.6b . . . and withdraw the filter assembly

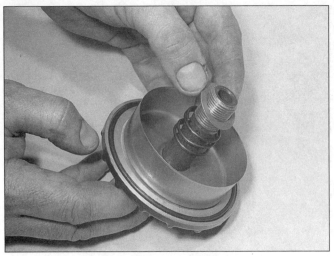

23.6c Remove the washer and spring from the bolt

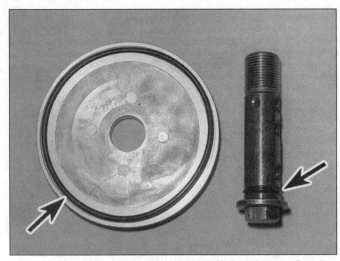

23.6d Check the cover and cover bolt O-rings (arrowed) and replace them if necessary

bolt from the cover and check the condition of its O-ring. Also check the cover O-ring, and replace them if they are damaged or deteriorated (see illustration).

7 Install the filter bolt through the cover and the filter seat, then fit the spring and the washer onto the bolt, then install the new filter using a twisting motion, making sure the rubber grommets in the filter remain in place (see illustration). Install the filter assembly into the engine and tighten the bolt to the specified torque setting (see illustration).

8 Refill the crankcase to the proper level using the recommended type and amount of oil (see *Daily (pre-ride) checks*). With the motorcycle held vertical, the oil level should lie between the upper and lower marks (550 models) or H and L lines (750 models) on the inspection window in the clutch cover (see *Daily (pre-ride) checks*). Install the filler cap. Start the engine and let it run for two or three minutes (make sure that the oil pressure light

extinguishes after a few seconds). Shut it off, wait a few minutes, then check the oil level. If necessary, add more oil to bring the level up to the high level line on the inspection window. Check around the drain plug and the oil filter cover for leaks.

9 The old oil drained from the engine cannot be re-used and should be disposed of properly. Check with your local refuse disposal company, disposal facility or environmental agency to see whether they will accept the used oil for recycling. Don't pour used oil into drains or onto the ground.

---

24 Fuel system - check

⚠️ *Warning: Petrol (gasoline) is extremely flammable, so make sure you take extra precautions when you work on any part of*

the fuel system. Don't smoke or allow open flames or bare light bulbs near the work area, and don't work in a garage where a natural gas-type appliance is present. If you spill any fuel on your skin, rinse it off immediately with soap and water. When you perform any kind of work on the fuel system, it is advisable to wear safety glasses and to have a fire extinguisher suitable for a Class B type fire (flammable liquids) on hand.

Check

1 Remove the fuel tank (see Chapter 3) and check the tank, the fuel tap, and the fuel hoses for signs of leakage, deterioration or damage; in particular check that there is no leakage from the fuel hoses. Replace any hoses which are cracked or deteriorated.

2 If the fuel tap is leaking, remove the tap and tighten the assembly screws on the back of the tap (see Chapter 3). If leakage persists

23.7a Assemble the components as shown . . .

23.7b . . . then install the assembly and tighten the bolt to the specified torque setting

remove the screws and disassemble the tap, noting how the components fit. Inspect all components for wear or damage. If any of the components are worn or damaged, check if they can be purchased separately - in certain cases, it may be necessary to purchase a new tap.

3 If the carburettor gaskets are leaking, the carburettors should be disassembled and rebuilt using new gaskets and seals (see Chapter 3).

Filter cleaning

4 Cleaning or replacement of the fuel filter is advised after a particularly high mileage has been covered. It is also necessary if fuel starvation is suspected.

5 The fuel filter is mounted in the tank and is integral with the fuel tap. Remove the fuel tank and the fuel tap (see Chapter 3). Clean the gauze filter to remove all traces of dirt and fuel sediment. Check the gauze for holes. If any are found, a new filter should be fitted (check for availability - it may be necessary to replace the whole tap). Check the condition of the O-ring and replace it if it is in any way damaged or deteriorated.

25 Cylinder head nuts - tightness check (ZR550 B and ZR750 C)

1 Kawasaki recommend that the cylinder head nuts are checked to ensure they are tightened to their correct torque settings. The engine must be completely cool for these maintenance procedures, so let the machine sit overnight before beginning.

2 Remove the valve cover (see Chapter 2).

3 On 550 models, the cylinder head is secured by twelve 8 mm domed nuts with plain washers and five 6 mm bolts, and the cylinder block by three 6 mm nuts. First slacken the bolts and nuts on the front and back of the cylinder head and block (see illustrations). The twelve domed nuts are numbered for identification (see illustration). Slacken the nuts evenly and a little at a time in a reverse of their numerical sequence until they are all slack. Using a torque wrench, now tighten the domed nuts evenly and a little at a time in numerical sequence to the torque setting specified at the beginning of the Chapter. When the nuts are correctly torqued,

tighten the bolts at the front and back of the cylinder head and the nuts at the front and back of the cylinder block to the specified torque setting.

4 On 750 models, the cylinder head is secured by twelve 10 mm domed nuts with plain washers and two 8 mm bolts, which are located inside the cam chain tunnel, one at the front and one at the back. The nuts and bolts are numbered for identification (see illustration). Slacken them evenly and a little at a time in a reverse of their numerical sequence until they are all slack. Using a torque wrench, now tighten the nuts evenly and a little at a time in numerical sequence to the torque settings specified at the beginning of the Chapter, noting that the 8 mm bolts have a lower setting than the 10 mm nuts.

5 Install the valve cover (see Chapter 2).

26 Suspension - checks

1 The suspension components must be maintained in top operating condition to

25.3a Remove the cylinder head front bolts (A) and cylinder block nut (B) . . .

25.3b . . . and the cylinder head rear bolts (A) and cylinder block nuts (B)

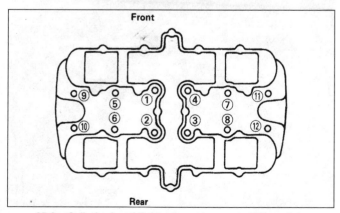

25.3c Cylinder head tightening sequence - 550 models

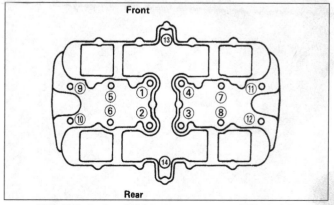

25.4 Cylinder head tightening sequence - 750 models

ensure rider safety. Loose, worn or damaged suspension parts decrease the motorcycle's stability and control.

Front suspension

2 While standing alongside the motorcycle, apply the front brake and push on the handlebars to compress the forks several times. See if they move up-and-down smoothly without binding. If binding is felt, the forks should be disassembled and inspected (see Chapter 5).

3 Inspect the area above the dust seal for signs of oil leakage, then carefully lever up the dust seal using a flat-bladed screwdriver and inspect the area around the fork seal **(see illustrations)**. If leakage is evident, the seal must be replaced (see Chapter 5).

4 Check the tightness of all suspension nuts and bolts to be sure none have worked loose.

Rear suspension

5 Inspect the rear shocks for fluid leakage and tightness of their mountings. If leakage is found, the shock should be replaced (see Chapter 5).

6 With the aid of an assistant to support the bike, compress the rear suspension several times. It should move up and down freely without binding. If any binding is felt, the worn or faulty component must be identified and replaced. The problem could be due to either the shock absorber or the swingarm components.

7 Position the motorcycle on its centre stand (where fitted), or support it using an auxiliary stand so that the rear wheel is off the ground. Grab the swingarm and rock it from side to side - there should be no discernible movement at the rear **(see illustration)**. If there's a little movement or a slight clicking can be heard, inspect the tightness of all the rear suspension mounting bolts and nuts, referring to the torque settings specified at the beginning of the Chapter, and re-check for movement. Next, grasp the top of the rear wheel and pull it upwards - there should be no discernible freeplay before the shock absorber

begins to compress **(see illustration)**. Any freeplay felt in either check indicates worn bearings in the swingarm, or worn shock absorber mountings. The worn components must be replaced (see Chapter 5).

8 To make an accurate assessment of the swingarm bearings, remove the rear wheel (see Chapter 6) and the shock absorbers (see Chapter 5). Grasp the rear of the swingarm with one hand and place your other hand at the junction of the swingarm and the frame. Try to move the rear of the swingarm from side-to-side. Any wear (play) in the bearings should be felt as movement between the swingarm and the frame at the front. If there is any play the swingarm will be felt to move forward and backward at the front (not from side-to-side). Next, move the swingarm up and down through its full travel. It should move freely, without any binding or rough spots. If any play in the swingarm is noted or if the swingarm does not move freely, the bearings must be removed for inspection or replacement (see Chapter 5).

26.3a **Lever up the dust seal . . .**

26.3b **. . . and check for signs of oil leakage**

26.7a **Checking for play . . .**

26.7b **. . . in the rear suspension**

27.1a Swingarm grease nipple - 750 models

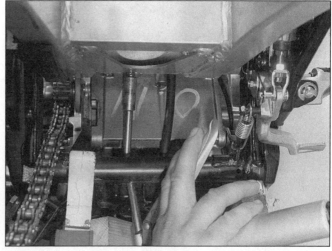

27.1b Applying grease to the 550 swingarm using a grease gun

27 Swingarm pivot and bearing - lubrication

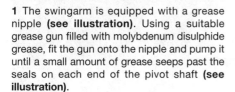

1 The swingarm is equipped with a grease nipple **(see illustration)**. Using a suitable grease gun filled with molybdenum disulphide grease, fit the gun onto the nipple and pump it until a small amount of grease seeps past the seals on each end of the pivot shaft **(see illustration)**.

28 Nuts and bolts - tightness check

1 Since vibration of the machine tends to loosen fasteners, all nuts, bolts, screws, etc. should be periodically checked for proper tightness.
2 Pay particular attention to the following:
   Spark plugs
   Engine oil drain plug and oil filter bolt
   Gearshift pedal bolt
   Footrest and stand bolts
   Engine mounting bolts
   Shock absorber mounting bolts
   Handlebar bolts
   Front axle and axle clamp bolts
   Front fork clamp bolts -
   (top and bottom yoke)
   Rear axle nut
   Swingarm pivot nut
   Brake caliper mounting bolts
   Brake hose banjo bolts and caliper bleed valves
   Brake disc bolts and rear sprocket nuts
   Exhaust system bolts/nuts

3 If a torque wrench is available, use it along with the torque specifications at the beginning of this, or other, Chapters.

Every 12 000 miles (20 000 km) or 2 years - ZR550 B & ZR750 C

Every 15 000 miles (24 000 km) or 2 years - ZR750 D

1

29 Air filter - replacement

1 Remove the old air filter as described in Section 21 and install a new one.

30 Brake fluid - change

1 The brake fluid should be replaced at the prescribed interval or whenever a master cylinder or caliper overhaul is carried out. Refer to the brake bleeding section in Chapter 6, noting that all old fluid must be pumped from the fluid reservoir and hydraulic line before filling with new fluid.

HAYNES HiNT *Old brake fluid is invariably much darker in colour than new fluid, making it easy to see when all old fluid has been expelled from the system.*

31 Steering head bearings - lubrication

1 Disassemble the steering head for re-greasing of the bearings. Refer to Chapter 5 for details.

32 Front forks - oil change (ZR750 D)

1 Fork oil degrades over a period of time, and will lose its damping qualities. The forks fitted to these machines are equipped with drain plugs, so that they do not have to be removed from the yokes to effect an oil change. Place the machine on its centre stand (if fitted) or else support it in an upright position using an auxiliary stand. Raise the front wheel off the ground using a jack and a block of wood under the engine. To be on the safe side, it is advisable to remove the fuel tank (see Chapter 3) to prevent the possibility of damage should a tool slip.

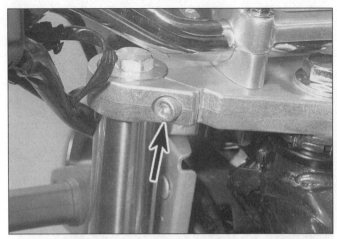

32.2a Slacken the fork clamp bolt (arrowed)

32.2b With the handlebars displaced, unscrew the fork top bolt

32.3 Remove the fork drain screw and allow all the oil to drain

32.5a Withdraw the spacer . . .

32.5b . . . the spring seat and the spring from the fork

32.6a Pour in the specified amount and type of oil . . .

32.6b . . . then measure the level of oil in the fork

2 Slacken, but do not remove, the fork clamp bolts in the top yoke **(see illustration)**. Displace the handlebars for access to the fork top bolts (see Chapter 5), then remove the top bolts **(see illustration)**.

 Slackening the fork clamp bolts in the top yoke before slackening the fork top bolts releases pressure on the top bolt. This makes it much easier to remove and helps to preserve the threads.

3 Place a suitable container under the drain screw of the fork being drained, then remove the screw and allow all the oil to drain **(see illustration)**. Pump the forks up and down to help expel all the oil; bear in mind that it could squirt out forcibly. Discard the drain screw sealing washer - a new one must be used.
4 When all the oil has drained, clean the drain screw threads and apply a suitable non-permanent thread locking compound to them. Install the screw using a new sealing washer and tighten it to the torque setting specified at the beginning of the Chapter.

5 Withdraw the spacer, spring seat and the spring from the tube, noting which way up they fit **(see illustrations)**. Compress the forks if necessary to access the components.
6 Slowly pour in the specified quantity of the specified grade of fork oil and pump the fork to distribute it evenly **(see illustration)**; the oil level should also be measured and adjustment made by adding or subtracting oil. Fully compress the fork and measure the fork oil level from the top of the tube **(see illustration)**. Add or subtract fork oil until the oil is at the level given in the Specifications.

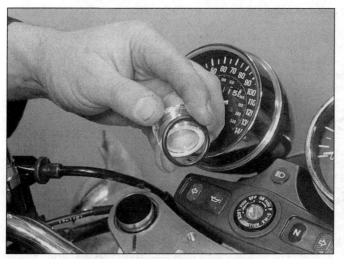

32.8a Fit a new O-ring onto the top bolt . . .

32.8b . . . and tighten it to the specified torque setting

7 Install the spring, followed by the spring seat and the spacer **(see illustrations 32.5b and a)**.

8 Fit a new O-ring to the fork top bolt and thread the bolt into the top of the fork tube **(see illustration)**. Screw the top bolt carefully into the fork tube making sure it is not cross-threaded, and tighten it to the specified torque setting **(see illustration)**. Also tighten the fork clamp bolts in the top yoke to the specified torque setting.

 Warning: *It will be necessary to compress the spring by pressing down on the spacer using the top bolt to engage the threads of the bolt with the fork tube. This is a potentially dangerous operation and should be performed with care, using an assistant if necessary. Wipe off any excess oil before starting to prevent the possibility of slipping.*

9 Install the handlebars (see Chapter 5) and the fuel tank (see Chapter 3).

TOOL TiP *Use a ratchet-type tool when installing the fork top bolt. This makes it unnecessary to remove the tool from the bolt whilst threading it in making it easier to maintain a downward pressure on the spring.*

Every 18 000 miles (30 000 km) or two years - ZR550 B & ZR750 C

 1

33 Front forks - oil change (ZR750 B and ZR750 C)

1 The procedure for changing the front fork oil is the same as for the other models (see Section 32).

Every two or four years - see schedule

34 Brake calipers and master cylinders - seal replacement

This task must be carried out every two years on ZR550 B and ZR750 C models, and every four years on ZR750 D models.
1 Refer to Chapter 6 and dismantle the components for seal replacement.

35 Brake hoses - replacement

This task must be carried out every four years.
1 The hoses should be replaced regardless of their condition.
2 Refer to Chapter 6 and disconnect the brake hoses from the master cylinders and calipers. Always replace the banjo union sealing washers with new ones.

36 Fuel hose - replacement

This task must be carried out every four years.
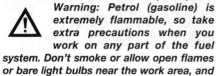 **Warning:** *Petrol (gasoline) is extremely flammable, so take extra precautions when you work on any part of the fuel system. Don't smoke or allow open flames or bare light bulbs near the work area, and*

don't work in a garage where a natural gas-type appliance is present. If you spill any fuel on your skin, rinse it off immediately with soap and water. When you perform any kind of work on the fuel system, it is advisable to wear safety glasses and have a fire extinguisher suitable for a Class B type fire (flammable liquids) on hand.

1 The hoses should be replaced regardless of their condition.

2 Remove the fuel tank (see Chapter 3). Disconnect the fuel hoses from the fuel tap and from the carburettors, noting the routing of each hose and where it connects (see Chapter 3 if required). It is advisable to make a sketch of the various hoses before removing them to ensure they are correctly installed.

3 Secure each new hose to its unions using new clamps. Run the engine and check for leaks before taking the bike out on the road.

Non-scheduled maintenance

37 Headlight aim - check and adjustment

Note: *An improperly adjusted headlight may cause problems for oncoming traffic or provide poor, unsafe illumination of the road ahead. Before adjusting the headlight aim, be sure to consult with local traffic laws and regulations - for UK models refer to MOT Test Checks in the Reference section.*

1 The headlight beam can adjusted both horizontally and vertically. Before making any adjustment, check that the tyre pressures are correct and the suspension is adjusted as required. Make any adjustments to the headlight aim with the machine on level ground, with the fuel tank half full and with an assistant sitting on the seat. If the bike is usually ridden with a passenger on the back, have a second assistant to do this.

2 Horizontal adjustment is made by turning the adjuster screw in the right-hand side of the headlight rim **(see illustration)**. Turn it clockwise to move the beam to the right, and anti-clockwise to move it to the left.

3 Vertical adjustment is made by turning the adjuster screw in the base of the headlight **(see illustration)**. Turn it clockwise to move the beam up, and anti-clockwise to move it down.

38 Wheel bearings - check

1 Place the motorcycle on its centre stand (where fitted) or support it upright using an auxiliary stand. Check for any play in the bearings by pushing and pulling the wheel against the hub. Also rotate the wheel and check that it rotates smoothly. If any play is detectable in the hub, or if the wheel does not rotate smoothly (and this is not due to brake or transmission drag), the wheel bearings must be removed and inspected for wear or damage (see Chapter 6).

39 Engine - cylinder compression check

1 Among other things, poor engine performance may be caused by leaking valves, incorrect valve clearances, a leaking head gasket, or worn pistons, rings and/or cylinder walls. A cylinder compression check will help pinpoint these conditions and can also indicate the presence of excessive carbon deposits in the cylinder heads.

2 The only tools required are a compression gauge and a spark plug wrench. A compression gauge with a threaded end for the spark plug hole is preferable to the type which requires hand pressure to maintain a tight seal. Depending on the outcome of the initial test, a squirt-type oil can may also be needed.

3 Make sure the valve clearances are correctly set (see Section 18) and that the cylinder head nuts are tightened to the correct torque setting (see Section 25).

4 Refer to *Fault Finding Equipment* in the Reference section for details of the compression test.

40 Engine - oil pressure check

1 To check the oil pressure, a suitable gauge and adapter piece (which screws into the crankcase) will be needed. Kawasaki provide a kit (part nos. 57001-164 and 57001-1278) for this purpose.

2 Warm the engine up to normal operating temperature then stop it.

3 Unscrew the oil gallery plug below the pulse generator assembly cover and swiftly screw the adapter into the crankcase threads **(see illustration)**. Connect the gauge to the adapter.

4 Start the engine and increase the engine speed to 4000 rpm whilst watching the gauge reading. The oil pressure should be similar to that given in the Specifications at the start of this Chapter.

5 If the pressure is significantly lower than the standard, either the pressure regulator is stuck open, the oil pump is faulty, the oil strainer or filter is blocked, or there is other engine damage. Begin diagnosis by checking the oil filter, strainer and regulator, then the oil pump (see Chapter 2). If those items check out okay, chances are the bearing oil clearances are excessive and the engine needs to be overhauled.

6 If the pressure is too high, either an oil passage is clogged, the regulator is stuck closed or the wrong grade of oil is being used.

7 Stop the engine and unscrew the gauge and adapter from the crankcase.

8 Install the oil gallery plug, and tighten it to the torque setting specified at the beginning of the Chapter. Check the oil level (see *Daily (pre-ride) checks*).

37.2 Headlight beam horizontal adjuster screw (arrowed)

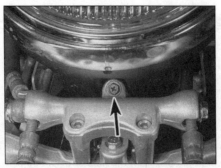

37.3 Headlight beam vertical adjuster screw (arrowed)

40.3 Remove the oil gallery plug (arrowed) and install the pressure gauge

Chapter 2
Engine, clutch and transmission

Contents

Degrees of difficulty

Easy, suitable for novice with little experience	**Fairly easy,** suitable for beginner with some experience	**Fairly difficult,** suitable for competent DIY mechanic	**Difficult,** suitable for experienced DIY mechanic	**Very difficult,** suitable for expert DIY or professional

Specifications

ZR550 models

General

Type	Four-stroke DOHC in-line four
Capacity	553 cc
Bore	58.0 mm
Stroke	52.4 mm
Compression ratio	9.5 to 1
Clutch	Wet multi-plate
Transmission	Six-speed constant mesh
Final drive	Chain and sprockets

Cylinder head

Warpage (max)	0.05 mm

Cylinder block

Bore	
Standard	58.000 to 58.012 mm
Wear limit (max)	58.10 mm
Cylinder compression	see Chapter 1

ZR550 models (continued)

Camshafts

	Standard	Service limit
Intake camshaft lobe height	36.23 to 36.37 mm	36.1 mm (min)
Exhaust camshaft lobe height	36.23 to 36.37 mm	36.1 mm (min)
Journal diameter	21.900 to 21.922 mm	21.87 mm (min)
Journal holder diameter	22.000 to 22.021 mm	22.08 mm (max)
Journal oil clearance	0.078 to 0.121 mm	0.21 mm (max)
Runout (max)	0.10 mm	
Camchain 21 pin length (see text)	127.0 to 127.4 mm	128.9 mm

Valves, guides and springs

Valve clearances	see Chapter 1	
Intake valve	**Standard**	**Service limit**
Stem diameter	5.475 to 5.490 mm	5.46 mm (min)
Guide bore diameter	5.500 to 5.512 mm	5.58 mm (max)
Stem-to-guide clearance	0.010 to 0.037 mm	0.12 mm (max)
Stem deflection (see text)	0.02 to 0.09 mm	0.24 mm (max)
Face thickness	0.85 to 1.15 mm	0.6 mm (min)
Seat width	0.5 to 1.0 mm	
Seat diameter	26.9 to 27.1 mm	
Stem runout	0.05 mm (max)	
Exhaust valve		
Stem diameter	5.455 to 5.470 mm	5.44 mm (min)
Guide bore diameter	5.500 to 5.512 mm	5.58 mm (max)
Stem-to-guide clearance	0.030 to 0.057 mm	0.14 mm (max)
Stem deflection (see text)	0.07 to 0.13 mm	0.28 mm (max)
Face thickness	0.85 to 1.15 mm	0.7 mm (min)
Seat width	0.5 to 1.0 mm	
Seat diameter	22.9 to 23.1 mm	
Stem runout (max)	0.05 mm	
Valve springs free length (intake and exhaust)		
Original parts		
Inner spring	36.7 mm	35.1 mm (min)
Outer spring	38.7 mm	37.1 mm (min)
Replacement parts		
Inner spring	37.25 mm	35.8 mm (min)
Outer spring	41.85 mm	40.2 mm (min)

Pistons

Piston diameter (measured 5.0 mm up from skirt, at 90° to piston pin axis)		
Standard	57.965 to 57.980 mm	
Service limit (min)	57.82 mm	
Piston-to-bore clearance	0.020 to 0.047 mm	
1st oversize	+ 0.5 mm	
2nd oversize	+ 1.0 mm	

Piston rings

	Standard	Service limit
End gap (installed)		
Top ring and 2nd ring	0.15 to 0.30 mm	0.60 mm (max)
Oil ring	0.20 to 0.70 mm	1.0 mm (max)
Piston ring thickness - top ring and 2nd ring	1.175 to 1.190 mm	1.1 mm (min)
Piston ring groove width		
Top ring	1.21 to 1.23 mm	1.31 mm (max)
2nd ring	1.23 to 1.25 mm	1.33 mm (max)
Ring-to-groove clearance		
Top ring	0.020 to 0.055 mm	0.16 mm (max)
2nd ring	0.040 to 0.075 mm	0.18 mm (max)
1st oversize	+ 0.5 mm	
2nd oversize	+ 1.0 mm	

Clutch

Friction plate	
Quantity	7
Thickness	
Standard	2.9 to 3.1 mm
Service limit (min)	2.8 mm
Warpage (max)	0.3 mm
Plain plate	
Quantity	6
Warpage (max)	0.3 mm

ZR550 models (continued)

Clutch (continued)

Spring free length
  Standard . . . . 32.6 mm
  Service limit (min) . . . . 31.7 mm

Transmission

Gear ratios (No. of teeth)
  Primary reduction . . . . 2.934 to 1 (27/23T x 65/26T)
  Final reduction
    UK models . . . . 2.375 to 1 (38/16T)
    US models . . . . 2.562 to 1 (41/16T)
  1st gear . . . . 2.571 to 1 (36/14T)
  2nd gear . . . . 1.777 to 1 (32/18T)
  3rd gear . . . . 1.380 to 1 (29/21T)
  4th gear . . . . 1.125 to 1 (27/24T)
  5th gear . . . . 0.961 to 1 (25/26T)
  6th gear . . . . 0.851 to 1 (23/27T)

Selector drum and forks

	Standard	Service limit
Selector fork-to-groove clearance	0.05 to 0.25 mm	0.45 mm (max)
Selector fork end thickness	4.9 to 5.0 mm	4.8 mm (min)
Selector fork groove width	5.05 to 5.15 mm	5.25 mm (max)
Selector fork guide pin diameter		
Input shaft	7.985 to 8.000 mm	7.9 mm (min)
Output shaft	7.9 to 8.0 mm	7.8 mm (min)
Selector drum groove width	8.05 to 8.20 mm	8.3 mm (max)

Crankshaft and bearings

	Standard	Service limit
Journal diameter	31.984 to 32.000 mm	31.96 mm (min)
Main bearing oil clearance	0.014 to 0.038 mm	0.08 mm
Runout (max)	0.05 mm (max)	
Side clearance	0.05 to 0.20 mm	0.40 mm
Primary chain slack	0 to 5 mm	25 mm

Connecting rods

	Standard	Service limit
Big-end side clearance	0.13 to 0.33 mm	0.5 mm (max)
Crankpin diameter	32.984 to 33.000 mm	32.97 mm (min)
Big-end oil clearance	0.035 to 0.059 mm	0.10 mm (max)

Lubrication system

Oil pressure . . . . see Chapter 1

Torque settings

Engine mounting bolts and nuts . . . . 39 Nm
Engine mounting bracket bolts . . . . 23 Nm
Pulse generator assembly cover bolts . . . . 10 Nm
Oil cooler hose union nuts . . . . 22 Nm
Oil cooler hose union bolts . . . . 8.8 Nm
Valve cover bolts . . . . 12 Nm
Cam chain tensioner mounting bolts . . . . 12 Nm
Cam chain tensioner cap bolt . . . . 5 Nm
Cam chain tensioner blade pivot bracket bolts . . . . 12 Nm
Camshaft cap bolts . . . . 12 Nm
Camshaft sprocket bolts . . . . 15 Nm
Cylinder head 8 mm nuts . . . . 25 Nm
Cylinder head 6 mm bolts . . . . 12 Nm
Cylinder block 6 mm nuts . . . . 9.8 Nm
Clutch nut . . . . 130 Nm
Clutch pressure plate bolts . . . . 8.8 Nm
Gearchange shaft centralising spring locating pin . . . . 20 Nm
Gearchange mechanism cover bolts . . . . 10 Nm
Starter clutch Allen bolts . . . . 34 Nm
Secondary shaft nut . . . . 59 Nm
Oil pressure regulator . . . . 15 Nm
Oil sump bolts . . . . 10 Nm
Crankcase 6 mm bolts . . . . 12 Nm
Crankcase 8 mm bolts . . . . 29 Nm
Connecting rod cap nuts . . . . 24 Nm

ZR750 models

General

Type	Four-stroke DOHC in-line four
Capacity	738 cc
Bore	66.0 mm
Stroke	54.0 mm
Compression ratio	9.5 to 1
Clutch	Wet multi-plate
Transmission	Five-speed constant mesh
Final drive	Chain and sprockets

Camshafts

	Standard	Service limit
Intake camshaft lobe height	36.245 to 36.353 mm	36.15 mm (min)
Exhaust camshaft lobe height	36.245 to 36.353 mm	36.15 mm (min)
Journal diameter	21.940 to 22.040 mm	21.91 mm (min)
Journal holder diameter	22.060 to 22.081 mm	22.14 mm (max)
Journal oil clearance	0.100 to 0.141 mm	0.23 mm (max)
Runout (max)	0.10 mm	
Camchain 21 pin length (see text)	127.0 to 127.36 mm	128.9 mm

Cylinder head

Warpage (max)	0.05 mm

Valves, guides and springs

	Standard	Service limit
Valve clearances	see Chapter 1	
Intake valve		
Stem diameter	6.95 to 6.97 mm	6.94 mm (min)
Guide bore diameter	7.000 to 7.015 mm	7.08 mm (max)
Stem-to-guide clearance	0.030 to 0.065 mm	0.14 mm (max)
Stem deflection (see text)	0.07 to 0.15 mm	0.30 mm (max)
Head thickness	0.80 to 1.20 mm	0.5 mm (min)
Seat width	0.5 to 1.0 mm	
Seat diameter	32.9 to 33.1 mm	
Stem runout (max)	0.05 mm	
Exhaust valve		
Stem diameter	6.95 to 6.97 mm	6.94 mm (min)
Guide bore diameter	7.000 to 7.015 mm	7.08 mm (max)
Stem-to-guide clearance	0.030 to 0.065 mm	0.14 mm (max)
Stem deflection (see text)	0.06 to 0.14 mm	0.28 mm (max)
Head thickness	0.80 to 1.20 mm	0.7 mm (min)
Seat width	0.5 to 1.0 mm	
Seat diameter	28.9 to 29.1 mm	
Stem runout (max)	0.05 mm	
Valve springs free length (intake and exhaust)		
Inner spring	37.25 mm	35.9 mm (min)
Outer spring	41.85 mm	40.3 mm (min)

Cylinder block

Bore	
Standard	66.005 to 66.017 mm
Wear limit (max)	66.10 mm
Cylinder compression	see Chapter 1

Pistons

Piston diameter (measured 5.0 mm up from skirt, at 90° to piston pin axis)	
Standard	65.951 to 65.966 mm
Service limit (min)	65.81 mm
Piston-to-bore clearance	0.039 to 0.066 mm
1st oversize	+ 0.5 mm
2nd oversize	+ 1.0 mm

Piston rings

	Standard	Service limit
End gap (installed)		
Top ring and 2nd ring	0.20 to 0.40 mm	0.70 mm (max)
Piston ring thickness		
Top ring	0.970 to 0.990 mm	0.90 mm (min)
2nd ring	1.170 to 1.190 mm	1.10 mm (min)

ZR750 models (continued)

Piston rings (continued)	Standard	Service limit
Piston ring groove width		
Top ring	1.02 to 1.04 mm	1.12 mm (max)
2nd ring	1.21 to 1.23 mm	1.31 mm (max)
Ring-to-groove clearance		
Top ring	0.030 to 0.070 mm	0.17 mm (max)
2nd ring	0.020 to 0.060 mm	0.16 mm (max)
1st oversize	+ 0.5 mm	
2nd oversize	+ 1.0 mm	

Clutch

Friction plate - C1, C2, C3 and C4 models
- Quantity 7
- Thickness
  - Standard . . . . 2.65 to 2.95 mm
  - Service limit (min) . . . . 2.5 mm
- Warpage (max) . . . . 0.3 mm

Friction plate - C5 and D1 models
- Type A plate
  - Quantity 2
  - Thickness . . . . not available
  - Warpage (max) . . . . 0.3 mm
- Type B plate
  - Quantity 5
  - Thickness . . . . not available
  - Warpage (max) . . . . 0.3 mm

Plain plate
- Quantity 6
- Warpage (max) . . . . 0.3 mm

Spring free length
- Standard . . . . 33.6 mm
- Service limit (min) . . . . 32.6 mm

Transmission

Gear ratios (No. of teeth)
- Primary reduction . . . . 2.550 to 1 (27/23T x 63/29T)
- Final reduction . . . . 2.600 to 1 (39/15T)
- 1st gear . . . . 2.333 to 1 (35/15T)
- 2nd gear . . . . 1.631 to 1 (31/19T)
- 3rd gear . . . . 1.272 to 1 (28/22T)
- 4th gear . . . . 1.040 to 1 (26/25T)
- 5th gear . . . . 0.875 to 1 (21/24T)

Selector drum and forks	Standard	Service limit
Selector fork-to-groove clearance	0.05 to 0.25 mm	0.45 mm (max)
Selector fork end thickness	4.9 to 5.0 mm	4.8 mm (min)
Selector fork groove width	5.05 to 5.15 mm	5.25 mm (max)
Selector fork guide pin diameter		
Input shaft fork	7.985 to 8.000 mm	7.9 mm (min)
Output shaft forks	7.9 to 8.0 mm	7.8 mm (min)
Selector drum groove width	8.05 to 8.20 mm	8.3 mm (max)

Crankshaft and bearings	Standard	Service limit
Journal diameter	35.984 to 36.000 mm	35.96 mm (min)
Main bearing oil clearance	0.020 to 0.044 mm	0.08 mm (max)
Runout (max)	0.05 mm	
Side clearance	0.05 to 0.15 mm	0.35 mm
Primary chain slack	0 to 5 mm	25 mm

Connecting rods	Standard	Service limit
Big-end side clearance	0.15 to 0.30 mm	0.48 mm (max)
Crankpin diameter	34.984 to 35.000 mm	34.97 mm (min)
Big-end oil clearance	0.036 to 0.066 mm	0.10 mm (max)

Lubrication system

Oil pressure . . . . see Chapter 1

2

ZR750 models (continued)

Torque settings

Engine mounting bolts and nuts	39 Nm
Engine mounting bracket bolts	23 Nm
Pulse generator assembly cover bolts	10 Nm
Oil cooler hose union nuts	22 Nm
Oil cooler hose union bolts	8.8 Nm
Valve cover bolts	12 Nm
Cam chain tensioner plunger bolt	10 Nm
Cam chain tensioner mounting bolts	10 Nm
Cam chain tensioner cap bolt	26 Nm
Camshaft cap bolts	12 Nm
Camshaft sprocket bolts	15 Nm
Cylinder head 10 mm nuts	39 Nm
Cylinder head 8 mm bolts	29 Nm
Clutch nut	130 Nm
Clutch pressure plate bolts	8.8 Nm
Gearchange shaft centralising spring locating pin	20 Nm
Gearchange mechanism cover bolts	10 Nm
Starter clutch Allen bolts	34 Nm
Secondary shaft nut	59 Nm
Oil pressure regulator	15 Nm
Oil sump bolts	10 Nm
Crankcase 6 mm bolts	12 Nm
Crankcase 8 mm bolts	29 Nm
Connecting rod cap nuts	36 Nm
Selector drum cam plunger bolt	25 Nm
Selector drum guide bolt	25 Nm

1 General information

The engine/transmission unit is an air-cooled in-line four. The valves (two per cylinder) are operated by double overhead camshafts which are chain driven off the crankshaft. The engine/transmission assembly is constructed from aluminium alloy. The crankcase is divided horizontally.

The crankcase incorporates a wet sump, pressure-fed lubrication system which uses a gear-driven, dual-rotor oil pump, an oil filter and by-pass valve assembly, a relief valve and an oil pressure switch.

Power from the crankshaft is transmitted via a Hy-Vo primary chain to the secondary shaft which runs behind the crankshaft. The secondary shaft carries the starter clutch assembly and provides gear drive to the clutch, which is of the wet, multi-plate type. From the clutch, power is transmitted directly to the input shaft of the transmission, which is a six-speed (550 models) or five-speed (750 models) constant-mesh unit.

2 Operations possible with the engine in the frame

The components and assemblies listed below can be removed without having to remove the engine/transmission assembly from the frame. If however, a number of areas require attention at the same time, removal of the engine is recommended.

Valve cover
Cam chain tensioner & cam chain guides
Camshafts
Cylinder head
Cylinder block, pistons and piston rings
Ignition rotor and pulse generator coil
Clutch
Gearchange mechanism (external parts)
Alternator
Starter clutch and idle gear
Engine sprocket
Oil sump, oil pump, oil strainer and oil pressure relief valve
Starter clutch
Starter motor

3 Operations requiring engine removal

It is necessary to remove the engine/transmission assembly from the frame and separate the crankcase halves to gain access to the following components.

Transmission shafts
Selector drum and forks
Crankshaft and bearings
Connecting rod big-ends and bearings
Cam chain
Primary chain

4 Major engine repair - general note

1 It is not always easy to determine when or if an engine should be completely overhauled, as there are a number of factors to be considered.

2 High mileage is not necessarily an indication that an overhaul is needed, while low mileage, on the other hand, does not preclude the need for an overhaul. Frequency of servicing is probably the single most important factor. An engine that has regular and frequent oil and filter changes, and other required maintenance, will most likely give many miles of reliable service. Conversely, a neglected engine, or one which has not been run in properly, may require an overhaul very early in its life.

3 Exhaust smoke and excessive oil consumption are both indications that piston rings and/or valve guides are in need of attention, although make sure that the fault is not due to oil leakage.

4 If the engine is making obvious knocking or rumbling noises, the connecting rod and/or main bearings are probably at fault.

5 Loss of power, rough running, excessive valve train noise and high fuel consumption rates may also point to the need for an overhaul, especially if they are all present at the same time. If a complete tune-up does not remedy the situation, major mechanical work is the only solution.

6 An engine overhaul generally involves restoring the internal parts to the specifications of a new engine. The piston rings and main and connecting rod bearings are usually replaced and the cylinder walls honed or, if necessary, re-bored during a major overhaul. Generally the valve seats are re-ground, since they are usually in less than perfect condition at this point. The end result should be a like new engine that will give as many trouble-free miles as the original.

5.5 Disconnect the negative lead wire at the connector

5.10 Make alignment marks then remove the bolt (arrowed) and slide the arm off the shaft

7 Before starting the engine overhaul, read through the related procedures to familiarise yourself with the scope and requirements of the job. Overhauling an engine is not all that difficult, but it is time consuming. Plan on the bike being tied up for a minimum of two weeks. Check on the availability of parts and make sure that any necessary special tools, equipment and supplies are obtained in advance.

8 Most work can be done with typical workshop hand tools, although some precision measuring tools are required for inspecting parts to determine if they must be replaced. Often a dealer will handle the inspection of parts and offer advice on reconditioning and replacement. As a general rule, time is the primary cost of an overhaul so it does not pay to install worn or substandard parts.

9 As a final note, to ensure maximum life and minimum trouble from a rebuilt engine, everything must be assembled with care in a spotlessly clean environment.

5 Engine -
removal and installation

Note: *The engine is very heavy. Engine removal and installation should be carried out with the aid of at least one assistant; personal injury or damage could occur if the engine falls or is dropped. A hydraulic or mechanical floor jack should be used to support and lower or raise the engine if possible.*

Removal

1 Position the bike on its centre stand or support it securely in an upright position using an auxiliary stand. Work can be made easier by raising the machine to a suitable working height on a hydraulic ramp or a suitable platform.

2 If the engine is dirty, particularly around its mountings, wash it thoroughly before starting

any major dismantling work. This will make work much easier and rule out the possibility of caked on lumps of dirt falling into some vital component.

3 Drain the engine oil and, if required, remove the oil filter (see Chapter 1).

4 Remove the seat and the side panels (see Chapter 7).

5 Disconnect the battery negative (-) lead (see Chapter 8). Trace the black/yellow wire connected to the battery negative lead and disconnect it at its connector **(see illustration)**. Feed the lead through to the engine and coil it on the crankcase, noting its routing.

6 Remove the fuel tank (see Chapter 3).

7 Remove the carburettors (see Chapter 3). Plug the engine intake manifolds with clean rag.

8 Disconnect all the spark plug leads from the plugs and secure them clear of the engine. If the leads are not already marked, make a note of the cylinder number for each lead.

9 On US models, release the air suction valve hose clamps and detach the hoses from their unions. Remove the valve with the hoses attached, noting the routing of each hose.

10 Unscrew the gearchange lever linkage arm pinch bolt and remove the arm from the shaft, noting any alignment marks **(see illustration)**. If no marks are visible, make

your own before removing the arm so that it can be correctly aligned with the shaft on installation.

11 Remove the front sprocket cover and the front sprocket (see Chapter 5).

12 Remove the clutch cable (see Section 19).

13 On 550 models, unscrew the two bolts securing the starter motor top cover and lift off the cover **(see illustration)**. Slacken the starter motor upper mounting bolt, then remove the lower cover **(see illustration)**.

14 Pull back the rubber cover on the starter motor terminal and disconnect the lead **(see illustration)**.

5.13a On 550 models, remove the starter motor top cover . . .

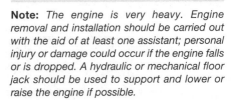

5.13b . . . and the starter motor lower cover

5.14 Pull back the rubber cover and disconnect the starter motor lead

2

5.15a The pulse generator cover assembly is secured by two bolts (arrowed)

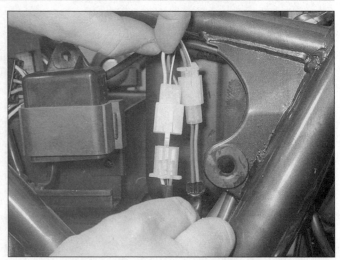

5.15b The pulse generator wiring connector is behind the right-hand side panel on 750 models

5.15c Oil pressure switch wiring connector (arrowed) - 550 models

5.16 Alternator wire connectors (A) - 550 models (750 models have a single block connector), sidestand switch wire connector (B), neutral switch wire connector (C)

15 Remove the ignition pulse generator coil assembly cover **(see illustration)**, then, on 750 models, disconnect the oil pressure switch wiring. Trace the ignition pulse generator wiring back and disconnect it at the ignition control unit (550 models - remove the unit for access to the connectors (refer to Chapter 4) or at the connector behind the right-hand side panel (750 models) **(see illustration)**. Release the wiring from any clips or ties, noting its routing, and coil it on top of the crankcase so that it does not impede engine removal. On 550 models, disconnect the oil pressure switch wiring from the switch on the left-hand side of the sump **(see illustration)**.

16 Trace the alternator wiring back from the alternator cover and disconnect it at the connector(s) **(see illustration)**. Release the wiring from any clips or ties, noting its routing. Also disconnect the sidestand switch wiring at

the connector and pull the neutral switch wiring connector off the switch.

17 Remove the ignition HT coils (refer to Chapter 4).

18 Remove the exhaust system (refer to Chapter 3).

19 Remove the oil cooler and hoses (see Section 7). Also remove the horn if required for improved clearance and access when removing the engine (see Chapter 8).

20 At this point, position an hydraulic or mechanical jack under the engine with a block of wood between the jack head and sump. Make sure that the jack is centrally positioned so that the engine will not topple in any direction when the last mounting bolt is removed. Take the weight of the engine on the jack.

21 Remove the engine front mounting nuts and bolts, then remove the nuts and bolts securing the right-hand front engine mounting

bracket to the frame downtube and remove the bracket, noting how it fits **(see illustrations)**.

22 Make sure that the engine is properly supported on the jack, and have an assistant

5.21a Engine front mounting bolt (A), mounting bracket bolts (B)

5.21b The bolts are secured by nuts on the inside

5.22b Rear mounting bracket bolts (arrowed) - 550 models

5.22a Engine rear mounting bolts (arrowed)

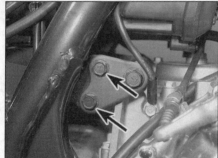

5.22c Rear mounting bracket bolts (arrowed) - 750 models

support it as well. Remove the nuts on the left-hand end of the lower and upper rear engine mounting bolts, then withdraw the bolts **(see illustration)**. Remove the bolts securing the right-hand rear engine mounting bracket to the frame and remove the bracket, noting how it fits **(see illustrations)**.

23 The engine can now be removed from the frame. Check that all wiring, cables and hoses are well clear, then manoeuvre the engine out of the right-hand side of the frame.

24 Check the condition of the front mounting bracket rubber dampers and replace them if they are damaged or deteriorated. Lubricate the new dampers with a soapy solution to aid installation.

Installation

25 Installation is the reverse of removal, noting the following points:

a) Make sure no wires, cables or hoses become trapped between the engine and the frame when installing the engine.

b) The engine mounting bolts are of different lengths. Make sure the correct bolt is installed in its correct location.

c) Install the rear engine mounting bolts from the right-hand side. The longer bolt is for the upper rear mounting, and the shorter for the lower rear mounting.

d) Do not fully tighten any of the bolts until they have all been installed. Make sure the brackets are correctly positioned.

e) Tighten the engine mounting bolt nuts, the mounting bracket bolt nuts and any other bolts and nuts to the torque settings specified at the beginning of the Chapter.

f) Use new gaskets on the exhaust pipe connections.

g) Align the marks made on the gearchange lever linkage arm and shaft when installing the arm onto the shaft, and tighten the pinch bolt securely.

h) Make sure all wires, cables and hoses are correctly routed and connected, and secured by any clips or ties.

i) Refill the engine with oil (see Chapter 1).

j) Adjust the drive chain freeplay (see Chapter 1).

k) Adjust the throttle cable freeplay, the clutch freeplay and the idle speed (see Chapter 1).

6 Engine disassembly and reassembly - general information

Disassembly

1 Before disassembling the engine, the external surfaces of the unit should be thoroughly cleaned and degreased. This will prevent contamination of the engine internals, and will also make working a lot easier and cleaner. A high flash-point solvent, such as paraffin (kerosene) can be used, or better still, a proprietary engine degreaser. Use old paintbrushes and toothbrushes to work the solvent into the various recesses of the engine casings. Take care to exclude solvent or water from the electrical components and intake and exhaust ports.

 Warning: The use of petrol (gasoline) as a cleaning agent should be avoided because of the risk of fire.

2 When clean and dry, arrange the unit on the workbench, leaving suitable clear area for working. Gather a selection of small containers and plastic bags so that parts can be grouped together in an easily identifiable manner. Some paper and a pen should be on hand to permit notes to be made and labels attached where necessary. A supply of clean rag is also required.

3 Before commencing work, read through the appropriate section so that some idea of the necessary procedure can be gained. When removing various engine components it should be noted that great force is seldom required, unless specified. In many cases, a component's reluctance to be removed is indicative of an incorrect approach or removal method. If in any doubt, re-check with the text.

4 An engine support stand made from short lengths of 2 x 4 bolted together into a rectangle will help support the engine **(see illustration)**. The perimeter of the mount should be just big enough to accommodate the sump within it so that the engine rests on its crankcase.

5 When disassembling the engine, keep "mated" parts together (including gears, cylinders, pistons, connecting rods, valves, etc. that have been in contact with each other during engine operation). These "mated" parts must be reused or replaced as an assembly.

6 Engine/transmission disassembly should be done in the following general order with reference to the appropriate Sections.

Remove the valve cover
Remove the cam chain tensioner and cam chain guide blades
Remove the camshafts
Remove the cylinder head
Remove the cylinder block
Remove the pistons
Remove the ignition rotor and pulse generator coil assembly (see Chapter 4)
Remove the clutch
Remove the gearchange mechanism external components
Remove the starter clutch and idle gear
Remove the alternator (see Chapter 8)
Remove the starter motor (see Chapter 8)

2

6.4 An engine support made from pieces of 2 x 4 inch wood

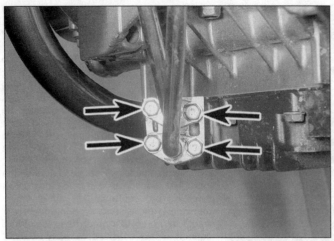

7.2a Each union is secured to the sump by two bolts (arrowed)

7.2b Separate the hose from the cooler by unscrewing the nut (arrowed)

7.3 The cooler is secured by three bolts (arrowed)

8.6 Note the locations of the different valve cover bolts as you remove them

Remove the oil sump
Remove the oil pump
Separate the crankcase halves
Remove the crankshaft and connecting rods
Remove the transmission shafts/gears
Remove the selector drum and forks

Reassembly

7 Reassembly is accomplished by reversing the general disassembly sequence.

7 Oil cooler and hoses - removal and installation

Note: *The oil cooler and its hoses can be removed with the engine in the frame.*

Removal

1 Drain the engine oil (see Chapter 1).
2 Unscrew the bolts securing each oil cooler hose union to the oil sump **(see illustration)**. Discard the O-rings as new ones must be

used. If required, unscrew the nut securing each hose union to the bottom of the cooler and detach the hoses **(see illustration)**. Discard the O-rings as new ones must be used.
3 Unscrew the three bolts securing the cooler to the frame, then carefully remove the cooler **(see illustration)**.

Installation

4 Installation is the reverse of removal. Always use new O-rings when installing the hoses. Tighten the hose union nuts and bolts to the torque settings specified at the beginning of the Chapter.

8 Valve cover - removal and installation

Note: *The valve cover can be removed with the engine in the frame. If the engine has been removed, ignore the steps which do not apply.*

Removal

1 Remove the seat and the side panels (see Chapter 7) and disconnect the battery negative (-) lead.
2 Remove the fuel tank (see Chapter 3).
3 On US models, release the air suction valve hose clamps and detach the hoses from their unions. Remove the valve with the hoses attached, noting the routing of each hose.
4 Disconnect the spark plug leads from the plugs and secure them clear of the engine. If the leads are not already marked, label each lead with its cylinder number.
5 Remove the ignition HT coils (Chapter 4). On 750 models, remove the horn (Chapter 8).
6 Unscrew the valve cover bolts and remove them, noting the positions of the different types of bolt **(see illustration)**.
7 Lift the valve cover off the cylinder head. If it is stuck, do not try to lever it off with a screwdriver; tap it gently around the sides with a rubber hammer or block of wood to dislodge it. Remove the gasket and the camshaft end plugs.

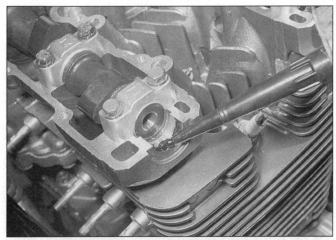

8.9a Apply a sealant to the cut-outs . . .

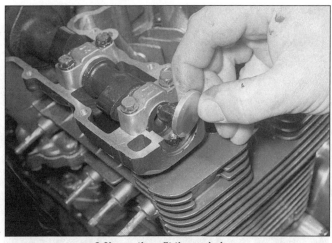

8.9b . . . then fit the end plugs

8.10 Lay a new gasket onto the cylinder head . . .

8.11 . . . then install the valve cover with the arrow facing forward

Installation

8 Examine the valve cover gasket and camshaft end plugs for signs of damage or deterioration and replace them if necessary. On 750 models, Kawasaki recommend that they are replaced as a matter of course.

9 Clean the mating surfaces of the cylinder head and the valve cover with lacquer thinner, acetone or brake system cleaner. Apply a silicone sealant to the cut-outs where the camshaft end plugs fit, then install the plugs with the flattened inner section facing up **(see illustrations)**.

10 Lay the gasket onto the cylinder head, making sure all the bolt holes align **(see illustration)**. On 750 models the tab on the gasket must be on the left-hand front portion of the cylinder head.

11 Position the valve cover on the cylinder head with the arrow on its raised centre section facing forward, making sure the gasket stays in place and the cover locates correctly **(see illustration)**. Install the cover bolts and tighten them to the specified torque.

12 Install the remaining components in the reverse order of removal.

9 Cam chain tensioner - removal, inspection and installation

Note: *The cam chain tensioner can be removed with the engine in the frame. If the engine has been removed, ignore the steps that don't apply.*

ZR550 B1 and B2 to frame no. 064686

Caution: Once you start to remove the tensioner bolts, you must remove the tensioner all the way and reset it before tightening the bolts. The tensioner extends itself and locks in place, so if you loosen the bolts partway and then retighten them, the tensioner or cam chain will be damaged. Do not rotate the crankshaft once the tensioner has been removed.

Removal

1 Remove the carburettors (see Chapter 3).

2 Slacken the tensioner cap bolt, then unscrew the two tensioner mounting bolts and withdraw the tensioner from the back of the cylinder block.

3 Remove the O-ring from the base of the tensioner or from the cylinder block and discard it as a new one must be used.

Inspection

4 Examine the tensioner components for signs of wear or damage.

5 Remove the tensioner cap bolt. Discard the O-ring as a new one must be used. Using a flat-bladed screwdriver, turn the slotted end of the tensioner clockwise to release the tension and allow the plunger to retract into the tensioner body. Remove the screwdriver and check that the tensioner plunger springs back out of the tensioner body.

6 If the tensioner is worn or damaged, or if the plunger is seized in the body or the spring mechanism broken, the tensioner must be replaced. The internal components of the tensioner are not available individually.

Installation

7 Fit a new O-ring onto the tensioner body.

2

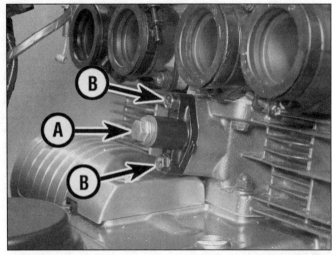

9.13 Tensioner spring cap bolt (A), tensioner mounting bolts (B)

9.14 Use the tab (arrowed) as a leverage point if necessary

8 If not already done, remove the tensioner cap bolt. Discard the O-ring as a new one must be used. Using a flat-bladed screwdriver, turn the slotted end of the tensioner clockwise to release the tension and allow the plunger to retract fully into the tensioner body. Keep the screwdriver located in the slotted end of the tensioner to prevent the plunger springing back out.

9 With the screwdriver still located, fit the tensioner into the cylinder block and install the tensioner mounting bolts. Tighten the bolts to the torque setting specified at the beginning of the Chapter.

10 Remove the screwdriver from the end of the tensioner. As the slotted end turns itself back, the tensioner automatically sets itself to the correct tension against the cam chain. It is advisable to remove the valve cover (see Section 8) and check that the cam chain is tensioned. If this is not the case, remove the pulse generator assembly cover and turn the crankshaft clockwise using a 17 mm socket on the timing rotor hex **(see illustrations 11.2a and b).**
Caution: DO NOT use the timing rotor bolt to turn the crankshaft - it may snap or strip out. Also be sure to turn the engine in its normal direction of rotation.
Set the rotor so that the T mark aligns with the static timing mark on the crankcase. If this does not cure the problem, remove the tensioner and check that it has been correctly installed. Also check that the valve timing marks are all correctly aligned (refer to Section 11).

11 Fit a new O-ring onto the tensioner cap bolt and tighten it to the specified torque.

12 Apply a smear of sealant to the crankcase joints on the pulse generator assembly cover mating surface **(see illustration 9.24a).** Install the pulse generator assembly cover using a new gasket and tighten its bolts to the specified torque setting **(see illustration 9.24b).** If removed, install the valve cover (see Section 8).

ZR550 B2 from frame no. 064687, B3, B4, B5 and B6
Caution: Once you start to remove the tensioner bolts, you must remove the tensioner all the way and reset it before tightening the bolts. The tensioner extends itself and locks in place, so if you loosen the bolts partway and then retighten them, the tensioner or cam chain will be damaged.

Removal
13 Unscrew the tensioner spring cap bolt and withdraw the spring from the tensioner body **(see illustration).**
14 Unscrew the two tensioner mounting bolts and withdraw the tensioner from the back of the cylinder block **(see illustration 9.13).** If it is difficult to remove, there is a little tab on the right-hand side of the tensioner which can be used as a leverage point **(see illustration).**
15 Remove the gasket from the base of the tensioner or from the cylinder block and discard it as a new one must be used.

Inspection
16 Examine the tensioner components for signs of wear or damage.
17 Release the ratchet mechanism from the tensioner plunger and check that the plunger

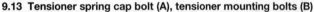

moves freely in and out of the tensioner body **(see illustrations 9.20a and b).**
18 If the tensioner or any of its components are worn or damaged, or if the plunger is seized in the body, the tensioner assembly must be replaced. Individual components are not available.

Installation
19 Unscrew the bolts securing the pulse generator assembly cover to the right-hand side of the engine **(see illustration 11.2a).** Turn the crankshaft in a clockwise direction with a 17 mm socket on the timing rotor hex **(see illustration 11.2b).** Alternatively, place the motorcycle on its centre stand (where fitted) or support it using an auxiliary stand so that the rear wheel is off the ground, then select a high gear and rotate the rear wheel by hand in its normal direction of rotation. This removes all the slack between the crankshaft and the camshaft in the front run of the chain and transfers it to the back run where it will be taken up by the tensioner.
Caution: DO NOT use the timing rotor bolt to turn the crankshaft - it may snap or strip out. Also be sure to turn the engine in its normal direction of rotation.
20 Release the ratchet mechanism and press the tensioner plunger all the way into the tensioner body **(see illustrations).**

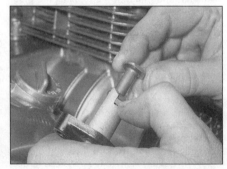

9.20a Release the ratchet (arrowed) . . .

9.20b . . . and press the plunger into the tensioner

9.21a Fit a new gasket on the tensioner . . .

9.21b . . . then install it with the arrow pointing up

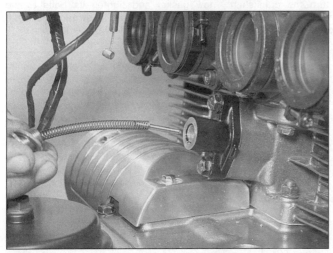

9.22 Install the spring into the tensioner and tighten the cap bolt to the specified torque setting

9.24a Apply sealant to the areas shown (arrowed) . . .

21 Place a new gasket on the tensioner body, then install it in the engine, making sure the arrow on the left-hand side of the tensioner faces up (see illustrations). Tighten the mounting bolts to the torque setting specified at the beginning of the Chapter.

22 Install a new sealing washer on the spring cap bolt. Install the spring and cap bolt and tighten the bolt to the specified torque setting (see illustration).

23 It is advisable to remove the valve cover (see Section 8) and check that the cam chain is tensioned. If it is slack, the tensioner piston did not release.

24 Apply a smear of sealant to the crankcase joints on the pulse generator assembly cover mating surface (see illustration). Install the pulse generator assembly cover using a new gasket and tighten its bolts to the specified torque setting (see illustration). If removed, install the valve cover (see Section 8).

ZR750

Caution: Once you start to remove the tensioner bolts, you must remove the

9.24b . . . then fit the cover using a new gasket

tensioner all the way and reset it before tightening the bolts. The tensioner extends itself and locks in place, so if you loosen the bolts partway and then retighten them, the tensioner or cam chain will be damaged. Do not rotate the crankshaft once the tensioner has been removed.

Removal

25 Remove the starter motor (see Chapter 8).

9.26 Unscrew the cap bolt and withdraw the spring and stopper

26 Unscrew the tensioner cap bolt from the side of the tensioner body and withdraw the stopper spring and stopper (see illustration).

27 Unscrew the two tensioner mounting bolts and withdraw the tensioner from the back of the cylinder block (see illustration 9.33).

28 Remove the gasket from the base of the tensioner or from the cylinder block and discard it as a new one must be used.

2

Inspection

29 Keeping your thumb on the plunger to prevent it from springing out, unscrew the plunger bolt from the side of the tensioner body **(see illustration)**. Remove the bolt and release the plunger, then remove it along with the plunger spring. Check that the plunger moves freely in and out of the tensioner body. If it does not, clean all components with solvent and apply molybdenum disulphide grease to all moving parts.

30 Examine the tensioner components for signs of wear or damage **(see illustration)**.

31 If the tensioner or any of its components are worn or damaged, or if the plunger is seized in the body, they must be replaced. Individual components are available.

Installation

32 Install the plunger spring and plunger into the tensioner, aligning the slot in the plunger with the plunger bolt hole **(see illustration)**. Press the plunger into the tensioner and install the plunger bolt and its washer, making sure the bolt end locates in the slot in the plunger **(see illustration 9.29)**. Tighten the bolt to the torque setting specified at the beginning of the Chapter.

33 Place a new gasket on the tensioner body, then install the tensioner, making sure the longer bolt is installed uppermost and with its aluminium washer **(see illustration)**. Tighten the mounting bolts gradually and evenly to the torque setting specified at the beginning of the Chapter.

34 Install the stopper into the tensioner with its tapered face up, making sure it fits against the tapered face of the plunger **(see illustration 9.26)**. The end of the stopper should protrude about 10 mm from the tensioner. If the stopper sticks out too far the tension has not been taken up by the plunger. If this is the case, remove the pulse generator assembly cover and turn the crankshaft clockwise using a 17 mm socket on the timing rotor hex **(see illustration 11.2a and b)**.

Caution: DO NOT use the timing rotor bolt to turn the crankshaft - it may snap or strip out. Also be sure to turn the engine in its normal direction of rotation.

Set the rotor so that the T mark aligns with the static timing mark on the crankcase. If this does not cure the problem, remove the tensioner and check that it has been correctly assembled. With the stopper correctly installed, install the spring and cap bolt with its washer **(see illustration 9.26)**. Tighten the cap bolt to the specified torque setting.

35 It is advisable to remove the valve cover (see Section 8) and check that the cam chain is tensioned and that the valve timing marks are all correctly aligned (see Section 11).

36 Apply a smear of sealant to the crankcase joints on the pulse generator assembly cover mating surface **(see illustration 9.24a)**. Install the pulse generator assembly cover using a new gasket and tighten its bolts to the specified torque **(see illustration 9.24b)**. If removed, install the valve cover (Section 8).

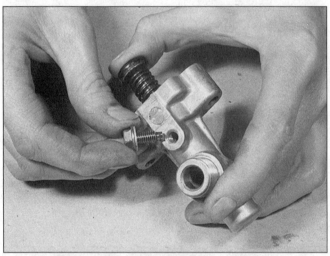

9.29 **Remove the plunger bolt and release the plunger**

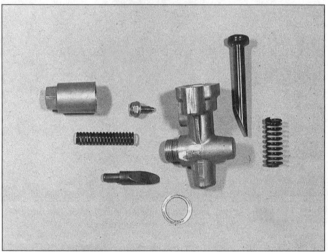

9.30 **Tensioner components - 750 models**

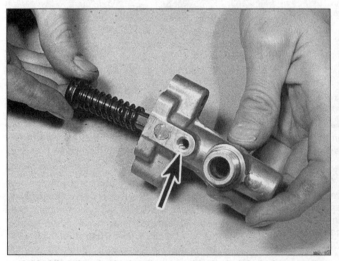

9.32 **Align the slot in the plunger with the bolt hole (arrowed)**

9.33 **Install the tensioner with the longer bolt and aluminium washer uppermost**

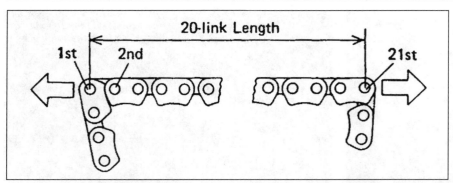

10.3 Measure the cam chain as shown to determine stretch

10.9 Fit the guide blade into the tunnel sideways and twist it round

10 Cam chain and blades - removal, inspection and installation

Note: *To remove the cam chain the engine must be removed from the frame and the crankcases separated. The tensioner blade and guide blade can be removed with the engine in the frame.*

Cam chain

Removal

1 Separate the crankcase halves (Section 24) and remove the crankshaft (see Section 27).
2 Slip the cam chain off the crankshaft.

Inspection

3 Pull the chain tight to remove any slack, then measure the length of 21 pins (from the centre of the 1st pin to the centre of the 21st pin) and compare the result with the service limit specified at the beginning of the Chapter **(see illustration)**. Take several measurements at different places in case the chain has worn unevenly. If any measurement exceeds the service limit, the chain must be replaced. If the chain is replaced, also replace the camshaft sprockets (see Section 11). The sprocket on the crankshaft should also be checked (see Section 27).

Installation

4 Slip the cam chain onto its sprocket on the crankshaft, making sure it is properly engaged.
5 Install the crankshaft (see Section 27).

Cam chain guide blade

Removal

6 Remove the cylinder head (see Section 12).
7 Lift the blade out of the front of the cam chain tunnel in the cylinder block, noting which way round it fits and how it locates.

Inspection

8 Examine the sliding surface of the guide for signs of wear or damage, and replace it if necessary.

Installation

9 Install the blade into the front of the cam chain tunnel in the cylinder block, making sure the sliding surface faces inwards and that it seats correctly in the cut-outs. On 550 models, install the blade sideways into the block and twist it round when it is in position **(see illustration)**.
10 Install the cylinder head (see Section 12).

Cam chain tensioner blade

Removal

11 Remove the cylinder block (Section 15).
12 On 550 models, remove the two bolts securing the tensioner blade pivot bracket to the crankcase and remove the blade, noting which way round it fits. If required, push out the pivot pin and separate the blade and the bracket.
13 On 750 models, lift the cam chain tensioner blade out of its cut-outs in the crankcase, noting which way round it fits **(see illustration 10.16)**. Take care not to lose the rubber dampers and pivot shaft which fits into the end of the blade.

Inspection

14 Examine the sliding surface of the tensioner blade for signs of wear or damage, and replace it if necessary. Check the condition of the pivot hardware and replace any components that are damaged or deteriorated.

Installation

15 On 550 models, if removed, install the bracket onto the end of the blade and slide the pin through to secure it. Install the blade onto the crankcase, making sure the sliding surface faces inwards, and tighten the bolts to the torque setting specified at the beginning of the Chapter.
16 On 750 models, if removed, install the pivot shaft into the blade so that the flat ends face up. Fit the rubber dampers with the UP mark facing up onto the flat ends and secure them with some adhesive. Install the blade into the crankcase, making sure the sliding surface faces inwards and the shaft ends locate in their cut-outs **(see illustration)**.
17 Install the cylinder block (see Section 15).

11 Camshafts and followers - removal, inspection and installation

Note: *The camshafts and followers can be removed with the engine in the frame.*

Removal

1 Remove the valve cover (see Section 8).
2 Unscrew the bolts securing the pulse generator coil cover to the right-hand side of the engine **(see illustration)**. The engine can be rotated by using a 17 mm socket on the timing rotor hex and turning it in a clockwise direction only **(see illustration)**.
Caution: DO NOT use the timing rotor bolt to turn the crankshaft - it may snap or strip out. Also be sure to turn the engine in its normal direction of rotation.
Alternatively, place the motorcycle on its centre stand (where fitted) or support it using an auxiliary stand so that the rear wheel is off the ground, then select a high gear and rotate the rear wheel by hand in its normal

10.16 Fit the tensioner blade into the crankcase as shown

11.2a The pulse generator assembly cover is secured by two bolts (arrowed)

2

11.2b Rotate the engine using a 17 mm socket on the timing rotor hex

11.2c Align the mark next to the T with the index mark (arrowed)

direction of rotation. Rotate the engine until the T mark on the rotor is aligned with the static timing mark on the crankcase **(see illustration)**, and so that the Z5EX (550 models) or Z7EX (750 models) mark on the exhaust camshaft sprocket points at the valve cover gasket mating surface on the front of the cylinder head **(see illustrations 11.24a and b)**. Check the positions of all the marks on the exhaust and intake sprockets. This is how they should be positioned for installation later. On 550 models, as the camshafts are identical, make an EX mark on the exhaust camshaft and an IN mark on the intake camshaft (or use tags or labels) so they can be readily identified for installation. On 750 models, the exhaust camshaft has a raised section to the right of the sprocket mounting flange. It is essential the shafts do not get mixed up.

3 Remove the cam chain tensioner (see Section 9).

4 Before disturbing the camshaft caps, check for the identification number on each cap which corresponds to the number marked close to it on the cylinder head **(see illustration)**. Also note the arrow on each cap which points to the front of the engine. These markings ensure that the caps can be matched up to their original journals on installation. If no markings are visible, mark your own using a suitable felt pen. If necessary, make a sketch of the layout as an aid for installation.

5 Unscrew the cap bolts for one of the camshafts, evenly and a little at a time and in a reverse of the tightening sequence **(see illustration 11.26b)**, until they are all loose, then unscrew the cap bolts for the other camshaft. Remove the bolts and lift off the camshaft caps. Retrieve the dowels from either the cap or the cylinder head if they are loose **(see illustration 11.26a)**.

Caution: If the bearing cap bolts aren't loosened evenly, the camshaft may bind.

6 Pull up on the cam chain and carefully guide one camshaft out. With the chain still held taut, remove the other camshaft.

7 While the camshafts are out, don't allow the chain to go slack - the chain may drop down and bind between the crankshaft and case, which could damage these components. Wire the chain to another component to prevent it from dropping. Also, cover the top of the cylinder head with a rag to prevent foreign objects from falling into the engine.

8 Obtain a container which is divided into eight compartments, and label each compartment with the location of its

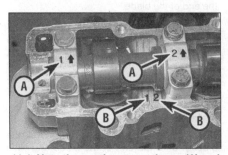

11.4 Note the number on each cap (A) and the corresponding number on the cylinder head (B). Arrow on each cap faces forward

11.8b ... and the shim from each valve

corresponding valve in the cylinder head and whether it belongs with an intake or an exhaust valve. Pick each follower and shim out of the cylinder head and store them in the corresponding compartment in the container **(see illustrations)**.

Inspection

9 Inspect the bearing surfaces of the head and the bearing caps and the corresponding journals on the camshaft. Look for score marks, deep scratches or for any evidence of spalling (a pitted appearance) **(see illustration)**.

11.8a Remove the follower ...

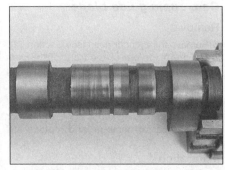

11.9 Check the journal surfaces of the camshaft for scratches or wear

11.10a Check the lobes of the camshaft for wear - here's an example of damage requiring camshaft repair or renewal

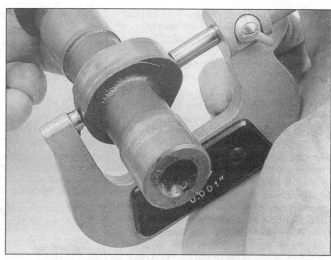

11.10b Measure the height of the camshaft lobes with a micrometer

10 Check the camshaft lobes for heat discoloration (blue appearance), score marks, chipped areas, flat spots and spalling **(see illustration)**. Measure the height of each lobe with a micrometer **(see illustration)** and compare the results to the minimum lobe height listed in this Chapter's Specifications. If damage is noted or wear is excessive, the camshaft must be replaced.

11 The sprocket must be removed before camshaft runout can be checked. Check the sprocket markings in relation to the sprocket holding bolts before removing the bolts and separating the sprocket from the camshaft **(see illustration 11.21a or b)**. Support each end of the camshaft on V-blocks, and measure

any runout using a dial gauge positioned with its tip against the sprocket mounting shoulder **(see illustration)**. If the runout exceeds the specified limit the camshaft must be replaced. Install the sprocket on the camshaft as described in Step 21.

12 Next, check the camshaft bearing oil clearances. Clean the camshafts, the bearing surfaces in the cylinder head and the bearing caps with a clean, lint-free cloth, then lay the camshafts in their correct place in the cylinder head, with the sprocket bolt heads facing the right-hand side of the engine and with the marks correctly aligned **(see illustration 11.24a and b)**. Make sure the exhaust camshaft is on the exhaust side of the engine,

and the intake camshaft is on the intake side of the engine. Engage the cam chain with the sprockets as you position the camshafts, so they don't turn as the bearing caps are tightened.

13 Cut eight strips of Plastigauge and lay one piece on each bearing journal, parallel with the camshaft centreline **(see illustration)**.

14 Make sure the camshaft cap dowels are installed **(see illustration 11.26a)**. Install the caps in their correct numbered positions and with the arrow on each cap pointing to the front of the engine **(see illustration 11.4)** and install the bolts. Tighten the bolts evenly and a little at a time in the sequence shown, to the torque listed in this Chapter's Specifications **(see illustration 11.26b)**. While doing this, DO NOT let the camshafts rotate!

15 Now unscrew the bolts, a little at a time, and carefully lift off the caps.

16 To determine the oil clearance, compare the crushed Plastigauge (at its widest point) on each journal to the scale printed on the Plastigauge container **(see illustration)**. Compare the results to this Chapter's Specifications. If the oil clearance is greater than specified, measure the diameter of the cam bearing journal with a micrometer **(see illustration)**. If the journal diameter is less

2

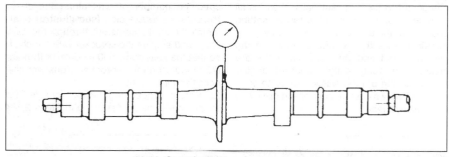

11.11 Camshaft runout measurement

11.13 Place a strip of Plastigauge on each bearing journal

11.16a Compare the width of the crushed Plastigauge to the scale provided with it to obtain the clearance

11.16b Measure the cam bearing journal with a micrometer

than the specified limit, replace the camshaft with a new one and recheck the clearance. If the clearance is still too great, or if the journal diameter was within limits, replace the cylinder head and camshaft caps with new parts.

Before replacing camshafts or the cylinder head and caps because of damage, check with local machine shops specialising in motorcycle engine work. In the case of the camshafts, it may be possible for cam lobes to be welded, reground and hardened, at a cost far lower than that of a new camshaft. If the bearing surfaces in the cylinder head are damaged, it may be possible for them to be bored out to accept bearing inserts. Due to the cost of a new cylinder head it is recommended that all options be explored before condemning it as trash!

17 Except in cases of oil starvation, the cam chain wears very little. If the chain has stretched beyond its limit (see Section 10), which makes it difficult to maintain proper tension, replace it with a new one.

18 Check the sprockets for wear, cracks and other damage, replacing them if necessary. If the sprockets are worn, the chain is also worn, and also the sprocket on the crankshaft (which can only be remedied by replacing the crankshaft). If wear this severe is apparent, the entire engine should be disassembled for inspection.

19 Inspect the outer surfaces of the cam followers for evidence of scoring or other damage. If a follower is in poor condition, it is probable that the bore in which it works is also damaged. Check for clearance between the followers and their bores. Whilst no specifications are given, if slack is excessive, replace the followers. If the bores are seriously out-of-round or tapered, the cylinder head and the followers must be replaced.

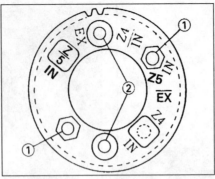

11.21a Sprocket details - 550 models

1 Bolt holes for intake camshaft
2 Bolt holes for exhaust camshaft

Installation

20 Lubricate each shim and its follower with engine oil and install them in the cylinder head, noting that the shim must be installed with its size marking downwards **(see illustrations 11.8b and a)**. **Note:** *It is most important that the shims and followers are returned to their original valves otherwise the valve clearances will be inaccurate.*

21 If removed, install each sprocket onto its camshaft. The sprockets are identical and can be interchanged, but are installed using different mounting holes **(see illustrations)**. Be sure to correctly identify each camshaft (see Step 2), then install the sprockets accordingly. Make sure they are installed correctly and with the marked side of each sprocket facing out otherwise the timing marks will not align. Apply a smear of a suitable non-permanent thread locking compound to the sprocket bolts, then install them and tighten them to the torque setting specified at the beginning of the Chapter.

22 Make sure the bearing surfaces in the cylinder head and the camshaft caps are clean, then apply a light coat of engine assembly lube or moly-based grease to each of them. Apply a coat of moly-based grease to the camshaft lobes.

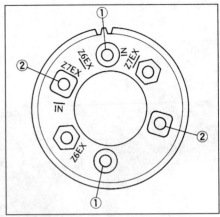

11.21b Sprocket details - 750 models

1 Bolt holes for intake camshaft
2 Bolt holes for exhaust camshaft

23 Check that the cam chain is engaged around the lower sprocket teeth on the crankshaft and that the crankshaft is positioned as described in Step 2. Next identify which is the exhaust camshaft and which is the intake (see Step 2). Install the exhaust camshaft through the cam chain. Position it so that the Z5EX mark (550 models) or Z7EX mark (750 models) on the sprocket points forwards and is flush with the top of the cylinder head mating surface **(see illustrations 11.24a and b)**. Keeping the front run of the chain taut engage the chain on the sprocket teeth.

24 Starting with the cam chain pin that is directly opposite the Z5EX mark (550 models) and slightly above the Z7EX mark (750 models) on the exhaust camshaft sprocket, count the specified number of pins along the chain towards the intake side **(see illustrations)**. Install the intake camshaft through the cam chain and engage the sprocket with the chain so that the Z5IN mark (550 models) or IN mark (750 models) on the sprocket aligns with the specified pins as shown.

25 Before proceeding further, check that everything aligns as described in Steps 2, 23

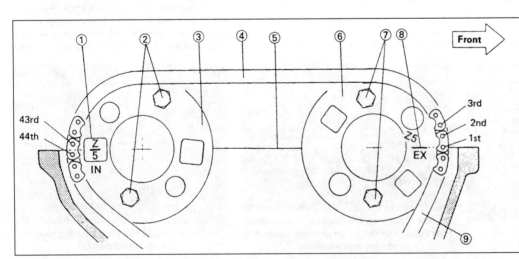

11.24a Camshaft timing details - 550 models

1 Z5IN mark
2 Sprocket bolts (intake)
3 Intake camshaft sprocket
4 Cam chain
5 Cylinder head gasket surface
6 Exhaust camshaft sprocket
7 Sprocket bolts (exhaust)
8 Z5EX mark
9 Pull this side of the chain taut

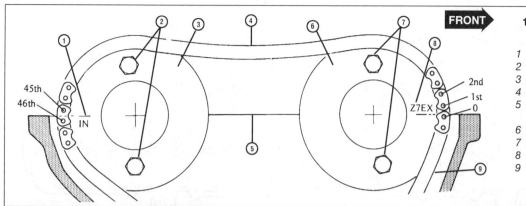

11.24b Camshaft timing details - 750 models

1 IN mark
2 Sprocket bolts (intake)
3 Intake camshaft sprocket
4 Cam chain
5 Cylinder head gasket surface
6 Exhaust camshaft sprocket
7 Sprocket bolts (exhaust)
8 Z7EX mark
9 Pull this side of the chain taut

11.26a Check that the camshaft cap dowels are installed

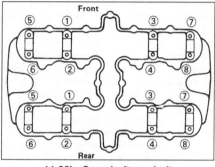

11.26b Camshaft cap bolt tightening sequence

11.26c Tighten the bolts to the specified torque setting

and 24. If it doesn't, the valve timing will be inaccurate and the valves will contact the pistons when the engine is turned over.

26 Oil the camshaft caps. Ensure the camshaft cap dowels are installed **(see illustration)**, then fit the caps, making sure they are in their proper positions as noted on removal (Step 4) **(see illustration 11.4)**. Tighten the cap bolts on one camshaft evenly and a little at a time in the sequence shown, until the specified torque setting is reached **(see illustrations)**. Repeat for the other camshaft. **Note:** *The cap bolts are of the high tensile type - don't use any other type of bolt..*
27 With all caps tightened down, check that the valve timing marks still align (see Steps 2, 23 and 24). Check that each camshaft is not pinched by turning the crankshaft a few degrees in each direction with a 17 mm socket on the timing rotor hex **(see illustration 11.2b)**.
Caution: If the marks are not aligned exactly as described, the valve timing will be incorrect and the valves may strike the pistons, causing extensive damage to the engine.
28 Install the cam chain tensioner (see Section 9).
29 Check the valve clearances (see Chapter 1).
30 The remainder of installation is the reverse of removal Apply a smear of sealant to the crankcase joints on the pulse generator assembly cover mating surface **(see illustration 9.24a)**. Install the pulse generator assembly cover using a new gasket and

tighten its bolts to the specified torque setting **(see illustration 9.24b)**. Install the valve cover (see Section 8).

12 Cylinder head - removal and installation

Caution: The engine must be completely cool before beginning this procedure or the cylinder head may become warped.
Note: *The cylinder head can be removed with the engine in the frame. If the engine has already been removed, ignore the steps which don't apply.*

Removal

1 Remove the carburettors (see Chapter 3).

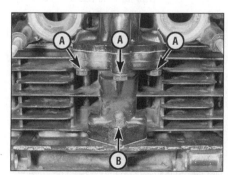

12.5a Remove the cylinder head front bolts (A) and cylinder block nut (B) . . .

2 Remove the exhaust system (see Chapter 3).
3 Remove the spark plugs (see Chapter 1).
4 Remove the camshafts (see Section 11).
5 On 550 models, the cylinder head is secured by twelve 8 mm domed nuts with plain washers and five 6 mm bolts, and the cylinder block by three 6 mm nuts. Unscrew the bolts and nuts on the front and back of the cylinder head and block **(see illustrations)**. The twelve domed nuts are numbered for identification **(see illustration)**. Slacken the nuts evenly and a little at a time in a **reverse** of their numerical sequence until they are all slack. Remove all the nuts and their washers, taking great care not to drop any of them into the crankcase.

6 On 750 models, the cylinder head is secured by twelve 10 mm domed nuts with plain washers and two 8 mm bolts, which are

12.5b . . . and the cylinder head rear bolts (A) and cylinder block nuts (B)

2

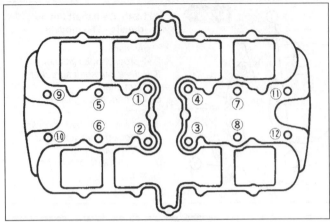

12.5c Cylinder head nut TIGHTENING sequence - 550 models

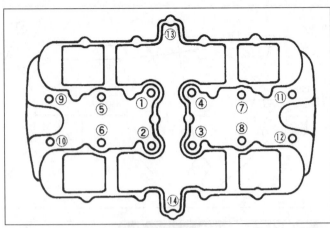

12.6 Cylinder head nut TIGHTENING sequence - 750 models

located inside the cam chain tunnel. The nuts and bolts are numbered for identification **(see illustration)**. Slacken them evenly and a little at a time in a **reverse** of their numerical sequence until they are all slack. Remove all the nuts and their washers, and the bolts, taking great care not to drop any of them into the crankcase.

7 Pull the cylinder head up off the studs. If it is stuck, tap around the joint faces of the cylinder head with a soft-faced mallet to free the head. Do not attempt to free the head by inserting a screwdriver between the head and cylinder block - you'll damage the sealing surfaces.

8 Lift the head off the block, passing the cam chain down through the tunnel as you do. Do not let the chain fall into the block - secure it with a piece of wire or metal bar to prevent it from doing so. Remove the old cylinder head gasket and the two oil nozzles and the O-rings which fit around them on each end of the block. Stuff a clean rag into the cam chain tunnel to prevent any debris falling into the engine. Discard the gasket and O-rings as new ones must be used.

9 If they are loose, remove the dowels from around the front outer studs **(see illustration)**. If either appears to be missing it is probably stuck in the underside of the cylinder head.

10 Check the cylinder head gasket and the mating surfaces on the cylinder head and block for signs of leakage, which could indicate warpage. Refer to Section 14 and check the flatness of the cylinder head.

11 Clean all traces of old gasket material from the cylinder head and block. If a scraper is used, take care not to scratch or gouge the soft aluminium. Be careful not to let any of the gasket material fall into the crankcase, the cylinder bores or the oil passages.

Installation

12 If removed, install the two dowels onto the front outer studs on the cylinder block **(see illustration 12.9)**. Lubricate the cylinder bores with engine oil.

13 Make sure the oil nozzles are clean and not blocked, then install them into each end of the cylinder block **(see illustration)**. Fit new O-rings around them **(see illustration)**. Make sure they are pressed into their recesses and are properly seated.

14 Ensure both cylinder head and block mating surfaces are clean, then lay the new head gasket in place on the cylinder block, making sure all the holes are correctly aligned and that the UP or HEAD letters on the gasket face up. Never re-use the old gasket.

15 Carefully lower the cylinder head over the studs and onto the block **(see illustration)**. It is helpful to have an assistant to pass the cam chain up through the tunnel and slip a piece of wire through it to prevent it falling back into the engine. Keep the chain taut to prevent it becoming disengaged from the crankshaft sprocket.

16 On 550 models, install the twelve 10 mm domed nuts with their plain washers and tighten them finger-tight. Now tighten the nuts evenly and a little at a time in their numerical sequence **(see illustration 12.5c)** to the torque setting specified at the beginning of the Chapter **(see illustration)**. When the nuts are correctly torqued, tighten the bolts at the front and back of the cylinder head and the nuts at the front and back of the cylinder block to the specified torque setting **(see illustration 12.5a and b)**.

12.9 Remove the dowel (arrowed) from each front outer stud if it is loose

12.13a Press each oil nozzle into its hole . . .

12.13b . . . and fit a new O-ring around it

12.15 Keep the cam chain taut when fitting the cylinder head

12.16 Tighten the cylinder head nuts in the correct sequence to the specified torque

17 On 750 models, install the twelve 10 mm domed nuts with their plain washers, and the two 8 mm bolts and tighten them finger-tight. Now tighten the nuts and bolts evenly and a little at a time in their numerical sequence **(see illustration 12.6)** to the torque settings specified at the beginning of the Chapter **(see illustration 12.16)**.
18 Install the camshafts (see Section 11) and the valve cover (see Section 8).
19 Install the spark plugs (see Chapter 1).
20 Install the exhaust system (see Chapter 3).
21 Install the carburettors (see Chapter 3).

13 Valves/valve seats/valve guides - servicing

1 Because of the complex nature of this job and the special tools and equipment required, most owners leave servicing of the valves, valve seats and valve guides to a professional.
2 The home mechanic can, however, remove the valves from the cylinder head, clean and check the components for wear and assess the extent of the work needed, and, unless a valve service is required, grind in the valves (see Section 14).
3 The dealer service department will remove the valves and springs, recondition or replace the valves and valve seats, replace the valve guides, check and replace the valve springs, spring retainers and collets/keepers (as necessary), replace the valve seals with new ones and reassemble the valve components.
4 After the valve service has been performed, the head will be in like-new condition. When the head is returned, be sure to clean it again very thoroughly before installation on the engine to remove any metal particles or abrasive grit that may still be present from the valve service operations. Use compressed air, if available, to blow out all the holes and passages.

14 Cylinder head and valves - disassembly, inspection and reassembly

1 As mentioned in the previous section, valve servicing, valve seat re-cutting and valve

guide replacement should be left to a Kawasaki dealer. However, disassembly, cleaning and inspection of the valves and related components can be done (if the necessary special tools are available) by the home mechanic. This way no expense is incurred if the inspection reveals that overhaul is not required at this time.
2 To disassemble the valve components without the risk of damaging them, a valve spring compressor is absolutely necessary. This special tool can usually be rented, but if it's not available, have a dealer service department or motorcycle repair shop handle the entire process of disassembly, inspection, service or repair (if required) and reassembly of the valves.

Disassembly

3 Before proceeding, arrange to label and store the valves along with their related components in such a way that they can be returned to their original locations without getting mixed up **(see illustration)**. An excellent way to do this is to make up a container which is divided into eight compartments, and then to label each with the identity of the valve and components which will be stored in it (ie the number of the cylinder, and intake or exhaust valve).

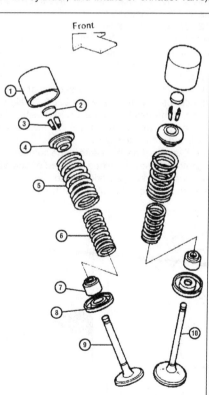

Front

14.3 Valve components

1	Follower	6	Inner spring
2	Shim	7	Stem seal
3	Collets (keepers)	8	Spring seat
4	Spring retainer	9	Exhaust valve
5	Outer spring	10	Intake valve

Alternatively, labelled plastic bags will do just as well.
4 If not already done, clean all traces of old gasket material from the cylinder head. If a scraper is used, take care not to scratch or gouge the soft aluminium. Gasket removing solvents, which work very well, are available at most motorcycle shops and auto parts stores. Carefully scrape all carbon deposits out of the combustion chamber area. A hand held wire brush or a piece of fine emery cloth can be used once the majority of deposits have been scraped away. Do not use a wire brush mounted in a drill motor, or one with extremely stiff bristles, as the head material is soft and may be eroded away or scratched by the wire brush.
5 Compress the valve spring on the first valve with a spring compressor, making sure it is correctly located onto each end of the valve assembly **(see illustration)**. Do not compress the springs any more than is absolutely necessary. Remove the collets, using either needle-nose pliers, tweezers, a magnet or a screwdriver with a dab of grease on it **(see illustration)**. Carefully release the valve spring compressor and remove the spring retainer, noting which way up it fits, the springs and the valve from the head **(see illustrations 14.27c, b and a)**. If the valve binds in the guide (won't

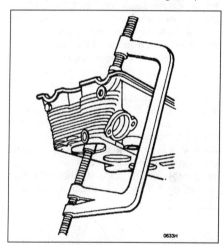

14.5a Compressing the valve springs with a valve spring compressor

14.5b Remove the collets with needle-nose pliers, tweezers, a magnet or a screwdriver with a dab of grease on it

2

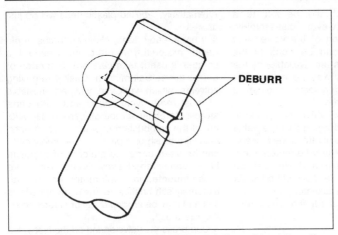

14.5c If the valve stem won't pull through the guide, deburr the area above the collet groove

14.13 Measure the valve seat width with a ruler (or for greater precision use a vernier caliper)

pull through), push it back into the head and deburr the area around the collet groove with a very fine file or whetstone **(see illustration)**.

6 Repeat the procedure for the remaining valves. Remember to keep the parts for each valve together and in order so they can be reinstalled in the same location.

7 Once the valves have been removed and labelled, pull the valve stem seals off the top of the valve guides with pliers and discard them (the old seals should never be reused), then remove the spring seats, noting which way up they fit **(see illustrations 14.26b and a)**.

8 Next, clean the cylinder head with solvent and dry it thoroughly. Compressed air will speed the drying process and ensure that all holes and recessed areas are clean.

9 Clean all of the valve springs, collets, retainers and spring seats with solvent and dry them thoroughly. Do the parts from one valve at a time so that no mixing of parts between valves occurs.

10 Scrape off any deposits that may have formed on the valve, then use a motorised

wire brush to remove deposits from the valve heads and stems. Again, make sure the valves do not get mixed up.

Inspection

11 Inspect the head very carefully for cracks and other damage. If cracks are found, a new head will be required. Check the cam bearing surfaces for wear and evidence of seizure. Check the camshafts and followers for wear as well (see Section 11).

12 Using a precision straight-edge and a feeler gauge set to the warpage limit listed in the specifications at the beginning of the Chapter, check the head gasket mating surface for warpage. Refer to *Tools and Workshop Tips* in the Reference section for details of how to check for use a straight-edge. If the head is warped, it must either be machined or, if warpage is excessive, replaced with a new one.

13 Examine the valve seats in the combustion chamber. If they are pitted, cracked or burned, the head will require work beyond the scope of the home mechanic. Measure the valve seat

width and compare it to this Chapter's Specifications **(see illustration)**. If it exceeds the service limit, or if it varies around its circumference, valve overhaul is required. If available, use Prussian blue to determine the extent of valve seat wear. Uniformly coat the seat with the Prussian blue, then install the valve and rotate it back and forth using a lapping tool. Remove the valve and check whether the ring of blue on the valve is uniform and continuous around the valve, and of the correct width as specified.

14 Clean the valve guides to remove any carbon build-up, then install the valve in its guide so that its face is 10 mm above the seat. Mount a dial gauge against the side of the valve as close to the cylinder head surface as possible and measure the amount of side clearance (wobble) between the valve stem and its guide in two perpendicular directions **(see illustration)**. If the clearance exceeds the limit specified, remove the valve and measure the valve stem diameter **(see illustration)**. Also measure the inside diameter of the guide

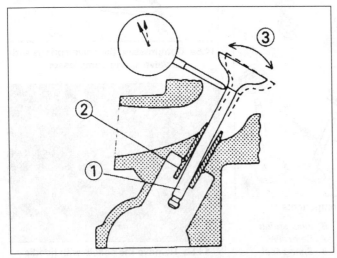

14.14a Measuring valve stem-to-guide clearance (wobble method)
1 Valve   2 Guide   3 Wobble

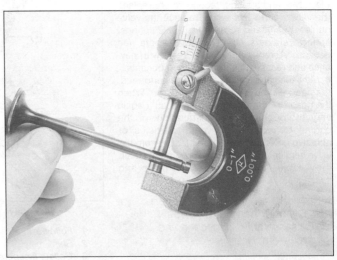

14.14b Measure the valve stem diameter with a micrometer

14.14c Insert a small hole gauge into the valve guide and expand it so there's a slight drag when it's pulled out

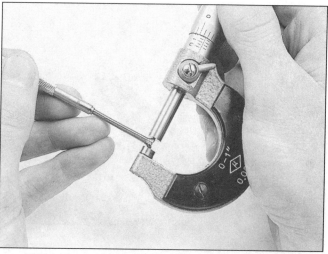

14.14d Measure the small hole gauge with a micrometer

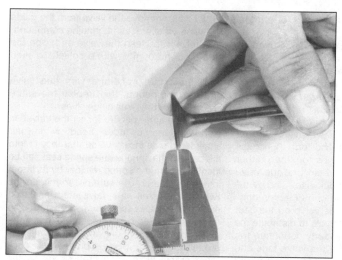

14.15 Measure the valve face thickness as shown

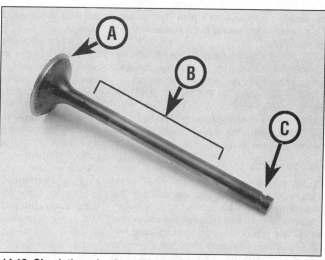

14.16 Check the valve face (A), stem (B) and collet groove (C) for signs of wear and damage

2

(at both ends and the centre of the guide) with a small hole gauge and micrometer **(see illustrations)**. The guides are measured at the ends and at the centre to determine if they are worn in a bell-mouth pattern (more wear at the ends). If the valve stem or guide is worn beyond its limit, it must be replaced.

15 Carefully inspect each valve face for cracks, pits and burned spots. Measure the valve face thickness and compare it to this Chapter's Specifications **(see illustration)**. If it exceeds the service limit, or if it varies around its circumference, valve overhaul is required.

16 Check the valve stem and the collet groove area for cracks **(see illustration)**. Rotate the valve and check for any obvious indication that it is bent. Check the end of the stem for pitting and excessive wear. The presence of any of the above conditions indicates the need for valve servicing.

17 Using V-blocks and a dial gauge, measure the valve stem runout and compare the results to the specifications **(see illustration)**. If the measurement exceeds the service limit specified, the valve must be replaced.

18 Check the end of each valve spring for

wear and pitting. Measure the spring free length and compare it to that listed in the specifications **(see illustration)**. If any spring is shorter than specified it has sagged and must be replaced. Also place the spring upright on a flat surface and check it for bend

14.17 Measure the valve stem runout using V-blocks and a dial gauge as shown

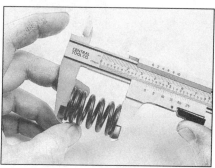

14.18a Measure the free length of the valve springs

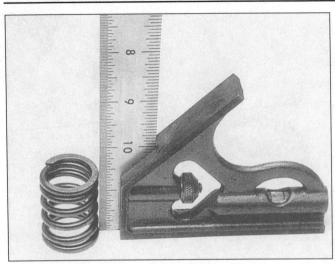

14.18b Check the valve springs for squareness

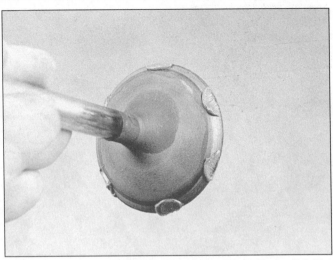

14.22 Apply the lapping compound very sparingly, in small dabs, to the valve face only

by placing a ruler against it **(see illustration)**. If the bend in any spring is excessive, it must be replaced.

19 Check the spring retainers and collets for obvious wear and cracks. Any questionable parts should not be reused, as extensive damage will occur in the event of failure during engine operation.

20 If the inspection indicates that no overhaul work is required, the valve components can be reinstalled in the head.

Reassembly

21 Unless a valve service has been performed, before installing the valves in the head they should be ground in (lapped) to ensure a positive seal between the valves and seats. This procedure requires coarse and fine valve grinding compound and a valve grinding tool. If a grinding tool is not available, a piece of rubber or plastic hose can be slipped over the valve stem (after the valve has been installed in the guide) and used to turn the valve.

22 Apply a small amount of coarse grinding compound to the valve face, then slip the valve into the guide **(see illustration)**. **Note:** *Make sure each valve is installed in its correct guide and be careful not to get any grinding compound on the valve stem.*

23 Attach the grinding tool (or hose) to the valve and rotate the tool between the palms of your hands. Use a back-and-forth motion (as though rubbing your hands together) rather than a circular motion (ie so that the valve rotates alternately clockwise and anti-clockwise rather than in one direction only) **(see illustration)**. Lift the valve off the seat and turn it at regular intervals to distribute the grinding compound properly. Continue the grinding procedure until the valve face and seat contact area is of uniform width and unbroken around the entire circumference of the valve face and seat **(see illustration)**.

24 Carefully remove the valve from the guide and wipe off all traces of grinding compound. Use solvent to clean the valve and wipe the seat area thoroughly with a solvent soaked cloth.

25 Repeat the procedure with fine valve grinding compound, then repeat the entire procedure for the remaining valves.

26 Lay the spring seats for all the valves in place in the cylinder head with their shouldered side facing up so that they fit into the base of the springs (the spring seat can be identified from the spring retainer by its larger internal diameter - be sure not to mix up the two), then install new valve stem seals on each of the guides **(see illustrations)**. Use an appropriate size deep socket to push the seals over the end of the valve guide until they are felt to clip into place. Don't twist or cock them, or they will not seal properly against the valve stems. Also, don't remove them again or they will be damaged.

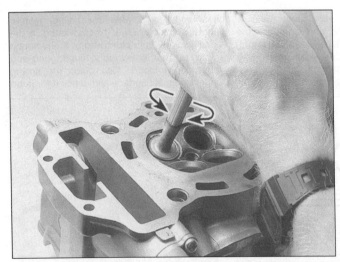

14.23a Rotate the valve grinding tool back and forth between the palms of your hands

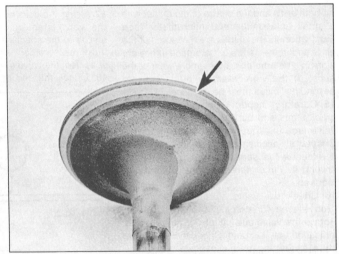

14.23b The face and seat should be the specified width and with a smooth, unbroken appearance (arrowed)

14.26a Install the spring seat, not confusing the spring seat with the spring retainer which goes on top of the springs

14.26b Fit the oil seal over the valve stem

14.27a Coat the valve stem with molybdenum disulphide grease and install the valve in its guide

14.27b Install the inner and outer springs with their closer wound coils at the bottom next to the head

14.27c Make sure the spring retainer is the correct way round

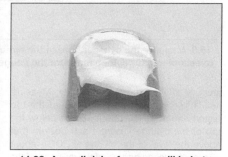

14.28 A small dab of grease will help to keep the collets in place on the valve while the spring is released

27 Coat the valve stems with molybdenum disulphide grease, then install one of them into its guide, rotating it slowly to avoid damaging the seal **(see illustration)**. Check that the valve moves up and down freely in the guide. Next, install the inner and outer springs, with their closer wound coils facing down into the cylinder head, followed by the spring retainer, with its larger shouldered side which fits into the top of the springs facing down, and with the shim cut-out facing up **(see illustrations)**.
28 Apply a small amount of grease to the collets to help hold them in place as the pressure is released from the springs **(see illustration)**. Compress the springs with the valve spring compressor and install the collets **(see illustration 14.5b)**. When compressing the springs, depress them only as far as is absolutely necessary to slip the collets into place. Make certain that the collets are securely locked in their retaining grooves.
29 Support the cylinder head on blocks so the valves can't contact the workbench top, then very gently tap each of the valve stems with a soft-faced hammer. This will help seat the collets in their grooves.

> **HAYNES HiNT** *Check for proper sealing of the valves by pouring a little solvent into each of the valve ports. If the solvent leaks past any valve into the combustion chamber area the valve grinding operation on that valve should be repeated.*

15 Cylinder block - removal, inspection and installation

Note: *The cylinder block can be removed with the engine in the frame.*

Removal

1 Remove the cylinder head (see Section 12). On 550 models, don't forget to remove the three 6 mm nuts which retain the block to the crankcase studs.
2 Hold the cam chain up and lift the cylinder block up to remove it from the studs, then pass the cam chain down through the tunnel. Do not let the chain fall into the crankcase - secure it with a piece of wire or metal bar to prevent it from doing so. If the block is stuck, tap around the joint faces of the block with a soft-faced mallet to free it from the crankcase, taking great care not to damage any of the cooling fins. Don't attempt to free the block by inserting a screwdriver between it and the crankcase - you'll damage the sealing surfaces. When the block is removed, stuff clean rags around the pistons to prevent anything falling into the crankcase.
3 Note the location of the oil nozzle on each end of the block mating surface on the crankcase. Remove the nozzles and their O-rings **(see illustration)**; discard the O-rings as new ones must be used.
4 Remove the gasket and, where a paper-based gasket has been used, clean all traces of old gasket material from the cylinder block

and crankcase mating surfaces. If a scraper is used, take care not to scratch or gouge the soft aluminium. Be careful not to let any of the gasket material fall into the crankcase or the oil passages.

Inspection

5 Do not attempt to separate the cylinder liners from the cylinder block.
6 Check the cylinder walls carefully for scratches and score marks. A rebore will be necessary to remove any deep scores.
7 No figure is given for block gasket face warpage, but a check can be performed as described for the cylinder head in Section 12. If warpage seems excessive, seek the advice of a bike engineering specialist.
8 Using telescoping gauges and a micrometer (see *Tools and Workshop Tips*), check the dimensions of each cylinder to assess the

15.3 Remove each oil nozzle and its O-ring
O-ring not fitted to 750 C5 and D1 models

2

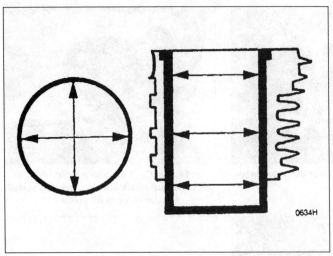

15.8 Measure the cylinder bore in the directions shown with a telescoping gauge, then measure the gauge with a micrometer

15.16 The cut-out in the gasket (arrowed) must be on the left-hand side - 550 models

amount of wear, taper and ovality. Measure near the top (but below the level of the top piston ring at TDC - about 10 mm below the top of the cylinder), centre and bottom (but above the level of the oil ring at BDC - about 20 mm above the bottom of the cylinder) of the bore, both parallel to and across the crankshaft axis **(see illustration)**. Calculate any differences between the measurements taken to determine any taper and ovality in the bore. Compare the results to the specifications at the beginning of the Chapter. If the cylinders are tapered, oval, or worn beyond the service limits, or badly scratched, scuffed or scored, have them rebored and honed by a Kawasaki dealer or bike engineering specialist. If the cylinders are rebored, they will require oversize pistons and rings.

9 If the precision measuring tools are not available, take the block to a Kawasaki dealer or specialist motorcycle repair shop for assessment and advice.

10 If the block and cylinders are in good condition and the piston-to-bore clearance is within specifications (see Section 16), the cylinders should be honed (de-glazed). To perform this operation you will need the proper size flexible hone with fine, or a bottle-brush type hone, plenty of light oil or honing oil, some clean rags and an electric drill motor.

11 Hold the block sideways (so that the bores are horizontal rather than vertical) in a vice with soft jaws or cushioned with wooden blocks. Mount the hone in the drill motor, compress the stones and insert the hone into the cylinder. Thoroughly lubricate the cylinder, then turn on the drill and move the hone up and down in the cylinder at a pace which produces a fine cross-hatch pattern on the cylinder wall with the lines intersecting at an angle of approximately 60°. Be sure to use plenty of lubricant and do not take off any more material than is necessary to produce the desired effect. Do not withdraw the hone

from the cylinder while it is still turning. Switch off the drill and continue to move it up and down in the cylinder until it has stopped turning, then compress the stones and withdraw the hone. Wipe the oil from the cylinder and repeat the procedure on the other cylinder. Remember, do not take too much material from the cylinder wall.

12 Wash the cylinders thoroughly with warm soapy water to remove all traces of the abrasive grit produced during the honing operation. Be sure to run a brush through the bolt holes and flush them with running water. After rinsing, dry the cylinders thoroughly and apply a thin coat of light, rust-preventative oil to all machined surfaces.

13 If you do not have the equipment or desire to perform the honing operation, take the block to a Kawasaki dealer or specialist motorcycle repair shop.

14 Check that all the cylinder head studs are tight in the crankcase. If any are loose, remove them, noting which fits where as they are of different lengths, then clean their threads. Apply a suitable non-permanent thread locking compound and tighten them securely.

Installation

15 Check that the mating surfaces of the cylinder block and crankcase are free from oil or pieces of old gasket.

16 Remove the rags from around the pistons, and lay the new base gasket in place on the crankcase making sure all the holes are correctly aligned and that the cut-out in one end of the gasket is on the left-hand side of the engine (550 models) **(see illustration)** or the UP letters on the gasket face up (750 models). Never re-use the old gasket. **Note:** *The gasket material on 750 C1 to C4 models was changed from paper-based to aluminium. If working on one of these models, always ensure that the aluminium gasket is fitted.*

17 Make sure the oil nozzles are clean and not

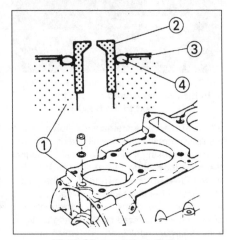

15.17 Oil nozzle installation

1	Cylinder block	4	O-ring -
2	Oil nozzle		all 550 models,
3	Gasket		and 750 C1 to C4

blocked, then install them into their holes in the crankcase making sure they are the correct way up **(see illustration)**. On all 550 models and 750 C1 to C4 models, fit a new O-ring around each oil nozzle.

18 If required, install piston ring clamps onto the pistons to ease their entry into the bores as the block is lowered. This is not essential as each cylinder has a good lead-in enabling the piston rings to be hand-fed into the bore. If possible, have an assistant to support the block while this is done.

> **HAYNES HiNT**
>
> *Rotate the crankshaft until the inner pistons are uppermost and feed them into the block first. This makes access to the lower pistons easier when compressing the rings and feeding them into the bores as they are on the outside.*

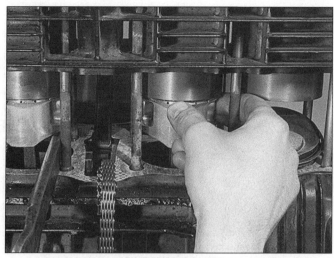

15.19 Make sure the pistons enter their bores squarely

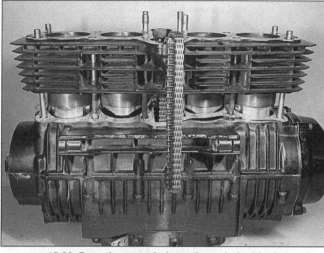

15.20 Pass the cam chain up through the block

19 Lubricate the cylinder bores, pistons and piston rings, and the connecting rod big and small-ends, with clean engine oil, then install the block down over the studs until the uppermost piston crowns fit into the bores **(see illustration)**. At this stage feed the cam chain up through the block and secure it in place with a piece of wire to prevent it from falling back down.

20 Gently push down on the cylinder block, making sure the pistons enter the bore squarely and do not get cocked sideways **(see illustration)**. If piston ring clamps are not being used, carefully compress and feed each ring into the bore as the block is lowered. If necessary, use a soft mallet to gently tap the block down, but do not use force if the block appears to be stuck as the pistons and/or rings will be damaged. If clamps are used, remove them once the pistons are in the bore.

21 When the pistons are correctly installed in the cylinders, press the block down onto the base gasket.

22 Install the cylinder head (see Section 11).

16 Pistons - removal, inspection and installation

Note: The pistons can be removed with the engine in the frame.

Removal

1 Remove the cylinder block (see Section 15).

2 Before removing the piston from the connecting rod, stuff a clean rag into the hole around the rod to prevent the circlips or anything else from falling into the crankcase. Use a sharp scribe or felt marker pen to write the cylinder identity on the crown of each piston (or on the skirt if the piston is dirty and going to be cleaned). Each piston should also have an arrow marked on its crown which should face forwards **(see illustration 16.3b)**. If this is not visible, mark the piston accordingly so that it can be installed the correct way round.

3 Carefully prise out the circlip on one side of

the piston using needle-nose pliers or a small flat-bladed screwdriver inserted into the notch **(see illustration)**. Push the piston pin out from the other side to free the piston from the connecting rod **(see illustration)**. Remove the other circlip and discard them as new ones

HAYNES HiNT *To prevent the circlip from pinging away or from dropping into the crankcase, pass a rod or screwdriver, whose diameter is greater than the gap between the circlip ends, through the piston pin - this will trap the circlip if it springs out.*

HAYNES HiNT *If a piston pin is a tight fit in the piston bosses, soak a rag in boiling water then wring it out and wrap it around the piston - this will expand the alloy piston sufficiently to release its grip on the pin.*

2

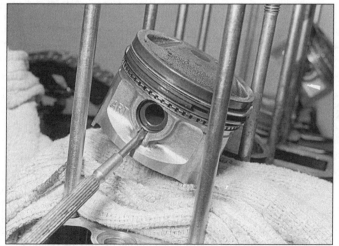

16.3a Remove the circlip using a pair of pliers or screwdriver inserted in the notch . . .

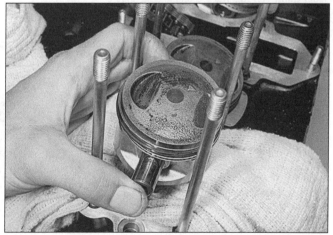

16.3b . . . then push the pin out from the other side and withdraw it from the piston. Note the arrow stamped into each piston crown which must face forward

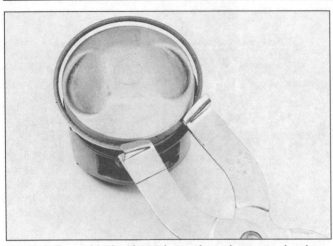

16.5 Removing the piston rings using a ring removal and installation tool

16.11 Measure the piston ring-to-groove clearance with a feeler gauge

must be used. When the piston has been removed, install its pin back into its bore so that related parts do not get mixed up. Rotate the crankshaft so that the best access is obtained for each piston.

Inspection

4 Before the inspection process can be carried out, the pistons must be cleaned and the old piston rings removed. Note that if the cylinders are being rebored, piston inspection can be overlooked as new ones will be fitted.

5 Using your thumbs or a piston ring removal and installation tool, carefully remove the rings from the pistons **(see illustration)**. Do not nick or gouge the pistons in the process. Carefully note in which groove each ring fits as they must be installed in their original positions if being re-used. The top ring is unmarked and can be installed either way up. The upper surface of the second (middle) ring is marked with a letter at one end; on 550 models, the ring is identified by the letter T, and on 750 models by the letter N **(see illustration 17.11a)**. The top and middle rings can also be identified by their different cross-section shape **(see illustration 17.11b)**.

6 Scrape all traces of carbon from the tops of the pistons. A hand-held wire brush or a piece of fine emery cloth can be used once most of the deposits have been scraped away. Do not, under any circumstances, use a wire brush mounted in a drill motor to remove deposits from the pistons; the piston material is soft and will be eroded away by the wire brush.

7 Use a piston ring groove cleaning tool to remove any carbon deposits from the ring grooves. If a tool is not available, a piece broken off an old ring will do the job. Be very careful to remove only the carbon deposits. Do not remove any metal and do not nick or gouge the sides of the ring grooves.

8 Once the deposits have been removed, clean the pistons with solvent and dry them thoroughly. If the identification previously

marked on the piston is cleaned off, be sure to re-mark it with the correct identity. Make sure the oil return holes below the oil ring groove are clear.

9 Carefully inspect each piston for cracks around the skirt, at the pin bosses and at the ring lands. Normal piston wear appears as even, vertical wear on the thrust surfaces of the piston and slight looseness of the top ring in its groove. If the skirt is scored or scuffed, the engine may have been suffering from overheating and/or abnormal combustion, which caused excessively high operating temperatures. The oil pump should be checked thoroughly. Also check that the circlip grooves are not damaged.

10 A hole in the piston crown, an extreme to be sure, is an indication that abnormal combustion (pre-ignition) was occurring. Burned areas at the edge of the piston crown are usually evidence of spark knock (detonation). If any of the above problems exist, the causes must be corrected or the damage will occur again.

11 Measure the piston ring-to-groove clearance by laying each piston ring in its groove and slipping a feeler gauge in beside it **(see illustration)**. Make sure you have the correct ring for the groove (see Step 5). Check the clearance at three or four locations around

the groove. If the clearance is greater than specified, replace both the piston and rings as a set. If new rings are being used, measure the clearance using the new rings. If the clearance is greater than that specified, the piston is worn and must be replaced.

12 Check the piston-to-bore clearance by measuring the bore (see Section 15) and the piston diameter. Make sure each piston is matched to its correct cylinder. Measure the piston 5.0 mm up from the bottom of the skirt and at 90° to the piston pin axis **(see illustration)**. Subtract the piston diameter from the bore diameter to obtain the clearance. If it is greater than the specified figure, the piston must be replaced (assuming the bore itself is within limits, otherwise a rebore is necessary).

13 Apply clean engine oil to the piston pin, insert it into the piston and check for any freeplay between the two **(see illustration)**.

14 If the pistons are to be replaced, ensure the correct size of piston is ordered. Kawasaki produce two oversize pistons as well as the standard piston. The oversize pistons available are: +0.5 mm and +1.00 mm. **Note:** *Oversize pistons usually have their relevant size stamped on top of the piston crown, eg a 0.50 mm oversize piston will be marked 0.50. Be sure to obtain the correct oversize rings for the pistons.*

16.12 Measure the piston diameter with a micrometer at the specified distance from the bottom of the skirt

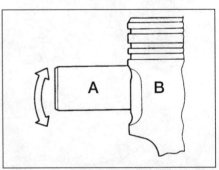

16.13 Slip the pin (A) into the piston (B) and try to rock it back and forth. If it's loose, replace the piston and pin

16.17 Install the circlip, making sure it is properly seated in its groove, with the open end away from the notch

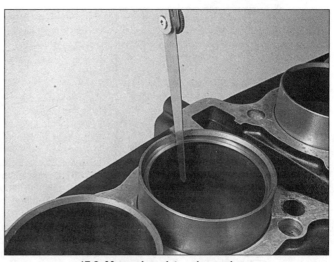

17.3 Measuring piston ring end gap

Installation

15 Inspect and install the piston rings (see Section 17).

16 Lubricate the piston pin, the piston pin bore and the connecting rod small-end bore with clean engine oil.

17 Install a new circlip in one side of the piston (do not re-use old circlips) **(see illustration)**. Line up the piston on its correct connecting rod, making sure the arrow on the piston crown faces forwards, and insert the piston pin from the other side **(see illustration 16.3b)**. Secure the pin with the other new circlip. When installing the circlips, compress them only just enough to fit them in the piston, and make sure they are properly seated in their grooves with the open end away from the removal notch.

17 Piston rings - inspection and installation

1 It is good practice to replace the piston rings when an engine is being overhauled. Before installing the new piston rings, the ring end gaps must be checked.

2 Lay out the pistons and the new ring sets so the rings will be matched with the same piston and cylinder during the end gap measurement procedure and engine assembly.

3 To measure the end gap, insert the top ring into the bottom of the first cylinder and square it up with the cylinder walls by pushing it in with the top of the piston. The ring should be close to the bottom edge of the cylinder. To measure the end gap, slip a feeler gauge between the ends of the ring and compare the measurement to the specifications at the beginning of the Chapter **(see illustration)**.

4 If the gap is larger or smaller than specified, double check to make sure that you have the correct rings before proceeding.

5 If the gap is too small, it must be enlarged or the ring ends may come in contact with each other during engine operation, which can cause serious damage. The end gap can be increased by filing the ring ends very carefully with a fine file. When performing this operation, file only from the outside in **(see illustration)**.

6 Excess end gap is not critical unless it is greater than 0.6 mm. Again, double check to make sure you have the correct rings for your engine and check that the bore is not worn.

7 Repeat the procedure for each ring that will be installed in the cylinders. Remember to keep the rings, pistons and cylinders matched up.

8 Once the ring end gaps have been checked/corrected, the rings can be installed on the pistons.

9 The oil control ring (lowest on the piston) is installed first. It is composed of three separate components, namely the expander and the upper and lower side rails. Slip the expander into the groove, then install the upper side rail. Do not use a piston ring installation tool on the oil ring side rails as they may be damaged. Instead, place one end of the side rail into the groove between the expander and the ring land. Hold it firmly in place and slide a finger around the piston while pushing the rail into the groove. Next, install the lower side rail in the same manner **(see illustrations)**. Make sure the ends of the expander do not overlap.

10 After the three oil ring components have been installed, check to make sure that both the upper and lower side rails can be turned smoothly in the ring groove.

11 The upper surface of each second (middle) ring is marked with a letter at one end, whilst the top rings are unmarked. On 550 models,

2

17.5 Ring end gap can be enlarged by clamping a file in a vice and filing the ring ends

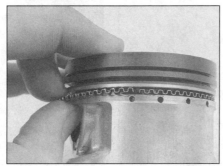

17.9a Install the oil ring expander in its groove . . .

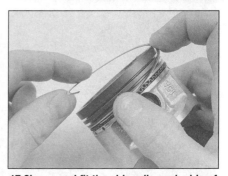

17.9b . . . and fit the side rails each side of it. The oil ring must be installed by hand

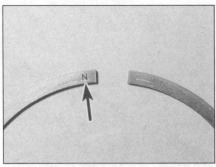

17.11a Note the letter (arrowed) which must face up

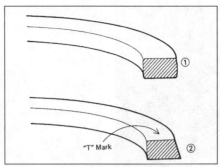

17.11b Compression ring cross-sections - 550 models

1 Top ring   2 Second ring

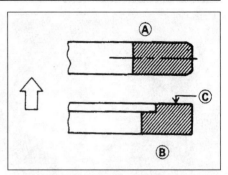

17.11c Compression ring cross-sections - 750 models

A Top ring   B Second ring   C "N" mark

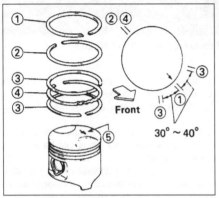

17.13 When installing the rings, stagger their end gaps as shown

1 Top ring	4 Oil ring expander
2 Second ring	5 Directional arrow
3 Oil ring side rails	

the ring is identified by the letter T, and on 750 models by the letter N **(see illustration)**. The second and top rings can also be identified by their different cross-section shape **(see illustrations)**. Install the second (middle) ring next. Make sure that the identification letter near the end gap is facing up. Fit the ring into the middle groove in the piston. Do not expand the ring any more than is necessary to slide it into place. To avoid breaking the ring, use a piston ring installation tool.

12 Finally, install the top ring in the same manner into the top groove in the piston. The top ring can be installed either way up.

13 Once the rings are correctly installed, check they move freely without snagging and stagger their end gaps as shown **(see illustration)**.

18 Clutch - removal, inspection and installation

Note: *The clutch can be removed with the engine in the frame.*

Removal

1 Drain the engine oil (refer to Chapter 1).
2 Disconnect the clutch cable (Section 19, Step 1).

3 Free the pulse generator coil and oil pressure switch wiring from any clamps on the clutch cover bolts, noting its routing. Working in a criss-cross pattern, evenly slacken the clutch cover retaining bolts, noting which size bolt fits where **(see illustrations)**. Rotate the clutch release lever towards the back of the machine and lift the cover away from the engine, being prepared to catch any residual oil which may be released as the cover is removed. Remove the gasket and discard it. Remove the two dowels from either the cover or the crankcase, if they are loose.

4 Working in a criss-cross pattern, gradually and evenly slacken the clutch pressure plate bolts until spring pressure is released **(see illustration)**. Remove the bolts and springs, then withdraw the pressure plate **(see illustrations 18.21b and a)**. Remove the release rod, and on 750 models the thrust washer and release bearing, from either the back of the pressure plate or the end of the input shaft **(see illustration 18.20)**. On 550 models the release bearing is fitted into the pressure plate and remains there unless being replaced **(see illustration 18.13)**.

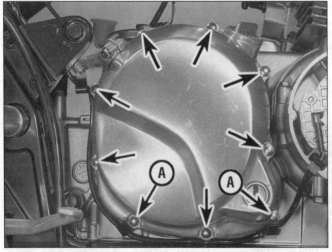

18.3a Clutch cover bolts (arrowed) - 550 models. Note the positions of the wiring clamps (A)

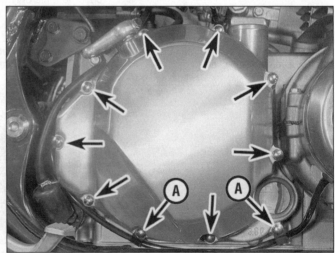

18.3b Clutch cover bolts (arrowed) - 750 models. Note the positions of the wiring clamps (A)

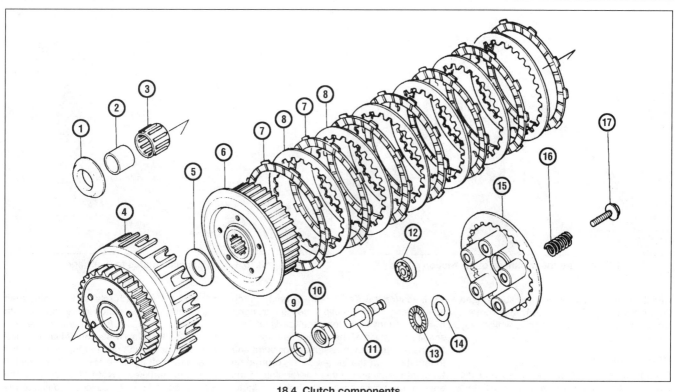

18.4 Clutch components

1	Inner thrust washer	6	Clutch centre
2	Spacer	7	Friction plates
3	Needle roller bearing	8	Plain plates
4	Clutch housing	9	Washer
5	Thrust washer	10	Clutch nut

11 Release rod
12 Release bearing (ball type) -
   550 models
13 Release bearing (needle type)
   - 750 models

14 Thrust washer - 750 models
15 Pressure plate
16 Spring
17 Pressure plate bolt

5 Grasp the complete set of clutch plates and remove them as a pack. Unless the plates are being replaced with new ones, keep them in their original order. If the plates are being separated, note that on 550 models the innermost plain plate is thicker than the outer ones, and on 750 C5 and D1 models the innermost and outermost friction plates differ from the rest.

6 To remove the clutch nut the input shaft must be locked. This can be done in several ways. If the engine is in the frame, engage 1st gear and have an assistant hold the rear brake on hard with the rear tyre in firm contact with the ground. Alternatively, the Kawasaki service tool (Pt. No. 57001-1243), or a similar home-made tool made from two strips of steel bent at the ends and bolted together in the

middle **(see Tool tip)**, can be used to stop the clutch centre from turning whilst the nut is slackened **(see illustration)**. Unscrew the nut and remove the washer from the input shaft. Discard the nut as a new one must be used.
7 Remove the clutch centre from the shaft, followed by the thrust washer **(see illustrations 18.18b and a)**.
8 Slide the clutch housing off the shaft, along

2

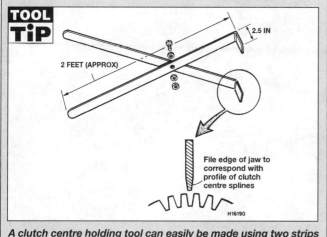

A clutch centre holding tool can easily be made using two strips of steel bent over at the ends and bolted together in the middle

18.6 Use the holding tool as shown when slackening the clutch nut

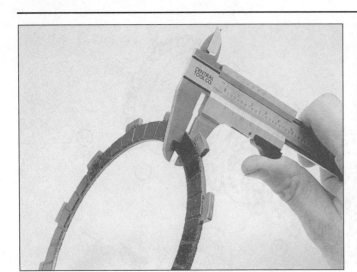

18.9 Measure the thickness of the friction plates

18.10 Check the plain plates for warpage

with the needle roller bearing and spacer **(see illustrations 18.17c, b and a)**. Also remove the inner thrust washer, noting which way round it fits **(see illustration 18.16)**.

Inspection

9 After an extended period of service the clutch friction plates will wear and promote clutch slip. Measure the thickness of each friction plate using a vernier caliper **(see illustration)**. If any plate has worn to or beyond the service limits given in the Specifications at the beginning of the Chapter, the friction plates must be replaced as a set. Also, if any of the plates smell burnt or are glazed, they must be replaced as a set.

10 The plain plates should not show any signs of excess heating (bluing). Check for warpage using a flat surface and feeler gauges **(see illustration)**. If any plate exceeds the maximum permissible amount of warpage, or shows signs of bluing, all plain plates must be replaced as a set.

11 Measure the free length of each clutch spring using a vernier caliper **(see illustration)**. If any spring is below the service limit specified, replace all the springs as a set.

12 Inspect the clutch assembly for burrs and indentations on the edges of the protruding tangs of the friction plates and/or slots in the edge of the housing with which they engage. Similarly check for wear between the inner tongues of the plain plates and the slots in the clutch centre. Wear of this nature will cause clutch drag and slow disengagement during gear changes, since the plates will snag when the pressure plate is lifted. With care a small amount of wear can be corrected by dressing with a fine file, but if this is excessive the worn components should be replaced.

13 Check the pressure plate, release bearing, release rod and thrust washer (750 models) for signs of roughness, wear or damage, and replace any parts as necessary. On 550 models, the release bearing fits into a housing in the pressure plate **(see illustration)**.

14 Check the clutch release lever and shaft mechanism in the clutch cover for smooth operation and any signs of wear or damage. If the shaft oil seal shows signs of leakage, or if the shaft bearings feels rough, withdraw the lever and shaft from the cover and replace the bearings and seal. **Note:** *Removal of the release shaft from the cover will damage the oil seal - always make sure the oil seal is replaced with a new one if the shaft is disturbed.* If the release lever is removed from the shaft, install it so that the punch mark on the shaft aligns with the mark on the lever as shown **(see illustrations)**. Apply grease to the oil seal lips and clean engine oil to the shaft and bearings.

Installation

15 Remove all traces of old gasket from the crankcase and clutch cover surfaces.

16 Slide the inner thrust washer, with its flat surface facing out, onto the end of the input shaft **(see illustration)**.

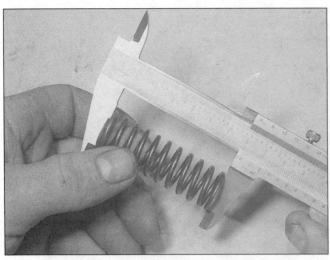

18.11 Measure the free length of the clutch springs

18.13 The release bearing on 550 models fit into the pressure plate

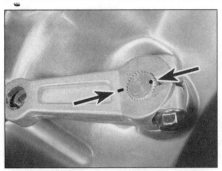

18.14a Clutch release lever alignment marks (arrowed) - 550 models

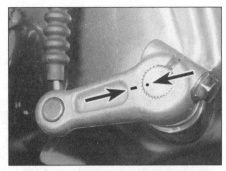

18.14b Clutch release lever alignment marks (arrowed) - 750 models

18.16 Install the inner thrust washer with the chamfered side facing in, flat side facing out

18.17a Slide the spacer . . .

18.17b . . . the needle roller bearing . . .

18.17c . . . and the clutch housing onto the input shaft

18.18a Slide the thrust washer . . .

18.18b . . . and the clutch centre onto the shaft

18.18c Fit the washer and the clutch nut . . .

17 Lubricate the spacer and needle roller bearing with clean engine oil and slide them onto the shaft **(see illustrations)**. Slide the clutch housing onto the shaft, making sure it engages correctly with the teeth on the primary drive gear **(see illustration)**.
18 Slide the thrust washer onto the shaft, then install the clutch centre, making sure it locates correctly onto the shaft splines **(see illustrations)**. Slide the clutch nut washer onto the shaft splines, then install a new clutch nut. Using the method employed on removal to prevent the input shaft turning, tighten the nut to the torque setting specified at the beginning of the Chapter **(see illustrations)**. **Note:** *Check that the clutch centre rotates freely after tightening.*
19 Coat each clutch plate with clean engine oil, then build up the plates in the clutch

housing, starting with a friction plate, then a plain plate and alternating friction and plain plates until all are installed **(see illustrations)**. On 550 models, note that one plain plate is

thicker than the rest and must be the first plain plate fitted. On 750 C5 and D1 models, note that two friction plates differ from the rest and must be the first and last fitted.

18.18d . . . and tighten the nut to the specified torque setting

18.19a Install a friction plate first . . .

2

18.19b . . . followed by a plain plate

18.20 Fit the release rod through the back of the pressure plate

18.21a Fit the pressure plate . . .

18.21b . . . then install the springs and bolts . . .

18.21c . . . and tighten them to the specified torque setting

18.22a Apply a smear of sealant to the areas arrowed

18.22b Fit the dowels (arrowed) if removed, and a new gasket

18.22c The cut-out (A) engages behind the head of the release rod (B)

18.22d Move the lever back when fitting the cover, then move it forwards to engage the release rod

20 Lubricate the release rod with molybdenum disulphide grease. On 750 models lubricate both sides of the release bearing and thrust washer with clean engine oil, then install them onto the release rod. Install the release rod into the back of the pressure plate so that the headed end protrudes from the front **(see illustration)**.

21 Install the pressure plate onto the clutch **(see illustration)**. Install the springs, then install the pressure plate bolts, and tighten them evenly in a criss-cross sequence to the specified torque setting **(see illustrations)**.

22 Apply a smear of silicone sealant to the area around the crankcase joints as shown **(see illustration)**. Check that the dowels are in place, then place a new gasket onto the crankcase **(see illustration)**. Install the clutch cover with the release lever pushed back, and tighten the cover bolts evenly in a criss-cross

sequence **(see illustrations)**. Move the release lever forward so that the cutout in the shaft end engages with the release rod. If the shaft is difficult to engage with the rod, pull up on the lever so that there is about 4 mm clearance between it and the clutch cover, and again move it forward to engage it. Make sure the pulse generator and oil pressure switch wiring is correctly routed and secured by its clamps **(see illustrations 18.3a and b)**.

23 Connect the clutch cable (see Section 19, Step 3).

24 Refill the engine with oil (see Chapter 1).

19 Clutch cable - removal and installation

1 Slide the rubber boot off the adjuster on the

lower end of the clutch cable **(see illustration)**. Fully slacken the upper nut and thread the lower nut off the end of the adjuster, then slide the adjuster down in the bracket to provide as much inner cable

19.1a Pull back the rubber boot . . .

19.1b . . . then slacken the upper nut and thread the nut off the adjuster

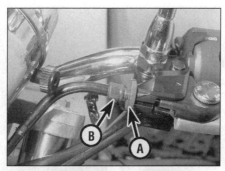

19.1c Slacken the lockwheel (A) and screw the adjuster (B) in

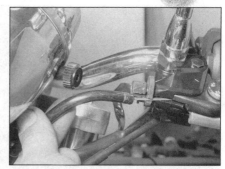

19.1d With the slots aligned, remove the outer cable from the adjuster . . .

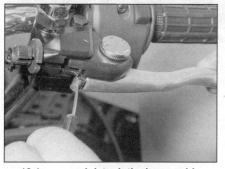

19.1e . . . and detach the inner cable nipple from the lever

19.1f Withdraw the adjuster from its bracket . . .

19.1g . . . and remove the cable end nipple from the lever

freeplay as possible **(see illustration)**. Fully slacken the lockwheel on the freeplay adjuster at the handlebar end of the cable, then screw the adjuster fully in **(see illustration)**. Align the slots in the adjuster and lockwheel with that in the lever bracket, then pull the outer cable end from the socket in the adjuster and release the inner cable from the lever **(see illustrations)**. Now release the lower end adjuster from its bracket and the end of the inner cable from the release lever on the clutch cover **(see illustrations)**.
2 Remove the cable from the machine, noting its routing.

HAYNES HiNT *Before removing the cable from the bike, tape the lower end of the new cable to the upper end of the old cable. Slowly pull the lower end of the old cable out, guiding the new cable down into position. Using this method will ensure the cable is routed correctly.*

3 Install the cable, making sure it is correctly routed. Apply grease to the ends of the inner cables. Fit the lower inner cable end into the release lever and the adjuster into the bracket on the clutch cover **(see illustrations 19.1g and f)**. Attach the upper end of the inner cable to the clutch lever, then align the slots in the adjuster and lockwheel with that in the lever bracket and fit the cable into the adjuster **(see illustrations 19.1e and d)**. Thread the nuts on the lower adjuster so that it is secure in the

bracket **(see illustrations 19.1b and a)**, then check and adjust the amount of clutch lever freeplay (see Chapter 1).

20 Gearchange mechanism (external parts) - removal, inspection and installation

Note: The gearchange mechanism external component parts can be removed with the engine in the frame.

Removal

1 Remove the engine (front) sprocket (see Chapter 5).
2 Remove the sidestand switch (Chapter 8). Also disconnect the neutral switch wiring connector from the gearchange mechanism cover.

20.3 The gearchange mechanism cover is secured by seven screws (550 models) or bolts (750 models)

3 Remove the screws (550 models) or bolts (750 models) securing the gearchange mechanism cover to the crankcase and remove the cover, noting which length screws or bolts fit where **(see illustration)**. Be prepared to catch any residue oil. Discard the gasket as a new one must be used. Remove the two dowels from either the cover or the crankcase if they are loose.
4 Note how the gearchange shaft centralising spring ends fit on each side of the locating pin in the crankcase, and how the selector arm and stopper arm engage with the pins in the end of the selector drum **(see illustration 20.10)**. Lift the selector arm and stopper arm off the selector drum, then withdraw the gearchange shaft from the crankcase.
5 If necessary, remove the screw securing the pin holder plate to the end of the selector drum, then remove the plate, noting which hole locates over the longer pin in the selector drum, and which hole in the drum the longer pin fits into. Mark the holes with a felt pen to ensure correct installation, otherwise the neutral light will not work correctly. Take care not to lose any of the pins.

Inspection

6 Inspect the shaft centralising spring for fatigue, wear or damage. If any is found, it must be replaced. Also check that the spring locating pin in the crankcase is securely tightened. If it is loose, remove it and apply a non-permanent thread locking compound to its threads, then tighten it to the torque setting specified at the beginning of the Chapter.

2

20.7 Replace the cover oil seals if necessary

20.10 The installed mechanism should be as shown

7 Check the gearchange shaft for straightness and damage to the splines. If the shaft is bent you can attempt to straighten it, but if the splines are damaged the shaft must be replaced. Also check the condition of the shaft oil seal in the cover. If it is damaged, deteriorated or shows signs of leakage it must be replaced with a new one. Lever out the old seal and drive the new one squarely into place, with its lip facing inward, using a seal driver or suitable socket. Similarly check the condition of the transmission output shaft oil seal **(see illustration)**.

8 Check the selector arm and stopper arm pawls, and the pins in the selector drum for wear and damage. Also check the arm return spring, and make sure it is correctly installed. Replace any components that are worn or damaged.

Installation

9 If removed, install the pins into the end of the selector drum, making sure the longer pin is fitted into the hole noted on removal. Install the holder onto the pins, then apply a non-permanent thread locking compound to the holder screw and tighten it securely.

10 If removed, slide the centralising spring onto the gearchange shaft and locate the spring ends either side of the pin on the arm. Smear clean engine oil over the shaft then guide it into place, lifting the selector arm and stopper arm onto the pins as you do, and making sure the centralising spring ends locate correctly on each side of the pins on the shaft arm and the crankcase **(see illustration)**.

11 Apply a smear of silicone sealant to the area where the cover fits over the crankcase joints. Also apply high-temperature grease to the lips of the gearchange shaft oil seal and the transmission output shaft oil seal in the cover.

12 If removed, install the gearchange mechanism cover dowels into the crankcase. Install the cover using a new gasket **(see illustration)**. On 750 models, apply a non-permanent thread locking compound to the longer cover bolts only, and tighten all bolts to the specified torque setting.

13 Temporarily install the gearchange lever onto the end of the shaft and check that the mechanism works correctly between neutral and first gear. Due to the positive neutral selector mechanism, which allows only

neutral to be selected from first gear unless the output shaft is rotating (ie the machine is moving), it is not possible to select each gear in turn.

14 Install the sidestand switch (see Chapter 8) and connect the neutral switch wiring connector.

15 Install the sprocket (see Chapter 5).

---

21 Starter clutch and idle/reduction gear - removal, inspection and installation

Note: *The starter clutch and idle gear assembly can be removed with the engine in the frame.*

Removal

1 Remove the clutch (see Section 18).

2 Remove the oil pump (see Section 23).

3 Before the secondary shaft is removed, check the primary chain slack by measuring the amount of up and down movement in the chain mid-way between the crankshaft and secondary shaft sprockets **(see illustration)**. If it exceeds the service limit specified, the

20.12 Fit the cover using a new gasket

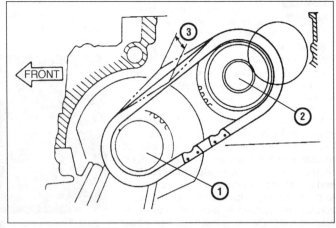

21.3 Primary chain wear measurement
1 Crankshaft   2 Secondary shaft   3 Primary chain slack

21.4 Unscrew the pinch bolt (arrowed) and slide the arm off the shaft

21.5a Engine sprocket cover bolts (arrowed) - 550 models

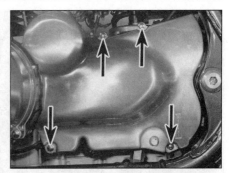

21.5b Engine sprocket cover bolts (arrowed) - 750 models

21.6 Remove the shaft bearing cap and discard its O-ring

21.8 On 750 models, remove the remaining screw securing the retainer plate and remove the plate

chain must be replaced. Rotate the crankshaft and repeat the measurement at various points along the chain. If chain slack is excessive, remove the chain as described in Section 27 and replace it with a new one.

4 Unscrew the gearchange linkage arm pinch bolt and remove the arm from the shaft, noting any alignment marks **(see illustration)**. If no marks are visible, make your own before removing the arm so that it can be correctly aligned with the shaft on installation.

5 Unscrew the bolts securing the engine sprocket cover to the crankcase and remove the cover **(see illustrations)**.

6 Remove the two screws securing the secondary shaft bearing cap and remove the cap **(see illustration)**. Discard the O-ring as a new one must be used. On 750 models, do not lose the wiring clamps.

7 To remove the secondary shaft nut it is necessary to stop the engine from turning. If the engine is in the frame, engage 1st gear and have an assistant hold the rear brake on hard with the rear tyre in firm contact with the ground. Alternatively, unscrew the bolts securing the alternator cover to the left-hand side of the engine and remove the cover. Discard the gasket as a new one must be

used. Using the Kawasaki service tool (Pt. No. 09920-34810), or a similar commercially available rotor holder to hold the alternator rotor, unscrew the secondary shaft nut.

8 On 750 models, working on the right-hand end of the secondary shaft, remove the remaining screw (the others secured the oil pump) securing the shaft bearing retainer plate and remove the plate **(see illustration)**.

9 Tap the left-hand end of the shaft with a hammer until the right-hand end bearing is

displaced from the crankcase, then withdraw the shaft from the right, supporting the starter clutch and damper assembly via the bottom of the crankcase as you do **(see illustrations)**. Note the sleeve fitted between the shaft and the left-hand bearing, and the thrust washer fitted between the starter clutch and the shaft's integral pinion. 750 models also have a needle roller bearing between the shaft and the starter driven gear hub, which might come out with the shaft but could stay inside the starter

2

21.9a Tap the left-hand end of the shaft . . .

21.9b . . . and withdraw it from the right (750 model with needle roller bearing shown)

21.9c Disengage the primary chain and remove the starter clutch assembly

21.10 Remove the E-clip (arrowed) to release the idle/reduction gear shaft

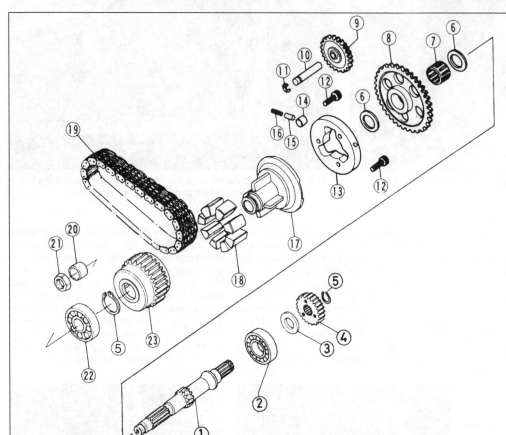

21.11 Secondary shaft and starter clutch components

1   Secondary shaft
2   Bearing
3   Thrust washer
4   Primary drive gear
5   Circlip
6   Thrust washer
7   Needle roller bearing
    (750 models)
8   Starter driven gear
9   Idle/reduction gear
10 Idle/reduction gear shaft
11 E-clip
12 Allen bolt
13 Starter clutch
14 Roller
15 Plunger
16 Spring
17 Damper hub
18 Damper rubbers
19 Primary chain
20 Bearing sleeve
21 Shaft nut
22 Bearing
23 Damper assembly
    sprocket

clutch. With the shaft removed, disengage the starter clutch assembly from the primary chain and remove it **(see illustration)**.

10 Remove the E-clip from the end of the idle/reduction gear shaft, then withdraw the shaft and remove the gear, noting which way round it fits **(see illustration)**.

Inspection

11 Install the starter driven gear into the starter clutch (if removed) and, with the clutch face down on a workbench, check that the gear rotates freely in an anti-clockwise direction and locks against the rotor in a clockwise direction **(see illustration)**. If it doesn't, replace the starter clutch.

12 Remove the needle bearing from the centre of the starter driven gear if it didn't come out with the secondary shaft (750 models only). Withdraw the starter driven gear from the starter clutch. If it appears stuck, rotate it anti-clockwise as you withdraw it to free it from the starter clutch. Note the thrust washer fitted between the driven gear and the damper assembly.

13 Check the bearing surface of the starter driven gear hub and the condition of the rollers inside the clutch body **(see illustration)**. If the bearing surface shows signs of excessive wear or the rollers are

21.13 Check the rollers and the hub of the gear they run on

21.14 Replace the springs and plungers if worn or damaged

21.16a Remove the circlip securing the damper assembly sprocket . . .

21.16b . . . and check the damper components

damaged, marked or flattened at any point, they should be replaced.

14 Remove the rollers and check the plungers and springs for signs of deformation or damage **(see illustration)**. Make sure the plungers move freely in their sockets.

15 Check that the three Allen bolts securing the starter clutch to the damper assembly hub are tight **(see illustration 21.13)**. If any are loose, unscrew all the bolts, then apply a suitable non-permanent thread locking compound to their threads and tighten them to the specified torque. Lubricate the starter clutch rollers with new engine oil.

16 Remove the circlip from the back of the damper assembly sprocket and withdraw the damper hub **(see illustration)**. Check the rubber damper segments for wear, damage and deterioration and replace them if necessary **(see illustration)**.

17 Examine the teeth of the starter idle/reduction gear and the corresponding teeth of the starter driven gear and starter

motor drive shaft. Replace the gears and/or starter motor if worn or chipped teeth are discovered on related gears. Also check the idle/reduction gear shaft for damage, and check that the gear is not a loose fit on the shaft. Replace the shaft if necessary.

18 Examine the secondary shaft bearings and replace them if necessary. The right-hand bearing will have been displaced with the secondary shaft and can be separated from the shaft by removing the circlip, primary drive gear and washer from the shaft end; draw the bearing off the shaft using a puller if necessary. Install the bearing on the secondary shaft using a drift or bearing driver which bears on the bearing's inner race only. The left-hand bearing can be driven out of the crankcase using a drift or bearing driver which bears on its outer race only. When installing the bearing make sure that it is positioned to the precise depth in its housing **(see illustration)**; use a drift or bearing driver which bears on the bearing's outer race only.

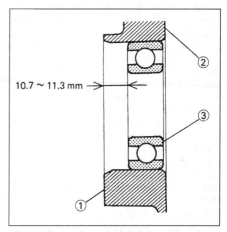

10.7 ~ 11.3 mm

2

21.18 Secondary shaft left-hand bearing installed depth

1 Crankcase outer surface
2 Crankcase inner surface
3 Bearing

21.21a Slide the shaft into the case and through the starter clutch/damper assembly

21.21b Bearing sleeve fits between secondary shaft and bearing

Installation

19 Lubricate the idle/reduction gear shaft with clean engine oil, then install the idle/reduction gear followed by its shaft, making sure the smaller pinion on the idle/reduction gear faces the left-hand side of the engine. Secure the shaft with the E-clip **(see illustration 21.10)**.

20 Fit the thrust washer into the starter clutch. Lubricate the hub of the starter driven gear with clean engine oil, then install the starter driven gear into the clutch, rotating it anti-clockwise as you do so to spread the rollers and allow the hub of the gear to enter. On 750 models, lubricate the needle bearing and fit it into the starter driven gear.

21 Slide the thrust washer onto the left-hand end of the secondary shaft. Manoeuvre the starter clutch assembly into the crankcase so that the starter driven gear faces the right-hand side of the engine and engage the sprocket with the primary chain **(see illustration 21.9c)**. Supporting the assembly, install the secondary shaft into the right-hand side of the crankcase and slide it through the starter clutch assembly and into the bearing in the left-hand side **(see illustration)**. Tap the right-hand end of the shaft with a hammer until the right-hand bearing is fully seated in the crankcase. Slide the bearing sleeve onto the left-hand end of the shaft and drive it into place between the shaft and the bearing **(see illustration)**.

22 Fit the nut onto the left-hand end of the shaft and, using the method employed on removal to prevent the shaft turning, tighten the nut to the torque setting specified at the beginning of the Chapter **(see illustration)**.

23 Install the remaining components in a reverse order of removal. Use a new O-ring on the shaft bearing cap and smear it with grease, and on 750 models, make sure the wiring clamps are fitted with the screws.

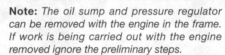

22 Oil sump and oil pressure regulator - removal, inspection and installation

Note: The oil sump and pressure regulator can be removed with the engine in the frame. If work is being carried out with the engine removed ignore the preliminary steps.

Removal

1 Remove the exhaust system (see Chapter 3).
2 Drain the engine oil (see Chapter 1).

21.22 Tighten the secondary shaft nut to the specified torque setting

22.3b ... and disconnect the oil pressure switch wiring (550 models)

3 Unscrew the bolts securing each oil cooler hose union to the oil sump **(see illustration)**. Discard the O-rings as new ones must be used. On 550 models (except the B4 model), disconnect the oil pressure switch wiring from the switch on the left-hand side of the sump **(see illustration)**.

4 Unscrew the sump bolts, slackening them evenly in a criss-cross sequence to prevent distortion. Remove the sump and its gasket **(see illustration)**. Discard the gasket as a new one must be used.

5 If required, unscrew the oil pressure

22.3a Remove the two bolts securing each hose union ...

22.4 Unscrew the bolts and remove the sump

22.5 The oil pressure regulator threads into the sump

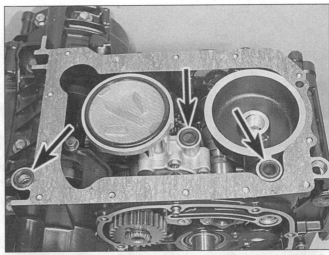

22.12a Fit the three small O-rings (arrowed) to the oil passages . . .

22.12b . . . and large O-ring (arrowed) around oil filter chamber

23.3 The oil pump is secured by two screws and a bolt (arrowed)

regulator from the sump and remove it **(see illustration)**.

6 Remove all traces of gasket from the sump and crankcase mating surfaces.

Inspection

7 Clean the sump, making sure all the oil passages are free of any debris.

8 Make sure the oil strainer is clean and remove any debris caught in the mesh. Inspect the strainer for any signs of wear or damage.

9 Clean the pressure regulator, and check that the plunger moves freely in the body. Inspect it for signs of wear or damage and replace it if necessary.

10 Remove the three oil passage O-rings and the oil filter chamber O-ring from the sump **(see illustrations 22.12a and b)**. Check their condition and replace them if they are in any way damaged or deteriorated. Install the new ones with the flat side facing the crankcase, and smear them with clean engine oil.

Installation

11 If removed, apply a small amount of non-permanent thread locking compound to the oil pressure regulator threads and tighten it to the torque setting specified at the beginning of the Chapter **(see illustration 22.5)**.

12 Lay a new gasket onto the sump (if the engine is in the frame) or onto the crankcase (if the engine has been removed and is positioned upside down on the work surface). Make sure the holes in the gasket align correctly with the bolt holes, and that all O-rings are installed **(see illustrations)**.

13 Position the sump onto the crankcase and install the sump bolts. Tighten the bolts evenly in a criss-cross pattern to the torque setting specified at the beginning of the Chapter.

14 Install the oil cooler hoses onto the sump using new O-rings smeared with oil, and tighten the bolts to the specified torque setting **(see illustration 22.3a)**. On 550 models, connect the oil pressure switch wiring **(see illustration 22.3b)**.

15 Install the exhaust system (see Chapter 3).

16 Fill the engine with the correct type and quantity of oil (see Chapter 1). Start the engine and check for leaks around the sump.

23 Oil pump - removal, inspection and installation

Note: *The oil pump can be removed with the engine in the frame. If work is being carried out with the engine removed ignore the preliminary steps.*

Removal

1 Remove the clutch (see Section 18).

2 Remove the oil sump (see Section 22).

3 The oil pump is secured by a bolt and two screws **(see illustration)**. The screws also secure the secondary shaft bearing retainer plate. Remove the bolt and the screws, noting how they are staked to the retainer plate, and remove the pump from below. On 550 models,

2

23.5a Remove the circlip and washer . . .

23.5b . . . and push the shaft through to expose the drive pin (arrowed)

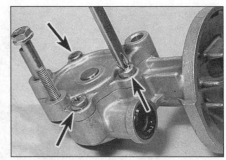

23.5c The cover is secured by three screws (arrowed)

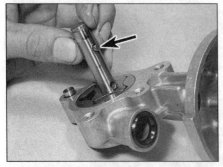

23.5d Withdraw the shaft and its second pin (arrowed) . . .

23.5e . . . then remove the rotors

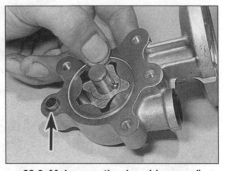

23.6 Make sure the dowel (arrowed) is fitted, and use a new gasket

remove the retainer plate with the screws (on 750 models, the plate is secured by three screws and therefore remains in situ). Remove the two dowels from either the crankcase or the pump if they are loose.

Inspection

4 Inspect the pump body for any obvious damage such as cracks or distortion, and check that the shaft rotates freely and without any side-to-side play or excessive endfloat.
5 Whilst the pump can be disassembled for cleaning and inspection and individual components replaced if required, Kawasaki provide no service specifications for rotor clearance and endfloat. To disassemble the pump, remove the circlip and washer from the cover end of the pump shaft **(see illustration)**. Push the shaft through the pump until the drive pin is clear of the driven gear, then remove the pin and slide the driven gear off the shaft **(see illustration)**. Remove the

three screws securing the pump cover, then remove the cover **(see illustration)**. Discard the gasket as a new one must be used, and remove the cover dowel if it is loose. Withdraw the drive shaft and its rotor pin **(see illustration)**, then remove the inner and outer rotors from the pump body, noting how they fit **(see illustration)**.
6 Inspect the rotors for scoring and wear. If any damage, scoring or uneven or excessive wear is evident, replace the components as required. Make sure all components are clean, then reassemble the pump applying clean oil to all components. Use a new cover gasket and make sure the cover dowel is fitted **(see illustration)**. Check that the shaft rotates freely and without any side-to-side play or excessive endfloat.
7 Make sure the oil strainer is clean and remove any debris caught in the mesh. Inspect the strainer for any signs of wear or damage and replace it if necessary.

Installation

8 If removed, fit the dowels into their holes in the crankcase, making sure they are secure **(see illustration)**.
9 Before installing the pump, prime it by pouring oil into the outlet and turning the shaft by hand. This ensures that oil is being pumped as soon as the engine is turned over.
10 Install the pump, making sure it is correctly located over the dowels **(see illustration)**. On 550 models, install the bearing retainer plate (on 750 models it is still in situ, retained by a single screw). Apply a suitable non-permanent thread locking compound to the threads of the retainer plate/pump screws and bolt, then tighten them securely **(see illustration 23.3)**. Using a centre punch, stake the screws against the retainer plate to lock them **(see illustration)**.
11 Install the sump (see Section 22) and the clutch (see Section 18).

23.8 Fit the pump dowels (arrowed) into the crankcase if removed

23.10a Locate the pump onto the dowels

23.10b Stake the screws against the plate using a centre punch

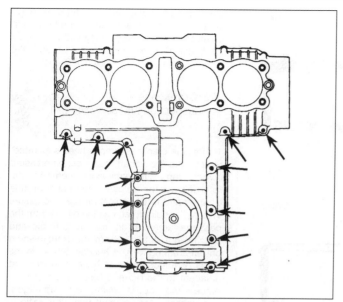

24.3 Upper crankcase half 6 mm bolts (arrowed)

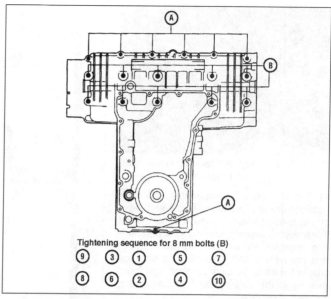

Tightening sequence for 8 mm bolts (B)

24.5 Lower crankcase half - 6 mm bolts (A), 8 mm bolts (B)

24 Crankcase -
separation and reassembly

Note: *When the engine is upside down (Steps 4 to 19), referrals to the right and left-hand ends or sides of the transmission shafts or components are made as though the engine is the correct way up. Therefore the right-hand end of a shaft or side of a crankcase will actually be on your left as you look down onto the underside of the crankcase assembly.*

Separation

1 To access the crankshaft, connecting rods, bearings and transmission components, the crankcase must be split into two parts.

2 To enable the crankcases to be separated, the engine must be removed from the frame (see Section 5). Before the crankcases can be separated, the cam chain tensioner, camshafts, cylinder head, cylinder block, ignition pulse generator coil assembly, clutch, gearchange mechanism (external components), alternator, starter motor, starter clutch and starter idle/reduction gear, oil sump and oil pump must be removed. See the relevant Sections or Chapters for details. **Note:** *If the crankcases are being separated to inspect or access the transmission components, or to inspect the crankshaft without removing it, the engine top-end components (cam chain tensioner, camshafts, cylinder head, cylinder block, pistons) can remain in situ. However, if removal of the crankshaft and connecting rod assemblies is intended, full disassembly of the top-end is necessary.*

3 Unscrew the thirteen 6 mm upper crankcase bolts **(see illustration)**. **Note:** *As*

each bolt is removed, store it in its relative position in a cardboard template of the crankcase halves. This will ensure all bolts are installed in the correct location on reassembly.*

4 Turn the engine upside down so that it rests on the cylinder head studs and the back of the upper crankcase half.

5 Unscrew the seven 6 mm lower crankcase bolts as shown **(see illustration)**.

6 Working in a **reverse** of the tightening sequence shown **(see illustration 24.5)**, slacken the ten 8 mm lower crankcase bolts a little a time until they are all finger-tight, then remove the bolts. **Note:** *As each bolt is removed, store it in its relative position in a cardboard template of the crankcase halves. This will ensure all bolts are installed in the correct location on reassembly.*

7 Carefully lift the lower crankcase half off the upper half, using either a soft hammer to tap around the joint or a screwdriver inserted into one of the leverage points cast into the crankcase, to initially separate the halves if necessary **(see illustration)**. There are three leverage points, one on either side of the

engine near the ends of the crankshaft as shown, and one at the back of the engine. **Note:** *If the halves do not separate easily, make sure all fasteners have been removed. Do not try and separate the halves by levering against the crankcase mating surfaces as they are easily scored and will leak oil. Use only the two leverage points.* The lower crankcase half will come away with the selector drum and selector forks, leaving the crankshaft and transmission shafts in the upper crankcase half.

8 Remove the two locating dowels from the crankcase if they are loose (they could be in either crankcase half), noting their locations **(see illustration)**.

9 Refer to Sections 25 to 31 for the removal and installation of the components housed within the crankcases.

Reassembly

Note: *Kawasaki advise that the 8 mm bolts should be replaced with new ones if they have already been removed five times before.*

10 Remove all traces of sealant from the crankcase mating surfaces.

24.7 Use a screwdriver in one of the leverage points to separate the crankcase halves

24.8 Remove the two dowels (arrowed) if they are loose

2

24.12 Generously lubricate the crankshaft main bearings

11 Ensure that all components and their bearings are in place in the upper and lower crankcase halves. Check that the transmission bearing locating pins and half-ring retainers are all correctly located, and that the oil jets and the rubber oil passage plug in the transmission input shaft right-hand bearing (upper crankcase half) have been installed, if removed.

12 Generously lubricate the transmission shafts, selector drum and forks, and the crankshaft, particularly around the bearings, with clean engine oil, then use a rag soaked in high flash-point solvent to wipe over the gasket surfaces of both halves to remove all traces of oil **(see illustration)**.

13 Install the two locating dowels in the upper crankcase half **(see illustration 24.8)**. Make sure that the gear selector drum is in the neutral position.

14 Apply a small amount of suitable sealant (Kawasaki-Bond 92104-002 or equivalent) to the mating surfaces of the crankcase halves as shown **(see illustration)**.

Caution: Do not apply an excessive amount of sealant as it will ooze out when the case halves are assembled and may obstruct oil passages. Do not apply the sealant on or too close to any of the oil passages, bearing inserts or bearing surfaces.

15 Check again that all components are in position, particularly that the bearing shells are still correctly located in the lower crankcase half. Carefully install the lower crankcase half down onto the upper crankcase half, making sure that the gear selector forks locate correctly into their grooves in the gears **(see illustration)**. Make

24.15 Fit the lower half down onto the upper half

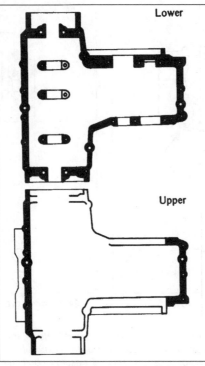

24.14 Apply sealant to the shaded areas

sure the dowels locate correctly into the lower crankcase half.

16 Check that the lower crankcase half is correctly seated. **Note:** *The crankcase halves should fit together without being forced. If the casings are not correctly seated, remove the lower crankcase half and investigate the problem. Do not attempt to pull them together using the crankcase bolts as the casing will crack and be ruined.*

17 Check that the transmission shafts rotate freely and independently in neutral. Due to the positive neutral selector mechanism, which allows only neutral to be selected from first gear unless the output shaft is rotating (ie the machine is moving), it is not possible to select each gear in turn and check the shafts.

18 Clean the threads of the ten 8 mm lower crankcase bolts and insert them in their original locations (see **Note** above). Secure all bolts finger-tight at first, then tighten the bolts a little at a time and in the numerical sequence shown to the torque setting specified at the beginning of the Chapter **(see illustrations 24.5)**.

19 Clean the threads of the seven 6 mm lower crankcase bolts and insert them in their original locations **(see illustration 24.5)**. Tighten all the bolts a little at a time to the specified torque setting.

20 Turn the engine over. Install the thirteen 6 mm upper crankcase bolts **(see illustration 24.3)**. Tighten all the bolts a little at a time to the specified torque setting.

21 With all crankcase fasteners tightened, check that the crankshaft and transmission shafts rotate smoothly and easily. If there are

any signs of undue stiffness, tight or rough spots, or of any other problem, the fault must be rectified before proceeding further.

22 Install all other removed assemblies in the reverse of the sequence given in Step 2.

25 Crankcase - inspection and servicing

1 After the crankcases have been separated, remove the crankshaft, bearings, oil pressure switch and transmission components, referring to the relevant Sections of this Chapter and to Chapter 8 for the oil pressure switch. If required, remove the oil jets from the passage adjacent to the middle big-end bearing cut-out and from the transmission output shaft right-hand bearing cut-out in the lower crankcase half. Note that the jet adjacent to the big-end bearing is staked in place and could easily be damaged, necessitating replacement **(see illustration)**. Also remove the rubber oil passage plug in the transmission input shaft right-hand bearing in the upper crankcase half if it is loose **(see illustration)**.

2 The crankcases should be cleaned thoroughly with new solvent and dried with compressed air. All oil passages and oil jets should be blown out with compressed air.

3 All traces of old gasket sealant should be removed from the mating surfaces. Minor damage to the surfaces can be cleaned up with a fine sharpening stone or grindstone.

Caution: Be very careful not to nick or gouge the crankcase mating surfaces, or

25.1a This oil nozzle is staked in place

25.1b Remove the rubber plug

oil leaks will result. Check both crankcase halves very carefully for cracks and other damage.

4 Small cracks or holes in aluminium castings may be repaired with an epoxy resin adhesive as a temporary measure. Permanent repairs can only be effected by argon-arc welding, and only a specialist in this process is in a position to advise on the economy or practical aspect of such a repair. If any damage is found that can't be repaired, replace the crankcase halves as a set.

5 Damaged threads can be economically reclaimed by using a diamond section wire insert, of the Helicoil type, which is easily fitted after drilling and re-tapping the affected thread.

 Refer to "Tools and Workshop Tips" in the Reference section for details of how to fit a thread insert, use screw and stud extractors and for gasket removal methods.

6 Sheared studs or screws can usually be removed with screw extractors, which consist of a tapered, left-thread screw of very hard steel. These are inserted into a pre-drilled hole in the stud, and usually succeed in dislodging the most stubborn stud or screw. If a problem arises which seems beyond your scope, it is worth consulting a professional engineering firm before condemning an otherwise sound casing. Many of these firms advertise regularly in the motorcycle press.

7 Check that all the cylinder head studs are tight in the crankcase halves. If any are loose, remove them, noting which fits where as they are of different lengths, then clean their threads. Apply a suitable non-permanent thread locking compound and tighten them securely.

8 If removed, install the jets into their correct locations and stake the jet adjacent to the big-end bearing in place, taking care not to deform the nozzle (see illustration 25.1a). Also install the rubber oil passage plug into the transmission input shaft right-hand bearing cut-out in the upper crankcase half if removed (see illustrations 25.1b). Install all other components and assemblies, referring to the relevant Sections of this Chapter and to Chapter 8, before reassembling the crankcase halves.

26 Main and connecting rod bearings - general information

1 Even though main and connecting rod bearings are generally replaced with new ones during the engine overhaul, the old bearings should be retained for close examination as they may reveal valuable information about the condition of the engine.

2 Bearing failure occurs mainly because of lack of lubrication, the presence of dirt or other foreign particles, overloading the engine and/or corrosion. Regardless of the cause of bearing failure, it must be corrected before the engine is reassembled to prevent it from happening again.

3 When examining the connecting rod bearings, remove them from the connecting rods and caps and lay them out on a clean surface in the same general position as their location on the crankshaft journals. This will enable you to match any noted bearing problems with the corresponding crankshaft journal.

4 Dirt and other foreign particles get into the engine in a variety of ways. It may be left in the engine during assembly or it may pass through filters or breathers. It may get into the oil and from there into the bearings. Metal chips from machining operations and normal engine wear are often present. Abrasives are sometimes left in engine components after reconditioning operations, especially when parts are not thoroughly cleaned using the proper cleaning methods. Whatever the source, these foreign objects often end up imbedded in the soft bearing material and are easily recognised. Large particles will not imbed in the bearing and will score or gouge the bearing and journal. The best prevention for this cause of bearing failure is to clean all parts thoroughly and keep everything spotlessly clean during engine reassembly. Frequent and regular oil and filter changes are also recommended.

5 Lack of lubrication or lubrication breakdown has a number of interrelated causes. Excessive heat (which thins the oil), overloading (which squeezes the oil from the bearing face) and oil leakage or throw off (from excessive bearing clearances, worn oil pump or high engine speeds) all contribute to lubrication breakdown. Blocked oil passages will also starve a bearing and destroy it. When lack of lubrication is the cause of bearing failure, the bearing material is wiped or extruded from the steel backing of the bearing. Temperatures may increase to the point where the steel backing and the journal turn blue from overheating.

 Refer to "Tools and Workshop Tips" for bearing fault finding and further information.

6 Riding habits can have a definite effect on bearing life. Full throttle low speed operation, or labouring the engine, puts very high loads on bearings, which tend to squeeze out the oil film. These loads cause the bearings to flex, which produces fine cracks in the bearing face (fatigue failure). Eventually the bearing material will loosen in pieces and tear away from the steel backing. Short trip riding leads to corrosion of bearings, as insufficient engine

heat is produced to drive off the condensed water and corrosive gases produced. These products collect in the engine oil, forming acid and sludge. As the oil is carried to the engine bearings, the acid attacks and corrodes the bearing material.

7 Incorrect bearing installation during engine assembly will lead to bearing failure as well. Tight fitting bearings which leave insufficient bearing oil clearances result in oil starvation. Dirt or foreign particles trapped behind a bearing insert result in high spots on the bearing which lead to failure.

8 To avoid bearing problems, clean all parts thoroughly before reassembly, double check all bearing clearance measurements and lubricate the new bearings with clean engine oil during installation.

27 Crankshaft - removal, inspection and installation

Note: *To remove the crankshaft the engine must be removed from the frame and the crankcases separated.*

Removal

1 Separate the crankcase halves (Section 24).

2 Before removing the crankshaft check the side clearance. Insert a feeler gauge between the crankshaft web and the no. 2 main bearing journal and record the clearance (see illustration). Compare the measurement with this Chapter's Specifications. If the clearance is excessive, replace the crankcase halves as a set.

3 Lift the crankshaft together with the connecting rods, cam chain and primary chain out of the upper crankcase half (see illustration). If the crankshaft appears stuck, tap it gently using a soft-faced mallet. Remove the oil seal from each end of the crankshaft and discard them as new ones must be used.

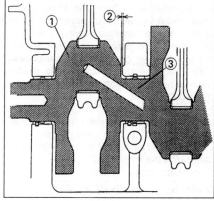

27.2 Crankshaft side clearance measurement

1 Crankshaft
2 Side clearance measurement
3 No. 2 main bearing journal

2

27.3 Lift the crankshaft out of the case

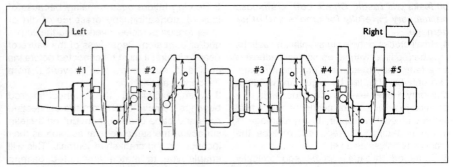

27.10a Crankshaft main bearing journal and crankpin journal size markings

□ *Main bearing journal diameter mark - 1 mark or unmarked*
O *Crankpin diameter mark - O or unmarked*

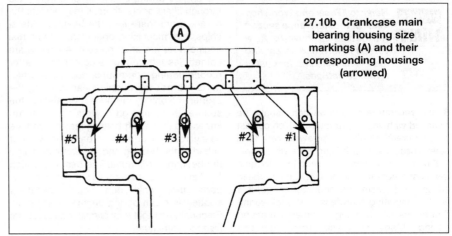

27.10b Crankcase main bearing housing size markings (A) and their corresponding housings (arrowed)

4 The main bearing shells can be removed from their cutouts by pushing their centres to the side, then lifting them out. Keep the bearing shells in order.

5 If required, remove the connecting rods from the crankshaft (see Section 28), and disengage the cam chain and primary chain from their sprockets.

Inspection

6 Clean the crankshaft with solvent, using a rifle-cleaning brush to scrub out the oil passages. If available, blow the crank dry with compressed air, and also blow through the oil passages. Check the cam chain sprocket and primary chain sprocket for wear or damage. If any of the sprocket teeth are excessively worn, chipped or broken, the crankshaft must be replaced. Similarly check the primary drive gear on the end of the secondary shaft.

7 Refer to Section 26 and examine the main bearings. If they are scored, badly scuffed or appear to have been seized, new bearings must be installed. Always replace the main bearings as a set. If they are badly damaged, check the corresponding crankshaft journal. Evidence of extreme heat, such as discoloration, indicates that lubrication failure has occurred. Be sure to thoroughly check the oil pump and pressure regulator as well as all oil holes and passages before reassembling the engine.

8 The crankshaft journals should be given a close visual examination, paying particular attention where damaged bearings have been discovered. If the journals are scored or pitted in any way a new crankshaft will be required. Note that undersizes are not available, precluding the option of re-grinding the crankshaft.

9 Place the crankshaft on V-blocks and check the runout at the main bearing journals using a dial gauge. Compare the reading to the maximum specified at the beginning of the Chapter. If the runout exceeds the limit, the crankshaft must be replaced.

Main bearing shell selection

10 Replacement bearing shells for the main bearings are supplied on a selected fit basis. Marks stamped on various components are used to identify the correct replacement bearings. The crankshaft main bearing journal size marks (either a 1 or no mark) are stamped

on the outside of the crankshaft webs **(see illustration)**. The corresponding main bearing housing size marks (either a O or no mark) are stamped into the front of the upper crankcase half **(see illustration)**.

11 A range of bearing shells is available. To select the correct bearing for a particular journal, using the table below cross-refer the main bearing journal size mark (stamped on the crank web) with the main bearing housing size mark (stamped on the crankcase) to determine the colour code of the bearing required. For example, if the journal size is 1, and the housing size is unmarked, then the bearing required is Black. The colour is marked on the side of the shell **(see illustration)**.

Crankcase housing code	Crankshaft journal code	
	1	None
O	Brown	Black
None	Black	Blue

Oil clearance check

12 Whether new bearing shells are being fitted or the original ones are being re-used, the main bearing oil clearance should be checked before the engine is reassembled.

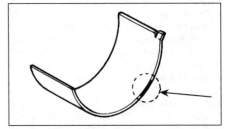

27.11 Bearing shell colour code location

13 Clean the backs of the bearing shells and the bearing housings in both crankcase halves.

14 Press the bearing shells into their cut-outs, ensuring that the tab on each shell engages in the notch in the crankcase **(see illustration)**. Make sure the bearings are fitted in the correct locations and take care not to touch any shell's bearing surface with your fingers.

15 Ensure the shells and crankshaft are clean and dry. Lay the crankshaft in position in the upper crankcase **(see illustration 27.3)**.

16 Cut several lengths of the appropriate size Plastigauge (they should be slightly shorter than the width of the crankshaft journal). Place a strand of Plastigauge on each (cleaned) journal **(see illustration)**. Make sure the crankshaft is not rotated.

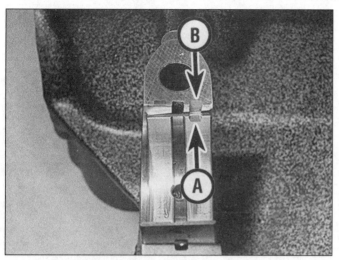

27.14 Make sure the tab (A) locates in the notch (B)

27.16 Lay a strip of Plastigauge (arrowed) on each journal parallel
to the crankshaft centreline

17 Carefully install the lower crankcase half on to the upper half. Make sure that the selector forks (if fitted) engage with their respective slots in the transmission gears as the halves are joined. Check that the lower crankcase half is correctly seated. **Note:** *Do not tighten the crankcase bolts if the casing is not correctly seated.* Install the lower crankcase 8 mm bolts **(see illustration 24.5)** in their original locations and tighten them a little at a time in the sequence shown to the torque setting specified at the beginning of the Chapter. Make sure that the crankshaft is not rotated as the bolts are tightened.

18 Slacken each bolt in reverse sequence starting at number 10 and working backwards to number 1. Slacken each bolt a little at a time until they are all finger-tight, then remove the bolts. Carefully lift off the lower crankcase half, making sure the Plastigauge is not disturbed.

19 Compare the width of the crushed Plastigauge on each crankshaft journal to the scale printed on the Plastigauge envelope to obtain the main bearing oil clearance **(see illustration)**. Compare the reading to the specifications at the beginning of the Chapter.

20 If the oil clearance falls into the specified

27.19 Measure the width of the crushed Plastigauge (be sure to use the correct scale - metric and imperial are included)

range, no bearing shell replacement is required (provided they are in good shape). If the clearance is more than the standard range, but within the service limit, refer to the marks on the case and the marks on the crankshaft and select new bearing shells (see Steps 10 and 11). Install the new shells and check the oil clearance once again (the new shells may bring bearing clearance within the specified range). Always replace all of the shells at the same time.

21 On completion carefully scrape away all traces of the Plastigauge material from the crankshaft journal and bearing shells; use a fingernail or other object which is unlikely to score them.

22 If the clearance is greater than the service limit listed in this Chapter's Specifications (even with replacement shells), measure the diameter of the crankshaft journals with a micrometer and compare your findings with this Chapter's Specifications. By measuring the diameter at a number of points around each journal's circumference, you'll be able to determine whether or not the journal is out-of-round. Also take a measurement at each end of the journal, near the crank throws, as well as in the middle, to determine if the journal is tapered. Replace the crankshaft if it is worn, tapered or out-of-round.

Installation

23 If removed, install the connecting rods onto the crankshaft (see Section 28), and engage the cam chain and primary chain onto their sprockets.

24 Clean the backs of the bearing shells and the bearing cut-outs in both crankcase halves. If new shells are being fitted, ensure that all traces of the protective grease are cleaned off using paraffin (kerosene). Wipe dry the shells and crankcase halves with a lint-free cloth. Make sure all the oil passages and holes are clear, and blow them through with compressed air if it is available.

25 Lubricate each shell, preferably with molybdenum paste, or if not available then with clean engine oil. Press the bearing shells into their locations. Make sure the tab on each shell engages in the notch in the casing **(see illustration 27.14)**. Make sure the bearings are fitted in the correct locations and take care not to touch any shell's bearing surface with your fingers.

26 Apply high temperature grease to the inner lip and silicone sealant to the outer lip of each crankshaft oil seal. Fit the seals so that the arrow marked on one side faces out and points in the normal direction of rotation of the crankshaft (with the engine the correct way up, the right-hand end of the crankshaft rotates clockwise as you look at it, and the left-hand end anti-clockwise).

27 Lower the crankshaft into position in the upper crankcase, feeding the cam chain down through its tunnel **(see illustration 27.3)**.

28 Reassemble the crankcase halves (see Section 24).

28 Connecting rods - removal, inspection and installation

Note: *To remove the connecting rods the engine must be removed from the frame and the crankcases separated.*

Removal

1 Remove the crankshaft (see Section 27).

2 Before removing the rods from the crankshaft, measure the side clearance on each rod with a feeler gauge **(see illustration)**. If the clearance on any rod is greater than the service limit listed in this Chapter's Specifications, replace the rod and recheck the clearance. If it is still too great, replace the crankshaft as well.

3 Using paint or a felt marker pen, mark the relevant cylinder identity on each connecting

28.2 Measure the connecting rod side clearance using a feeler gauge

28.4 Unscrew the nuts and remove the cap

rod and bearing. Mark across the cap-to-connecting rod join and note which side of the rod faces the front of the engine to ensure that the cap and rod are fitted the correct way around on reassembly. Note that the letter already across the rod and cap indicates rod weight - each left-hand or right-hand pair of rods should have the same letter for proper balance **(see illustration 28.8)**.

4 Unscrew the big-end cap nuts and separate the connecting rod, cap and both bearing shells from the crankpin **(see illustration)**. Do not remove the bolts from the connecting rods. Keep the rod, cap, nuts and (if they are to be reused) the bearing shells together in their correct positions to ensure correct installation.

Inspection

5 Check the connecting rods for cracks, bend or twist and other obvious damage. Have the rods checked for twist and bend by a Kawasaki dealer if you are in doubt about their straightness.

6 If not already done (see Section 16), apply clean engine oil to the piston pin, insert it into the connecting rod small-end and check for freeplay between the two **(see illustration)**.

7 Refer to Section 26 and examine the connecting rod bearing shells. If they are scored, badly scuffed or appear to have seized, new shells must be installed. Always replace the shells in the connecting rods as a set. If they are badly damaged, check the corresponding crankpin. Evidence of extreme heat, such as discoloration, indicates that lubrication failure has occurred. Be sure to thoroughly check the oil pump and pressure regulator as well as all oil holes and passages before reassembling the engine.

Bearing shell selection

8 Replacement bearing shells for the big-end bearings are supplied on a selected fit basis. Marks stamped on various components are used to identify the correct replacement bearings. The crankpin journal size marks (either a O or no mark) are stamped on the crankshaft web **(see illustration 27.10a)**. The

connecting rod size mark (either a O or no mark) is marked around the weight letter on the flat face of the connecting rod and cap **(see illustration)**.

9 A range of bearing shells is available. To select the correct bearing for a particular big-end, using the table below cross-refer the crankpin journal size mark (stamped on the web) with the connecting rod size mark (stamped on the rod) to determine the colour code of the bearing required. For example, if the connecting rod size is O, and the crankpin is unmarked, then the bearing required is Blue. The colour is marked on the side of the shell **(see illustration 27.11)**.

	Crankpin code	
	O	None
Connecting rod code		
O	Black	Blue
None	Brown	Black

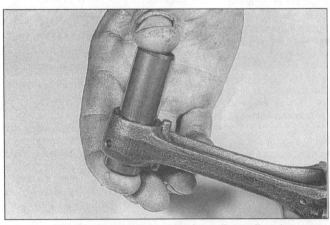

28.6 Slip the piston pin into the rod's small-end and rock it back and forth to check for looseness

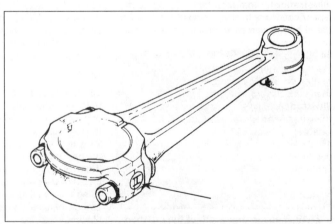

28.8 Connecting rod weight group letter and size marking (O or no mark)

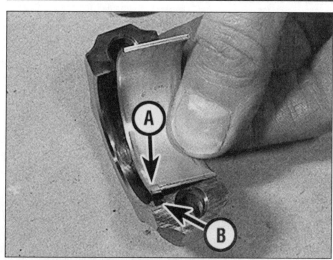

28.12 Make sure the tab (A) locates in the notch (B)

28.21 Tighten the cap nuts to the specified torque setting

Oil clearance check

10 Whether new bearing shells are being fitted or the original ones are being re-used, the connecting rod bearing oil clearance should be checked prior to reassembly.

11 Clean the backs of the bearing shells and the bearing locations in both the connecting rod and cap.

12 Press the bearing shells into their locations, ensuring that the tab on each shell engages the notch in the connecting rod/cap **(see illustration)**. Make sure the bearings are fitted in the correct locations and take care not to touch any shell's bearing surface with your fingers.

13 Cut a length of the appropriate size Plastigauge (it should be slightly shorter than the width of the crankpin) **(see illustration 27.16)**. Place a strand of Plastigauge on the (cleaned) crankpin journal and fit the (clean) connecting rod, shells and cap. Make sure the cap is fitted the correct way around so the previously made markings align, and that the rod is facing the right way, and tighten the bearing cap nuts to the torque setting specified at the beginning of the Chapter, whilst ensuring that the connecting rod does not rotate. Slacken the cap nuts and remove the connecting rod, again taking great care not to rotate the crankshaft.

14 Compare the width of the crushed Plastigauge on the crankpin to the scale printed on the Plastigauge envelope to obtain the connecting rod bearing oil clearance **(see illustration 27.19)**. Compare the reading to the specifications at the beginning of the Chapter.

15 If the clearance is within the range listed in this Chapter's Specifications and the bearings are in perfect condition, they can be reused. If the clearance is beyond the service limit, replace the bearing shells with new ones (see Steps 8 and 9). Check the oil clearance once again (the new shells may be thick enough to bring bearing clearance within the specified

range). Always replace all of the inserts at the same time.

16 If the clearance is still greater than the service limit listed in this Chapter's Specifications, measure the diameter of the crankpin journal with a micrometer and compare your findings with this Chapter's Specifications. Also, by measuring the diameter at a number of points around the journal's circumference, you'll be able to determine whether or not the journal is out-of-round. Also take a measurement at each end of the journal, near the crank throws, as well as in the middle, to determine if the journal is tapered.

17 If any journal has worn down past the service limit, replace the crankshaft.

18 Repeat the bearing selection procedure for the remaining connecting rods.

19 On completion carefully scrape away all traces of the Plastigauge material from the crankpin and bearing shells using a fingernail or other object which is unlikely to score the shells.

Installation

20 Install the bearing shells in the connecting rods and caps, aligning the notch in the bearing with the groove in the rod or cap **(see illustration 28.12)**. Lubricate the shells, preferably with molybdenum paste, or if not available with clean engine oil, and assemble each connecting rod on its correct crankpin so that the previously made matchmarks align and the rods face the right way **(see illustration 28.4)**. Tighten the nuts finger-tight at this stage. Check to make sure that all components have been returned to their original locations using the marks made on disassembly.

21 Tighten the bearing cap nuts to the torque setting specified at the beginning of the Chapter **(see illustration)**.

22 Check that the rods rotate smoothly and freely on the crankpin. If there are any signs of

roughness or tightness, remove the rods and re-check the bearing clearance. Sometimes tapping the bottom of the connecting rod cap will relieve tightness, but if in doubt, recheck the clearances.

23 Install the crankshaft (see Section 27).

29 Transmission shafts - removal and installation

Note: *To remove the transmission shafts the engine must be removed from the frame and the crankcases separated.*

Note: *Referrals to the right and left-hand ends of the transmission shafts are made as though the engine is the correct way up, even though throughout this procedure it is upside down. Therefore the right-hand end of a shaft will actually be on your left as you look down onto the underside of the upper crankcase assembly.*

Removal

1 Separate the crankcase halves (Section 24).

2 Lift the input shaft and output shaft out of the crankcase, noting their relative positions in the crankcase and how they fit together **(see illustration)**. If they are stuck, use a soft-

29.2 Lift the shafts out of the crankcase (550 six-speed transmission shown)

2

29.5a Install the caged ball bearing half-ring retainers . . .

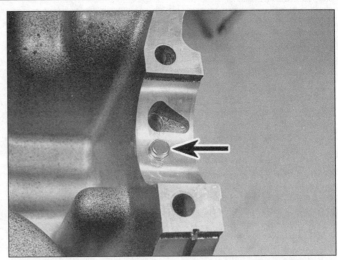

29.5b . . . and the needle bearing dowel pins (arrowed)

29.6 Install the output shaft . . .

29.7 . . . and the input shaft (750 five-speed transmission shown)

faced hammer and gently tap on the ends of the shafts to free them.

3 Remove the caged-ball bearing half-ring retainers and the needle bearing dowel pins from the upper crankcase half, noting how they fit **(see illustrations 29.5a and b)**. If they are not in their slots or holes in the crankcase, remove them from the bearings themselves on the shafts.

4 If necessary, the input shaft and output shaft can be disassembled and inspected for wear or damage (see Section 30).

Installation

5 Install the caged ball bearing half-ring retainers into their slots in the upper crankcase half, and install the needle bearing dowels into their holes **(see illustrations)**.

6 Lower the output shaft into position in the crankcase half, making sure the hole in the needle bearing engages correctly with the dowel, and the groove in the caged-ball bearing engages correctly with the bearing half-ring retainer **(see illustration)**. On 750 models,

check that the 1st gear pinion on the right-hand end of the shaft rotates freely without any drag (remove the input shaft before making this check). If drag is felt, remove the needle bearing outer race from the right-hand end of the shaft, then remove the circlip and needle bearing and replace the plain washer behind it with a thinner one. The standard washer is 1 mm thick. Replacements are available either 0.7 mm or 0.5 mm thick.

7 Lower the input shaft into position in the upper crankcase, making sure the hole in the needle bearing engages correctly with the dowel, and the groove in the caged-ball bearing engages correctly with the bearing half-ring retainer **(see illustration)**. On 750 models, check that the shaft rotates freely without any drag. If drag is felt, remove the needle bearing outer race from the left-hand end of the shaft, then remove the circlip and needle bearing and replace the washer behind it with a thinner one. The standard washer is 1 mm thick. Replacements are available either 0.7 mm or 0.5 mm thick.

8 Make sure both transmission shafts are correctly seated and their related pinions are correctly engaged.

Caution: If the caged-ball bearing retainers or needle bearing dowel pins are not correctly engaged, the crankcase halves will not seat correctly.

9 Position the gears in the neutral position and check the shafts are free to rotate easily and independently (ie the input shaft can turn whilst the output shaft is held stationary) before proceeding further.

10 Reassembly the crankcase halves (see Section 24).

30 Transmission shafts - disassembly, inspection and reassembly

Note: *Referrals to the right and left-hand ends of the transmission shafts are made as though they are installed in the engine and the engine is the correct way up.*

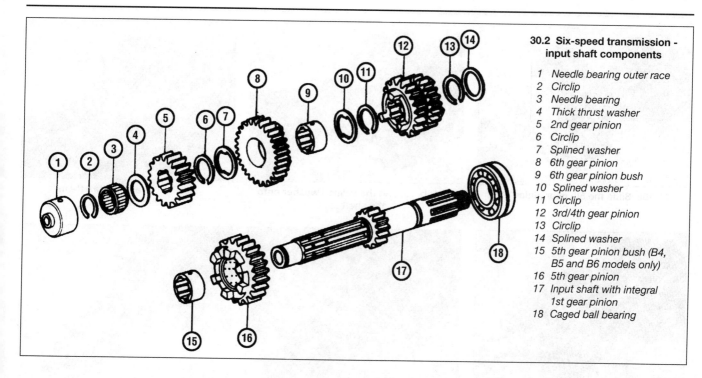

30.2 Six-speed transmission - input shaft components

1   Needle bearing outer race
2   Circlip
3   Needle bearing
4   Thick thrust washer
5   2nd gear pinion
6   Circlip
7   Splined washer
8   6th gear pinion
9   6th gear pinion bush
10 Splined washer
11 Circlip
12 3rd/4th gear pinion
13 Circlip
14 Splined washer
15 5th gear pinion bush (B4, B5 and B6 models only)
16 5th gear pinion
17 Input shaft with integral 1st gear pinion
18 Caged ball bearing

1 Remove the transmission shafts from the upper crankcase half (see Section 29). Always disassemble the transmission shafts separately to avoid mixing up the components.

ZR550 models - six-speed transmission

Input shaft disassembly

 HAYNES HiNT *When disassembling the transmission shafts, place the parts on a long rod or thread a wire through them to keep them in order and facing the proper direction.*

2 Remove the needle bearing outer race from the left-hand end of the shaft, then remove the circlip and slide the needle bearing and thick thrust washer and the 2nd gear pinion off the shaft (see illustration).
3 Remove the circlip securing the 6th gear pinion, then slide the splined washer, the 6th gear pinion and its bush, and the splined washer off the shaft.
4 Remove the circlip securing the combined 3rd/4th gear pinion, then slide the pinion off the shaft.
5 Remove the circlip securing the 5th gear pinion, then slide the splined washer and 5th gear pinion off the shaft, along with its bush (B4, B5 and B6 models only).
6 The 1st gear pinion is integral with the shaft.

Input shaft inspection

7 Wash all of the components in clean solvent and dry them off.

8 Check the gear teeth for cracking chipping, pitting and other obvious wear or damage. Any pinion that is damaged as such must be replaced.
9 Inspect the dogs and the dog holes in the gears for cracks, chips, and excessive wear especially in the form of rounded edges. Make sure mating gears engage properly. Replace the paired gears as a set if necessary.
10 Check for signs of scoring or bluing on the pinions, bushes and shaft. This could be caused by overheating due to inadequate lubrication. Check that all the oil holes and passages are clear. Replace any damaged pinions or bushes.
11 Check that each pinion moves freely on the shaft or bush but without undue freeplay. Check that each bush moves freely on the shaft but without undue freeplay.
12 The shaft is unlikely to sustain damage unless the engine has seized, placing an unusually high loading on the transmission, or the machine has covered a very high mileage. Check the surface of the shaft, especially where a pinion turns on it, and replace the shaft if it has scored or picked up, or if there are any cracks. Place the shaft on V-blocks and check the runout at the shaft centre using a dial gauge. Damage of any kind can only be cured by replacement.
13 Check the caged-ball bearing for play or roughness, and that it is a tight fit on the shaft. Replace the bearing if it is worn, loose or damaged, using a bearing puller to remove it (see illustration). If one is not available, you could try carefully levering it off using a pair of tyre levers, though it is preferable to take the shaft to a Kawasaki dealer. Install the bearing using a press. Install the needle roller bearing

onto the shaft, and check it for play or roughness. Replace the bearing if it is worn or damaged.
14 Check the washers and replace any that are bent or appear weakened or worn. Discard all the circlips as new ones must be used.

Input shaft reassembly

15 During reassembly, apply molybdenum paste or engine oil to the mating surfaces of the shaft, pinions and bushes. Install the bushes with their oil hole aligned with the hole in the shaft. When installing the circlips, do not expand the ends any further than is necessary, and install them so that the chamfered side faces the pinion it secures and the open ends are in a gap between splines (see illustrations in Fasteners section of Tools and Workshop Tips in the Reference section of this manual).

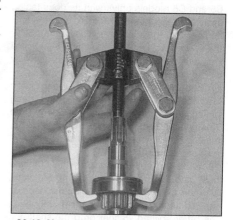

30.13 Use a puller to remove the bearing

2

30.16a Slide the 5th gear pinion . . .

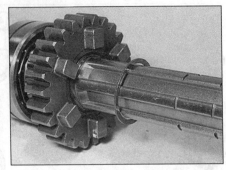

30.16b . . . and the splined washer onto the shaft . . .

30.16c . . . and secure them with the circlip

30.17a Slide the 3rd/4th gear pinion onto the shaft . . .

30.17b . . . and secure it with circlip (A), then slide the splined washer (B) . . .

30.18a . . . the 6th gear bushing . . .

30.18b . . . the 6th gear pinion . . .

30.18c . . . and the splined washer onto the shaft . . .

30.18d . . . and secure them with the circlip

16 Slide the 5th gear pinion and its bush (B4, B5 and B6 models only), with its dogs facing away from the integral 1st gear, onto the left-hand end of the shaft (see illustration). Slide the splined washer onto the shaft, then install the circlip, making sure that it locates correctly in the groove in the shaft (see illustrations).

17 Slide the combined 3rd/4th gear pinion onto the shaft, so that the smaller (3rd gear) pinion faces the 5th gear pinion dogs (see illustration). Secure it in place with the circlip, making sure it is properly seated in its groove (see illustration).

18 Slide the splined washer, the 6th gear bush and the 6th gear pinion onto the shaft, with the pinion dog holes facing the dogs on the 4th gear pinion (see illustrations). Slide the other splined washer onto the shaft and secure the 6th gear pinion with the circlip,

30.19a Slide the 2nd gear pinion . . .

making sure it locates correctly in the groove in the shaft (see illustrations).

19 Slide the 2nd gear pinion onto the shaft, followed by the thick thrust washer and the needle bearing (see illustrations). Secure the

30.19b . . . the thick thrust washer . . .

bearing with the circlip, making sure it locates correctly in the groove, then fit the bearing outer race (see illustrations).

20 Check that all components have been correctly installed.

30.19c . . . and the needle bearing onto the shaft . . .

30.19d . . . and secure them with the circlip . . .

30.19e . . . then slide the outer race over the bearing

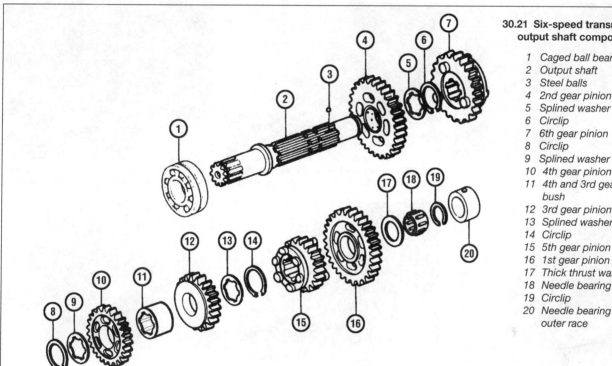

30.21 Six-speed transmission - output shaft components

1 Caged ball bearing
2 Output shaft
3 Steel balls
4 2nd gear pinion
5 Splined washer
6 Circlip
7 6th gear pinion
8 Circlip
9 Splined washer
10 4th gear pinion
11 4th and 3rd gear bush
12 3rd gear pinion
13 Splined washer
14 Circlip
15 5th gear pinion
16 1st gear pinion
17 Thick thrust washer
18 Needle bearing
19 Circlip
20 Needle bearing outer race

2

Output shaft disassembly

21 Remove the needle bearing outer race from the right-hand end of the shaft, then remove the circlip and slide the needle bearing, the thick thrust washer and the 1st gear pinion off the shaft **(see illustration)**.

22 To remove the 5th gear pinion it is necessary to displace the steel balls for the positive neutral system from the slots in the shaft and into the holes in the pinion using centrifugal force. Support the shaft vertically with the 5th gear pinion facing down and hold it above a soft container padded with rags into which the pinion and balls can drop when the shaft is rotated. Holding the shaft by any of the freely rotating pinions, spin the shaft as hard as possible while keeping it as vertical as possible **(see illustration)**. When the balls are flung out of their slots and into the holes in the pinion, the pinion should drop off the shaft. Take care not to lose the balls.

23 Remove the circlip securing the 3rd gear pinion, then slide the splined washer, the 3rd gear pinion, the 4th gear pinion, the 3rd and 4th gear pinion bush and the splined washer off the shaft.

30.22 Hold the output shaft as shown and spin it hard to release the 5th gear pinion

24 Remove the circlip securing the 6th gear pinion, then slide the pinion off the shaft.
25 Remove the circlip securing the 2nd gear pinion, then slide the splined washer and the 2nd gear pinion off the shaft.

Output shaft inspection

26 Refer to Steps 7 to 14 above.

Output shaft reassembly

27 During reassembly, apply molybdenum paste or engine oil to the mating surfaces of the shaft, pinions and bush. Install the bush with its oil hole aligned with the hole in the shaft. When installing the circlips, do not expand the ends any further than is necessary, and install them so that the chamfered side faces the pinion it secures and the open ends are in a gap between (see illustrations in Fasteners section of *Tools and Workshop Tips* in the Reference section of this manual).

30.28a Slide the 2nd gear pinion . . .

30.28b . . . and the splined washer
onto the shaft . . .

30.28c . . . and secure them
with the circlip

30.29a Slide the 6th gear pinion
onto the shaft . . .

30.29b . . . secure it with the circlip, then
slide the splined washer onto the shaft

30.30a Slide the 4th/3rd gear bush onto
the shaft, then slide the 4th gear pinion . . .

30.30b . . . and the 3rd gear pinion
onto the bush . . .

30.30c . . . then slide on the
splined washer . . .

30.30d . . . and secure it with the circlip

28 Slide the 2nd gear pinion onto the shaft, followed by the splined washer, and secure them in place with the circlip, making sure it is properly seated in its groove **(see illustrations)**.
29 Slide the 6th gear pinion onto the shaft with its selector fork groove facing away from the 2nd gear pinion, and secure it in place with the circlip, making sure it is properly seated in its groove **(see illustrations)**.
30 Slide the spline washer, followed by the 4th and 3rd gear bushing onto the shaft, then slide the 4th gear pinion and the 3rd gear pinion onto the bushing, followed by the spline washer, and secure them with the circlip, making sure it is properly seated in its groove **(see illustrations)**.
31 The 5th gear pinion has six drillings, three of which are narrower on the outside of the pinion (in the selector fork groove) **(see illustration)**. Fit one of the positive neutral

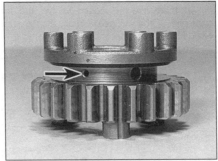

30.31a Identify the three holes with the
narrower diameter (arrowed) . . .

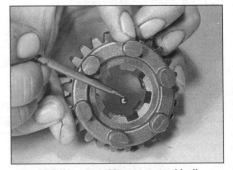

30.31b . . . and insert a steel ball
into each of them

system balls into each of the holes with the narrower outside diameter **(see illustration)**. To stop them from continuously rolling out, squirt some clean engine oil into each of the

drillings after the ball has been installed. Do not use grease as the balls will stick too much and the neutral system will not work. Holding the shaft vertical and the pinion flat, slide the

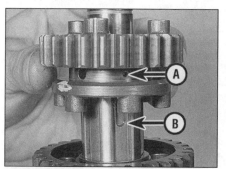

30.31c Align the holes with the balls (A) with the groove in the shaft (B) and fit the 5th gear pinion as shown

30.32a Slide the 1st gear pinion . . .

30.32b . . . the thick thrust washer . . .

30.32c . . . and the needle bearing onto the shaft . . .

30.32d . . . and secure them with the circlip . . .

30.32e . . . then slide the outer race over the bearing

pinion onto the shaft with the selector fork groove facing the 3rd gear pinion and so that the drillings with the balls align with the slots in the shaft (see illustration). Check that the balls have located themselves in the slot in the shaft, thereby locking the pinion, by trying to slide the pinion off the shaft again.

32 Slide the 1st gear pinion onto the shaft, followed by the thick thrust washer and the needle bearing (see illustrations). Secure the bearing with the circlip, making sure it locates correctly in the groove, then fit the bearing outer race (see illustrations).

33 Check that all components have been correctly installed.

ZR750 - five-speed transmission

Input shaft disassembly

 HAYNES HiNT *When disassembling the transmission shafts, place the parts on a long rod or thread a wire through them to keep them in order and facing the proper direction.*

34 Remove the needle bearing outer race from the left-hand end of the shaft, then remove the circlip and slide the needle bearing, plain washer, the 2nd gear pinion, the 5th gear pinion and its bush, and the thrust washer off the shaft (see illustration).

35 Remove the circlip securing the 3rd gear pinion, then slide the pinion off the shaft.

36 Remove the circlip securing the 4th gear pinion, then slide the thrust washer and the pinion off the shaft.

37 The 1st gear pinion is integral with the shaft.

Input shaft inspection

38 Wash all of the components in clean solvent and dry them off.

39 Check the gear teeth for cracking, chipping, pitting and other obvious wear or

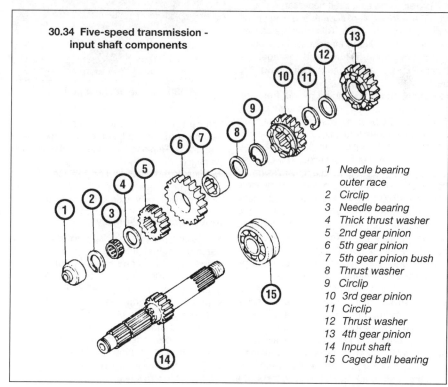

30.34 Five-speed transmission - input shaft components

1 Needle bearing outer race
2 Circlip
3 Needle bearing
4 Thick thrust washer
5 2nd gear pinion
6 5th gear pinion
7 5th gear pinion bush
8 Thrust washer
9 Circlip
10 3rd gear pinion
11 Circlip
12 Thrust washer
13 4th gear pinion
14 Input shaft
15 Caged ball bearing

2

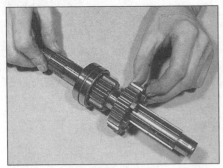

30.47a Slide the 4th gear pinion . . .

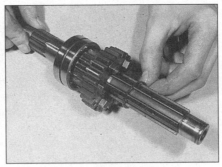

30.47b . . . and the thrust washer onto the shaft . . .

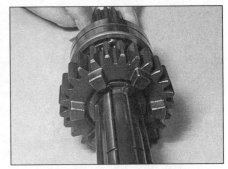

30.47c . . . and secure them with the circlip

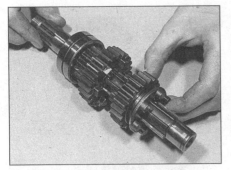

30.48a Slide the 3rd gear pinion onto the shaft . . .

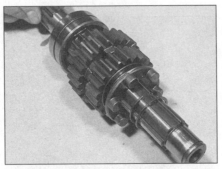

30.48b . . . and secure it with the circlip, then slide the thrust washer . . .

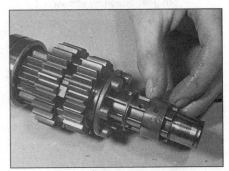

30.49a . . . the 5th gear bush . . .

30.49b . . . the 5th gear pinion . . .

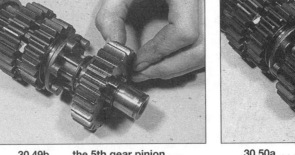

30.50a . . . the 2nd gear pinion . . .

damage. Any pinion that is damaged as such must be replaced.

40 Inspect the dogs and the dog holes in the gears for cracks, chips, and excessive wear especially in the form of rounded edges. Make sure mating gears engage properly. Replace the paired gears as a set if necessary.

41 Check for signs of scoring or bluing on the pinions, bush and shaft. This could be caused by overheating due to inadequate lubrication. Check that all the oil holes and passages are clear. Replace any damaged pinions or the bush.

42 Check that each pinion moves freely on the shaft or bush but without undue freeplay. Check that the bush moves freely on the shaft but without undue freeplay.

43 The shaft is unlikely to sustain damage unless the engine has seized, placing an unusually high loading on the transmission, or the machine has covered a very high mileage. Check the surface of the shaft, especially where a pinion turns on it, and replace the shaft if it has scored or picked up, or if there are any cracks. Place the shaft on V-blocks and check the runout at the shaft centre using a dial gauge. Damage of any kind can only be cured by replacement.

44 Check the caged-ball bearing for play or roughness, and that it is a tight fit on the shaft. Replace the bearing if it is worn, loose or damaged, using a bearing puller to remove it **(see illustration 30.13)**. If one is not available, you could try carefully levering it off using a pair of tyre levers, though it is preferable to take the shaft to a Kawasaki dealer. Install the

bearing using a press. Install the needle roller bearing onto the shaft, and check it for play or roughness. Replace the bearing if it is worn or damaged.

45 Check the washers and replace any that are bent or appear weakened or worn. Discard all the circlips as new ones must be used.

Input shaft reassembly

46 During reassembly, apply molybdenum paste or engine oil to the mating surfaces of the shaft, pinions and bush. Install the bush with its oil hole aligned with the hole in the shaft. When installing the circlips, do not expand the ends any further than is necessary, and install them so that the chamfered side faces the pinion it secures and the open ends are in a gap between splines (see illustrations in Fasteners section of *Tools and Workshop Tips* in the Reference section of this manual).

47 Slide the 4th gear pinion, with its dogs facing away from the integral 1st gear, onto the left-hand end of the shaft, followed by the thrust washer **(see illustrations)**. Install the circlip, making sure that it locates correctly in the groove in the shaft **(see illustration)**.

48 Slide the 3rd gear pinion onto the shaft with its selector fork groove facing away from the 4th gear pinion **(see illustration)**. Secure it in place with the circlip, making sure it is properly seated in its groove **(see illustration)**.

49 Slide the thrust washer onto the shaft, followed by the 5th gear pinion and its bush, making sure the dog holes in the pinion face the dogs on the 3rd gear pinion, and the oil hole in the bush aligns with the hole in the shaft **(see illustrations)**.

50 Slide the 2nd gear pinion onto the shaft, followed by the plain washer and the needle bearing **(see illustrations)**. Secure the bearing with the circlip, making sure it locates

30.50b ... the thick thrust washer ...

30.50c ... and the needle bearing onto the shaft

30.50d Secure the needle bearing with the circlip ...

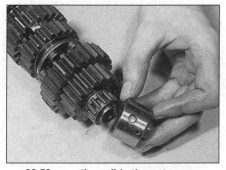

30.50e ... then slide the outer race over the bearing

correctly in the groove, then fit the bearing outer race **(see illustrations)**.
51 Check that all components have been correctly installed.

Output shaft disassembly

52 Remove the needle bearing outer race from the left-hand end of the shaft, then remove the circlip and slide the needle bearing, thick thrust washer and the 1st gear pinion off the shaft **(see illustration)**.
53 To remove the 4th gear pinion it is necessary to displace the steel balls for the positive neutral system from the slots in the shaft and into the holes in the pinion using centrifugal force. Support the shaft vertically

with the 4th gear pinion facing down and hold it above a container padded with rags into which the pinion and balls can drop when the shaft is rotated. Holding the shaft by any of the freely rotating pinions, spin the shaft as hard as possible while keeping it as vertical as possible **(see illustration)**. When the balls are flung out of their slots and into the holes in the pinion, the pinion should drop off the shaft **(see illustration)**. Take care not to lose the balls.
54 Remove the circlip securing the 3rd gear pinion, then slide the splined washer, the pinion and the splined washer off the shaft.
55 Remove the circlip securing the 5th gear pinion, then slide the pinion off the shaft.
56 Remove the circlip securing the 2nd gear pinion, then slide the splined washer and the 2nd gear pinion off the shaft.

Output shaft inspection

57 Refer to Steps 38 to 45 above.

Output shaft reassembly

58 During reassembly, apply molybdenum paste or engine oil to the mating surfaces of the shaft, pinions and bushings. Install the bushings with their oil hole aligned with the hole in the shaft. When installing the circlips, do not expand the ends any further than is necessary, and install them so that the chamfered side faces the pinion it secures and the open ends are in a gap between splines **(see illustration 30.15)**.
59 Slide the 2nd gear pinion onto the shaft, followed by the splined washer, and secure

30.53a Hold the output shaft as shown and spin it hard ...

30.53b ... to release the 4th gear pinion

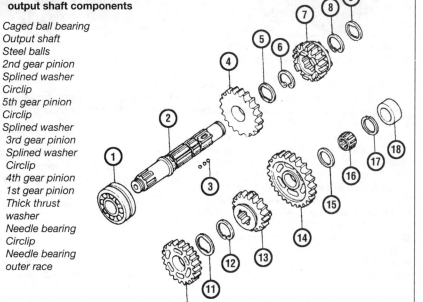

30.52 Five-speed transmission - output shaft components

1 Caged ball bearing
2 Output shaft
3 Steel balls
4 2nd gear pinion
5 Splined washer
6 Circlip
7 5th gear pinion
8 Circlip
9 Splined washer
10 3rd gear pinion
11 Splined washer
12 Circlip
13 4th gear pinion
14 1st gear pinion
15 Thick thrust washer
16 Needle bearing
17 Circlip
18 Needle bearing outer race

30.59a Slide the 2nd gear pinion . . .

30.59b . . . and the thrust washer onto the shaft, and secure them with the circlip

30.60a Slide the 5th gear pinion onto the shaft . . .

30.60b . . . and secure it with the circlip, then slide the splined washer . . .

30.61a . . . the 3rd gear pinion . . .

30.61b . . . and the splined washer onto the shaft, and secure them with the circlip

30.63a Slide the 1st gear pinion, thick thrust washer . . .

30.63b . . . and needle bearing onto the shaft, and secure them with the circlip . . .

30.63c . . . then fit the outer race over the bearing

them in place with the circlip, making sure it is properly seated in its groove **(see illustrations)**.
60 Slide the 5th gear pinion onto the shaft with its selector fork groove facing away from the 2nd gear pinion and secure it with the circlip, making sure it is properly seated in its groove **(see illustrations)**.
61 Slide the splined washer followed by the 3rd gear pinion onto the shaft, followed by the splined washer, and secure them in place with the circlip, making sure it is properly seated in its groove **(see illustrations)**.
62 The 4th gear pinion has six drillings, three of which are narrower on the outside of the pinion (in the selector fork groove) **(see illustration 30.31a)**. Fit one of the positive neutral system balls into each of the holes with the narrower outside diameter **(see illustration 30.31b)**. To stop them from continuously rolling out, squirt some clean

engine oil into each of the drillings after the ball has been installed. Do not use grease as the balls will stick too much and the neutral system will not work. Holding the shaft vertical and the pinion flat, slide the pinion onto the shaft with the selector fork groove facing the 3rd gear pinion and so that the drillings with the balls align with the slots in the shaft **(see illustration 30.31c)**. Check that the balls have located themselves in the slot in the shaft, thereby locking the pinion, by trying to slide the pinion off the shaft again.
63 Slide the 1st gear pinion onto the shaft, followed by the thick thrust washer and the needle bearing, and secure the bearing with the circlip, making sure it locates correctly in the groove **(see illustrations)**. Fit the outer race over the bearing **(see illustration)**.
64 Check that all components have been correctly installed.

31 Selector drum and forks - removal, inspection and installation

Note: *Access can be gained to the gearchange mechanism (external components) with the engine in the frame and the clutch removed (see Section 20). All other operations require the engine to be removed and the crankcases to be separated.*

Removal

1 Separate the crankcase halves (refer to Section 24). The selector drum and forks are housed inside the lower half.
2 Before removing the selector forks, note the position of each and which way round they fit as an aid to installation.

31.3a Withdraw the shaft (arrowed) . . .

31.3b . . . and remove the two forks

31.4a Remove the split pin (arrowed) . . .

31.4b . . . and withdraw the guide pin

31.5 Bend back the lockwasher tab (arrowed) and remove the bolt

31.6 Unscrew the cam plunger bolt and remove it with the spring and plunger

31.7 Remove the circlip securing the cam, then slide the cam (arrowed) off the drum

31.8 Withdraw the drum, sliding the fork off as you do, noting which way round it fits (550 models shown)

3 Supporting the selector forks on the fork shaft, withdraw the shaft from the left-hand side of the crankcase, then remove the forks **(see illustrations)**. Once removed from the crankcase, slide the forks back onto the shaft in their correct order and way round.

4 Remove the split pin from the top of the guide pin on the selector fork which fits around the selector drum **(see illustration)**. Discard the split pin as a new one must be used. Withdraw the guide pin **(see illustration)**.

5 Bend back the tab on the lockwasher securing the selector drum guide bolt, then

unscrew the bolt **(see illustration)**. Discard the lockwasher if the tab is weakened or damaged.

6 Unscrew the cam plunger bolt and remove it with its spring and plunger **(see illustration)**.

7 Remove the circlip securing the cam to the right-hand end of the drum **(see illustration)**. Remove the cam, noting how the pin in the drum locates in the slot in the cam **(see illustration 31.17b)**. Remove the pin for safekeeping if it is loose.

8 Withdraw the selector drum from the left-hand side of the crankcase, sliding the selector

fork off the drum as you do. On 550 models, the longer side of the fork boss faces the left-hand end of the drum **(see illustration)**. On 750 models, the longer side of the fork boss faces the right-hand end of the drum **(see illustration 31.16)**.

Inspection

9 Inspect the selector forks for any signs of wear or damage, especially around the fork ends where they engage with the groove in the pinion. Check that each fork fits correctly in its pinion groove. Check closely to see if the

2

31.10a Measure the fork-to groove clearance using a feeler gauge

31.10b Measure the thickness of the fork end . . .

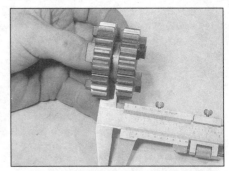

31.10c . . . and the width of the groove

31.14 Check the needle bearing in the crankcase

31.16 Ensure the fork is fitted the correct way round for your model (see text)

31.17a Fit the pin into the drum (arrowed) . . .

31.17b . . . then locate the slot in the cam over the pin

31.18 Align the drum so the plunger fits into the neutral detent (arrowed)

forks are bent. If the forks are in any way damaged they must be replaced.

10 With the fork engaged with its pinion groove, measure the fork-to-groove clearance using a feeler gauge, and compare the result to the specifications at the beginning of the Chapter (see illustration). If the clearance exceeds the service limit specified, measure the thickness of the fork ends and the width of the groove and compare the readings to the specifications (see illustrations). Replace whichever components are worn beyond their specifications.

11 Check that the forks fit correctly on their shaft. They should move freely with a light fit but no appreciable freeplay. Check that the fork shaft holes in the crankcases are not worn or damaged.

12 The selector fork shaft can be checked for trueness by rolling it along a flat surface. A bent rod will cause difficulty in selecting gears and make the gearchange action heavy. Replace the shaft if it is bent.

13 Inspect the selector drum grooves and selector fork guide pins for signs of wear or damage. Measure the width of each groove and the diameter of the corresponding fork guide pin and compare the results to the specifications. If any component is worn beyond its service limit or is damaged, it must be replaced.

14 Check that the selector drum needle bearing rotates freely and has no sign of freeplay between it and the crankcase (see illustration). Replace the bearing if necessary. Drift it out of the crankcase, noting

that once it has been removed it cannot be re-used. Draw or drive the new bearing onto place, making sure it enters squarely.

15 Make sure the cam plunger moves freely in the plunger bolt, and that the spring is not worn or damaged.

Installation

16 Slide the drum halfway into the crankcase, then fit the input shaft selector fork over the drum. On 550 models, the fork must be fitted so that the longer side of the fork boss faces the left-hand end of the drum (see illustration 31.8). On 750 models, the fork must be fitted so that the longer side of the fork boss faces the right-hand end of drum (see illustration). Slide the drum all the way home, then fit the fork guide pin into the fork, making sure it enters the middle groove

in the drum, and secure it with a new split pin (see illustrations 31.4b and a).

17 If removed, fit the cam locating pin into the hole in the drum (see illustration). Slide the cam onto the right-hand end of the drum, making sure the slot in the cam locates over the pin (see illustration). Secure the cam with the circlip, making sure it is properly seated in its groove (see illustration 31.7).

18 Fit the spring and plunger into the cam plunger bolt, then fit the bolt into the bottom of the crankcase and tighten it securely (see illustration 31.6). On 750 models, a torque setting is specified (see the beginning of the Chapter). Align the selector drum so that the neutral detent in the cam faces down and the plunger locates in it (see illustration).

19 Install the selector drum guide bolt and its lockwasher into the bottom of the crankcase, making sure the bolt end fits into the guide

31.19 Fit the guide bolt with its tab washer

groove in the drum **(see illustration)**. Tighten the bolt securely, then bend up the tab on the washer to secure it **(see illustration 31.5)**. On 750 models, a torque setting is specified (see the beginning of the Chapter).

20 Lubricate the selector fork shaft with clean engine oil and slide it into its bore in the crankcase, making sure the E-clip is fitted to the left-hand end **(see illustration 31.3a)**. As the shaft is installed, fit each output shaft selector fork in turn, making sure the longer side of each fork boss faces the left-hand side, and that the guide pins locate in the outer tracks in the selector drum **(see illustration 31.3b)**.

21 Reassemble the crankcase halves (see Section 24).

32 Initial start-up after overhaul

1 Make sure the engine oil level is correct (see *Daily (pre-ride) checks*).

2 Pull the plug caps off the spark plugs and insert a spare spark plug into each cap. Position the spare plugs so that their bodies are earthed (grounded) against the engine. Turn the ignition switch ON and make sure the kill switch is in the RUN position, then crank the engine over with the starter until the oil pressure light goes off (which indicates that oil pressure exists). Turn off the ignition. Remove the spare spark plugs and reconnect the plug caps.

3 Make sure there is fuel in the tank, then turn the fuel tap to the ON position and operate the choke.

4 Start the engine and allow it to run at a moderately fast idle until it reaches operating temperature.

⚠️ *Warning: If the oil pressure light doesn't go off, or it comes on while the engine is running, stop the engine immediately.*

5 Check carefully for oil leaks and make sure the transmission and controls, especially the brakes, function properly before road testing the machine. Refer to Section 33 for the recommended running-in procedure.

6 Upon completion of the road test, and after the engine has cooled down completely, recheck the valve clearances (see Chapter 1) and check the engine oil level (see *Daily (pre-ride) checks*).

33 Recommended running-in procedure

1 Treat the machine gently for the first few miles to make sure oil has circulated throughout the engine and any new parts installed have started to seat.

2 Even greater care is necessary if the engine has been rebored or a new crankshaft has been installed. In the case of a rebore, the bike will have to be run in as when new. This means greater use of the transmission and a restraining hand on the throttle until at least 500 miles (800 km) have been covered. There's no point in keeping to any set speed limit - the main idea is to keep from labouring the engine and to gradually increase performance up to the 500 mile (800 km) mark. These recommendations can be lessened to an extent when only a new crankshaft is installed. Experience is the best guide, since it's easy to tell when an engine is running freely. The following maximum engine speed limitations, which Kawasaki provide for new motorcycles, can be used as a guide.

3 If a lubrication failure is suspected, stop the engine immediately and try to find the cause. If an engine is run without oil, even for a short period of time, severe damage will occur.

Running-in recommendations

Up to 500 miles (800 km)	4000 rpm max	Vary throttle position/speed
500 to 1000 miles (800 to 1600 km)	6000 rpm max	Vary throttle position/speed. Use full throttle for short bursts
Over 1000 miles (1600 km)	10 000 rpm max	Do not exceed tachometer red line

2

Chapter 3
Fuel and exhaust systems

Contents

Degrees of difficulty

| Easy, suitable for novice with little experience | | Fairly easy, suitable for beginner with some experience | | Fairly difficult, suitable for competent DIY mechanic | | Difficult, suitable for experienced DIY mechanic | | Very difficult, suitable for expert DIY or professional | |

Specifications

Fuel
Grade .... Unleaded, minimum 91 RON (Research Octane Number)
Fuel tank capacity (inc. reserve)
  550 models .... 15 litres
  750 models .... 17 litres
Fuel tank reserve capacity
  550 models .... 3.2 litres
  750 models .... 3.0 litres

Carburettors
550 models
  Type .... Keihin CVK30
  Bore .... 30 mm
750 models
  Type .... Keihin CVK32
  Bore .... 32 mm

Carburettor adjustments
Pilot screw setting (turns out)
  550 (UK) .... 1 3/4 to 2 1/4 turns out
  750 C1, C2, C3 and C4 models (UK) .... 1 5/8 turns out
  750 C5 and D1 models (UK) .... 1 1/2 turns out
  All US models .... Pre-set
Float height .... 15.0 to 17.0 mm
Fuel level .... 0.5 mm below to 1.5 mm above float bowl mating surface
Idle speed .... see Chapter 1
Synchronisation vacuum .... see Chapter 1

3

Jet sizes - 550 models

Pilot jet 35
Pilot air jet 160
Needle jet 6
Jet needle N67J
Main jet
  Cylinders 1 and 4 108
  Cylinders 2 and 3 110
Main air jet 100
Starter jet 52

Jet sizes - 750 models

Pilot jet 35
Pilot air jet . . . . not available
Needle jet . . . . not available
Jet needle
  C1, C2, C3 and C4 models N52S
  C5 and D1 models
    Cylinders 1 and 4 . . . . N1GK
    Cylinders 2 and 3 . . . . N2NZ
Main jet
  C1, C2, C3 and C4 models
    Cylinders 1 and 4 88
    Cylinders 2 and 3 92
  C5 and D1 models
    Cylinders 1 and 4 82
    Cylinders 2 and 3 85
Main air jet 100
Starter jet . . . . not available

Torque setting

Cylinder head intake adapter bolts . . . . 12 Nm

---

1 General information and precautions

General information

The fuel system consists of the fuel tank, the fuel tap and filter, the carburettors, fuel hoses and control cables.

The fuel tap incorporates a filter which sits inside the tank.

The carburettors used on all models are CV types. For cold starting, a choke lever mounted on the left-handlebar and connected by a cable controls an enrichment circuit in the carburettor.

All except US ZR550 B1 and B2 models have a fuel gauge operated by a level sensor inside the tank.

UK ZR550 B4, B5 and B6 models, and UK ZR750 C3, C4, C5 and D1 models are fitted as standard with a carburettor heating system; this may have been subsequently fitted on earlier models.

Air is drawn into the carburettors via an air filter which is housed under the fuel tank.

The exhaust system on 550 models is a one piece four-into-one design, and on 750 models a three piece four-into-two.

Many of the fuel system service procedures are considered routine maintenance items and for that reason are included in Chapter 1.

Precautions

 Warning: Petrol (gasoline) is extremely flammable, so take extra precautions when you work on any part of the fuel system. Don't smoke or allow open flames or bare light bulbs near the work area, and don't work in a garage where a natural gas-type appliance is present. If you spill any fuel on your skin, rinse it off immediately with soap and water. When you perform any kind of work on the fuel system, wear safety glasses and have a fire extinguisher suitable for a class B type fire (flammable liquids) on hand.

Always perform service procedures in a well-ventilated area to prevent a build-up of fumes.

Never work in a building containing a gas appliance with a pilot light, or any other form of naked flame. Ensure there are no naked light bulbs or any sources of flame or sparks nearby.

Do not smoke (or allow anyone else to smoke) while in the vicinity of petrol (gasoline) or of components containing it. Remember the possible presence of vapour from these sources and move well clear before smoking.

Check all electrical equipment belonging to the house, garage or workshop where work is being undertaken (see the Safety first! section of this manual). Remember that certain electrical appliances such as drills, cutters etc. create sparks in the normal course of operation and must not be used near petrol

(gasoline) or any component containing it. Again, remember the possible presence of fumes before using electrical equipment.

Always mop up any spilt fuel and safely dispose of the rag used.

Any stored fuel that is drained off during servicing work must be kept in sealed containers that are suitable for holding petrol (gasoline), and clearly marked as such; the containers themselves should be kept in a safe place. Note that this last point applies equally to the fuel tank if it is removed from the machine; also remember to keep its cap closed at all times.

Read the Safety first! section of this manual carefully before starting work.

Owners of machines used in the US, particularly California, should note that their machines must comply at all times with Federal or State legislation governing the permissible levels of noise and of pollutants such as unburnt hydrocarbons, carbon monoxide etc. that can be emitted by those machines. All vehicles offered for sale must comply with legislation in force at the date of manufacture and must not subsequently be altered in any way which will affect their emission of noise or of pollutants.

In practice, this means that adjustments may not be made to any part of the fuel, ignition or exhaust systems by anyone who is not authorised or mechanically qualified to do so, or who does not have the tools, equipment

2.3 The tank is secured to the bracket by two bolts

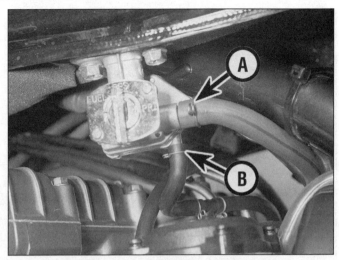

2.4a Raise the tank and detach the fuel hose (A) and the vacuum hose (B) from the tap . . .

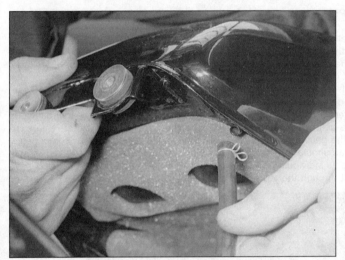

2.4b . . . and the water drain hose from its union

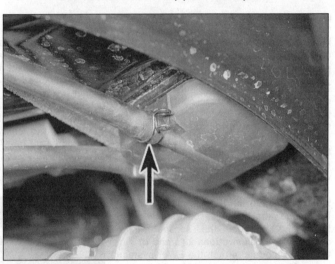

2.4c Detach the fuel level sensor overflow hose (arrowed) . . .

and data necessary to properly carry out the task. Also if any part of these systems is to be replaced it must be replaced with only genuine Kawasaki components or by components which are approved under the relevant legislation. The machine must never be used with any part of these systems removed, modified or damaged.

2 Fuel tank and fuel tap -
removal and installation

 Warning: Refer to the precautions given in Section 1 before starting work.

Fuel tank

Removal

1 Make sure the fuel tap is turned to the ON position and the fuel cap is secure.

2 Remove the seat and the side panels (see Chapter 7), then disconnect the battery, negative (-) terminal first.
3 Unscrew the bolts securing the rear of the tank to the tank bracket on the frame **(see illustration)**.
4 Draw the tank back slightly and raise it up at the rear, then release the clamps securing the fuel hose and the vacuum hose to the tap and detach the hoses **(see illustration)**. Also detach the water drain hose from its union on the underside of the tank **(see illustration)**. On models with a fuel gauge, also detach the sensor overflow drain hose and disconnect the sensor wiring at the connector **(see illustrations)**. On California models, detach the EVAP system hoses. Plug the fuel return hose (red) to prevent fuel flowing into the canister. Label the hoses to prevent confusion on installation.
5 Remove the tank by carefully drawing it back and away from the bike. Take care not to

lose the mounting rubbers from the front of the tank and from between the sides of the tank and the frame, noting how they fit.
6 Inspect the tank mounting rubbers for signs of damage or deterioration and replace them if necessary. Also inspect the rubbers on the fuel tank mounting bracket. If necessary,

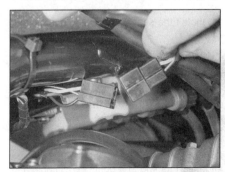

2.4d . . . and disconnect the sensor wiring

3

2.6 The tank bracket is secured by two bolts (arrowed)

2.7 Carefully manoeuvre the tank into position

unscrew the two bolts securing the bracket to the frame and remove the bracket **(see illustration)**. Replace the rubbers if necessary.

Installation

7 If removed, install the tank mounting bracket and tighten the bracket bolts securely **(see illustration 2.6)**. Check that the front and side tank rubbers are fitted, then carefully lower the fuel tank into position, making sure the rubbers remain in place **(see illustration)**.

8 With the tank raised at the rear, attach the water drain hose, the fuel hose and the vacuum hose to their unions **(see illustrations 2.4b and a)**. On models with a fuel gauge, attach the sensor overflow drain hose and connect the sensor wiring connector **(see illustrations 2.4c and d)**. On California models, attach the EVAP system hoses. Make sure all hoses are fitted fully onto their unions and secured by their clamps. Lower the tank and check that it is properly seated and is not pinching any control cables or wires. Check that there is no sign of fuel leakage.

9 Install the tank mounting bolts and tighten them securely **(see illustration)**.

10 Connect the battery, fitting the negative (-) terminal last. Start the engine and check that there is no sign of fuel leakage, then shut if off.

11 Install the seat and the side panels (see Chapter 7).

Fuel tap

Removal

12 The tap should not be removed unnecessarily due to the possibility of damaging the O-ring or the filter, and the tap should not be dismantled.

13 Remove the fuel tank as described above. Connect a drain hose to the fuel hose union and insert its end in a container suitable and large enough for storing the petrol (gasoline).

Turn the fuel tap to the PRI position, and allow the tank to fully drain.

14 Unscrew the two bolts securing the tap to the tank and withdraw the tap assembly **(see illustrations)**. Check the condition of the O-ring **(see illustration)**. If it is in good condition it can be re-used. If it is in any way deteriorated or damaged it must be replaced.

15 Clean the gauze filters using a high flash-point solvent to remove all traces of dirt and fuel sediment. Check the gauze for holes. If any are found, a new tap should be fitted as the filters are not available individually. Flush high flash-point solvent through the tap with

the lever in all positions, then blow it through with compressed air.

16 If the fuel tap is leaking, tightening the assembly screws on the front and back of the tap may help **(see illustrations)**. If leakage persists, remove the screws and disassemble the tap, noting how the components fit. Clean all components using a high flash-point solvent and inspect them for wear or damage. Replace the O-rings and gasket, whatever their condition. If any of the other components are worn or damaged, or if the tap is still leaking with new O-rings and gasket, a new tap must be fitted.

2.9 Tighten the tank mounting bolts securely

2.14a Unscrew the bolts . . .

2.14b . . . and remove the tap

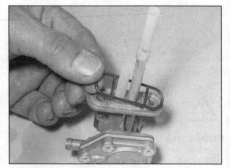

2.14c Check the condition of the O-ring and replace it if necessary

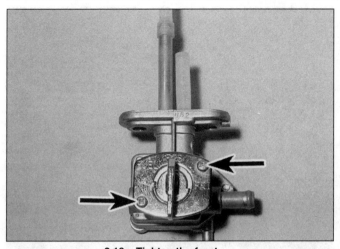

2.16a Tighten the front . . .

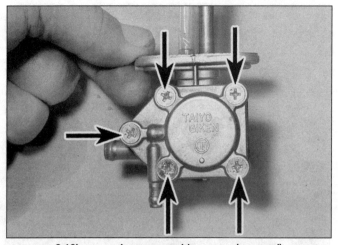

2.16b . . . and rear assembly screws (arrowed)

Installation

17 Check the condition of the tap mounting bolt nylon washers and replace them if damaged or deteriorated. Do not use steel washers.
18 Install the fuel tap into the tank, using a new O-ring if necessary, and tighten its bolts securely **(see illustrations 2.14c, b and a)**.
19 Install the fuel tank (see above).

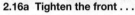

3 Fuel tank - cleaning and repair

1 All repairs to the fuel tank should be carried out by a professional who has experience in this critical and potentially dangerous work. Even after cleaning and flushing of the fuel system, explosive fumes can remain and ignite during repair of the tank.
2 If the fuel tank is removed from the bike, it should not be placed in an area where sparks or open flames could ignite the fumes coming out of the tank. Be especially careful inside garages where a natural gas-type appliance is located, because the pilot light could cause an explosion.
3 Flush and clean the tank using a high flash-point solvent. Make sure none of the hose unions are blocked.

4 Idle fuel/air mixture adjustment - general information

1 Due to the increased emphasis on controlling motorcycle exhaust emissions, certain governmental regulations have been formulated which directly affect the carburation of this machine. In order to comply with the regulations, the carburettors on US models are sealed so they can't be tampered with. The pilot screws on other models are accessible, but the use of an exhaust gas analyser is the only accurate way to adjust the

idle fuel/air mixture and be sure the machine doesn't exceed the emissions regulations.
2 The pilot screws are set to their correct position by the manufacturer and should not be adjusted unless it is necessary to do so for a carburettor overhaul. If the screws are adjusted they should be reset to the settings specified at the beginning of the Chapter.
3 If the engine runs extremely rough at idle or continually stalls, and if a carburettor overhaul does not cure the problem, take the motorcycle to a Kawasaki dealer equipped with an exhaust gas analyser. They will be able to properly adjust the idle fuel/air mixture to achieve a smooth idle and restore low speed performance.

5 Carburettor overhaul - general information

1 Poor engine performance, hesitation, hard starting, stalling, flooding and backfiring are all signs that major carburettor maintenance may be required.
2 Keep in mind that many so-called carburettor problems are really not carburettor problems at all, but mechanical problems within the engine or ignition system malfunctions. Try to establish for certain that the carburettors are in need of maintenance before beginning a major overhaul.
3 Check the fuel filter, the fuel hoses, the intake manifold joint clamps, the air filter, the ignition system, the spark plugs and carburettor synchronisation before assuming that a carburettor overhaul is required.
4 Most carburettor problems are caused by dirt particles, varnish and other deposits which build up in and block the fuel and air passages. Also, in time, gaskets and O-rings shrink or deteriorate and cause fuel and air leaks which lead to poor performance.
5 When overhauling the carburettors, disassemble them completely and clean the parts thoroughly with a carburettor cleaning

solvent and dry them with filtered, unlubricated compressed air. Blow through the fuel and air passages with compressed air to force out any dirt that may have been loosened but not removed by the solvent. Once the cleaning process is complete, reassemble the carburettor using new gaskets and O-rings.
6 Before disassembling the carburettors, make sure you have a carburettor rebuild kit (which will include all necessary O-rings and other parts), some carburettor cleaner, a supply of clean rags, some means of blowing out the carburettor passages and a clean place to work. It is recommended that only one carburettor be overhauled at a time to avoid mixing up parts.

6 Carburettors - removal and installation

> ⚠ **Warning: Refer to the precautions given in Section 1 before starting work.**

Removal

1 Remove the fuel tank and its bracket (see Section 2).
2 On 550 models, carefully pull each air filter housing end cover away from the housing **(see illustration)**.

6.2 Remove the air filter housing end covers

3

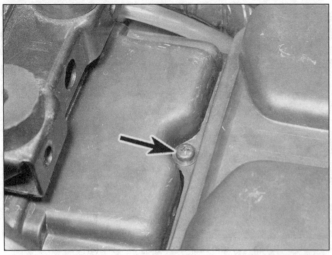

6.3 Remove the screw (arrowed) and lift out the rear section of the housing

6.4 Slide the spring bands (arrowed) back off the carburettors

6.5 Disconnect the carburettor heater system wiring connector

6.6a Slacken each clamp screw (arrowed) to release the carburettors . . .

3 Remove the screw securing the rear section of the air filter housing to the front section, then lift the rear section out **(see illustration)**.

4 Slide back the spring bands securing the air filter housing rubbers to the carburettor intakes **(see illustration)**. Manoeuvre the air filter housing backwards so that the rubbers detach from the carburettor intakes and provide clearance for the carburettors to be removed.

5 On UK ZR550 B4, B5 and B6 models and UK ZR750 C3, C4, C5 and D1 models, trace the carburettor heater wiring and disconnect it at the connector **(see illustration)**.

6 Slacken the clamps securing the carburettors to the cylinder head intake adapters and ease the carburettors off the adapters, noting how they fit **(see illustration)**. Manoeuvre the carburettors out of the frame, noting the routing of the various hoses, and support them on the frame or engine for removal of the cables **(see illustration)**.

Note: *Keep the carburettors upright to prevent fuel spillage from the float chambers and the possibility of the piston diaphragms being damaged.*

7 Detach the throttle cables from the carburettors (see Section 10).

6.6b . . . and ease them off the adapters and out of the frame

8 Detach the choke cable from the carburettors (see Section 11).

9 Place a suitable container below the float chambers then slacken the drain screws and drain all the fuel from the carburettors. Once all the fuel has been drained, tighten the drain screws securely.

10 If necessary, unscrew the screws securing the intake adapters to the cylinder head and remove the adapters and O-rings, noting how they fit. Discard the O-rings as new ones must be used. Note that the cylinder number for each adapter is marked at the top of the intake duct - they are not interchangeable and must be installed correctly.

Installation

11 Installation is the reverse of removal, noting the following.

a) *Check for cracks or splits in the cylinder head intake adapters and air filter housing rubbers, and replace them if necessary.*

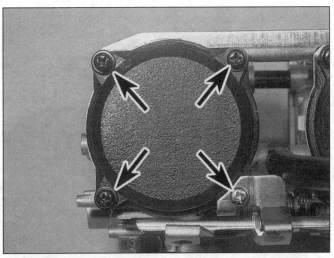

7.2a Remove the screws (arrowed) and lift off the top cover . . .

7.2b . . . then remove the spring

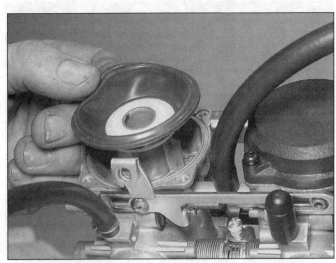

7.3 Carefully remove the diaphragm and piston assembly

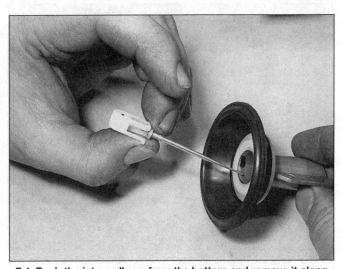

7.4 Push the jet needle up from the bottom and remove it along with the spring seat if not already removed

b) If removed, make sure the intake adapters are installed correctly using new O-rings (see Step 10). Apply a non-permanent thread locking compound to the bolt threads and tighten to the specified torque.

c) Make sure the air filter housing and the cylinder head intake adapters are fully engaged with the carburettors and their retaining springs or clamps are secure.

d) Make sure all hoses are correctly routed and secured, and not trapped or kinked.

e) On UK ZR550 B4, B5 and B6 models and UK ZR750 C3, C4, C5 and D1 models, do not forget to connect the carburettor heater wiring connectors.

f) Check the operation of the choke and throttle cables and adjust them as necessary (see Chapter 1).

g) Check idle speed and carburettor synchronisation and adjust as necessary (see Chapter 1).

7 Carburettors - disassembly, cleaning and inspection

Warning: Refer to the precautions given in Section 1 before starting work.

Disassembly

1 Remove the carburettors from the machine as described in the previous Section. **Note:** *Do not separate the carburettors unless this is absolutely necessary; each carburettor can be dismantled sufficiently for all normal cleaning and adjustments while still in place on the mounting brackets. Dismantle the carburettors separately to avoid interchanging parts, or else store the parts from each in marked containers.*

2 Unscrew and remove the top cover retaining screws **(see illustration)**. Lift off the cover and remove the spring from inside the piston **(see illustration)**. The spring seat may come out with the spring - if not, it will come out with the jet needle (Step 4).

3 Carefully peel the diaphragm away from its sealing groove in the carburettor and withdraw the diaphragm and piston assembly, noting which way round it fits **(see illustration)**. *Caution: Do not use a sharp instrument to displace the diaphragm as it is easily damaged.*

4 Push the jet needle up from the bottom of the piston and withdraw it from the top **(see illustration)**. Take care not to lose the spring seat, if not already removed.

5 Where fitted, remove the screw securing the carburettor heater bracket and pull the heater out of the carburettor body **(see illustration)**.

6 Remove the screws securing the float chamber to the base of the carburettor and

3

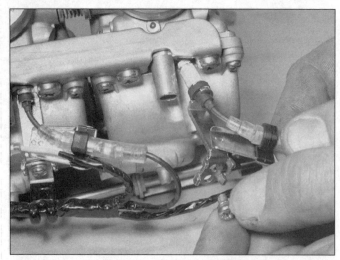

7.5 Remove the heater bracket screw and pull out the heater

7.6a The float chamber is secured by four screws (arrowed)

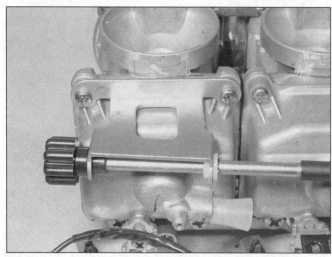

7.6b Note the throttle stop screw bracket secured to the float chamber on the no. 1 carburettor on 550 models

7.7 Withdraw the float pivot pin and remove the float assembly

remove the float chamber, noting how it fits **(see illustration)**. Remove the rubber gasket and discard it as a new one must be used. On 550 models, note that two of the float chamber screws on the no. 1 carburettor also secure the throttle stop screw bracket **(see illustration)**.

7 Using a pair of thin-nose pliers, carefully withdraw the float pivot pin **(see illustration)**. If necessary, carefully displace the pin using a suitable small punch or a nail. Remove the float assembly, noting how it fits **(see illustration 9.6b)**. Unhook the needle valve from the tab on the float, noting how it fits **(see illustration 9.6a)**.

8 Unscrew and remove the main jet from the base of the needle jet holder **(see illustration)**. 9 Unscrew and remove the needle jet holder **(see illustration)**. With the holder removed the needle jet may come out if it is loose - if it does, note which way round it fits **(see illustration 9.4a)**.

10 Unscrew and remove the pilot jet **(see illustration)**.

7.8 Unscrew and remove the main jet (arrowed)

7.9 Unscrew and remove the needle jet holder (arrowed)

7.10 Unscrew and remove the pilot jet (arrowed)

7.11 Unscrew and remove the pilot screw (arrowed)

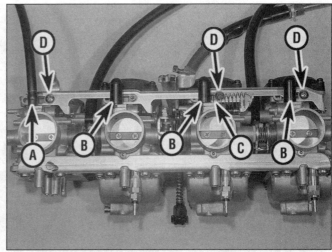

7.12 Detach the vacuum hose (A) and remove the caps (B).
Unhook the spring (C), then remove the three linkage
bar screws (D) and lift off the bar

11 On UK models, the pilot screw can be removed from the carburettor, but note that its setting will be disturbed (see *Haynes Hint*). Unscrew and remove the pilot screw along with its spring, washer and O-ring **(see illustration)**. Discard the O-ring as a new one must be used.

To record the pilot screw's current setting, turn the screw in until it seats lightly, counting the number of turns necessary to achieve this, then fully unscrew it. On installation, the screw is simply backed out the number of turns you've recorded.

12 Detach the vacuum hose and remove the vacuum blanking caps, then unhook the choke linkage bar return spring from the vacuum take-off adapter **(see illustration)**. Remove the three screws securing the linkage bar to the carburettors, then remove the outer plastic washers **(see illustration 9.1d)**. Lift off the bar, noting how it fits, and remove the inner plastic washers **(see illustrations 9.1c, b and a)**.
13 Unscrew the choke plunger nut and withdraw the plunger and spring from the carburettor body, noting how they fit. Take care not to lose the spring when removing the nut.

Cleaning

Caution: Use only a petroleum based solvent for carburettor cleaning. Don't use caustic cleaners.
14 Submerge the metal components in the solvent for approximately thirty minutes (or longer, if the directions recommend it).
15 After the carburettor has soaked long enough for the cleaner to loosen and dissolve most of the varnish and other deposits, use a

nylon-bristled brush to remove the stubborn deposits. Rinse it again, then dry it with compressed air.
16 Use a jet of compressed air to blow out all of the fuel and air passages in the main and upper body, not forgetting the air jets in the carburettor intake **(see illustration)**.
Caution: Never clean the jets or passages with a piece of wire or a drill bit, as they will be enlarged, causing the fuel and air metering rates to be upset.

Inspection

17 Check the operation of the choke plunger. If it doesn't move smoothly, inspect the needle on the end of the choke plunger, the spring and the plunger linkage bar. Replace any component that is worn, damaged or bent.
18 If removed from the carburettor, check the tapered portion of the pilot screw and the spring and O-ring for wear or damage. Replace them if necessary.
19 Check the carburettor body, float chamber and top cover for cracks, distorted sealing surfaces and other damage. If any defects are found, replace the faulty component, although replacement of the entire carburettor will probably be necessary

7.16 Do not forget the air passages
in the intakes (arrowed)

(check with a Kawasaki dealer on the availability of separate components).
20 Check the piston diaphragm for splits, holes and general deterioration. Holding it up to a light will help to reveal problems of this nature.
21 Insert the piston in the carburettor body and check that it moves up-and-down smoothly. Check the surface of the piston for wear. If it's worn excessively or doesn't move smoothly in the guide, replace the components as necessary.
22 Check the jet needle for straightness by rolling it on a flat surface such as a piece of glass. Replace it if it's bent or if the tip is worn.
23 Check the tip of the float needle valve and the valve seat. If either has grooves or scratches in it, or is in any way worn, they must be replaced as a set.
24 Operate the throttle shaft to make sure the throttle butterfly valve opens and closes smoothly. If it doesn't, cleaning the throttle linkage may help. Otherwise, replace the carburettor.
25 Check the floats for damage. This will usually be apparent by the presence of fuel inside one of the floats. If the floats are damaged, they must be replaced.

8 Carburettors -
  separation and joining

Warning: Refer to the precautions given in Section 1 before proceeding

Separation

1 The carburettors do not need to be separated for normal overhaul. If you need to separate them (to replace a carburettor body, for example), refer to the following procedure.

3

8.4 Note the arrangement of the various linkage and synchronisation springs (arrowed) before separation

2 Remove the carburettors from the machine (see Section 6). Mark the body of each carburettor with its cylinder location to ensure that it is positioned correctly on reassembly.
3 Disconnect the fuel tap vacuum hose and remove the blanking caps or hoses (UK models), or EVAP and suction valve hoses or blanking caps as appropriate (US and California models) from the take-off stubs on the carburettors. Make a note of which hoses fit where. Unhook the choke linkage bar return spring **(see illustration 7.12 and 9.1e)**. Remove the three screws securing the linkage bar to the carburettors, then remove the outer plastic washers **(see illustration 9.1d)**. Lift off the bar, noting how it fits, and remove the inner plastic washers **(see illustrations 9.1c, b and a)**.
4 Make a note of how the throttle return

springs, linkage assembly and carburettor synchronisation springs are arranged to ensure that they are fitted correctly on reassembly **(see illustration)**. Also note the arrangement of the various hoses and their unions. On 550 models, depending on which carburettors are being separated, remove the two screws on the no. 1 carburettor float chamber securing the throttle stop screw bracket **(see illustration 7.6b)**.
5 Remove the screws securing the carburettors to the two mounting brackets and remove the brackets **(see illustrations)**. The carburettors are assembled using a thread-locking compound which may make the bracket screws difficult to remove.
6 Carefully separate the carburettors. Retrieve the synchronisation springs and note the fitting of the various fuel hose T-pieces

and joining pipes and vent hose T-pieces as they are separated. Discard their O-rings as new ones must be used.

Joining

7 Assembly is the reverse of the disassembly procedure, noting the following.
 a) *Make sure the fuel hose T-pieces and joining pipes and the air vent hose T-pieces are correctly and securely installed with new O-rings.*
 b) *Install the synchronisation springs after the carburettors are joined together. Make sure they are correctly and squarely seated* **(see illustration 8.4)**.
 c) *Apply a suitable non-permanent thread-locking compound to the carburettor bracket screws and tighten them securely.*
 d) *Check the operation of both the choke and throttle linkages ensuring that both operate smoothly and return quickly under spring pressure before installing the carburettors on the machine.*
 e) *Install the carburettors (see Section 6) and check carburettor synchronisation and idle speed (see Chapter 1).*

9 Carburettors - reassembly, float height and fuel level check

 Warning: Refer to the precautions given in Section 1 before proceeding.

Reassembly and float height check

Note: *When reassembling the carburettors, be sure to use all new O-rings and seals. Do not overtighten the carburettor jets and screws as they are easily damaged.*
1 Install the choke plunger and spring into the carburettor body and tighten the nut to

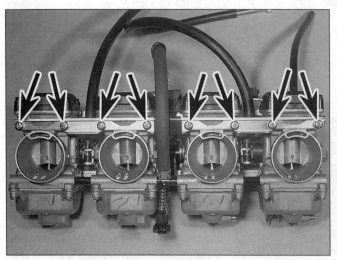

8.5a Unscrew the upper mounting bracket screws (arrowed) ...

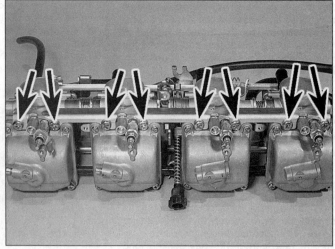

8.5b ... and the lower mounting bracket screws (arrowed) (600 type shown)

9.1a Fit the inner plastic washers . . .

9.1b . . . and the linkage bar . . .

9.1c . . . making sure it locates correctly onto each plunger

9.1d Install the screws with the outer plastic washers

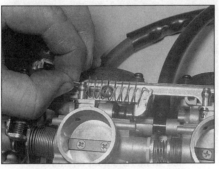

9.1e Hook the spring around the take-off adapter . . .

9.1f . . . then fit the caps and the vacuum hose

secure it. Install the choke linkage bar inner plastic washers, then fit the bar onto the plungers, making sure the slots locate

9.3 Install the pilot jet . . .

9.4b . . . the needle jet holder . . .

correctly behind the nipple on the end of each choke plunger (see illustrations). Install the outer plastic washers and secure the linkage

9.4a . . . the needle jet (if removed) . . .

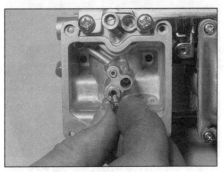

9.5 . . . and the main jet

bar in place with the screws (see illustration). Hook the return spring to the vacuum take-off adapter, then fit the cap (see illustration).

2 Install the pilot screw (if removed) along with its spring, washer and O-ring, turning it in until it seats lightly (see illustration 7.11). Now, turn the screw out the number of turns previously recorded, or as specified at the beginning of the Chapter.

3 Install the pilot jet (see illustration).

4 If removed, fit the needle jet into the carburettor with its tapered (smaller) end first (see illustration). Screw the needle jet holder into the carburettor (see illustration).

5 Install the main jet into the needle jet holder (see illustration).

6 Hook the float needle valve onto the tab on the float assembly, then position the float assembly in the carburettor and install the pin, making sure it is secure (see illustrations).

7 To check the float height, hold the carburettor so the float hangs down, then tilt it back until the needle valve is just seated, but not so far that the needle's spring-loaded tip is compressed. Measure the height of the bottom of the float above the gasket face (with the gasket removed) with an accurate ruler (see illustration). The correct setting should be as given in the Specifications at the beginning of the Chapter. If it is incorrect, adjust the float height by carefully bending the float tab a little at a time until the correct height is obtained. Repeat the procedure for both carburettors.

3

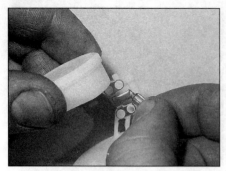

9.6a Fit the needle valve onto its tab
on the float . . .

9.6b . . . making sure the needle valve fits
into the seat (arrowed) . . .

9.6c . . . then install the float
and fit the pivot pin

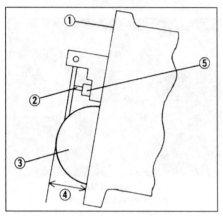

9.7 Float height measurement

1	Carburettor	3	Float
	body gasket face	4	Float height
2	Needle valve tip	5	Needle valve

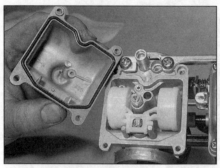

9.8 Install the float chamber
using a new gasket

9.11 Install the diaphragm assembly with
the indent in the piston facing the air
intake side

8 With the float height checked, fit a new gasket to the float chamber, making sure it is seated properly in its groove, then install the chamber on the carburettor and tighten its screws securely **(see illustration)**.

9 Where fitted, fit the carburettor heater into the carburettor body and mount the bracket on the float chamber **(see illustration 7.5)**.

10 Install the jet needle and spring seat into the diaphragm assembly **(see illustration 7.4)**.

11 Insert the diaphragm assembly into the piston guide with the indent on the piston facing the intake side of the carburettor **(see illustration)**. Lightly push the piston down, ensuring the needle is correctly aligned with the needle jet. Press the diaphragm outer edge into its groove, making sure it is correctly seated. Check the diaphragm is not creased, and that the piston moves smoothly up and down in the guide.

12 Install the spring into the diaphragm assembly, making sure it locates correctly onto the spring seat, then fit the top cover, making sure the top of the spring fits over the lug in the middle of the cover, and tighten its screws securely **(see illustration)**.

13 Checking the fuel level is advised before the carburettors are installed (see Step 15 on).

14 Install the carburettors (see Section 6).

Fuel level check

15 Lightly clamp the carburettor assembly in the jaws of a vice. Make sure the vice jaws are lined with wood. Set the fuel tank next to the vice, but at an elevation that is higher than the carburettors (resting on a box, for example). Connect a hose from the fuel tap to the fuel inlet fitting on the carburettor assembly - make sure the fuel tap is in the ON or RES position.

16 Attach Kawasaki service tool no. 57001-1017 to the drain fitting on the bottom of one of the carburettor float chambers (all four will be checked) **(see illustration)**. This is a clear plastic tube graduated in millimetres. An alternative is to use a length of clear plastic tubing and an accurate ruler. Hold the graduated tube (or the free end of the clear plastic tube) against the carburettor body, as

9.12 Install the top cover, making sure the
spring is correctly located top and bottom

shown in the accompanying illustration. If the Kawasaki tool is being used, raise the zero mark to a point several millimetres above the bottom edge of the carburettor main body. If a piece of clear plastic tubing is being used, make a mark on the tubing at a point several millimetres above the bottom edge of the carburettor main body.

17 Unscrew the drain screw at the bottom of the float chamber a couple of turns, then turn

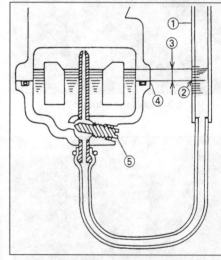

9.16 Fuel level measurement

1	Fuel level gauge	4	Bottom edge of
2	Gauge zero mark		carburettor body
3	Fuel level	5	Drain screw

the fuel tap to the PRI position - fuel will flow into the tube. Wait for the fuel level to stabilise, then slowly lower the tube until the zero mark is level with the bottom edge of the carburettor body. **Note:** *Don't lower the zero mark below the bottom edge of the carburettor then bring it back up - the reading won't be accurate.*

18 Measure the distance between the mark and top of the fuel level in the tube or gauge. This distance is the fuel level - write it down on a piece of paper, screw in the drain screw, turn the fuel tap to the On or Reserve position, then move on to the next carburettor and check it the same way.

19 Compare your fuel level readings to the value listed in this Chapter's Specifications. If the fuel level in any carburettor is not correct, remove the float chamber and bend the tang up or down (see Step 7), as necessary, then recheck the fuel level. **Note:** *Bending the tang up increases the float height and lowers the fuel level - bending it down decreases the float height and raises the fuel level.*

20 After the fuel level for each carburettor has been adjusted, install the carburettor assembly (see Section 6).

10 Throttle cables - removal and installation

> **Warning: Refer to the precautions given in Section 1 before proceeding.**

Removal

1 Remove the carburettors (see Section 6, Steps 1 to 6).

2 Lift the lower end of the cable out of its mounting bracket and detach the inner cable from the throttle cam **(see illustration)**. Repeat for the other cable. Keep the carburettors upright to prevent fuel spillage.

3 Remove the handlebar switch/throttle pulley housing screws and separate the halves **(see illustrations)**. Remove the cable elbows from the housing, noting how they fit and hook the cable ends out of the pulley **(see illustration)**. Mark each cable to ensure it is connected correctly on installation.

4 Remove the cables from the machine noting the correct routing of each cable.

Installation

5 Install the cables making sure they are correctly routed. The cables must not interfere with any other component and should not be kinked or bent sharply.

6 Lubricate the end of each inner cable with multi-purpose grease and attach them to the pulley **(see illustration 10.3c)**. Install the cables into the throttle pulley housing, making sure the accelerator cable is at the front and the decelerator is at the back. Assemble the housing, aligning its locating pin with the hole in the front of the handlebar **(see illustration 10.3b)**. Install the retaining screws, and tighten them securely.

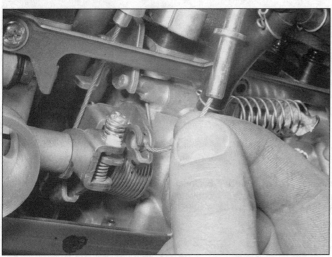

10.2 Lift the outer cable out of its bracket and detach the inner cable nipple from the cam

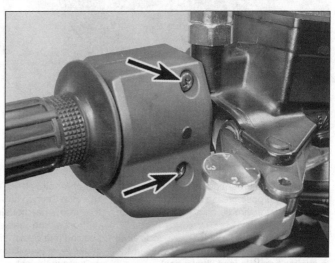

10.3a The switch housing is secured by two screws (arrowed)

10.3b Separate switch halves and displace the cable elbows . . .

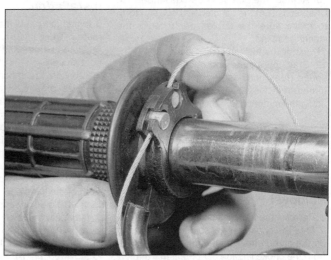

10.3c . . . then detach the cable ends from the pulley

3

10.8 Cables should be correctly located in the throttle cam and bracket

11.2a Pull the outer cable out of its bracket . . .

11.2b . . . and detach the inner cable nipple

11.3a Separate the switch halves . . .

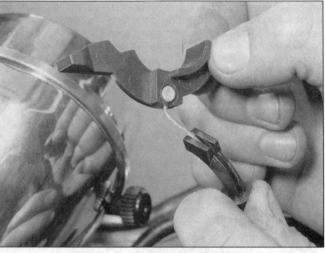

11.3b . . . and remove the cable and lever

7 Lubricate the lower end of each inner cable with multi-purpose grease and attach them to the carburettor throttle cam **(see illustration 10.2)**.
8 Make sure the cables are correctly connected and locate the outer cables in the mounting brackets **(see illustration)**.
9 Install the carburettors (see Section 6).
10 Adjust the cables as described in Chapter 1. Turn the handlebars back and forth to make sure the cables don't cause the steering to bind.
11 Install the fuel tank (see Section 2).
12 Start the engine and check that the idle speed does not rise as the handlebars are turned. If it does, correct the problem before riding the motorcycle.

11 Choke cable - removal and installation

Removal

1 Remove the fuel tank (see Section 2).
2 Free the choke outer cable from its bracket on the carburettor and detach the inner cable from the choke linkage bar **(see illustrations)**.
3 Unscrew the two left-hand side handlebar

switch/choke lever housing screws and separate the two halves, noting how the lever fits into the housing **(see illustration)**. Withdraw the cable and lever from the housing and detach the cable nipple from the choke lever **(see illustration)**.
4 Remove the cable from the machine noting its correct routing.

Installation

5 Install the cable making sure it is correctly routed. The cable must not interfere with any other component and should not be kinked or bent sharply.
6 Lubricate the upper cable nipple with multi-purpose grease. Attach the nipple to the choke lever **(see illustration 11.3b)**, then install the lever and cable in the switch/choke lever housing, making sure the cable elbow is correctly fitted **(see illustration)**. Fit the two halves of the housing onto the handlebar, making sure the lever fits correctly, and the pin in the front half locates in the hole in the front of the handlebar **(see illustration 11.3a)**. Install the screws and tighten them securely.
7 Lubricate the lower cable nipple with multi-purpose grease and attach it to the choke linkage bar on the carburettor **(see illustration 11.2b)**. Fit the outer cable into its bracket **(see illustration 11.2a)**.

8 Check the operation and adjustment of the choke cable (see Chapter 1).
9 Install the fuel tank (see Section 2).

12 Air filter housing - removal and installation

Removal

1 Remove the fuel tank (see Section 2).
2 Remove the carburettors (see Section 6).
3 On UK models with a carburettor heater system, disconnect the atmospheric

11.6 Check that the cable elbow is correctly fitted in the switch housing

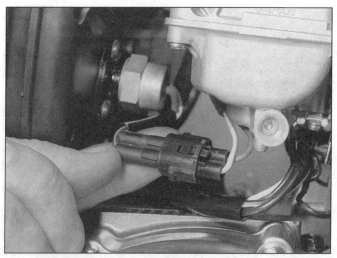

12.3 Disconnect the atmospheric temperature sensor wiring connector

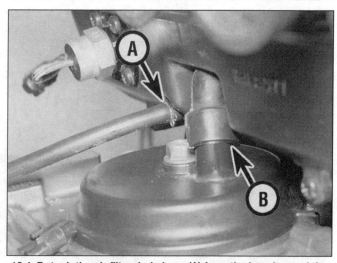

12.4 Detach the air filter drain hose (A) from the housing and the breather hose (B) from the breather cover

12.5 Manoeuvre the housing out of the frame

13.1 Remove the silencer mounting bolt and nut

temperature sensor wiring connector **(see illustration)**.

4 Release the clamp securing the air filter drain hose to the bottom of the front of the air filter housing, then detach the hose from its union **(see illustration)**. Also release the clamp securing the engine breather hose to the breather on the top of the crankcase and detach the hose.

5 Manoeuvre the air filter housing forwards and out of the frame **(see illustration)**.

Installation

6 Installation is the reverse of removal.

13 Exhaust system -
 removal and installation

⚠ *Warning: If the engine has been running the exhaust system will be very hot. Let the system cool before carrying out any work.*

550 models

Removal

1 Unscrew and remove the silencer mounting nut and bolt **(see illustration)**.

2 Support the system, unscrew the downpipe clamp nuts from the cylinder head, then remove the system **(see illustrations)**. Note

13.2a Unscrew the downpipe clamp nuts (arrowed) . . .

how the half-ring retainers locate against the head of each pipe and are taped in place **(see illustration)**. Remove the gasket from each port in the cylinder head and discard them; new ones must be used **(see illustration 13.4)**.

3 Check the rubber dampers in the silencer mounting points; if damaged or deteriorated replace them with new ones.

13.2b . . . and remove the system

3

13.2c Note how the half-ring retainers fit

13.4 Fit a new gasket into each port

13.5 Butt the clamps against the half-ring retainers

13.7 Slacken the clamp bolt (arrowed) . . .

Installation

4 Fit a new gasket into each of the cylinder head ports **(see illustration)**. Apply a smear of grease to the gaskets to keep them in place whilst fitting the downpipe if necessary.

5 Manoeuvre the system into position so that the head of each downpipe is located in its port in the cylinder head **(see illustration 13.2b)**. Fit the clamps onto the studs, making sure the half-ring retainers are installed and the clamps butt up against them, then install the clamp nuts finger-tight to hold the system in place **(see illustration)**. Supporting the system, align the silencer mounting bracket at the rear and install the bolt with its washer but do not yet tighten the nut **(see illustration 13.1)**. Now tighten the flange nuts securely, then tighten the silencer nut.

6 Run the engine until it is warmed up and check the system for leaks. Allow the engine to cool then retighten all the clamp nuts and the silencer nut.

750 models

Silencers

7 Slacken the clamp on the joint between the silencer and the downpipe **(see illustration)**.
8 Unscrew and remove the silencer mounting nut and bolt, then release the silencer from the exhaust downpipe assembly using a twisting motion **(see illustration)**.

13.8 . . . and remove mounting nut and bolt

9 Inspect the bushes for signs of damage and replace them if necessary. Remove the sealing ring from either the end of the silencer or inside the downpipe assembly and check it for damage. Replace it if necessary.
10 Install the silencer into the downpipe assembly, using a new sealing ring if required, and making sure it is pushed fully home **(see illustration)**. Align the silencer mounting

13.10 Use a new sealing ring if required

bracket at the rear then install the bolt from the inside. Tighten the clamp bolt and the silencer nut securely **(see illustrations 13.7 and 13.8)**.

11 Run the engine until it is warmed up and check the system for leaks. Allow the engine to cool then retighten the clamp bolts and silencer nuts.

Downpipe assembly

12 Remove the silencers (see above).

13 Supporting the assembly, unscrew the downpipe clamp nuts from the cylinder head, then remove the assembly from the machine **(see illustration 13.2a)**. Note how the half-ring retainers locate against the head of each pipe and are taped in place **(see illustration 13.2c)**.

14 Remove the gasket from each port in the cylinder head and check them for damage. Replace them if necessary.

15 Fit the gasket into each of the cylinder head ports **(see illustration 13.4)**. Apply a thin smear of grease to the gaskets to keep them in place whilst fitting the downpipe if necessary.

16 Manoeuvre the system into position so that the head of each downpipe is located in its port in the cylinder head **(see illustration 13.2b)**. Fit the clamps onto the studs with the notch in the clamp facing down, making sure the half-ring retainers are installed and the clamps butt up against them, then install the clamp nuts and tighten them securely **(see illustration 13.5)**.

17 Install the silencers (see above).

18 Run the engine until it is warmed up and check the system for leaks. Allow the engine to cool then retighten all the clamp bolts and silencer nuts.

Complete system

19 Unscrew and remove the silencer mounting nuts and bolts **(see illustration 13.8)**.

20 Supporting the system, unscrew the downpipe clamp nuts from the cylinder head then remove the system from the machine **(see illustration 13.2a)**. Note how the half-ring retainers locate against the head of each pipe and are taped in place **(see illustration 13.2c)**.

21 Remove the gasket from each port in the cylinder head and check them for damage. Replace them if necessary.

22 Fit a new gasket into each of the cylinder head ports **(see illustration 13.4)**. Apply a smear of grease to the gaskets to keep them in place whilst fitting the downpipe if necessary.

23 Manoeuvre the system into position so that the head of each downpipe is located in its port in the cylinder head **(see illustration 13.2b)**. Fit the clamps onto the studs with the notch in the clamp facing down, making sure the half-ring retainers are installed and the clamps butt up against them, then install the clamp nuts finger-tight to hold the system in place **(see illustration 13.5)**. Supporting the system, align the silencer mounting brackets at the rear and install the bolts with their

washers but do not yet tighten the nut **(see illustration 13.8)**. Now tighten the flange nuts securely, then tighten the silencer nut.

24 Run the engine until it is warmed up and check the system for leaks. Allow the engine to cool then retighten all the clamp nuts and the silencer nuts.

14 Evaporative emission control (EVAP) system (California models) - general information

1 The EVAP system prevents the escape of fuel vapours into the atmosphere and functions as follows **(see illustration)**.

2 Whilst the engine is stopped, vapour emitted by the evaporation of fuel in the tank passes through a vent hose to the top of the separator where some of it condenses and passes through the separator into the pump unit, but the majority passes into the canister. Vapour emitted from the carburettor float chambers passes through a vent hose directly to the canister. From there it can only escape to the atmosphere by passing through the activated charcoal which traps the vapour completely.

3 When the engine is started all vapour stored in the canister is purged via the purge hose into the air filter housing where it passes into the engine for burning in the normal way. At the same time a simple pump, operated by

the vacuum from no. 3 carburettor intake stub, returns all liquid fuel in the separator to the fuel tank via the return hose.

4 The fuel tank filler cap has a one way valve which allows air into the tank as the volume of fuel decreases, but prevents any fuel vapour from escaping.

5 The system is not adjustable and can be tested only by a Kawasaki dealer. Checks which can be performed by the owner are given in Chapter 1.

15 Air suction valves (US models) - general information

1 The US models incorporate an air injection system designed to enhance the burning of hydrocarbons in the exhaust gases, thus reducing toxic emissions. The system employs a modified cylinder head and valve cover, in which air is drawn through a reed valve arrangement to the exhaust ports.

2 The system is automatic in operation and except for the reed valve check described in Chapter 1, should not require attention. The most likely fault is that unfiltered air may be drawn into the system through a damaged air filter element or leaking hose, making tickover unstable and reducing engine power. Backfiring or other unusual noises may be apparent.

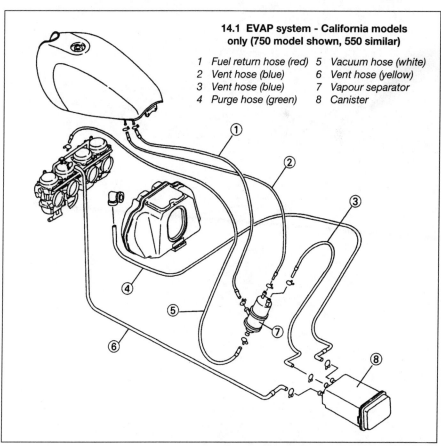

14.1 EVAP system - California models only (750 model shown, 550 similar)

1	*Fuel return hose (red)*	*5*	*Vacuum hose (white)*
2	*Vent hose (blue)*	*6*	*Vent hose (yellow)*
3	*Vent hose (blue)*	*7*	*Vapour separator*
4	*Purge hose (green)*	*8*	*Canister*

3

Chapter 4
Ignition system

Contents

Degrees of difficulty

| Easy, suitable for novice with little experience | | Fairly easy, suitable for beginner with some experience | | Fairly difficult, suitable for competent DIY mechanic | | Difficult, suitable for experienced DIY mechanic | | Very difficult, suitable for expert DIY or professional | |

Specifications

General information
Cylinder identification .... 1 - 2 - 3 - 4, from left to right
Firing order .... 1 - 2 - 4 - 3
Spark plugs .... see Chapter 1

Ignition timing
550 models
UK models .... 12.5° BTDC @ 1200 rpm to 35° BTDC @ 7000 rpm
US models .... 13° BTDC @ 1200 rpm to 36° BTDC @ 7000 rpm
750 models
UK models .... 12.5° BTDC @ 1100 rpm to 35° BTDC @ 7000 rpm
US models .... 12.5° BTDC @ 1300 rpm to 35° BTDC @ 7000 rpm

Pulse generator coil
Resistance
550 models .... 380 to 560 ohms
750 models .... 350 to 540 ohms
Air gap
550 models .... 0.4 to 0.6 mm
750 models .... not available

Ignition HT coils
Primary winding resistance
550 models .... 2.30 to 3.50 ohms
750 models .... 2.61 to 3.19 ohms
Secondary winding resistance (with plug cap removed)
550 models .... 12.0 to 18.0 K ohms
750 models .... 13.5 to 16.5 K ohms
Arcing distance
550 models .... min 6 mm
750 models .... min 7 mm

Torque settings
Pulse generator coil mounting plate screws .... 2.9 Nm
Timing rotor bolt .... 25 Nm
Pulse generator assembly cover bolts .... 10 Nm

4

1 General information

All models are fitted with a fully transistorised electronic ignition system, which due to its lack of mechanical parts is totally maintenance-free. The system comprises a rotor, pulse generator coil, ignition control unit and ignition HT coils (refer to the wiring diagrams at the end of Chapter 8 for details).

The triggers on the rotor, which is fitted to the right-hand end of the crankshaft, magnetically operate the pulse generator coil as the crankshaft rotates. The pulse generator coil sends a signal to the ignition control unit which then supplies the ignition HT coils with the power necessary to produce a spark at the plugs.

The system uses two HT coils mounted on the frame tubes under the fuel tank. The left-hand coil supplies nos. 1 and 4 cylinder spark plugs and the right-hand coil supplies nos. 2 and 3 cylinder plugs.

The system incorporates an electronic advance system controlled by signals generated by the rotor and the pulse generator coil.

The system incorporates a safety interlock circuit which will cut the ignition if the sidestand is lowered whilst the engine is running and in gear, or if a gear is selected whilst the engine is running and the sidestand is down.

Because of their nature, the individual ignition system components can be checked but not repaired. If ignition system troubles occur, and the faulty component can be isolated, the only cure for the problem is to replace the part with a new one. Keep in mind that most electrical parts, once purchased, cannot be returned. To avoid unnecessary expense, make very sure the faulty component has been positively identified before buying a replacement part.

2 Ignition system - check

Caution: The energy levels in electronic systems can be very high. On no account should the ignition be switched on whilst the plugs or plug caps are being held. Shocks from the HT circuit can be most unpleasant. Secondly, it is vital that the engine is not turned over or run with any of the plug caps removed, and that the plugs are soundly earthed (grounded) when the system is checked for sparking. The ignition system components can be seriously damaged if the HT circuit becomes isolated.

1 As no means of adjustment is available, any failure of the system can be traced to failure of a system component or a simple wiring fault.

Of the two possibilities, the latter is by far the most likely. In the event of failure, check the system in a logical fashion, as described below.

2 Disconnect the HT leads from the spark plugs. Connect each lead to a spare spark plug and lay each plug on the engine with the threads contacting the engine. If necessary, hold each spark plug with an insulated tool.

 Warning: Do not remove any of the spark plugs from the engine to perform this check - atomised fuel being pumped out of an open spark plug hole could ignite, causing severe injury!

3 Having observed the above precautions, check that the kill switch is in the RUN position, turn the ignition switch ON and turn the engine over on the starter motor. If the system is in good condition a regular, fat blue spark should be evident at each plug electrode. If the spark appears thin or yellowish, or is non-existent, further investigation will be necessary. Before proceeding further, turn the ignition off and remove the key as a safety measure.

4 The ignition system must be able to produce a spark which is capable of jumping a particular size gap. Kawasaki specify that a healthy system should produce a spark capable of jumping 6 mm (550 models) or 7 mm (750 models). A simple testing tool can be made to test the minimum gap across which the spark will jump **(see Tool Tip)**.

5 Connect one of the spark plug HT leads from one coil to the protruding electrode on the test tool, and clip the tool to a good earth (ground) on the engine or frame. Check that the kill switch is in the RUN position, turn the ignition switch ON and turn the engine over on the starter motor. If the system is in good condition a regular, fat blue spark should be seen to jump the gap between the nail ends. Repeat the test for the other coil. If the test results are good the entire ignition system can

TOOL TiP

A simple spark gap testing tool can be made from a block of wood, a large alligator clip and two nails, one of which is fashioned so that a spark plug cap or bare HT lead end can be connected to its end. Make sure the gap between the two nail ends is the same as specified.

be considered good. If the spark appears thin or yellowish, or is non-existent, further investigation will be necessary.

6 Ignition faults can be divided into two categories, namely those where the ignition system has failed completely, and those which are due to a partial failure. The likely faults are listed below, starting with the most probable source of failure. Work through the list systematically, referring to the subsequent sections for full details of the necessary checks and tests. **Note:** *Before checking the following items ensure that the battery is fully charged and that all fuses are in good condition.*

 a) *Loose, corroded or damaged wiring connections, broken or shorted wiring between any of the component parts of the ignition system (see Chapter 8).*
 b) *Faulty HT lead or spark plug cap, faulty spark plug, dirty, worn or corroded plug electrodes, or incorrect gap between electrodes.*
 c) *Faulty ignition switch or engine kill switch (see Chapter 8).*
 d) *Faulty neutral or sidestand switch (see Chapter 8).*
 e) *Faulty pulse generator coil or damaged rotor.*
 f) *Faulty ignition HT coil(s).*
 g) *Faulty ignition control unit.*

7 If the above checks don't reveal the cause of the problem, have the ignition system tested by a Kawasaki dealer. Kawasaki produce special testers which can perform a complete diagnostic analysis of the ignition system.

3 Ignition HT coils - check, removal and installation

Check

1 In order to determine conclusively that the ignition coils are defective, they should be tested by a Kawasaki dealer equipped with the special diagnostic tester.

2 However, the coils can be checked visually (for cracks and other damage) and the primary and secondary coil resistance can be measured with a multimeter. If the coils are undamaged, and if the resistance readings are as specified at the beginning of the Chapter, they are probably capable of proper operation.

3 Remove the seat (see Chapter 7) and disconnect the battery negative (-) lead. To gain access to the coils, remove the fuel tank (see Chapter 3). The coils are mounted on the frame tubes **(see illustration 3.10)**.

4 Disconnect the primary circuit electrical connectors from the coil being tested and the HT leads from the spark plugs **(see illustration)**. Mark the locations of all wires and leads before disconnecting them.

5 Set the meter to the ohms x 1 scale and measure the resistance between the primary circuit terminals **(see illustration)**. This will

3.4 Disconnect the primary circuit connectors

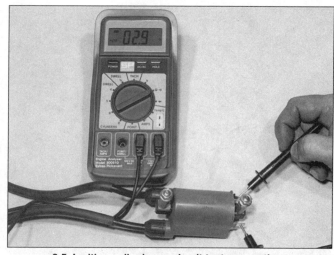

3.5 Ignition coil primary circuit test connections

give a resistance reading of the primary windings and should be consistent with the value given in the Specifications at the beginning of the Chapter.

6 To check the condition of the secondary windings, set the meter to the K ohm scale. Unscrew the spark plug caps from the ends of the HT leads **(see illustration)**. Connect one meter probe to one HT lead and the other probe to the other lead **(see illustration)**. If the reading obtained is not within the range shown in the Specifications, it is likely that the coil is defective.

7 Should either of the above checks not produce the expected result, have your findings confirmed on the diagnostic tester (see Step 1). If the coil is confirmed to be faulty, it must be replaced; the coil is a sealed unit and cannot therefore be repaired.

> **HAYNES HiNT** *An inaccurate secondary winding reading could be due to an HT lead breakdown or poor connection between the HT lead and coil. Unscrew the lead connection at the coil and make the secondary winding test across the HT lead terminals - the reading should be slightly less than the specified figure.*

Removal

8 Remove the seat (see Chapter 7) and disconnect the battery negative (-) lead, then remove the fuel tank (see Chapter 3).

9 The coils are mounted on the frame tubes **(see illustration 3.10)**. Disconnect the primary circuit electrical connectors from the coils **(see illustration 3.4)** and disconnect the HT leads from the spark plugs. Mark the locations of all wires and leads before disconnecting them.

10 Unscrew the two nuts securing each coil, noting the earth (ground) terminal secured by the front nut for the left-hand coil, and remove the coils **(see illustration)**. Note the routing of the HT leads.

Installation

11 Installation is the reverse of removal. Install the coils with the HT leads facing forward. Make sure the wiring connectors and HT leads are securely connected.

---

4 Pulse generator coil assembly - check, removal and installation

Check

1 Remove the seat (see Chapter 7) and disconnect the battery negative (-) lead. On

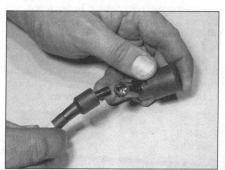

3.6a Unscrew the cap from the lead

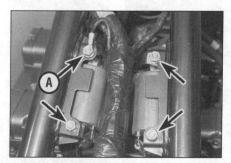

3.10 Each coil is secured by two nuts (arrowed). Note the earth terminal secured by one of the nuts (A)

750 models, also remove the right-hand side panel (see Chapter 7).

2 Trace the ignition pulse generator wiring back and disconnect it at the ignition control unit (550 models - remove the unit for access to the connectors - see Section 5) or at the connector behind the right-hand side panel (750 models) **(see illustration)**. Using a multimeter set to the ohms x 100 scale, measure the resistance between the black and yellow terminals on the coil side of the connector.

3 Compare the reading obtained with that given in the Specifications at the beginning of this Chapter. The pulse generator coil must be replaced if the reading obtained differs greatly

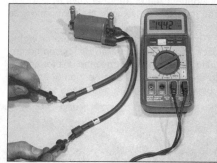

3.6b Ignition coil secondary circuit test

4.2 On 750 models the wiring connector is behind the right-hand side panel

4

4.7 The pulse generator assembly cover is secured by two bolts (arrowed)

4.9 The assembly mounting plate is secured by three screws (arrowed)

from that given, particularly if the meter indicates a short circuit (no measurable resistance) or an open circuit (infinite, or very high resistance).

4 If the pulse generator coil is thought to be faulty, first check that this is not due to a damaged or broken wire from the coil to the connector; pinched or broken wires can usually be repaired. Note that the pulse generator coil is not available individually but comes as an assembly along with the mounting plate and wiring.

Removal

5 Remove the seat (see Chapter 7) and disconnect the battery negative (-) lead. On 750 models, also remove the right-hand side panel (see Chapter 7).

6 Trace the ignition pulse generator wiring back and disconnect it at the ignition control unit (550 models - remove the unit for access to the connectors - see Section 5) or at the connector behind the right-hand side panel

(750 models) **(see illustration 4.2)**. Free the wiring from any clips or ties and feed it through to the coil.

7 Unscrew the bolts securing the pulse generator assembly cover to the right-hand side of the crankcase **(see illustration)**. Remove the cover. Discard the gasket as a new one must be used.

8 On 750 models, remove the screw securing the wire to the terminal on the oil pressure switch and detach the wire.

9 Remove the three screws securing the pulse generator coil assembly mounting plate to the crankcase **(see illustration)**. Remove the rubber wiring grommet from its recess in the crankcase cover, then remove the coil assembly, noting how it fits.

10 Examine the rotor for signs of damage and replace it if necessary. To remove the rotor, use a 17 mm spanner on the rotor hex to counter-hold it, and unscrew the bolt in the centre of the rotor which secures it to the end of the crankshaft **(see illustration)**. Remove

the rotor, noting how the pin in the end of the crankshaft locates in the slot in the rotor.

Installation

11 If removed, install the timing rotor onto the end of the crankshaft, making sure the slot in the rotor locates correctly over the pin in the end of the crankshaft. Using a 17 mm spanner to counter-hold the rotor, install the rotor bolt and tighten it to the torque setting specified at the beginning of the Chapter **(see illustration)**.

12 Apply a smear of sealant to the rubber wiring seal and fit it into its recess in the crankcase, then mount the pulse generator coil assembly and tighten the mounting screws to the specified torque setting **(see illustrations)**.

13 On 750 models, connect the oil pressure switch wire to its terminal on the switch and tighten the screw securely.

14 Apply a smear of sealant to the crankcase joints on the pulse generator assembly cover

4.10 Counter-hold the outer hex on the rotor and unscrew the centre bolt

4.11 Tighten the rotor bolt to the specified torque setting

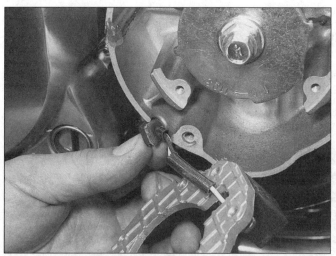

4.12a Fit the grommet into its cut-out . . .

4.12b . . . and secure the assembly with its screws

4.14a Apply a smear of sealant to the areas shown (arrowed)

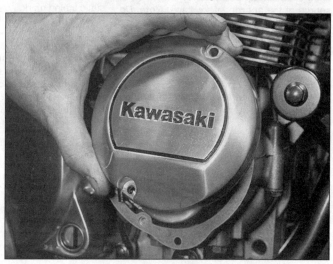

4.14b Install the cover using a new gasket

mating surface **(see illustration)**. Install the pulse generator assembly cover using a new gasket and tighten its bolts to the specified torque setting **(see illustration)**.

15 Route the wiring up to the connector and reconnect it **(see illustration 4.2)**. Secure the wiring in its clips or ties.

16 Reconnect the battery negative (-) lead and install the seat and side panel (750 models) (see Chapter 7).

---

5 Ignition control unit - check, removal and installation

Check

1 If the tests shown in the preceding Sections have failed to isolate the cause of an ignition fault, it is likely that the ignition control unit itself is faulty. No test details are available with which the unit can be tested on home workshop equipment. Take the machine to a Kawasaki dealer for testing.

Removal

2 Remove the seat (see Chapter 7) and the battery (see Chapter 8).

3 The ignition control unit is mounted behind the battery **(see illustration)**.

4 Remove the ignition control unit from its rubber sleeve, or lift the sleeve and unit together off the sleeve's mounting lugs.

5.3 The control unit is mounted behind the battery

Disconnect the two wiring connectors from the ignition control unit remove the unit **(see illustration)**.

Installation

5 Installation is the reverse of removal. Make sure the wiring connectors are correctly and securely connected.

5.4 Disconnect the two wiring connectors (arrowed) and remove the unit

4

6 Ignition timing - general information and check

General information

1 Since no provision exists for adjusting the ignition timing and since no component is subject to mechanical wear, there is no need for regular checks; only if investigating a fault such as a loss of power or a misfire, should the ignition timing be checked.

2 The ignition timing is checked dynamically (engine running) using a stroboscopic lamp. The inexpensive neon lamps should be adequate in theory, but in practice may produce a pulse of such low intensity that the timing mark remains indistinct. If possible, one of the more precise xenon tube lamps should be used, powered by an external source of the appropriate voltage. **Note:** *Do not use the machine's own battery as an incorrect reading may result from stray impulses within the machine's electrical system.*

Check

3 Warm the engine up to normal operating temperature then stop it.

4 Unscrew the bolts securing the pulse generator assembly cover to the right-hand side crankcase cover **(see illustration 4.7)**. Discard the gasket as a new one must be used.

5 The timing mark on the rotor is the line next to the letter F which indicates the firing point at idle speed for cylinder nos. 1 and 4 **(see illustration)**. The static timing mark with which this should align is the protrusion on the case.

 The rotor timing mark can be highlighted with white paint to make it more visible under the stroboscope light.

6 Connect the timing light to the no. 1 cylinder HT lead as described in the manufacturer's instructions.

7 Start the engine and aim the light at the static timing mark.

8 With the machine idling at the specified speed, the timing mark F should align with the static timing mark.

9 Slowly increase the engine speed whilst observing the timing mark. The timing mark should move anti-clockwise, increasing in relation to the engine speed until it reaches full advance (no identification mark).

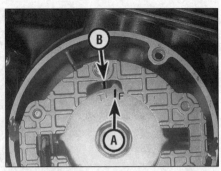

6.5 Ignition rotor timing mark (A) and static mark (B)

10 As already stated, there is no means of adjustment of the ignition timing on these machines. If the ignition timing is incorrect, or suspected of being incorrect, one of the ignition system components is at fault, and the system must be tested as described in the preceding Sections of this Chapter.

11 When the check is complete, apply a smear of sealant to the crankcase joints on the pulse generator assembly cover mating surface **(see illustration 4.14a)**. Install the pulse generator assembly cover using a new gasket and tighten its bolts to the specified torque setting **(see illustration 4.14b)**.

Chapter 5
Frame, suspension and final drive

Contents

Degrees of difficulty

Easy, suitable for novice with little experience	**Fairly easy,** suitable for beginner with some experience	**Fairly difficult,** suitable for competent DIY mechanic	**Difficult,** suitable for experienced DIY mechanic	**Very difficult,** suitable for expert DIY or professional

Specifications

Front forks

Fork oil type	SAE 10W20 fork oil
Fork oil capacity	
550 models	
Oil change	350 cc
Following fork overhaul (completely dry)	408 to 416 cc
750 models	
C1 and C2 models	
Oil change	400 cc
Following fork overhaul (completely dry)	466 to 474 cc
C3, C4 and C5 models	
Oil change	417 cc
Following fork overhaul (completely dry)	490 cc
D1 model	
Oil change	400 cc
Following fork overhaul (completely dry)	463 to 471 cc
Fork oil level*	
550 models	96 to 100 mm*
750 models	
C1 and C2 models	108 to 112 mm*
C3, C4 and C5 models	88 to 92 mm*
D1 model	111 to 115 mm*

Oil level is measured from the top of the tube with the fork spring removed and the tube fully compressed in the slider.

5

Front forks (continued)

Fork spring free length (min)
  550 models
    Standard .... 395.5 mm
    Service limit (min) .... 387 mm
  750 models
    C1 and C2 models
      Standard .... 402.5 mm
      Service limit .... 394 mm
    C3, C4 and C5 models
      Standard .... 396.5 mm
      Service limit .... 389 mm
    D1 model
      Standard .... 391.5 mm
      Service limit .... 384 mm

Final drive

Chain freeplay and wear limit .... see Chapter 1
Chain size, no. of links
  550 UK models .... 520 O-ring type, 106 links
  550 US and Canada models .... 520 O-ring type, 108 links
  750 models .... 525 O-ring type, 106 links
Front sprocket diameter - 750 models
  Standard .... 65.58 to 65.78 mm
  Service limit .... 64.9 mm
Rear sprocket diameter - 750 models
  Standard .... 187.02 to 187.52 mm
  Service limit .... 186.7 mm
Rear sprocket warpage - all models
  Standard .... less than 0.4 mm
  Service limit .... 0.5 mm

Torque settings

Brake pedal pivot bolt
  550 models .... 10 Nm
  750 models .... 9 Nm
Gearchange lever pivot bolt .... 23 Nm
Handlebar clamp bolts .... 23 Nm
Fork clamp bolts
  550 models .... 21 Nm
  750 models .... 20 Nm
Fork top bolt .... 23 Nm
Damper rod Allen bolt
  550 models .... 29 Nm
  750 models .... 61 Nm
Steering stem bolt .... 39 Nm
Rear shock absorber lower mounting bolt and nut .... 39 Nm
Swingarm pivot bolt nut
  550 models .... 93 Nm
  750 models .... 109 Nm
Brake torque arm nuts
  550 models .... 32 Nm
  750 models .... 34 Nm
Front sprocket bolts - 550 models .... 10 Nm
Front sprocket nut - 750 models .... 125 Nm
Rear sprocket nuts .... 74 Nm

1 General information

All models use a full cradle twin spar steel frame.

Front suspension is by a pair of conventional oil-damped telescopic forks which are non-adjustable.

At the rear, a box-section aluminium swingarm acts on twin shock absorbers with remote reservoirs. The shock absorbers are adjustable for pre-load and both compression and rebound damping.

The drive to the rear wheel is by chain. A rubber damper system (often called a 'cush drive') is fitted between the rear wheel coupling and the wheel.

2 Frame - inspection and repair

1 The frame should not require attention unless accident damage has occurred. In most cases, frame replacement is the only satisfactory remedy for such damage. A few frame specialists have the jigs and other equipment necessary for straightening the frame to the required standard of accuracy, but even then there is no simple way of assessing to what extent the frame may have been over stressed.

2 After the machine has accumulated a lot of miles, the frame should be examined closely for signs of cracking or splitting at the welded joints. Loose engine mount bolts can cause ovaling or fracturing of the mounting tabs. Minor damage can often be repaired by welding, depending on the extent and nature of the damage.

3 Remember that a frame which is out of alignment will cause handling problems. If misalignment is suspected as the result of an accident, it will be necessary to strip the machine completely so the frame can be thoroughly checked.

3 Footrests, brake pedal and gearchange lever - removal and installation

Footrests

Removal

1 Remove the E-clip from the bottom of the footrest pivot pin, then withdraw the pivot pin and remove the footrest (see illustrations). On the front footrests, note the fitting of the return spring. On the rear footrests, note the fitting of the two interlocking plates and the spring (see illustration).

Installation

2 Installation is the reverse of removal.

Brake pedal

Removal

3 Unhook the brake pedal return spring and the brake light switch spring from the brake pedal (see illustration).

4 Remove the split pin from the clevis pin securing the brake pedal to the master cylinder pushrod (see illustration). Remove the clevis pin and separate the pedal from the pushrod.

5 Unscrew the pivot bolt securing the brake pedal to the footrest bracket and remove the pedal (see illustration). On 550 models, note how the brake light switch lever fits.

Installation

6 Installation is the reverse of removal. Check the operation of the rear brake light switch and the height of the brake pedal (see Chapter 1).

Gearchange lever

Removal

7 Unscrew the gearchange lever linkage arm pinch bolt and remove the arm from the shaft, noting any alignment marks (see illustration). If no marks are visible, make your own before removing the arm so that it can be correctly aligned with the shaft on installation.

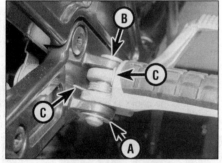

3.1a Remove the E-clip (A) and withdraw the pivot pin (B). Note how the spring ends (C) locate

3.1b Rear footrest assembly

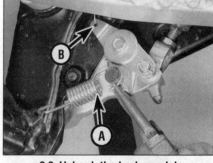

3.3 Unhook the brake pedal return spring (A) and the brake light switch spring (B) - 550 model shown

3.4 Remove the split pin and withdraw the clevis pin (arrowed)

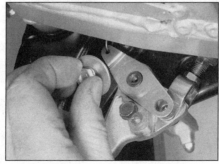

3.5 Remove the pivot bolt, detach the pushrod and slide the pedal off

3.7 Remove the pinch bolt (arrowed) and slide the arm off the shaft

5

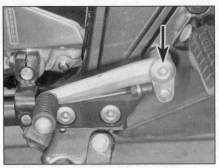

3.8 Remove the pivot bolt (arrowed) and remove the lever and linkage

3.10a Align the previously made marks and install the pinch bolt

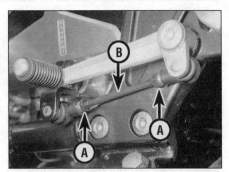

3.10b Slacken the locknuts (A) and turn the rod (B) to adjust lever height

8 Unscrew the pivot bolt securing the gearchange lever to the footrest bracket and remove the lever and linkage assembly **(see illustration)**.

9 If required, slacken the linkage rod locknuts and thread the lever off the rod. Note the how far the rod is threaded into the lever as this determines the height of the lever relative to the footrest.

Installation

10 Installation is the reverse of removal. Align the marks made on the gearchange lever linkage arm and shaft when installing the arm onto the shaft, and tighten the pinch bolt securely **(see illustration)**. Adjust the gear lever height as required by slackening the rod locknuts and screwing the rod in or out of the lever and linkage arm **(see illustration)**. Tighten the locknuts securely on completion.

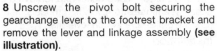

4 Stands -
removal and installation

Centre stand (750 models only)

1 The centre stand is secured in the frame by two pivot bolts. Support the bike on its

sidestand and unhook the centre stand spring, then unscrew the nuts, withdraw the bolts and remove the stand **(see illustration)**.

2 Inspect the stand and pivot bolts for signs of wear and replace them if necessary. Apply a smear of grease to the bolts and fit the stand back on the bike, tightening the bolts securely. Reconnect the return spring.

3 Make sure the spring is in good condition and capable of holding the stand up when not in use. A broken or weak spring is an obvious safety hazard.

Sidestand

4 The sidestand is attached to a bracket on the frame. A spring anchored to the bracket ensures that the stand is held in the retracted or extended position.

5 Support the bike on its centre stand if fitted, or support it using an auxiliary stand.

6 Unhook the stand spring and unscrew the nut from the pivot bolt **(see illustration)**. Withdraw the pivot bolt to free the stand from its bracket.

7 On installation apply grease to the pivot bolt shank and tighten the bolt securely. Reconnect the sidestand spring and check that the return spring holds the stand securely up when not in use - an accident is almost

certain to occur if the stand extends while the machine is in motion.

8 For check and replacement of the side stand switch see Chapter 8.

5 Handlebars and levers -
removal and installation

Handlebars

Removal

Note: If required, the handlebars can be displaced for access to the fork top bolts or the steering stem nut without removing the switch housings and the front brake master cylinder assembly and the clutch lever assembly.

1 Remove the screws securing both the left- and right-hand switch housings to the handlebar, noting how the top mating surfaces of the switch housings align with the top mating surfaces of the brake master cylinder and clutch lever assembly clamps, then separate the switch halves. Detach the throttle cables from the throttle pulley and note how the choke lever fits (see Chapter 3 if required), then remove the housings from the

4.1 Unhook the stand spring, then unscrew the nuts and withdraw the bolts

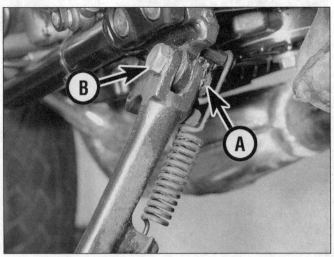

4.6 Unhook the spring, then unscrew the nut (A) and withdraw the bolt (B)

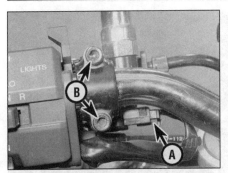

5.3 Disconnect the clutch switch wiring connector (A) and unscrew the clamp bolts (B)

5.4a The handlebar clamp is secured by four bolts (arrowed)

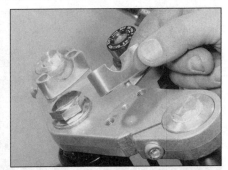

5.4b The pin in the base of the lower clamp locates in the hole in the yoke, and the flat end of the clamp faces forward

5.6a Align the punch mark (arrowed) with the clamp mating surfaces

5.6b Note the UP mark on the clamp which points upwards

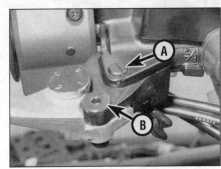

5.7 Lever main pivot bolt (A), span adjuster pivot bolt (B)

handlebar, noting how they fit (see Chapter 8 if required). There is no need to disconnect the switch housing wiring at its connector blocks.

2 Disconnect the brake light switch wiring connectors from the underside of the master cylinder. Unscrew the two clamp bolts securing the front brake master cylinder assembly to the handlebar and lift the assembly away (see Chapter 6 if required). There is no need to disconnect the hose from the master cylinder. Support the assembly in an upright position and so that no strain is placed on the hose.

3 Disconnect the clutch switch connector from the underside of the lever bracket **(see illustration)**. Unscrew the two clamp bolts securing the clutch lever assembly to the handlebar and lift the assembly away.

4 Unscrew the bolts securing the handlebar clamp and remove the clamp top and the handlebars **(see illustration)**. Note the punch mark on the back of the handlebar which aligns with the rear mating surfaces of the clamp. Remove the clamp bottoms, noting which way round they fit and how they locate **(see illustration)**.

5 If necessary, unscrew the handlebar end-weight retaining screws, then remove the weights from the end of the handlebars. If replacing the grips, it may be necessary to slit them using a sharp knife as they are adhered to the throttle twist (right-hand) and the handlebar (left-hand).

Installation

6 Installation is the reverse of removal, noting the following.

  a) *Align the handlebars so that the punch mark on the rear of the handlebar aligns with the rear mating surfaces of the clamp (see illustration). Tighten the front handlebar clamp bolts to the torque setting specified at the beginning of the Chapter, then tighten the rear bolts to the specified torque. There should be a gap between the rear clamp mating surfaces.*

  b) *Make sure the front brake master cylinder clamp is installed with the UP mark facing up, and so that the top clamp mating surfaces align with the top mating surfaces of the switch housings (see illustration). Tighten the upper clamp bolt first, then the lower bolt, to the torque setting specified at the beginning of the Chapter. There should be a gap between the lower clamp mating surfaces.*

  c) *If removed, apply a suitable non-permanent thread-locking compound to the handlebar end-weight retaining screws. If new grips are being fitted, secure them using a suitable adhesive.*

Levers

Removal

7 To remove the complete front brake lever or clutch lever assembly from the master cylinder, unscrew the main pivot bolt locknut, then withdraw the bolt and remove the lever assembly **(see illustration)**. If working on the clutch lever, slip the cable end out of the lever as it is withdrawn.

8 To remove the lever blade from the pivot assembly, unscrew the span adjuster pivot bolt locknut, then withdraw the bolt and remove the lever blade **(see illustration 5.7)**.

Installation

9 Installation is the reverse of removal. Apply grease to the pivot bolt shafts and to the contact areas between the lever and its bracket. Grease the clutch cable end and fit it into the lever before installing the lever in its bracket. If necessary, back off clutch cable adjustment to allow the cable to be reconnected (see Chapter 1).

5

6 Forks -
    removal and installation

Removal

1 Remove the front wheel (see Chapter 6).

2 Remove the front mudguard as described in Chapter 7.

3 On 750 models, unscrew the bolts securing the brake hose clamps and speedometer cable guide to the forks **(see illustration)**.

6.3 Hose guide and cable guide bolt (arrowed) - 750 models

6.4 Top yoke fork clamp bolt (arrowed). Note the alignment of the fork with the top yoke as an aid to installation

4 Slacken, but do not remove, the fork clamp bolts in the top yoke **(see illustration)**. If the forks are to be disassembled, it is advisable to slacken the fork top bolts at this stage. Displace the handlebars if required for improved access to the top bolts (Section 5).

 Slackening the fork clamp bolts in the top yoke before slackening the fork top bolts releases pressure on the top bolt. This makes it much easier to remove and helps to preserve the threads.

5 Note the position of the top of the fork tubes relative to the top yoke so that they are installed in the same position **(see illustration 6.4)**. Slacken but do not remove the fork clamp bolts in the bottom yoke, and remove the forks by twisting them and pulling them downwards **(see illustration)**.

 If the fork legs are seized in the yokes, spray the area with penetrating oil and allow time for it to soak in before trying again.

Installation

6 Remove all traces of corrosion from the fork tubes and the yokes and slide the forks up through the bottom yoke and the top yoke so that they align with the top yoke as noted on removal **(see illustration 6.4)**.
7 Tighten the fork clamp bolts in the bottom yoke to the torque setting specified at the beginning of the Chapter **(see illustration 6.5)**. If the fork legs have been dismantled or if the fork oil has been changed, the fork top bolts should now be tightened to the specified torque setting. Now tighten the fork clamp bolts in the top yoke to the specified torque setting. Install the handlebars if displaced.

8 If the forks were disassembled, install the axle nut into the bottom of the left-hand fork **(see illustration)**, but do not tighten the axle nut clamp bolt until the wheel has been installed and the axle has been tightened to the correct torque. Install the front mudguard (see Chapter 7) and the front wheel (see Chapter 6). On 750 models, install the brake hose clamps onto the forks and tighten their bolts securely.
9 Check the operation of the front forks and brakes before taking the machine out on the road.

7 Forks - disassembly, inspection and reassembly

Disassembly

1 Always dismantle the fork legs separately to avoid interchanging parts and thus causing an

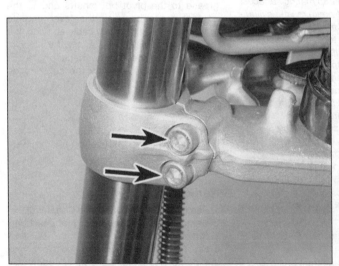

6.5 Bottom yoke fork clamp bolts (arrowed)

6.8 Fit the axle nut into the bottom of the left-hand fork

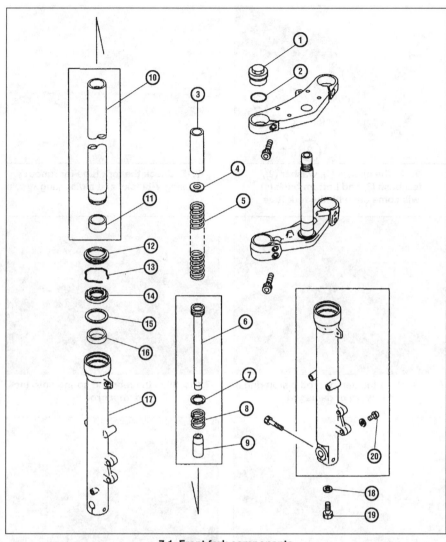

7.1 Front fork components

1	Top bolt	6	Damper rod	11	Bottom bush	16	Top bush
2	O-ring	7	Piston ring	12	Dust seal	17	Fork slider
3	Spacer	8	Rebound spring	13	Retaining clip	18	Sealing washer
4	Spring seat	9	Damper rod seat	14	Oil seal	19	Damper rod bolt
5	Spring	10	Fork tube	15	Washer	20	Oil drain screw

bolt, slacken the axle nut clamp bolt in the base of the fork slider and remove the axle nut **(see illustration 6.8)**. Compress the fork tube in the slider so that the spring exerts maximum pressure on the damper rod head, then have an assistant slacken the damper rod bolt in the base of the fork slider.

3 If the fork top bolt was not slackened with the fork in situ, carefully clamp the fork tube in a vice, taking care not to overtighten or score its surface, and slacken the top bolt.

4 Unscrew the fork top bolt from the top of the fork tube.

⚠️ **Warning: The fork spring is pressing on the fork top bolt with considerable pressure. Unscrew the bolt very carefully, keeping a downward pressure on it and release it slowly as it is likely to spring clear. It is advisable to wear some form of eye and face protection when carrying out this operation.**

5 Slide the fork tube down into the slider and withdraw the spacer, spring seat and the spring from the tube, noting which way up they fit **(see illustrations 7.26c, b and a)**.

6 Invert the fork leg over a suitable container and pump the fork vigorously to expel as much fork oil as possible.

7 Remove the slackened damper rod bolt and its copper sealing washer from the bottom of the slider. Discard the sealing washer as a new one must be used on reassembly. If the damper rod bolt was not slackened before dismantling the fork, it may be necessary to re-install the spring, spring seat, spacer and top bolt to prevent the damper rod from turning. Alternatively, a length of wooden doweling pressed hard into the damper rod head quite often suffices. **Note:** *A damper rod holding tool can be purchased from Kawasaki dealers (see Step 20).*

8 Invert the fork and withdraw the damper rod from inside the fork tube. Remove the rebound spring from the damper rod **(see illustration)**.

9 Carefully prise out the dust seal from the top of the slider to gain access to the oil seal retaining clip **(see illustration)**. Discard the dust seal as a new one must be used.

10 Carefully remove the retaining clip, taking care not to scratch the surface of the tube **(see illustration)**.

accelerated rate of wear. Store all components in separate, clearly-marked containers **(see illustration)**.

2 Before dismantling the fork, it is advised that the damper rod bolt be slackened at this stage. To access the left-hand fork damper

5

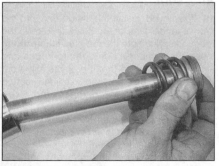

7.8 Withdraw the damper rod and rebound spring from the tube

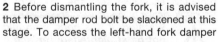

7.9 Prise out the dust seal using a flat-bladed screwdriver

7.10 Prise out the retaining clip using a flat-bladed screwdriver

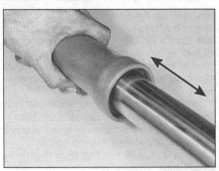

7.11 To separate the fork tube and slider, pull apart firmly several times - the slide hammer effect will pull the tubes apart

7.12 The oil seal (1), washer (2), top bush (3) and bottom bush (4) will come out with the fork tube

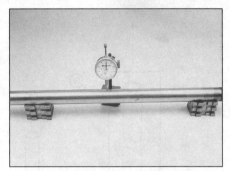

7.15 Check the fork tube for runout using V-blocks and a dial gauge

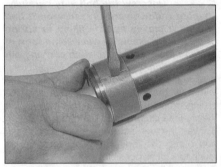

7.17 Ease the bottom bush ends apart using a flat-bladed screwdriver

7.18 Replace the damper rod piston ring if it is worn or damaged

7.19a Slide the rebound spring onto the damper rod

11 To separate the tube from the slider it will be necessary to displace the top bush and oil seal. The bottom bush should not pass through the top bush, and this can be used to good effect. Push the tube gently inwards until it stops against the damper rod seat. Take care not to do this forcibly or the seat may be damaged. Then pull the tube sharply outwards until the bottom bush strikes the top bush. Repeat this operation until the top bush and seal are tapped out of the slider **(see illustration)**.

12 With the tube removed, slide off the oil seal and its washer, followed by the top bush, noting which way up they fit **(see illustration)**. Discard the oil seal as a new one must be used.

Caution: Do not remove the bottom bush from the tube unless it is to be replaced.

13 Tip the damper rod seat out of the slider, noting which way up it fits.

Inspection

14 Clean all parts in solvent and blow them dry with compressed air, if available. Check the fork tube for score marks, scratches, flaking of the chrome finish and excessive or abnormal wear. Look for dents in the tube and replace the tube in both forks if any are found. Check the fork seal seat for nicks, gouges and scratches. If damage is evident, leaks will occur.

15 Check the fork tube for runout using V-blocks and a dial gauge **(see illustration)**. No

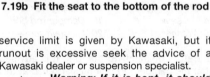
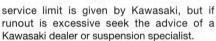

7.19b Fit the seat to the bottom of the rod

service limit is given by Kawasaki, but if runout is excessive seek the advice of a Kawasaki dealer or suspension specialist.

⚠️ *Warning: If it is bent, it should not be straightened; replace it with a new one.*

16 Check the spring for cracks and other damage. Measure the spring free length using a steel rule and compare the measurement to the specifications at the beginning of the Chapter. If it is defective or sagged below the service limit, replace the springs in both forks with new ones. Never replace only one spring. Also check the rebound spring.

17 Examine the working surfaces of the two bushes; if worn or scuffed they must be replaced. To remove the bottom bush from the fork tube, prise it apart at the slit using a screwdriver and slide it off **(see illustration)**. Make sure the new one seats properly.

7.20a Slide the tube into the slider

18 Check the damper rod and its piston ring for damage and wear, and replace them if necessary **(see illustration)**.

Reassembly

19 If removed, install the piston ring into the groove in the damper rod head, then slide the rebound spring onto the rod **(see illustration)**. Insert the damper rod into the fork tube and slide it into place so that it projects fully from the bottom of the tube, then install the seat on the bottom of the damper rod **(see illustration)**.

20 Oil the fork tube and bottom bush with the specified fork oil and insert the assembly into the slider **(see illustration)**. Fit a new copper sealing washer to the damper rod bolt and apply a few drops of a suitable non-permanent thread-locking compound, then

7.20b Apply a thread-locking compound to the damper rod bolt and use a new sealing washer

7.21a Install the top bush . . .

7.21b . . . followed by the washer

7.22 Make sure the oil seal is the correct way up

7.23 Install the retaining clip . . .

7.24 . . . followed by the dust seal

7.25a Pour the oil into the top of the tube

7.25b Measure the oil level with the fork held vertical

install the bolt into the bottom of the slider **(see illustration)**. Tighten the bolt to the specified torque setting. If the damper rod rotates inside the tube, temporarily install the fork spring and top bolt (see Steps 26 and 27) and compress the fork to hold the damper rod. Alternatively, a length of wood doweling pressed hard into the damper rod head quite often suffices. **Note:** *If neither method succeeds in holding the damper rod, obtain the Kawasaki service tool adapter (pt. no. 57001-1057) and handle (pt. no. 57001-183).*

21 Push the fork tube fully into the slider, then oil the top bush and slide it down over the tube **(see illustration)**. Press the bush squarely into its recess in the slider as far as possible, then install the oil seal washer **(see illustration)**. Either use the service tool (pt. no. 57001-1219) or a suitable piece of tubing

to tap the bush fully into place; the tubing must be slightly larger in diameter than the fork tube and slightly smaller in diameter than the bush recess in the slider. Take care not to scratch the fork tube during this operation; it is best to make sure that the fork tube is pushed fully into the slider so that any accidental scratching is confined to the area above the oil seal.

22 When the bush is seated fully and squarely in its recess in the slider, (remove the washer to check, wipe the recess clean, then reinstall the washer), install the new oil seal. Smear the seal's lips with fork oil and slide it over the tube so that its markings face upwards and drive the seal into place as described in Step 21 until the retaining clip groove is visible above the seal.**(see illustration)**.

23 Once the seal is correctly seated, fit the retaining clip, making sure it is correctly located in its groove **(see illustration)**.

24 Lubricate the lips of the new dust seal then slide it down the fork tube and press it into position **(see illustration)**.

25 Slowly pour in the specified quantity of the specified grade of fork oil and pump the fork to distribute it evenly **(see illustration)**; the oil level should also be measured and adjustment made by adding or subtracting oil. Fully compress the fork tube into the slider and measure the fork oil level from the top of the tube **(see illustration)**. Add or subtract fork oil until the oil is at the level specified in the Specifications Section of this Chapter.

26 Clamp the slider in a vice via the brake caliper mounting lugs, taking care not to overtighten and damage them. Pull the fork

5

7.26a Install the spring . . .

7.26b . . . followed by the spring seat . . .

7.26c . . . and the spacer

tube out of the slider as far as possible then install the spring with its closer-wound coils at the top, followed by the spring seat and the spacer **(see illustrations)**.

27 Fit a new O-ring onto the fork top bolt if the old one is in any way damaged or deteriorated. Thread the bolt into the top of the fork tube.

 Warning: It will be necessary to compress the spring by pressing it down using the top bolt in order to engage the threads of the top bolt with the fork tube. This is a potentially dangerous operation and should be performed with care, using an assistant if necessary. Wipe off any excess oil before starting to prevent the possibility of slipping.

28 Keep the fork tube fully extended whilst pressing on the spring. Screw the top bolt carefully into the fork tube making sure it is not cross-threaded. **Note:** The top bolt can be tightened to the specified torque setting at this stage if the tube is held between the padded jaws of a vice, but do not risk distorting the tube by doing so. A better method is to tighten the top bolt when the fork has been installed in the bike and is securely held in the bottom yoke.

29 Install the forks (see Section 6).

 Use a ratchet-type tool when installing the fork top bolt. This makes it unnecessary to remove the tool from the bolt whilst threading it in, thus making it easier to maintain a downward pressure on the spring.

8 Steering stem -
removal and installation

Removal

1 Remove the fuel tank (see Chapter 3)

2 Unscrew the bolts securing the brake hose union to the bottom yoke **(see illustration)**; there is no need to disconnect the hydraulic hoses.

3 Remove the headlight and its bracket (see Chapter 8).

4 Remove the handlebars (see Section 5).

5 Remove the instrument cluster (see Chapter 8).

6 Remove the front forks (see Section 6).

7 Remove the steering stem bolt and washer **(see illustration)**. Lift the top yoke off the steering stem.

8 Supporting the bottom yoke, unscrew the locknut and adjuster ring using a suitable C-spanner, then remove the bearing cover from the steering stem (the adjuster ring has a collar which fits into the bearing cover, so they will probably come away together) **(see illustration)**. Push up on the bottom yoke to displace the O-ring from between the stem and the bearing, then remove the O-ring and discard it as a new one must be used **(see illustration)**.

9 Gently lower the bottom yoke and steering stem out of the frame **(see illustration 8.12a)**.

10 Remove the upper bearing from the top of the steering head **(see illustration)**. Remove all traces of old grease from the bearings and races and check them for wear or damage as described in Section 9. **Note:** Do not attempt to remove the races from the frame or the lower bearing from the steering stem unless they are to be replaced.

8.2 The brake hose union is secured by two bolts

8.7 Unscrew the steering stem bolt and remove the washer

8.8a Remove the locknut (A), adjuster ring (B) and the bearing cover (C)

8.8b Displace the O-ring and discard it

8.10 Remove the upper bearing

8.11 Apply grease liberally to the bearings

8.12a Lift the steering stem up into the head

8.12b Fit the bearing cover . . .

8.12c . . . the adjuster ring . . .

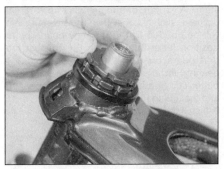

8.12d . . . and the locknut

8.13 Fit the top yoke onto the steering stem

8.14 Tighten the steering stem bolt to the specified torque setting

Installation

11 Smear a liberal quantity of grease on the bearing races in the frame. Work grease well into both the upper and lower bearings **(see illustration)**.
12 Carefully lift the steering stem/bottom yoke up through the frame **(see illustration)**. Install the upper bearing in the top of the steering head, then fit the new O-ring **(see illustration 8.8b)**. Install the bearing cover and thread the adjuster ring, with its stepped side facing down, and locknut on the steering stem **(see illustrations)**. Tighten the adjuster ring as required until all freeplay in the forks is removed, yet the steering is able to move freely from side to side. The object is to set the adjuster ring so that the bearings are under a very light loading, just enough to remove any freeplay. Tighten the locknut against the adjuster ring finger-tight only. Turn the steering stem through its full lock five or six times, then recheck for freeplay. Check

and adjust the bearings as described in Chapter 1 after installation is complete.
Caution: Take great care not to apply excessive pressure because this will cause premature failure of the bearings.
13 Install the top yoke onto the steering stem **(see illustration)**. Install the steering stem bolt and its washer and tighten it finger-tight only at this stage **(see illustration 8.7)**. Temporarily install one of the forks to align the top and bottom yokes, and secure it by tightening the bottom yoke clamp bolts only.
14 Tighten the steering stem bolt to the specified torque setting **(see illustration)**.
15 Install the front forks (see Section 6).
16 Install the remaining components and assemblies in a reverse of the removal procedure, referring to the relevant Sections and Chapters.
17 Carry out a check of the steering head bearing freeplay as described in Chapter 1, and if necessary re-adjust.

9 Steering head bearings - inspection and replacement

Inspection

1 Remove the steering stem (see Section 8).
2 Remove all traces of old grease from the bearings and races and check them for wear or damage.
3 The races should be polished and free from indentations. Inspect the bearing rollers for signs of wear, damage or discoloration, and examine the bearing roller retainer cage for signs of cracks or splits. Spin the bearings by hand. They should spin freely and smoothly. If there are any signs of wear on any of the above components both upper and lower bearing assemblies must be replaced as a set. Only remove the races if they need to be replaced - do not re-use them once they have been removed.

Replacement

4 The races are an interference fit in the steering head and can be tapped from position with a suitable drift **(see illustration)**. Tap firmly and evenly around each race to ensure that it is driven out squarely. It may prove advantageous to curve the end of the drift slightly to improve access.
5 Alternatively, remove the races using a slide-hammer type bearing extractor; these can often be hired from tool shops.

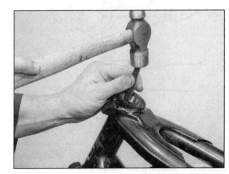

9.4 Drive the bearing races out with a brass drift as shown

5

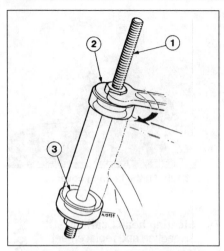

9.6 Drawbolt arrangement for fitting steering stem bearing races

1 Long bolt or threaded bar
2 Thick washer
3 Guide for lower race

6 Press the new races into the head using a drawbolt arrangement **(see illustration)**, or by using a large diameter tubular drift. Ensure that the drawbolt washer or drift (as applicable) bears only on the outer edge of the race and does not contact the working surface. Alternatively, have the races installed by a Kawasaki dealer equipped with the bearing race installing tools.

 Installation of new head bearing races is made much easier if the races are left overnight in the freezer. This causes them to contract slightly making them a looser fit.

7 To remove the lower bearing from the steering stem, clamp the stem in a vice and use two flat-bladed screwdrivers placed on opposite sides of the race to work it free, using blocks of wood to protect the yoke **(see illustration)**. If the bearing is firmly in place it will be necessary to use a bearing puller, or in extreme circumstances to split the bearing's inner section **(see illustration)**.

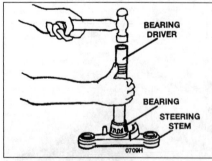

9.8 Drive the new bearing on using a suitable bearing driver or a length of pipe that bears only against the inner race and not against the rollers or cage

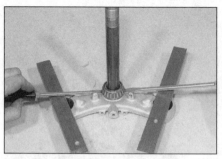

9.7a Remove the lower bearing as shown . . .

8 Fit the new lower bearing onto the steering stem. A length of tubing with an internal diameter slightly larger than the steering stem will be needed to tap the new bearing into position **(see illustration)**. Ensure that the drift bears only on the inner edge of the bearing and does not contact the rollers, or better still fit a washer between the bearing and the tubing to protect the bearing.
9 Install the steering stem (see Section 8).

10 Rear shock absorbers -
removal, inspection and installation

Removal

1 Place the machine on its centre stand or support it upright using an auxiliary stand. If both shock absorbers are to be removed at the same time, position a support under the rear wheel so that it does not drop when the

10.3a Right-hand shock absorber lower mounting

10.4a Unscrew the upper mounting bolt . . .

9.7b . . . or remove it using a bearing puller

second shock is removed, but also making sure that the weight of the machine is off the rear suspension so that the shocks are not compressed. Alternatively, remove only one shock at a time.
2 On 550 models, remove the exhaust system, and on 750 models, remove the silencer on the side which the shock is being removed from (remove both silencers if both shocks are being removed) (see Chapter 3).
3 Remove the shock absorber lower mounting bolt. The right-hand shock absorber bolt threads into a nut, whilst the left-hand shock bolt threads into the chain guard bracket **(see illustrations)**. When removing the right-hand shock, counter-hold the bolt and unscrew the nut. Swing the shock rearwards until the bottom clears the mounting bracket on the swingarm.
4 Supporting the shock absorber, unscrew and remove the upper mounting bolt and washer, then remove the shock **(see illustrations)**.

10.3b Left-hand shock absorber lower mounting

10.4b . . . and remove the shock absorber

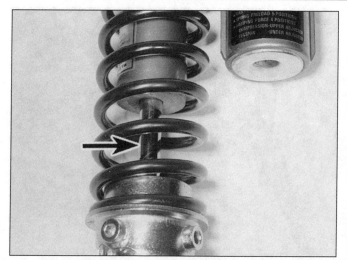

10.6 Inspect the damper rod (arrowed) for pitting and leakage . . .

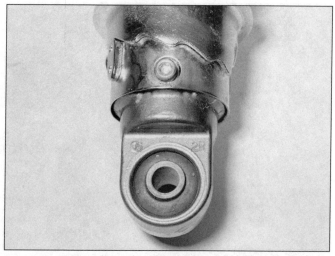

10.7 . . . and the bushes for wear and deterioration

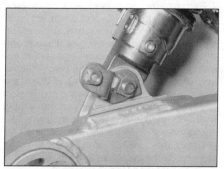

10.10 Make sure the chain guard bracket is correctly aligned

11.1a Spring pre-load adjuster - 550 models

11.1b Spring pre-load adjuster - 750 models

Inspection

5 Inspect the shock absorber for obvious physical damage and the coil spring for looseness, cracks or signs of fatigue.

6 Inspect the damper rod for signs of bending, pitting and oil leakage **(see illustration)**.

7 Inspect the pivot hardware at the top and bottom of the shock for wear or damage **(see illustration)**.

8 If the shock absorber is in any way damaged or worn it must be replaced. Individual replacement components are not available.

9 Kawasaki specify releasing the nitrogen gas pressure before discarding the shock absorber. To do this, remove the cap from the base of the reservoir, then, using a screwdriver or other suitable tool, depress the valve until all the nitrogen is released. If in doubt, take the shocks to a dealer for disposal.

⚠️ *Warning: Do not point the valve towards you when releasing the nitrogen - it is under considerable pressure, and an oil mist will also be released.*

Installation

10 Installation is the reverse of removal, noting the following.

a) *Apply multi-purpose lithium grease to the pivot points.*

b) *Install the upper mounting bolt first, but do not tighten it until the lower mounting bolt is installed.*

c) *If the chain guard has been removed, make sure the chain guard bracket is correctly positioned **(see illustration)**.*

d) *Tighten the lower mounting bolt (left-hand side) and nut (right-hand side) to the torque setting specified at the beginning of the Chapter.*

e) *Adjust the suspension as required (see Section 11).*

f) *Check the operation of the suspension before taking the machine on the road.*

11 Rear shock absorbers - adjustment

Caution: Always ensure that both shock absorber settings are the same. Uneven

settings will upset the handling of the machine and could cause it to become unstable.

Spring pre-load

1 Pre-load adjustment is made using a suitable slim bar (one of the Phillips screwdrivers provided in the toolkit will do) inserted into one of the holes in the pre-load adjuster ring on the bottom (550 models) or top (750 models) of the shock **(see illustrations)**. There are five positions, each indicated by a step in the adjuster ring. Align the step required with the adjustment stopper.

2 On 550 models, to increase the pre-load, turn the spring seat anti-clockwise (towards the front of the bike). To decrease the pre-load, turn the spring seat clockwise. Position 2 is the standard setting for a rider of average build, riding solo.

3 On 750 models, to increase the pre-load, turn the spring seat clockwise (towards the front of the bike). To decrease the pre-load, turn the spring seat anti-clockwise. Position 2 is the standard setting for a rider of average build, riding solo.

5

11.4 Compression damping adjuster

11.6 Rebound damping adjuster

Compression damping

4 Compression damping adjustment is made by turning the adjuster on the top of the shock absorber **(see illustration)**. There are four positions. Position 1 is the softest setting, position 4 the hardest.

5 Turn the adjuster until the number required aligns with the index mark on the shock. Do not set the adjuster in between any of the positions. Position 1 is the standard setting.

Rebound damping

6 Rebound damping adjustment is made by turning the adjuster on the bottom of the shock absorber **(see illustration)**. There are four positions, denoted by Roman numerals. Position I is the softest setting, position IIII the hardest.

7 Turn the adjuster until the number required is visible and clicks into position. Do not set the adjuster in between any of the positions. Position I is the standard setting.

12 Swingarm -
removed and installation

Removal

Note: *Before removing the swingarm, it is advisable to perform the swingarm checks described in Chapter 1, Section 26.*

1 On 550 models, remove the exhaust system, and on 750 models, remove the silencers (see Chapter 3).

2 Remove the rear wheel (see Chapter 6).

3 Remove the nut and the bolt securing the brake torque arm to the swingarm and lift the torque arm off the swingarm **(see illustration)**. Support the brake caliper, caliper bracket and torque arm assembly so that it does not impede removal of the swingarm, making sure that no strain is placed on the hose.

4 Unhook the lower end of the brake light switch spring and position the spring out of the way.

5 Supporting the swingarm, remove the rear shock absorber lower mounting bolts (see Section 10). Also remove the chainguard if required (see Chapter 7).

6 Before removing the swingarm it is advisable to re-check for play in the bearings. Any problems which may have been overlooked with the checks made with the wheel and shock absorbers in place (see Chapter 1) are highlighted with these components removed.

7 Remove the swingarm end caps **(see illustration)**. Unscrew the nut on the left-hand end of the swingarm pivot bolt, and on 750 models remove the washer **(see illustration)**. With the aid of an assistant to support the swingarm if required, drift the pivot bolt out and withdraw it from the right-hand side of the frame **(see illustration)**. Note the positions of any breather and drain pipes and move them aside if necessary, then manoeuvre the swingarm out of the back of the machine.

8 Check the condition of the chain slider on the front of the swingarm and replace it if it is worn or damaged **(see illustration)**.

12.3 Remove the brake torque arm bolt and lift the arm off

12.7a Remove the end cap . . .

12.7b . . . then unscrew the nut . . .

12.7c . . . and withdraw the pivot bolt

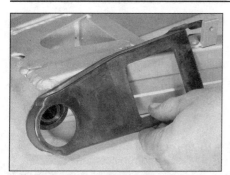

12.8 Replace the chain slider if worn or damaged

9 Inspect all components for wear or damage (see Section 13).

Installation

10 Installation is the reverse of removal, noting the following.

a) Remove the grease seal from each bearing and withdraw the inner sleeve from the swingarm, then lubricate the bearings with molybdenum disulphide grease *(see illustrations 13.4a and b and 13.5)*. Fit the sleeve and the seals back into the bearings. Also lubricate the pivot bolt and the shock absorber pivot bolt shanks with molybdenum disulphide grease.

b) Loop the drive chain over the swingarm as it is offered up to the frame *(see illustration)*. Make sure that the chain slider is fitted to the swingarm and that any breather and drain pipes are correctly positioned.

c) Tighten the swingarm pivot bolt nut to the torque setting specified at the beginning of the Chapter *(see illustration)*.

d) Tighten the brake torque arm nut to the specified torque setting.

e) Tighten the shock absorber bolts to the specified torque setting.

f) Check the operation of the rear suspension before taking the machine on the road.

13 Swingarm - inspection and bearing replacement

Inspection

1 Thoroughly clean all components, removing all traces of dirt, corrosion and grease.

2 Inspect all components closely, looking for obvious signs of wear such as heavy scoring, and cracks or distortion due to accident damage. Any damaged or worn component must be replaced.

3 Check the swingarm pivot bolt for straightness by rolling it on a flat surface such as a piece of plate glass (first wipe off all old grease and remove any corrosion using fine emery cloth). If the equipment is available, place the bolt in V-blocks and measure the runout using a dial indicator. If the bolt is bent or the runout is excessive, replace it.

Bearing replacement

4 Remove the grease seal from each bearing and withdraw the inner sleeve from the swingarm **(see illustrations)**. Inspect them and the bearings for signs of wear or damage and replace them if necessary.

5 Worn bearings can be drifted out of their bores, but note that removal will destroy them; new bearings should be obtained before work commences. The new bearings should be pressed or drawn into their bores rather than driven into position. Fit the bearings with the marked side facing out, and apply plenty of molybdenum disulphide grease **(see illustration)**.

HAYNES HINT *Refer to "Tools and Workshop Tips" in the Reference section for details of how to make up a bearing drawbolt.*

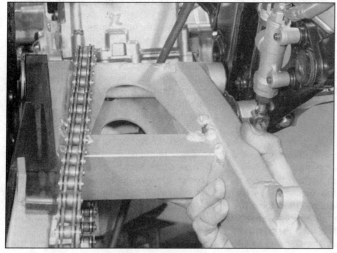

12.10a Do not forget to loop the chain around the swingarm

12.10b Tighten the swingarm nut to the specified torque setting

5

13.4a Remove the grease seals . . .

13.4b . . . and withdraw the inner sleeve

13.5 Liberally grease the bearings

14.2a Unscrew the pinch bolt (arrowed) and slide the arm off the shaft

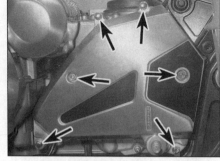

14.2b Engine sprocket cover bolts (arrowed) - 550 models

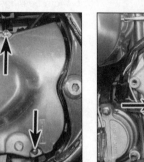

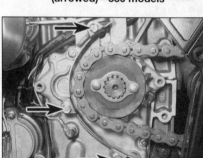

14.2c Engine sprocket cover bolts (arrowed) - 750 models

14.2d The chain guard is secured by three bolts (arrowed)

14 Drive chain - removal, cleaning and installation

Removal

Note: *The original equipment drive chain fitted to all models is an endless chain. Removal requires the removal of the swingarm as detailed below, or if the necessary chain breaking and joining tool is available, the chain can be separated and rejoined (see Tools and Workshop Tips in the Reference section).*

 Warning: NEVER install a drive chain which uses a clip-type master (split) link.

1 Remove the swingarm (see Section 12).
2 Unscrew the gearchange linkage arm pinch bolt and remove the arm from the shaft, noting any alignment marks **(see illustration)**.

If no marks are visible, make your own before removing the arm so that it can be correctly aligned with the shaft on installation. Unscrew the bolts securing the engine sprocket cover to the crankcase and remove it **(see illustrations)**. On 550 models, unscrew the three bolts securing the front sprocket chain guide and remove the guide **(see illustration)**.
3 Slip the chain off the front sprocket and remove it from the bike.

Cleaning

4 Soak the chain in paraffin (kerosene) for approximately five or six minutes.
Caution: Don't use gasoline (petrol), solvent, cleaning fluids, or high-pressure water. Remove the chain, wipe it off, then blow dry it with compressed air immediately. The entire process shouldn't take longer than ten minutes - if it does, the O-rings in the chain rollers could be damaged.

Installation

5 Installation is the reverse of removal. On completion adjust and lubricate the chain following the procedures described in Chapter 1.
Caution: Use only the recommended lubricant.

15 Sprockets - check and replacement

Check

1 Unscrew the gearchange linkage arm pinch bolt and remove the arm from the shaft, noting any alignment marks **(see illustration 14.2a)**. If no marks are visible, make your own before removing the arm so that it can be correctly aligned with the shaft on installation. Unscrew the bolts securing the engine sprocket cover to the crankcase and remove the cover **(see illustrations 14.2b and c)**.
2 Check the wear pattern on both sprockets **(see illustration)**. If the sprocket teeth are worn excessively, replace the chain and both sprockets as a set. Whenever the sprockets are inspected, the drive chain should be inspected also (see Chapter 1). If you are replacing the chain, replace the sprockets as well.
3 Place the machine on its centre stand, or support it using an auxiliary stand so that the rear wheel is off the ground. Check the amount of sprocket warpage using a dial gauge mounted against the outside of the sprocket next to the chain **(see illustration)**. Spin the wheel and record the amount of warpage indicated. If the amount exceeds the service limit specified, replace the sprocket.
4 On 750 models, use a vernier caliper to measure the diameter of each sprocket from the base of the sprocket teeth (you may need to remove the wheel to carry out this check successfully). If the diameter is less than the service limits specified, replace the sprocket.
5 Adjust and lubricate the chain following the procedures described in Chapter 1.
Caution: Use only the recommended lubricant.

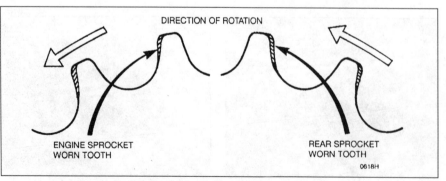

DIRECTION OF ROTATION

ENGINE SPROCKET WORN TOOTH

REAR SPROCKET WORN TOOTH

0618H

15.2 Check the sprocket teeth for wear

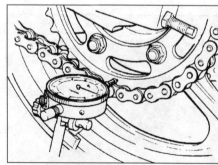

15.3 Measuring sprocket warpage with a dial gauge

15.8 On 550 models, the sprocket is secured by two bolts (arrowed)

15.9 On 750 models, bend back the lockwasher tab (arrowed) and unscrew the nut

Replacement

Front sprocket

6 Unscrew the gearchange linkage arm pinch bolt and remove the arm from the shaft, noting any alignment marks **(see illustration 14.2a)**. If no marks are visible, make your own before removing the arm so that it can be correctly aligned with the shaft on installation. Unscrew the bolts securing the engine sprocket cover to the crankcase and remove the cover **(see illustration 14.2b and c)**.

7 Install the gearchange linkage arm onto the shaft and shift the transmission into gear, then have an assistant sit on the seat and apply the rear brake. This will lock the transmission and enable you to slacken and remove the engine sprocket bolts or nut.

8 On 550 models, unscrew the bolts, then turn the sprocket plate slightly anti-clockwise until the splines in the plate align with those on the shaft and remove the plate **(see illustration)**.

9 On 750 models, bend back the tab on the sprocket nut lockwasher, then unscrew the sprocket nut and remove it with the lockwasher. Check the condition of the lockwasher and renew it if weakened or damaged.

10 Slide the sprocket and chain off the shaft, then slip the sprocket out of the chain **(see illustration)**. If the chain is too tight to allow the sprocket to be slid off the shaft, slacken the chain adjusters to provide some freeplay (see Chapter 1), or, if the rear sprocket is being replaced as well, remove the rear wheel.

11 Engage the new sprocket with the chain and slide it on the shaft. On 550 models, fit the sprocket with the stepped inner circle facing in.

12 On 550 models install the sprocket plate on the shaft until it is in its slot, then turn it slightly clockwise until its holes align with

those in the sprocket **(see illustrations)**. Install the sprocket bolts and, using the method employed on removal to prevent the transmission from turning, tighten them to the torque setting specified at the beginning of the Chapter **(see illustration)**.

13 On 750 models, install the sprocket nut with its lockwasher and, using the method employed on removal to prevent the transmission from turning, tighten it to the torque setting specified at the beginning of the Chapter. Bend up the tabs on the lockwasher to secure the nut **(see illustration)**.

15.10 Slide the sprocket off the shaft and out of the chain

15.12a Slide the sprocket plate onto the shaft . . .

15.12b . . . then turn it to align the bolt holes

15.12c Tighten the sprocket bolts to the specified torque setting

15.13 Bend up a lockwasher tab to lock the nut

5

15.16 The sprocket is secured by six nuts (arrowed)

16.2 Lift the sprocket coupling out of the wheel . . .

14 Install the sprocket cover and the gearchange linkage arm, aligning the marks **(see illustrations 14.2c, b and a)**. Adjust and lubricate the chain following the procedures described in Chapter 1.

Rear sprocket

15 Remove the rear wheel (see Chapter 6).
16 Unscrew the nuts securing the sprocket to the wheel coupling, then remove the sprocket, noting which way round it fits **(see illustration)**.
17 Before installing the new rear sprocket, check the wheel coupling and damper assembly components (see Section 16).
18 Install the sprocket onto the coupling with the stamped mark facing out, then tighten the sprocket nuts to the torque setting specified at the beginning of the Chapter.
19 Install the rear wheel (see Chapter 6).
20 Adjust and lubricate the chain following the procedures described in Chapter 1.

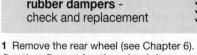

16 Rear wheel coupling/ rubber dampers - check and replacement

1 Remove the rear wheel (see Chapter 6).
Caution: Do not lay the wheel down on the disc as it could become warped. Lay the wheel on wooden blocks so that the disc is off the ground.
2 Lift the sprocket coupling away from the wheel leaving the rubber dampers in position in the wheel **(see illustration)**. Note the spacer inside the coupling. Check the coupling for cracks or any obvious signs of damage. Also check the sprocket studs for wear or damage.
3 Lift the rubber damper segments from the wheel and check them for cracks, hardening and general deterioration **(see illustration)**. Replace the rubber dampers as a set if necessary.

16.3 . . . and check the damper segments for wear and deterioration

4 Checking and replacement procedures for the sprocket coupling bearing are described in Chapter 6.
5 Installation is the reverse of removal. Make sure the spacer is correctly installed in the coupling.
6 Install the rear wheel (see Chapter 6).

Chapter 6
Brakes, wheels and tyres

Contents

Degrees of difficulty

Easy, suitable for novice with little experience	**Fairly easy,** suitable for beginner with some experience	**Fairly difficult,** suitable for competent DIY mechanic 	**Difficult,** suitable for experienced DIY mechanic	**Very difficult,** suitable for expert DIY or professional

Specifications

Brakes

Brake fluid type . . . . DOT 4
Brake pad friction material thickness
  550 models
    Front
      Standard . . . . 4.35 mm
      Service limit . . . . 1.0 mm
    Rear
      Standard . . . . 4.3 mm
      Service limit . . . . 1.0 mm
  750 models - front and rear
    Standard . . . . 4.5 mm
    Service limit . . . . 1.0 mm
Disc minimum thickness
  Front
    Standard . . . . 4.3 to 4.6 mm
    Service limit . . . . 4.0 mm
  Rear
    550 models
      Standard . . . . 4.8 to 5.1 mm
      Service limit . . . . 4.5 mm
    750 models
      Standard . . . . 5.8 to 6.1 mm
      Service limit . . . . 5.0 mm
Disc maximum runout (front and rear, all models)
  Standard . . . . less than 0.2 mm
  Service limit . . . . 0.3 mm

Wheels

Maximum wheel runout (front and rear)
  Axial (side-to-side) . . . . 0.5 mm
  Radial (out-of-round) . . . . 0.8 mm
Axle runout (front and rear)
  Standard . . . . less than 0.05 mm
  Service limit . . . . 0.2 mm

6

Tyres

Tyre pressures and tread depth	see *Daily (pre-ride) checks*
Tyre sizes - 550 models	
Front	110/80 - 17
Rear	140/70 - 18
Tyre sizes - 750 models	
Front	120/70 - 17
Rear	150/70 - 17

Refer to the owners handbook, the tyre information label, or a Kawasaki dealer for approved tyre brands and speed rating.

Torque settings

Front brake caliper mounting bolts	
550 models	32 Nm
750 models	34 Nm
Front brake master cylinder clamp bolts	
550 models	11 Nm
750 models	8.8 Nm
Brake hose banjo bolts	25 Nm
Brake disc bolts	23 Nm
Rear brake caliper mounting bolts	
550 models	25 Nm
750 models	34 Nm
Brake torque arm nuts	
550 models	32 Nm
750 models	34 Nm
Rear brake master cylinder bolts	23 Nm
Front axle	88 Nm
Front axle clamp bolts	
550 models	20 Nm
750 models	34 Nm
Rear axle nut	88 Nm
Chain adjuster clamp bolts	39 Nm

1 General information

All models covered in this manual are fitted with cast alloy wheels, except the ZR750 D model, which has spoked wheels. Tubeless tyres are used on the cast wheels, and tubed tyres on spoked wheels.

Both front and rear brakes are hydraulically operated disc brakes. On 550 models, the front has dual sliding calipers with twin pistons, the rear on B1, B2 and B3 models has a single sliding caliper with twin pistons, and the rear on B4, B5 and B6 models has a single sliding caliper with single piston. On 750 models, the front has dual sliding calipers with twin pistons, and the rear has a single sliding caliper with twin pistons.

Caution: Disc brake components rarely require disassembly. Do not disassemble components unless absolutely necessary. If a hydraulic brake line is loosened, the entire system must be disassembled, drained, cleaned and then properly filled and bled upon reassembly. Do not use solvents on internal brake components. Solvents will cause the seals to swell and distort. Use only clean brake fluid or denatured alcohol for cleaning. Use care when working with brake fluid as it can injure your eyes and it will damage painted surfaces and plastic parts.

2 Front brake pads - replacement

⚠️ *Warning: The dust created by the brake system may contain asbestos, which is harmful to your health. Never blow it out with compressed air and don't inhale any of it. An approved filtering mask should be worn when working on the brakes.*

1 On all except ZR750 D models, unscrew the brake caliper mounting bolts and slide the caliper off the disc **(see illustration 3.2a)**. Remove the outer pad from the caliper body, noting how the protrusion on each end of the pad locates against the guide **(see illustration)**.

2.1a Remove the outer pad . . .

Slide the caliper in on its sliders until the inner pad can be lifted off its guide pins on the caliper mounting bracket **(see illustration)**. Also note how the pad spring is fitted and remove it if required.

2 On ZR750 D models, unscrew the brake caliper mounting bolts and slide the caliper off the disc. Remove the R-pin from the end of the pad retaining pin, then withdraw the pad pin. Remove the outer pad from the caliper body, noting how the protrusion on the end of the pad locates against the guide. Lift the inner pad off its guide pin on the caliper mounting bracket, noting how it fits.

3 Inspect the surface of each pad for contamination and check that the friction material has not worn beyond its service limit. If either pad is worn down to, or beyond, the

2.1b . . . then slide the caliper fully in until the inner pad can be lifted off the pins

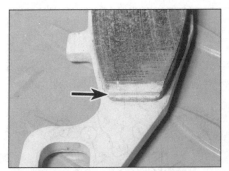

2.3 Brake pad wear indicator step (arrowed)

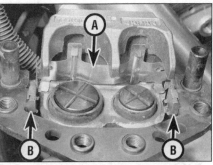

2.9a Make sure the spring (A) and guides (B) are correctly positioned

2.9b Locate the outer pad ends as shown

service limit wear step, line or groove (ie they are no longer visible), fouled with oil or grease, or heavily scored or damaged by dirt and debris, both pads must be replaced as a set **(see illustration)**. If you are in doubt about the amount of friction material left, measure the thickness of the material. If it is 1 mm or less, the pads must be replaced. Note that it is not possible to degrease the friction material; if the pads are contaminated in any way they must be replaced.

4 If the pads are in good condition clean them carefully, using a fine wire brush which is completely free of oil and grease to remove all traces of road dirt and corrosion. Using a pointed instrument, clean out the grooves in the friction material and dig out any embedded particles of foreign matter. Any areas of glazing may be removed using emery cloth.

5 Check the brake disc condition (Section 4).

6 On ZR750 D models, remove all traces of corrosion from the pad pin. Inspect the pin for signs of damage and replace if necessary.

7 Push the pistons as far back into the caliper as possible using hand pressure only **(see illustration 7.11)**. Due to the increased friction material thickness of new pads, it may be necessary to remove the master cylinder reservoir cover and diaphragm and siphon out some fluid.

8 Smear the backs of the pads and the shank of the pad pin (ZR750 D models only) with copper-based grease, making sure that none gets on the front or sides of the pads.

9 On all except ZR750 D models, installation of the pads is the reverse of removal. Make sure the pad spring and guides are correctly positioned **(see illustration)**. Insert the pads into the caliper so that the friction material of each pad will be facing the disc. Make sure the protrusion on each end of the outer pad locates correctly against its guide **(see illustration)**.

10 On ZR750 D models, installation of the pads and pad pin is the reverse of removal. Make sure the pad spring and guide are correctly positioned. Insert the pads into the caliper so that the friction material of each pad will be facing the disc. Make sure the protrusion on the outer pad locates correctly against the guide. Make sure the pad pin passes through each pad and secure it with the R-pin.

11 Install the caliper on the brake disc making sure the pads sit squarely either side of the disc **(see illustration 3.13)**.

12 Install the caliper mounting bolts, and tighten them to the torque setting specified at the beginning of this Chapter **(see illustration 3.14)**.

13 Top up the master cylinder reservoir if necessary (see *Daily (pre-ride) checks*), and replace the reservoir cover and diaphragm if removed.

14 Operate the brake lever several times to bring the pads into contact with the disc. Check the master cylinder fluid level (see *Daily (pre-ride) checks*) and the operation of the brake before riding the motorcycle.

3 Front brake calipers - removal, overhaul and installation

⚠️ *Warning: If a caliper indicates the need for an overhaul (usually due to leaking fluid or sticky operation), all old brake fluid should be flushed from the system. Also, the dust created by the brake system may contain asbestos, which is harmful to your health. Never blow it out with compressed air and don't inhale any of it. An approved filtering mask should be worn when working on the brakes. Do not, under any circumstances, use petroleum-based solvents to clean brake parts. Use clean brake fluid, brake cleaner or denatured alcohol only.*

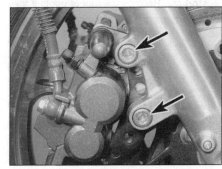

3.2a Brake caliper mounting bolts (arrowed)

Removal

1 Remove the brake hose banjo bolt, noting its position on the caliper and separate the hose from the caliper **(see illustration)**. Plug the hose end or wrap a plastic bag tightly around it to minimise fluid loss and prevent dirt entering the system. Discard the sealing washers as new ones must be used on installation. **Note:** *If you are overhauling the caliper and don't have a source of compressed air to blow out the pistons, just loosen the banjo bolt at this stage and retighten it lightly. The bike's hydraulic system can then be used to force the pistons out of the body once the pads have been removed. Disconnect the hose once the pistons have been sufficiently displaced.*

2 Unscrew the caliper mounting bolts, and slide the caliper away from the disc **(see illustration)**. Remove the brake pads. On all except ZR750 D models, remove the piston insulator pieces **(see illustration)**.

3.1 Note the brake hose alignment before unscrewing the banjo bolt (arrowed)

3.2b Remove the insulator piece from each piston

6

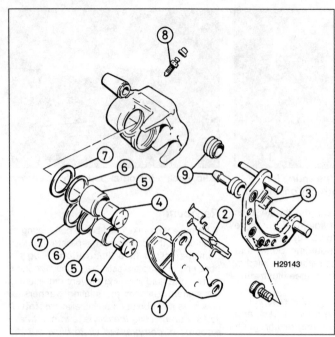

3.3a Front brake caliper components - all models except ZR750 D

1 Brake pads
2 Pad spring
3 Outer pad guides
4 Piston insulator piece
5 Piston
6 Dust seal
7 Piston seal
8 Bleed valve
9 Slider pin boot

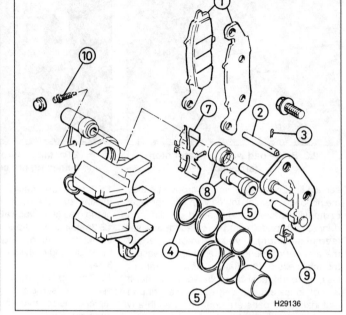

3.3b Front brake caliper components - ZR750 D models

1 Brake pads
2 Pad pin
3 R-pin
4 Piston seal
5 Dust seal
6 Piston
7 Pad spring
8 Slider pin boot
9 Outer pad guide
10 Bleed valve

Overhaul

3 Clean the exterior of the caliper with denatured alcohol or brake system cleaner **(see illustrations)**.

4 Remove the pistons from the caliper body, either by pumping them out by operating the front brake lever until the pistons are displaced, or by forcing them out using compressed air. Note that on all except 750 D1 models, two sizes of piston are used, and that different size seals are used accordingly. Mark each piston head and caliper body with a felt marker to ensure that the pistons can be matched to their original bores on reassembly. If the compressed air method is used, place a wad of rag between the pistons and the caliper to act as a cushion, then use compressed air directed into the fluid inlet to force the pistons out of the body. Use only low pressure to ease the pistons out and make sure both pistons are displaced at the same time. If the air pressure is too high and the pistons are forced out, the caliper and/or pistons may be damaged.

⚠ **Warning: Never place your fingers in front of the pistons in an attempt to catch or protect them when applying compressed air, as serious injury could result.**

5 Using a wooden or plastic tool, remove the dust seals from the caliper bores and discard them **(see illustration)**. New seals must be used on installation. If a metal tool is being used, take great care not to damage the caliper bores.

6 Remove and discard the piston seals in the same way.

7 Clean the pistons and bores with denatured alcohol, clean brake fluid or brake system cleaner. If compressed air is available, use it to dry the parts thoroughly (make sure it's filtered and unlubricated).

Caution: Never use a petroleum-based solvent to clean brake parts.

8 Inspect the caliper bores and pistons for signs of corrosion, nicks and burrs and loss of plating. If surface defects are present, the caliper assembly must be replaced. Check that the caliper body is able to slide freely on the mounting bracket slider pins. If seized due to corrosion, separate the two components and clean off all traces of corrosion and hardened grease. Apply a smear of copper or silicone-based grease to the mounting bracket slider pins and reassemble the two components **(see illustration)**. Replace the rubber boots if they

are damaged or deteriorated **(see illustration)**. If the caliper is in bad shape the master cylinder should also be checked.

9 Lubricate the new piston seals with clean brake fluid and install them in their grooves in

3.5 Remove the dust seal with a plastic or wooden tool (a pencil works well) to avoid damage to the bore and seal groove

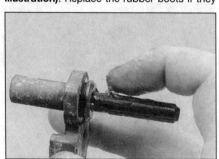

3.8a Apply a little of the specified grease to the slider pins on the caliper bracket

3.8b Replace the slider boots if necessary

3.13 Install the caliper . . .

3.14 . . . and tighten the bolts to the specified torque setting

the caliper bores. Note that on all except ZR750 D models, two sizes of bore and piston are used, and care must therefore be taken to ensure that the correct size seals are fitted to the correct bores. The same applies when fitting the new dust seals and pistons.

10 Lubricate the new dust seals with clean brake fluid and install them in their grooves in the caliper bores.

11 Lubricate the pistons with clean brake fluid and install them closed-end first into the caliper bores. Using your thumbs, push the pistons all the way in, making sure they enter the bore squarely **(see illustration 7.11)**.

Installation

12 On all except ZR750 D models, install the piston centre pieces **(see illustration 3.2b)**.Install the brake pads (see Section 2).

13 Install the caliper on the brake disc making sure the pads sit squarely either side of the disc **(see illustration)**.

14 Install the caliper mounting bolts, and tighten them to the torque setting specified at the beginning of this Chapter **(see illustration)**.

15 Connect the brake hose to the caliper, using new sealing washers on each side of the fitting. Position the hose so that it fits into its slot in the caliper **(see illustration 3.1)**.

Tighten the banjo bolt to the torque setting specified at the beginning of the Chapter.

16 Fill the fluid reservoir to the maximum level line with the specified brake fluid **(see illustration 5.24)** and bleed the hydraulic system as described in Section 11.

17 Check for leaks and thoroughly test the operation of the brake before riding the motorcycle.

4 Front brake disc - inspection, removal and installation

Inspection

1 Visually inspect the surface of the disc for score marks and other damage. Light scratches are normal after use and won't affect brake operation, but deep grooves and heavy score marks will reduce braking efficiency and accelerate pad wear. If a disc is badly grooved it must be machined or replaced.

2 To check disc runout, position the bike on its centre stand or an auxiliary stand, and support it so that the front wheel is raised off the ground. Turn the handlebars so that the steering is on full lock either way. Mount a dial

gauge to a fork leg, with the plunger on the gauge touching the surface of the disc about 10 mm (1/2 inch) from the outer edge **(see illustration)**. Rotate the wheel and watch the gauge needle, comparing the reading with the limit listed in the Specifications at the beginning of the Chapter. If the runout is greater than the service limit, check the wheel bearings for play (see Chapter 1). If the bearings are worn, replace them (Section 16) and repeat this check. If the disc runout is still excessive, it will have to be replaced, although machining by a competent engineering shop may be possible.

3 The disc must not be machined or allowed to wear down to a thickness less than the service limit as listed in this Chapter's Specifications and as marked on the disc itself **(see illustration)**. The thickness of the disc can be checked with a micrometer **(see illustration)**. If the thickness of the disc is less than the service limit, it must be replaced.

Removal

4 Remove the wheel (see Section 14).
Caution: Do not lay the wheel down and allow it to rest on the disc - the disc could become warped. Set the wheel on wood blocks so the disc doesn't support the weight of the wheel.

6

4.2 Set up a dial gauge with the probe contacting the brake disc, then rotate the wheel to check for runout

4.3a The minimum disc thickness is marked on the disc

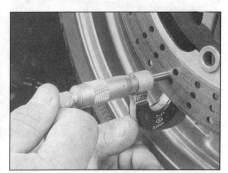

4.3b Using a micrometer to measure disc thickness

4.5 The disc is secured by five bolts (arrowed)

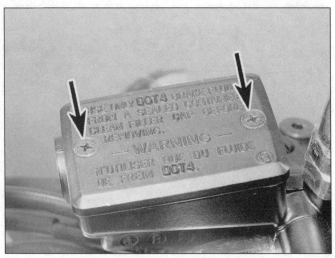

5.4 Slacken the reservoir cover screws (arrowed)

5 Mark the relationship of the disc to the wheel, so it can be installed in the same position. Unscrew the disc retaining bolts, loosening them a little at a time in a criss-cross pattern to avoid distorting the disc, then remove the disc from the wheel **(see illustration)**.

Installation

6 Install the disc on the wheel, aligning the previously applied matchmarks (if you're reinstalling the original disc). The arrow marked on the disc must be on the outside and point in the direction of normal wheel rotation **(see illustration 8.4)**.

7 Install the disc bolts and tighten them in a criss-cross pattern evenly and progressively to the torque setting specified at the beginning of the Chapter. Clean off all grease from the brake disc(s) using acetone or brake system cleaner. If a new brake disc has been installed, remove any protective coating from its working surfaces.

8 Install the front wheel (see Section 14).

9 Operate the brake lever several times to bring the pads into contact with the disc. Check the operation of the brakes carefully before riding the bike.

---

5 Front brake master cylinder - removal, overhaul and installation

1 If the master cylinder is leaking fluid, or if the lever does not produce a firm feel when the brake is applied, and bleeding the brakes does not help (see Section 11), and the hydraulic hoses are all in good condition, then master cylinder overhaul is recommended.

2 Before disassembling the master cylinder, read through the entire procedure and make sure that you have the correct rebuild kit. Also, you will need some new, clean brake fluid of the recommended type, some clean rags and internal circlip pliers. **Note:** *To*

prevent damage to the paint from spilled brake fluid, always cover the fuel tank when working on the master cylinder.
Caution: Disassembly, overhaul and reassembly of the brake master cylinder must be done in a spotlessly clean work area to avoid contamination and possible failure of the brake hydraulic system components.

Removal

3 Remove the rear view mirror (Chapter 7).

4 Loosen, but do not remove, the screws holding the reservoir cover in place **(see illustration)**.

5 Disconnect the electrical connectors from the brake light switch **(see illustration)**.

6 Remove the front brake lever (Chapter 5).

7 Pull back the rubber cover on the brake hose banjo bolt, then unscrew the bolt and separate the hose from the master cylinder, noting its alignment **(see illustration)**. Discard the two sealing washers as they must be

5.5 Disconnect the brake light switch electrical connectors (arrowed)

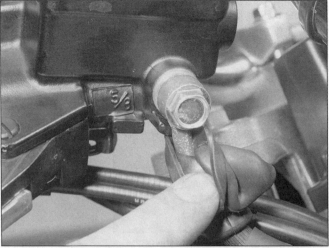

5.7 Peel back the rubber boot to expose the brake hose banjo bolt. Note the alignment of the hose

5.8 Front brake master cylinder clamp bolts (arrowed)

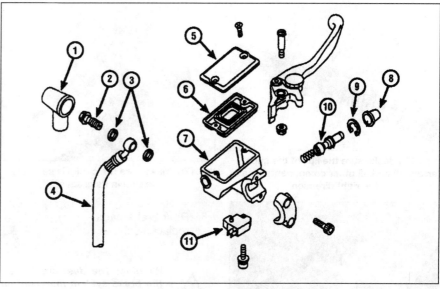

5.9 Front brake master cylinder components

1 Rubber boot	5 Reservoir cover and	8 Rubber dust boot
2 Brake hose banjo bolt	diaphragm plate	9 Circlip
3 Sealing washers	6 Rubber diaphragm	10 Piston assembly & spring
4 Brake hose	7 Reservoir	11 Brake light switch

replaced with new ones. Wrap the end of the hose in a clean rag and suspend it in an upright position or bend it down carefully and place the open end in a clean container. The objective is to prevent excessive loss of brake fluid, fluid spills and system contamination.

8 Unscrew the master cylinder clamp bolts, then lift the master cylinder and reservoir away from the handlebar, noting how the top mating surfaces of the clamp align with the top mating surfaces of the switch housing **(see illustration)**.

Caution: Do not tip the master cylinder upside down or brake fluid will run out.

Overhaul

9 Remove the reservoir cover retaining screws and lift off the cover, the diaphragm plate and the rubber diaphragm **(see illustration)**. Drain the brake fluid from the reservoir into a suitable container. Wipe any remaining fluid out of the reservoir with a clean rag.

10 Unscrew the screw securing the brake light switch to the bottom of the master cylinder and remove the switch **(see illustration)**.

11 Carefully remove the dust boot from the end of the piston **(see illustration)**.

12 Using circlip pliers, remove the circlip and slide out the piston assembly and the spring, noting how they fit **(see illustration)**. Lay the parts out in the proper order to prevent confusion during reassembly **(see illustration)**.

13 Clean all parts with clean brake fluid or denatured alcohol. If compressed air is available, use it to dry the parts thoroughly (make sure it's filtered and unlubricated).

Caution: Do not, under any circumstances, use a petroleum-based solvent to clean brake parts.

14 Check the master cylinder bore for corrosion, scratches, nicks and score marks. If damage or wear is evident, the master cylinder must be replaced with a new one. If the master cylinder is in poor condition, then the calipers should be checked as well. Check that the fluid inlet and outlet ports in the master cylinder are clear.

15 The piston assembly and spring are included in the rebuild kit. Use all of the new parts, regardless of the apparent condition of the old ones.

16 Install the spring in the master cylinder with its wider end first so that its tapered end faces the piston.

17 Lubricate the components with clean brake fluid and install the assembly into the master cylinder, ensuring all the components are the correct way round **(see illustration)**.

5.10 The brake light switch is secured by a single screw (arrowed)

5.12a . . . then depress the piston and remove the circlip using a pair of internal circlip pliers

Make sure the lips on the cup seals do not turn inside out when they are slipped into the bore. Depress the piston and install the new circlip, ensuring it locates in the master cylinder groove **(see illustration)**.

18 Install the rubber dust boot, making sure the lip is seated correctly in the piston groove.

5.11 Remove the rubber boot from the end of the master cylinder piston . . .

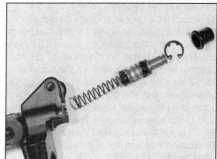

5.12b Lay out the internal parts as shown, even if new parts are being used, to avoid confusion on reassembly

6

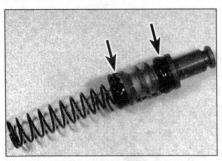

5.17a Make sure the lips of the cups (arrowed) and all other components face in the right direction

5.17b Make sure the circlip is securely seated in its groove

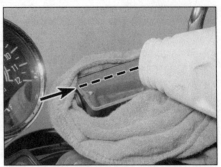

5.24 Fill the reservoir to the maximum line (arrowed) with the specified fluid

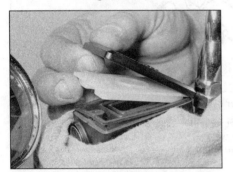

5.25 Fit the diaphragm, plate and cover

19 Install the brake light switch.
20 Inspect the reservoir cover rubber diaphragm and replace if damaged or deteriorated.

Installation

21 Attach the master cylinder to the handlebar and fit the clamp with its UP mark facing up **(see illustration 5.8)**. Align the top mating surfaces of the clamp with the top mating surfaces of the switch housing, then tighten the upper bolt first then the lower bolt to the torque setting specified at the beginning of the Chapter. There should be a gap between the lower clamp mating surfaces.
22 Connect the brake hose to the master cylinder, using new sealing washers on each side of the union, and aligning the hose as noted on removal **(see illustration 5.7)**. Tighten the banjo bolt to the torque setting specified at the beginning of this Chapter.
23 Install the brake lever (see Chapter 5).
24 Fill the fluid reservoir to the maximum level line with the specified brake fluid **(see illustration)**. Refer to Section 11 of this Chapter and bleed the air from the system.
25 Fit the rubber diaphragm, making sure it is correctly seated, the diaphragm plate and the cover onto the master cylinder reservoir, and tighten the screws securely **(see illustration)**.
26 Connect the brake light switch wiring **(see illustration 5.5)** and install the rear view mirror (see Chapter 7).

6 Rear brake pads - replacement

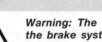

⚠️ *Warning: The dust created by the brake system may contain asbestos, which is harmful to your health. Never blow it out with compressed air and don't inhale any of it. An approved filtering mask should be worn when working on the brakes.*

1 On ZR550 B1, B2 and B3 and all 750 models, unscrew the brake caliper mounting bolts and slide the caliper off the disc **(see illustration 7.2b)**. Remove the outer pad from the caliper body, noting how the protrusion on each end of the pad locates against the guide **(see illustration 2.1a)**. Slide the caliper in on its sliders until the inner pad can be lifted off its guide pins on the caliper mounting bracket **(see illustration 2.1b)**. Also take note of how

the pad spring is fitted and remove if required.
2 On ZR550 B4, B5 and B6 models, unscrew the brake caliper mounting bolts and slide the caliper off the disc **(see illustration 7.2a)**. Remove the R-pin from the end of the pad retaining pin, then withdraw the pad pin **(see illustrations)**. Lift the inner pad and slide it off its guide pin on the caliper mounting bracket, noting how it fits **(see illustration)**. Remove the outer pad from the caliper body, noting how the pad locates against the guide and the bracket **(see illustration)**. On B4 models to frame no. 024010, remove the shim from the back of the inner pad, noting which way round it fits.
3 Inspect the surface of each pad for contamination and check that the friction material has not worn beyond its service limit. If either pad is worn down to, or beyond, the service limit wear step, line or groove (ie they are no longer visible), fouled with oil or grease, or heavily scored or damaged by dirt and debris, both pads must be replaced. If you are

6.2a Remove the R-pin . . .

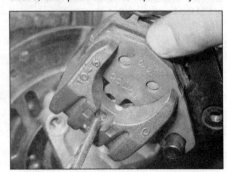

6.2b . . . and withdraw the pad pin

6.2c Lift the inner pad and slide it off the pin . . .

6.2d . . . then remove the outer pad, noting how its protrusions (arrowed) locate

6.10a Make sure the pad spring (arrowed) . . .

6.10b . . . and guide (arrowed) are correctly positioned

in doubt about the amount of friction material left, measure the thickness of the material. If it is 1 mm or less, the pads must be replaced. Note that it is not possible to degrease the friction material; if the pads are contaminated in any way they must be replaced.

4 If the pads are in good condition clean them carefully, using a fine wire brush which is completely free of oil and grease to remove all traces of road dirt and corrosion. Using a pointed instrument, clean out the grooves in the friction material and dig out any embedded particles of foreign matter. Any areas of glazing may be removed using emery cloth.

5 Check the brake disc condition (Section 4).

6 On ZR550 B4, B5 and B6 models, remove all traces of corrosion from the pad pin. Inspect the pin for signs of damage and replace if necessary.

7 Push the piston(s) as far back into the caliper as possible using hand pressure only **(see illustration 7.11)**. Due to the increased friction material thickness of new pads, it may be necessary to remove the master cylinder reservoir cover and diaphragm and siphon out some fluid.

8 Smear the backs of the pads and the shank of the pad pin (ZR550 B4, B5 and B6 models only) with copper-based grease, making sure none gets on the front or sides of the pads.

9 On ZR550 B1, B2 and B3 and all 750 models, installation of the pads is the reverse of removal. Make sure the pad spring and guides are correctly positioned **(see illustration 2.9a)**. Insert the pads into the caliper so that the friction material of each pad will be facing the disc. Make sure the protrusion on each end of the outer pad locates correctly against its guide **(see illustration 2.9b)**.

10 On 550 B4, B5 and B6 models, installation of the pads and pad pin is the reverse of removal. Make sure the pad spring and guide are correctly positioned **(see illustrations)**. Make sure the outer pad locates correctly against the guide and the bracket **(see illustration 6.2d)**. Insert the pads into the caliper so that the friction material of each pad will be facing the disc **(see illustration 6.2c)**. On B4 models to frame no. 024010, fit the shim onto the back of the inner pad with the open end facing back. Make sure the pad

pin passes through each pad and secure it with the R-pin **(see illustrations 6.2b and a)**.

11 Install the caliper on the brake disc making sure the pads sit squarely either side of the disc **(see illustration 7.13)**.

12 Install the caliper mounting bolts, and tighten them to the specified torque **(see illustration 7.14b)**.

13 Top up the master cylinder reservoir if necessary (see *Daily (pre-ride) checks*), and replace the reservoir cover and diaphragm if removed.

14 Operate the brake lever several times to bring the pads into contact with the disc. Check the master cylinder fluid level (see *Daily (pre-ride) checks*) and the operation of the brake before riding the motorcycle.

7 Rear brake caliper - removal, overhaul and installation

⚠ **Warning: If a caliper needs an overhaul (usually due to leaking fluid or sticky operation), all old brake fluid should be flushed from the system. Also, the dust created by the brake system may contain asbestos, which is harmful to your health. Never blow it out with compressed air and don't inhale any of it. An approved filtering mask should be worn when working on the brakes. Do not, under any circumstances, use petroleum-based solvents to clean brake parts. Use clean brake fluid, brake cleaner or denatured alcohol only.**

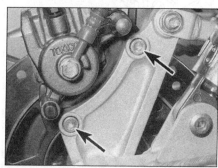

7.2a Rear brake caliper mounting bolts (arrowed) - ZR550 B4, B5 and B6 models

Removal

1 Remove the brake hose banjo bolt, noting its position on the caliper and separate the hose from the caliper **(see illustration)**. Plug the hose end or wrap a plastic bag tightly around it to minimise fluid loss and prevent dirt entering the system. Discard the sealing washers as new ones must be used on installation. **Note:** *If you are planning to overhaul the caliper and don't have a source of compressed air to blow out the pistons, just loosen the banjo bolt at this stage and retighten it lightly. The bike's hydraulic system can then be used to force the pistons out of the body once the pads have been removed. Disconnect the hose once the pistons have been sufficiently displaced.*

2 Unscrew the caliper mounting bolts, and slide the caliper away from the disc **(see illustrations)**. Remove the brake pads (see Section 6), and the piston insulator piece(s) **(see illustration 3.2b)**.

Overhaul

3 Clean the exterior of the caliper with denatured alcohol or brake system cleaner **(see illustrations)**.

4 Remove the pistons from the caliper body, either by pumping them out by operating the front brake lever until the pistons are displaced, or by forcing them out using compressed air. Note that on 750 models, two sizes of piston are used, and that different size seals are used accordingly. Mark each piston head and caliper body with a felt marker to ensure that the pistons can be

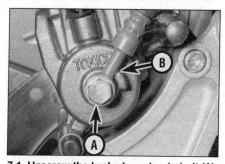

7.1 Unscrew the brake hose banjo bolt (A), noting its alignment with the lug (B) - ZR550 B4, B5 and B6 type shown

7.2b Rear brake caliper mounting bolts (arrowed) - 750 models

6

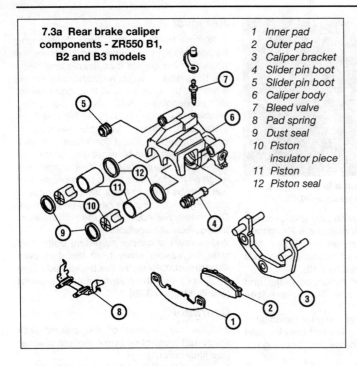

7.3a Rear brake caliper components - ZR550 B1, B2 and B3 models

1 Inner pad
2 Outer pad
3 Caliper bracket
4 Slider pin boot
5 Slider pin boot
6 Caliper body
7 Bleed valve
8 Pad spring
9 Dust seal
10 Piston insulator piece
11 Piston
12 Piston seal

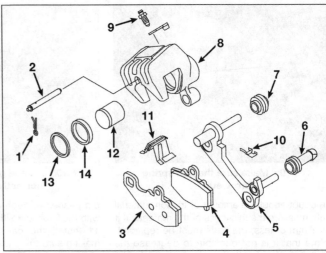

7.3b Rear brake caliper components - ZR550 B4, B5 & B6 models

1 R-pin	6 Slider pin boot	11 Pad spring
2 Pad pin	7 Slider pin boot	12 Piston
3 Inner pad	8 Caliper body	13 Dust seal
4 Outer pad	9 Bleed valve	14 Piston seal
5 Caliper bracket	10 Pad guide	

matched to their original bores on reassembly. If the compressed air method is used, place a wad of rag between the pistons and the caliper to act as a cushion, then use compressed air directed into the fluid inlet to force the pistons out of the body. Use only low pressure to ease the pistons out and make sure both pistons are displaced at the same time. If the air pressure is too high and the pistons are forced out, the caliper and/or pistons may be damaged.

Warning: Never place your fingers in front of the pistons in an attempt to catch or protect them when applying compressed air, as serious injury could result.

5 Using a wooden or plastic tool, remove the dust seals from the caliper bores and discard them **(see illustration 3.5)**. New seals must be used on installation. If a metal tool is being used, take great care not to damage the caliper bores.

6 Remove and discard the piston seals in the same way.
7 Clean the pistons and bores with denatured alcohol, clean brake fluid or brake system cleaner. If compressed air is available, use it to dry the parts thoroughly (make sure it's filtered and unlubricated).

Caution: Do not, under any circumstances, use a petroleum-based solvent to clean brake parts.

8 Inspect the caliper bores and pistons for signs of corrosion, nicks and burrs and loss of plating. If surface defects are present, the caliper assembly must be replaced. Check that the caliper body is able to slide freely on the mounting bracket slider pins. If seized due to corrosion, separate the two components and clean off all traces of corrosion and hardened grease. Apply a smear of copper or silicone-based grease to the mounting bracket slider pins and reassemble the two components **(see illustration 3.8a)**. Replace the rubber boots if they are damaged or deteriorated **(see illustration 3.8b)**. If the caliper is in bad shape the master cylinder should also be checked.

9 Lubricate the new piston seals with clean brake fluid and install them in their grooves in the caliper bores. Note that on 750 models, two sizes of bore and piston are used, and care must therefore be taken to ensure that the correct size seals are fitted to the correct bores. The same applies when fitting the new dust seals and pistons.

10 Lubricate the new dust seals with clean brake fluid and install them in their grooves in the caliper bores.

11 Lubricate the pistons with clean brake fluid and install them closed-end first into the caliper bores. Using your thumbs, push the

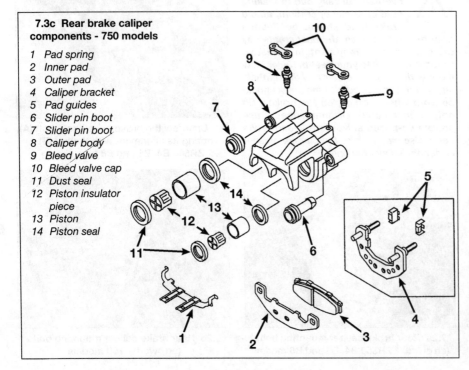

7.3c Rear brake caliper components - 750 models

1 Pad spring
2 Inner pad
3 Outer pad
4 Caliper bracket
5 Pad guides
6 Slider pin boot
7 Slider pin boot
8 Caliper body
9 Bleed valve
10 Bleed valve cap
11 Dust seal
12 Piston insulator piece
13 Piston
14 Piston seal

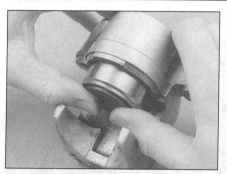

7.11 Push the piston squarely into the bore

7.13 Mount the caliper onto the disc . . .

7.14a . . . then install the bolts . . .

7.14b . . . and tighten them to the specified torque setting

pistons all the way in, making sure they enter the bore squarely **(see illustration)**.

Installation

12 On all except ZR550 B4, B5 and B6 models, install the piston insulator pieces **(see illustration 3.2b)**. Install the brake pads (see Section 6).
13 Install the caliper on the brake disc making sure the pads sit squarely either side of the disc **(see illustration)**.
14 Install the caliper mounting bolts, and tighten them to the specified torque **(see illustrations)**.

15 Connect the brake hose to the caliper, using new sealing washers on each side of the fitting. Position the hose as noted on removal **(see illustrations 7.1 and 7.2b)**. Tighten the banjo bolt to the torque setting specified at the beginning of the Chapter.
16 Fill the fluid reservoir to the upper level line with the specified brake fluid **(see illustration 5.24)** and bleed the hydraulic system as described in Section 11.
17 Check very carefully for leaks and thoroughly test the operation of the brake, preferably before taking the machine out on the road.

8 Rear brake disc - inspection, removal and installation

Inspection

1 Refer to Section 4 of this Chapter, noting that the dial gauge should be attached to the swingarm.

Removal

2 Remove the rear wheel with reference to Section 15.
3 Mark the relationship of the disc to the wheel so it can be installed in the same position. Unscrew the disc retaining bolts, loosening them a little at a time in a criss-cross pattern to avoid distorting the disc, and remove the disc **(see illustration)**.

Installation

4 Position the disc on the wheel, aligning the previously applied matchmarks (if you're reinstalling the original disc). The arrow marked on the disc must be on the outside and point in the direction of normal wheel rotation **(see illustration)**.
5 Install the disc bolts and tighten them in a criss-cross pattern evenly and progressively to the torque setting specified at the beginning of this Chapter. Clean off all grease from the brake disc using acetone or brake system cleaner. If a new brake disc has been installed, remove any protective coating from its working surfaces.
6 Install the rear wheel with reference to Section 15.
7 Operate the brake pedal several times to bring the pads into contact with the disc. Check the operation of the brake, preferably before taking the machine out on the road.

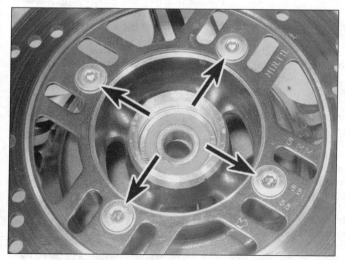

8.3 The disc is secured by four bolts (arrowed)

8.4 The arrow must point in the direction of normal rotation

6

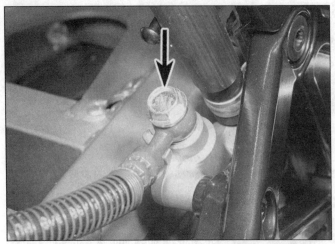

9.4a Rear master cylinder banjo bolt (arrowed) - 550 models. Note the alignment of the hose

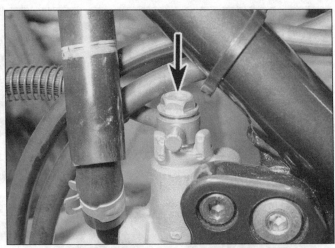

9.4b Rear master cylinder banjo bolt (arrowed) - 750 models. Note the alignment of the hose

9.5 Rear master cylinder reservoir

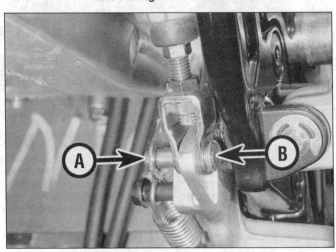

9.6 Remove the split pin (A), withdraw the clevis pin (B), and separate the pushrod from the pedal

9 Rear brake master cylinder - removal, overhaul and installation

1 If the master cylinder is leaking fluid, or if the lever does not produce a firm feel when the brake is applied, and bleeding the brakes does not help (see Section 11), and the hydraulic hoses are all in good condition, then master cylinder overhaul is recommended.

2 Before disassembling the master cylinder, read through the entire procedure and make sure that you have the correct rebuild kit. Also, you will need some new, clean brake fluid of the recommended type, some clean rags and internal circlip pliers. **Note:** *To prevent damage to the paint from spilled brake fluid, always cover surrounding painted surfaces when working on the master cylinder.* **Caution: *Disassembly, overhaul and reassembly of the brake master cylinder must be done in a spotlessly clean work area to avoid contamination and possible***

failure of the brake hydraulic system components.

Removal

3 Remove the seat and the right-hand side panel (see Chapter 7).

4 Unscrew the brake hose banjo bolt and separate the brake hose from the master cylinder, noting its alignment **(see illustrations)**. Discard the two sealing washers as they must be replaced with new ones. Wrap the end of the hose in a clean rag and suspend the hose in an upright position or bend it down carefully and place the open end in a clean container. The objective is to prevent excessive loss of brake fluid, fluid spills and system contamination.

5 Unscrew the master cylinder fluid reservoir cap and remove the diaphragm plate and diaphragm **(see illustration)**. Separate the fluid reservoir hose from the elbow on the master cylinder by releasing the hose clamp, and allow the fluid to drain from the reservoir into a suitable container.

6 Remove the split pin from the clevis pin securing the brake pedal to the master cylinder pushrod **(see illustration)**. Withdraw the clevis pin and separate the pedal from the pushrod. Discard the split pin as a new one must be used.

7 Unscrew the two bolts securing the master cylinder to the bracket **(see illustration)**.

9.7 The master cylinder is secured by two bolts (arrowed)

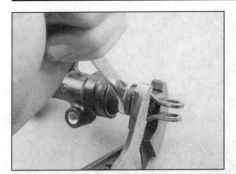

9.9 Hold the clevis with a pair of pliers and slacken the locknut

8 If required, unscrew the nut and remove the bolt securing the reservoir to the frame, then remove the reservoir with its hose.

Overhaul

9 If necessary, slacken the clevis locknut, then unscrew the clevis with its nut and locknut and remove them from the pushrod **(see illustration)**.

10 Dislodge the rubber dust boot from the base of the master cylinder to reveal the pushrod retaining circlip **(see illustrations)**.

11 Depress the pushrod and, using internal circlip pliers, remove the circlip **(see illustration)**. Slide out the piston assembly and spring. If they are difficult to remove, apply low pressure compressed air to the fluid outlet. Lay the parts out in the proper order to prevent confusion during reassembly.

12 Clean all of the parts with clean brake fluid or denatured alcohol.

Caution: **Do not, under any circumstances, use a petroleum-based solvent to clean brake parts.** *If compressed air is available, use it to dry the parts thoroughly (make sure it's filtered and unlubricated).*

13 Check the master cylinder bore for corrosion, scratches, nicks and score marks. If damage is evident, the master cylinder must be replaced with a new one. If the master cylinder is in poor condition, then the caliper should be checked as well.

14 If required, remove the fluid reservoir hose elbow circlip and detach the elbow from the master cylinder **(see illustration)**. Discard the

9.10a Rear brake master cylinder components

1 Split pin
2 Clevis pin
3 Master cylinder mounting bolt
4 Master cylinder
5 Circlip
6 Reservoir hose elbow
7 O-ring
8 Pushrod
9 Rubber dust boot
10 Circlip
11 Piston assembly
12 Spring
13 Hose clamp
14 Reservoir hose
15 Reservoir cap
16 Diaphragm plate
17 Rubber diaphragm
18 Reservoir
19 Reservoir mounting bolt
20 Banjo bolt
21 Sealing washer
22 Brake hose

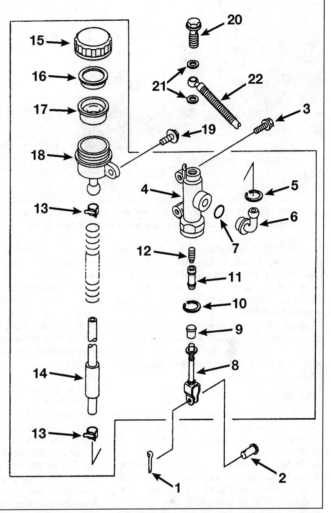

O-ring as a new one must be used. Inspect the reservoir hose for cracks or splits and replace if necessary.

15 The piston assembly and spring are included in the rebuild kit. Use all of the new parts, regardless of the apparent condition of the old ones.

16 Install the spring in the master cylinder with its wider end first so that its tapered end faces the piston.

17 Lubricate the piston components with clean brake fluid and install the assembly into the master cylinder, ensuring all components are the correct way round **(see illustration)**. Ensure the cup seal lips do not turn inside out when they are slipped into the bore.

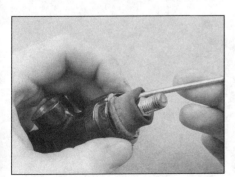

9.10b Remove the dust boot from the pushrod

9.11 Depress the pushrod and remove the circlip from the cylinder bore

9.14 Remove the circlip securing the reservoir hose elbow

6

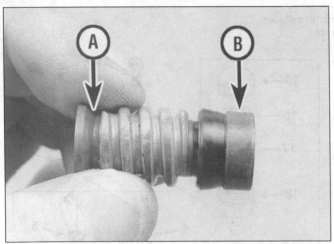

9.17 Make sure the piston assembly is installed with the inner end (A) facing in, and the outer end (B) facing out

9.20 Use a new O-ring for the reservoir hose elbow

18 Install and depress the pushrod, then install a new circlip, making sure it is properly seated in the groove **(see illustration 9.11)**.

19 Install the rubber dust boot, making sure the lip is seated properly in the groove **(see illustration 9.10b)**.

20 If removed, fit a new O-ring into the fluid reservoir hose elbow socket **(see illustration)**, then install the elbow into the master cylinder and secure it with its circlip **(see illustration 9.14)**.

Installation

21 If removed, install the clevis locknut, the clevis and its nut onto the master cylinder pushrod end, but do not yet tighten the locknut.

22 Install the master cylinder onto the footrest bracket and tighten its mounting bolts to the torque setting specified at the beginning of the Chapter **(see illustration 9.7)**.

23 If removed, secure the fluid reservoir to the frame with its retaining bolt. Ensure that the hose is correctly routed, then connect it to

the elbow on the master cylinder and secure it with the clamp. Check that the hose is secure and clamped at the reservoir end as well. If the clamps have weakened, use new ones.

24 Connect the brake hose banjo bolt to the master cylinder, using a new sealing washer on each side of the banjo union. Ensure that the hose is positioned as noted on removal **(see illustrations 9.4a and b)** and tighten the banjo bolt to the specified torque setting.

25 Align the brake pedal with the master cylinder pushrod clevis, then slide in the clevis pin and secure it using a new split pin **(see illustration 9.6)**. If the clevis position on the pushrod was disturbed during overhaul, re-set the brake pedal to its specified height (see Chapter 1, Section 13).

26 Tighten the clevis locknut securely.

27 Fill the fluid reservoir to the upper level line with the specified brake fluid **(see illustration 9.5)** and bleed the system following the procedure in Section 11.

28 Check the operation of the brake carefully before riding the motorcycle.

10 Brake hoses and unions - inspection and replacement

Inspection

1 Brake hose condition should be checked regularly and the hoses replaced at the specified interval (see Chapter 1).

2 Twist and flex the rubber hoses while looking for cracks, bulges and seeping fluid **(see illustration)**. Check extra carefully around the areas where the hoses connect with the banjo fittings, as these are common areas for hose failure.

3 Inspect the metal banjo union fittings connected to the brake hoses. If the fittings are rusted, scratched or cracked, replace them.

Replacement

4 The brake hoses have banjo union fittings on each end **(see illustration)**. Cover the surrounding area with plenty of rags and

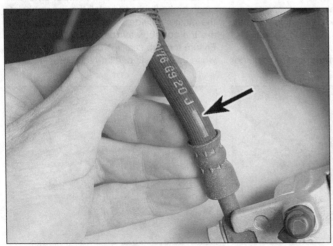

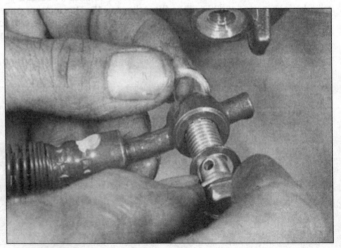

10.2 Flex the brake hoses and check for cracks, bulges and leaking fluid

10.4 Remove the banjo bolt and separate the hose from the caliper; there is a sealing washer on each side of the fitting

11.6a Brake caliper bleed valve

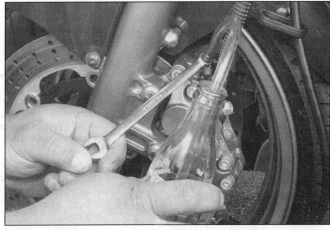

11.6b To bleed the brakes, you need a spanner, a short section of clear tubing, and a clear container half-filled with brake fluid

unscrew the banjo bolt on each end of the hose, noting its alignment. Free the hose from any clips or guides and remove the hose. Discard the sealing washers.

5 Position the new hose, making sure it isn't twisted or otherwise strained and that it is passed through any clips or guides, and abut the tab on the hose union with the lug on the component casting, where present. Otherwise align the hose as noted on removal. Install the banjo bolts, using new sealing washers on both sides of the unions, and tighten them to the torque setting specified at the beginning of this Chapter. Make sure they are correctly aligned and routed clear of all moving components.

6 Flush the old brake fluid from the system, refill with the recommended fluid (see *Daily (pre-ride) checks*) and bleed the air from the system (see Section 11). Check the operation of the brakes carefully before riding the motorcycle.

11 Brake system bleeding

1 Bleeding the brakes is simply the process of removing all the air bubbles from the brake fluid reservoirs, the hoses and the brake calipers. Bleeding is necessary whenever a brake system hydraulic connection is loosened, when a component or hose is replaced, or when the master cylinder or caliper is overhauled. Leaks in the system may also allow air to enter, but leaking brake fluid will reveal their presence and warn you of the need for repair.

2 To bleed the brakes, you will need some new, clean DOT 4 brake fluid, a length of clear vinyl or plastic tubing, a small container partially filled with clean brake fluid, some rags and a spanner to fit the brake caliper bleed valves.

3 Cover the fuel tank and other painted components to prevent damage in the event that brake fluid is spilled.

4 If bleeding the rear brake, remove the right-hand side panel for access to the fluid reservoir.

5 Remove the reservoir cap/cover, diaphragm plate and diaphragm and slowly pump the brake lever or pedal a few times, until no air bubbles can be seen floating up from the holes in the bottom of the reservoir. Doing this bleeds the air from the master cylinder end of the line. Loosely refit the reservoir cap/cover.

6 Pull the dust cap off the bleed valve (see illustration). Attach one end of the clear vinyl or plastic tubing to the bleed valve and submerge the other end in the brake fluid in the container (see illustration).

7 Remove the reservoir cap/cover and check the fluid level. Do not allow the fluid level to drop below the lower mark during the bleeding process.

8 Carefully pump the brake lever or pedal three or four times and hold it in (front) or down (rear) while opening the caliper bleed valve. When the valve is opened, brake fluid will flow out of the caliper into the clear tubing and the lever will move toward the handlebar or the pedal will move down.

9 Retighten the bleed valve, then release the brake lever or pedal gradually. Repeat the process until no air bubbles are visible in the brake fluid leaving the caliper and the lever or pedal is firm when applied. On completion, disconnect the bleeding equipment, then tighten the bleed valve to the torque setting specified at the beginning of the chapter and install the dust cap. In the case of the front brakes, always go on to bleed the other

> **HAYNES HINT**
> *If it's not possible to produce a firm feel to the lever or pedal the fluid may be aerated. Let the brake fluid in the system stabilise for a few hours and then repeat the procedure when the tiny bubbles in the system have settled out.*

caliper, and on the 750 rear caliper, also bleed the system via the other bleed valve on the caliper.

10 Install the diaphragm and cap/cover assembly, wipe up any spilled brake fluid and check the entire system for leaks.

12 Wheels - inspection and repair

1 In order to carry out a proper inspection of the wheels, it is necessary to support the bike upright so that the wheel being inspected is raised off the ground. Position the motorcycle on its centre stand or an auxiliary stand. Clean the wheels thoroughly to remove mud and dirt that may interfere with the inspection procedure or mask defects. Make a general check of the wheels and tyres as described in Chapter 1.

2 Attach a dial gauge to the fork slider or the swingarm and position its stem against the side of the rim (see illustration). Spin the

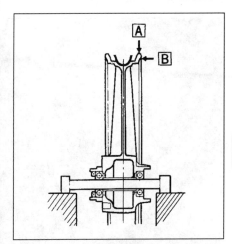

12.2 Check the wheel for radial (out-of-round) runout (A) and axial (side-to-side) runout (B)

wheel slowly and check the axial (side-to-side) runout of the rim. In order to accurately check radial (out of round) runout with the dial gauge, the wheel would have to be removed from the machine, and the tyre from the wheel. With the axle clamped in a vice and the dial gauge positioned on the top of the rim, the wheel can be rotated to check the runout.

3 An easier, though slightly less accurate, method is to attach a stiff wire pointer to the fork slider or the swingarm and position the end a fraction of an inch from the wheel (where the wheel and tyre join). If the wheel is true, the distance from the pointer to the rim will be constant as the wheel is rotated. **Note:** *If wheel runout is excessive, check the wheel bearings very carefully before replacing the wheel.*

4 The wheels should also be visually inspected for cracks, flat spots on the rim and other damage. On all cast alloy wheels, look very closely for dents in the area where the tyre bead contacts the rim. Dents in this area may prevent complete sealing of the tyre against the rim, which leads to deflation of the tyre over a period of time. If damage is evident, or if runout in either direction is excessive, the wheel will have to be replaced with a new one. Never attempt to repair a damaged cast alloy wheel.

5 On spoke wheel models, check for loose or broken spokes. Tapping the spokes with a screwdriver is the best guide to their tension. A loose spoke will make a dull flat note compared to a tight one. Loose spokes must be tightened by turning the nipple at the spoke end in an anti-clockwise direction. Always check for runout after altering the tension in any of the spokes. Small irregularities can be corrected by adjusting the spokes in the affected area, although a certain amount of practice is necessary to prevent over-correction. If the wheel runout continues to be excessive, take the wheel to a professional wheel builder for inspection and adjustment.

13 Wheels - alignment check

1 Misalignment of the wheels, which may be due to a cocked rear wheel or a bent frame or fork yokes, can cause strange and possibly serious handling problems. If the frame or yokes are at fault, repair by a frame specialist or replacement with new parts are the only alternatives.

2 To check the alignment you will need an assistant, a length of string or a perfectly straight piece of wood and a ruler. A plumb bob or other suitable weight will also be required.

3 In order to make a proper check of the wheels it is necessary to support the bike in an upright position, either on its centre stand or on an auxiliary stand. Measure the width of both tyres at their widest points. Subtract the smaller measurement from the larger measurement, then divide the difference by two. The result is the amount of offset that should exist between the front and rear tyres on both sides.

4 If a string is used, have your assistant hold one end of it about halfway between the floor and the rear axle, touching the rear sidewall of the tyre.

5 Run the other end of the string forward and pull it tight so that it is roughly parallel to the floor. Slowly bring the string into contact with the front sidewall of the rear tyre, then turn the front wheel until it is parallel with the string. Measure the distance from the front tyre sidewall to the string.

6 Repeat the procedure on the other side of the motorcycle. The distance from the front tyre sidewall to the string should be equal on both sides.

7 As was previously pointed out, a perfectly straight length of wood may be substituted for the string. The procedure is the same.

8 If the distance between the string and tyre is greater on one side, or if the rear wheel appears to be cocked, check that the drive chain adjuster alignment marks are the same on each side of the swingarm (see Chapter 1)..

9 If the front-to-back alignment is correct, the wheels still may be out of alignment vertically.

10 Using the plumb bob, or other suitable weight, and a length of string, check the rear wheel to make sure it is vertical. To do this, hold the string against the tyre upper sidewall and allow the weight to settle just off the floor. When the string touches both the upper and lower tyre sidewalls and is perfectly straight, the wheel is vertical. If it is not, place thin spacers under one leg of the stand.

11 Once the rear wheel is vertical, check the front wheel in the same manner. If both wheels are not perfectly vertical, the frame and/or major suspension components are bent.

14 Front wheel - removal and installation

Removal

1 Unscrew the knurled ring securing the speedometer cable to its drive housing on the left-hand side of the wheel hub, and detach the cable **(see illustration)**.

2 Remove the left-hand brake caliper mounting bolts and slide the caliper off the disc **(see illustration 3.2a)**. Support the caliper with a piece of wire or a bungee cord so that no strain is placed on its hydraulic hose. There is no need to disconnect the hose from the caliper.

3 Slacken the axle clamp bolt on the bottom of the right-hand side fork, then slacken the axle itself (right-hand end), while counter-holding the axle nut on the left-hand end **(see illustration)**.

14.1 Unscrew the knurled ring (arrowed) and detach the cable

14.3 Axle clamp bolt (A), axle (B)

14.5 Support the wheel and withdraw the axle

14.6a Remove the spacer . . .

14.6b . . . and the speedometer drive housing

14.13 Tighten the axle . . .

14.14 . . . and the axle clamp bolt to the specified torque setting

4 Position the motorcycle on its centre stand or on an auxiliary stand and support it under the crankcase so that the front wheel is off the ground. Always make sure the motorcycle is properly supported.

5 Support the wheel, then fully unscrew the axle and withdraw it from the right-hand side and carefully lower the wheel **(see illustration)**.

6 Remove the wheel spacer from the right-hand side of the wheel, noting which way round it fits, and the speedometer drive housing from the left **(see illustrations)**. **Note:** *Do not operate the front brake lever with the wheel removed.*

Caution: Don't lay the wheel down and allow it to rest on the disc - the disc could become warped. Set the wheel on wood blocks so the disc doesn't support the weight of the wheel.

7 Check the axle for straightness by rolling it on a flat surface such as a piece of plate glass (first wipe off all old grease and remove any corrosion using fine emery cloth). If the equipment is available, place the axle in V-blocks and measure the runout using a dial gauge. If the axle is bent or the runout exceeds the limit specified, replace it.

8 Check the condition of the wheel bearings and bearing seals (see Section 16).

Installation

9 Clean the speedometer drive components and apply grease to the drive gears. Fit the speedometer drive housing to the wheel's left-hand side, aligning its driven gear tabs with the slots in the drive unit in the hub **(see illustration 14.6b)**.

10 Apply a smear of grease to the inside and ends of the wheel spacer and to the lips of the bearing seal in the hub, then fit the spacer into the wheel **(see illustration 14.6a)**.

11 Manoeuvre the wheel into position. Apply a thin coat of grease to the axle.

12 Lift the wheel, making sure the spacer remains in place, and slide the axle into position from the right-hand side **(see illustration 14.5)**. Align the speedometer drive housing so that its lug fits into the slot on the inside of the fork slider.

13 Counter-holding the axle nut on the left-hand end of the axle, tighten the axle to the torque setting specified at the beginning of the Chapter **(see illustration)**.

14 Tighten the axle clamp bolt on the right-hand side fork to the specified torque setting **(see illustration)**. If the axle nut clamp bolt was slackened, also tighten that to the specified torque setting.

15 Install the brake caliper, making sure the pads sit squarely on either side of the disc. Tighten the caliper mounting bolts to the torque setting specified at the beginning of the Chapter **(see illustrations 3.13 and 3.14)**.

16 Pass the speedometer cable through its guides (if withdrawn), then connect the cable to the drive housing and securely tighten its knurled ring **(see illustration)**.

17 Apply the front brake a few times to bring the pads back into contact with the discs. Move the motorcycle off its stand, apply the front brake and pump the front forks a few times to settle all components in position.

18 Check for correct operation of the front brake before riding the motorcycle.

15 Rear wheel - removal and installation

Removal

1 Position the motorcycle on its centre stand or an auxiliary stand. Remove the chain guard (see Chapter 7).

14.16 Fit the speedometer cable into the drive housing

6

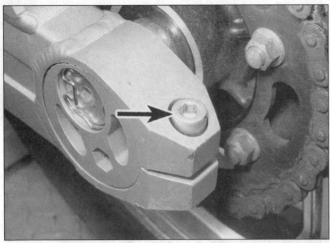

15.2a Slacken the clamp bolts (arrowed) . . .

15.2b . . . and turn the adjuster using an Allen key

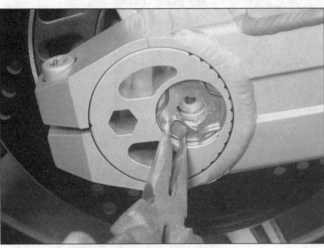

15.3a Remove the retaining clip . . .

15.3b . . . and unscrew the axle nut

2 Slacken each chain adjuster clamp bolt, then rotate each adjuster using a 12 mm Allen key to provide the maximum amount of slack in the drive chain **(see illustrations)**. You will probably find that as you turn one adjuster the other adjuster turns as well. Make sure that each adjuster is in the same position relative to the cutout in each side of the swingarm, then retighten the clamp bolts.
3 Remove the retaining clip from the axle nut

on the right-hand end of the axle **(see illustration)**. Unscrew the axle nut and remove the washer **(see illustration)**.
4 Remove the retaining clip from the left-hand end of the axle. Support the wheel then withdraw the axle from the left-hand side, then lower the wheel to the ground **(see illustration)**. Note how the axle passes through the spacer in the caliper mounting bracket. The brake torque arm should support

the caliper assembly in position. If it doesn't, check that the torque arm nuts are tightened to the specified torque setting. Otherwise, support the assembly so that no strain is placed on the hose.
5 Disengage the chain from the sprocket and remove the wheel from the swingarm. Remove the spacers from both sides of the wheel, noting which way round they fit **(see illustrations)**. If required for safekeeping, also

15.4 Support the wheel and withdraw the axle

15.5a Remove the left-hand spacer . . .

15.5b . . . and the right-hand spacer from the wheel

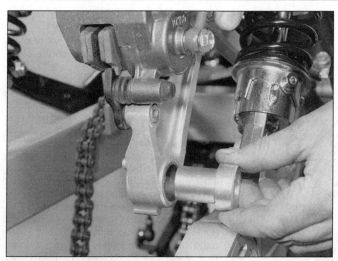

15.9 Fit the spacer into the caliper bracket if removed

15.10a Engage the chain around the sprocket

15.10b Make sure the disc fits correctly between the brake pads

15.11 Tighten the axle nut to the specified torque setting

remove the spacer from the caliper bracket (see illustration 15.9).

Caution: Do not lay the wheel down and allow it to rest on the disc or the sprocket - they could become warped. Set the wheel on wood blocks so the disc or the sprocket doesn't support the weight of the wheel. Do not operate the brake pedal with the wheel removed.

6 Check the axle for straightness by rolling it on a flat surface such as a piece of plate glass (if the axle is corroded, first remove the corrosion with fine emery cloth). If the equipment is available, place the axle in V-blocks and measure the runout using a dial gauge. If the axle is bent or the runout exceeds the limit specified at the beginning of the Chapter, replace it.

7 Check the condition of the wheel bearings and bearing seals (see Section 16).

Installation

8 Apply a thin coat of grease to the lips of each bearing seal, and also to the spacers.

Using a 12 mm Allen key in each of the chain adjusters, rotate them so that the axle hole is well forward in the swingarm (about 9 o'clock); ensure that the same adjuster mark aligns with the cutout on each side of the swingarm, then tighten the adjuster clamp bolts to the specified torque setting.

9 Install the spacers into the wheel (see illustrations 15.5a and b). If removed, also fit the spacer into the brake caliper bracket (see illustration). Manoeuvre the wheel so that it is in between the ends of the swingarm and apply a thin coat of grease to the axle.

10 Engage the drive chain with the sprocket and lift the wheel into position (see illustration). Make sure the spacers remain correctly in place, and that the brake disc fits squarely into the caliper with the pads positioned correctly each side of the disc (see illustration).

11 Install the axle from the left (see illustration 15.4). Check that everything is correctly aligned, then fit the axle nut (see

illustration 15.3b) and tighten it to the specified torque setting, counter-holding the axle head on the other side of the wheel (see illustration). Fit the retaining clips onto each end of the axle, making sure they fit correctly into their grooves (see illustration 15.3a).

12 Adjust the chain slack as described in Chapter 1.

13 Operate the brake pedal several times to bring the pads into contact with the disc. Check the operation of the rear brake carefully before riding the bike.

16 Wheel bearings - removal, inspection and installation

6

Front wheel bearings

Note: *Always replace the wheel bearings in pairs. Never replace the bearings individually. Avoid using a high pressure cleaner on the wheel bearing area.*

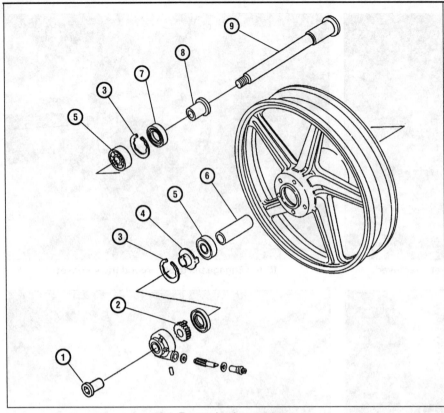

16.1 Front wheel components

1	Axle nut	3	Circlip	5	Bearing	8	Spacer
2	Speedometer	4	Speedometer	6	Bearing spacer	9	Axle
	drive gear housing		drive	7	Grease seal		

1 Remove the wheel (see Section 14) **(see illustration)**.

2 Set the wheel on blocks so as not to allow the weight of the wheel to rest on the brake disc.

3 Using a flat-bladed screwdriver, remove the grease seal from the right-hand side of the wheel **(see illustration)**. Discard the seal if it is in any way damaged or deteriorated as a new one should be used. Kawasaki recommend using new ones as a matter of course. Using a pair of internal circlip pliers, remove the circlip securing the wheel bearing in the hub **(see illustration)**. Turn the wheel over and remove the circlip from the other side, then remove the speedometer drive **(see illustration)**.

4 Using a metal rod (preferably a brass drift punch) inserted through the centre of the left-hand bearing, tap evenly around the inner race of the right-hand bearing to drive it from the hub **(see illustrations)**. The bearing spacer will also come out.

5 Lay the wheel on its other side so that the remaining bearing faces down. Drive the bearing out of the wheel using the same technique as above.

> **HAYNES HiNT** *Refer to Tools and Workshop Tips in the Reference section for more information about bearings.*

6 If the bearings are of the unsealed type or are only sealed on one side, clean them with a high flash-point solvent (one which won't

16.3a Lever out the grease seal using a flat-bladed screwdriver . . .

16.3b . . . then remove the circlip on each side of the wheel . . .

16.3c . . . and remove the speedometer drive (arrowed)

16.4a Using a drift to knock out the bearings

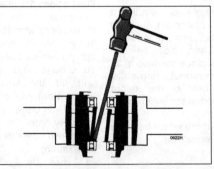

16.4b Locate the drift as shown when driving out the bearing

16.9a Using a socket to drive in the bearings

16.9b Press in the grease seal

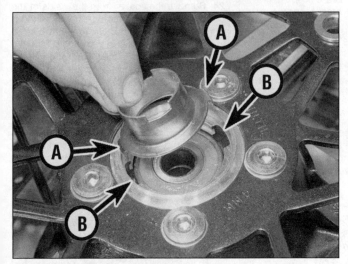

16.10a The tabs (A) on the speedometer drive locate in the slots (B) in the wheel

16.10b Make sure the circlip is properly seated

leave any residue) and blow them dry with compressed air (don't let the bearings spin as you dry them). Apply a few drops of oil to the bearing. **Note:** *If the bearing is sealed on both sides don't attempt to clean it.*

7 Hold the outer race of the bearing and rotate the inner race - if the bearing doesn't turn smoothly, has rough spots or is noisy, replace it with a new one.

8 If the bearing is good and can be re-used, wash it in solvent once again and dry it, then pack the bearing with high melting-point grease. Kawasaki recommend that the bearings and circlips should be renewed if they are removed.

9 Thoroughly clean the hub area of the wheel. First install the right-hand bearing into its recess in the hub, with the marked or sealed side facing outwards. Using the old bearing (if new ones are being fitted), a bearing driver or a socket large enough to contact the outer race of the bearing, drive it in until it's completely seated **(see illustration)**. Fit the

circlip, making sure it is correctly seated in its groove **(see illustration 16.3b)**. Apply a smear of grease to the lips of the bearing seal, and press it into the right-hand side of the wheel using your fingers, a seal or bearing driver, a suitable socket or a flat piece of wood **(see illustration)**.

10 Turn the wheel over and install the bearing spacer. Drive the left-hand bearing into place as described above. Fit the speedometer drive into the hub, making sure the tabs on the drive locate in the slots in the hub, then fit the circlip, making sure it is correctly seated in its groove **(see illustrations)**.

11 Clean off all grease from the brake discs using acetone or brake system cleaner then install the wheel (see Section 14).

Rear wheel bearings

12 Remove the rear wheel (see Section 15). Lift the rear sprocket and sprocket coupling assembly out of the wheel, noting how it fits **(see illustrations)**.

13 Set the wheel on blocks so as not to allow the weight of the wheel to rest on the brake disc.

14 Using a flat-bladed screwdriver, prise out the grease seal from the right-hand side of the wheel **(see illustration 16.3a)**. Discard the seal if it is in any way damaged or deteriorated as a new one should be used. Kawasaki recommend using new ones as a matter of course. Using a pair of internal circlip pliers, remove the circlip securing the wheel bearing in the hub **(see illustration 16.3b)**.

15 Using a metal rod (preferably a brass drift punch) inserted through the centre of the right-hand bearing, tap evenly around the inner race of the left-hand bearing to drive it from the hub **(see illustrations 16.4a and b)**. The bearing spacer will also come out.

16 Lay the wheel on its other side so that the remaining bearing faces down. Drive the bearing out of the wheel using the same technique as above.

17 If the bearings are of the unsealed type or

6

16.12b Lift the sprocket coupling out of the wheel

16.12a **Rear wheel components**

1 *Retaining ring*
2 *Axle*
3 *Spacer (left)*
4 *Damper segments*
5 *Bearing*
6 *Bearing spacer*
7 *Circlip*
8 *Grease seal*
9 *Spacer (right)*
10 *Brake caliper bracket spacer*
11 *Washer*
12 *Axle nut*

Sprocket coupling bearing

23 Remove the rear wheel (see Section 15). Lift the sprocket and sprocket coupling assembly out of the wheel, noting how it fits **(see illustration 16.12b)**.

24 Remove the spacer from the inside of the coupling bearing, noting which way round it fits **(see illustrations)**. Using a flat-bladed screwdriver, prise out the grease seal from the outside of the coupling **(see illustration)**. If the seal appears stuck, make sure the tip of the screwdriver is not catching under the circlip. Discard the seal if it is in any way damaged or deteriorated as a new one should be used. Kawasaki recommend using new ones as a matter of course. Using a pair of internal circlip pliers, remove the circlip securing the wheel bearing in the hub **(see illustration)**.

25 Support the coupling on blocks of wood and drive the bearing out from the inside

are only sealed on one side, clean them with a high flash-point solvent (one which won't leave any residue) and blow them dry with compressed air (don't let the bearings spin as you dry them). Apply a few drops of oil to the bearing. **Note:** *If the bearing is sealed on both sides don't attempt to clean it.*

18 Hold the outer race of the bearing and rotate the inner race - if the bearing doesn't turn smoothly, has rough spots or is noisy, replace it with a new one.

19 If the bearing is good and can be re-used, wash it in solvent once again and dry it, then pack the bearing with high melting-point grease. Kawasaki recommend that the bearings and circlip should be renewed if they are removed.

20 Thoroughly clean the hub area of the wheel. First install the right-hand side bearing into its recess in the hub, with the marked or sealed side facing outwards. Using the old bearing (if new ones are being fitted), a bearing driver or a socket large enough to contact the outer race of the bearing, drive it in squarely until it's completely seated **(see illustration 16.9a)**. Fit the circlip, making sure it is correctly seated in its groove **(see illustration 16.3b)**. Apply a smear of grease to the lips of the bearing seal, and press it into the right-hand side of the wheel using your fingers, a seal or bearing driver, a suitable socket or a flat piece of wood **(see illustration 16.9b)**.

21 Turn the wheel over and install the bearing spacer. Drive the left-hand side bearing into place as described above.

22 Clean off all grease from the brake disc using acetone or brake system cleaner. Install the rear sprocket and sprocket coupling assembly onto the wheel, then install the wheel (see Section 15).

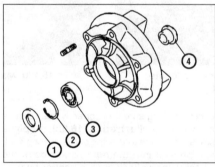

16.24a Sprocket coupling components

1 *Grease seal*   3 *Bearing*
2 *Circlip*   4 *Spacer*

16.24b Remove the spacer from inside the coupling

16.24c Lever out the grease seal using a flat-bladed screwdriver . . .

16.24d . . . then remove the circlip

16.25 Drive the bearing out from the inside

16.29a Drive the bearing in until seated

16.29b Install the circlip, then press in the grease seal

using a socket located on the bearing inner race **(see illustration)**. Do not remove the bearing unless a new one is being installed.

26 If the bearing is of the unsealed type or is only sealed on one side, clean it with a high flash-point solvent (one which won't leave any residue) and blow it dry with compressed air (don't let the bearing spin as you dry it). Apply a few drops of oil to the bearing. **Note:** *If the bearing is sealed on both sides don't attempt to clean it.*

27 Hold the outer race of the bearing and rotate the inner race - if the bearing doesn't turn smoothly, has rough spots or is noisy, replace it with a new one.

28 If the bearing is good and can be re-used, wash it in solvent once again and dry it, then pack the bearing with high melting-point grease. Kawasaki recommend that the bearing and circlip should be renewed if they are removed.

29 Thoroughly clean the bearing recess then install the bearing into the recess in the coupling, with the marked or sealed side facing out. Using the old bearing (if a new one is being fitted), a bearing driver or a socket large enough to contact the outer race of the bearing, drive it in until it is completely seated **(see illustration)**. Fit the circlip, making sure it is correctly seated in its groove **(see illustration 16.24d)**. Apply a smear of grease to the lips of the bearing seal, and press it into the right-hand side of the wheel using your fingers, a seal or bearing driver, a suitable socket or a flat piece of wood **(see illustration)**.

30 Install the spacer into the inside of the coupling, making sure it is the correct way round **(see illustration 16.24b)**. Install the sprocket coupling assembly onto the wheel **(see illustration 16.12b)**, then install the wheel (see Section 15).

17 Tyres - general information and fitting

General information

1 The cast wheels fitted to ZR550 and ZR750 C models are designed to take tubeless tyres only. The spoked wheels fitted to ZR750 D models use tubed tyres only.
2 Refer to the *Daily (pre-ride) checks* at the beginning of this manual for tyre maintenance.

Fitting new tyres

3 When selecting new tyres, refer to the tyre information label and the tyre options listed in the owners handbook. Ensure that front and rear tyre types are compatible, the correct size and correct speed rating; if necessary seek advice from a Kawasaki dealer or tyre fitting specialist **(see illustration)**.

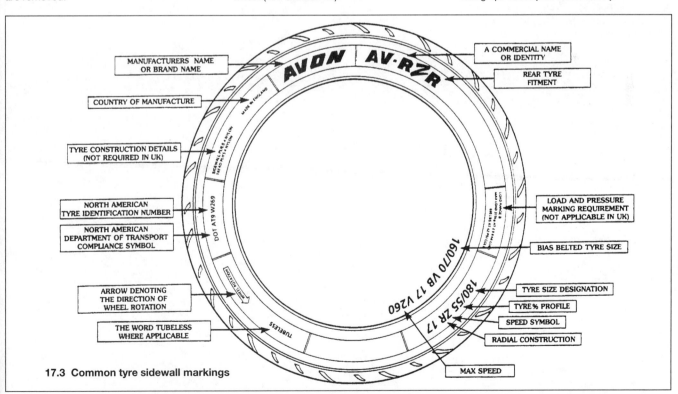

17.3 Common tyre sidewall markings

MANUFACTURERS NAME OR BRAND NAME
COUNTRY OF MANUFACTURE
TYRE CONSTRUCTION DETAILS (NOT REQUIRED IN UK)
NORTH AMERICAN TYRE IDENTIFICATION NUMBER
NORTH AMERICAN DEPARTMENT OF TRANSPORT COMPLIANCE SYMBOL
ARROW DENOTING THE DIRECTION OF WHEEL ROTATION
THE WORD TUBELESS WHERE APPLICABLE
A COMMERCIAL NAME OR IDENTITY
REAR TYRE FITMENT
LOAD AND PRESSURE MARKING REQUIREMENT (NOT APPLICABLE IN UK)
BIAS BELTED TYRE SIZE
TYRE SIZE DESIGNATION
TYRE % PROFILE
SPEED SYMBOL
RADIAL CONSTRUCTION
MAX SPEED

6

4 It is recommended that tyres are only ever fitted by a motorcycle tyre specialist rather than attempted in the home workshop. This is particularly relevant in the case of tubeless tyres because the force required to break the seal between the wheel rim and tyre bead is substantial, and is usually beyond the capabilities of an individual working with normal tyre levers. Additionally, the specialist will be able to balance the wheels after tyre fitting.

5 In the case of tubeless tyres, note that punctured tyres can in some cases be repaired, but again, this should not be attempted in the home workshop. Kawasaki also recommend that a repaired tyre should not be used at speeds above 60 mph (100 kmh) for the first 24 hrs after the repair, and thereafter not above 110 mph (180 kmh). If a puncture occurs on a tubed tyre it is advisable to have a new inner tube fitted.

Chapter 7
Bodywork

Contents

Degrees of difficulty

Easy, suitable for novice with little experience	Fairly easy, suitable for beginner with some experience	Fairly difficult, suitable for competent DIY mechanic	Difficult, suitable for experienced DIY mechanic	Very difficult, suitable for expert DIY or professional

1 General information

This Chapter covers the procedures necessary to remove and install the body parts. Since many service and repair operations on these motorcycles require the removal of the body parts, the procedures are grouped here and referred to from other Chapters.

In the case of damage to the body parts, it is usually necessary to remove the broken component and replace it with a new (or used) one. The material that the body panels are composed of doesn't lend itself to conventional repair techniques. There are however some shops that specialise in "plastic welding", so it may be worthwhile seeking the advice of one of these specialists before consigning an expensive component to the bin.

When attempting to remove any body panel, first study it closely, noting any fasteners and associated fittings, to be sure of returning everything to its correct place on installation. In some cases the aid of an assistant will be required when removing panels, to help avoid the risk of damage to paintwork. Once the evident fasteners have been removed, try to withdraw the panel as described but DO NOT FORCE IT - if it will not release, check that all fasteners have been removed and try again. Where a panel engages another by means of tabs, be careful not to break the tab or its mating slot or to damage the paintwork. Remember that a few moments of patience at this stage will save you a lot of money in replacing broken panels!

When installing a body panel, first study it closely, noting any fasteners and associated fittings removed with it, to be sure of returning everything to its correct place. Check that all fasteners are in good condition, including all trim nuts or clips and damping/rubber mounts; any of these must be replaced if faulty before the panel is reassembled. Check also that all mounting brackets are straight and repair or replace them if necessary before attempting to install the panel. Where assistance was required to remove a panel, make sure your assistant is on hand to install it.

Carefully settle the panel in place, following the instructions provided, and check that it engages correctly with its partners (where applicable) before tightening any of the fasteners. Where a panel engages another by means of tabs, be careful not to break the tab or its mating slot. Note that a small amount of lubricant (liquid soap or similar) applied to the mounting rubbers of the side panels will assist the panel retaining pegs to engage without the need for undue pressure.

Tighten the fasteners securely, but be careful not to overtighten any of them or the panel may break (not always immediately) due to the uneven stress.

2 Rear view mirrors - removal and installation

Removal

1 Unscrew the mirror using the lower nut on the base of the mirror mounting and remove it from the handlebar (see illustration).

Installation

2 Install the mirror into its mounting and screw it in until it is fully home and tight. To adjust the position of the mirror, counter-hold the lower nut and slacken the upper nut, then move the mirror until it is as required, then tighten the upper nut against the lower nut.

3 Seat - removal and installation

Removal

1 Insert the ignition key into the seat lock which is located under the left-hand side panel and turn it clockwise to unlock the seat (see illustration).

2.1 Unscrew the mirror using a spanner on the nut (arrowed)

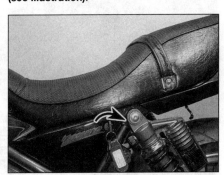

3.1 Turn the key clockwise to unlock the seat

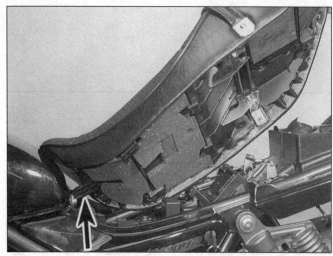

3.3 Locate the tab (arrowed) under the fuel tank

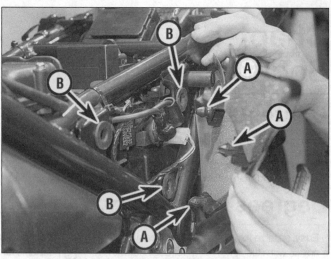

4.2 Each side panel is secured by three pegs (A) which locate in the grommets (B)

2 Lift the rear of the seat and draw it back and away from the bike. Note how the tab at the front of the seat locates under the tank mounting bracket, and how the seat locates onto the locking rail.

Installation

3 Locate the tab at the front of the seat under the fuel tank mounting bracket **(see illustration)**. Align the seat at the rear and push down on it to engage the latches.

4 Side panels -
removal and installation

Removal

1 Remove the seat (see Section 3).
2 Each side panel is secured by three pegs which are a press-fit into rubber grommets on the frame. Gently pull each panel away from the frame to release the pegs from the grommets **(see illustration)**. Do not force or bend the panel while removing it.

Installation

3 Installation is the reverse of removal.

> **HAYNES HINT** *A smear of liquid soap applied to the mounting grommets will help the side panel and rear cover pegs engage without the need for undue pressure.*

5 Front mudguard -
removal and installation

Removal

1 Remove the front wheel for improved access, if required (see Chapter 6).
2 Carefully pull the press-fit brake hose guides from the mudguard, where fitted **(see illustration)**. Unscrew the four bolts securing the mudguard to the forks, noting the position of the brake hose and/or speedometer cable guide **(see illustration)**. Carefully remove the mudguard from between the forks, noting how it fits.

Installation

3 Installation is the reverse of removal.

6 Chain guard -
removal and installation

Removal

1 Unscrew the three screws securing the chain guard to the swingarm and remove the guard, noting how it fits **(see illustration)**.

Installation

2 Installation is the reverse of removal.

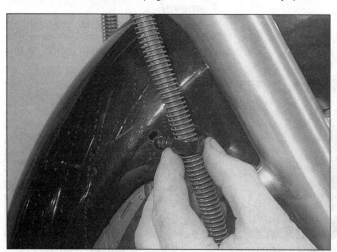

5.2a Pull the hose guides out of the mudguard

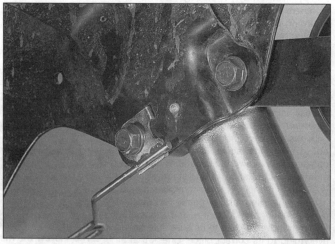

5.2b The mudguard is secured to each fork by two bolts

6.1 The chain guard is secured by three screws (arrowed)

7.2 The grab-rail is secured by two bolts (arrowed)

7.3a The rear cover is secured by two screws (arrowed) . . .

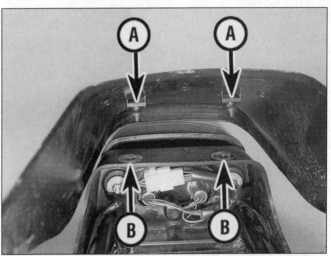

7.3b . . . and two pegs (A) which locate in the grommets (B)

7 Rear cover and grab-rail - removal and installation

Removal

1 Remove the seat (see Section 3).
2 On 750 models, remove the two bolts securing the passenger grab-rail, then remove the rail **(see illustration)**.

3 The rear cover is secured by two screws at the front ends, and by two pegs which are a press-fit into grommets on the top of the tail light assembly **(see illustrations)**. Remove the two screws, then carefully lift the cover off the tail light until the pegs are free.

Installation

4 Installation is the reverse of removal (see **Haynes Hint** on previous page).

7

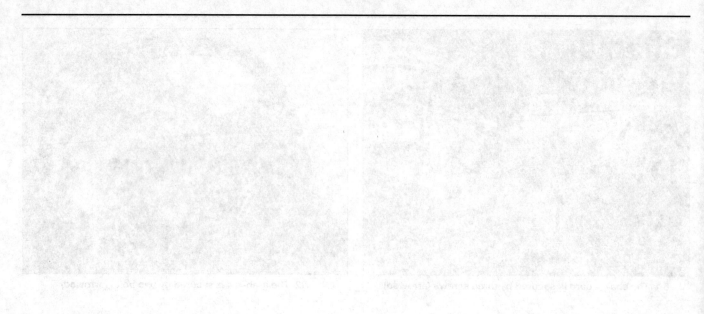

Chapter 8
Electrical system

Contents

Degrees of difficulty

Easy, suitable for novice with little experience		Fairly easy, suitable for beginner with some experience		Fairly difficult, suitable for competent DIY mechanic		Difficult, suitable for experienced DIY mechanic		Very difficult, suitable for expert DIY or professional	

Specifications

Battery
Capacity
  ZR550 B1, B2, B3 and B4 models 12V, 12Ah
  All other models .... 12V, 10Ah MF (maintenance-free)
Electrolyte specific gravity - ZR550 B1, B2, B3 and B4 models ...... 1.280 at 20°C

Fuses
Main 30A
Headlight 10A
Tail light 10A
Turn signal (later models only) 10A
Ignition (later models only) 10A
Horn (later models only) 10A
Accessories
  ZR550 (all models), ZR750 C1, C2 (UK)
    and ZR750 C1 to C3 (US/Canada) 10A
  ZR750 C3, C4, C5, D1 (UK), ZR750 C4 (Canada) 15A

Bulbs
Headlight .... 60/55 W H4 halogen
Sidelight (UK only) 4W
Brake/taillight
  UK models 21/5W
  US models 27/8W
Turn signal lights
  UK models 21W
  US models 23/8W

Bulbs (continued)

Instrument lights - US ZR550 B1 and B2
Speedometer and tachometer	3W
Warning lights	3.4W

Instrument lights - all other models
Speedometer	1.7W
Tachometer and warning lights	3W

Fuel level sender

Resistance
Fuel tank full	4 to 10 ohms
Fuel tank empty	90 to 100 ohms

Carburettor heater system

Heater resistance	11 to 20 ohms

Atmospheric temperature sensor resistance
Rising temperature	from zero to infinite between 7 and 13°C
Falling temperature	from infinite to zero above 3°C

Oil temperature sensor resistance
Rising temperature	from zero to infinite between 37 and 43°C
Falling temperature	from infinite to zero above 33°C

Carburettor temperature sensor resistance
at 9°C	2.9 K ohms
at 10°C	2.2 to 5.2 K ohms
at 12°C	3.0 to 7.2 K ohms
at 25°C	43 K ohms

Starter motor

Brush length
Standard	12.0 to 12.5 mm
Service limit	
550 models	8.5 mm
750 models	6.0 mm

Commutator diameter
Standard	27.98 to 28.02 mm
Service limit	27.0 mm

Alternator

Type	Three phase ac

Rated current output
550 models	17A at 10,000 rpm
750 models	20A at 8000 rpm

Rated voltage output
550 models	min 45V at 4000 rpm
750 models	min 31V at 4000 rpm
Charging (regulated) voltage	14.0 to 15.0V

Stator coil resistance
550 models	0.36 to 0.54 ohms
750 models	0.05 to 0.70 ohms

Regulator/rectifier

Regulated voltage	14.0 to 15.0 V

Torque settings

Front brake master cylinder clamp bolts
550 models	11 Nm
750 models	8.8 Nm
Oil pressure switch	15 Nm
Neutral switch	15 Nm
Starter motor mounting bolts (750 models)	10 Nm

Alternator rotor bolt
550 models	69 Nm
750 models	125 Nm

Alternator stator bolts
550 models	12 Nm
750 models	8 Nm

1 General information

All models have a 12-volt electrical system. The components include a three-phase alternator unit and regulator/rectifier unit.

The regulator maintains the charging system output within the specified range to prevent overcharging, and the rectifier converts the ac (alternating current) output of the alternator to dc (direct current) to power the lights and other components and to charge the battery. The alternator rotor is mounted on the left-hand end of the crankshaft.

The starter motor is mounted on the crankcase behind the cylinders. The starting system includes the motor, the battery, the relay and the various wires and switches. If the engine stop switch and the ignition (main) switch are both in the "Run" or "On" position, the starter relay allows the starter motor to operate only if the transmission is in neutral (neutral switch on) or, if the transmission is in gear, if the clutch lever is pulled into the handlebar (clutch switch on) and the sidestand is up.

Note: *Keep in mind that electrical parts, once purchased, cannot be returned. To avoid any unnecessary expense, make very sure that the faulty component has been positively identified before buying a replacement part.*

2 Electrical fault finding

⚠️ *Warning: To prevent the risk of short circuits, the ignition (main) switch must always be "OFF" and the battery negative (–) terminal should be disconnected before any of the bike's other electrical components are disturbed. Don't forget to reconnect the terminal securely once work is finished or if battery power is needed for circuit testing.*

1 A typical electrical circuit consists of an electrical component, the switches, relays, etc. related to that component and the wiring and connectors that hook the component to both the battery and the frame. To aid in locating a problem in any electrical circuit, refer to the wiring diagrams at the end of this Chapter.

2 Before tackling any troublesome electrical circuit, first study the wiring diagram (see end of Chapter) thoroughly to get a complete picture of what makes up that individual circuit. Trouble spots, for instance, can often be narrowed down by noting if other components related to that circuit are operating properly or not. If several

components or circuits fail at one time, chances are the fault lies in the fuse or earth connection, as several circuits often are routed through the same fuse and earth.

3 Electrical problems often stem from simple causes, such as loose or corroded connections or a blown fuse. Prior to any electrical fault finding, always visually check the condition of the fuse, wires and connections in the problem circuit. Intermittent failures can be especially frustrating, since you can't always duplicate the failure when it's convenient to test. In such situations, a good practice is to clean and check all of the connections in the affected circuit, whether or not they appear to be good. All of the connections and wires should also be wiggled to check for looseness which can cause intermittent failure.

4 If testing instruments are going to be utilised, use the wiring diagrams at the end of this Chapter to plan where you will make the necessary connections in order to accurately pinpoint the trouble spot.

5 The basic tools needed for electrical fault finding include a battery and bulb test circuit, a continuity tester, a test light, and a jumper wire. A multimeter capable of reading volts, ohms and amps is also very useful as an alternative to the above, and is necessary for performing more extensive tests and checks. Full details on the use of this test equipment are given in the *Fault Finding Equipment* section at the end of the manual.

3 Battery - removal, installation, inspection and maintenance

Caution: Be extremely careful when handling or working around the battery. The electrolyte is very caustic and an explosive gas (hydrogen) is given off when the battery is charging.

Removal and installation

1 Remove the seat (see Chapter 7). On 750 models, also remove the fuel tank and the tank bracket, then remove the two screws securing the air filter cover to the filter housing and lift off the cover (see Chapter 3) **(see illustration)**. On ZR550 B5 and B6 models, remove either of the side panels and unhook the rubber battery strap.

2 Unscrew the terminal screws and disconnect the leads from the battery, disconnecting the negative (–) terminal first, and noting that the positive (+) terminal has an insulating cover which must be pulled back **(see illustration)**. On ZR550 B1, B2, B3 and B4 models, disconnect the vent hose from the side of the battery. Unhook the rubber strap and lift the battery out of its box **(see illustrations)**.

3 On installation, clean the battery terminals and lead ends with a wire brush or knife and emery paper. Reconnect the leads, connecting the positive (+) terminal first, then

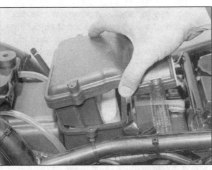

3.1 On 750 models, remove the air filter cover to access the battery

3.2a Pull back the insulating cover to access the positive (+) terminal

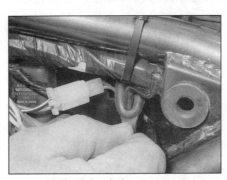

3.2b Unhook the strap . . .

3.2c . . . and remove the battery

8

fit the insulating cover over the positive (+) terminal **(see illustration 3.2a)**. On ZR550 B1, B2, B3 and B4 models, connect the vent hose to the side of the battery. Install the remaining components in a reverse of the removal procedure.

HAYNES HiNT *Battery corrosion can be kept to a minimum by applying a layer of petroleum jelly to the terminals after the cables have been connected.*

Inspection and maintenance

4 The battery fitted to ZR550 B1, B2, B3 and B4 models is of the conventional lead/acid type, requiring regular checks of the electrolyte level (see Chapter 1) in addition to those detailed below. The battery fitted to all other models is of the maintenance-free (sealed) type, therefore requiring no regular checking/topping-up of the electrolyte level. However, the following checks should still be regularly performed.

5 Check the battery terminals and leads for tightness and corrosion. If corrosion is evident, unscrew the terminal screws and disconnect the leads from the battery, disconnecting the negative (–) terminal first, and clean the terminals and lead ends with a wire brush or knife and emery paper. Reconnect the leads, connecting the negative (–) terminal last, and apply a thin coat of petroleum jelly to the connections to slow further corrosion.

6 The battery case should be kept clean to prevent current leakage, which can discharge the battery over a period of time (especially when it sits unused). Wash the outside of the case with a solution of baking soda and water. Rinse the battery thoroughly, then dry it.

7 Look for cracks in the case and replace the battery if any are found. If acid has been spilled on the frame or battery holder, neutralise it with a baking soda and water solution, dry it thoroughly, then touch up any damaged paint. On ZR550 B1, B2, B3 and B4 models, make sure that the battery vent hose is routed correctly and is not kinked or pinched.

8 If the motorcycle sits unused for long periods of time, disconnect the cables from the battery terminals, negative (–) terminal first. Refer to Section 4 and charge the battery once every month to six weeks.

9 The condition of the battery can be assessed by measuring the voltage present at the battery terminals. Connect the voltmeter positive (+) probe to the battery positive (+) terminal and the negative (–) probe to the battery negative (–) terminal. When fully charged there should be more than 12.5 volts present. If the voltage falls below 12.0 volts the battery must be removed, disconnecting the negative (–) terminal first, and recharged as described below in Section 4.

4 Battery - charging

Caution: Be extremely careful when handling or working around the battery. The electrolyte is very caustic and an explosive gas (hydrogen) is given off when the battery is charging.

1 Remove the battery (see Section 3). Connect the charger to the battery, making sure that the positive (+) lead on the charger is connected to the positive (+) terminal on the battery, and the negative (–) lead is connected to the negative (–) terminal.

2 On ZR550 B1, B2, B3 and B4 models with a conventional battery, Kawasaki recommend that the battery is charged at a maximum rate of 1.2 amps for 10 hours. A specific gravity check can be made to determine when the battery is fully charged (refer to *Fault Finding Equipment* in the Reference section for details of specific gravity checks).

3 On all other models equipped with a sealed maintenance-free battery, Kawasaki recommend the battery is charged according to its current state. Use a multimeter set to dc volts to measure the voltage of the battery.

a) *If the voltage is 12.6 V or more, the battery does not need charging.*

b) *If the voltage is between 11.5 and 12.6 V, charge the battery at 1.2 A for between 10 and 5 hours, according to the voltage measured.*

c) *If the voltage is below 11.5 V, an initial high voltage input of about 25 V will be required for approximately five minutes before the battery will accept any charge. The charging current will drop, and the voltage should then be reduced until the charging current is as recommended. If the current does not drop, a new battery is required.*

4 Exceeding the figures can cause the battery to overheat, buckling the plates and rendering it useless. Few owners will have access to an expensive current-controlled charger, so if a normal domestic charger is used check that after a possible initial peak, the charge rate falls to a safe level **(see illustration)**. If the battery becomes hot during charging **stop**. Further charging will cause damage. On ZR550 B1, B2,

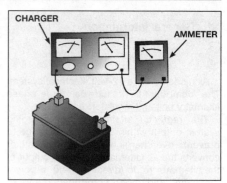

4.4 If the charger doesn't have ammeter built in, connect one in series as shown. DO NOT connect the ammeter between the battery terminals or it will be ruined

B3 and B4 models check the electrolyte level after charging and replenish if necessary (see Chapter 1). **Note:** *In emergencies the battery can be charged at a higher rate of around 4.0 or 5.0 amps for a period of 1 hour. However, this is not recommended and the low amp charge is by far the safer method of charging the battery.*

5 If the recharged battery discharges rapidly if left disconnected it is likely that an internal short caused by physical damage or sulphation has occurred. A new battery will be required. A sound item will tend to lose its charge at about 1% per day.

6 Install the battery (see Section 3).

7 If the motorcycle sits unused for long periods of time, charge the battery once every month to six weeks and leave it disconnected.

5 Fuses - check and replacement

1 The electrical system is protected by fuses of different ratings. All fuses are housed in the fusebox, which is located within the junction box under the seat **(see illustration)**. The junction box also contains the starter circuit relay and diode, and on US models the headlight relay, which should also be tested in the event of electrical problems (refer to Section 25).

2 To access the fuses, remove the seat (see Chapter 7) and unclip the fusebox lid **(see illustration)**.

5.1 The junction box is under the seat

5.2 Unclip the lid to access the fuses

5.3a The fuses are a push fit

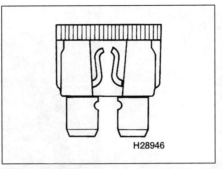

5.3b A blown fuse can be identified by a break in its element

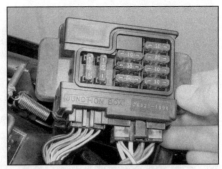

5.5a Remove the junction box and disconnect the wiring connectors

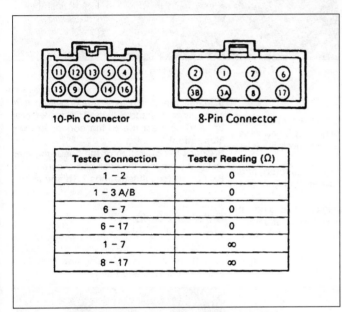

Tester Connection	Tester Reading (Ω)
1 – 2	0
1 – 3 A/B	0
6 – 7	0
6 – 17	0
1 – 7	∞
8 – 17	∞

5.5b Fuse circuit testing - ZR550 B1 to B5 and ZR750 C1 to C4 models

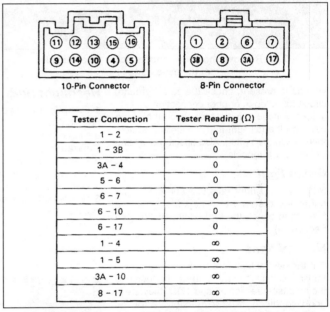

Tester Connection	Tester Reading (Ω)
1 – 2	0
1 – 3B	0
3A – 4	0
5 – 6	0
6 – 7	0
6 – 10	0
6 – 17	0
1 – 4	∞
1 – 5	∞
3A – 10	∞
8 – 17	∞

5.5c Fuse circuit testing - ZR550 B6, ZR750 C5 and D1 models

3 The fuses can be removed and checked visually. If you can't pull the fuse out with your fingertips, use a pair of needle-nose pliers **(see illustration)**. A blown fuse is easily identified by a break in the element **(see illustration)**. Each fuse is clearly marked with its rating and must only be replaced by a fuse of the correct rating. A spare fuse of each rating is housed in the fusebox. If a spare fuse is used, always replace it so that a spare of each rating is carried on the bike at all times.

Caution: Never put in a fuse of a higher rating or bridge the terminals with any other substitute, however temporary it may be. Serious damage may be done to the circuit, or a fire may start.

4 If a fuse blows, be sure to check the wiring circuit very carefully for evidence of a short-circuit. Look for bare wires and chafed, melted or burned insulation. If the fuse is replaced before the cause is located, the new fuse will blow immediately.

5 Occasionally a fuse will blow or cause an open-circuit for no obvious reason. Corrosion of the fuse ends and fusebox terminals may

occur and cause poor fuse contact. If this happens, remove the corrosion with a wire brush or emery paper, then spray the fuse end and terminals with electrical contact cleaner. To determine whether any of the fusebox circuitry is faulty, slide the junction box out of its holder and disconnect the wiring connectors **(see illustration)**. Using the tables shown, check for continuity between the various terminals as indicated **(see illustrations)**.

---

6 Lighting system - check

1 The battery provides power for operation of the headlight, tail light, brake light and instrument cluster lights. If none of the lights operate, always check battery voltage before proceeding. Low battery voltage indicates either a faulty battery or a defective charging system. Refer to Section 3 for battery checks and Sections 32 and 33 for charging system tests. Also, check the condition of the fuses.

Headlight

2 If the headlight fails to work, first check the fuse with the ignition ON (see Section 5), and then the bulb (see Section 7). If they are both good, use jumper wires to connect the bulb directly to the battery terminals. If the light comes on, the problem lies in the wiring or one of the switches in the circuit. Refer to Section 20 for the switch testing procedures, and also the wiring diagrams at the end of this Chapter. On US models, a headlight relay is incorporated in the junction box circuitry, and there is no headlight switch incorporated in the handlebar switches. The headlight comes on automatically when the ignition is switched on and the engine is running, but will extinguish when the starter button is pressed. To check the headlight relay in the junction box, see Section 25.

Tail light

3 If the tail light fails to work, check the bulbs and the bulb terminals first, then the fuse, then check for battery voltage on the supply side of the tail light wiring connector. If

8

7.1a Remove the screw and its collar on each side of the headlight . . .

7.1b . . . and ease the rim out of the shell

voltage is present, check the earth (ground) circuit for an open or poor connection.

4 If no voltage is indicated, check the wiring between the tail light and the ignition switch, then check the switch. Also check the lighting switch on UK models.

Brake light

5 If the brake light fails to work, check the bulbs and the bulb terminals first, then the fuse, then check the brake light switch (see Section 14).

Neutral light

6 If the neutral light fails to operate when the transmission is in neutral, check the fuse and the bulb (see Sections 5 and 17). If they are in good condition, refer to Section 22 for the neutral switch check and replacement procedures.

Oil pressure warning light

7 If the oil pressure warning light fails to operate when the engine is not running, check the fuse and the bulb (see Sections 5 and 17). If they are in good condition, refer to Section 18 for the oil pressure switch check.

Instrument lights

8 See Section 17.

7 Headlight bulb and sidelight bulb - replacement

Note: *The headlight bulb is of the quartz-halogen type. Do not touch the bulb glass as skin acids will shorten the bulb's service life. If the bulb is accidentally touched, it should be wiped carefully when cold with a rag soaked in methylated spirit (stoddard solvent) and dried before fitting.*

⚠ *Warning: Allow the bulb time to cool before removing it if the headlight has just been on.*

Headlight bulb

1 Remove the two screws securing the headlight rim to the headlight shell, and ease the rim out of the shell, noting how it fits **(see illustrations)**.
2 Disconnect the wiring connector and remove the rubber dust cover, noting how it fits **(see illustration)**.
3 Release the bulb retaining clip, noting how it fits, then remove the bulb **(see illustrations)**.
4 Fit the new bulb, bearing in mind the **Note** at the start of this Section. Ensure the tabs on the bulb fit correctly in the slots in the bulb housing, and secure it with the retaining clip.

7.2 Disconnect the headlight wiring connector and remove the rubber cover

7.3b . . . and remove the bulb

5 Install the dust cover, making sure it is correctly seated and with the TOP mark facing up, and connect the wiring connector **(see illustration)**.
6 Check the operation of the headlight, then install the rim into the shell and secure it with the screws **(see illustrations 7.1b and a)**.

Sidelight bulb

7 Remove the two screws securing the headlight rim to the headlight shell, and ease the rim out of the shell, noting how it fits **(see illustrations 7.1a and b)**.

7.3a Release the clip . . .

7.5 Fit the cover with the TOP mark uppermost

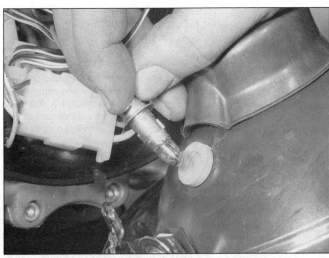

7.8a Pull the bulbholder out of the headlight . . .

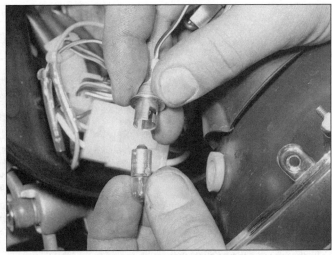

7.8b . . . and remove the bulb

8 Pull the bulbholder out of its socket in the base of the headlight **(see illustration)**. Push the bulb down and twist it anti-clockwise to release it from the bulbholder **(see illustration)**.
9 Install the new bulb in the bulbholder, then install the bulbholder by pressing it in.
10 Check the operation of the sidelight, then install the headlight rim into the shell and secure it with the screws **(see illustrations 7.1b and a)**.

8 Headlight assembly - removal and installation

Removal

1 Remove the two screws securing the headlight rim to the headlight shell, and ease the rim out of the shell, noting how it fits **(see illustrations 7.1a and b)**.

2 Disconnect the wiring connectors from the headlight bulb **(see illustration 7.2)**, and the sidelight bulb **(see illustration)**.
3 To remove the headlight shell, first unscrew the bolts securing the brake hose union to the bottom yoke, thereby freeing the vertical beam adjuster **(see illustration)**. Free the wiring inside the shell from any clamps, then disconnect any wiring connectors necessary and ease the wiring out the back of the shell. Unscrew the nuts on the inside of the shell and remove the bolts securing the shell to the brackets and remove the shell **(see illustration)**.
4 If necessary, unscrew the bolts securing the brackets to the support frame and remove the brackets, with the turn signal assemblies attached or removed as required (Section 12). To remove the support frame, first remove the instrument cluster (see Section 15), then unscrew the bolt securing the frame to the bottom yoke and remove the frame, noting how it fits **(see illustration)**.

> **HAYNES HINT** *When disconnecting wiring, label the connectors to avoid confusion on reconnection.*

Installation

5 Installation is the reverse of removal. Make sure all the wiring is correctly connected and secured. Check the operation of the headlight and sidelight. Check the headlight aim (see Chapter 1).

9 Tail light bulbs - replacement

1 Unscrew the two screws securing the tail light lens and remove the lens **(see illustration)**.

8.2 Disconnect the sidelight bulb wiring connectors (arrowed)

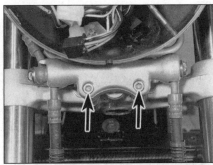

8.3a Remove the brake hose union bolts (arrowed) to release the headlight adjuster bracket

8.3b Unscrew the nuts and remove the bolts

8.4 The support frame is secured to the bottom yoke by a single bolt

8

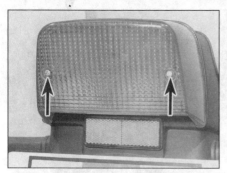

9.1 The tail light lens is secured by two screws (arrowed)

2 Push the bulb in and twist it anti-clockwise to remove it **(see illustration)**. Check the socket terminals for corrosion and clean them if necessary. Line up the pins of the new bulb with the slots in the socket, then push the bulb in and turn it clockwise until it locks into place. **Note:** *The pins on the bulb are offset so it can only be installed one way. It is a good idea to use a paper towel or dry cloth when handling the new bulb to prevent injury if the bulb should break and to increase bulb life.*

3 Install the lens onto the tail light, making sure the sealing rubber is correctly seated, and secure it with the screws. Do not overtighten the lens screws as the lens is easily cracked.

4 Install the seat (see Chapter 7).

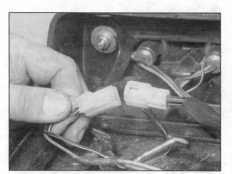

10.2 Disconnect the tail light wiring connector

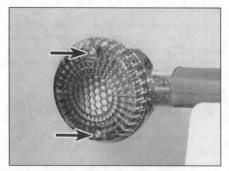

11.1 The turn signal lens is secured by two screws (arrowed)

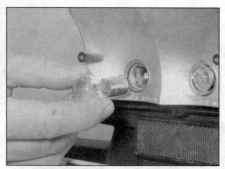

9.2 Push the bulb in and twist it anti-clockwise to remove it

10 Tail light assembly - removal and installation

Removal

1 Remove the seat and the rear cover (see Chapter 7).
2 Trace the tail light wiring back from the tail light and disconnect it at the connector **(see illustration)**.
3 Unscrew the two nuts securing the tail light assembly and carefully remove it from the bike **(see illustration)**. Note the wiring clamp fitted with each nut.

Installation

4 Installation is the reverse of removal. Check the operation of the tail light and the brake light.

10.3 The tail light assembly is secured by two nuts (arrowed)

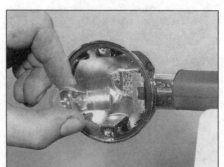

11.2 Push the bulb in and twist it anti-clockwise to remove it

11 Turn signal bulbs - replacement

1 Remove the two screws securing the lens to the turn signal assembly and remove the lens, noting which way round it fits **(see illustration)**. Remove the rubber gasket and check it for damage or deterioration. Replace it if necessary.
2 Push the bulb into the holder and twist it anti-clockwise to remove it **(see illustration)**. Check the socket terminals for corrosion and clean them if necessary. Line up the pins of the new bulb with the slots in the socket, then push the bulb in and turn it clockwise until it locks into place. **Note:** *It is a good idea to use a paper towel or dry cloth when handling the new bulb to prevent injury if the bulb should break and to increase bulb life.*
3 Install the lens back onto the cover, using a new gasket if required, and tighten the retaining screws **(see illustration)**. Take care not to overtighten the screws as the lens is easily cracked.

> **HAYNES HiNT** *If the socket contacts are dirty or corroded, scrape them clean and spray with electrical contact cleaner before a new bulb is installed.*

12 Turn signal assemblies - removal and installation

Front

Removal

1 Remove the two screws securing the headlight rim to the headlight shell, and ease the rim out of the shell, noting how it fits **(see illustrations 7.1a and b)**.
2 Trace the turn signal wiring back from the turn signal and disconnect it at the connectors inside the headlight shell **(see illustration)**. Pull the wiring through to the turn signal mounting, noting its routing.

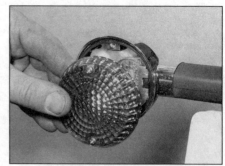

11.3 Make sure the rubber gasket is properly seated when fitting the cover

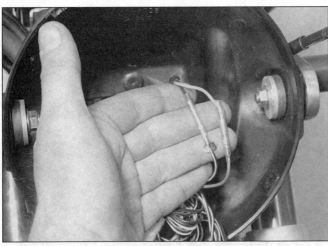

12.2 The front turn signal wiring connectors are inside the headlight shell

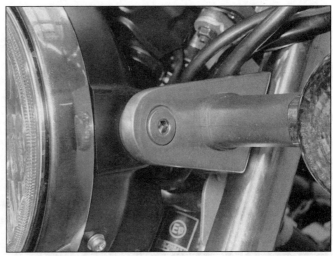

12.3 The nut is on the inside of the headlight bracket

3 Unscrew the nut securing the turn signal assembly to the headlight bracket and carefully remove the assembly, taking care not to snag the wiring connectors as you draw them through the mounting hole **(see illustration)**.

Installation

4 Installation is the reverse of removal. Make sure the wiring is correctly routed and securely connected. Check the operation of the turn signals.

Rear

Removal

5 Remove the seat (see Chapter 7). Trace the turn signal wiring back from the turn signal and disconnect it at the connector **(see illustration)**. Pull the wiring through to the turn signal mounting, releasing it from any clips and noting its routing.

6 Unscrew the nut securing the turn signal assembly to the mudguard and carefully remove the assembly, taking care not to snag the wiring connectors as you draw them through the mounting hole **(see illustration)**.

Installation

7 Installation is the reverse of removal. Make sure the wiring is correctly routed and securely connected. Check the operation of the turn signals.

13 Turn signal circuit - check

1 The battery provides power for operation of the turn signal lights, so if they do not operate, always check the battery voltage first. Low battery voltage indicates either a faulty battery or a defective charging system. Refer to Section 3 for battery checks and Sections 32 and 33 for charging system tests. Also, check the fuse (see Section 5) and the switch (see Section 20).

2 Most turn signal problems are the result of a burned out bulb or corroded socket. This is especially true when the turn signals function properly in one direction, but fail to flash in the other direction. Check the bulbs and the sockets (see Section 11), and make sure that the bulbs are of the correct wattage.

3 If the bulbs and sockets are good, check the turn signal relay, which is mounted behind the left-hand side panel **(see illustration)**. Remove the side panel for access (see Chapter 7). Disconnect the relay wiring connector and check for voltage by connecting the positive (+) probe of a multimeter to the turn signal relay brown (early models) or orange/green (later models) wire, and the negative (–) probe to the

orange wire. With the ignition ON and the turn signal switch placed first to the right and then to the left side, there should be battery voltage in each case. Turn the ignition OFF when the check is complete. Also check for continuity between the relay terminals. There should be continuity (zero or close to zero resistance). If a resistance reading of more than a few ohms is shown, replace the relay.

4 If no power was present at the relay, check the wiring from the relay to the ignition (main) switch for continuity.

5 If power was present at the relay, using the appropriate wiring diagram at the end of this Chapter, check the wiring between the relay, turn signal switch and turn signal lights for continuity. If the wiring and switch are sound, replace the relay with a new one.

14 Brake light switches - check and replacement

Circuit check

1 Before checking any electrical circuit, check the bulb (see Section 9) and fuse (see Section 5).

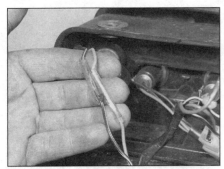

12.5 Disconnect the turn signal wiring connectors

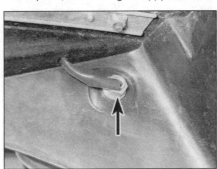

12.6 The nut (arrowed) is on the inside of the mudguard

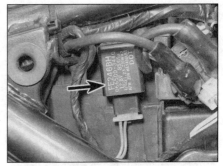

13.3 The turn signal relay is behind the left-hand side panel

14.5 Disconnect the front brake switch wiring connectors (arrowed)

14.6 The switch is secured by a single screw (arrowed)

2 Using a multimeter or test light connected to a good earth (ground), check for voltage at the brake light switch wiring connector brown wire **(see illustration 14.5 or 14.8b)**. If there's no voltage present, check the wire between the switch and the ignition switch (see the *wiring diagrams* at the end of this Chapter).

3 If voltage is available, touch the probe of the test light to the other terminal (blue wire) of the switch, then pull the brake lever in or depress the brake pedal; the connector must be joined for this check. If no reading is obtained or the test light doesn't light up, replace the switch.

4 If a reading is obtained or the test light does light, check the wiring between the switch and the brake lights (see the *wiring diagrams* at the end of this Chapter).

Switch replacement

Front brake lever switch

5 Disconnect the wiring connectors from the switch **(see illustration)**.

6 Remove the single screw securing the switch to the bottom of the front brake master cylinder and remove the switch **(see**

illustration). It may be necessary to slacken the brake master cylinder lower clamp bolt and rotate the assembly on the handlebar until the screw is clear of the cables before it can be accessed with a screwdriver. If so, tighten the clamp bolt to the torque setting specified on completion.

7 Installation is the reverse of removal. The switch isn't adjustable.

Rear brake pedal switch

8 The switch is mounted on the inside of the frame above the master cylinder **(see illustration)**. Trace the wiring from the top of the switch and disconnect it at the wiring connector behind the right-hand side panel **(see illustration)**. Remove the side panel for access (see Chapter 7).

9 Detach the upper end of the switch spring from the switch, then unscrew the switch **(see illustration)**.

10 Installation is the reverse of removal. Make sure the brake light is activated just before the rear brake pedal takes effect. If adjustment is necessary, hold the switch and turn the adjusting nut on the switch body until the brake light is activated when required.

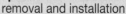

15 Instrument cluster and speedometer cable - removal and installation

Instrument cluster

Removal

1 Remove the two screws securing the headlight rim to the headlight shell, and ease the rim out of the shell, noting how it fits **(see illustrations 7.1a and b)**. Trace the wiring back from the instrument cluster and disconnect it at the connectors inside the headlight shell. Release the wiring from any clips or ties.

2 Unscrew the speedometer cable retaining ring from the back of the speedometer and detach the cable **(see illustration 15.5)**.

3 Unscrew the two nuts securing the instrument cluster to the underside of the top yoke and carefully remove the assembly from the yoke, taking care not to snag the wiring and noting its routing **(see illustration)**.

Installation

4 Installation is the reverse of removal. Make sure that the speedometer cable and wiring connectors are correctly routed and secured.

14.8a Rear brake light switch (arrowed)

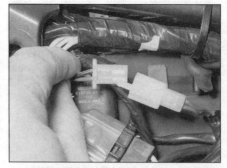

14.8b Disconnect the wiring at the connector behind the right-hand side panel

14.9 Detach the spring from the switch

15.3 The instrument cluster is secured by two nuts (arrowed)

15.5 Unscrew the knurled ring securing the cable to the speedometer (arrowed) . . .

15.6 . . . and the drive housing (arrowed)

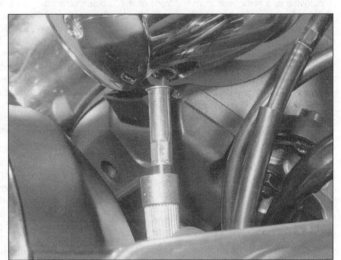

15.9 Make sure the inner cable locates correctly in the speedometer . . .

Speedometer cable

Removal

5 Unscrew the speedometer cable retaining ring from the rear of the instrument cluster and detach the cable **(see illustration)**.
6 Unscrew the retaining ring securing the lower end of the cable to the drive housing on the left-hand side of the front wheel **(see illustration)**.
7 Withdraw the cable from its guide(s) and remove it from the bike, noting its correct routing.

Installation

8 Route the cable correctly and install it in its retaining guide(s).
9 Connect the cable upper end to the instrument cluster and tighten the retaining ring securely **(see illustration)**.
10 Connect the cable lower end to the drive

housing and tighten the retaining ring securely **(see illustration)**.
11 Check that the cable doesn't restrict steering movement or interfere with any other components.

15.10 . . . and the drive housing

16 Instruments -
check and replacement

Speedometer

Check

1 Special instruments are required to properly check the operation of this meter. If it is believed to be faulty, take the motorcycle to a Kawasaki dealer for assessment.

Replacement

2 Remove the instrument cluster (Section 15).
3 On US ZR550 B1 and B2 models, remove the screws securing the rear cover and remove the cover. Remove the nuts securing the mounting bracket and remove the bracket. Turn the odometer trip knob anti-

8

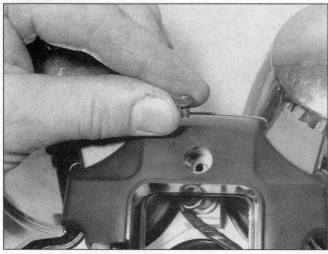

16.4a Remove the screw securing the rear cover

16.4b Speedometer mounting nut (A),
tachometer mounting nut (B)

clockwise and remove it from the front of the cluster. Remove the three screws on the back of the cluster which secure the front cover and remove the front cover. Remove the two screws securing the speedometer to the back cover and lift the speedometer out.

4 On all other models, remove the single screw securing the instrument cluster rear cover and remove the cover **(see illustration)**. Remove the nut securing the speedometer to the bracket and lift it off the bracket, noting how the small lug locates in the hole in the bracket **(see illustration)**. Unscrew the single screw securing the casing and withdraw the speedometer from the casing, then remove the bulbholders **(see illustrations 16.10a and b, and 17.1a)**.

5 Installation is the reverse of removal. Make sure the cable is correctly and securely connected.

Tachometer

Check

6 First check all the wiring in the tachometer circuit for faults (see the *wiring diagrams* at the end of this Chapter). If the wiring is all good, then the tachometer is probably faulty. Remove the fuel tank (see Chapter 3). Disconnect the black wire from the primary circuit terminal on the ignition coil for nos. 1 and 4 cylinders. Turn the ignition switch ON. Connect an insulated jumper wire between the coil black wire and the positive (+) terminal of the battery. The tachometer needle should flick off its rest. If it doesn't. the tachometer is faulty.

7 Special instruments are required to properly check the operation of this meter. If it is believed to be faulty, take the motorcycle to a Kawasaki dealer for assessment.

Replacement

8 Remove the instrument cluster (Section 15). Disconnect the single wiring connector between the tachometer wiring and the warning light panel wiring.

9 On US ZR550 B1 and B2 models, remove the screws securing the rear cover and remove the cover. Remove the nuts securing the mounting bracket and remove the bracket. Turn the odometer trip knob anti-clockwise and remove it from the front of the cluster. Remove the tachometer wiring screws and detach the wires, carefully noting the position of each wire. Remove the three screws on the back of the cluster which secure the front cover and remove the front cover. Remove the screws securing the tachometer to the back cover and lift the tachometer out.

10 On all other models, remove the single screw securing the instrument cluster rear cover and remove the cover **(see illustration 16.4a)**. Remove the nut securing the tachometer to the bracket and lift it off the bracket, noting how the small lug locates in the hole in the bracket **(see illustration 16.4b)**. Unscrew the single screw securing the casing and withdraw the tachometer from the casing **(see illustrations)**. Remove the tachometer wiring screws and detach the wires, carefully noting the position of each wire. Also remove the bulbholders **(see illustration 17.1a)**.

11 Installation is the reverse of removal. Make sure the wires are correctly and securely connected.

Fuel gauge (all models except US ZR550 B1 and B2)

Check

12 Remove the seat (see Chapter 7). Trace the fuel level sender wiring from the underside of the fuel tank and disconnect it at the connector (remove the tank mounting bolts and raise the tank at the rear, or remove the tank for improved access if required - see Chapter 3) **(see illustration)**.

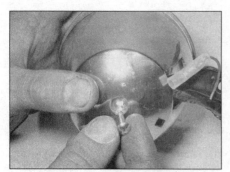

16.10a Remove the screw . . .

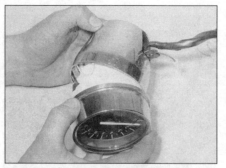

16.10b . . . and withdraw the instrument from the casing

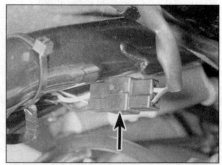

16.12 Disconnect the fuel level sender wiring connector (arrowed)

17.1a Remove the bulbholder from the instrument . . .

17.1b . . . and pull the bulb from the holder

13 Connect an insulated jumper wire between the white/yellow and black/yellow terminals on the wiring loom side of the connector. With the ignition switched ON, the fuel gauge should read F (full), and with the ignition switched OFF it should read E (empty). If it doesn't, check the wiring between the connector and the gauge, and check for voltage at the brown wire on the back of the fuel gauge. If the wiring is good, then the gauge is faulty.

14 If the gauge reads correctly when tested, check the fuel level sender inside the fuel tank (see Section 26).

Replacement

15 The fuel gauge is integral with the tachometer. Refer to the tachometer replacement procedure above. If the fuel gauge is faulty, the entire tachometer must be replaced.

17 Instrument and warning light bulbs - replacement

Instrument bulbs

1 To replace the instrument illumination bulbs, remove the relevant instrument (see Section 16). Gently pull the bulbholder out of the instrument, then pull the bulb out of the bulbholder **(see illustrations)**. Carefully push the new bulb into the holder and the holder into the instrument, then install the instrument back into the casing or the casing onto the instrument (see Section 16).

Warning bulbs

2 To replace the warning light bulbs on US ZR550 B1 and B2 models, remove the instrument cluster (see Section 15), then remove the rear cover. Pull the relevant bulbholder out of the back of the panel. Gently pull the bulb out of the bulbholder. Carefully push the new bulb into position,

then push the bulbholder back into the rear of the panel.

3 To replace the warning light bulbs on all other models, remove the instrument cluster (see Section 15), then remove the single screw securing the rear cover **(see illustration 16.4a)**. Remove the three small screws securing the warning light panel to the cluster, then separate the panel, noting how the small lugs fit into the holes **(see illustrations)**. Pull the relevant bulbholder out of the back of the panel, then gently pull the bulb out of the bulbholder **(see illustrations)**. Carefully push the new bulb into position, then push the bulbholder back into the rear of the panel.

18 Oil pressure switch - check, removal and installation

Check

1 The oil pressure warning light should come on when the ignition (main) switch is turned ON and extinguish a few seconds after the engine is started. If the oil pressure light comes on whilst the engine is running, stop the engine immediately and carry out an oil pressure check as described in Chapter 1.

2 If the oil pressure warning light does not

17.3a Remove the screws (arrowed) . . .

17.3b . . . and lift the panel off the cluster

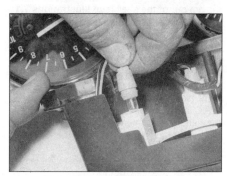

17.3c Remove the bulbholder from the panel . . .

17.3d . . . and the bulb from the holder

8

18.8 Oil pressure switch - 550 models except B4

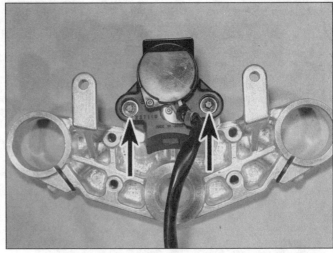

19.8 The switch is secured by two Torx bolts (arrowed)

come on when the ignition is turned on, check the bulb (see Section 17) and fuse (see Section 5).

3 The oil pressure switch is screwed into the sump near the oil filter cover on all 550 models except UK B4 models **(see illustration 18.8)**, and into the right-hand side of the crankcase below the pulse generator assembly on 750 models and UK 550 B4 models - remove the pulse generator assembly cover for access. Remove the screw (where fitted) and detach the wiring connector from the switch. With the ignition switched ON, earth (ground) the wire on the crankcase and check that the warning light comes on. If the light comes on, the switch is defective and must be replaced.

4 If the light still does not come on, check for voltage at the wire terminal using a test light with the ignition switched ON. If there is no voltage present, check the wire between the switch, the instrument cluster and fusebox for continuity (see the *wiring diagrams* at the end of this Chapter).

5 If the warning light comes on whilst the engine is running, yet the oil pressure is satisfactory, remove the wire from the oil pressure switch. With the wire detached and the ignition switched ON the light should be out. If it is illuminated, the wire between the switch and instrument cluster must be earthed (grounded) at some point. If the wiring is good, the switch must be assumed faulty and replaced.

Removal

6 Drain the engine oil (see Chapter 1).

7 The oil pressure switch is screwed into the sump near the oil filter cover on all 550 models except UK B4 models, and into the right-hand side of the crankcase below the pulse generator assembly on 750 models and UK ZR550 B4 models - remove the pulse generator assembly cover for access. Discard the gasket as a new one must be used.

8 Detach the wiring connector from the switch **(see illustration)**.

9 Unscrew the oil pressure switch and withdraw it from the sump or crankcase.

Installation

10 Apply a suitable silicone sealant (Kawasaki Bond or equivalent) to the threads of the switch, then install it in the crankcase and tighten it to the torque setting specified at the beginning of the Chapter.

11 On 750 models and UK ZR550 B4 models, install the pulse generator assembly cover using a new gasket and tighten the bolts securely.

12 Fill the engine with the correct type and quantity of oil as described in Chapter 1.

19 Ignition (main) switch - check, removal and installation

Note: *To prevent the risk of short circuits, disconnect the battery negative (–) lead before making any ignition (main) switch checks.*

Check

1 Remove the two screws securing the headlight rim to the headlight shell, and ease the rim out of the shell **(see illustrations 7.1a and b)**. Trace the ignition (main) switch wiring back from the base of the switch and disconnect it at the connector in the headlight shell.

2 Using an ohmmeter or a continuity tester, check the continuity of the connector terminal pairs (see the *wiring diagrams* at the end of this Chapter). Continuity should exist between the terminals connected by a solid line on the diagram when the switch is in the indicated position.

3 If the switch fails any of the tests, replace it.

Removal

4 Remove the instrument cluster (Section 15).

5 Remove the handlebars (see Chapter 5).

6 Trace the ignition switch wiring and disconnect it at the connector (see Step 1).

7 Slacken the fork clamp bolts in the top yoke, then remove the steering stem bolt and washer. Lift the top yoke off the steering stem.

8 Remove the two Torx-head bolts to free the ignition switch from the top yoke **(see illustration)**. In the event that special security bolts have been used, which have shear-off heads, their heads must be drilled off.

Installation

9 Install the switch onto the top yoke. Using new special Torx bolts, tighten them until either the tool slips round on the bolt head, or until the bolt head sheers off.

10 The remainder of installation is the reverse of removal. Tighten the steering stem bolt and the fork clamp bolts in the top yoke to the torque settings specified at the beginning of Chapter 5. Make sure all wiring is correctly connected and secured by any clips or ties.

20 Handlebar switches - check

1 Generally speaking, the switches are reliable and trouble-free. Most troubles, when they do occur, are caused by dirty or corroded contacts, but wear and breakage of internal parts is a possibility that should not be overlooked. If breakage does occur, the entire switch and related wiring harness will have to be replaced with a new one, since individual parts are not available.

2 The switches can be checked for continuity using an ohmmeter or a continuity test light. Always disconnect the battery negative (–) cable, which will prevent the possibility of a short circuit, before making the checks.

3 Trace the wiring harness of the switch in question back to its connectors and

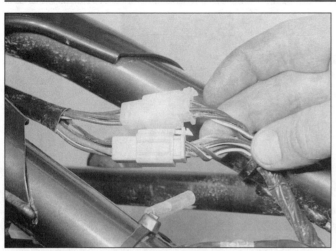

21.1 Right-hand side handlebar switch wiring connectors

21.5 Left-hand side handlebar switch wiring connectors

disconnect them. The connectors located below the fuel tank. Remove the tank for access (see Chapter 3).

4 Using the ohmmeter or test light, check for continuity between the terminals of the switch harness with the switch in the various positions (ie switch off - no continuity, switch on - continuity) (see the *wiring diagrams* at the end of this Chapter).

5 If the continuity check indicates a problem exists, refer to Section 21, remove the switch and spray the switch contacts with electrical contact cleaner. If they are accessible, the contacts can be scraped clean with a knife or polished with crocus cloth. If switch components are damaged or broken, it will be obvious when the switch is disassembled.

21 Handlebar switches - removal and installation

Right-hand handlebar switch

Removal

1 If the switch is to be removed from the bike, rather than just displaced from the handlebar, trace the wiring harness back from the switch to the wiring connectors and disconnect them. The connectors are located below the

fuel tank (see illustration). Remove the tank for access (see Chapter 3). Work back along the harness, freeing it from all the relevant clips and ties, whilst noting its correct routing.

2 Disconnect the two wires from the brake light switch (see illustration 14.5).

3 Remove the throttle cables from the switch (see Chapter 3 - this procedure incorporates switch removal).

Installation

4 Installation is the reverse of removal. Make sure the locating pin in the front half of the switch fits into hole in the front of the handlebar. Refer to Chapter 3 for installation of the throttle cables.

Left-hand handlebar switch

Removal

5 If the switch is to be removed from the bike, rather than just displaced from the handlebar, trace the wiring harness back from the switch to the wiring connectors and disconnect them; the connectors are located below the fuel tank (see illustration). Remove the tank for access (see Chapter 3). Work back along the harness, freeing it from all the relevant clips and ties, whilst noting its correct routing.

6 Disconnect the clutch switch wiring connector (see illustration 24.2).

7 Remove the choke cable from the switch (see Chapter 3 - this procedure incorporates switch removal).

Installation

8 Installation is the reverse of removal. Make sure the locating pin in the front half of the switch fits into hole in the front of the handlebar. Refer to Chapter 3 for installation of the choke cable.

22 Neutral switch - check, removal and installation

Check

1 Before checking the electrical circuit, check the bulb (see Section 17) and fuse (see Section 5).

2 The switch is located in the left-hand side of the crankcase, behind the engine sprocket cover. Unscrew the gearchange linkage arm pinch bolt and remove the arm from the shaft, noting any alignment marks (see illustration). If no marks are visible, make your own before removing the arm so that it can be correctly aligned with the shaft on installation. Unscrew the bolts securing the engine sprocket cover to the crankcase and remove the cover (see illustrations). Detach the wiring connector

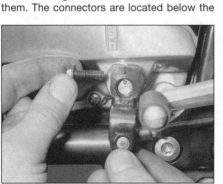

22.2a Remove the pinch bolt and slide the arm off the shaft

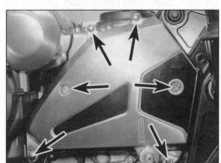

22.2b Engine sprocket cover bolts (arrowed) - 550 models

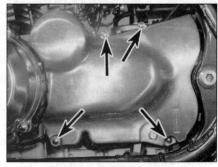

22.2c Engine sprocket cover bolts (arrowed) - 750 models

8

22.7 Disconnect the neutral switch wiring connector

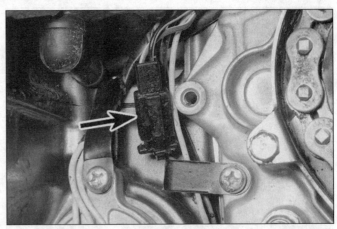

23.2 Disconnect the sidestand switch wiring connector

from the neutral switch **(see illustration 22.7)**. Make sure the transmission is in neutral.

3 With the connector disconnected and the ignition switched ON, the neutral light should be out. If not, the wire between the connector and instrument cluster must be earthed (grounded) at some point.

4 Using an ohmmeter or continuity tester, check for continuity between the switch and the crankcase. With the transmission in neutral, there should be continuity. With the transmission in gear, there should be no continuity. If the tests prove otherwise, then either the switch is faulty or the neutral pin has been incorrectly installed in the selector drum (this is only likely if the gearchange selector drum pin holder plate has been removed).

5 If the continuity tests prove the switch is good, switch the ignition ON and check for voltage at the wire terminal using a test light. If there's no voltage present, check the wire between the switch, the instrument cluster and fusebox (see the *wiring diagrams* at the end of this Chapter). If the wiring is all good, remove the selector drum pin holder plate (see Chapter 2, Section 20) and check that the longer neutral pin is correctly positioned in the drum, and that the pin fits into the correct hole in the holder plate. With the transmission in neutral, the pin should align with the contact on the neutral switch.

Removal

6 Unscrew the gearchange linkage arm pinch bolt and remove the arm from the shaft, noting any alignment marks **(see illustration 22.2a)**. If no marks are visible, make your own before removing the arm so that it can be correctly aligned with the shaft on installation. Unscrew the engine sprocket cover bolts, and remove the cover **(see illustrations 22.2b and c)**.

7 Detach the wiring connector from the neutral switch **(see illustration)**. Make sure the transmission is in neutral.

8 Unscrew the switch and remove it.

Installation

9 Install the switch and tighten it to the specified torque.

10 Reconnect the switch wiring connector **(see illustration 22.7)**.

11 Check the operation of the neutral light.

12 Install the sprocket cover and the gearchange linkage arm, aligning the marks made on removal.

---

23 Sidestand switch - check and replacement

Check

1 The sidestand switch is mounted on the frame just ahead of the sidestand pivot **(see illustration 23.8)**. The switch is part of the safety circuit which prevents or stops the engine running if the transmission is in gear whilst the sidestand is down, and prevents the engine from starting if the transmission is in gear unless the sidestand is up, and unless the clutch is pulled in. Before checking the electrical circuit, check the fuse (see Section 5).

2 Unscrew the gearchange linkage arm pinch bolt and remove the arm from the shaft, noting any alignment marks **(see illustration 22.2a)**. If no marks are visible, make your own before removing the arm so that it can be correctly aligned with the shaft on installation. Unscrew the bolts securing the engine sprocket cover to the crankcase and remove the cover **(see illustrations 22.2b or c)**. Trace the wiring back from the switch to its connector and disconnect it **(see illustration)**.

3 Check the operation of the switch using an ohmmeter or continuity test light. Connect the meter to the green/white and black/yellow wires on the switch side of the connector. With the sidestand up there should be continuity (zero resistance) between the terminals, and with the stand down there should be no continuity (infinite resistance).

4 If the switch does not perform as expected, it is defective and must be replaced.

5 If the switch is good, check the junction box and other components in the starter circuit as described in the relevant sections of this

Chapter. If all components are good, check the wiring between the various components (see the *wiring diagrams* at the end of this book).

> **HAYNES HINT** *Sidestand switch troubles may be caused by a sticking switch plunger due to the ingress of road dirt - peel back the rubber gaiter and spray the plunger with a water dispersant aerosol.*

Replacement

6 The sidestand switch is mounted on the frame just ahead of the sidestand pivot. Unscrew the gearchange linkage arm pinch bolt and remove the arm from the shaft, noting any alignment marks **(see illustration 22.2a)**. If no marks are visible, make your own before removing the arm so that it can be correctly aligned with the shaft on installation. Unscrew the bolts securing the engine sprocket cover to the crankcase and remove the cover **(see illustrations 22.2b or c)**.

7 Trace the wiring back from the switch to its connector and disconnect it **(see illustration 23.2)**. Work back along the switch wiring, freeing it from any relevant retaining clips and ties, noting its correct routing.

8 Unscrew the two bolts securing the switch to the frame **(see illustration)**.

23.8 The sidestand switch is secured by two bolts (arrowed)

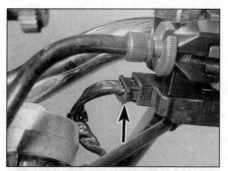

24.2 Disconnect the clutch switch wiring connector (arrowed)

9 Fit the new switch to the frame and install the retaining screws, tightening them securely.
10 Make sure the wiring is correctly routed up to the connector and retained by all the necessary clips and ties.
11 Reconnect the wiring connector and check the operation of the sidestand switch.

24 Clutch switch -
check and replacement

Check

1 The clutch switch is situated on the base of the clutch lever bracket. The switch is part of the safety circuit which prevents or stops the engine running if the transmission is in gear whilst the sidestand is down, and prevents the engine from starting if the transmission is in gear unless the sidestand is up, and unless the clutch is pulled in.
2 To check the switch, disconnect the wiring connector from the switch (see illustration). Connect the probes of an ohmmeter or a continuity test light to the black and black/yellow wire terminals on the switch. With the clutch lever pulled in, there should be continuity (zero resistance). With the clutch lever out, there should be no continuity (infinite resistance). Now connect the meter probes between the black and black/red wire terminals on the switch. With the clutch lever pulled in, there should be no continuity (infinite resistance). With the clutch lever out, there should be continuity (no resistance).
3 If the switch is good, check the junction box and other components in the starter circuit as described in the relevant sections of this Chapter. If all components are good, check the wiring between the various components (see the *wiring diagrams* at the end of this book).

Replacement

4 Disconnect the wiring connector from the clutch switch (see illustration 24.2). Unscrew the two screws securing the switch to the bottom of the clutch lever bracket and remove the switch.

5 Installation is the reverse of removal. The switch isn't adjustable.

25 Junction box -
check and replacement

Check

1 Remove the seat (see Chapter 7).
2 The junction box contains the starter circuit relay, the diodes, and on US models the headlight relay, as well as the fusebox. The starter circuit relay and diodes are part of the safety circuit which prevents or stops the engine running if the transmission is in gear whilst the sidestand is down, and prevents the engine from starting if the transmission is in gear unless the sidestand is up, and unless the clutch is pulled in. Slide the junction box out of its holder and disconnect the wiring connectors (see illustration).
3 Using an ohmmeter or continuity tester and a 12 V battery with auxiliary leads, connect the meter probes and the battery leads (when

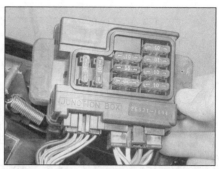

25.2 Remove the junction box and disconnect the wiring connectors

specified) to the relay terminals on the junction box connectors as indicated (see illustrations). Use an ohmmeter or continuity tester to check the diodes. If the results achieved after all terminal pairs have been tested as indicated do not agree with the results specified in the tables, the junction box is probably faulty - have your findings confirmed by a Kawasaki dealer before buying a replacement.

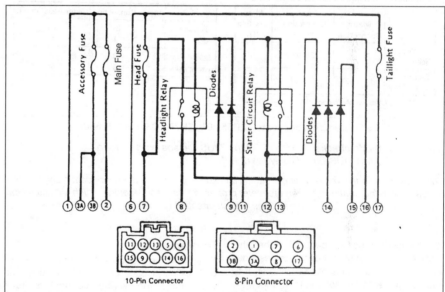

	Meter Connection	Battery Connection + −	Meter Reading (Ω)
Headlight Relay	*7 – 8	*9 – 13	0
Starter Circuit Relay	11 – 13	11 – 12	0

Relay Inspection (with the battery connected)

	Meter Connection	Meter Reading (Ω)
Headlight Relay	*7 – 8	∞
	*7 – 13	∞
Starter Circuit Relay	11 – 13	∞
	12 – 13	∞

Relay Inspection (with the battery disconnected)

(*) : U.S. and Canadian Models only

25.3a Junction box tests - ZR550 B1 to B5 and ZR750 C1 to C4 models

Diode checks   8 to 13 (US/Canada only)   15 to 14
9 to 13 (US/Canada only)   12 to 14   16 to 14

When testing diodes, the resistance reading should be low in one direction (continuity) and ten times as high (no continuity) when the meter probes are reversed. A diode which indicates high or low readings in each direction has failed.

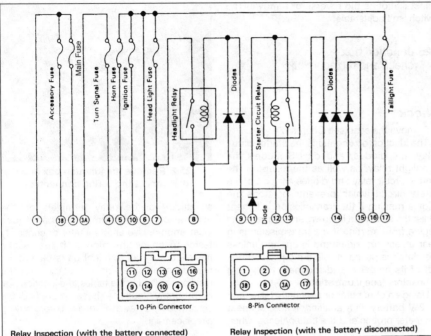

26 Fuel level sender -
check and replacement

10-Pin Connector

8-Pin Connector

Relay Inspection (with the battery connected)

	Meter Connection	Battery Connection +	Battery Connection −	Meter Reading (Ω)
Headlight Relay	*7 –8	*9 – 13		0
Starter Circuit Relay	11 – 13	11 – 12		0

(*) : U.S. and Canadian Models only

Relay Inspection (with the battery disconnected)

	Meter Connection	Meter Reading (Ω)
Headlight Relay	*7 – 8	∞
	*7 – 13	∞
Starter Circuit Relay	11 – 13	∞
	12 – 13	∞

25.3b Junction box tests - ZR550 B6, ZR750 C5 and D1 models

Diode checks

9 to 13 (US/Canada only)	8 to 13 (US/Canada only) 15 to 14
	12 to 14 16 to 14

When testing diodes, the resistance reading should be low in one direction (continuity) and ten times as high (no continuity) when the meter probes are reversed. A diode which indicates high or low readings in each direction has failed.

4 If the junction box is good, check the other components in the starter circuit as described in the relevant sections of this Chapter. If all the components are satisfactory, check the wiring between the various components (refer to the *wiring diagrams* at the end of this Chapter).

Replacement

5 Remove the seat (see Chapter 7).
6 Slide the junction box out of its holder and disconnect the wiring connectors **(see illustration 25.2)**. Install the new box and make sure the connectors are secure.
7 Install the seat (see Chapter 7).

⚠️ *Warning: Petrol (gasoline) is extremely flammable, so take extra precautions when you work on any part of the fuel system. Don't smoke or allow open flames or bare light bulbs near the work area, and don't work in a garage where a natural gas-type appliance is present. If you spill any fuel on your skin, rinse it off immediately with soap and water. When you perform any kind of work on the fuel system, wear safety glasses and have a fire extinguisher suitable for a class B type fire (flammable liquids) on hand.*

Check

1 Remove the seat (see Chapter 7). Trace the fuel level sender wiring from the underside of the fuel tank and disconnect it at the connector (remove the tank mounting bolts and raise the tank at the rear, or remove the tank for improved access if required - see Chapter 3) **(see illustration 16.12)**.
2 Using an ohmmeter set to ohms x 100 scale, connect the probes to the terminals on the sender side of the connector. Check the resistance reading with the tank empty and full. Compare the readings with those listed in the specifications at the beginning of the Chapter. Alternatively, remove the sender from the tank (see Steps 4 and 5 below) and, with the meter connected as above, manually move the float up and down to emulate the different positions **(see illustrations)**.
3 If the readings taken differ to those listed in the specifications, replace the sender.

Replacement

4 Drain and remove the fuel tank (see Chapter 3).
5 Prise off the sender cover using a flat-bladed screwdriver **(see illustration)**. Unscrew the bolts securing the sender to the base of the tank and withdraw it **(see illustration)**. Discard the gasket as a new one must be used.
6 Install the sender by reversing the removal process, using a new gasket **(see illustration)**.

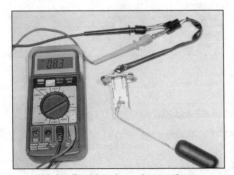

26.2a Fuel level sender testing - FULL position

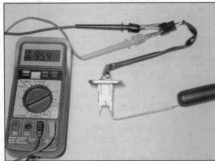

26.2b Fuel level sender testing - EMPTY position

26.5a Prise off the cover . . .

26.5b ... then unscrew the bolts ...

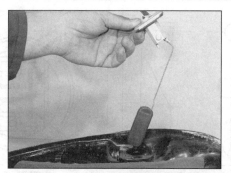

26.5c ... and withdraw the sender

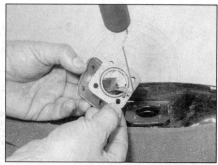

26.6 Use a new gasket on installation

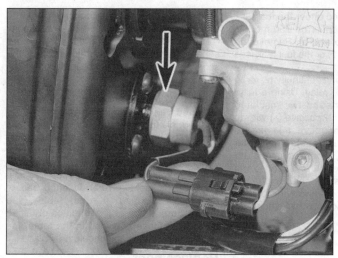

27.3a Atmospheric temperature sensor (arrowed)
and its wiring connector

27.3b Carburettor temperature sensor (arrowed)

27 Carburettor heater system (UK later models only) - check and replacement

Check

1 The carburettor heater system fitted to UK ZR550 B4, B5 and B6 models, and to UK ZR750 C3, C4, C5 and D1 models incorporates a heater unit in each carburettor body, an atmospheric temperature sensor in the air filter housing and a relay. The ZR750 C3 and C4 models also have an oil temperature sensor and relay, and ZR550 B5 and B6 and ZR750 C5 and D1 models have a carburettor temperature sensor and a system control unit.

Heater unit

2 To check the heater unit in the carburettor, disconnect the wiring connector from the heater being tested and the black/yellow wire from the earth terminal. Using a multimeter set to the ohms x 10 scale, touch the positive (+) probe to the heater terminal and the negative (–) probe to the earth terminal on the carburettor body. If the reading obtained is not within the range specified at the beginning of the Chapter, replace the heater. Repeat the check for the remaining heaters.

Sensors

3 To check the atmospheric temperature sensor, the oil temperature sensor and the carburettor temperature sensor, disconnect the wiring connector and unscrew the sensor. The atmospheric temperature sensor is threaded into the front of the air filter housing **(see illustration)**, the oil temperature sensor is threaded into the crankcase below the pulse generator assembly cover, and the carburettor temperature sensor is threaded into the no. 2 carburettor in place of one of the joining bracket screws **(see illustration)**.

4 Fill a small heatproof container with water (for the atmospheric and carburettor sensors) or oil (for the oil temperature sensor) and place it on a stove. Using an ohmmeter, connect the positive (+) probe of the meter to the terminal on the sensor, and the negative (–) probe to the body of the sensor. Using some wire or other support suspend the sensor in the water or oil so that just the sensing portion and the threads are submerged. Also place a thermometer capable of reading temperatures up to 50°C in the water or oil so that its bulb is close to the sensor **(see illustration)**. **Note:** *None of the components should be allowed to directly touch the container.* Heat the water or oil over a low flame, stirring it gently. The

temperatures required for testing the sensor are not high, so avoid applying excessive heat.

⚠ *Warning: This must be done very carefully to avoid the risk of personal injury.*

5 Referring to the specifications at the beginning of the Chapter for the sensor being tested, check whether the resistance reading

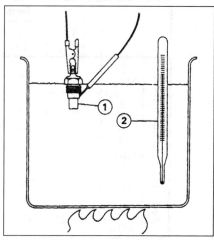

27.4 Sensor test set-up
1 Sensor   2 Thermometer

8

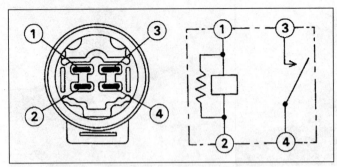

27.7a Atmospheric temperature sensor relay test
Terminal numbers shown

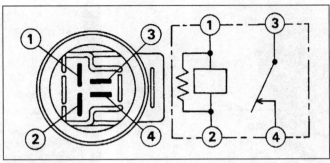

27.7b Oil temperature sensor relay test
Terminal numbers shown

specified is obtained at the temperature specified. When the required temperature has been reached, turn off the heat and check that the correct reading is obtained as the temperature falls. If the meter readings obtained are different, or they are obtained at different temperatures, then the sensor is faulty and must be replaced.

Relay

6 To check the atmospheric temperature sensor and oil temperature sensor relay, disconnect the wiring connector from the relay and identify the terminal numbers which should be marked on the relay terminals. The relay is mounted behind the right-hand side panel on 550 models, and under the fuel tank behind the regulator/rectifier on 750 models **(see illustrations 27.9a and b)**. Remove the side panel (see Chapter 7) or the fuel tank (see Chapter 3) for access.

7 Connect the probes of a continuity tester to terminals 3 and 4 of the relay. Using a fully-charged 12 volt battery and two insulated jumper wires, connect the positive (+) wire to terminal 1 and the negative (–) wire to terminal 2 **(see illustrations)**. The meter should show continuity (zero resistance) for the atmospheric temperature sensor, or no continuity (infinite resistance) for the oil temperature sensor. Disconnect the battery leads. The meter should now show no continuity (infinite resistance) for the atmospheric temperature sensor, or continuity (zero resistance) for the oil temperature sensor. If the readings obtained differ, the sensor is faulty and should be replaced.

Control unit

8 To check the system control unit, which is mounted behind the ignition control unit on 550 models (necessitating its removal - see Chapter 4) and behind the left-hand side panel on 750 models, disconnect the wiring connector **(see illustrations 27.10a and b)**.
9 Using a multimeter set to the K ohms scale, connect the meter probes to each pair of terminals specified in the table **(see illustration)**. If any of the readings obtained differ from those specified in the table, the control unit is faulty and should be replaced.

Replacement

10 The carburettor heater system fitted to UK ZR550 B4, B5 and B6 models, and to UK ZR750 C3, C4, C5 and D1 models incorporates a heater unit in each carburettor body, an atmospheric temperature sensor in the air filter housing and a relay. ZR750 C3 and C4 models also have an oil temperature sensor and relay, and ZR550 B5 and B6 and ZR750 C5 and D1 models have a carburettor temperature sensor and a system control unit.
11 To remove the heater unit in the carburettor, disconnect the wiring connector from the heater being removed, then remove the screw securing the heater bracket and pull the heater out of the carburettor body **(see illustration)**.

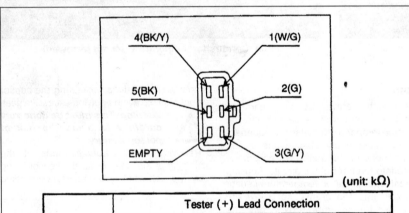

(unit: kΩ)

		Tester (+) Lead Connection				
		1 (W/G)	2 (G)	3 (G/Y)	4 (BK/Y)	5 (BK)
Tester (–) Lead Connection	1 (W/G)	–	7 ~ 28	∞	6.5 ~ 28	17 ~ 80
	2 (G)	∞	–	∞	∞	∞
	3 (G/Y)	6 ~ 26	9.5 ~ 40	–	9.5 ~ 40	24 ~ 150
	4 (BK/Y)	4.4 ~ 19	1.4 ~ 6	∞	–	6.5 ~ 28
	5 (BK)	13 ~ 60	10 ~ 45	∞	6.5 ~ 28	–

27.9 System control unit test

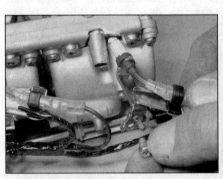

27.11 Remove the bracket screw and withdraw the heater

27.13a Sensor relay - 550 models

27.13b Sensor relay - 750 models

27.13c Disconnect the relay wiring connector and remove the relay

27.14a System control unit - 550 models

27.14b System control unit - 750 models

12 The atmospheric temperature sensor is threaded into the front of the air filter housing **(see illustration 27.3a)**, the oil temperature sensor is threaded into the crankcase below the pulse generator assembly cover, and the carburettor temperature sensor is threaded into the no. 2 carburettor in place of one of the joining bracket screws **(see illustration 27.3b)**. Disconnect the wiring connector and unscrew the sensor (in the case of the oil temperature sensor, first drain the engine oil - see Chapter 1).

13 The relay is mounted behind the right-hand side panel on 550 models, and under the fuel tank behind the regulator/rectifier on 750 models **(see illustrations)**. Remove the side panel (see Chapter 7) or the fuel tank (see Chapter 3) for access. Disconnect the relay wiring connector and remove the relay **(see illustration)**.

14 The system control unit is mounted behind the ignition control unit on 550 models and behind the left-hand side panel on 750 models **(see illustrations)**. Remove the ignition control unit (see Chapter 4) or the side panel (see Chapter 7). Disconnect the wiring at the connector and pull the unit and its rubber sleeve off its mounting lugs.

15 Installation is the reverse of removal. Make sure all wiring connectors are secure.

Apply a silicone sealant to the threads of the oil temperature sensor.

28 Horn - check and replacement

Check

1 The horn is mounted in front of the engine below the steering head.
2 Unplug the wiring connectors from the horn **(see illustration)**. Using two jumper wires,

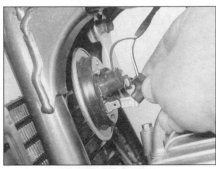

28.2 Disconnect the horn wiring connectors

apply battery voltage directly to the terminals on the horn. If the horn sounds, check the switch (see Section 21) and the wiring between the switch and the horn (see the *wiring diagrams* at the end of this Chapter).
3 If the horn doesn't sound, replace it.

Replacement

4 The horn is mounted in front of the engine below the steering head.
5 Unplug the wiring connectors from the horn **(see illustration 28.2)**, then unscrew the bolts securing the horn bracket and remove the horn from the bike **(see illustration)**.

28.5 The horn bracket is secured by two bolts (arrowed)

8

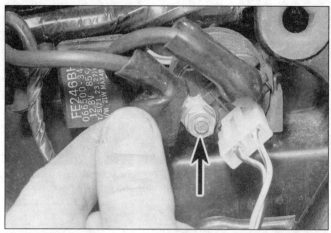

29.2 Detach the starter motor lead (arrowed) from the relay

29.4 Starter relay test meter (A) and battery (B) connections

6 Install the horn and securely tighten the bolts. Connect the wiring connectors to the horn.

29 Starter relay -
check and replacement

Check

1 If the starter circuit is faulty, first check the fuse (see Section 5).
2 The starter relay is located behind the left-hand side panel. Remove the side panel for access (see Chapter 7). Pull back the rubber cover on the starter motor lead, then unscrew the nut securing the starter motor lead to its terminal and disconnect the lead **(see illustration)**. Making sure that the disconnected lead is well clear of its terminal, switch the ignition ON and ensure the engine kill switch is in the RUN position, the transmission is in neutral and the clutch pulled in, then press the starter switch. The relay should click.
3 If the relay doesn't click, switch off the ignition and remove the relay as described below; test it as follows.
4 With the relay removed from the bike, set a multimeter to the ohms x 1 scale and connect it across the relay's starter motor and battery

lead terminals. Using a fully-charged 12 volt battery and two insulated jumper wires, connect the positive (+) terminal of the battery to the yellow/red wire terminal of the relay, and the negative (–) terminal to the black/yellow wire terminal of the relay **(see illustration)**. At this point the relay should click and the multimeter read 0 ohms (continuity). If this is the case the relay is proved good. If the relay does not click when battery voltage is applied and indicates no continuity (infinite resistance) across its terminals, it is faulty and must be replaced.
5 If the relay is good, check for battery voltage between the yellow/red wire and the black/yellow wire when the starter button is pressed. Check the other components in the starter circuit as described in the relevant sections of this Chapter. If all components are good, check the wiring between the various components (see the *wiring diagrams* at the end of this book).

Replacement

6 Remove the seat and the left-hand side panel (see Chapter 7).
7 Disconnect the battery terminals, remembering to disconnect the negative (–) terminal first.
8 Disconnect the relay wiring connector, then unscrew the two nuts securing the starter motor and battery leads to the relay and

detach the leads **(see illustration)**. Remove the relay with its rubber sleeve from its mounting lugs on the frame.
9 Installation is the reverse of removal, ensuring the terminal screws are securely tightened. Connect the negative (–) lead last when reconnecting the battery.

30 Starter motor -
removal and installation

Removal

1 Remove the seat (see Chapter 7). Disconnect the battery negative (–) lead.
2 On 550 models, unscrew the two bolts securing the starter motor top cover and lift off the cover **(see illustration)**. Slacken the upper starter motor mounting bolt, then remove the lower cover **(see illustration)**.
3 On 750 models, unscrew the gearchange linkage arm pinch bolt and remove the arm from the shaft, noting any alignment marks **(see illustration 22.2a)**. If no marks are visible, make your own before removing the arm so that it can be correctly aligned with the shaft on installation. Unscrew the bolts securing the engine sprocket cover to the crankcase and remove the cover **(see illustration 22.2c)**. Unscrew the two bolts

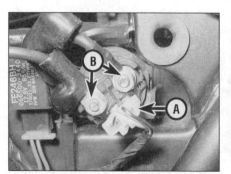

29.8 Disconnect the wiring connector (A), unscrew the nuts (B) and detach the leads

30.2a Unscrew the bolts (arrowed) and remove the top cover . . .

30.2b . . . then slacken the upper mounting bolt and remove the lower cover

30.3 Removing the top cover on 750 models

30.4 Unscrew the nut and detach the starter motor lead

30.5 Unscrew the mounting bolts . . .

30.6 . . . and remove the starter

securing the starter motor top cover, noting how the collar and rubber damper fit, and remove the cover **(see illustration)**.

4 Peel back the rubber cover and unscrew the nut securing the starter cable to the motor **(see illustration)**.

5 Unscrew the two bolts securing the starter motor to the crankcase **(see illustration)**.

6 Slide the starter motor out from the crankcase and remove it from the machine **(see illustration)**.

7 Remove the O-ring on the end of the starter motor and discard it; a new one must be used.

Installation

8 Install a new O-ring on the end of the starter motor and ensure it is seated in its groove **(see illustration)**. Apply a smear of engine oil to the O-ring to aid installation. Make sure that the mating surfaces between the starter motor mounting points and the crankcase are clean to ensure a good earth (ground).

9 Manoeuvre the motor into position and slide it into the crankcase **(see illustration 30.6)**. Ensure that the starter motor teeth mesh correctly with those of the starter idle/reduction gear.

10 Install the starter motor bolts. On 550 models, tighten only the lower bolt, leaving the upper one slack for the lower cover. On 750 models, tighten both bolts to the torque setting specified at the beginning of the Chapter.

11 Connect the starter cable to the motor and secure it with the nut **(see illustration 30.4)**. Make sure the rubber cover is correctly seated over the terminal.

12 On 550 models, install the lower cover so that the front mounting fits around the upper

starter motor bolt **(see illustration 30.2b)**. Tighten the bolt to secure the cover. Install the upper cover and tighten its bolts.

13 On 750 models, install the top cover, making sure the rubber damper and collar are correctly fitted, then install the bolts **(see illustration 30.3)**. Install the sprocket cover and the gearchange linkage arm, aligning the marks made previously, and tighten the pinch bolt securely **(see illustration)**.

14 Connect the battery negative (–) lead and install the seat.

30.8 Fit a new O-ring (arrowed)

30.13 Install the engine sprocket cover

8

31.2 Note the alignment marks between the main housing and the covers

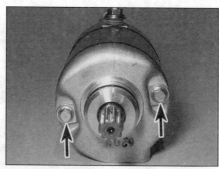

31.3a Starter motor long bolts (arrowed) - 550 models

31.3b Starter motor long bolts (arrowed) - 750 models

31.6a Unscrew the nut (arrowed) and remove the washers . . .

31.6b . . . then remove the brushplate assembly

31 Starter motor - disassembly, inspection and reassembly

Disassembly

1 Remove the starter motor (see Section 30).
2 Note the alignment marks between the main housing and the front and rear covers as an aid to installation, or make some of your own if they are difficult to see (see illustration). Also make a mark to identify which way up the housing fits.
3 Unscrew the two long bolts and withdraw them from the starter motor (see illustrations). Discard their O-rings (550 models only) as new ones must be used. Remove the rear cover from the motor along with its O-ring. Discard the O-ring as a new one must be used. Remove the shims from the rear end of the armature shaft or from inside the rear cover.
4 Remove the front cover from the motor along with its O-ring. Discard the O-ring as a new one must be used. On 550 models, remove the washer(s) from the front end of the armature shaft and the seal protector from inside the front cover, noting their correct fitted locations (see illustration 31.19a). On

750 models, remove the dividing plate, noting how the notch in its perimeter locates over the lug on the inside of the main housing (see illustration 31.19c). Also note the locating pin between the ring gear and the front cover, and take care not to lose it (see illustration 31.19d). The notch in the perimeter of the front cover also locates over the lug on the inside of the main housing. Remove the shims from the front end of the armature shaft.
5 Withdraw the armature from the main housing.
6 Noting the correct fitted location of each component, unscrew the terminal nut and remove the insulating washers (see illustration). On US/Canada ZR750 C1, C2 and C3 models, remove the brushplate assembly and terminal bolt from the main housing. On all other models, remove the brushplate assembly and terminal bolt from the rear cover (see illustration).
7 Lift the brush springs and slide the brushes out from their holders, noting how they fit.

Inspection

8 The parts of the starter motor that are most likely to require attention are the brushes. Measure the length of the brushes and compare the results to the brush length listed

in this Chapter's Specifications (see illustration). If any of the brushes are worn beyond the service limit, replace the brush assembly with a new one. If the brushes are not worn excessively, nor cracked, chipped, or otherwise damaged, they may be re-used. Also check the brush springs, making sure they provide a firm pressure on the brush when installed.
9 Inspect the commutator bars on the armature for scoring, scratches and discoloration (see illustration). The commutator can be cleaned and polished with crocus cloth, but do not use sandpaper or

31.8 Measure the length of each brush

31.9 Check the commutator bars as described

emery paper. After cleaning, wipe away any residue with a cloth soaked in electrical system cleaner or denatured alcohol. Clean out the mica grooves between the commutator bars. Measure the diameter of the commutator and compare it to the specifications. If the commutator has worn to below its service limit, the armature must be replaced.

10 Using an ohmmeter or a continuity test light, check for continuity between the commutator bars **(see illustration)**. Continuity should exist between each bar and all of the others. Also, check for continuity between the commutator bars and the armature shaft **(see illustration)**. There should be no continuity (infinite resistance) between the commutator and the shaft. If the checks indicate otherwise, the armature is defective.

11 Check for continuity between each brush and the terminal bolt. There should be continuity (zero resistance). Check for continuity between the terminal bolt and the housing (when assembled). There should be no continuity (infinite resistance).

12 Check the front end of the armature shaft for worn, cracked, chipped and broken teeth. If the shaft is damaged or worn, replace the armature. On 750 models, similarly check the ring gear in the front cover and the drive pinion on the front of the cover. The drive pinion is secured by a circlip, and the chamfered side of the pinion teeth must face out **(see illustration)**.

13 Inspect the end covers for signs of cracks or wear. Inspect the magnets in the main housing and the housing itself for cracks.

14 Inspect the insulating washers and front cover oil seal (550 models) for signs of damage and replace them if necessary.

Reassembly

15 Slide the brushes back into position in their holders on the brushplate and, on all except US ZR750 C1, C2 and C3 models, place the brush spring ends onto the brushes. On US ZR750 C1, C2 and C3 models, locate the spring end onto the top of the brush holder so that there is no pressure on the spring. This makes installation of the armature much easier.

16 Fit the inner rubber insulator on the terminal bolt, then insert the bolt through the rear cover (main housing on US ZR750 C1, C2 and C3 models) and install the brushplate assembly in the rear cover (main housing on US ZR750 C1, C2 and C3 models) making sure its tab is correctly located in the slot in the cover or housing **(see illustration)**. Fit the O-ring and the washers over the terminal and secure it with the nut.

17 On all except US ZR750 C1, C2 and C3 models, slide the shims over the rear end of the armature shaft **(see illustration)**. Insert the armature into the offset opening in the brushplate, locating the commutator bars against the brushes, then press the brushes back into the holders until the armature shaft

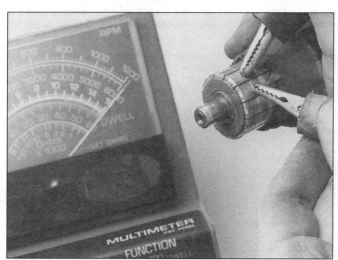

31.10a Continuity should exist between the commutator bars

31.10b There should be no continuity between the commutator bars and the armature shaft

31.12 Check the drive pinion on 750 models

31.16 Install the brushplate and terminal bolt and fit the washers as shown

31.17a Fit the shims onto the shaft . . .

8

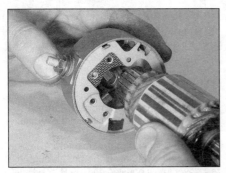

31.17b ... then install the armature in the rear housing ...

31.17c ... and locate the commutator against the brushes

31.18a Fit new O-rings onto the main housing ...

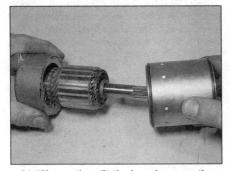

31.18b ... then fit the housing over the armature ...

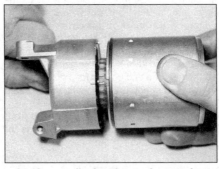

31.18c ... aligning the marks noted or made on removal

31.19a On 550 models, fit the washers onto the shaft and the seal protector onto the front cover

end locates in its hole in the cover **(see illustrations)**. Take care not to damage the brushes. On US ZR750 C1, C2 and C3 models, insert the armature into the main housing, then locate the spring ends onto the brushes so that the brushes are pressed onto the commutator. On all models, check that each brush is securely pressed against the commutator by its spring and is free to move easily in its holder.

18 Fit a new O-ring onto each end of the main housing **(see illustration)**. On all except US ZR750 C1, C2 and C3 models, slide the housing over the armature, aligning the marks made on disassembly **(see illustration)**. On US ZR750 C1, C2 and C3 models, slide the shims over the rear end of the armature shaft, then fit the end cover onto the main housing, aligning the marks made on disassembly.

19 On 550 models, apply a smear of grease to the lips of the front cover oil seal. Fit the washer(s) onto the shaft and the seal protector onto the front cover, making sure that the tabs on the seal protector locate correctly **(see illustration)**. Install the cover, aligning the marks made on removal. On 750 models, fit the shims onto the front end of the armature shaft, then fit the dividing plate, locating the notch in its perimeter over the lug on the inside of the main housing. Check that the locating pin is installed in the notch between the perimeter of the ring gear and the front cover **(see illustration)**. Fit the front cover onto the housing, aligning the lug on the inside of the main housing with the notch in the perimeter of the ring gear **(see illustration)**.

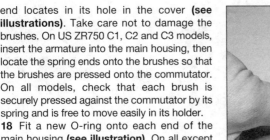

31.19b On 750 models, fit the washers onto the shaft ...

31.19c ... then install the dividing plate, aligning the notch with the lug (arrowed)

31.19d Make sure the locating pin is in place ...

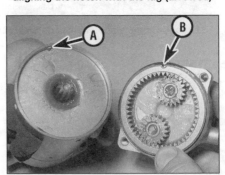

31.19e ... then fit the front cover, aligning the lug (A) with the notch (B)

20 On 550 models, slide the lockwasher and a new O-ring onto each of the long bolts **(see illustration)**. On all models, check the marks made on removal are aligned, then install the long bolts and tighten them securely **(see illustration)**. On 550 models, make sure the

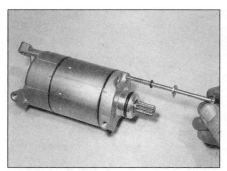

31.20a On 550 models, do not forget the O-ring and washer on each long bolt

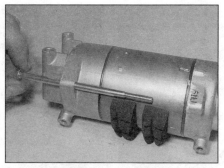

31.20b On 750 models, the long bolts run outside the housing

flat side of the lockwasher locates correctly against the body of the rear cover **(see illustration 31.3a)**.

21 Install the starter motor (see Section 30).

32 Charging system testing - general information and precautions

1 If the performance of the charging system is suspect, the system as a whole should be checked first, followed by testing of the individual components. **Note:** *Before beginning the checks, make sure the battery is fully charged and that all system connections are clean and tight.*

2 Checking the output of the charging system and the performance of the various components within the charging system requires the use of a multimeter (with voltage, current and resistance checking facilities).

3 When making the checks, follow the procedures carefully to prevent incorrect connections or short circuits, as irreparable damage to electrical system components may result if short circuits occur.

4 If a multimeter is not available, the job of checking the charging system should be left to a Kawasaki dealer.

33 Charging system - testing

1 If the machine's charging system is thought to be faulty, perform the following checks.

Leakage test

2 Remove the seat (see Chapter 7) and disconnect the lead from the battery negative (–) terminal.

3 Set the multimeter to the mA (milli Amps) function and connect its negative (–) probe to the battery negative (–) terminal, and positive (+) probe to the disconnected negative (–) lead **(see illustration)**. With the meter connected like this the reading should not exceed 0.1 mA.

4 If the reading exceeds the specified amount it is likely that there is a short circuit in the wiring. Thoroughly check the wiring between the various components (see the *wiring diagrams* at the end of this book).

5 If the reading is below the specified amount, the leakage rate is satisfactory. Disconnect the meter and reconnect the negative (–) lead to the battery, tightening it securely, Check the alternator output as described below.

Output test

Regulated output test

6 Remove the seat (see Chapter 7). Start the engine and warm it up to normal operating temperature then stop the engine.

7 Connect a multimeter set to the 0 - 20 volts dc scale (voltmeter) across the terminals of the battery (positive (+) lead to battery positive (+) terminal, negative (–) lead to battery negative (–) terminal). Start the engine, then turn on the lights (UK models) and note the reading obtained at idle speed - it should be just under battery voltage (12V). Increase engine speed and note the voltage reading - it should vary between 14 to 15V. Stop the engine and disconnect the meter when testing is complete. If the voltage is outside these limits, check the unregulated output of the alternator (see below), and the regulator (see Section 35). **Note:** *If the voltage is low, it is more likely that the alternator is faulty. If the voltage is above 15 volts, it is more likely that the regulator is faulty.*

> **HAYNES HiNT** *Clues to a faulty regulator are constantly blowing bulbs, with brightness varying considerably with engine speed, and battery overheating, necessitating frequent topping up of the electrolyte level.*

8 Carry out the above test with the headlight turned off and note the readings. On US/Canada the headlight wire connector must be detached from the back of the headlight unit to turn off the headlight.

Unregulated output test

9 Unscrew the gearchange linkage arm pinch bolt and remove the arm from the shaft, noting any alignment marks **(see illustration 22.2a)**. If no marks are visible, make your own before removing the arm so that it can be correctly aligned with the shaft on installation. Unscrew the bolts securing the engine sprocket cover to the crankcase and remove the cover **(see illustrations 22.2b or c)**.

10 Trace the alternator wiring from the base of the alternator cover and disconnect it at the connector(s) **(see illustrations)**. Using a multimeter set to 0 - 250 V ac range, connect the meter probes between two of the yellow wires from the alternator. Start the engine and increase its speed to 4000 rpm. Check the voltage output and compare it to the minimum specified at the beginning of the Chapter.

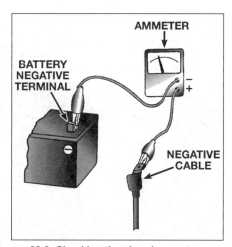

33.3 Checking the charging system leakage rate. Connect the meter as shown

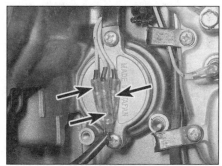

33.10a Alternator wiring connectors (arrowed) - 550 models

33.10b Alternator wiring connector (arrowed) - 750 models

8

33.14 Testing stator coil resistance

34.3 The alternator cover is secured by four bolts (arrowed)

11 Stop the engine, then connect the meter to another pair of yellow wires and repeat the test. Stop the engine then test across the remaining pair of yellow wires. If any of the three readings are below the minimum specified, check the stator coil resistance (see below). If the readings are good, check the regulator (see Section 35).

Alternator stator coil test

12 Unscrew the gearchange linkage arm pinch bolt and remove the arm from the shaft, noting any alignment marks **(see illustration 22.2a)**. If no marks are visible, make your own before removing the arm so that it can be correctly aligned with the shaft on installation. Unscrew the bolts securing the engine sprocket cover to the crankcase and remove the cover **(see illustrations 22.2b or c)**.

13 Trace the alternator wiring from the base of the alternator cover and disconnect it at the connector(s) **(see illustrations 33.9a or b)**.

14 Using multimeter set to the ohms x 1 scale, check the resistance between each of the wires on the alternator side of the connector, taking a total of three readings **(see illustration)**. Also check for continuity between each terminal and earth (ground). If the stator coil windings are in good condition there should be the resistance specified between each of the terminals, and no continuity (infinite resistance) between any of the terminals and ground (earth). If not, the alternator stator coil assembly is at fault and should be replaced. If the resistance readings are as specified but the alternator output is low when tested as above, the rotor magnets have probably weakened. **Note:** *Before condemning the stator coils, check the fault is not due to damaged wiring between the connector and coils.*

34 Alternator - removal and installation

Removal

1 Unscrew the gearchange linkage arm pinch bolt and remove the arm from the shaft, noting any alignment marks **(see illustration 22.2a)**. If no marks are visible, make your own before removing the arm so that it can be correctly aligned with the shaft on installation. Unscrew the bolts securing the engine sprocket cover to the crankcase and remove the cover **(see illustrations 22.2b or c)**.

2 Trace the alternator wiring from the base of the alternator cover and disconnect it at the connector(s) **(see illustrations 33.10a or b)**. Release the wiring from any clips or ties.

3 Unscrew the alternator cover retaining bolts and lift the cover away from the engine **(see illustration)**. The stator is mounted inside the cover. Remove the gasket and discard it. Remove the two dowels from either the cover or the crankcase, if they are loose.

4 To remove the rotor bolt, the rotor must be held against rotation. If a rotor holding strap or tool is not available, place the transmission in gear and have an assistant apply the rear brake. Unscrew the bolt **(see illustration)**.

34.4 Alternator rotor bolt (arrowed)

5 To remove the rotor from the shaft it is necessary to use a rotor puller. The Kawasaki special tools (pt. no. 57001-1099 for 550 models, and pt. nos. 57001-1151 and 57001-1216 for 750 models), or a commercially available rotor puller can be used (making sure it has the correct thread on it). Screw the puller into the rotor thread, and using the method employed earlier to stop the rotor from turning, tighten the puller until the rotor is displaced from the shaft.

> **HAYNES HINT** *A smart tap on the head of the puller will usually succeed in breaking any corrosion free between the rotor and crankshaft taper.*

6 To remove the stator from the crankcase cover, unscrew the three bolts securing the stator and the screws securing the wiring clamp, then remove the assembly from the cover, noting the routing of the wiring and how the rubber grommet fits **(see illustration)**.

Installation

7 De-grease the tapered portion of the crankshaft and the corresponding surface in the rotor using a suitable solvent. Make sure

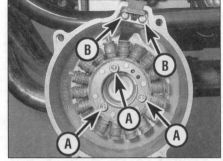

34.6 Stator bolts (A), wiring clamp screws (B)

34.9 Install the cover using a new gasket

35.1a Regulator/rectifier wiring connector (arrowed) - later 550 models

35.1b Regulator/rectifier wiring connector (arrowed) - 750 models

that no metal objects have attached themselves to the magnet on the inside of the rotor then install the rotor onto the crankshaft. Install the rotor bolt and, using the method employed on removal to stop the rotor from turning, tighten it to the torque setting specified at the beginning of the Chapter.

8 Install the stator into the cover, aligning the rubber wiring grommet with the groove in the cover. Apply a suitable non-permanent thread-locking compound to the stator bolt threads, then install the bolts and tighten them to the specified torque setting. Apply a suitable sealant to the wiring grommet, then install it into the cutout in the cover. Install the wiring clamp and secure it with the screws **(see illustration 34.6)**.

9 Make sure the dowels are fitted, then install the alternator cover using a new gasket **(see illustration)**. Tighten the cover bolts evenly in a criss-cross sequence.

10 Reconnect the wiring at the connector(s), making sure it is correctly routed, and secure it with any clips or ties **(see illustrations 33.10a or b)**.

11 Install the sprocket cover and the gearchange lever, aligning the marks made on removal.

35 Regulator/rectifier unit - check and replacement

Check

1 The regulator/rectifier is mounted behind the right-hand side panel on early 550 models, below the battery tray above the front of the swingarm on later 550 models, and under the fuel tank on 750 models **(see illustrations 35.6a and b)**. Remove the right-hand side panel (see Chapter 7) or the fuel tank (see Chapter 3) as required. Trace the wiring from the regulator/rectifier unit and disconnect it at the connector, or disconnect the wiring connector from the unit, according to model **(see illustrations)**.

2 To test the rectifier circuit, use a multimeter set to the appropriate resistance scale and check the resistance between the various terminals of the regulator/rectifier connectors

as shown in the table **(see illustration)**. If the readings do not compare closely with those shown in the accompanying table the regulator/rectifier unit can be considered faulty. **Note:** *The use of certain multimeters could lead to false readings being obtained. Therefore, if the above check shows the regulator/rectifier unit to be faulty take the unit to a Kawasaki dealer for confirmation of its condition before replacing it.*

3 To test the regulator circuit, three fully charged 12 V batteries, each with a set of auxiliary leads, and a test light are required (see below). If these are not available, carry out a charging system test (see Section 33). If the conditions arise from that test that indicate a faulty regulator, take it to a Kawasaki dealer for further testing. Clues to a faulty regulator are constantly blowing bulbs, with brightness varying considerably with

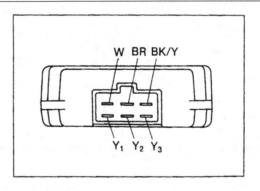

No.	Connections		Reading	Meter
	Meter (+) to	Meter (−) to		Range
1	Y₁			
2	Y₂	W	∞	
3	Y₃			
4	Y₁			
5	Y₂	BK/Y		× 10 Ω
6	Y₃		0 ~	or
7		Y₁	½ scale	× 100 Ω
8	W	Y₂		
9		Y₃		
10		Y₁		
11	BK/Y	Y₂	∞	
12		Y₃		

35.2 Rectifier circuit test connections

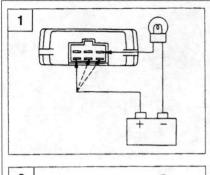

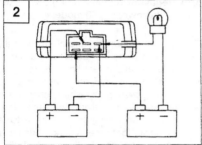

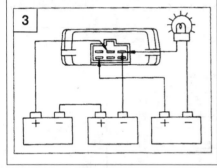

35.4 Regulator circuit tests (see text)

35.6a Regulator/rectifier (arrowed) - later 550 models

35.6b Regulator/rectifier - 750 models

engine speed, and battery overheating, necessitating frequent topping up of the electrolyte level (where possible).

4 Referring to the three circuit diagrams shown, set each circuit up in turn **(see illustration)**. Where dotted lines are shown to the yellow terminals on the connector, check the circuit for each of the terminals in turn using the same lead, thereby taking three readings for each circuit. In the first test circuit, the bulb should not light up. In the second test circuit, the bulb should not light up. In the third test circuit, the bulb should light up. If any of the tests prove otherwise, the regulator/rectifier is faulty and must be replaced.

5 The tests outlined above are not foolproof. If the test results indicate that the unit is good, and all other components in the charging circuit have been checked and proven good, but there is still a problem, the regulator/rectifier may well be faulty. If this is the case, either take the unit to a Kawasaki dealer for testing, or substitute the suspect unit with one that is known to be good and recheck the system.

Replacement

6 The regulator/rectifier is mounted behind the right-hand side panel on early 550 models, below the battery tray above the front of the swingarm on later 550 models, and under the fuel tank on 750 models **(see illustrations)**. Remove the right-hand side panel (see Chapter 7) or the fuel tank (see Chapter 3) as required. Trace the wiring from the regulator/rectifier unit and disconnect it at the connector, or disconnect the wiring connector from the unit, according to model **(see illustrations 34.1a or b)**.

7 Unscrew the two bolts or screws securing the unit and remove it.

8 Install the new unit and tighten its mountings securely. Connect the wiring at the connector.

9 Install the right-hand side panel (see Chapter 7) or fuel tank (see Chapter 3) as required.

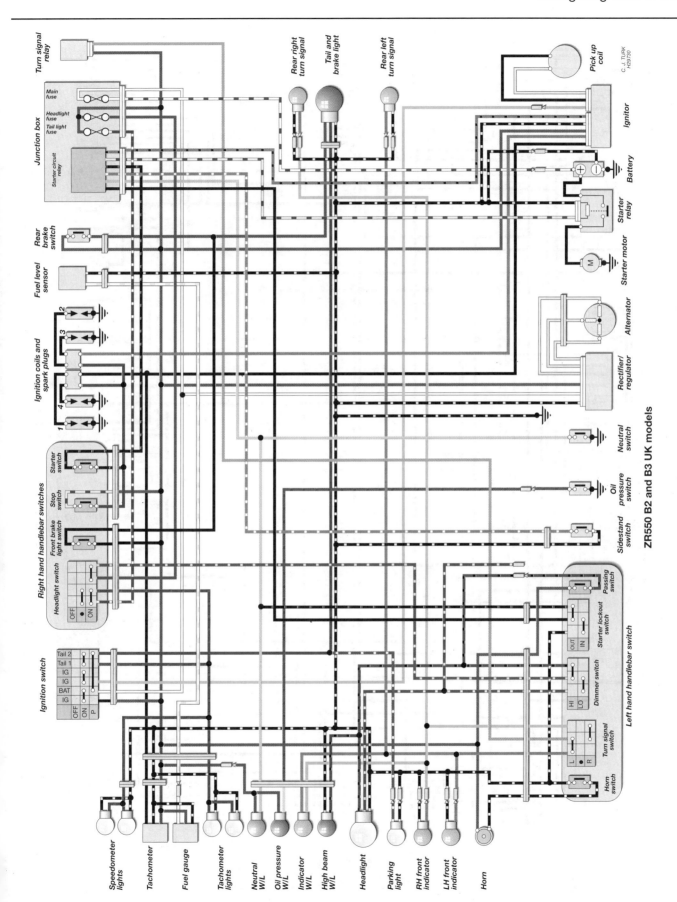

Turn signal relay

Junction box

Main fuse

Headlight fuse

Tail light fuse

Starter circuit relay

Rear brake switch

Fuel level sensor

Ignition coils and spark plugs

Right hand handlebar switches

Starter switch

Stop switch

Front brake light switch

Headlight switch

OFF
ON

Ignition switch

Tail 2
Tail 1
IG
IG
BAT
IG
OFF
ON
P

Rear right turn signal

Tail and brake light

Rear left turn signal

Pick up coil

Ignitor

Battery

Starter relay

Starter motor

Alternator

Rectifier/ regulator

Neutral switch

Oil pressure switch

Sidestand switch

Passing switch

Starter lockout switch

OUT
IN

Dimmer switch

HI
LO

Turn signal switch

L   R

Horn switch

Left hand handlebar switch

C. J. TURK
H29730

ZR550 B2 and B3 UK models

Speedometer lights

Tachometer

Fuel gauge

Tachometer lights

Neutral W/L

Oil pressure W/L

Indicator W/L

High beam W/L

Headlight

Parking light

RH front indicator

LH front indicator

Horn

8

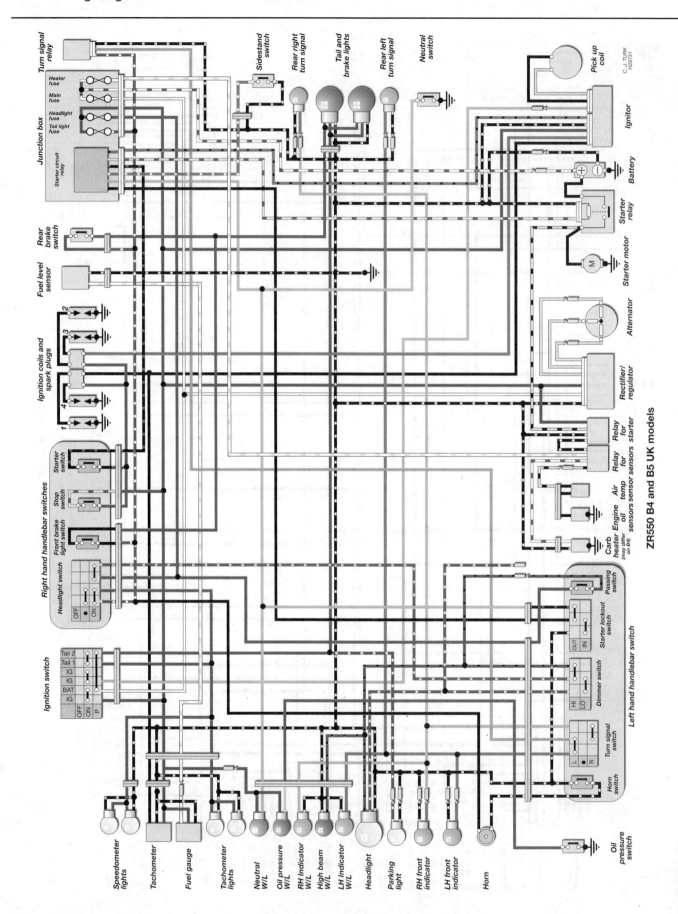

Junction box

- Turn signal relay
- Heater fuse
- Main fuse
- Headlight fuse
- Tail light fuse
- Starter circuit relay

Sidestand switch
Rear right turn signal
Tail and brake lights
Rear left turn signal
Neutral switch
Pick up coil
Ignitor
Battery
Starter relay
Starter motor

Rear brake switch
Fuel level sensor

Alternator
Rectifier/regulator

Ignition coils and spark plugs

Relay for starter
Relay for sensors
Carb heater (may differ on B4) sensors
Engine oil sensors
Air temp sensors

Right hand handlebar switches
- Starter switch
- Stop switch
- Front brake light switch
- Headlight switch (OFF • ON)

ZR550 B4 and B5 UK models

Ignition switch
	Tail 2	Tail 1	IG	IG	BAT	IG
OFF						
ON						
P						

Passing switch
Starter lockout switch (OUT / IN)
Dimmer switch (HI / LO)
Turn signal switch (L / R)
Horn switch

Left hand handlebar switch

Speedometer lights
Tachometer
Fuel gauge
Tachometer lights
Neutral W/L
Oil pressure W/L
RH Indicator W/L
High beam W/L
LH Indicator W/L
Headlight
Parking light
RH front indicator
LH front indicator
Horn
Oil pressure switch

C. J. TURK
H29731

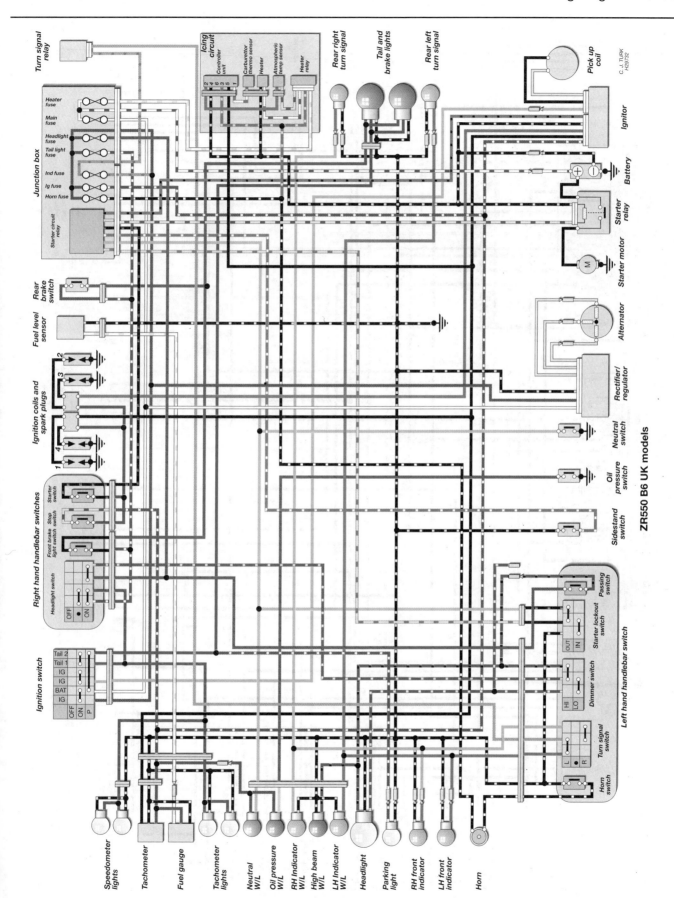

Turn signal relay

Heater fuse
Main fuse
Headlight fuse
Tail light fuse
Ind fuse
Ig fuse
Horn fuse

Junction box

Starter circuit relay

Rear brake switch

Fuel level sensor

Ignition coils and spark plugs

Right hand handlebar switches

Starter switch
Stop switch
Front brake light switch

Headlight switch

OFF
ON

Ignition switch

Tail 2
Tail 1
IG
IG
BAT
IG

OFF
ON
P

Icing circuit

Controller unit
Carburetor thermo sensor
Heater
Atmospheric temp sensor
Heater relay

Rear right turn signal
Tail and brake lights
Rear left turn signal

Pick up coil

Ignitor

Battery

Starter relay

Starter motor

Alternator

Rectifier/regulator

Neutral switch

Oil pressure switch

Sidestand switch

C. J. TURK
H29732

ZR550 B6 UK models

Passing switch
Starter lockout switch
OUT
IN
Dimmer switch
HI
LO
Turn signal switch
L
R
Horn switch

Left hand handlebar switch

Speedometer lights
Tachometer
Fuel gauge
Tachometer lights
Neutral W/L
Oil pressure W/L
RH Indicator W/L
High beam W/L
LH Indicator W/L
Headlight
Parking light
RH front indicator
LH front indicator
Horn

8

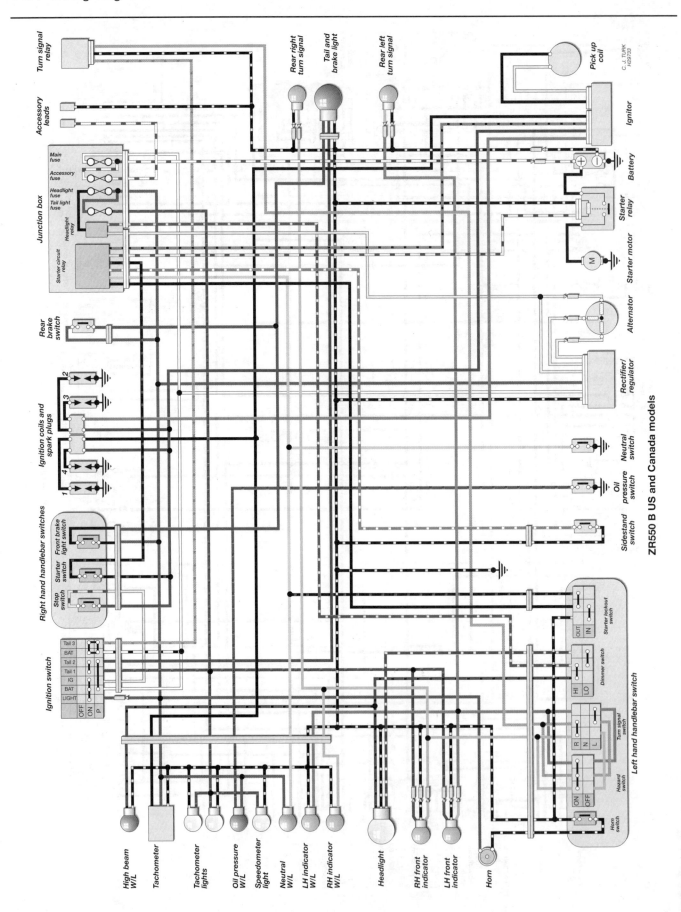

ZR550 B US and Canada models

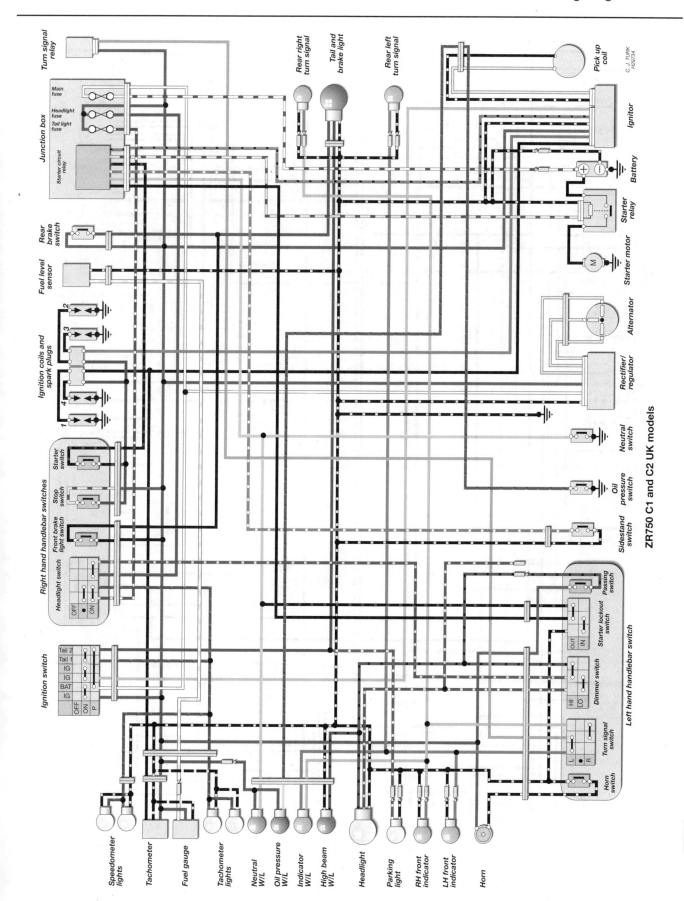

Turn signal relay

Junction box
Main fuse
Headlight fuse
Tail light fuse
Starter circuit relay

Rear brake switch

Fuel level sensor

Ignition coils and spark plugs
2
3
4
1

Right hand handlebar switches
Starter switch
Stop switch
Front brake light switch
Headlight switch
OFF
ON

Ignition switch
Tail 2
Tail 1
IG
IG
BAT
IG
OFF
ON
P

Rear right turn signal

Tail and brake light

Rear left turn signal

Pick up coil

Ignitor

C.J.TURK
H29734

Battery

Starter relay

Starter motor

Alternator

Rectifier/ regulator

Neutral switch

Oil pressure switch

Sidestand switch

Passing switch

Starter lockout switch
OUT
IN

Dimmer switch
HI
LO

Turn signal switch
L
R

Horn switch

Left hand handlebar switch

ZR750 C1 and C2 UK models

Speedometer lights
Tachometer
Fuel gauge
Tachometer lights
Neutral W/L
Oil pressure W/L
Indicator W/L
High beam W/L
Headlight
Parking light
RH front indicator
LH front indicator
Horn

8

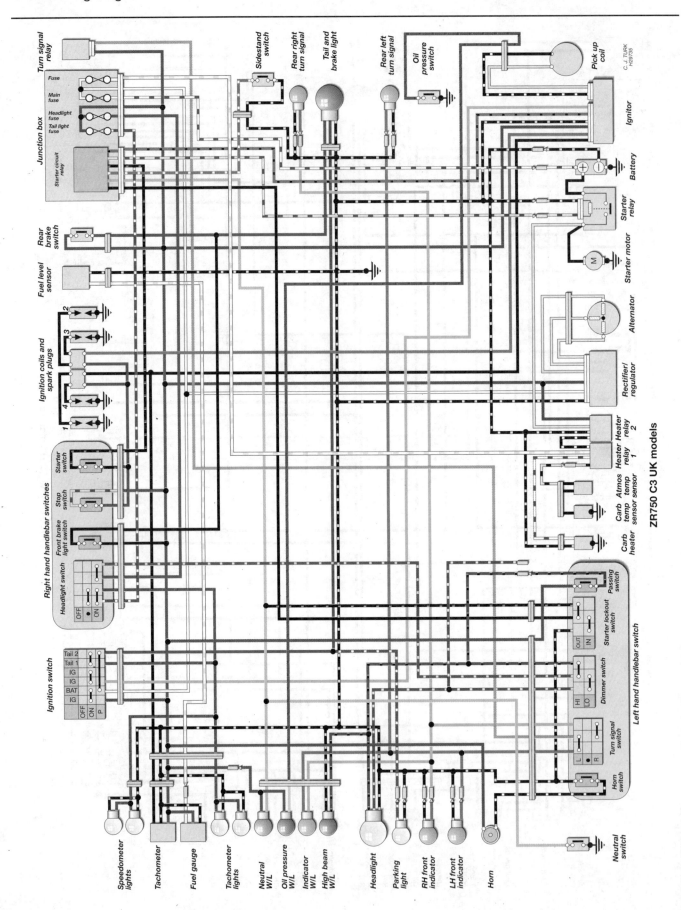

Turn signal relay

Junction box
- Fuse
- Main fuse
- Headlight fuse
- Tail light fuse
- Starter circuit relay

Sidestand switch

Rear right turn signal

Tail and brake light

Rear left turn signal

Oil pressure switch

Pick up coil

Ignitor

Battery

Starter relay

Starter motor

Rear brake switch

Fuel level sensor

Alternator

Ignition coils and spark plugs

Rectifier/ regulator

Heater relay 1 Heater relay 2

Carb temp sensor Atmos temp sensor

Right hand handlebar switches
- Starter switch
- Stop switch
- Front brake light switch
- Headlight switch
- OFF • ON

Carb heater

ZR750 C3 UK models

Passing switch

Starter lockout switch
- OUT / IN

Ignition switch
- Tail 2
- Tail 1
- IG
- IG
- BAT
- IG
- OFF ON P.

Dimmer switch
- HI / LO

Left hand handlebar switch

Turn signal switch
- L / R

Horn switch

Speedometer lights

Tachometer

Fuel gauge

Tachometer lights

Neutral W/L

Oil pressure W/L

Indicator W/L

High beam W/L

Headlight

Parking light

RH front indicator

LH front indicator

Horn

Neutral switch

C. J. TURK
H29735

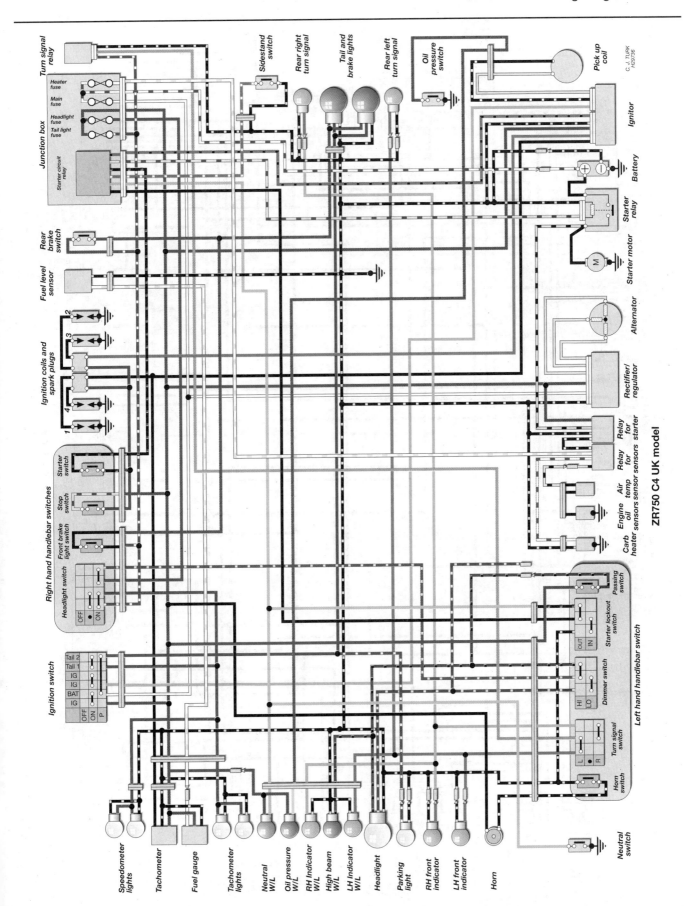

ZR750 C4 UK model

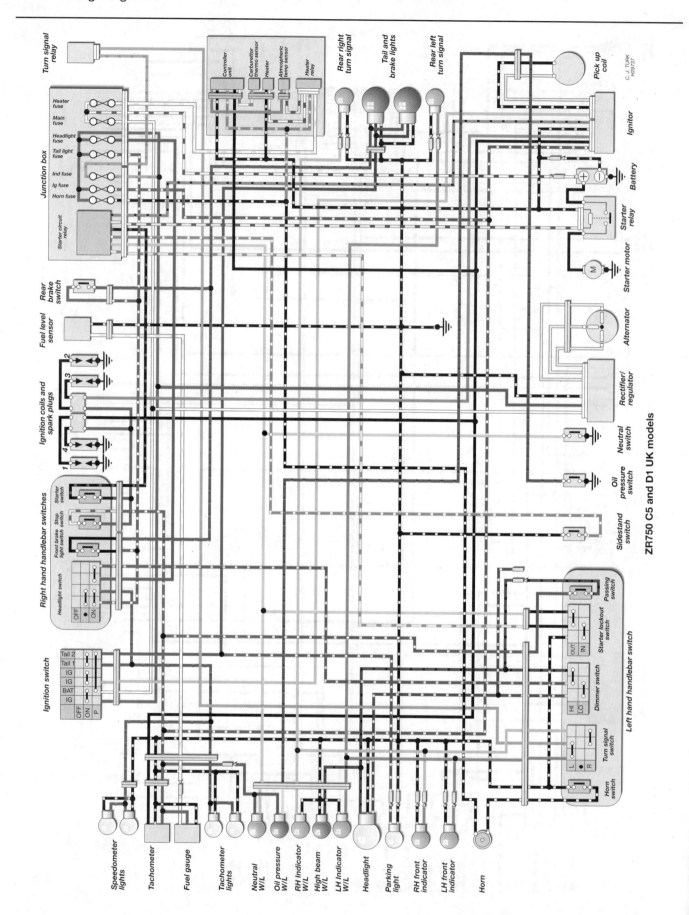

ZR750 C5 and D1 UK models

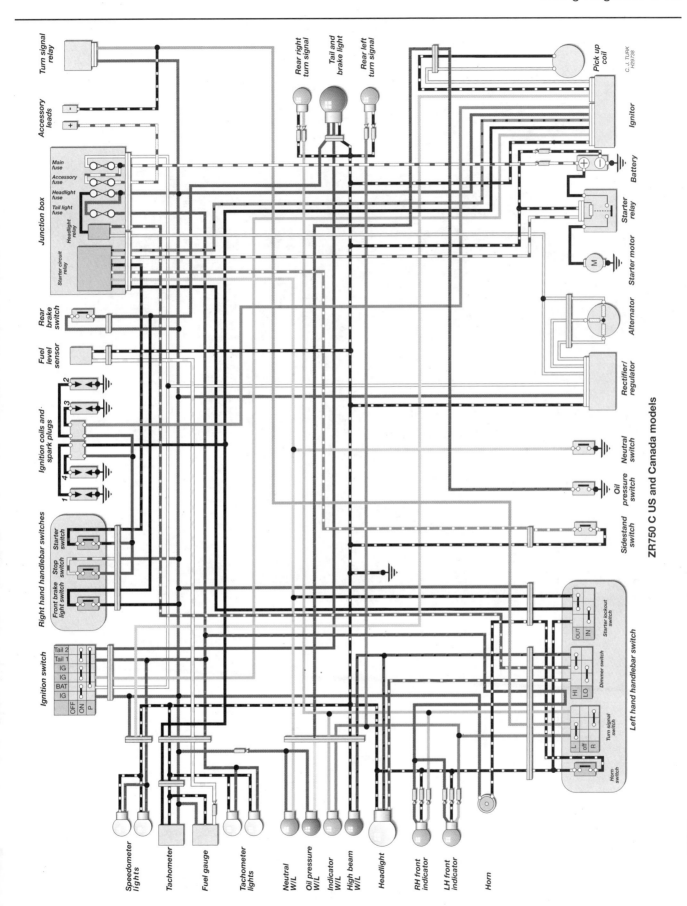

ZR750 C US and Canada models

8

Notes

Dimensions and Weights

550 models

Wheelbase
  UK models . . . . .1435 mm
  US models . . . . .1440 mm
Overall length
  UK models . . . . .2080 mm
  US models . . . . .2100 mm
Overall width . . . . .755 mm
Overall height . . . . .1095 mm
Seat height . . . . .770 mm
Minimum ground clearance . . . . .120 mm
Weight (dry)
  UK models . . . . .179 kg
  US models . . . . .178 kg

750 models

Wheelbase . . . . .1455 mm
Overall length . . . . .2105 mm
Overall width . . . . .770 mm
Overall height . . . . .1095 mm
Seat height . . . . .780 mm
Minimum ground clearance . . . . .150 mm
Weight (dry)
  C models . . . . .201 kg
  D models . . . . .212 kg

Buying tools

A toolkit is a fundamental requirement for servicing and repairing a motorcycle. Although there will be an initial expense in building up enough tools for servicing, this will soon be offset by the savings made by doing the job yourself. As experience and confidence grow, additional tools can be added to enable the repair and overhaul of the motorcycle. Many of the specialist tools are expensive and not often used so it may be preferable to hire them, or for a group of friends or motorcycle club to join in the purchase.

As a rule, it is better to buy more expensive, good quality tools. Cheaper tools are likely to wear out faster and need to be renewed more often, nullifying the original saving.

> ⚠️ **Warning: To avoid the risk of a poor quality tool breaking in use, causing injury or damage to the component being worked on, always aim to purchase tools which meet the relevant national safety standards.**

The following lists of tools do not represent the manufacturer's service tools, but serve as a guide to help the owner decide which tools are needed for this level of work. In addition, items such as an electric drill, hacksaw, files, soldering iron and a workbench equipped with a vice, may be needed. Although not classed as tools, a selection of bolts, screws, nuts, washers and pieces of tubing always come in useful.

For more information about tools, refer to the Haynes *Motorcycle Workshop Practice TechBook* (Bk. No. 3470).

Manufacturer's service tools

Inevitably certain tasks require the use of a service tool. Where possible an alternative tool or method of approach is recommended, but sometimes there is no option if personal injury or damage to the component is to be avoided. Where required, service tools are referred to in the relevant procedure.

Service tools can usually only be purchased from a motorcycle dealer and are identified by a part number. Some of the commonly-used tools, such as rotor pullers, are available in aftermarket form from mail-order motorcycle tool and accessory suppliers.

Maintenance and minor repair tools

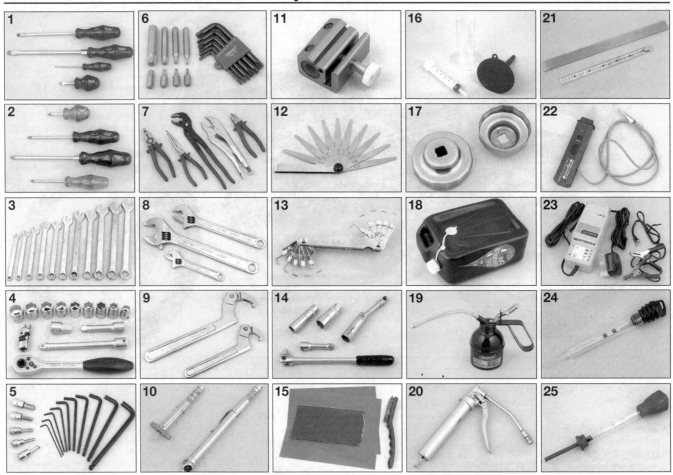

1 *Set of flat-bladed screwdrivers*
2 *Set of Phillips head screwdrivers*
3 *Combination open-end and ring spanners*
4 *Socket set (3/8 inch or 1/2 inch drive)*
5 *Set of Allen keys or bits*
6 *Set of Torx keys or bits*
7 *Pliers, cutters and self-locking grips (Mole grips)*
8 *Adjustable spanners*
9 *C-spanners*
10 *Tread depth gauge and tyre pressure gauge*
11 *Cable oiler clamp*
12 *Feeler gauges*
13 *Spark plug gap measuring tool*
14 *Spark plug spanner or deep plug sockets*
15 *Wire brush and emery paper*
16 *Calibrated syringe, measuring vessel and funnel*
17 *Oil filter adapters*
18 *Oil drainer can or tray*
19 *Pump type oil can*
20 *Grease gun*
21 *Straight-edge and steel rule*
22 *Continuity tester*
23 *Battery charger*
24 *Hydrometer (for battery specific gravity check)*
25 *Anti-freeze tester (for liquid-cooled engines)*

Repair and overhaul tools

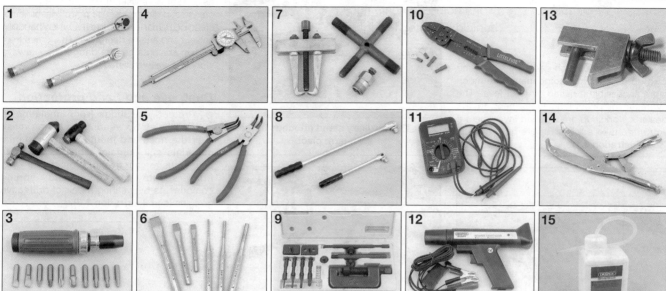

1 Torque wrench
(small and mid-ranges)
2 Conventional, plastic or
soft-faced hammers
3 Impact driver set

4 Vernier gauge
5 Circlip pliers (internal and
external, or combination)
6 Set of cold chisels
and punches

7 Selection of pullers
8 Breaker bars
9 Chain breaking/
riveting tool set

10 Wire stripper and
crimper tool
11 Multimeter (measures
amps, volts and ohms)
12 Stroboscope (for
dynamic timing checks)

13 Hose clamp
(wingnut type shown)
14 Clutch holding tool
15 One-man brake/clutch
bleeder kit

Specialist tools

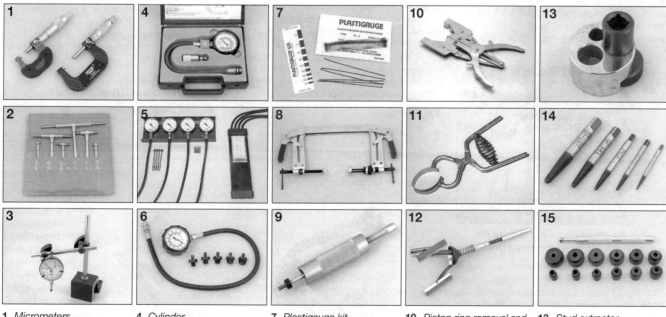

1 Micrometers
(external type)
2 Telescoping gauges
3 Dial gauge

4 Cylinder
compression gauge
5 Vacuum gauges (left) or
manometer (right)
6 Oil pressure gauge

7 Plastigauge kit
8 Valve spring compressor
(4-stroke engines)
9 Piston pin drawbolt tool

10 Piston ring removal and
installation tool
11 Piston ring clamp
12 Cylinder bore hone
(stone type shown)

13 Stud extractor
14 Screw extractor set
15 Bearing driver set

1 Workshop equipment and facilities

The workbench

● Work is made much easier by raising the bike up on a ramp - components are much more accessible if raised to waist level. The hydraulic or pneumatic types seen in the dealer's workshop are a sound investment if you undertake a lot of repairs or overhauls **(see illustration 1.1)**.

1.1 Hydraulic motorcycle ramp

● If raised off ground level, the bike must be supported on the ramp to avoid it falling. Most ramps incorporate a front wheel locating clamp which can be adjusted to suit different diameter wheels. When tightening the clamp, take care not to mark the wheel rim or damage the tyre - use wood blocks on each side to prevent this.
● Secure the bike to the ramp using tie-downs **(see illustration 1.2)**. If the bike has only a sidestand, and hence leans at a dangerous angle when raised, support the bike on an auxiliary stand.

1.2 Tie-downs are used around the passenger footrests to secure the bike

● Auxiliary (paddock) stands are widely available from mail order companies or motorcycle dealers and attach either to the wheel axle or swingarm pivot **(see illustration 1.3)**. If the motorcycle has a centrestand, you can support it under the crankcase to prevent it toppling whilst either wheel is removed **(see illustration 1.4)**.

1.3 This auxiliary stand attaches to the swingarm pivot

1.4 Always use a block of wood between the engine and jack head when supporting the engine in this way

Fumes and fire

● Refer to the Safety first! page at the beginning of the manual for full details. Make sure your workshop is equipped with a fire extinguisher suitable for fuel-related fires (Class B fire - flammable liquids) - it is not sufficient to have a water-filled extinguisher.
● Always ensure adequate ventilation is available. Unless an exhaust gas extraction system is available for use, ensure that the engine is run outside of the workshop.
● If working on the fuel system, make sure the workshop is ventilated to avoid a build-up of fumes. This applies equally to fume build-up when charging a battery. Do not smoke or allow anyone else to smoke in the workshop.

Fluids

● If you need to drain fuel from the tank, store it in an approved container marked as suitable for the storage of petrol (gasoline) **(see illustration 1.5)**. Do not store fuel in glass jars or bottles.

1.5 Use an approved can only for storing petrol (gasoline)

● Use proprietary engine degreasers or solvents which have a high flash-point, such as paraffin (kerosene), for cleaning off oil, grease and dirt - never use petrol (gasoline) for cleaning. Wear rubber gloves when handling solvent and engine degreaser. The fumes from certain solvents can be dangerous - always work in a well-ventilated area.

Dust, eye and hand protection

● Protect your lungs from inhalation of dust particles by wearing a filtering mask over the nose and mouth. Many frictional materials still contain asbestos which is dangerous to your health. Protect your eyes from spouts of liquid and sprung components by wearing a pair of protective goggles **(see illustration 1.6)**.

1.6 A fire extinguisher, goggles, mask and protective gloves should be at hand in the workshop

● Protect your hands from contact with solvents, fuel and oils by wearing rubber gloves. Alternatively apply a barrier cream to your hands before starting work. If handling hot components or fluids, wear suitable gloves to protect your hands from scalding and burns.

What to do with old fluids

● Old cleaning solvent, fuel, coolant and oils should not be poured down domestic drains or onto the ground. Package the fluid up in old oil containers, label it accordingly, and take it to a garage or disposal facility. Contact your local authority for location of such sites or ring the oil care hotline.

OIL CARE

FOLLOW THE CODE

OIL BANK LINE
0800 66 33 66

Note: It is antisocial and illegal to dump oil down the drain. To find the location of your local oil recycling bank, call this number free.

In the USA, note that any oil supplier must accept used oil for recycling.

2 Fasteners -
screws, bolts and nuts

Fastener types and applications

Bolts and screws

● Fastener head types are either of hexagonal, Torx or splined design, with internal and external versions of each type **(see illustrations 2.1 and 2.2)**; splined head fasteners are not in common use on motorcycles. The conventional slotted or Phillips head design is used for certain screws. Bolt or screw length is always measured from the underside of the head to the end of the item **(see illustration 2.11)**.

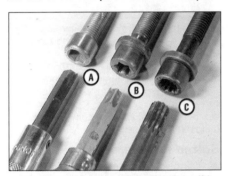

2.1 Internal hexagon/Allen (A), Torx (B) and splined (C) fasteners, with corresponding bits

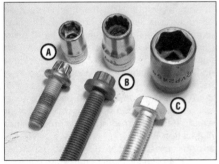

2.2 External Torx (A), splined (B) and hexagon (C) fasteners, with corresponding sockets

● Certain fasteners on the motorcycle have a tensile marking on their heads, the higher the marking the stronger the fastener. High tensile fasteners generally carry a 10 or higher marking. Never replace a high tensile fastener with one of a lower tensile strength.

Washers **(see illustration 2.3)**

● Plain washers are used between a fastener head and a component to prevent damage to the component or to spread the load when torque is applied. Plain washers can also be used as spacers or shims in certain assemblies. Copper or aluminium plain washers are often used as sealing washers on drain plugs.

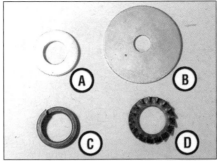

2.3 Plain washer (A), penny washer (B), spring washer (C) and serrated washer (D)

● The split-ring spring washer works by applying axial tension between the fastener head and component. If flattened, it is fatigued and must be renewed. If a plain (flat) washer is used on the fastener, position the spring washer between the fastener and the plain washer.

● Serrated star type washers dig into the fastener and component faces, preventing loosening. They are often used on electrical earth (ground) connections to the frame.

● Cone type washers (sometimes called Belleville) are conical and when tightened apply axial tension between the fastener head and component. They must be installed with the dished side against the component and often carry an OUTSIDE marking on their outer face. If flattened, they are fatigued and must be renewed.

● Tab washers are used to lock plain nuts or bolts on a shaft. A portion of the tab washer is bent up hard against one flat of the nut or bolt to prevent it loosening. Due to the tab washer being deformed in use, a new tab washer should be used every time it is disturbed.

● Wave washers are used to take up endfloat on a shaft. They provide light springing and prevent excessive side-to-side play of a component. Can be found on rocker arm shafts.

Nuts and split pins

● Conventional plain nuts are usually six-sided **(see illustration 2.4)**. They are sized by thread diameter and pitch. High tensile nuts carry a number on one end to denote their tensile strength.

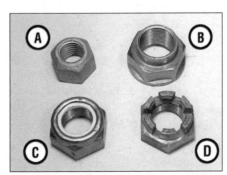

2.4 Plain nut (A), shouldered locknut (B), nylon insert nut (C) and castellated nut (D)

● Self-locking nuts either have a nylon insert, or two spring metal tabs, or a shoulder which is staked into a groove in the shaft - their advantage over conventional plain nuts is a resistance to loosening due to vibration. The nylon insert type can be used a number of times, but must be renewed when the friction of the nylon insert is reduced, ie when the nut spins freely on the shaft. The spring tab type can be reused unless the tabs are damaged. The shouldered type must be renewed every time it is disturbed.

● Split pins (cotter pins) are used to lock a castellated nut to a shaft or to prevent slackening of a plain nut. Common applications are wheel axles and brake torque arms. Because the split pin arms are deformed to lock around the nut a new split pin must always be used on installation - always fit the correct size split pin which will fit snugly in the shaft hole. Make sure the split pin arms are correctly located around the nut **(see illustrations 2.5 and 2.6)**.

2.5 Bend split pin (cotter pin) arms as shown (arrows) to secure a castellated nut

2.6 Bend split pin (cotter pin) arms as shown to secure a plain nut

Caution: If the castellated nut slots do not align with the shaft hole after tightening to the torque setting, tighten the nut until the next slot aligns with the hole - never slacken the nut to align its slot.

● R-pins (shaped like the letter R), or slip pins as they are sometimes called, are sprung and can be reused if they are otherwise in good condition. Always install R-pins with their closed end facing forwards **(see illustration 2.7)**.

2.7 Correct fitting of R-pin. Arrow indicates forward direction

Circlips (see illustration 2.8)

● Circlips (sometimes called snap-rings) are used to retain components on a shaft or in a housing and have corresponding external or internal ears to permit removal. Parallel-sided (machined) circlips can be installed either way round in their groove, whereas stamped circlips (which have a chamfered edge on one face) must be installed with the chamfer facing away from the direction of thrust load **(see illustration 2.9)**.

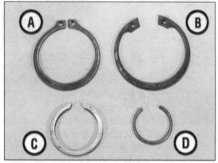

2.8 External stamped circlip (A), internal stamped circlip (B), machined circlip (C) and wire circlip (D)

● Always use circlip pliers to remove and install circlips; expand or compress them just enough to remove them. After installation, rotate the circlip in its groove to ensure it is securely seated. If installing a circlip on a splined shaft, always align its opening with a shaft channel to ensure the circlip ends are well supported and unlikely to catch **(see illustration 2.10)**.

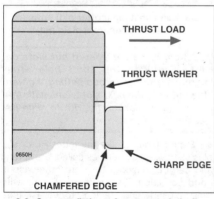

THRUST LOAD

THRUST WASHER

SHARP EDGE

CHAMFERED EDGE

0650H

2.9 Correct fitting of a stamped circlip

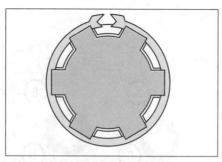

2.10 Align circlip opening with shaft channel

● Circlips can wear due to the thrust of components and become loose in their grooves, with the subsequent danger of becoming dislodged in operation. For this reason, renewal is advised every time a circlip is disturbed.

● Wire circlips are commonly used as piston pin retaining clips. If a removal tang is provided, long-nosed pliers can be used to dislodge them, otherwise careful use of a small flat-bladed screwdriver is necessary. Wire circlips should be renewed every time they are disturbed.

Thread diameter and pitch

● Diameter of a male thread (screw, bolt or stud) is the outside diameter of the threaded portion **(see illustration 2.11)**. Most motorcycle manufacturers use the ISO (International Standards Organisation) metric system expressed in millimetres, eg M6 refers to a 6 mm diameter thread. Sizing is the same for nuts, except that the thread diameter is measured across the valleys of the nut.

● Pitch is the distance between the peaks of the thread **(see illustration 2.11)**. It is expressed in millimetres, thus a common bolt size may be expressed as 6.0 x 1.0 mm (6 mm thread diameter and 1 mm pitch). Generally pitch increases in proportion to thread diameter, although there are always exceptions.

● Thread diameter and pitch are related for conventional fastener applications and the accompanying table can be used as a guide. Additionally, the AF (Across Flats), spanner or socket size dimension of the bolt or nut **(see illustration 2.11)** is linked to thread and pitch specification. Thread pitch can be measured with a thread gauge **(see illustration 2.12)**.

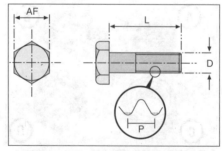

AF

L

D

P

2.11 Fastener length (L), thread diameter (D), thread pitch (P) and head size (AF)

2.12 Using a thread gauge to measure pitch

AF size	Thread diameter x pitch (mm)
8 mm	M5 x 0.8
8 mm	M6 x 1.0
10 mm	M6 x 1.0
12 mm	M8 x 1.25
14 mm	M10 x 1.25
17 mm	M12 x 1.25

● The threads of most fasteners are of the right-hand type, ie they are turned clockwise to tighten and anti-clockwise to loosen. The reverse situation applies to left-hand thread fasteners, which are turned anti-clockwise to tighten and clockwise to loosen. Left-hand threads are used where rotation of a component might loosen a conventional right-hand thread fastener.

Seized fasteners

● Corrosion of external fasteners due to water or reaction between two dissimilar metals can occur over a period of time. It will build up sooner in wet conditions or in countries where salt is used on the roads during the winter. If a fastener is severely corroded it is likely that normal methods of removal will fail and result in its head being ruined. When you attempt removal, the fastener thread should be heard to crack free and unscrew easily - if it doesn't, stop there before damaging something.

● A smart tap on the head of the fastener will often succeed in breaking free corrosion which has occurred in the threads **(see illustration 2.13)**.

● An aerosol penetrating fluid (such as WD-40) applied the night beforehand may work its way down into the thread and ease removal. Depending on the location, you may be able to make up a Plasticine well around the fastener head and fill it with penetrating fluid.

2.13 A sharp tap on the head of a fastener will often break free a corroded thread

● If you are working on an engine internal component, corrosion will most likely not be a problem due to the well lubricated environment. However, components can be very tight and an impact driver is a useful tool in freeing them **(see illustration 2.14)**.

2.14 Using an impact driver to free a fastener

● Where corrosion has occurred between dissimilar metals (eg steel and aluminium alloy), the application of heat to the fastener head will create a disproportionate expansion rate between the two metals and break the seizure caused by the corrosion. Whether heat can be applied depends on the location of the fastener - any surrounding components likely to be damaged must first be removed **(see illustration 2.15)**. Heat can be applied using a paint stripper heat gun or clothes iron, or by immersing the component in boiling water - wear protective gloves to prevent scalding or burns to the hands.

2.15 Using heat to free a seized fastener

● As a last resort, it is possible to use a hammer and cold chisel to work the fastener head unscrewed **(see illustration 2.16)**. This will damage the fastener, but more importantly extreme care must be taken not to damage the surrounding component.

Caution: Remember that the component being secured is generally of more value than the bolt, nut or screw - when the fastener is freed, do not unscrew it with force, instead work the fastener back and forth when resistance is felt to prevent thread damage.

2.16 Using a hammer and chisel to free a seized fastener

Broken fasteners and damaged heads

● If the shank of a broken bolt or screw is accessible you can grip it with self-locking grips. The knurled wheel type stud extractor tool or self-gripping stud puller tool is particularly useful for removing the long studs which screw into the cylinder mouth surface of the crankcase or bolts and screws from which the head has broken off **(see illustration 2.17)**. Studs can also be removed by locking two nuts together on the threaded end of the stud and using a spanner on the lower nut **(see illustration 2.18)**.

2.17 Using a stud extractor tool to remove a broken crankcase stud

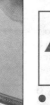

2.18 Two nuts can be locked together to unscrew a stud from a component

● A bolt or screw which has broken off below or level with the casing must be extracted using a screw extractor set. Centre punch the fastener to centralise the drill bit, then drill a hole in the fastener **(see illustration 2.19)**. Select a drill bit which is approximately half to three-quarters the

2.19 When using a screw extractor, first drill a hole in the fastener . . .

diameter of the fastener and drill to a depth which will accommodate the extractor. Use the largest size extractor possible, but avoid leaving too small a wall thickness otherwise the extractor will merely force the fastener walls outwards wedging it in the casing thread.

● If a spiral type extractor is used, thread it anti-clockwise into the fastener. As it is screwed in, it will grip the fastener and unscrew it from the casing **(see illustration 2.20)**.

2.20 . . . then thread the extractor anti-clockwise into the fastener

● If a taper type extractor is used, tap it into the fastener so that it is firmly wedged in place. Unscrew the extractor (anti-clockwise) to draw the fastener out.

⚠ *Warning: Stud extractors are very hard and may break off in the fastener if care is not taken - ask an engineer about spark erosion if this happens.*

● Alternatively, the broken bolt/screw can be drilled out and the hole retapped for an oversize bolt/screw or a diamond-section thread insert. It is essential that the drilling is carried out squarely and to the correct depth, otherwise the casing may be ruined - if in doubt, entrust the work to an engineer.

● Bolts and nuts with rounded corners cause the correct size spanner or socket to slip when force is applied. Of the types of spanner/socket available always use a six-point type rather than an eight or twelve-point type - better grip

2.21 Comparison of surface drive ring spanner (left) with 12-point type (right)

is obtained. Surface drive spanners grip the middle of the hex flats, rather than the corners, and are thus good in cases of damaged heads **(see illustration 2.21)**.

● Slotted-head or Phillips-head screws are often damaged by the use of the wrong size screwdriver. Allen-head and Torx-head screws are much less likely to sustain damage. If enough of the screw head is exposed you can use a hacksaw to cut a slot in its head and then use a conventional flat-bladed screwdriver to remove it. Alternatively use a hammer and cold chisel to tap the head of the fastener around to slacken it. Always replace damaged fasteners with new ones, preferably Torx or Allen-head type.

A dab of valve grinding compound between the screw head and screw-driver tip will often give a good grip.

Thread repair

● Threads (particularly those in aluminium alloy components) can be damaged by overtightening, being assembled with dirt in the threads, or from a component working loose and vibrating. Eventually the thread will fail completely, and it will be impossible to tighten the fastener.

● If a thread is damaged or clogged with old locking compound it can be renovated with a thread repair tool (thread chaser) **(see illustrations 2.22 and 2.23)**; special thread

2.22 A thread repair tool being used to correct an internal thread

2.23 A thread repair tool being used to correct an external thread

chasers are available for spark plug hole threads. The tool will not cut a new thread, but clean and true the original thread. Make sure that you use the correct diameter and pitch tool. Similarly, external threads can be cleaned up with a die or a thread restorer file **(see illustration 2.24)**.

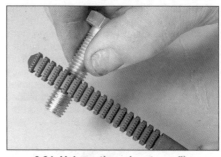

2.24 Using a thread restorer file

● It is possible to drill out the old thread and retap the component to the next thread size. This will work where there is enough surrounding material and a new bolt or screw can be obtained. Sometimes, however, this is not possible - such as where the bolt/screw passes through another component which must also be suitably modified, also in cases where a spark plug or oil drain plug cannot be obtained in a larger diameter thread size.

● The diamond-section thread insert (often known by its popular trade name of Heli-Coil) is a simple and effective method of renewing the thread and retaining the original size. A kit can be purchased which contains the tap, insert and installing tool **(see illustration 2.25)**. Drill out the damaged thread with the size drill specified **(see illustration 2.26)**. Carefully retap the thread **(see illustration 2.27)**. Install the

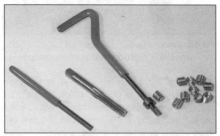

2.25 Obtain a thread insert kit to suit the thread diameter and pitch required

2.26 To install a thread insert, first drill out the original thread . . .

2.27 . . . tap a new thread . . .

2.28 . . . fit insert on the installing tool . . .

2.29 . . . and thread into the component . . .

2.30 . . . break off the tang when complete

insert on the installing tool and thread it slowly into place using a light downward pressure **(see illustrations 2.28 and 2.29)**. When positioned between a 1/4 and 1/2 turn below the surface withdraw the installing tool and use the break-off tool to press down on the tang, breaking it off **(see illustration 2.30)**.

● There are epoxy thread repair kits on the market which can rebuild stripped internal threads, although this repair should not be used on high load-bearing components.

Thread locking and sealing compounds

● Locking compounds are used in locations where the fastener is prone to loosening due to vibration or on important safety-related items which might cause loss of control of the motorcycle if they fail. It is also used where important fasteners cannot be secured by other means such as lockwashers or split pins.

● Before applying locking compound, make sure that the threads (internal and external) are clean and dry with all old compound removed. Select a compound to suit the component being secured - a non-permanent general locking and sealing type is suitable for most applications, but a high strength type is needed for permanent fixing of studs in castings. Apply a drop or two of the compound to the first few threads of the fastener, then thread it into place and tighten to the specified torque. Do not apply excessive thread locking compound otherwise the thread may be damaged on subsequent removal.

● Certain fasteners are impregnated with a dry film type coating of locking compound on their threads. Always renew this type of fastener if disturbed.

● Anti-seize compounds, such as copper-based greases, can be applied to protect threads from seizure due to extreme heat and corrosion. A common instance is spark plug threads and exhaust system fasteners.

3 Measuring tools and gauges

Feeler gauges

● Feeler gauges (or blades) are used for measuring small gaps and clearances **(see illustration 3.1)**. They can also be used to measure endfloat (sideplay) of a component on a shaft where access is not possible with a dial gauge.

● Feeler gauge sets should be treated with care and not bent or damaged. They are etched with their size on one face. Keep them clean and very lightly oiled to prevent corrosion build-up.

3.1 Feeler gauges are used for measuring small gaps and clearances - thickness is marked on one face of gauge

● When measuring a clearance, select a gauge which is a light sliding fit between the two components. You may need to use two gauges together to measure the clearance accurately.

Micrometers

● A micrometer is a precision tool capable of measuring to 0.01 or 0.001 of a millimetre. It should always be stored in its case and not in the general toolbox. It must be kept clean and never dropped, otherwise its frame or measuring anvils could be distorted resulting in inaccurate readings.

● External micrometers are used for measuring outside diameters of components and have many more applications than internal micrometers. Micrometers are available in different size ranges, eg 0 to 25 mm, 25 to 50 mm, and upwards in 25 mm steps; some large micrometers have interchangeable anvils to allow a range of measurements to be taken. Generally the largest precision measurement you are likely to take on a motorcycle is the piston diameter.

● Internal micrometers (or bore micrometers) are used for measuring inside diameters, such as valve guides and cylinder bores. Telescoping gauges and small hole gauges are used in conjunction with an external micrometer, whereas the more expensive internal micrometers have their own measuring device.

External micrometer

Note: *The conventional analogue type instrument is described. Although much easier to read, digital micrometers are considerably more expensive.*

● Always check the calibration of the micrometer before use. With the anvils closed (0 to 25 mm type) or set over a test gauge (for

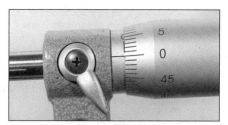

3.2 Check micrometer calibration before use

the larger types) the scale should read zero **(see illustration 3.2)**; make sure that the anvils (and test piece) are clean first. Any discrepancy can be adjusted by referring to the instructions supplied with the tool. Remember that the micrometer is a precision measuring tool - don't force the anvils closed, use the ratchet (4) on the end of the micrometer to close it. In this way, a measured force is always applied.

● To use, first make sure that the item being measured is clean. Place the anvil of the micrometer (1) against the item and use the thimble (2) to bring the spindle (3) lightly into contact with the other side of the item **(see illustration 3.3)**. Don't tighten the thimble down because this will damage the micrometer - instead use the ratchet (4) on the end of the micrometer. The ratchet mechanism applies a measured force preventing damage to the instrument.

● The micrometer is read by referring to the linear scale on the sleeve and the annular scale on the thimble. Read off the sleeve first to obtain the base measurement, then add the fine measurement from the thimble to obtain the overall reading. The linear scale on the sleeve represents the measuring range of the micrometer (eg 0 to 25 mm). The annular scale

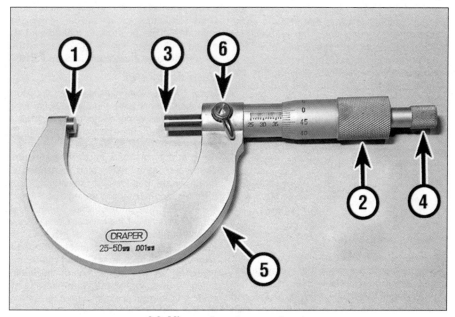

3.3 Micrometer component parts

1	Anvil	3	Spindle	5	Frame
2	Thimble	4	Ratchet	6	Locking lever

on the thimble will be in graduations of 0.01 mm (or as marked on the frame) - one full revolution of the thimble will move 0.5 mm on the linear scale. Take the reading where the datum line on the sleeve intersects the thimble's scale. Always position the eye directly above the scale otherwise an inaccurate reading will result.

In the example shown the item measures 2.95 mm **(see illustration 3.4)**:

Linear scale	2.00 mm
Linear scale	0.50 mm
Annular scale	0.45 mm
Total figure	**2.95 mm**

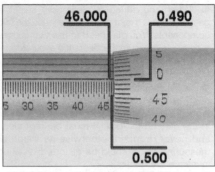

3.5 Micrometer reading of 46.99 mm on linear and annular scales . . .

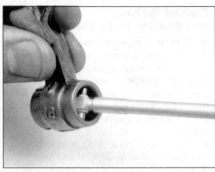

3.7 Expand the telescoping gauge in the bore, lock its position . . .

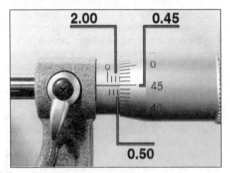

3.4 Micrometer reading of 2.95 mm

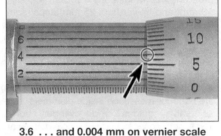

3.6 . . . and 0.004 mm on vernier scale

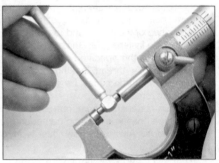

3.8 . . . then measure the gauge with a micrometer

Most micrometers have a locking lever (6) on the frame to hold the setting in place, allowing the item to be removed from the micrometer.
● Some micrometers have a vernier scale on their sleeve, providing an even finer measurement to be taken, in 0.001 increments of a millimetre. Take the sleeve and thimble measurement as described above, then check which graduation on the vernier scale aligns with that of the annular scale on the thimble **Note:** *The eye must be perpendicular to the scale when taking the vernier reading - if necessary rotate the body of the micrometer to ensure this.* Multiply the vernier scale figure by 0.001 and add it to the base and fine measurement figures.

In the example shown the item measures 46.994 mm **(see illustrations 3.5 and 3.6)**:

Linear scale (base)	46.000 mm
Linear scale (base)	00.500 mm
Annular scale (fine)	00.490 mm
Vernier scale	00.004 mm
Total figure	**46.994 mm**

Internal micrometer

● Internal micrometers are available for measuring bore diameters, but are expensive and unlikely to be available for home use. It is suggested that a set of telescoping gauges and small hole gauges, both of which must be used with an external micrometer, will suffice for taking internal measurements on a motorcycle.
● Telescoping gauges can be used to

measure internal diameters of components. Select a gauge with the correct size range, make sure its ends are clean and insert it into the bore. Expand the gauge, then lock its position and withdraw it from the bore **(see illustration 3.7)**. Measure across the gauge ends with a micrometer **(see illustration 3.8)**.
● Very small diameter bores (such as valve guides) are measured with a small hole gauge. Once adjusted to a slip-fit inside the component, its position is locked and the gauge withdrawn for measurement with a micrometer **(see illustrations 3.9 and 3.10)**.

Vernier caliper

Note: *The conventional linear and dial gauge type instruments are described. Digital types are easier to read, but are far more expensive.*
● The vernier caliper does not provide the precision of a micrometer, but is versatile in being able to measure internal and external diameters. Some types also incorporate a depth gauge. It is ideal for measuring clutch plate friction material and spring free lengths.
● To use the conventional linear scale vernier, slacken off the vernier clamp screws (1) and set its jaws over (2), or inside (3), the item to be measured **(see illustration 3.11)**. Slide the jaw into contact, using the thumb-wheel (4) for fine movement of the sliding scale (5) then tighten the clamp screws (1). Read off the main scale (6) where the zero on the sliding scale (5) intersects it, taking the whole number to the left of the zero; this provides the base measurement. View along the sliding scale and select the division which

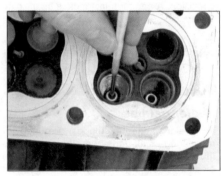

3.9 Expand the small hole gauge in the bore, lock its position . . .

3.10 . . . then measure the gauge with a micrometer

lines up exactly with any of the divisions on the main scale, noting that the divisions usually represents 0.02 of a millimetre. Add this fine measurement to the base measurement to obtain the total reading.

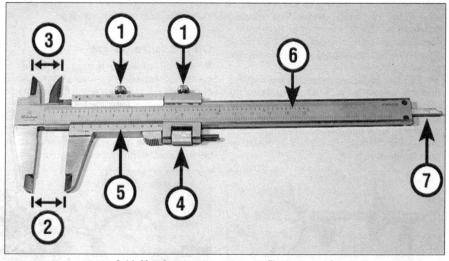

3.11 Vernier component parts (linear gauge)

1 Clamp screws 3 Internal jaws 5 Sliding scale 7 Depth gauge
2 External jaws 4 Thumbwheel 6 Main scale

In the example shown the item measures 55.92 mm **(see illustration 3.12)**:

Base measurement	55.00 mm
Fine measurement	00.92 mm
Total figure	**55.92 mm**

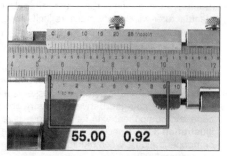

3.12 Vernier gauge reading of 55.92 mm

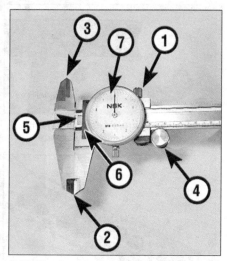

3.13 Vernier component parts (dial gauge)

1 Clamp screw 5 Main scale
2 External jaws 6 Sliding scale
3 Internal jaws 7 Dial gauge
4 Thumbwheel

● Some vernier calipers are equipped with a dial gauge for fine measurement. Before use, check that the jaws are clean, then close them fully and check that the dial gauge reads zero. If necessary adjust the gauge ring accordingly. Slacken the vernier clamp screw (1) and set its jaws over (2), or inside (3), the item to be measured **(see illustration 3.13)**. Slide the jaws into contact, using the thumbwheel (4) for fine movement. Read off the main scale (5) where the edge of the sliding scale (6) intersects it, taking the whole number to the left of the zero; this provides the base measurement. Read off the needle position on the dial gauge (7) scale to provide the fine measurement; each division represents 0.05 of a millimetre. Add this fine measurement to the base measurement to obtain the total reading.

In the example shown the item measures 55.95 mm **(see illustration 3.14)**:

Base measurement	55.00 mm
Fine measurement	00.95 mm
Total figure	**55.95 mm**

3.14 Vernier gauge reading of 55.95 mm

Plastigauge

● Plastigauge is a plastic material which can be compressed between two surfaces to measure the oil clearance between them. The width of the compressed Plastigauge is measured against a calibrated scale to determine the clearance.

● Common uses of Plastigauge are for measuring the clearance between crankshaft journal and main bearing inserts, between crankshaft journal and big-end bearing inserts, and between camshaft and bearing surfaces. The following example describes big-end oil clearance measurement.

● Handle the Plastigauge material carefully to prevent distortion. Using a sharp knife, cut a length which corresponds with the width of the bearing being measured and place it carefully across the journal so that it is parallel with the shaft **(see illustration 3.15)**. Carefully install both bearing shells and the connecting rod. Without rotating the rod on the journal tighten its bolts or nuts (as applicable) to the specified torque. The connecting rod and bearings are then disassembled and the crushed Plastigauge examined.

3.15 Plastigauge placed across shaft journal

● Using the scale provided in the Plastigauge kit, measure the width of the material to determine the oil clearance **(see illustration 3.16)**. Always remove all traces of Plastigauge after use using your fingernails.

Caution: Arriving at the correct clearance demands that the assembly is torqued correctly, according to the settings and sequence (where applicable) provided by the motorcycle manufacturer.

3.16 Measuring the width of the crushed Plastigauge

Dial gauge or DTI (Dial Test Indicator)

● A dial gauge can be used to accurately measure small amounts of movement. Typical uses are measuring shaft runout or shaft endfloat (sideplay) and setting piston position for ignition timing on two-strokes. A dial gauge set usually comes with a range of different probes and adapters and mounting equipment.

● The gauge needle must point to zero when at rest. Rotate the ring around its periphery to zero the gauge.

● Check that the gauge is capable of reading the extent of movement in the work. Most gauges have a small dial set in the face which records whole millimetres of movement as well as the fine scale around the face periphery which is calibrated in 0.01 mm divisions. Read off the small dial first to obtain the base measurement, then add the measurement from the fine scale to obtain the total reading.

In the example shown the gauge reads 1.48 mm **(see illustration 3.17)**:

Base measurement	1.00 mm
Fine measurement	0.48 mm
Total figure	**1.48 mm**

3.17 Dial gauge reading of 1.48 mm

● If measuring shaft runout, the shaft must be supported in vee-blocks and the gauge mounted on a stand perpendicular to the shaft. Rest the tip of the gauge against the centre of the shaft and rotate the shaft slowly whilst watching the gauge reading **(see illustration 3.18)**. Take several measurements along the length of the shaft and record the

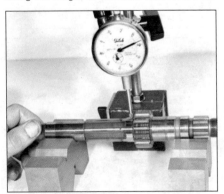

3.18 Using a dial gauge to measure shaft runout

maximum gauge reading as the amount of runout in the shaft. **Note:** *The reading obtained will be total runout at that point - some manufacturers specify that the runout figure is halved to compare with their specified runout limit.*

● Endfloat (sideplay) measurement requires that the gauge is mounted securely to the surrounding component with its probe touching the end of the shaft. Using hand pressure, push and pull on the shaft noting the maximum endfloat recorded on the gauge **(see illustration 3.19)**.

3.19 Using a dial gauge to measure shaft endfloat

● A dial gauge with suitable adapters can be used to determine piston position BTDC on two-stroke engines for the purposes of ignition timing. The gauge, adapter and suitable length probe are installed in the place of the spark plug and the gauge zeroed at TDC. If the piston position is specified as 1.14 mm BTDC, rotate the engine back to 2.00 mm BTDC, then slowly forwards to 1.14 mm BTDC.

Cylinder compression gauges

● A compression gauge is used for measuring cylinder compression. Either the rubber-cone type or the threaded adapter type can be used. The latter is preferred to ensure a perfect seal against the cylinder head. A 0 to 300 psi (0 to 20 Bar) type gauge (for petrol/gasoline engines) will be suitable for motorcycles.

● The spark plug is removed and the gauge either held hard against the cylinder head (cone type) or the gauge adapter screwed into the cylinder head (threaded type) **(see illustration 3.20)**. Cylinder compression is measured with the engine turning over, but not running - carry out the compression test as described in

3.20 Using a rubber-cone type cylinder compression gauge

Fault Finding Equipment. The gauge will hold the reading until manually released.

Oil pressure gauge

● An oil pressure gauge is used for measuring engine oil pressure. Most gauges come with a set of adapters to fit the thread of the take-off point **(see illustration 3.21)**. If the take-off point specified by the motorcycle manufacturer is an external oil pipe union, make sure that the specified replacement union is used to prevent oil starvation.

3.21 Oil pressure gauge and take-off point adapter (arrow)

● Oil pressure is measured with the engine running (at a specific rpm) and often the manufacturer will specify pressure limits for a cold and hot engine.

Straight-edge and surface plate

● If checking the gasket face of a component for warpage, place a steel rule or precision straight-edge across the gasket face and measure any gap between the straight-edge and component with feeler gauges **(see illustration 3.22)**. Check diagonally across the component and between mounting holes **(see illustration 3.23)**.

3.22 Use a straight-edge and feeler gauges to check for warpage

3.23 Check for warpage in these directions

- Checking individual components for warpage, such as clutch plain (metal) plates, requires a perfectly flat plate or piece or plate glass and feeler gauges.

4 Torque and leverage

What is torque?

- Torque describes the twisting force about a shaft. The amount of torque applied is determined by the distance from the centre of the shaft to the end of the lever and the amount of force being applied to the end of the lever; distance multiplied by force equals torque.
- The manufacturer applies a measured torque to a bolt or nut to ensure that it will not slacken in use and to hold two components securely together without movement in the joint. The actual torque setting depends on the thread size, bolt or nut material and the composition of the components being held.
- Too little torque may cause the fastener to loosen due to vibration, whereas too much torque will distort the joint faces of the component or cause the fastener to shear off. Always stick to the specified torque setting.

Using a torque wrench

- Check the calibration of the torque wrench and make sure it has a suitable range for the job. Torque wrenches are available in Nm (Newton-metres), kgf m (kilograms-force metre), lbf ft (pounds-feet), lbf in (inch-pounds). Do not confuse lbf ft with lbf in.
- Adjust the tool to the desired torque on the scale (see illustration 4.1). If your torque wrench is not calibrated in the units specified, carefully convert the figure (see Conversion Factors). A manufacturer sometimes gives a torque setting as a range (8 to 10 Nm) rather than a single figure - in this case set the tool midway between the two settings. The same torque may be expressed as 9 Nm ± 1 Nm. Some torque wrenches have a method of locking the setting so that it isn't inadvertently altered during use.

4.1 Set the torque wrench index mark to the setting required, in this case 12 Nm

- Install the bolts/nuts in their correct location and secure them lightly. Their threads must be clean and free of any old locking compound. Unless specified the threads and flange should be dry - oiled threads are necessary in certain circumstances and the manufacturer will take this into account in the specified torque figure. Similarly, the manufacturer may also specify the application of thread-locking compound.
- Tighten the fasteners in the specified sequence until the torque wrench clicks, indicating that the torque setting has been reached. Apply the torque again to double-check the setting. Where different thread diameter fasteners secure the component, as a rule tighten the larger diameter ones first.
- When the torque wrench has been finished with, release the lock (where applicable) and fully back off its setting to zero - do not leave the torque wrench tensioned. Also, do not use a torque wrench for slackening a fastener.

Angle-tightening

- Manufacturers often specify a figure in degrees for final tightening of a fastener. This usually follows tightening to a specific torque setting.
- A degree disc can be set and attached to the socket (see illustration 4.2) or a protractor can be used to mark the angle of movement on the bolt/nut head and the surrounding casting (see illustration 4.3).

4.2 Angle tightening can be accomplished with a torque-angle gauge . . .

4.3 . . . or by marking the angle on the surrounding component

Loosening sequences

- Where more than one bolt/nut secures a component, loosen each fastener evenly a little at a time. In this way, not all the stress of the joint is held by one fastener and the components are not likely to distort.
- If a tightening sequence is provided, work in the REVERSE of this, but if not, work from the outside in, in a criss-cross sequence (see illustration 4.4).

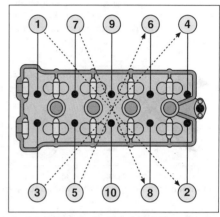

4.4 When slackening, work from the outside inwards

Tightening sequences

- If a component is held by more than one fastener it is important that the retaining bolts/nuts are tightened evenly to prevent uneven stress build-up and distortion of sealing faces. This is especially important on high-compression joints such as the cylinder head.
- A sequence is usually provided by the manufacturer, either in a diagram or actually marked in the casting. If not, always start in the centre and work outwards in a criss-cross pattern (see illustration 4.5). Start off by securing all bolts/nuts finger-tight, then set the torque wrench and tighten each fastener by a small amount in sequence until the final torque is reached. By following this practice,

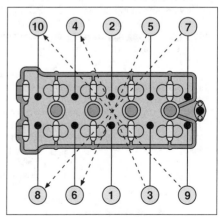

4.5 When tightening, work from the inside outwards

the joint will be held evenly and will not be distorted. Important joints, such as the cylinder head and big-end fasteners often have two- or three-stage torque settings.

Applying leverage

● Use tools at the correct angle. Position a socket wrench or spanner on the bolt/nut so that you pull it towards you when loosening. If this can't be done, push the spanner without curling your fingers around it **(see illustration 4.6)** - the spanner may slip or the fastener loosen suddenly, resulting in your fingers being crushed against a component.

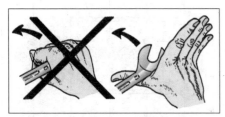

4.6 If you can't pull on the spanner to loosen a fastener, push with your hand open

● Additional leverage is gained by extending the length of the lever. The best way to do this is to use a breaker bar instead of the regular length tool, or to slip a length of tubing over the end of the spanner or socket wrench.
● If additional leverage will not work, the fastener head is either damaged or firmly corroded in place (see *Fasteners*).

5 Bearings

Bearing removal and installation

Drivers and sockets

● Before removing a bearing, always inspect the casing to see which way it must be driven out - some casings will have retaining plates or a cast step. Also check for any identifying markings on the bearing and if installed to a certain depth, measure this at this stage. Some roller bearings are sealed on one side - take note of the original fitted position.
● Bearings can be driven out of a casing using a bearing driver tool (with the correct size head) or a socket of the correct diameter. Select the driver head or socket so that it contacts the outer race of the bearing, not the balls/rollers or inner race. Always support the casing around the bearing housing with wood blocks, otherwise there is a risk of fracture. The bearing is driven out with a few blows on the driver or socket from a heavy mallet. Unless access is severely restricted (as with wheel bearings), a pin-punch is not recommended unless it is moved around the bearing to keep it square in its housing.

● The same equipment can be used to install bearings. Make sure the bearing housing is supported on wood blocks and line up the bearing in its housing. Fit the bearing as noted on removal - generally they are installed with their marked side facing outwards. Tap the bearing squarely into its housing using a driver or socket which bears only on the bearing's outer race - contact with the bearing balls/rollers or inner race will destroy it **(see illustrations 5.1 and 5.2)**.
● Check that the bearing inner race and balls/rollers rotate freely.

5.1 Using a bearing driver against the bearing's outer race

5.2 Using a large socket against the bearing's outer race

Pullers and slide-hammers

● Where a bearing is pressed on a shaft a puller will be required to extract it **(see illustration 5.3)**. Make sure that the puller clamp or legs fit securely behind the bearing and are unlikely to slip out. If pulling a bearing

5.3 This bearing puller clamps behind the bearing and pressure is applied to the shaft end to draw the bearing off

off a gear shaft for example, you may have to locate the puller behind a gear pinion if there is no access to the race and draw the gear pinion off the shaft as well **(see illustration 5.4)**.

> *Caution: Ensure that the puller's centre bolt locates securely against the end of the shaft and will not slip when pressure is applied. Also ensure that puller does not damage the shaft end.*

5.4 Where no access is available to the rear of the bearing, it is sometimes possible to draw off the adjacent component

● Operate the puller so that its centre bolt exerts pressure on the shaft end and draws the bearing off the shaft.
● When installing the bearing on the shaft, tap only on the bearing's inner race - contact with the balls/rollers or outer race with destroy the bearing. Use a socket or length of tubing as a drift which fits over the shaft end **(see illustration 5.5)**.

5.5 When installing a bearing on a shaft use a piece of tubing which bears only on the bearing's inner race

● Where a bearing locates in a blind hole in a casing, it cannot be driven or pulled out as described above. A slide-hammer with knife-edged bearing puller attachment will be required. The puller attachment passes through the bearing and when tightened expands to fit firmly behind the bearing **(see illustration 5.6)**. By operating the slide-hammer part of the tool the bearing is jarred out of its housing **(see illustration 5.7)**.
● It is possible, if the bearing is of reasonable weight, for it to drop out of its housing if the casing is heated as described opposite. If this

5.6 Expand the bearing puller so that it locks behind the bearing . . .

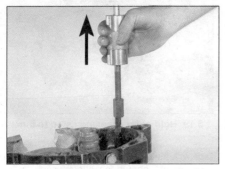

5.7 . . . attach the slide hammer to the bearing puller

method is attempted, first prepare a work surface which will enable the casing to be tapped face down to help dislodge the bearing - a wood surface is ideal since it will not damage the casing's gasket surface. Wearing protective gloves, tap the heated casing several times against the work surface to dislodge the bearing under its own weight **(see illustration 5.8)**.

5.8 Tapping a casing face down on wood blocks can often dislodge a bearing

● Bearings can be installed in blind holes using the driver or socket method described above.

Drawbolts

● Where a bearing or bush is set in the eye of a component, such as a suspension linkage arm or connecting rod small-end, removal by drift may damage the component. Furthermore, a rubber bushing in a shock absorber eye cannot successfully be driven out of position. If access is available to a engineering press, the task is straightforward. If not, a drawbolt can be fabricated to extract the bearing or bush.

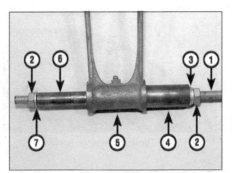

5.9 Drawbolt component parts assembled on a suspension arm

1 Bolt or length of threaded bar
2 Nuts
3 Washer (external diameter greater than tubing internal diameter)
4 Tubing (internal diameter sufficient to accommodate bearing)
5 Suspension arm with bearing
6 Tubing (external diameter slightly smaller than bearing)
7 Washer (external diameter slightly smaller than bearing)

5.10 Drawing the bearing out of the suspension arm

● To extract the bearing/bush you will need a long bolt with nut (or piece of threaded bar with two nuts), a piece of tubing which has an internal diameter larger than the bearing/bush, another piece of tubing which has an external diameter slightly smaller than the bearing/bush, and a selection of washers **(see illustrations 5.9 and 5.10)**. Note that the pieces of tubing must be of the same length, or longer, than the bearing/bush.
● The same kit (without the pieces of tubing) can be used to draw the new bearing/bush back into place **(see illustration 5.11)**.

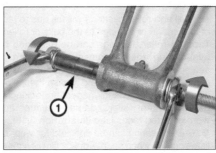

5.11 Installing a new bearing (1) in the suspension arm

Temperature change

● If the bearing's outer race is a tight fit in the casing, the aluminium casing can be heated to release its grip on the bearing. Aluminium will expand at a greater rate than the steel bearing outer race. There are several ways to do this, but avoid any localised extreme heat (such as a blow torch) - aluminium alloy has a low melting point.
● Approved methods of heating a casing are using a domestic oven (heated to 100°C) or immersing the casing in boiling water **(see illustration 5.12)**. Low temperature range localised heat sources such as a paint stripper heat gun or clothes iron can also be used **(see illustration 5.13)**. Alternatively, soak a rag in boiling water, wring it out and wrap it around the bearing housing.

> ⚠ **Warning: All of these methods require care in use to prevent scalding and burns to the hands. Wear protective gloves when handling hot components.**

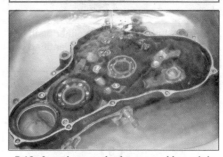

5.12 A casing can be immersed in a sink of boiling water to aid bearing removal

5.13 Using a localised heat source to aid bearing removal

● If heating the whole casing note that plastic components, such as the neutral switch, may suffer - remove them beforehand.
● After heating, remove the bearing as described above. You may find that the expansion is sufficient for the bearing to fall out of the casing under its own weight or with a light tap on the driver or socket.
● If necessary, the casing can be heated to aid bearing installation, and this is sometimes the recommended procedure if the motorcycle manufacturer has designed the housing and bearing fit with this intention.

● Installation of bearings can be eased by placing them in a freezer the night before installation. The steel bearing will contract slightly, allowing easy insertion in its housing. This is often useful when installing steering head outer races in the frame.

Bearing types and markings

● Plain shell bearings, ball bearings, needle roller bearings and tapered roller bearings will all be found on motorcycles (see illustrations 5.14 and 5.15). The ball and roller types are usually caged between an inner and outer race, but uncaged variations may be found.

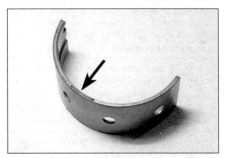

5.14 Shell bearings are either plain or grooved. They are usually identified by colour code (arrow)

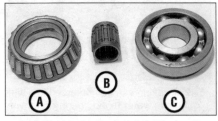

5.15 Tapered roller bearing (A), needle roller bearing (B) and ball journal bearing (C)

● Shell bearings (often called inserts) are usually found at the crankshaft main and connecting rod big-end where they are good at coping with high loads. They are made of a phosphor-bronze material and are impregnated with self-lubricating properties.

● Ball bearings and needle roller bearings consist of a steel inner and outer race with the balls or rollers between the races. They require constant lubrication by oil or grease and are good at coping with axial loads. Taper roller bearings consist of rollers set in a tapered cage set on the inner race; the outer race is separate. They are good at coping with axial loads and prevent movement along the shaft - a typical application is in the steering head.

● Bearing manufacturers produce bearings to ISO size standards and stamp one face of the bearing to indicate its internal and external diameter, load capacity and type (see illustration 5.16).

● Metal bushes are usually of phosphor-bronze material. Rubber bushes are used in suspension mounting eyes. Fibre bushes have also been used in suspension pivots.

5.16 Typical bearing marking

Bearing fault finding

● If a bearing outer race has spun in its housing, the housing material will be damaged. You can use a bearing locking compound to bond the outer race in place if damage is not too severe.

● Shell bearings will fail due to damage of their working surface, as a result of lack of lubrication, corrosion or abrasive particles in the oil (see illustration 5.17). Small particles of dirt in the oil may embed in the bearing material whereas larger particles will score the bearing and shaft journal. If a number of short journeys are made, insufficient heat will be generated to drive off condensation which has built up on the bearings.

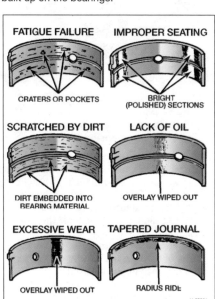

5.17 Typical bearing failures

● Ball and roller bearings will fail due to lack of lubrication or damage to the balls or rollers. Tapered-roller bearings can be damaged by overloading them. Unless the bearing is sealed on both sides, wash it in paraffin (kerosene) to remove all old grease then allow it to dry. Make a visual inspection looking to dented balls or rollers, damaged cages and worn or pitted races (see illustration 5.18).

● A ball bearing can be checked for wear by listening to it when spun. Apply a film of light oil to the bearing and hold it close to the ear - hold the outer race with one hand and spin the inner

5.18 Example of ball journal bearing with damaged balls and cages

5.19 Hold outer race and listen to inner race when spun

race with the other hand (see illustration 5.19). The bearing should be almost silent when spun; if it grates or rattles it is worn.

6 Oil seals

Oil seal removal and installation

● Oil seals should be renewed every time a component is dismantled. This is because the seal lips will become set to the sealing surface and will not necessarily reseal.

● Oil seals can be prised out of position using a large flat-bladed screwdriver (see illustration 6.1). In the case of crankcase seals, check first that the seal is not lipped on the inside, preventing its removal with the crankcases joined.

6.1 Prise out oil seals with a large flat-bladed screwdriver

● New seals are usually installed with their marked face (containing the seal reference code) outwards and the spring side towards the fluid being retained. In certain cases, such as a two-stroke engine crankshaft seal, a double lipped seal may be used due to there being fluid or gas on each side of the joint.

● Use a bearing driver or socket which bears only on the outer hard edge of the seal to install it in the casing - tapping on the inner edge will damage the sealing lip.

Oil seal types and markings

● Oil seals are usually of the single-lipped type. Double-lipped seals are found where a liquid or gas is on both sides of the joint.
● Oil seals can harden and lose their sealing ability if the motorcycle has been in storage for a long period - renewal is the only solution.
● Oil seal manufacturers also conform to the ISO markings for seal size - these are moulded into the outer face of the seal (see illustration 6.2).

6.2 These oil seal markings indicate inside diameter, outside diameter and seal thickness

7 Gaskets and sealants

Types of gasket and sealant

● Gaskets are used to seal the mating surfaces between components and keep lubricants, fluids, vacuum or pressure contained within the assembly. Aluminium gaskets are sometimes found at the cylinder joints, but most gaskets are paper-based. If the mating surfaces of the components being joined are undamaged the gasket can be installed dry, although a dab of sealant or grease will be useful to hold it in place during assembly.
● RTV (Room Temperature Vulcanising) silicone rubber sealants cure when exposed to moisture in the atmosphere. These sealants are good at filling pits or irregular gasket faces, but will tend to be forced out of the joint under very high torque. They can be used to replace a paper gasket, but first make sure that the width of the paper gasket is not essential to the shimming of internal components. RTV sealants should not be used on components containing petrol (gasoline).
● Non-hardening, semi-hardening and hard setting liquid gasket compounds can be used with a gasket or between a metal-to-metal joint. Select the sealant to suit the application: universal non-hardening sealant can be used on virtually all joints; semi-hardening on joint faces which are rough or damaged; hard setting sealant on joints which require a permanent bond and are subjected to high temperature and pressure. **Note:** *Check first if the paper gasket has a bead of sealant*

impregnated in its surface before applying additional sealant.
● When choosing a sealant, make sure it is suitable for the application, particularly if being applied in a high-temperature area or in the vicinity of fuel. Certain manufacturers produce sealants in either clear, silver or black colours to match the finish of the engine. This has a particular application on motorcycles where much of the engine is exposed.
● Do not over-apply sealant. That which is squeezed out on the outside of the joint can be wiped off, whereas an excess of sealant on the inside can break off and clog oilways.

Breaking a sealed joint

● Age, heat, pressure and the use of hard setting sealant can cause two components to stick together so tightly that they are difficult to separate using finger pressure alone. Do not resort to using levers unless there is a pry point provided for this purpose (see illustration 7.1) or else the gasket surfaces will be damaged.
● Use a soft-faced hammer (see illustration 7.2) or a wood block and conventional hammer to strike the component near the mating surface. Avoid hammering against cast extremities since they may break off. If this method fails, try using a wood wedge between the two components.

> **Caution: If the joint will not separate, double-check that you have removed all the fasteners.**

7.1 If a pry point is provided, apply gently pressure with a flat-bladed screwdriver

7.2 Tap around the joint with a soft-faced mallet if necessary - don't strike cooling fins

Removal of old gasket and sealant

● Paper gaskets will most likely come away complete, leaving only a few traces stuck on

Most components have one or two hollow locating dowels between the two gasket faces. If a dowel cannot be removed, do not resort to gripping it with pliers - it will almost certainly be distorted. Install a close-fitting socket or Phillips screwdriver into the dowel and then grip the outer edge of the dowel to free it.

the sealing faces of the components. It is imperative that all traces are removed to ensure correct sealing of the new gasket.
● Very carefully scrape all traces of gasket away making sure that the sealing surfaces are not gouged or scored by the scraper (see illustrations 7.3, 7.4 and 7.5). Stubborn deposits can be removed by spraying with an aerosol gasket remover. Final preparation of

7.3 Paper gaskets can be scraped off with a gasket scraper tool . . .

7.4 . . . a knife blade . . .

7.5 . . . or a household scraper

7.6 Fine abrasive paper is wrapped around a flat file to clean up the gasket face

7.7 A kitchen scourer can be used on stubborn deposits

the gasket surface can be made with very fine abrasive paper or a plastic kitchen scourer **(see illustrations 7.6 and 7.7).**

● Old sealant can be scraped or peeled off components, depending on the type originally used. Note that gasket removal compounds are available to avoid scraping the components clean; make sure the gasket remover suits the type of sealant used.

8 Chains

Breaking and joining final drive chains

● Drive chains for all but small bikes are continuous and do not have a clip-type connecting link. The chain must be broken using a chain breaker tool and the new chain securely riveted together using a new soft rivet-type link. Never use a clip-type connecting link instead of a rivet-type link, except in an emergency. Various chain breaking and riveting tools are available, either as separate tools or combined as illustrated in the accompanying photographs - read the instructions supplied with the tool carefully.

> ⚠ **Warning: The need to rivet the new link pins correctly cannot be overstressed - loss of control of the motorcycle is very likely to result if the chain breaks in use.**

● Rotate the chain and look for the soft link. The soft link pins look like they have been

8.1 Tighten the chain breaker to push the pin out of the link . . .

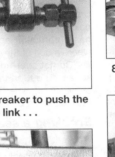

8.2 . . . withdraw the pin, remove the tool . . .

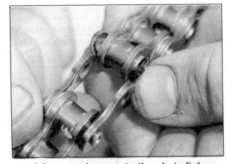

8.3 . . . and separate the chain link

deeply centre-punched instead of peened over like all the other pins **(see illustration 8.9)** and its sideplate may be a different colour. Position the soft link midway between the sprockets and assemble the chain breaker tool over one of the soft link pins **(see illustration 8.1).** Operate the tool to push the pin out through the chain **(see illustration 8.2).** On an O-ring chain, remove the O-rings **(see illustration 8.3).** Carry out the same procedure on the other soft link pin.

> **Caution: Certain soft link pins (particularly on the larger chains) may require their ends to be filed or ground off before they can be pressed out using the tool.**

● Check that you have the correct size and strength (standard or heavy duty) new soft link - do not reuse the old link. Look for the size marking on the chain sideplates **(see illustration 8.10).**

● Position the chain ends so that they are engaged over the rear sprocket. On an O-ring

8.4 Insert the new soft link, with O-rings, through the chain ends . . .

8.5 . . . install the O-rings over the pin ends . . .

8.6 . . . followed by the sideplate

chain, install a new O-ring over each pin of the link and insert the link through the two chain ends **(see illustration 8.4).** Install a new O-ring over the end of each pin, followed by the sideplate (with the chain manufacturer's marking facing outwards) **(see illustrations 8.5 and 8.6).** On an unsealed chain, insert the link through the two chain ends, then install the sideplate with the chain manufacturer's marking facing outwards.

● Note that it may not be possible to install the sideplate using finger pressure alone. If using a joining tool, assemble it so that the plates of the tool clamp the link and press the sideplate over the pins **(see illustration 8.7).** Otherwise, use two small sockets placed over

8.7 Push the sideplate into position using a clamp

8.8 Assemble the chain riveting tool over one pin at a time and tighten it fully

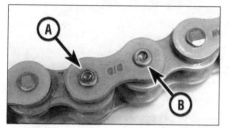

8.9 Pin end correctly riveted (A), pin end unriveted (B)

the rivet ends and two pieces of the wood between a G-clamp. Operate the clamp to press the sideplate over the pins.

● Assemble the joining tool over one pin (following the maker's instructions) and tighten the tool down to spread the pin end securely **(see illustrations 8.8 and 8.9)**. Do the same on the other pin.

> ⚠ **Warning: Check that the pin ends are secure and that there is no danger of the sideplate coming loose. If the pin ends are cracked the soft link must be renewed.**

Final drive chain sizing

● Chains are sized using a three digit number, followed by a suffix to denote the chain type **(see illustration 8.10)**. Chain type is either standard or heavy duty (thicker sideplates), and also unsealed or O-ring/X-ring type.

● The first digit of the number relates to the pitch of the chain, ie the distance from the centre of one pin to the centre of the next pin **(see illustration 8.11)**. Pitch is expressed in eighths of an inch, as follows:

8.10 Typical chain size and type marking

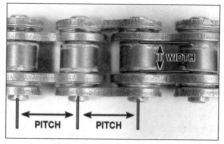

8.11 Chain dimensions

Sizes commencing with a 4 (eg 428) have a pitch of 1/2 inch (12.7 mm)
Sizes commencing with a 5 (eg 520) have a pitch of 5/8 inch (15.9 mm)
Sizes commencing with a 6 (eg 630) have a pitch of 3/4 inch (19.1 mm)

● The second and third digits of the chain size relate to the width of the rollers, again in imperial units, eg the 525 shown has 5/16 inch (7.94 mm) rollers **(see illustration 8.11)**.

9 Hoses

Clamping to prevent flow

● Small-bore flexible hoses can be clamped to prevent fluid flow whilst a component is worked on. Whichever method is used, ensure that the hose material is not permanently distorted or damaged by the clamp.

a) A brake hose clamp available from auto accessory shops **(see illustration 9.1)**.
b) A wingnut type hose clamp **(see illustration 9.2)**.

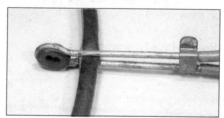

9.1 Hoses can be clamped with an automotive brake hose clamp . . .

9.2 . . . a wingnut type hose clamp . . .

c) Two sockets placed each side of the hose and held with straight-jawed self-locking grips **(see illustration 9.3)**.
d) Thick card each side of the hose held between straight-jawed self-locking grips **(see illustration 9.4)**.

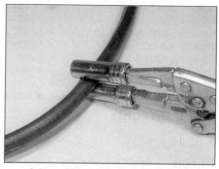

9.3 . . . two sockets and a pair of self-locking grips . . .

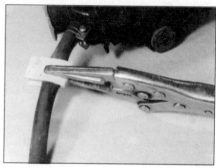

9.4 . . . or thick card and self-locking grips

Freeing and fitting hoses

● Always make sure the hose clamp is moved well clear of the hose end. Grip the hose with your hand and rotate it whilst pulling it off the union. If the hose has hardened due to age and will not move, slit it with a sharp knife and peel its ends off the union **(see illustration 9.5)**.

● Resist the temptation to use grease or soap on the unions to aid installation; although it helps the hose slip over the union it will equally aid the escape of fluid from the joint. It is preferable to soften the hose ends in hot water and wet the inside surface of the hose with water or a fluid which will evaporate.

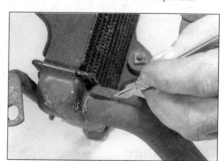

9.5 Cutting a coolant hose free with a sharp knife

Conversion Factors

Length (distance)

Inches (in)	x 25.4 = Millimetres (mm)	x 0.0394 = Inches (in)
Feet (ft)	x 0.305 = Metres (m)	x 3.281 = Feet (ft)
Miles	x 1.609 = Kilometres (km)	x 0.621 = Miles

Volume (capacity)

Cubic inches (cu in; in³)	x 16.387 = Cubic centimetres (cc; cm³)	x 0.061 = Cubic inches (cu in; in³)
Imperial pints (Imp pt)	x 0.568 = Litres (l)	x 1.76 = Imperial pints (Imp pt)
Imperial quarts (Imp qt)	x 1.137 = Litres (l)	x 0.88 = Imperial quarts (Imp qt)
Imperial quarts (Imp qt)	x 1.201 = US quarts (US qt)	x 0.833 = Imperial quarts (Imp qt)
US quarts (US qt)	x 0.946 = Litres (l)	x 1.057 = US quarts (US qt)
Imperial gallons (Imp gal)	x 4.546 = Litres (l)	x 0.22 = Imperial gallons (Imp gal)
Imperial gallons (Imp gal)	x 1.201 = US gallons (US gal)	x 0.833 = Imperial gallons (Imp gal)
US gallons (US gal)	x 3.785 = Litres (l)	x 0.264 = US gallons (US gal)

Mass (weight)

Ounces (oz)	x 28.35 = Grams (g)	x 0.035 = Ounces (oz)
Pounds (lb)	x 0.454 = Kilograms (kg)	x 2.205 = Pounds (lb)

Force

Ounces-force (ozf; oz)	x 0.278 = Newtons (N)	x 3.6 = Ounces-force (ozf; oz)
Pounds-force (lbf; lb)	x 4.448 = Newtons (N)	x 0.225 = Pounds-force (lbf; lb)
Newtons (N)	x 0.1 = Kilograms-force (kgf; kg)	x 9.81 = Newtons (N)

Pressure

Pounds-force per square inch (psi; lbf/in²; lb/in²)	x 0.070 = Kilograms-force per square centimetre (kgf/cm²; kg/cm²)	x 14.223 = Pounds-force per square inch (psi; lbf/in²; lb/in²)
Pounds-force per square inch (psi; lbf/in²; lb/in²)	x 0.068 = Atmospheres (atm)	x 14.696 = Pounds-force per square inch (psi; lbf/in²; lb/in²)
Pounds-force per square inch (psi; lbf/in²; lb/in²)	x 0.069 = Bars	x 14.5 = Pounds-force per square inch (psi; lbf/in²; lb/in²)
Pounds-force per square inch (psi; lbf/in²; lb/in²)	x 6.895 = Kilopascals (kPa)	x 0.145 = Pounds-force per square inch (psi; lbf/in²; lb/in²)
Kilopascals (kPa)	x 0.01 = Kilograms-force per square centimetre (kgf/cm²; kg/cm²)	x 98.1 = Kilopascals (kPa)
Millibar (mbar)	x 100 = Pascals (Pa)	x 0.01 = Millibar (mbar)
Millibar (mbar)	x 0.0145 = Pounds-force per square inch (psi; lbf/in²; lb/in²)	x 68.947 = Millibar (mbar)
Millibar (mbar)	x 0.75 = Millimetres of mercury (mmHg)	x 1.333 = Millibar (mbar)
Millibar (mbar)	x 0.401 = Inches of water (inH₂O)	x 2.491 = Millibar (mbar)
Millimetres of mercury (mmHg)	x 0.535 = Inches of water (inH₂O)	x 1.868 = Millimetres of mercury (mmHg)
Inches of water (inH₂O)	x 0.036 = Pounds-force per square inch (psi; lbf/in²; lb/in²)	x 27.68 = Inches of water (inH₂O)

Torque (moment of force)

Pounds-force inches (lbf in; lb in)	x 1.152 = Kilograms-force centimetre (kgf cm; kg cm)	x 0.868 = Pounds-force inches (lbf in; lb in)
Pounds-force inches (lbf in; lb in)	x 0.113 = Newton metres (Nm)	x 8.85 = Pounds-force inches (lbf in; lb in)
Pounds-force inches (lbf in; lb in)	x 0.083 = Pounds-force feet (lbf ft; lb ft)	x 12 = Pounds-force inches (lbf in; lb in)
Pounds-force feet (lbf ft; lb ft)	x 0.138 = Kilograms-force metres (kgf m; kg m)	x 7.233 = Pounds-force feet (lbf ft; lb ft)
Pounds-force feet (lbf ft; lb ft)	x 1.356 = Newton metres (Nm)	x 0.738 = Pounds-force feet (lbf ft; lb ft)
Newton metres (Nm)	x 0.102 = Kilograms-force metres (kgf m; kg m)	x 9.804 = Newton metres (Nm)

Power

Horsepower (hp)	x 745.7 = Watts (W)	x 0.0013 = Horsepower (hp)

Velocity (speed)

Miles per hour (miles/hr; mph)	x 1.609 = Kilometres per hour (km/hr; kph)	x 0.621 = Miles per hour (miles/hr; mph)

Fuel consumption*

Miles per gallon (mpg)	x 0.354 = Kilometres per litre (km/l)	x 2.825 = Miles per gallon (mpg)

Temperature

Degrees Fahrenheit = (°C x 1.8) + 32   Degrees Celsius (Degrees Centigrade; °C) = (°F - 32) x 0.56

It is common practice to convert from miles per gallon (mpg) to litres/100 kilometres (l/100km), where mpg x l/100 km = 282

A number of chemicals and lubricants are available for use in motorcycle maintenance and repair. They include a wide variety of products ranging from cleaning solvents and degreasers to lubricants and protective sprays for rubber, plastic and vinyl.

● **Contact point/spark plug cleaner** is a solvent used to clean oily film and dirt from points, grime from electrical connectors and oil deposits from spark plugs. It is oil free and leaves no residue. It can also be used to remove gum and varnish from carburettor jets and other orifices.

● **Carburettor cleaner** is similar to contact point/spark plug cleaner but it usually has a stronger solvent and may leave a slight oily reside. It is not recommended for cleaning electrical components or connections.

● **Brake system cleaner** is used to remove grease or brake fluid from brake system components (where clean surfaces are absolutely necessary and petroleum-based solvents cannot be used); it also leaves no residue.

● **Silicone-based lubricants** are used to protect rubber parts such as hoses and grommets, and are used as lubricants for hinges and locks.

● **Multi-purpose grease** is an all purpose lubricant used wherever grease is more practical than a liquid lubricant such as oil. Some multi-purpose grease is coloured white and specially formulated to be more resistant to water than ordinary grease.

● **Gear oil** (sometimes called gear lube) is a specially designed oil used in transmissions and final drive units, as well as other areas where high friction, high temperature lubrication is required. It is available in a number of viscosities (weights) for various applications.

● **Motor oil**, of course, is the lubricant specially formulated for use in the engine. It normally contains a wide variety of additives to prevent corrosion and reduce foaming and wear. Motor oil comes in various weights (viscosity ratings) of from 5 to 80. The recommended weight of the oil depends on the seasonal temperature and the demands on the engine. Light oil is used in cold climates and under light load conditions; heavy oil is used in hot climates and where high loads are encountered. Multi-viscosity oils are designed to have characteristics of both light and heavy oils and are available in a number of weights from 5W-20 to 20W-50.

● **Petrol additives** perform several functions, depending on their chemical makeup. They usually contain solvents that help dissolve gum and varnish that build up on carburettor and inlet parts. They also serve to break down carbon deposits that form on the inside surfaces of the combustion chambers. Some additives contain upper cylinder lubricants for valves and piston rings.

● **Brake and clutch fluid** is a specially formulated hydraulic fluid that can withstand the heat and pressure encountered in brake/clutch systems. Care must be taken that this fluid does not come in contact with painted surfaces or plastics. An opened container should always be resealed to prevent contamination by water or dirt.

● **Chain lubricants** are formulated especially for use on motorcycle final drive chains. A good chain lube should adhere well and have good penetrating qualities to be effective as a lubricant inside the chain and on the side plates, pins and rollers. Most chain lubes are either the foaming type or quick drying type and are usually marketed as sprays. Take care to use a lubricant marked as being suitable for O-ring chains.

● **Degreasers** are heavy duty solvents used to remove grease and grime that may accumulate on engine and frame components. They can be sprayed or brushed on and, depending on the type, are rinsed with either water or solvent.

● **Solvents** are used alone or in combination with degreasers to clean parts and assemblies during repair and overhaul. The home mechanic should use only solvents that are non-flammable and that do not produce irritating fumes.

● **Gasket sealing compounds** may be used in conjunction with gaskets, to improve their sealing capabilities, or alone, to seal metal-to-metal joints. Many gasket sealers can withstand extreme heat, some are impervious to petrol and lubricants, while others are capable of filling and sealing large cavities. Depending on the intended use, gasket sealers either dry hard or stay relatively soft and pliable. They are usually applied by hand, with a brush, or are sprayed on the gasket sealing surfaces.

● **Thread locking compound** is an adhesive locking compound that prevents threaded fasteners from loosening because of vibration. It is available in a variety of types for different applications.

● **Moisture dispersants** are usually sprays that can be used to dry out electrical components such as the fuse block and wiring connectors. Some types can also be used as treatment for rubber and as a lubricant for hinges, cables and locks.

● **Waxes and polishes** are used to help protect painted and plated surfaces from the weather. Different types of paint may require the use of different types of wax polish. Some polishes utilise a chemical or abrasive cleaner to help remove the top layer of oxidised (dull) paint on older vehicles. In recent years, many non-wax polishes (that contain a wide variety of chemicals such as polymers and silicones) have been introduced. These non-wax polishes are usually easier to apply and last longer than conventional waxes and polishes.

About the MOT Test

In the UK, all vehicles more than three years old are subject to an annual test to ensure that they meet minimum safety requirements. A current test certificate must be issued before a machine can be used on public roads, and is required before a road fund licence can be issued. Riding without a current test certificate will also invalidate your insurance.

For most owners, the MOT test is an annual cause for anxiety, and this is largely due to owners not being sure what needs to be checked prior to submitting the motorcycle for testing. The simple answer is that a fully roadworthy motorcycle will have no difficulty in passing the test.

This is a guide to getting your motorcycle through the MOT test. Obviously it will not be possible to examine the motorcycle to the same standard as the professional MOT tester, particularly in view of the equipment required for some of the checks. However, working through the following procedures will enable you to identify any problem areas before submitting the motorcycle for the test.

It has only been possible to summarise the test requirements here, based on the regulations in force at the time of printing. Test standards are becoming increasingly stringent, although there are some exemptions for older vehicles. More information about the MOT test can be obtained from the TSO publications, *How Safe is your Motorcycle* and *The MOT Inspection Manual for Motorcycle Testing*.

Many of the checks require that one of the wheels is raised off the ground. If the motorcycle doesn't have a centre stand, note that an auxiliary stand will be required. Additionally, the help of an assistant may prove useful.

Certain exceptions apply to machines under 50 cc, machines without a lighting system, and Classic bikes - if in doubt about any of the requirements listed below seek confirmation from an MOT tester prior to submitting the motorcycle for the test.

Check that the frame number is clearly visible.

> **HAYNES HINT**
> *If a component is in borderline condition, the tester has discretion in deciding whether to pass or fail it. If the motorcycle presented is clean and evidently well cared for, the tester may be more inclined to pass a borderline component than if the motorcycle is scruffy and apparently neglected.*

Electrical System

Lights, turn signals, horn and reflector

✔ With the ignition on, check the operation of the following electrical components. **Note:** *The electrical components on certain small-capacity machines are powered by the generator, requiring that the engine is run for this check.*

a) Headlight and tail light. Check that both illuminate in the low and high beam switch positions.

b) Position lights. Check that the front position (or sidelight) and tail light illuminate in this switch position.

c) Turn signals. Check that all flash at the correct rate, and that the warning light(s) function correctly. Check that the turn signal switch works correctly.

d) Hazard warning system (where fitted). Check that all four turn signals flash in this switch position.

e) Brake stop light. Check that the light comes on when the front and rear brakes are independently applied. Models first used on or after 1st April 1986 must have a brake light switch on each brake.

f) Horn. Check that the sound is continuous and of reasonable volume.

✔ Check that there is a red reflector on the rear of the machine, either mounted separately or as part of the tail light lens.

✔ Check the condition of the headlight, tail light and turn signal lenses.

Headlight beam height

✔ The MOT tester will perform a headlight beam height check using specialised beam setting equipment **(see illustration 1)**. This equipment will not be available to the home mechanic, but if you suspect that the headlight is incorrectly set or may have been maladjusted in the past, you can perform a rough test as follows.

✔ Position the bike in a straight line facing a brick wall. The bike must be off its stand, upright and with a rider seated. Measure the height from the ground to the centre of the headlight and mark a horizontal line on the wall at this height. Position the motorcycle 3.8 metres from the wall and draw a vertical

Headlight beam height checking equipment

line up the wall central to the centreline of the motorcycle. Switch to dipped beam and check that the beam pattern falls slightly lower than the horizontal line and to the left of the vertical line **(see illustration 2)**.

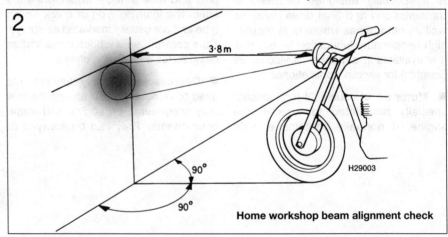

3·8 m

90°

90°

H29003

Home workshop beam alignment check

Exhaust System and Final Drive

Exhaust

✔ Check that the exhaust mountings are secure and that the system does not foul any of the rear suspension components.
✔ Start the motorcycle. When the revs are increased, check that the exhaust is neither holed nor leaking from any of its joints. On a linked system, check that the collector box is not leaking due to corrosion.

✔ Note that the exhaust decibel level ("loudness" of the exhaust) is assessed at the discretion of the tester. If the motorcycle was first used on or after 1st January 1985 the silencer must carry the BSAU 193 stamp, or a marking relating to its make and model, or be of OE (original equipment) manufacture. If the silencer is marked NOT FOR ROAD USE, RACING USE ONLY or similar, it will fail the MOT.

Final drive

✔ On chain or belt drive machines, check that the chain/belt is in good condition and does not have excessive slack. Also check that the sprocket is securely mounted on the rear wheel hub. Check that the chain/belt guard is in place.
✔ On shaft drive bikes, check for oil leaking from the drive unit and fouling the rear tyre.

Steering and Suspension

Steering

✔ With the front wheel raised off the ground, rotate the steering from lock to lock. The handlebar or switches must not contact the fuel tank or be close enough to trap the rider's hand. Problems can be caused by damaged lock stops on the lower yoke and frame, or by the fitting of non-standard handlebars.
✔ When performing the lock to lock check, also ensure that the steering moves freely without drag or notchiness. Steering movement can be impaired by poorly routed cables, or by overtight head bearings or worn bearings. The tester will perform a check of the steering head bearing lower race by mounting the front wheel on a surface plate, then performing a lock to

lock check with the weight of the machine on the lower bearing (see illustration 3).
✔ Grasp the fork sliders (lower legs) and attempt to push and pull on the forks (see

Front wheel mounted on a surface plate for steering head bearing lower race check

illustration 4). Any play in the steering head bearings will be felt. Note that in extreme cases, wear of the front fork bushes can be misinterpreted for head bearing play.
✔ Check that the handlebars are securely mounted.
✔ Check that the handlebar grip rubbers are secure. They should by bonded to the bar left end and to the throttle cable pulley on the right end.

Front suspension

✔ With the motorcycle off the stand, hold the front brake on and pump the front forks up and down (see illustration 5). Check that they are adequately damped.

Checking the steering head bearings for freeplay

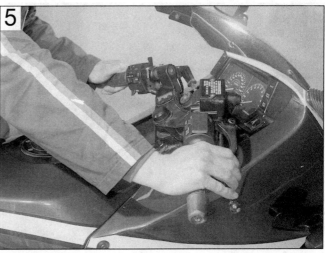

Hold the front brake on and pump the front forks up and down to check operation

Inspect the area around the fork dust seal for oil leakage (arrow)

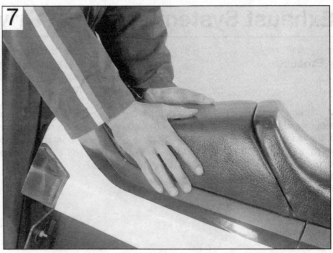

Bounce the rear of the motorcycle to check rear suspension operation

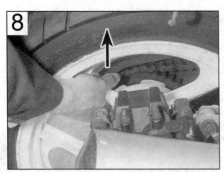

Checking for rear suspension linkage play

✔ Inspect the area above and around the front fork oil seals **(see illustration 6)**. There should be no sign of oil on the fork tube (stanchion) nor leaking down the slider (lower leg). On models so equipped, check that there is no oil leaking from the anti-dive units.

✔ On models with swingarm front suspension, check that there is no freeplay in the linkage when moved from side to side.

Rear suspension

✔ With the motorcycle off the stand and an assistant supporting the motorcycle by its handlebars, bounce the rear suspension **(see illustration 7)**. Check that the suspension components do not foul on any of the cycle parts and check that the shock absorber(s) provide adequate damping.

✔ Visually inspect the shock absorber(s) and check that there is no sign of oil leakage from its damper. This is somewhat restricted on certain single shock models due to the location of the shock absorber.

✔ With the rear wheel raised off the ground, grasp the wheel at the highest point and attempt to pull it up **(see illustration 8)**. Any play in the swingarm pivot or suspension linkage bearings will be felt as movement. **Note:** *Do not confuse play with actual suspension movement.* Failure to lubricate suspension linkage bearings can lead to bearing failure **(see illustration 9)**.

✔ With the rear wheel raised off the ground, grasp the swingarm ends and attempt to move the swingarm from side to side and forwards and backwards - any play indicates wear of the swingarm pivot bearings **(see illustration 10)**.

Worn suspension linkage pivots (arrows) are usually the cause of play in the rear suspension

Grasp the swingarm at the ends to check for play in its pivot bearings

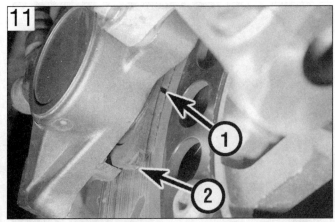

Brake pad wear can usually be viewed without removing the caliper. Most pads have wear indicator grooves (1) and some also have indicator tangs (2)

On drum brakes, check the angle of the operating lever with the brake fully applied. Most drum brakes have a wear indicator pointer and scale.

Brakes, Wheels and Tyres

Brakes

✔ With the wheel raised off the ground, apply the brake then free it off, and check that the wheel is about to revolve freely without brake drag.

✔ On disc brakes, examine the disc itself. Check that it is securely mounted and not cracked.

✔ On disc brakes, view the pad material through the caliper mouth and check that the pads are not worn down beyond the limit **(see illustration 11)**.

✔ On drum brakes, check that when the brake is applied the angle between the operating lever and cable or rod is not too great **(see illustration 12)**. Check also that the operating lever doesn't foul any other components.

✔ On disc brakes, examine the flexible hoses from top to bottom. Have an assistant hold the brake on so that the fluid in the hose is under pressure, and check that there is no sign of fluid leakage, bulges or cracking. If there are any metal brake pipes or unions, check that these are free from corrosion and damage. Where a brake-linked anti-dive system is fitted, check the hoses to the anti-dive in a similar manner.

✔ Check that the rear brake torque arm is secure and that its fasteners are secured by self-locking nuts or castellated nuts with split-pins or R-pins **(see illustration 13)**.

✔ On models with ABS, check that the self-check warning light in the instrument panel works.

✔ The MOT tester will perform a test of the motorcycle's braking efficiency based on a calculation of rider and motorcycle weight. Although this cannot be carried out at home, you can at least ensure that the braking systems are properly maintained. For hydraulic disc brakes, check the fluid level, lever/pedal feel (bleed of air if its spongy) and pad material. For drum brakes, check adjustment, cable or rod operation and shoe lining thickness.

Wheels and tyres

✔ Check the wheel condition. Cast wheels should be free from cracks and if of the built-up design, all fasteners should be secure. Spoked wheels should be checked for broken, corroded, loose or bent spokes.

✔ With the wheel raised off the ground, spin the wheel and visually check that the tyre and wheel run true. Check that the tyre does not foul the suspension or mudguards.

✔ With the wheel raised off the ground, grasp the wheel and attempt to move it about the axle (spindle) **(see illustration 14)**. Any play felt here indicates wheel bearing failure.

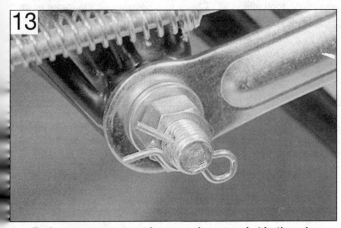

Brake torque arm must be properly secured at both ends

Check for wheel bearing play by trying to move the wheel about the axle (spindle)

Checking the tyre tread depth

Tyre direction of rotation arrow can be found on tyre sidewall

Castellated type wheel axle (spindle) nut must be secured by a split pin or R-pin

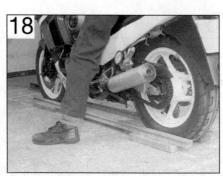

Two straightedges are used to check wheel alignment

✔ Check the tyre tread depth, tread condition and sidewall condition **(see illustration 15)**.
✔ Check the tyre type. Front and rear tyre types must be compatible and be suitable for road use. Tyres marked NOT FOR ROAD USE, COMPETITION USE ONLY or similar, will fail the MOT.

✔ If the tyre sidewall carries a direction of rotation arrow, this must be pointing in the direction of normal wheel rotation **(see illustration 16)**.
✔ Check that the wheel axle (spindle) nuts (where applicable) are properly secured. A self-locking nut or castellated nut with a split-pin or R-pin can be used **(see illustration 17)**.
✔ Wheel alignment is checked with the motorcycle off the stand and a rider seated. With the front wheel pointing straight ahead, two perfectly straight lengths of metal or wood and placed against the sidewalls of both tyres **(see illustration 18)**. The gap each side of the front tyre must be equidistant on both sides. Incorrect wheel alignment may be due to a cocked rear wheel (often as the result of poor chain adjustment) or in extreme cases, a bent frame.

General checks and condition

✔ Check the security of all major fasteners, bodypanels, seat, fairings (where fitted) and mudguards.

✔ Check that the rider and pillion footrests, handlebar levers and brake pedal are securely mounted.

✔ Check for corrosion on the frame or any load-bearing components. If severe, this may affect the structure, particularly under stress.

Sidecars

A motorcycle fitted with a sidecar requires additional checks relating to the stability of the machine and security of attachment and swivel joints, plus specific wheel alignment (toe-in) requirements. Additionally, tyre and lighting requirements differ from conventional motorcycle use. Owners are advised to check MOT test requirements with an official test centre.

Preparing for storage

Before you start

If repairs or an overhaul is needed, see that this is carried out now rather than left until you want to ride the bike again.

Give the bike a good wash and scrub all dirt from its underside. Make sure the bike dries completely before preparing for storage.

Engine

● Remove the spark plug(s) and lubricate the cylinder bores with approximately a teaspoon of motor oil using a spout-type oil can **(see illustration 1)**. Reinstall the spark plug(s). Crank the engine over a couple of times to coat the piston rings and bores with oil. If the bike has a kickstart, use this to turn the engine over. If not, flick the kill switch to the OFF position and crank the engine over on the starter **(see illustration 2)**. If the nature on the ignition system prevents the starter operating with the kill switch in the OFF position,

remove the spark plugs and fit them back in their caps; ensure that the plugs are earthed (grounded) against the cylinder head when the starter is operated **(see illustration 3)**.

> ⚠️ **Warning: It is important that the plugs are earthed (grounded) away from the spark plug holes otherwise there is a risk of atomised fuel from the cylinders igniting.**

> **HAYNES HiNT**
> *On a single cylinder four-stroke engine, you can seal the combustion chamber completely by positioning the piston at TDC on the compression stroke.*

● Drain the carburettor(s) otherwise there is a risk of jets becoming blocked by gum deposits from the fuel **(see illustration 4)**.

● If the bike is going into long-term storage, consider adding a fuel stabiliser to the fuel in the tank. If the tank is drained completely, corrosion of its internal surfaces may occur if left unprotected for a long period. The tank can be treated with a rust preventative especially for this purpose. Alternatively, remove the tank and pour half a litre of motor oil into it, install the filler cap and shake the tank to coat its internals with oil before draining off the excess. The same effect can also be achieved by spraying WD40 or a similar water-dispersant around the inside of the tank via its flexible nozzle.

● Make sure the cooling system contains the correct mix of antifreeze. Antifreeze also contains important corrosion inhibitors.

● The air intakes and exhaust can be sealed off by covering or plugging the openings. Ensure that you do not seal in any condensation; run the engine until it is hot,

Squirt a drop of motor oil into each cylinder

Flick the kill switch to OFF . . .

. . . and ensure that the metal bodies of the plugs (arrows) are earthed against the cylinder head

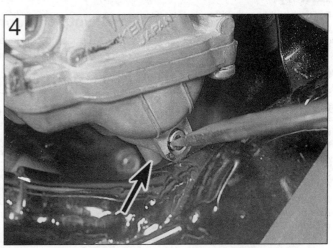

Connect a hose to the carburettor float chamber drain stub (arrow) and unscrew the drain screw

Exhausts can be sealed off with a plastic bag

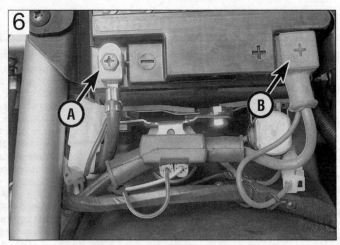

Disconnect the negative lead (A) first, followed by the positive lead (B)

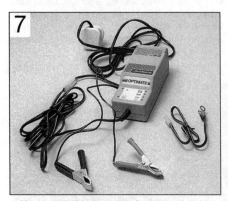

Use a suitable battery charger - this kit also assess battery condition

then switch off and allow to cool. Tape a piece of thick plastic over the silencer end(s) **(see illustration 5)**. Note that some advocate pouring a tablespoon of motor oil into the silencer(s) before sealing them off.

Battery

● Remove it from the bike - in extreme cases of cold the battery may freeze and crack its case **(see illustration 6)**.

● Check the electrolyte level and top up if necessary (conventional refillable batteries). Clean the terminals.
● Store the battery off the motorcycle and away from any sources of fire. Position a wooden block under the battery if it is to sit on the ground.
● Give the battery a trickle charge for a few hours every month **(see illustration 7)**.

Tyres

● Place the bike on its centrestand or an auxiliary stand which will support the motorcycle in an upright position. Position wood blocks under the tyres to keep them off the ground and to provide insulation from damp. If the bike is being put into long-term storage, ideally both tyres should be off the ground; not only will this protect the tyres, but will also ensure that no load is placed on the steering head or wheel bearings.
● Deflate each tyre by 5 to 10 psi, no more or the beads may unseat from the rim, making subsequent inflation difficult on tubeless tyres.

Pivots and controls

● Lubricate all lever, pedal, stand and

footrest pivot points. If grease nipples are fitted to the rear suspension components, apply lubricant to the pivots.
● Lubricate all control cables.

Cycle components

● Apply a wax protectant to all painted and plastic components. Wipe off any excess, but don't polish to a shine. Where fitted, clean the screen with soap and water.
● Coat metal parts with Vaseline (petroleum jelly). When applying this to the fork tubes, do not compress the forks otherwise the seals will rot from contact with the Vaseline.
● Apply a vinyl cleaner to the seat.

Storage conditions

● Aim to store the bike in a shed or garage which does not leak and is free from damp.
● Drape an old blanket or bedspread over the bike to protect it from dust and direct contact with sunlight (which will fade paint). This also hides the bike from prying eyes. Beware of tight-fitting plastic covers which may allow condensation to form and settle on the bike.

Getting back on the road

Engine and transmission

● Change the oil and replace the oil filter. If this was done prior to storage, check that the oil hasn't emulsified - a thick whitish substance which occurs through condensation.
● Remove the spark plugs. Using a spout-type oil can, squirt a few drops of oil into the cylinder(s). This will provide initial lubrication as the piston rings and bores comes back into contact. Service the spark plugs, or fit new ones, and install them in the engine.

● Check that the clutch isn't stuck on. The plates can stick together if left standing for some time, preventing clutch operation. Engage a gear and try rocking the bike back and forth with the clutch lever held against the handlebar. If this doesn't work on cable-operated clutches, hold the clutch lever back against the handlebar with a strong elastic band or cable tie for a couple of hours **(see illustration 8)**.
● If the air intakes or silencer end(s) were blocked off, remove the bung or cover used.
● If the fuel tank was coated with a rust

Hold clutch lever back against the handlebar with elastic bands or a cable tie

preventative, oil or a stabiliser added to the fuel, drain and flush the tank and dispose of the fuel sensibly. If no action was taken with the fuel tank prior to storage, it is advised that the old fuel is disposed of since it will go off over a period of time. Refill the fuel tank with fresh fuel.

Frame and running gear

● Oil all pivot points and cables.
● Check the tyre pressures. They will definitely need inflating if pressures were reduced for storage.
● Lubricate the final drive chain (where applicable).
● Remove any protective coating applied to the fork tubes (stanchions) since this may well destroy the fork seals. If the fork tubes weren't protected and have picked up rust spots, remove them with very fine abrasive paper and refinish with metal polish.
● Check that both brakes operate correctly. Apply each brake hard and check that it's not possible to move the motorcycle forwards, then check that the brake frees off again once released. Brake caliper pistons can stick due to corrosion around the piston head, or on the sliding caliper types, due to corrosion of the slider pins. If the brake doesn't free after repeated operation, take the caliper off for examination. Similarly drum brakes can stick

due to a seized operating cam, cable or rod linkage.
● If the motorcycle has been in long-term storage, renew the brake fluid and clutch fluid (where applicable).
● Depending on where the bike has been stored, the wiring, cables and hoses may have been nibbled by rodents. Make a visual check and investigate disturbed wiring loom tape.

Battery

● If the battery has been previously removal and given top up charges it can simply be reconnected. Remember to connect the positive cable first and the negative cable last.
● On conventional refillable batteries, if the battery has not received any attention, remove it from the motorcycle and check its electrolyte level. Top up if necessary then charge the battery. If the battery fails to hold a charge and a visual checks show heavy white sulphation of the plates, the battery is probably defective and must be renewed. This is particularly likely if the battery is old. Confirm battery condition with a specific gravity check.
● On sealed (MF) batteries, if the battery has not received any attention, remove it from the motorcycle and charge it according to the information on the battery case - if the battery fails to hold a charge it must be renewed.

Starting procedure

● If a kickstart is fitted, turn the engine over a couple of times with the ignition OFF to distribute oil around the engine. If no kickstart is fitted, flick the engine kill switch OFF and the ignition ON and crank the engine over a couple of times to work oil around the upper cylinder components. If the nature of the ignition system is such that the starter won't work with the kill switch OFF, remove the spark plugs, fit them back into their caps and earth (ground) their bodies on the cylinder head. Reinstall the spark plugs afterwards.
● Switch the kill switch to RUN, operate the choke and start the engine. If the engine won't start don't continue cranking the engine - not only will this flatten the battery, but the starter motor will overheat. Switch the ignition off and try again later. If the engine refuses to start, go through the fault finding procedures in this manual. **Note:** *If the bike has been in storage for a long time, old fuel or a carburettor blockage may be the problem. Gum deposits in carburettors can block jets - if a carburettor cleaner doesn't prove successful the carburettors must be dismantled for cleaning.*

● Once the engine has started, check that the lights, turn signals and horn work properly.

● Treat the bike gently for the first ride and check all fluid levels on completion. Settle the bike back into the maintenance schedule.

This Section provides an easy reference-guide to the more common faults that are likely to afflict your machine. Obviously, the opportunities are almost limitless for faults to occur as a result of obscure failures, and to try and cover all eventualities would require a book. Indeed, a number have been written on the subject.

Successful troubleshooting is not a mysterious 'black art' but the application of a bit of knowledge combined with a systematic and logical approach to the problem. Approach any troubleshooting by first accurately identifying the symptom and then checking through the list of possible causes, starting with the simplest or most obvious and progressing in stages to the most complex.

Take nothing for granted, but above all apply liberal quantities of common sense.

The main symptom of a fault is given in the text as a major heading below which are listed the various systems or areas which may contain the fault. Details of each possible cause for a fault and the remedial action to be taken are given, in brief, in the paragraphs below each heading. Further information should be sought in the relevant Chapter.

1 Engine doesn't start or is difficult to start

☐ Starter motor doesn't rotate
☐ Starter motor rotates but engine does not turn over
☐ Starter works but engine won't turn over (seized)
☐ No fuel flow
☐ Engine flooded
☐ No spark or weak spark
☐ Compression low
☐ Stalls after starting
☐ Rough idle

2 Poor running at low speed

☐ Spark weak
☐ Fuel/air mixture incorrect
☐ Compression low
☐ Poor acceleration

3 Poor running or no power at high speed

☐ Firing incorrect
☐ Fuel/air mixture incorrect
☐ Compression low
☐ Knocking or pinking
☐ Miscellaneous causes

4 Overheating

☐ Engine overheats
☐ Firing incorrect
☐ Fuel/air mixture incorrect
☐ Compression too high
☐ Engine load excessive
☐ Lubrication inadequate
☐ Miscellaneous causes

5 Clutch problems

☐ Clutch slipping
☐ Clutch not disengaging completely

6 Gearchanging problems

☐ Doesn't go into gear, or lever doesn't return
☐ Jumps out of gear
☐ Overshifts

7 Abnormal engine noise

☐ Knocking or pinking
☐ Piston slap or rattling
☐ Valve noise
☐ Other noise

8 Abnormal driveline noise

☐ Clutch noise
☐ Transmission noise
☐ Final drive noise

9 Abnormal frame and suspension noise

☐ Front end noise
☐ Shock absorber noise
☐ Brake noise

10 Oil pressure light comes on

☐ Engine lubrication system
☐ Electrical system

11 Excessive exhaust smoke

☐ White smoke
☐ Black smoke
☐ Brown smoke

12 Poor handling or stability

☐ Handlebar hard to turn
☐ Handlebar shakes or vibrates excessively
☐ Handlebar pulls to one side
☐ Poor shock absorbing qualities

13 Braking problems

☐ Brakes are spongy, don't hold
☐ Brake lever or pedal pulsates
☐ Brakes drag

14 Electrical problems

☐ Battery dead or weak
☐ Battery overcharged

1 Engine doesn't start or is difficult to start

Starter motor doesn't rotate

- [ ] Engine kill switch OFF.
- [ ] Fuse blown. Check fuse (Chapter 8).
- [ ] Battery voltage low. Check and recharge battery (Chapter 8).
- [ ] Starter motor defective. Make sure the wiring to the starter is secure. Make sure the starter relay clicks when the start button is pushed. If the relay clicks, then the fault is in the wiring or motor.
- [ ] Starter relay faulty. Check it using the procedure in Chapter 8.
- [ ] Starter switch not contacting. The contacts could be wet, corroded or dirty. Disassemble and clean the switch (Chapter 8).
- [ ] Wiring open or shorted. Check all wiring connections and harnesses to make sure that they are dry, tight and not corroded. Also check for broken or frayed wires that can cause a short to ground (earth) (see wiring diagram, Chapter 8).
- [ ] Ignition (main) switch defective. Check the switch according to the procedure in Chapter 8. Replace the switch with a new one if it is defective.
- [ ] Engine kill switch defective. Check for wet, dirty or corroded contacts. Clean or replace the switch as necessary (Chapter 8).
- [ ] Faulty neutral or side stand switch. Check the wiring to each switch and the switch itself according to the procedures in Chapter 8.
- [ ] Faulty starter circuit relay or diode. Check the junction box according to the procedure in Chapter 8.

Starter motor rotates but engine does not turn over

- [ ] Starter clutch defective. Inspect and repair or replace (Chapter 2).
- [ ] Damaged idle/reduction gear or starter gears. Inspect and replace the damaged parts (Chapter 2).

Starter works but engine won't turn over (seized)

- [ ] Seized engine caused by one or more internally damaged components. Failure due to wear, abuse or lack of lubrication. Damage can include seized valves, followers, camshafts, pistons, crankshaft, connecting rod bearings, or transmission gears or bearings. Refer to Chapter 2 for engine disassembly.

No fuel flow

- [ ] No fuel in tank.
- [ ] Main fuel cock filter clogged. Remove the fuel cock and clean it and the filter (Chapter 3).
- [ ] Fuel line clogged. Pull the fuel line loose and carefully blow through it.
- [ ] Float needle valve clogged. For both of the valves to be clogged, either a very bad batch of fuel with an unusual additive has been used, or some other foreign material has entered the tank. Many times after a machine has been stored for many months without running, the fuel turns to a varnish-like liquid and forms deposits on the inlet needle valves and jets. The carburettors should be removed and overhauled if draining the float chambers doesn't solve the problem (Chapter 3).

Engine flooded

- [ ] Float height incorrect. Check and adjust as necessary (Chapter 3).
- [ ] Float needle valve worn or stuck open. A piece of dirt, rust or other debris can cause the valve to seat improperly, causing excess fuel to be admitted to the float chamber. In this case, the float chamber should be cleaned and the needle valve and seat inspected. If the needle and seat are worn, then the leaking will persist and the parts should be replaced with new ones (Chapter 3).
- [ ] Starting technique incorrect. Under normal circumstances (i.e., if all the carburettor functions are sound) the machine should start with little or no throttle. When the engine is cold, the choke should be operated and the engine started without opening the throttle.

When the engine is at operating temperature, only a very slight amount of throttle should be necessary. If the engine is flooded hold the throttle open while cranking the engine. This will allow additional air to reach the cylinders.

No spark or weak spark

- [ ] Ignition switch OFF.
- [ ] Engine kill switch turned to the OFF position.
- [ ] Battery voltage low. Check and recharge the battery as necessary (Chapter 8).
- [ ] Spark plugs dirty, defective or worn out. Locate reason for fouled plugs using spark plug condition chart and follow the plug maintenance procedures (Chapter 1).
- [ ] Spark plug caps or secondary (HT) wiring faulty. Check condition. Replace either or both components if cracks or deterioration are evident (Chapter 4).
- [ ] Spark plug caps not making good contact. Make sure that the plug caps fit snugly over the plug ends.
- [ ] Ignition control unit defective. Check the unit, referring to Chapter 4 for details.
- [ ] Pulse generator coil defective. Check the coil, referring to Chapter 4 for details.
- [ ] Ignition HT coil(s) defective. Check the coils, referring to Chapter 4 for details.
- [ ] Ignition or kill switch shorted. This is usually caused by water, corrosion, damage or excessive wear. The switches can be disassembled and cleaned with electrical contact cleaner. If cleaning does not help, replace the switches (Chapter 8).
- [ ] Wiring shorted or broken between:
  - a) Ignition (main) switch and engine kill switch (or blown fuse)
  - b) Ignition control unit and engine kill switch
  - c) Ignition control unit and ignition HT coils
  - d) Ignition HT coils and spark plugs
  - e) Ignition control unit and pulse generator coil
- [ ] Make sure that all wiring connections are clean, dry and tight. Look for chafed and broken wires (Chapters 4 and 8).

Compression low

- [ ] Spark plugs loose. Remove the plugs and inspect their threads. Reinstall and tighten to the specified torque (Chapter 1).
- [ ] Cylinder head not sufficiently tightened down. If the cylinder head is suspected of being loose, then there's a chance that the gasket or head is damaged if the problem has persisted for any length of time. The head bolts should be tightened to the proper torque in the correct sequence (Chapter 2).
- [ ] Improper valve clearance. This means that the valve is not closing completely and compression pressure is leaking past the valve. Check and adjust the valve clearances (Chapter 1).
- [ ] Cylinder and/or piston worn. Excessive wear will cause compression pressure to leak past the rings. This is usually accompanied by worn rings as well. A top-end overhaul is necessary (Chapter 2).
- [ ] Piston rings worn, weak, broken, or sticking. Broken or sticking piston rings usually indicate a lubrication or carburation problem that causes excess carbon deposits or seizures to form on the pistons and rings. Top-end overhaul is necessary (Chapter 2).
- [ ] Piston ring-to-groove clearance excessive. This is caused by excessive wear of the piston ring lands. Piston replacement is necessary (Chapter 2).
- [ ] Cylinder head gasket damaged. If the head is allowed to become loose, or if excessive carbon build-up on the piston crown and combustion chamber causes extremely high compression, the head gasket may leak. Retorquing the head is not always sufficient to restore the seal, so gasket replacement is necessary (Chapter 2).

1 Engine doesn't start or is difficult to start (continued)

☐ Cylinder head warped. This is caused by overheating or improperly tightened head bolts. Machine shop resurfacing or head replacement is necessary (Chapter 2).

☐ Valve spring broken or weak. Caused by component failure or wear; the springs must be replaced (Chapter 2).

☐ Valve not seating properly. This is caused by a bent valve (from over-revving or improper valve adjustment), burned valve or seat (improper carburation) or an accumulation of carbon deposits on the seat (from carburation or lubrication problems). The valves must be cleaned and/or replaced and the seats serviced if possible (Chapter 2).

Stalls after starting

☐ Improper choke action. Make sure the choke linkage shaft is getting a full stroke and staying in the out position (Chapter 3).

☐ Ignition malfunction (Chapter 4).

☐ Carburettor malfunction (Chapter 3).

☐ Fuel contaminated. The fuel can be contaminated with either dirt or water, or can change chemically if the machine is allowed to sit for several months or more. Drain the tank and float chambers (Chapter 3).

2 Poor running at low speeds

Spark weak

☐ Battery voltage low. Check and recharge battery (Chapter 8).

☐ Spark plugs fouled, defective or worn out (Chapter 1).

☐ Spark plug cap or HT wiring defective (Chapters 1 and 4).

☐ Spark plug caps not making contact.

☐ Incorrect spark plugs. Wrong type, heat range or cap configuration. Check and install correct plugs (Chapter 1).

☐ Ignition control defective (Chapter 4).

☐ Pulse generator coil defective (Chapter 4).

☐ Ignition HT coil(s) defective (Chapter 4).

Fuel/air mixture incorrect

☐ Pilot screws out of adjustment (Chapter 3).

☐ Pilot jet or air passage clogged. Remove and overhaul the carburettors (Chapter 3).

☐ Air bleed holes clogged. Remove carburettor and blow out all passages (Chapter 3).

☐ Air filter clogged, poorly sealed or missing (Chapter 1).

☐ Air filter housing poorly sealed. Look for cracks, holes or loose clamps and replace or repair defective parts (Chapter 3).

☐ Fuel level too high or too low. Check the float height (Chapter 3).

☐ Carburettor intake manifolds loose. Check for cracks, breaks, tears or loose clamps. Replace the rubber intake manifold joints if split or perished (Chapter 3).

Compression low

☐ Spark plugs loose. Remove the plugs and inspect their threads. Reinstall and tighten to the specified torque (Chapter 1).

☐ Cylinder head not sufficiently tightened down. If the cylinder head is suspected of being loose, then there's a chance that the gasket or head is damaged if the problem has persisted for any length of time. The head bolts should be tightened to the proper torque in the correct sequence (Chapter 2).

☐ Improper valve clearance. This means that the valve is not closing completely and compression pressure is leaking past the valve. Check and adjust the valve clearances (Chapter 1).

☐ Cylinder and/or piston worn. Excessive wear will cause compression pressure to leak past the rings. This is usually accompanied by worn rings as well. A top-end overhaul is necessary (Chapter 2).

☐ Intake air leak. Check for loose carburettor-to-intake manifold connections, loose or missing vacuum gauge adapter caps, or loose carburettor tops (Chapter 3).

☐ Engine idle speed incorrect. Turn idle adjusting screw until the engine idles at the specified rpm (Chapter 1).

Rough idle

☐ Ignition malfunction (Chapter 4).

☐ Idle speed incorrect (Chapter 1).

☐ Carburettors not synchronised. Adjust carburettors with vacuum gauge or manometer set (Chapter 1).

☐ Carburettor malfunction (Chapter 3).

☐ Fuel contaminated. The fuel can be contaminated with either dirt or water, or can change chemically if the machine is allowed to sit for several months or more. Drain the tank and float chambers (Chapter 3).

☐ Intake air leak. Check for loose carburettor-to-intake manifold connections, loose or missing vacuum gauge adapter caps, or loose carburettor tops (Chapter 3).

☐ Air filter clogged. Replace the air filter element (Chapter 1).

☐ Piston rings worn, weak, broken, or sticking. Broken or sticking piston rings usually indicate a lubrication or carburation problem that causes excess carbon deposits or seizures to form on the pistons and rings. Top-end overhaul is necessary (Chapter 2).

☐ Piston ring-to-groove clearance excessive. This is caused by excessive wear of the piston ring lands. Piston replacement is necessary (Chapter 2).

☐ Cylinder head gasket damaged. If the head is allowed to become loose, or if excessive carbon build-up on the piston crown and combustion chamber causes extremely high compression, the head gasket may leak. Retorquing the head is not always sufficient to restore the seal, so gasket replacement is necessary (Chapter 2).

☐ Cylinder head warped. This is caused by overheating or improperly tightened head bolts. Machine shop resurfacing or head replacement is necessary (Chapter 2).

☐ Valve spring broken or weak. Caused by component failure or wear; the springs must be replaced (Chapter 2).

☐ Valve not seating properly. This is caused by a bent valve (from over-revving or improper valve adjustment), burned valve or seat (improper carburation) or an accumulation of carbon deposits on the seat (from carburation or lubrication problems). The valves must be cleaned and/or replaced and the seats serviced if possible (Chapter 2).

Poor acceleration

☐ Carburettors leaking or dirty. Overhaul the carburettors (Chapter 3).

☐ Timing not advancing. Faulty pulse generator coil or ignitor unit (Chapter 4).

☐ Carburettors not synchronised. Adjust them with a vacuum gauge set or manometer (Chapter 1).

☐ Engine oil viscosity too high. Using a heavier oil than that recommended in Chapter 1 can damage the oil pump or lubrication system and cause drag on the engine.

☐ Brakes dragging. Usually caused by debris which has entered the brake piston seals, or from a warped disc or bent axle. Repair as necessary (Chapter 6).

3 Poor running or no power at high speed

Firing incorrect

☐ Air filter restricted. Clean or replace filter (Chapter 1).
☐ Spark plugs fouled, defective or worn out (Chapter 1).
☐ Spark plug cap or HT wiring defective (Chapters 1 and 4).
☐ Spark plug caps not making contact. Make sure they are properly connected.
☐ Incorrect spark plugs. Wrong type, heat range or cap configuration. Check and install correct plugs (Chapter 1).
☐ Ignition control unit defective (Chapter 4).
☐ Pulse generator coil defective (Chapter 4).
☐ Ignition HT coil(s) defective (Chapter 4).

Fuel/air mixture incorrect

☐ Air bleed holes clogged. Remove carburettor and blow out all passages (Chapter 3).
☐ Air filter clogged, poorly sealed or missing (Chapter 1).
☐ Air filter housing poorly sealed. Look for cracks, holes or loose clamps and replace or repair defective parts (Chapter 3).
☐ Fuel level too high or too low. Check the float height (Chapter 3).
☐ Carburettor intake manifolds loose. Check for cracks, breaks, tears or loose clamps. Replace the rubber intake manifold joints if split or perished (Chapter 3).
☐ Jet needle incorrectly positioned or worn Check and adjust or replace (Chapter 3).
☐ Main jet clogged. Dirt, water or other contaminants can clog the main jets. Clean the fuel tap filter, the in-line filter, the float chamber area, and the jets and carburettor orifices (Chapter 3).
☐ Main jet wrong size. The standard jetting is for sea level atmospheric pressure and oxygen content. Check jet size (Chapter 3).
☐ Throttle shaft-to-carburettor body clearance excessive. Overhaul carburettors, replacing worn parts or complete carburettor if necessary (Chapter 3).

Compression low

☐ Spark plugs loose. Remove the plugs and inspect their threads. Reinstall and tighten to the specified torque (Chapter 1).
☐ Cylinder head not sufficiently tightened down. If the cylinder head is suspected of being loose, then there's a chance that the gasket or head is damaged if the problem has persisted for any length of time. The head bolts should be tightened to the proper torque in the correct sequence (Chapter 2).
☐ Improper valve clearance. This means that the valve is not closing completely and compression pressure is leaking past the valve. Check and adjust the valve clearances (Chapter 1).
☐ Cylinder and/or piston worn. Excessive wear will cause compression pressure to leak past the rings. This is usually accompanied by worn rings as well. A top-end overhaul is necessary (Chapter 2).
☐ Piston rings worn, weak, broken, or sticking. Broken or sticking piston rings usually indicate a lubrication or carburation problem that causes excess carbon deposits or seizures to form on the pistons and rings. Top-end overhaul is necessary (Chapter 2).

☐ Piston ring-to-groove clearance excessive. This is caused by excessive wear of the piston ring lands. Piston replacement is necessary (Chapter 2).
☐ Cylinder head gasket damaged. If the head is allowed to become loose, or if excessive carbon build-up on the piston crown and combustion chamber causes extremely high compression, the head gasket may leak. Retorquing the head is not always sufficient to restore the seal, so gasket replacement is necessary (Chapter 2).
☐ Cylinder head warped. This is caused by overheating or improperly tightened head bolts. Machine shop resurfacing or head replacement is necessary (Chapter 2).
☐ Valve spring broken or weak. Caused by component failure or wear; the springs must be replaced (Chapter 2).
☐ Valve not seating properly. This is caused by a bent valve (from over-revving or improper valve adjustment), burned valve or seat (improper carburation) or an accumulation of carbon deposits on the seat (from carburation or lubrication problems). The valves must be cleaned and/or replaced and the seats serviced if possible (Chapter 2).

Knocking or pinging

☐ Carbon build-up in combustion chamber. Use of a fuel additive that will dissolve the adhesive bonding the carbon particles to the crown and chamber is the easiest way to remove the build-up. Otherwise, the cylinder head will have to be removed and decarbonized (Chapter 2).
☐ Incorrect or poor quality fuel. Old or improper grades of fuel can cause detonation. This causes the piston to rattle, thus the knocking or pinging sound. Drain old fuel and always use the recommended fuel grade (Chapter 3).
☐ Spark plug heat range incorrect. Uncontrolled detonation indicates the plug heat range is too hot. The plug in effect becomes a glow plug, raising cylinder temperatures. Install the proper heat range plug (Chapter 1).
☐ Improper air/fuel mixture. This will cause the cylinder to run hot, which leads to detonation. Clogged jets or an air leak can cause this imbalance (Chapter 3).

Miscellaneous causes

☐ Throttle valve doesn't open fully. Adjust the throttle grip freeplay (Chapter 1).
☐ Clutch slipping. May be caused by loose or worn clutch components. Overhaul clutch (Chapter 2).
☐ Timing not advancing. Ignition control unit faulty (Chapter 4).
☐ Engine oil viscosity too high. Using a heavier oil than the one recommended in Chapter 1 can damage the oil pump or lubrication system and cause drag on the engine.
☐ Brakes dragging. Usually caused by debris which has entered the brake piston seals, or from a warped disc or bent axle. Repair as necessary.

4 Overheating

Firing incorrect

☐ Spark plugs fouled, defective or worn out (Chapter 1).
☐ Incorrect spark plugs (Chapter 1).
☐ Faulty ignition HT coils (Chapter 4).

Fuel/air mixture incorrect

☐ Main jet clogged. Dirt, water and other contaminants can clog the main jets. Clean the fuel tap filter, the fuel pump in-line filter, the float chamber area and the jets and carburettor orifices (Chapter 3).
☐ Main jet wrong size. The standard jetting is for sea level atmospheric pressure and oxygen content. Check jet size (Chapter 3).
☐ Air filter clogged, poorly sealed or missing (Chapter 1).
☐ Air filter housing poorly sealed. Look for cracks, holes or loose clamps and replace or repair (Chapter 3).
☐ Fuel level too low. Check float height (Chapter 3).
☐ Carburettor intake manifolds loose. Check for cracks, breaks, tears or loose clamps. Replace the rubber intake manifold joints if split or perished (Chapter 3).

Compression too high

☐ Carbon build-up in combustion chamber. Use of a fuel additive that will dissolve the adhesive bonding the carbon particles to the piston crown and chamber is the easiest way to remove the build-up. Otherwise, the cylinder head will have to be removed and decarbonized (Chapter 2).
☐ Improperly machined head surface or installation of incorrect gasket during engine assembly (Chapter 2).

Engine load excessive

☐ Clutch slipping. Can be caused by damaged, loose or worn clutch components. Overhaul clutch (Chapter 2).

☐ Engine oil level too high. The addition of too much oil will cause pressurisation of the crankcase and inefficient engine operation. Check Specifications and drain to proper level (Chapter 1).
☐ Engine oil viscosity too high. Using a heavier oil than the one recommended in Chapter 1 can damage the oil pump or lubrication system as well as cause drag on the engine.
☐ Brakes dragging. Usually caused by debris which has entered the brake piston seals, or from a warped disc or bent axle. Repair as necessary.
☐ Excessive friction in moving engine parts due to inadequate lubrication, worn bearings or incorrect assembly. Overhaul engine (Chapter 2).

Lubrication inadequate

☐ Engine oil level too low. Friction caused by intermittent lack of lubrication or from oil that is overworked can cause overheating. The oil provides a definite cooling function in the engine. Check the oil level (Chapter 1).
☐ Poor quality engine oil or incorrect viscosity or type. Oil is rated not only according to viscosity but also according to type. Some oils are not rated high enough for use in this engine. Check the Specifications section and change to the correct oil (Chapter 1).
☐ Worn oil pump or clogged oil passages. Check oil pump and clean passages (Chapter 2).

Miscellaneous causes

☐ Engine cooling fins clogged with debris.
☐ Modification to exhaust system. Most aftermarket exhaust systems cause the engine to run leaner, which make them run hotter. When installing an accessory exhaust system, always rejet the carburettors.

5 Clutch problems

Clutch slipping

☐ Cable freeplay insufficient. Check and adjust cable (Chapter 1).
☐ Friction plates worn or warped. Overhaul the clutch assembly (Chapter 2).
☐ Plain plates warped (Chapter 2).
☐ Clutch springs broken or weak. Old or heat-damaged (from slipping clutch) springs should be replaced with new ones (Chapter 2).
☐ Clutch release mechanism defective. Replace any defective parts (Chapter 2).
☐ Clutch centre or housing unevenly worn. This causes improper engagement of the plates. Replace the damaged or worn parts (Chapter 2).

Clutch not disengaging completely

☐ Cable freeplay excessive. Check and adjust cable (Chapter 1).
☐ Clutch plates warped or damaged. This will cause clutch drag, which in turn will cause the machine to creep. Overhaul the clutch assembly (Chapter 2).

☐ Clutch spring tension uneven. Usually caused by a sagged or broken spring. Check and replace the springs as a set (Chapter 2).
☐ Engine oil deteriorated. Old, thin, worn out oil will not provide proper lubrication for the plates, causing the clutch to drag. Replace the oil and filter (Chapter 1).
☐ Engine oil viscosity too high. Using a heavier oil than recommended in Chapter 1 can cause the plates to stick together, putting a drag on the engine. Change to the correct weight oil (Chapter 1).
☐ Clutch housing seized on mainshaft. Lack of lubrication, severe wear or damage can cause the guide to seize on the shaft. Overhaul of the clutch, and perhaps transmission, may be necessary to repair the damage (Chapter 2).
☐ Clutch release mechanism defective. Overhaul the clutch cover components (Chapter 2).
☐ Loose clutch centre nut. Causes drum and centre misalignment putting a drag on the engine. Engagement adjustment continually varies. Overhaul the clutch assembly (Chapter 2).

6 Gearchanging problems

Doesn't go into gear or lever doesn't return

☐ Clutch not disengaging. See above.
☐ Selector fork(s) bent or seized. Often caused by dropping the machine or from lack of lubrication. Overhaul the transmission (Chapter 2).
☐ Gear(s) stuck on shaft. Most often caused by a lack of lubrication or excessive wear in transmission bearings and bushings. Overhaul the transmission (Chapter 2).
☐ Gear selector drum binding. Caused by lubrication failure or excessive wear. Replace the drum and bearing (Chapter 2).
☐ Gearchange lever return spring weak or broken (Chapter 2).
☐ Gearchange lever or linkage arm broken. Splines stripped out of lever or shaft, caused by allowing the lever to get loose or from dropping the machine. Replace necessary parts (Chapter 2).

☐ Gearchange mechanism stopper arm broken or worn. Full engagement and rotary movement of shift drum results. Replace the arm (Chapter 2).
☐ Selector/stopper arm spring broken. Allows arms to float, causing sporadic shift operation. Replace spring (Chapter 2).

Jumps out of gear

☐ Selector fork(s) worn. Overhaul the transmission (Chapter 2).
☐ Gear groove(s) worn. Overhaul the transmission (Chapter 2).
☐ Gear dogs or dog slots worn or damaged. The gears should be inspected and replaced. No attempt should be made to service the worn parts (Chapter 2).

Overshifts

☐ Selector/stopper arm spring weak or broken (Chapter 2).
☐ Gearchange shaft return spring post broken or distorted (Chapter 2).

7 Abnormal engine noise

Knocking or pinging

☐ Carbon build-up in combustion chamber. Use of a fuel additive that will dissolve the adhesive bonding the carbon particles to the piston crown and chamber is the easiest way to remove the build-up. Otherwise, the cylinder head will have to be removed and decarbonized (Chapter 2).
☐ Incorrect or poor quality fuel. Old or improper fuel can cause detonation. This causes the pistons to rattle, thus the knocking or pinging sound. Drain the old fuel and always use the recommended grade fuel (Chapter 3).
☐ Spark plug heat range incorrect. Uncontrolled detonation indicates that the plug heat range is too hot. The plug in effect becomes a glow plug, raising cylinder temperatures. Install the proper heat range plug (Chapter 1).
☐ Improper air/fuel mixture. This will cause the cylinders to run hot and lead to detonation. Clogged jets or an air leak can cause this imbalance (Chapter 3).

Piston slap or rattling

☐ Cylinder-to-piston clearance excessive. Caused by improper assembly. Inspect and overhaul top-end parts (Chapter 2).
☐ Connecting rod bent. Caused by over-revving, trying to start a badly flooded engine or from ingesting a foreign object into the combustion chamber. Replace the damaged parts (Chapter 2).
☐ Piston pin or piston pin bore worn or seized from wear or lack of lubrication. Replace damaged parts (Chapter 2).
☐ Piston ring(s) worn, broken or sticking. Overhaul the top-end (Chapter 2).
☐ Piston seizure damage. Usually from lack of lubrication or overheating. Replace the pistons and bore the cylinders, as necessary (Chapter 2).

☐ Connecting rod upper or lower end clearance excessive. Caused by excessive wear or lack of lubrication. Replace worn parts (Chapter 2).

Valve noise

☐ Incorrect valve clearances. Adjust the clearances (Chapter 1).
☐ Valve spring broken or weak. Check and replace weak valve springs (Chapter 2).
☐ Camshaft or cylinder head worn or damaged. Lack of lubrication at high rpm is usually the cause of damage. Insufficient oil or failure to change the oil at the recommended intervals are the chief causes. Since there are no replaceable bearings in the head, the head itself will have to be replaced if there is excessive wear or damage (Chapter 2).

Other noise

☐ Cylinder head gasket leaking (Chapter 1).
☐ Exhaust pipe leaking at cylinder head connection. Caused by improper fit of pipe(s) or loose exhaust flange. All exhaust fasteners should be tightened evenly and carefully. Failure to do this will lead to a leak (Chapter 3).
☐ Crankshaft runout excessive. Caused by a bent crankshaft (from over-revving) or damage from an upper cylinder component failure. Can also be attributed to dropping the machine on either of the crankshaft ends (Chapter 2).
☐ Engine mounting bolts loose. Tighten all engine mount bolts (Chapter 2).
☐ Crankshaft bearings worn (Chapter 2).
☐ Cam chain tensioner defective. Replace (Chapter 2).
☐ Cam chain, sprockets or guides worn (Chapter 2).

8 Abnormal driveline noise

Clutch noise

- [ ] Clutch housing/friction plate clearance excessive (Chapter 2).
- [ ] Loose or damaged clutch pressure plate and/or bolts (Chapter 2).

Transmission noise

- [ ] Bearings worn. Also includes the possibility that the shafts are worn. Overhaul the transmission (Chapter 2).
- [ ] Gears worn or chipped (Chapter 2).
- [ ] Metal chips jammed in gear teeth. Probably pieces from a broken clutch, gear or shift mechanism that were picked up by the gears. This will cause early bearing failure (Chapter 2).

- [ ] Engine oil level too low. Causes a howl from transmission. Also affects engine power and clutch operation (Chapter 1).

Final drive noise

- [ ] Chain not adjusted properly (Chapter 1).
- [ ] Front or rear sprocket loose. Tighten fasteners (Chapter 5).
- [ ] Sprockets worn. Replace sprockets (Chapter 5).
- [ ] Rear sprocket warped. Replace sprockets (Chapter 5).
- [ ] Wheel coupling damper worn. Replace damper (Chapter 5).

9 Abnormal frame and suspension noise

Front end noise

- [ ] Low fluid level or improper viscosity oil in forks. This can sound like spurting and is usually accompanied by irregular fork action (Chapter 5).
- [ ] Spring weak or broken. Makes a clicking or scraping sound. Fork oil, when drained, will have a lot of metal particles in it (Chapter 5).
- [ ] Steering head bearings loose or damaged. Clicks when braking. Check and adjust or replace as necessary (Chapters 1 and 5).
- [ ] Fork yokes loose. Make sure all clamp pinch bolts are tight (Chapter 5).
- [ ] Fork tube bent. Good possibility if machine has been dropped. Replace tube with a new one (Chapter 5).
- [ ] Front axle or axle clamp bolt loose. Tighten them to the specified torque (Chapter 6).

Shock absorber noise

- [ ] Fluid level incorrect. Indicates a leak caused by defective seal. Shock will be covered with oil. Replace shock or seek advice on repair from a Kawasaki dealer (Chapter 5).
- [ ] Defective shock absorber with internal damage. This is in the body of the shock and can't be remedied. The shock must be replaced with a new one (Chapter 5).

- [ ] Bent or damaged shock body. Replace the shock with a new one (Chapter 5).
- [ ] Loose or worn mountings. Check and replace as needed (Chapter 5).

Brake noise

- [ ] Squeal caused by pad shim not installed or positioned correctly (Chapter 6).
- [ ] Squeal caused by dust on brake pads. Usually found together with glazed pads. Clean using brake cleaning solvent (Chapter 6).
- [ ] Contamination of brake pads. Oil, brake fluid or dirt causing brake to chatter or squeal. Clean or replace pads (Chapter 6).
- [ ] Pads glazed. Caused by excessive heat from prolonged use or from contamination. Do not use sandpaper, emery cloth, carborundum cloth or any other abrasive to roughen the pad surfaces as abrasives will stay in the pad material and damage the disc. A very fine flat file can be used, but pad replacement is suggested as a cure (Chapter 6).
- [ ] Disc warped. Can cause a chattering, clicking or intermittent squeal. Usually accompanied by a pulsating lever and uneven braking. Replace the disc (Chapter 6).
- [ ] Loose or worn wheel bearings. Check and replace as needed (Chapter 6).

10 Oil pressure light comes on

Engine lubrication system

- [ ] Engine oil pump defective, blocked oil strainer gauze or failed relief valve. Carry out oil pressure check (Chapter 2).
- [ ] Engine oil level low. Inspect for leak or other problem causing low oil level and add recommended oil (Chapter 1).
- [ ] Engine oil viscosity too low. Very old, thin oil or an improper weight of oil used in the engine. Change to correct oil (Chapter 1).
- [ ] Camshaft or journals worn. Excessive wear causing drop in oil pressure. Replace cam and/or cylinder head. Abnormal wear

could be caused by oil starvation at high rpm from low oil level or improper weight or type of oil (Chapter 1).
- [ ] Crankshaft and/or bearings worn. Same problems as paragraph 4. Check and replace crankshaft and/or bearings (Chapter 2).

Electrical system

- [ ] Oil pressure switch defective. Check the switch according to the procedure in Chapter 8. Replace it if it is defective.
- [ ] Oil pressure indicator light circuit defective. Check for pinched, shorted, disconnected or damaged wiring (Chapter 8).

11 Excessive exhaust smoke

White smoke

- [ ] Piston oil ring worn. The ring may be broken or damaged, causing oil from the crankcase to be pulled past the piston into the combustion chamber. Replace the rings with new ones (Chapter 2).
- [ ] Cylinders worn, cracked, or scored. Caused by overheating or oil starvation. The cylinders will have to be rebored and new pistons installed (Chapter 2).
- [ ] Valve oil seal damaged or worn. Replace oil seals with new ones (Chapter 2).
- [ ] Valve guide worn. Perform a complete valve job (Chapter 2).
- [ ] Engine oil level too high, which causes the oil to be forced past the rings. Drain oil to the proper level (Chapter 1).
- [ ] Head gasket broken between oil return and cylinder. Causes oil to be pulled into the combustion chamber. Replace the head gasket and check the head for warpage (Chapter 2).
- [ ] Abnormal crankcase pressurisation, which forces oil past the rings. Clogged ventilation system or breather hose (Chapter 2).

Black smoke

- [ ] Air filter clogged. Clean or replace the element (Chapter 1).

- [ ] Main jet too large or loose. Compare the jet size to the Specifications (Chapter 3).
- [ ] Choke cable or linkage shaft stuck, causing fuel to be pulled through choke circuit (Chapter 3).
- [ ] Fuel level too high. Check and adjust the float height(s) as necessary (Chapter 3).
- [ ] Float needle valve held off needle seat. Clean the float chambers and fuel line and replace the needles and seats if necessary (Chapter 3).

Brown smoke

- [ ] Main jet too small or clogged. Lean condition caused by wrong size main jet or by a restricted orifice. Clean float chambers and jets and compare jet size to Specifications (Chapter 3).
- [ ] Fuel flow insufficient. Float needle valve stuck closed due to chemical reaction with old fuel. Float height incorrect. Restricted fuel line. Clean line and float chamber and adjust floats if necessary (Chapter 3).
- [ ] Carburettor intake manifold clamps loose (Chapter 3).
- [ ] Air filter poorly sealed or not installed (Chapter 1).

12 Poor handling or stability

Handlebar hard to turn

- [ ] Steering head bearing adjuster nut too tight. Check adjustment (Chapter 1).
- [ ] Bearings damaged. Roughness can be felt as the bars are turned from side-to-side. Replace bearings and races (Chapter 5).
- [ ] Races dented or worn. Denting results from wear in only one position (e.g., straight ahead), from a collision or hitting a pothole or from dropping the machine. Replace races and bearings (Chapter 5).
- [ ] Steering stem lubrication inadequate. Causes are grease getting hard from age or being washed out by high pressure car washes. Disassemble steering head and repack bearings (Chapter 5).
- [ ] Steering stem bent. Caused by a collision, hitting a pothole or by dropping the machine. Replace damaged part. Don't try to straighten the steering stem (Chapter 5).
- [ ] Front tire air pressure too low (Chapter 1).

Handlebar shakes or vibrates excessively

- [ ] Tyres worn or out of balance (Chapter 6).
- [ ] Swingarm bearings worn. Replace worn bearings (Chapter 5).
- [ ] Rim(s) warped or damaged. Inspect wheels for runout (Chapter 6).
- [ ] Wheel bearings worn. Worn front or rear wheel bearings can cause poor tracking. Worn front bearings will cause wobble (Chapter 6).
- [ ] Handlebar clamp bolts loose (Chapter 5).
- [ ] Fork yoke bolts loose. Tighten them to the specified torque (Chapter 5).
- [ ] Engine mounting bolts loose. Will cause excessive vibration with increased engine rpm (Chapter 2).

Handlebar pulls to one side

- [ ] Frame bent. Definitely suspect this if the machine has been dropped. May or may not be accompanied by cracking near the bend. Replace the frame (Chapter 5).
- [ ] Wheels out of alignment. Caused by improper location of axle spacers or from bent steering stem or frame (Chapter 5).
- [ ] Swingarm bent or twisted. Caused by age (metal fatigue) or impact damage. Replace the arm (Chapter 5).
- [ ] Steering stem bent. Caused by impact damage or by dropping the motorcycle. Replace the steering stem (Chapter 5).
- [ ] Fork tube bent. Disassemble the forks and replace the damaged parts (Chapter 5).
- [ ] Fork oil level uneven. Check, add or drain as necessary (Chapter•1).

Poor shock absorbing qualities

- [ ] Too hard:
  - a) Fork oil level excessive (Chapter 5).
  - b) Fork oil viscosity too high. Use a lighter oil (see the Specifications in Chapter 5).
  - c) Fork tube bent. Causes a harsh, sticking feeling (Chapter 5).
  - d) Shock shaft or body bent or damaged (Chapter 5).
  - e) Fork internal damage (Chapter 5).
  - f) Shock internal damage.
  - g) Tire pressure too high (Chapter 1).
- [ ] Too soft:
  - a) Fork or shock oil insufficient and/or leaking (Chapter 5).
  - b) Fork oil level too low (Chapter 5).
  - c) Fork oil viscosity too light (Chapter 5).
  - d) Fork springs weak or broken (Chapter 5).
  - e) Shock internal damage or leakage (Chapter 5).

13 Braking problems

Brakes are spongy, don't hold

☐ Air in brake line. Caused by inattention to master cylinder fluid level or by leakage. Locate problem and bleed brakes (Chapter 6).
☐ Pad or disc worn (Chapters 1 and 6).
☐ Brake fluid leak. Causes air in brake line. Locate problem and bleed brakes (Chapter 6).
☐ Contaminated pads. Caused by contamination with oil, grease, brake fluid, etc. Clean or replace pads. Clean disc thoroughly with brake cleaner (Chapter 6).
☐ Brake fluid deteriorated. Fluid is old or contaminated. Drain system, replenish with new fluid and bleed the system (Chapter 6).
☐ Master cylinder internal parts worn or damaged causing fluid to bypass (Chapter 6).
☐ Master cylinder bore scratched by foreign material or broken spring. Repair or replace master cylinder (Chapter 6).
☐ Disc warped. Replace disc (Chapter 6).

Brake lever or pedal pulsates

☐ Disc warped. Replace disc (Chapter 6).

☐ Axle bent. Replace axle (Chapter 6).
☐ Brake caliper bolts loose (Chapter 6).
☐ Brake caliper sliders damaged or sticking, causing caliper to bind. Lubricate the sliders or replace them if they are corroded or bent (Chapter 6).
☐ Wheel warped or otherwise damaged (Chapter 6).
☐ Wheel bearings damaged or worn (Chapter 6).

Brakes drag

☐ Master cylinder piston seized. Caused by wear or damage to piston or cylinder bore (Chapter 6).
☐ Lever balky or stuck. Check pivot and lubricate (Chapter 6).
☐ Brake caliper binds. Caused by inadequate lubrication or damage to caliper sliders (Chapter 6).
☐ Brake caliper piston seized in bore. Caused by wear or ingestion of dirt past deteriorated seal (Chapter 6).
☐ Brake pad damaged. Pad material separated from backing plate. Usually caused by faulty manufacturing process or from contact with chemicals. Replace pads (Chapter 6).
☐ Pads improperly installed (Chapter 6).

14 Electrical problems

Battery dead or weak

☐ Battery faulty. Caused by sulphated plates which are shorted through sedimentation. Also, broken battery terminal making only occasional contact (Chapter 8).
☐ Battery cables making poor contact (Chapter 1).
☐ Load excessive. Caused by addition of high wattage lights or other electrical accessories.
☐ Ignition (main) switch defective. Switch either grounds (earths) internally or fails to shut off system. Replace the switch (Chapter 8).
☐ Regulator/rectifier defective (Chapter 8).

☐ Alternator stator coil open or shorted (Chapter 8).
☐ Wiring faulty. Wiring grounded (earthed) or connections loose in ignition, charging or lighting circuits (Chapter 8).

Battery overcharged

☐ Regulator/rectifier defective. Overcharging is noticed when battery gets excessively warm (Chapter 8).
☐ Battery defective. Replace battery with a new one (Chapter 8).
☐ Battery amperage too low, wrong type or size. Install manufacturer's specified amp-hour battery to handle charging load (Chapter 8).

Checking engine compression

● Low compression will result in exhaust smoke, heavy oil consumption, poor starting and poor performance. A compression test will provide useful information about an engine's condition and if performed regularly, can give warning of trouble before any other symptoms become apparent.

● A compression gauge will be required, along with an adapter to suit the spark plug hole thread size. Note that the screw-in type gauge/adapter set up is preferable to the rubber cone type.

● Before carrying out the test, first check the valve clearances as described in Chapter 1.

1 Run the engine until it reaches normal operating temperature, then stop it and remove the spark plug(s), taking care not to scald your hands on the hot components.

2 Install the gauge adapter and compression gauge in No. 1 cylinder spark plug hole **(see illustration 1)**.

Screw the compression gauge adapter into the spark plug hole, then screw the gauge into the adapter

3 On kickstart-equipped motorcycles, make sure the ignition switch is OFF, then open the throttle fully and kick the engine over a couple of times until the gauge reading stabilises.

4 On motorcycles with electric start only, the procedure will differ depending on the nature of the ignition system. Flick the engine kill switch (engine stop switch) to OFF and turn the ignition switch ON; open the throttle fully and crank the engine over on the starter motor for a couple of revolutions until the gauge reading stabilises. If the starter will not operate with the kill switch OFF, turn the ignition switch OFF and refer to the next paragraph.

5 Install the spark plugs back into their suppressor caps and arrange the plug electrodes so that their metal bodies are earthed (grounded) against the cylinder head; this is essential to prevent damage to the ignition system as the engine is spun over **(see illustration 2)**. Position the plugs well

All spark plugs must be earthed (grounded) against the cylinder head

away from the plug holes otherwise there is a risk of atomised fuel escaping from the combustion chambers and igniting. As a safety precaution, cover the top of the valve cover with rag. Now turn the ignition switch ON and kill switch ON, open the throttle fully and crank the engine over on the starter motor for a couple of revolutions until the gauge reading stabilises.

6 After one or two revolutions the pressure should build up to a maximum figure and then stabilise. Take a note of this reading and on multi-cylinder engines repeat the test on the remaining cylinders.

7 The correct pressures are given in Chapter 2 Specifications. If the results fall within the specified range and on multi-cylinder engines all are relatively equal, the engine is in good condition. If there is a marked difference between the readings, or if the readings are lower than specified, inspection of the top-end components will be required.

8 Low compression pressure may be due to worn cylinder bores, pistons or rings, failure of the cylinder head gasket, worn valve seals, or poor valve seating.

9 To distinguish between cylinder/piston wear and valve leakage, pour a small quantity of oil into the bore to temporarily seal the piston rings, then repeat the compression tests **(see illustration 3)**. If the readings show

Bores can be temporarily sealed with a squirt of motor oil

a noticeable increase in pressure this confirms that the cylinder bore, piston, or rings are worn. If, however, no change is indicated, the cylinder head gasket or valves should be examined.

10 High compression pressure indicates excessive carbon build-up in the combustion chamber and on the piston crown. If this is the case the cylinder head should be removed and the deposits removed. Note that excessive carbon build-up is less likely with the used on modern fuels.

Checking battery open-circuit voltage

 Warning: The gases produced by the battery are explosive - never smoke or create any sparks in the vicinity of the battery. Never allow the electrolyte to contact your skin or clothing - if it does, wash it off and seek immediate medical attention.

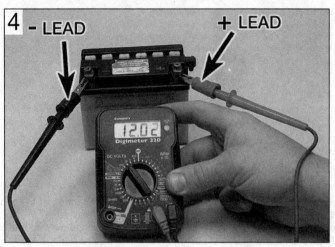

Measuring open-circuit battery voltage

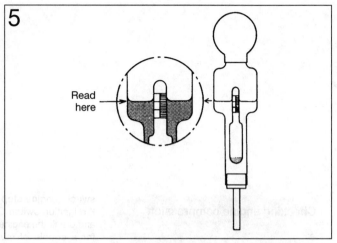

Float-type hydrometer for measuring battery specific gravity

● Before any electrical fault is investigated the battery should be checked.

● You'll need a dc voltmeter or multimeter to check battery voltage. Check that the leads are inserted in the correct terminals on the meter, red lead to positive (+ve), black lead to negative (-ve). Incorrect connections can damage the meter.

● A sound fully-charged 12 volt battery should produce between 12.3 and 12.6 volts across its terminals (12.8 volts for a maintenance-free battery). On machines with a 6 volt battery, voltage should be between 6.1 and 6.3 volts.

1 Set a multimeter to the 0 to 20 volts dc range and connect its probes across the battery terminals. Connect the meter's positive (+ve) probe, usually red, to the battery positive (+ve) terminal, followed by the meter's negative (-ve) probe, usually black, to the battery negative terminal (-ve) **(see illustration 4)**.

2 If battery voltage is low (below 10 volts on a 12 volt battery or below 4 volts on a six volt battery), charge the battery and test the voltage again. If the battery repeatedly goes flat, investigate the motorcycle's charging system.

Checking battery specific gravity (SG)

Warning: The gases produced by the battery are explosive - never smoke or create any sparks in the vicinity of the battery. Never allow the electrolyte to contact your skin or clothing - if it does, wash it off and seek immediate medical attention.

● The specific gravity check gives an indication of a battery's state of charge.

● A hydrometer is used for measuring specific gravity. Make sure you purchase one

which has a small enough hose to insert in the aperture of a motorcycle battery.

● Specific gravity is simply a measure of the electrolyte's density compared with that of water. Water has an SG of 1.000 and fully-charged battery electrolyte is about 26% heavier, at 1.260.

● Specific gravity checks are not possible on maintenance-free batteries. Testing the open-circuit voltage is the only means of determining their state of charge.

1 To measure SG, remove the battery from the motorcycle and remove the first cell cap. Draw

Digital multimeter can be used for all electrical tests

Battery-powered continuity tester

some electrolyte into the hydrometer and note the reading **(see illustration 5)**. Return the electrolyte to the cell and install the cap.

2 The reading should be in the region of 1.260 to 1.280. If SG is below 1.200 the battery needs charging. Note that SG will vary with temperature; it should be measured at 20°C (68°F). Add 0.007 to the reading for every 10°C above 20°C, and subtract 0.007 from the reading for every 10°C below 20°C. Add 0.004 to the reading for every 10°F above 68°F, and subtract 0.004 from the reading for every 10°F below 68°F.

3 When the check is complete, rinse the hydrometer thoroughly with clean water.

Checking for continuity

● The term continuity describes the uninterrupted flow of electricity through an electrical circuit. A continuity check will determine whether an **open-circuit** situation exists.

● Continuity can be checked with an ohmmeter, multimeter, continuity tester or battery and bulb test circuit **(see illustrations 6, 7 and 8)**.

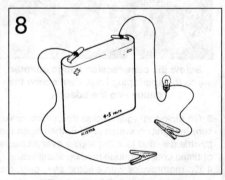

Battery and bulb test circuit

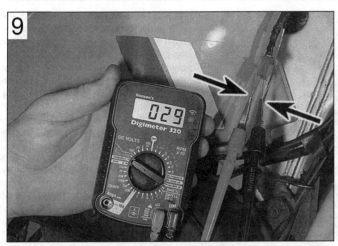

Continuity check of front brake light switch using a meter - note split pins used to access connector terminals

Continuity check of rear brake light switch using a continuity tester

● All of these instruments are self-powered by a battery, therefore the checks are made with the ignition OFF.

● As a safety precaution, always disconnect the battery negative (-ve) lead before making checks, particularly if ignition switch checks are being made.

● If using a meter, select the appropriate ohms scale and check that the meter reads infinity (∞). Touch the meter probes together and check that meter reads zero; where necessary adjust the meter so that it reads zero.

● After using a meter, always switch it OFF to conserve its battery.

Switch checks

1 If a switch is at fault, trace its wiring up to the wiring connectors. Separate the wire connectors and inspect them for security and condition. A build-up of dirt or corrosion here will most likely be the cause of the problem - clean up and apply a water dispersant such as WD40.

2 If using a test meter, set the meter to the ohms x 10 scale and connect its probes across the wires from the switch **(see illustration 9)**. Simple ON/OFF type switches, such as brake light switches, only have two

wires whereas combination switches, like the ignition switch, have many internal links. Study the wiring diagram to ensure that you are connecting across the correct pair of wires. Continuity (low or no measurable resistance - 0 ohms) should be indicated with the switch ON and no continuity (high resistance) with it OFF.

3 Note that the polarity of the test probes doesn't matter for continuity checks, although care should be taken to follow specific test procedures if a diode or solid-state component is being checked.

4 A continuity tester or battery and bulb circuit can be used in the same way. Connect its probes as described above **(see illustration 10)**. The light should come on to indicate continuity in the ON switch position, but should extinguish in the OFF position.

Wiring checks

● Many electrical faults are caused by damaged wiring, often due to incorrect routing or chaffing on frame components.

● Loose, wet or corroded wire connectors can also be the cause of electrical problems, especially in exposed locations.

1 A continuity check can be made on a single length of wire by disconnecting it at each end

and connecting a meter or continuity tester across both ends of the wire **(see illustration 11)**.

2 Continuity (low or no resistance - 0 ohms) should be indicated if the wire is good. If no continuity (high resistance) is shown, suspect a broken wire.

Checking for voltage

● A voltage check can determine whether current is reaching a component.

● Voltage can be checked with a dc voltmeter, multimeter set on the dc volts scale, test light or buzzer **(see illustrations 12 and 13)**. A meter has the advantage of being able to measure actual voltage.

● When using a meter, check that its leads are inserted in the correct terminals on the meter, red to positive (+ve), black to negative (-ve). Incorrect connections can damage the meter.

● A voltmeter (or multimeter set to the dc volts scale) should always be connected in parallel (across the load). Connecting it in series will destroy the meter.

● Voltage checks are made with the ignition ON.

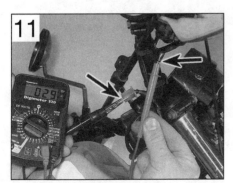

Continuity check of front brake light switch sub-harness

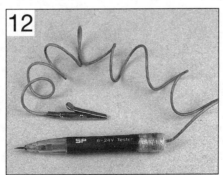

A simple test light can be used for voltage checks

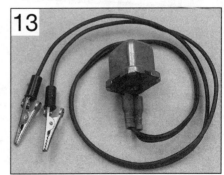

A buzzer is useful for voltage checks

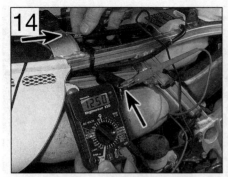

Checking for voltage at the rear brake light power supply wire using a meter . . .

1 First identify the relevant wiring circuit by referring to the wiring diagram at the end of this manual. If other electrical components share the same power supply (ie are fed from the same fuse), take note whether they are working correctly - this is useful information in deciding where to start checking the circuit.

2 If using a meter, check first that the meter leads are plugged into the correct terminals on the meter (see above). Set the meter to the dc volts function, at a range suitable for the battery voltage. Connect the meter red probe (+ve) to the power supply wire and the black probe to a good metal earth (ground) on the motorcycle's frame or directly to the battery negative (-ve) terminal **(see illustration 14)**. Battery voltage should be shown on the meter

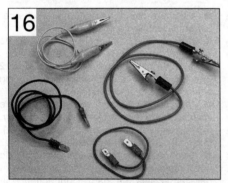

A selection of jumper wires for making earth (ground) checks

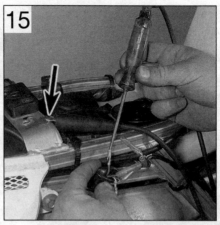

. . . or a test light - note the earth connection to the frame (arrow)

with the ignition switched ON.

3 If using a test light or buzzer, connect its positive (+ve) probe to the power supply terminal and its negative (-ve) probe to a good earth (ground) on the motorcycle's frame or directly to the battery negative (-ve) terminal **(see illustration 15)**. With the ignition ON, the test light should illuminate or the buzzer sound.

4 If no voltage is indicated, work back towards the fuse continuing to check for voltage. When you reach a point where there is voltage, you know the problem lies between that point and your last check point.

Checking the earth (ground)

● Earth connections are made either directly to the engine or frame (such as sensors, neutral switch etc. which only have a positive feed) or by a separate wire into the earth circuit of the wiring harness. Alternatively a short earth wire is sometimes run directly from the component to the motorcycle's frame.

● Corrosion is often the cause of a poor earth connection.

● If total failure is experienced, check the security of the main earth lead from the negative (-ve) terminal of the battery and also the main earth (ground) point on the wiring harness. If corroded, dismantle the connection and clean all surfaces back to bare metal.

1 To check the earth on a component, use an insulated jumper wire to temporarily bypass its earth connection **(see illustration 16)**. Connect one end of the jumper wire between the earth terminal or metal body of the component and the other end to the motorcycle's frame.

2 If the circuit works with the jumper wire installed, the original earth circuit is faulty. Check the wiring for open-circuits or poor connections. Clean up direct earth connections, removing all traces of corrosion and remake the joint. Apply petroleum jelly to the joint to prevent future corrosion.

Tracing a short-circuit

● A short-circuit occurs where current shorts to earth (ground) bypassing the circuit components. This usually results in a blown fuse.

● A short-circuit is most likely to occur where the insulation has worn through due to wiring chafing on a component, allowing a direct path to earth (ground) on the frame.

1 Remove any bodypanels necessary to access the circuit wiring.

2 Check that all electrical switches in the circuit are OFF, then remove the circuit fuse and connect a test light, buzzer or voltmeter (set to the dc scale) across the fuse terminals. No voltage should be shown.

3 Move the wiring from side to side whilst observing the test light or meter. When the test light comes on, buzzer sounds or meter shows voltage, you have found the cause of the short. It will usually shown up as damaged or burned insulation.

4 Note that the same test can be performed on each component in the circuit, even the switch.

A

ABS (Anti-lock braking system) A system, usually electronically controlled, that senses incipient wheel lockup during braking and relieves hydraulic pressure at wheel which is about to skid.

Aftermarket Components suitable for the motorcycle, but not produced by the motorcycle manufacturer.

Allen key A hexagonal wrench which fits into a recessed hexagonal hole.

Alternating current (ac) Current produced by an alternator. Requires converting to direct current by a rectifier for charging purposes.

Alternator Converts mechanical energy from the engine into electrical energy to charge the battery and power the electrical system.

Ampere (amp) A unit of measurement for the flow of electrical current. Current = Volts ÷ Ohms.

Ampere-hour (Ah) Measure of battery capacity.

Angle-tightening A torque expressed in degrees. Often follows a conventional tightening torque for cylinder head or main bearing fasteners **(see illustration)**.

Angle-tightening cylinder head bolts

Antifreeze A substance (usually ethylene glycol) mixed with water, and added to the cooling system, to prevent freezing of the coolant in winter. Antifreeze also contains chemicals to inhibit corrosion and the formation of rust and other deposits that would tend to clog the radiator and coolant passages and reduce cooling efficiency.

Anti-dive System attached to the fork lower leg (slider) to prevent fork dive when braking hard.

Anti-seize compound A coating that reduces the risk of seizing on fasteners that are subjected to high temperatures, such as exhaust clamp bolts and nuts.

API American Petroleum Institute. A quality standard for 4-stroke motor oils.

Asbestos A natural fibrous mineral with great heat resistance, commonly used in the composition of brake friction materials. Asbestos is a health hazard and the dust created by brake systems should never be inhaled or ingested.

ATF Automatic Transmission Fluid. Often used in front forks.

ATU Automatic Timing Unit. Mechanical device for advancing the ignition timing on early engines.

ATV All Terrain Vehicle. Often called a Quad.

Axial play Side-to-side movement.

Axle A shaft on which a wheel revolves. Also known as a spindle.

B

Backlash The amount of movement between meshed components when one component is held still. Usually applies to gear teeth.

Ball bearing A bearing consisting of a hardened inner and outer race with hardened steel balls between the two races.

Bearings Used between two working surfaces to prevent wear of the components and a build-up of heat. Four types of bearing are commonly used on motorcycles: plain shell bearings, ball bearings, tapered roller bearings and needle roller bearings.

Bevel gears Used to turn the drive through 90°. Typical applications are shaft final drive and camshaft drive **(see illustration)**.

Bevel gears are used to turn the drive through 90°

BHP Brake Horsepower. The British measurement for engine power output. Power output is now usually expressed in kilowatts (kW).

Bias-belted tyre Similar construction to radial tyre, but with outer belt running at an angle to the wheel rim.

Big-end bearing The bearing in the end of the connecting rod that's attached to the crankshaft.

Bleeding The process of removing air from an hydraulic system via a bleed nipple or bleed screw.

Bottom-end A description of an engine's crankcase components and all components contained there-in.

BTDC Before Top Dead Centre in terms of piston position. Ignition timing is often expressed in terms of degrees or millimetres BTDC.

Bush A cylindrical metal or rubber component used between two moving parts.

Burr Rough edge left on a component after machining or as a result of excessive wear.

C

Cam chain The chain which takes drive from the crankshaft to the camshaft(s).

Canister The main component in an evaporative emission control system (California market only); contains activated charcoal granules to trap vapours from the fuel system rather than allowing them to vent to the atmosphere.

Castellated Resembling the parapets along the top of a castle wall. For example, a castellated wheel axle or spindle nut.

Catalytic converter A device in the exhaust system of some machines which converts certain pollutants in the exhaust gases into less harmful substances.

Charging system Description of the components which charge the battery, ie the alternator, rectifer and regulator.

Circlip A ring-shaped clip used to prevent endwise movement of cylindrical parts and shafts. An internal circlip is installed in a groove in a housing; an external circlip fits into a groove on the outside of a cylindrical piece such as a shaft. Also known as a snap-ring.

Clearance The amount of space between two parts. For example, between a piston and a cylinder, between a bearing and a journal, etc.

Coil spring A spiral of elastic steel found in various sizes throughout a vehicle, for example as a springing medium in the suspension and in the valve train.

Compression Reduction in volume, and increase in pressure and temperature, of a gas, caused by squeezing it into a smaller space.

Compression damping Controls the speed the suspension compresses when hitting a bump.

Compression ratio The relationship between cylinder volume when the piston is at top dead centre and cylinder volume when the piston is at bottom dead centre.

Continuity The uninterrupted path in the flow of electricity. Little or no measurable resistance.

Continuity tester Self-powered bleeper or test light which indicates continuity.

Cp Candlepower. Bulb rating commonly found on US motorcycles.

Crossply tyre Tyre plies arranged in a criss-cross pattern. Usually four or six plies used, hence 4PR or 6PR in tyre size codes.

Cush drive Rubber damper segments fitted between the rear wheel and final drive sprocket to absorb transmission shocks **(see illustration)**.

Cush drive rubbers dampen out transmission shocks

D

Degree disc Calibrated disc for measuring piston position. Expressed in degrees.

Dial gauge Clock-type gauge with adapters for measuring runout and piston position. Expressed in mm or inches.

Diaphragm The rubber membrane in a master cylinder or carburettor which seals the upper chamber.

Diaphragm spring A single sprung plate often used in clutches.

Direct current (dc) Current produced by a dc generator.

Decarbonisation The process of removing carbon deposits - typically from the combustion chamber, valves and exhaust port/system.

Detonation Destructive and damaging explosion of fuel/air mixture in combustion chamber instead of controlled burning.

Diode An electrical valve which only allows current to flow in one direction. Commonly used in rectifiers and starter interlock systems.

Disc valve (or rotary valve) A induction system used on some two-stroke engines.

Double-overhead camshaft (DOHC) An engine that uses two overhead camshafts, one for the intake valves and one for the exhaust valves.

Drivebelt A toothed belt used to transmit drive to the rear wheel on some motorcycles. A drivebelt has also been used to drive the camshafts. Drivebelts are usually made of Kevlar.

Driveshaft Any shaft used to transmit motion. Commonly used when referring to the final driveshaft on shaft drive motorcycles.

E

Earth return The return path of an electrical circuit, utilising the motorcycle's frame.

ECU (Electronic Control Unit) A computer which controls (for instance) an ignition system, or an anti-lock braking system.

EGO Exhaust Gas Oxygen sensor. Sometimes called a Lambda sensor.

Electrolyte The fluid in a lead-acid battery.

EMS (Engine Management System) A computer controlled system which manages the fuel injection and the ignition systems in an integrated fashion.

Endfloat The amount of lengthways movement between two parts. As applied to a crankshaft, the distance that the crankshaft can move side-to-side in the crankcase.

Endless chain A chain having no joining link. Common use for cam chains and final drive chains.

EP (Extreme Pressure) Oil type used in locations where high loads are applied, such as between gear teeth.

Evaporative emission control system Describes a charcoal filled canister which stores fuel vapours from the tank rather than allowing them to vent to the atmosphere. Usually only fitted to California models and referred to as an EVAP system.

Expansion chamber Section of two-stroke engine exhaust system so designed to improve engine efficiency and boost power.

F

Feeler blade or gauge A thin strip or blade of hardened steel, ground to an exact thickness, used to check or measure clearances between parts.

Final drive Description of the drive from the transmission to the rear wheel. Usually by chain or shaft, but sometimes by belt.

Firing order The order in which the engine cylinders fire, or deliver their power strokes, beginning with the number one cylinder.

Flooding Term used to describe a high fuel level in the carburettor float chambers, leading to fuel overflow. Also refers to excess fuel in the combustion chamber due to incorrect starting technique.

Free length The no-load state of a component when measured. Clutch, valve and fork spring lengths are measured at rest, without any preload.

Freeplay The amount of travel before any action takes place. The looseness in a linkage, or an assembly of parts, between the initial application of force and actual movement. For example, the distance the rear brake pedal moves before the rear brake is actuated.

Fuel injection The fuel/air mixture is metered electronically and directed into the engine intake ports (indirect injection) or into the cylinders (direct injection). Sensors supply information on engine speed and conditions.

Fuel/air mixture The charge of fuel and air going into the engine. See **Stoichiometric ratio**.

Fuse An electrical device which protects a circuit against accidental overload. The typical fuse contains a soft piece of metal which is calibrated to melt at a predetermined current flow (expressed as amps) and break the circuit.

G

Gap The distance the spark must travel in jumping from the centre electrode to the side electrode in a spark plug. Also refers to the distance between the ignition rotor and the pickup coil in an electronic ignition system.

Gasket Any thin, soft material - usually cork, cardboard, asbestos or soft metal - installed between two metal surfaces to ensure a good seal. For instance, the cylinder head gasket seals the joint between the block and the cylinder head.

Gauge An instrument panel display used to monitor engine conditions. A gauge with a movable pointer on a dial or a fixed scale is an analogue gauge. A gauge with a numerical readout is called a digital gauge.

Gear ratios The drive ratio of a pair of gears in a gearbox, calculated on their number of teeth.

Glaze-busting see **Honing**

Grinding Process for renovating the valve face and valve seat contact area in the cylinder head.

Gudgeon pin The shaft which connects the connecting rod small-end with the piston. Often called a piston pin or wrist pin.

H

Helical gears Gear teeth are slightly curved and produce less gear noise that straight-cut gears. Often used for primary drives.

Installing a Helicoil thread insert in a cylinder head

Helicoil A thread insert repair system. Commonly used as a repair for stripped spark plug threads **(see illustration)**.

Honing A process used to break down the glaze on a cylinder bore (also called glaze-busting). Can also be carried out to roughen a rebored cylinder to aid ring bedding-in.

HT (High Tension) Description of the electrical circuit from the secondary winding of the ignition coil to the spark plug.

Hydraulic A liquid filled system used to transmit pressure from one component to another. Common uses on motorcycles are brakes and clutches.

Hydrometer An instrument for measuring the specific gravity of a lead-acid battery.

Hygroscopic Water absorbing. In motorcycle applications, braking efficiency will be reduced if DOT 3 or 4 hydraulic fluid absorbs water from the air - care must be taken to keep new brake fluid in tightly sealed containers.

I

lbf ft Pounds-force feet. An imperial unit of torque. Sometimes written as ft-lbs.

lbf in Pound-force inch. An imperial unit of torque, applied to components where a very low torque is required. Sometimes written as in-lbs.

IC Abbreviation for Integrated Circuit.

Ignition advance Means of increasing the timing of the spark at higher engine speeds. Done by mechanical means (ATU) on early engines or electronically by the ignition control unit on later engines.

Ignition timing The moment at which the spark plug fires, expressed in the number of crankshaft degrees before the piston reaches the top of its stroke, or in the number of millimetres before the piston reaches the top of its stroke.

Infinity (∞) Description of an open-circuit electrical state, where no continuity exists.

Inverted forks (upside down forks) The sliders or lower legs are held in the yokes and the fork tubes or stanchions are connected to the wheel axle (spindle). Less unsprung weight and stiffer construction than conventional forks.

J

JASO Quality standard for 2-stroke oils.

Joule The unit of electrical energy.

Journal The bearing surface of a shaft.

K

Kickstart Mechanical means of turning the engine over for starting purposes. Only usually fitted to mopeds, small capacity motorcycles and off-road motorcycles.

Kill switch Handebar-mounted switch for emergency ignition cut-out. Cuts the ignition circuit on all models, and additionally prevent starter motor operation on others.

km Symbol for kilometre.

kmh Abbreviation for kilometres per hour.

L

Lambda (λ) sensor A sensor fitted in the exhaust system to measure the exhaust gas oxygen content (excess air factor).

Lapping see **Grinding**.
LCD Abbreviation for Liquid Crystal Display.
LED Abbreviation for Light Emitting Diode.
Liner A steel cylinder liner inserted in a aluminium alloy cylinder block.
Locknut A nut used to lock an adjustment nut, or other threaded component, in place.
Lockstops The lugs on the lower triple clamp (yoke) which abut those on the frame, preventing handlebar-to-fuel tank contact.
Lockwasher A form of washer designed to prevent an attaching nut from working loose.
LT Low Tension Description of the electrical circuit from the power supply to the primary winding of the ignition coil.

M

Main bearings The bearings between the crankshaft and crankcase.
Maintenance-free (MF) battery A sealed battery which cannot be topped up.
Manometer Mercury-filled calibrated tubes used to measure intake tract vacuum. Used to synchronise carburettors on multi-cylinder engines.
Micrometer A precision measuring instrument that measures component outside diameters **(see illustration)**.

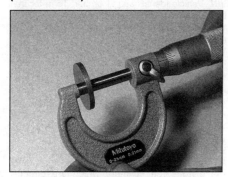

Tappet shims are measured with a micrometer

MON (Motor Octane Number) A measure of a fuel's resistance to knock.
Monograde oil An oil with a single viscosity, eg SAE80W.
Monoshock A single suspension unit linking the swingarm or suspension linkage to the frame.
mph Abbreviation for miles per hour.
Multigrade oil Having a wide viscosity range (eg 10W40). The W stands for Winter, thus the viscosity ranges from SAE10 when cold to SAE40 when hot.
Multimeter An electrical test instrument with the capability to measure voltage, current and resistance. Some meters also incorporate a continuity tester and buzzer.

N

Needle roller bearing Inner race of caged needle rollers and hardened outer race. Examples of uncaged needle rollers can be found on some engines. Commonly used in rear suspension applications and in two-stroke engines.
Nm Newton metres.
NOx Oxides of Nitrogen. A common toxic pollutant emitted by petrol engines at higher temperatures.

O

Octane The measure of a fuel's resistance to knock.
OE (Original Equipment) Relates to components fitted to a motorcycle as standard or replacement parts supplied by the motorcycle manufacturer.
Ohm The unit of electrical resistance. Ohms = Volts ÷ Current.
Ohmmeter An instrument for measuring electrical resistance.
Oil cooler System for diverting engine oil outside of the engine to a radiator for cooling purposes.
Oil injection A system of two-stroke engine lubrication where oil is pump-fed to the engine in accordance with throttle position.
Open-circuit An electrical condition where there is a break in the flow of electricity - no continuity (high resistance).
O-ring A type of sealing ring made of a special rubber-like material; in use, the O-ring is compressed into a groove to provide the sealing action.
Oversize (OS) Term used for piston and ring size options fitted to a rebored cylinder.
Overhead cam (sohc) engine An engine with single camshaft located on top of the cylinder head.
Overhead valve (ohv) engine An engine with the valves located in the cylinder head, but with the camshaft located in the engine block or crankcase.
Oxygen sensor A device installed in the exhaust system which senses the oxygen content in the exhaust and converts this information into an electric current. Also called a Lambda sensor.

P

Plastigauge A thin strip of plastic thread, available in different sizes, used for measuring clearances. For example, a strip of Plastigauge is laid across a bearing journal. The parts are assembled and dismantled; the width of the crushed strip indicates the clearance between journal and bearing.
Polarity Either negative or positive earth (ground), determined by which battery lead is connected to the frame (earth return). Modern motorcycles are usually negative earth.
Pre-ignition A situation where the fuel/air mixture ignites before the spark plug fires. Often due to a hot spot in the combustion chamber caused by carbon build-up. Engine has a tendency to 'run-on'.
Pre-load (suspension) The amount a spring is compressed when in the unloaded state. Preload can be applied by gas, spacer or mechanical adjuster.
Premix The method of engine lubrication on older two-stroke engines. Engine oil is mixed with the petrol in the fuel tank in a specific ratio. The fuel/oil mix is sometimes referred to as "petroil".
Primary drive Description of the drive from the crankshaft to the clutch. Usually by gear or chain.
PS Pfedestärke - a German interpretation of BHP.
PSI Pounds-force per square inch. Imperial measurement of tyre pressure and cylinder pressure measurement.
PTFE Polytetrafluoroethylene. A low friction substance.

Pulse secondary air injection system A process of promoting the burning of excess fuel present in the exhaust gases by routing fresh air into the exhaust ports.

Q

Quartz halogen bulb Tungsten filament surrounded by a halogen gas. Typically used for the headlight **(see illustration)**.

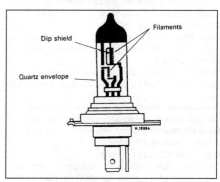

Quartz halogen headlight bulb construction

R

Rack-and-pinion A pinion gear on the end of a shaft that mates with a rack (think of a geared wheel opened up and laid flat). Sometimes used in clutch operating systems.
Radial play Up and down movement about a shaft.
Radial ply tyres Tyre plies run across the tyre (from bead to bead) and around the circumference of the tyre. Less resistant to tread distortion than other tyre types.
Radiator A liquid-to-air heat transfer device designed to reduce the temperature of the coolant in a liquid cooled engine.
Rake A feature of steering geometry - the angle of the steering head in relation to the vertical **(see illustration)**.

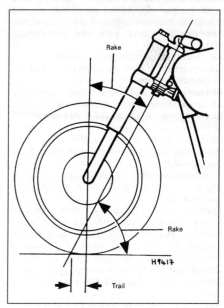

Steering geometry

Rebore Providing a new working surface to the cylinder bore by boring out the old surface. Necessitates the use of oversize piston and rings.

Rebound damping A means of controlling the oscillation of a suspension unit spring after it has been compressed. Resists the spring's natural tendency to bounce back after being compressed.

Rectifier Device for converting the ac output of an alternator into dc for battery charging.

Reed valve An induction system commonly used on two-stroke engines.

Regulator Device for maintaining the charging voltage from the generator or alternator within a specified range.

Relay A electrical device used to switch heavy current on and off by using a low current auxiliary circuit.

Resistance Measured in ohms. An electrical component's ability to pass electrical current.

RON (Research Octane Number) A measure of a fuel's resistance to knock.

rpm revolutions per minute.

Runout The amount of wobble (in-and-out movement) of a wheel or shaft as it's rotated. The amount a shaft rotates 'out-of-true'. The out-of-round condition of a rotating part.

S

SAE (Society of Automotive Engineers) A standard for the viscosity of a fluid.

Sealant A liquid or paste used to prevent leakage at a joint. Sometimes used in conjunction with a gasket.

Service limit Term for the point where a component is no longer useable and must be renewed.

Shaft drive A method of transmitting drive from the transmission to the rear wheel.

Shell bearings Plain bearings consisting of two shell halves. Most often used as big-end and main bearings in a four-stroke engine. Often called bearing inserts.

Shim Thin spacer, commonly used to adjust the clearance or relative positions between two parts. For example, shims inserted into or under tappets or followers to control valve clearances. Clearance is adjusted by changing the thickness of the shim.

Short-circuit An electrical condition where current shorts to earth (ground) bypassing the circuit components.

Skimming Process to correct warpage or repair a damaged surface, eg on brake discs or drums.

Slide-hammer A special puller that screws into or hooks onto a component such as a shaft or bearing; a heavy sliding handle on the shaft bottoms against the end of the shaft to knock the component free.

Small-end bearing The bearing in the upper end of the connecting rod at its joint with the gudgeon pin.

Spalling Damage to camshaft lobes or bearing journals shown as pitting of the working surface.

Specific gravity (SG) The state of charge of the electrolyte in a lead-acid battery. A measure of the electrolyte's density compared with water.

Straight-cut gears Common type gear used on gearbox shafts and for oil pump and water pump drives.

Stanchion The inner sliding part of the front forks, held by the yokes. Often called a fork tube.

Stoichiometric ratio The optimum chemical air/fuel ratio for a petrol engine, said to be 14.7 parts of air to 1 part of fuel.

Sulphuric acid The liquid (electrolyte) used in a lead-acid battery. Poisonous and extremely corrosive.

Surface grinding (lapping) Process to correct a warped gasket face, commonly used on cylinder heads.

T

Tapered-roller bearing Tapered inner race of caged needle rollers and separate tapered outer race. Examples of taper roller bearings can be found on steering heads.

Tappet A cylindrical component which transmits motion from the cam to the valve stem, either directly or via a pushrod and rocker arm. Also called a cam follower.

TCS Traction Control System. An electronically-controlled system which senses wheel spin and reduces engine speed accordingly.

TDC Top Dead Centre denotes that the piston is at its highest point in the cylinder.

Thread-locking compound Solution applied to fastener threads to prevent slackening. Select type to suit application.

Thrust washer A washer positioned between two moving components on a shaft. For example, between gear pinions on gearshaft.

Timing chain See **Cam Chain.**

Timing light Stroboscopic lamp for carrying out ignition timing checks with the engine running.

Top-end A description of an engine's cylinder block, head and valve gear components.

Torque Turning or twisting force about a shaft.

Torque setting A prescribed tightness specified by the motorcycle manufacturer to ensure that the bolt or nut is secured correctly. Undertightening can result in the bolt or nut coming loose or a surface not being sealed. Overtightening can result in stripped threads, distortion or damage to the component being retained.

Torx key A six-point wrench.

Tracer A stripe of a second colour applied to a wire insulator to distinguish that wire from another one with the same colour insulator. For example, Br/W is often used to denote a brown insulator with a white tracer.

Trail A feature of steering geometry. Distance from the steering head axis to the tyre's central contact point.

Triple clamps The cast components which extend from the steering head and support the fork stanchions or tubes. Often called fork yokes.

Turbocharger A centrifugal device, driven by exhaust gases, that pressurises the intake air. Normally used to increase the power output from a given engine displacement.

TWI Abbreviation for Tyre Wear Indicator. Indicates the location of the tread depth indicator bars on tyres.

U

Universal joint or U-joint (UJ) A double-pivoted connection for transmitting power from a driving to a driven shaft through an angle. Typically found in shaft drive assemblies.

Unsprung weight Anything not supported by the bike's suspension (ie the wheel, tyres, brakes, final drive and bottom (moving) part of the suspension).

V

Vacuum gauges Clock-type gauges for measuring intake tract vacuum. Used for carburettor synchronisation on multi-cylinder engines.

Valve A device through which the flow of liquid, gas or vacuum may be stopped, started or regulated by a moveable part that opens, shuts or partially obstructs one or more ports or passageways. The intake and exhaust valves in the cylinder head are of the poppet type.

Valve clearance The clearance between the valve tip (the end of the valve stem) and the rocker arm or tappet/follower. The valve clearance is measured when the valve is closed. The correct clearance is important - if too small the valve won't close fully and will burn out, whereas if too large noisy operation will result.

Valve lift The amount a valve is lifted off its seat by the camshaft lobe.

Valve timing The exact setting for the opening and closing of the valves in relation to piston position.

Vernier caliper A precision measuring instrument that measures inside and outside dimensions. Not quite as accurate as a micrometer, but more convenient.

VIN Vehicle Identification Number. Term for the bike's engine and frame numbers.

Viscosity The thickness of a liquid or its resistance to flow.

Volt A unit for expressing electrical "pressure" in a circuit. Volts = current x ohms.

W

Water pump A mechanically-driven device for moving coolant around the engine.

Watt A unit for expressing electrical power. Watts = volts x current.

Wear limit see **Service limit**

Wet liner A liquid-cooled engine design where the pistons run in liners which are directly surrounded by coolant **(see illustration)**.

Wet liner arrangement

Wheelbase Distance from the centre of the front wheel to the centre of the rear wheel.

Wiring harness or loom Describes the electrical wires running the length of the motorcycle and enclosed in tape or plastic sheathing. Wiring coming off the main harness is usually referred to as a sub harness.

Woodruff key A key of semi-circular or square section used to locate a gear to a shaft. Often used to locate the alternator rotor on the crankshaft.

Wrist pin Another name for gudgeon or piston pin.

Note: *References throughout this index are in the form - "Chapter number" • "page number"*

Haynes Motorcycle Manuals – The Complete List

Title	Book No.
BMW	
BMW 2-valve Twins (70 - 96)	0249
BMW K100 & 75 2-valve Models (83 - 96)	1373
BMW R850 & R1100 4-valve Twins (93 - 97)	3466
BSA	
BSA Bantam (48 - 71)	0117
BSA Unit Singles (58 - 72)	0127
BSA Pre-unit Singles (54 - 61)	0326
BSA A7 & A10 Twins (47 - 62)	0121
BSA A50 & A65 Twins (62 - 73)	0155
DUCATI	
Ducati 600, 750 & 900 2-valve V-Twins (91 - 96)	3290
HARLEY-DAVIDSON	
Harley-Davidson Sportsters (70 - 99)	0702
Harley-Davidson Big Twins (70 - 99)	0703
HONDA	
Honda NB, ND, NP & NS50 Melody (81 - 85) ◊	0622
Honda NE/NB50 Vision & SA50 Vision Met-in (85 - 95) ◊	1278
Honda MB, MBX, MT & MTX50 (80 - 93)	0731
Honda C50, C70 & C90 (67 - 99)	0324
Honda CR80R & CR125R (86 - 97)	2220
Honda XR80R & XR100R (85 - 96)	2218
Honda XL/XR 80, 100, 125, 185 & 200 2-valve Models (78 - 87)	0566
Honda CB100N & CB125N (78 - 86) ◊	0569
Honda H100 & H100S Singles (80 - 92) ◊	0734
Honda CB/CD125T & CM125C Twins (77 - 88) ◊	0571
Honda CG125 (76 - 99) ◊	0433
Honda NS125 (86 - 93) ◊	3056
Honda MBX/MTX125 & MTX200 (83 - 93) ◊	1132
Honda CD/CM185 200T & CM250C 2-valve Twins (77 - 85)	0572
Honda XL/XR 250 & 500 (78 - 84)	0567
Honda XR250L, XR250R & XR400R (86 - 97)	2219
Honda CB250 & CB400N Super Dreams (78 - 84) ◊	0540
Honda CR250R & CR500R (86 - 97)	2222
Honda Elsinore 250 (73 - 75)	0217
Honda CBR400RR Fours (88 - 99)	3552
Honda VFR400 (NC30) & RVF400 (NC35) V-Fours (89 - 98)	3496
Honda CB400 & CB550 Fours (73 - 77)	0262
Honda CX/GL500 & 650 V-Twins (78 - 86)	0442
Honda CBX550 Four (82 - 86) ◊	0940
Honda XL600R & XR600R (83 - 96)	2183
Honda CBR600F1 & 1000F Fours (87 - 96)	1730
Honda CBR600F2 & F3 Fours (91 - 98)	2070
Honda CB650 sohc Fours (78 - 84)	0665
Honda NTV600 & 650 V-Twins (88 - 96)	3243
Honda Shadow VT600 & 750 (USA) (88 - 99)	2312
Honda CB750 sohc Four (69 - 79)	0131
Honda V45/65 Sabre & Magna (82 - 88)	0820
Honda VFR750 & 700 V-Fours (86 - 97)	2101
Honda VFR800 V-Fours (97 - 00)	3703
Honda CB750 & CB900 dohc Fours (78 - 84)	0535
Honda CBR900RR FireBlade (92 - 99)	2161
Honda ST1100 Pan European V-Fours (90 - 97)	3384
Honda Shadow VT1100 (USA) (85 - 98)	2313
Honda GL1000 Gold Wing (75 - 79)	0309
Honda GL1100 Gold Wing (79 - 81)	0669
Honda Gold Wing 1200 (USA) (84 - 87)	2199
Honda Gold Wing 1500 (USA) (88 - 98)	2225
KAWASAKI	
Kawasaki AE/AR 50 & 80 (81 - 95)	1007

Title	Book No.
Kawasaki KC, KE & KH100 (75 - 99)	1371
Kawasaki KMX125 & 200 (86 - 96) ◊	3046
Kawasaki 250, 350 & 400 Triples (72 - 79)	0134
Kawasaki 400 & 440 Twins (74 - 81)	0281
Kawasaki 400, 500 & 550 Fours (79 - 91)	0910
Kawasaki EN450 & 500 Twins (Ltd/Vulcan) (85 - 93)	2053
Kawasaki EX & ER500 (GPZ500S & ER-5) Twins (87 - 99)	2052
Kawasaki ZX600 (Ninja ZX-6, ZZ-R600) Fours (90 - 97)	2146
Kawasaki ZX-6R Ninja Fours (95 - 98)	3541
Kawasaki ZX600 (GPZ600R, GPX600R, Ninja 600R & RX) & ZX750 (GPX750R, Ninja 750R) Fours (85 - 97)	1780
Kawasaki 650 Four (76 - 78)	0373
Kawasaki 750 Air-cooled Fours (80 - 91)	0574
Kawasaki ZR550 & 750 Zephyr Fours (90 - 97)	3382
Kawasaki ZX750 (Ninja ZX-7 & ZXR750) Fours (89 - 96)	2054
Kawasaki 900 & 1000 Fours (73 - 77)	0222
Kawasaki ZX900, 1000 & 1100 Liquid-cooled Fours (83 - 97)	1681
MOTO GUZZI	
Moto Guzzi 750, 850 & 1000 V-Twins (74 - 78)	0339
MZ	
MZ ETZ Models (81 - 95) ◊	1680
NORTON	
Norton 500, 600, 650 & 750 Twins (57 - 70)	0187
Norton Commando (68 - 77)	0125
PIAGGIO	
Piaggio (Vespa) Scooters (91 - 98)	3492
SUZUKI	
Suzuki GT, ZR & TS50 (77 - 90) ◊	0799
Suzuki TS50X (83 - 99) ◊	1599
Suzuki 100, 125, 185 & 250 Air-cooled Trail bikes (79 - 89)	0797
Suzuki GP100 & 125 Singles (78 - 93) ◊	0576
Suzuki GS, GN, GZ & DR125 Singles (82 - 99) ◊	0888
Suzuki 250 & 350 Twins (68 - 78)	0120
Suzuki GT250X7, GT200X5 & SB200 Twins (78 - 83) ◊	0469
Suzuki GS/GSX250, 400 & 450 Twins (79 - 85)	0736
Suzuki GS500E Twin (89 - 97)	3238
Suzuki GS550 (77 - 82) & GS750 Fours (76 - 79)	0363
Suzuki GS/GSX550 4-valve Fours (83 - 88)	1133
Suzuki GSX-R600 & 750 (96 - 99)	3553
Suzuki GSF600 & 1200 Bandit Fours (95 - 97)	3367
Suzuki GS850 Fours (78 - 88)	0536
Suzuki GS1000 Four (77 - 79)	0484
Suzuki GSX-R750, GSX-R1100 (85 - 92), GSX600F, GSX750F, GSX1100F (Katana) Fours (88 - 96)	2055
Suzuki GS/GSX1000, 1100 & 1150 4-valve Fours (79 - 88)	0737
TRIUMPH	
Triumph Tiger Cub & Terrier (52 - 68)	0414
Triumph 350 & 500 Unit Twins (58 - 73)	0137
Triumph Pre-Unit Twins (47 - 62)	0251
Triumph 650 & 750 2-valve Unit Twins (63 - 83)	0122
Triumph Trident & BSA Rocket 3 (69 - 75)	0136
Triumph Triples & Fours (carburettor engines) (91 - 99)	2162
VESPA	
Vespa P/PX125, 150 & 200 Scooters (78 - 95)	0707
Vespa Scooters (59 - 78)	0126
YAMAHA	
Yamaha DT50 & 80 Trail Bikes (78 - 95) ◊	0800
Yamaha T50 & 80 Townmate (83 - 95) ◊	1247
Yamaha YB100 Singles (73 - 91) ◊	0474

Title	Book No.
Yamaha RS/RXS100 & 125 Singles (74 - 95)	0331
Yamaha RD & DT125LC (82 - 87) ◊	0887
Yamaha TZR125 (87 - 93) & DT125R (88 - 95) ◊	1655
Yamaha TY50, 80, 125 & 175 (74 - 84) ◊	0464
Yamaha XT & SR125 (82 - 96)	1021
Yamaha 250 & 350 Twins (70 - 79)	0040
Yamaha XS250, 360 & 400 sohc Twins (75 - 84)	0378
Yamaha RD250 & 350LC Twins (80 - 82)	0803
Yamaha RD350 YPVS Twins (83 - 95)	1158
Yamaha RD400 Twin (75 - 79)	0333
Yamaha XT, TT & SR500 Singles (75 - 83)	0342
Yamaha XZ550 Vision V-Twins (82 - 85)	0821
Yamaha FJ, FZ, XJ & YX600 Radian (84 - 92)	2100
Yamaha XJ600S (Diversion, Seca II) & XJ600N Fours (92 - 99)	2145
Yamaha YZF600R Thundercat & FZS600 Fazer (96 - 99)	3702
Yamaha 650 Twins (70 - 83)	0341
Yamaha XJ650 & 750 Fours (80 - 84)	0738
Yamaha XS750 & 850 Triples (76 - 85)	0340
Yamaha TDM850, TRX850 & XTZ750 (89 - 99)	3540
Yamaha FZR600, 750 & 1000 Fours (87 - 96)	2056
Yamaha XV V-Twins (81 - 96)	0802
Yamaha XJ900F Fours (83 - 94)	3239
Yamaha FJ1100 & 1200 Fours (84 - 96)	2057
ATVS	
Honda ATC70, 90, 110, 185 & 200 (71 - 85)	0565
Honda TRX300 Shaft Drive ATVs (88 - 95)	2125
Honda TRX300EX & TRX400EX ATVs (93 - 99)	2318
Polaris ATVs (85 to 97)	2302
Yamaha YT, YFM, YTM & YTZ ATVs (80 - 85)	1154
Yamaha YFS200 Blaster ATV (88 - 98)	2317
Yamaha YFB250 Timberwolf ATV (92 - 96)	2217
Yamaha YFM350 Big Bear and ER ATVs (87 - 95)	2126
Yamaha Warrior and Banshee ATVs (87 - 99)	2314
ATV Basics	10450
TECHNICAL TITLES	
Motorcycle Basics Manual	1083
MOTORCYCLE TECHBOOKS	
Motorcycle Electrical TechBook (3rd Edition)	3471
Motorcycle Fuel Systems TechBook	3514
Motorcycle Workshop Practice TechBook (2nd Edition)	3470

◊ = not available in the USA   **Bold type** = *Superbike*

The manuals on this page are available through good motorcycle dealers and accessory shops.
In case of difficulty, contact: **Haynes Publishing**
(UK) +44 1963 440635   (USA) +1 805 4986703
(FR) +33 1 47 78 50 50   (SV) +46 18 124016
(Australia/New Zealand) +61 3 9763 8100

MCL08.09/99

Preserving Our Motoring Heritage

> *The Model J Duesenberg Derham Tourster. Only eight of these magnificent cars were ever built – this is the only example to be found outside the United States of America*

Almost every car you've ever loved, loathed or desired is gathered under one roof at the Haynes Motor Museum. Over 300 immaculately presented cars and motorbikes represent every aspect of our motoring heritage, from elegant reminders of bygone days, such as the superb Model J Duesenberg to curiosities like the bug-eyed BMW Isetta. There are also many old friends and flames. Perhaps you remember the 1959 Ford Popular that you did your courting in? The magnificent 'Red Collection' is a spectacle of classic sports cars including AC, Alfa Romeo, Austin Healey, Ferrari, Lamborghini, Maserati, MG, Riley, Porsche and Triumph.

A Perfect Day Out

Each and every vehicle at the Haynes Motor Museum has played its part in the history and culture of Motoring. Today, they make a wonderful spectacle and a great day out for all the family. Bring the kids, bring Mum and Dad, but above all bring your camera to capture those golden memories for ever. You will also find an impressive array of motoring memorabilia, a comfortable 70 seat video cinema and one of the most extensive transport book shops in Britain. The Pit Stop Cafe serves everything from a cup of tea to wholesome, home-made meals or, if you prefer, you can enjoy the large picnic area nestled in the beautiful rural surroundings of Somerset.

> *John Haynes O.B.E., Founder and Chairman of the museum at the wheel of a Haynes Light 12.*

< *The 1936 490cc sohc-engined International Norton – well known for its racing success*

The Museum is situated on the A359 Yeovil to Frome road at Sparkford, just off the A303 in Somerset. It is about 40 miles south of Bristol, and 25 minutes drive from the M5 intersection at Taunton.
Open 9.30am - 5.30pm (10.00am - 4.00pm Winter) 7 days a week, *except Christmas Day, Boxing Day and New Years Day*
Special rates available for schools, coach parties and outings Charitable Trust No. 292048

TECHNIQUES AND EXERCISES

TECHNIQUES AND EXERCISES
Acrylic
PAINTING

JOSÉ M. PARRAMÓN

*The guides at the end of the book are numbered in the margin and
designed to be cut with a paper* cutter.

Overall manager: José M. Parramón Vilasaló
Texts: José M. Parramón and Gabriel Martin
Editing, layout and design: Lema Publications, S.L.
Cover: Award and Lema Publications, S.L.
Editorial manager: José M. Parramón Homs
Editor: Eva Mª Durán
Original title: Pintando al Óleo
Translation: Mike Roberts
Coordination: Eduardo Hernández

Photography and Photosetting: Novasis, S.A.L.

First edition: March 2000
© José M. Parramón Vilasaló
© Exclusive publishing rights: Lema Publications, S.L.
Published and distributed by Lema Publications, S.L.
Gran Via de les Corts Catalanes, 8-10, 1st 5th A
08902 L'Hospitalet de Llobregat (Barcelona)

ISBN 84-95323-33-8
Printed in Spain

Index

Acrylic, also known as plastic paint, is one of the most recently discovered pictorial techniques. It was in the twenties when several Mexican painters began to experiment with a new pictorial medium, as resistant as it was fluid, that would allow them to produce huge mural paintings, exposed to severe weather conditions. This type of painting, still in a phase of experimentation, had to combine the material characteristics of watercolor with the opacity of oil paint, surpassing both techniques in terms of drying power. After a long period of experimentation, a new coloring substance which was called acrylic or plastic paint was obtained. It's a type of tempera paint, the only difference being that the glue that forms part of it is made from polymers (vinyl or acrylic).

This discovery had an important impact miles away, in New York, where many local artists realized that these paints could be used not only for mural paintings but were also appropriate for other types of painting. After long years of perfecting the technique, acrylic paint started to be sold in the United States in the fifties. This new paint was well received by the artists of the time and it played an important role in the new stylistic changes that postwar painting was about to undergo in the United States, comparable in Europe to the impact the appearance of oil paint had in Flanders. The fact that it was inexpensive, had a pasty consistency and could be bought in large quantities, made it possible for artists like **De Kooning**, **Jackson Pollock** or **Noland** to produce works of a very large format, applying spurts of paint or impastos onto the surface without having to wait months for the paint to dry, as had always been the case with oil paint. This new procedure granted artists more freedom, fluidity and spontaneity. On this subject **Pollock** said, *"When I paint, I have a general notion of what I have in my hands. I can control the flow of the paint: nothing is accidental... I am not afraid to make changes, to destroy the image... because the painting has a life of its own. I try to let it manifest itself"*. The use of acrylics made it possible for another abstract painter, **Morris Louis**, to apply colors onto his canvases without priming them first, something that would have been an extremely delicate operation with oil paint since the excess oil could eventually rot the canvas. In the mid-sixties, acrylics also flooded the European market, where they were equally well-received and soon began to be used by the main artists. This can

1

be seen in the interest shown by Jean Dubuffet when he wrote, *"My relationship with the material I use is that of a dancer with his partner, the jockey with his horse, the fortune-teller with her tarot cards. It is therefore possible to understand the interest I feel for a new material and my impatience to try it out"*.

Also in the mid-sixties, pop-art adopted acrylic paint as one of its symbols. This movement was an absolutely western cultural manifestation that grew under the capitalist and technological conditions of the industrial society. And what could be better than to use a newly created paint, fruit of the artificial, together with the deep-rooted influence of artistic language to express the new artistic spirit? And that's precisely what the generation of artists made up of **Jasper Jones**, **Andy Warhol**, **Roy Lichtenstein**, **Claes Oldenburg** and **Peter Blake** did.

Although several decades have gone by since those first experiments, today both amateur and professional painters still have some reservations about using acrylic paint.

That is why its real possibilities are yet unknown and people erroneously consider it a coarse imitation of watercolor or oil paints. And although it is true that acrylics can imitate the effects pro-

Fig. 1. **In the Open,** *by Teresa Trol (artist's private collection). Acrylic is a medium which can be used to work with glazes and to achieve paintings as realistic as this one, with effects that are reminiscent of photography.*
Fig. 2. **Marilyn,** *by Andy Warhol. By mixing acrylic paint with mediums, the artist was able to create new chromatic effects using fluorescent colors which are impossible to obtain with oil paint.*
Fig. 3. **Free form,** *by Jackson Pollock (Modern Art Museum, New York). This painting is a clear example of the versatility of the medium, which makes it possible to apply paint in spurts, squirted directly from the tube onto the surface using the technique known as extrusion.*

duced by other paints, it also has a character of its own.

Moreover, it is a highly polyvalent material, for it is equally appropriate for large-scale paintings as it is for reduced and delicate floral studies or miniatures, and can be used both on exterior and interior surfaces, applied on walls, canvases or paper and combined with other painting and drawing materials in mixed techniques and collages. Where can you find another method with as many qualities? I am sure that this book will help you to discover this "new" pictorial medium. However, you should not limit yourself to merely learning what you consider to be sufficient. On the contrary, you should feel impelled to play with your work materials, to try it all, for the possibilities of each of the techniques described in this book can't be understood completely unless you experiment with them by putting them into practice. You need to learn by trial and error.

Let yourself be encouraged by the exercises we suggest in the second part of this book and which are accompanied by outline-guides so that you can do them more easily. Experimenting with new techniques and procedures is important even for established painters who are experts in their craft. Otherwise, their work becomes more and more repetitive and routine. I am sure that you will find painting with acrylics a pleasing and gratifying experience.

Gabriel Martín Roig
Art critic

Fig. 1. An artist who knows his materials will be able to tell how acrylic paints, which can be worked with both as impastos and glazes reminiscent of the effects created with watercolors, will respond. Here is an example of the latter, namely this Still life, painted by Carlant (artist's private collection).

ACRYLICS: COMPOSITION AND MATERIALS

Acrylic is a recently-discovered synthetic paint that makes it possible to combine oil paint and watercolor techniques. It is an emulsion made with acrylic-vinyl polymers. Now specialized stores have an incredible range of paints, paintbrushes, mediums and an assortment of objects for painting with acrylics. Before you start painting, it would be a good idea to study the materials, that is, the composition and the quality of the colors, and also to take several indications into account that will help you know what to choose depending on your needs. For this reason, in the following chapters we offer instructions about basic aspects, such as the choice of a support and the paintbrushes, what the palette should be like and what the different mediums are for.

Quality and Composition

Acrylic paint is an industrial derivative of plastic, a new synthetic pictorial medium that in addition to possessing all the advantages of traditional mediums like watercolor or oil paint, dries very quickly. The base for its elaboration consists of an emulsion of very small resin particles in water. The pigments used for acrylics are the same as those used to make oil paints or watercolors, the difference can be found in the agglutinants, which are polymeric. That is why acrylic paint is so resistant. The acrylic particles, unlike those found in oil paint, are desiccant, that is, they dry rapidly as a result of the evaporation of the water contained in the agglutinant. As the water evaporates, the resin particles amalgamate and form a rather compact film of paint. When the pictorial surface has dried it acts as a plastic coating which is impossible to remove, and yet the layer of color remains flexible due to the large amount of resin that it contains. Flexibility is one of the main advantages of acrylics. The surface onto which the washes are applied can be cut, bent or folded without the danger of cracking, unless the paint was applied too thickly.

In comparison with oil paint, acrylic colors are more luminous, but also more artificial. This is most evident in the red, yellow and orange tones which acquire a very bright, almost fluorescent appearance.

Acrylics get darker as they dry since the solvent in which the pigment is suspended is white when it's wet but turns transparent when it dries. Normally, this is not a problem, but it can affect the relation between the colors when the dry brush or sfumato technique is used on top of a layer of paint that has already dried.

Fig. 1. Acrylic is a highly versatile medium that offers a wide range of very bright colors with high covering power.
Fig. 2. There are different qualities of acrylics on the market. It's a question of knowing what to choose depending on the needs and economy of each person.
Fig. 3. The variety of brushstrokes and lines, as well as mixing and blending of colors this medium provides can be seen in this work, **The stream,** *painted by Grau Carod (artist's private collection).*

This procedure can be used to work with washes as well as opaque colors. And since errors can be corrected by painting on top of it, it's probably the best medium for those who are learning to paint. As far as its mixtures are concerned, it can be mixed with a large variety of mediums, which increase its versatility as well as its expressive qualities.

Just like oil paints or watercolors, acrylic colors are sold in quality sets for artists and economical ones for students. Their price depends on the initial cost of the pigments and which of these two categories they belong to.

Although some uncompromising traditionalists still reject their use, acrylics are becoming more and more popular among painters at all levels.

Fig. 4A, B & C. The consistency of acrylics makes working with delicate washes as well as thick creamy impastos possible.

Fig. 5. As a result, acrylics are a medium that imitates the quality of both watercolors and oil paints perfectly.

Fig. 6. The medium can be adapted to fit a diversity of styles and tendencies, from the most academic and realistic painting to more spontaneous and freer compositions like this **Pond,** *painted by Miguel Olivares (artist's private collection).*

Color Range

The color range of acrylic paints is somewhat limited if we compare it to oil paints or watercolors, since some pigments cannot by mixed correctly with the agglutinant, that is, with the resin, and therefore tend to congeal. In these cases alternative pigments are used, so that colors like emerald green can be replaced by others that serve the same function. The technology of acrylic paint is still very young and there are enormous differences between the various brands. Those that are not as good can be distinguished, among other things, by their tendency to dry more quickly.

Acrylic paint is sold in different formats:

Tubes. They have a smooth and creamy consistency, especially appropriate for impasto techniques. Nevertheless, their capacity is limited since the paints are sold in sizes that do not exceed 8 fluid ounces. Therefore, they are not appropriate for painting works which have large formats (fig. 1).

Plastic jars. The consistency of paints sold in plastic jars is smoother and more fluid and they dissolve more easily in water, which makes this the most appropriate format for working with glazes which imitate watercolors. The paints form a thin film when they dry which is a bit matter than that of the paints sold in tubes. A wide variety of sizes can be found on the market ranging from 2 fluid ounces to almost 35 fluid ounces. Colors such as white or black are sold in even larger jars that can hold up to a gallon of paint (fig. 3).

Jar with a nozzle. These are jars that instead of a screw-on cap finish in a nozzle or opening that allows paint to be pressed out of the tube directly onto the pictorial surface or the palette. They have the disadvantage that the paint on the nozzle dries if it is not covered tightly and obstructs the flow of the paint. In these cases it is necessary to clear the canal with a toothpick or a metal point (fig. 4).

Liquid acrylic. Similar to bottles of Chinese ink, liquid acrylic comes provided with a dropper. It's made with an alkaline resin which gives it a considerable dying power. Due to its liquid consistency, it's appropriate for working with a reservoir-nib pen or a reed (fig. 2).

Fig. 1. More and more artists have stopped using tubes as they contain a small quantity of paint and besides, if the tip paint on the dries they are difficult to unscrew.

Fig. 2. Liquid acrylics are very common among illustrators and designers due to their dying power.

Fig. 3. Jars of acrylic paint are the containers that hold the largest amount of paint, although the consistency is not as thick as that of the paint sold in tubes.

Fig. 4. Jars with a nozzle are probably the most popular format. Their nozzle in the shape of a funnel or a sleeve keeps the paint from drying (unless the jars are left open) and makes it possible to measure out the contents. Their consistency is also creamier.

The Basic Palette

It is best to begin with a reduced number of colors until you know exactly what you want to achieve with this technique. Most artists that specialize in one thematic field or pictorial procedure almost always use the same colors adding one or two depending on the subject matter they want to paint, incorporating more shades of blue if the painting is to be a seascape and more greens and browns if the painting is to be a landscape.

The choice of colors is a very personal question. In any case, here are the colors I consider should be on a beginner's palette.

—**Cadmium red**
—**Carmine**
—**Ultramarine blue**
—**Cobalt blue**
—**Cadmium orange**
—**Cadmium yellow**
—**Viridian**
—**Chrome green**
—**Burnt sienna**
—**Yellow ocher**
—**Raw umber**
—**White**
—**Ivory black**

In general, you need a larger amount of white than of the other colors so it is best to buy a larger tube of it.

Sometimes the names of the colors vary depending on the manufacturer, so when in doubt, ask your local supplier. Another solution is to have a color chart (if possible, one that is painted by hand) which the specialized art supply stores usually provide for free to those customers who ask for it. It is the best source of information available on the range, quality, resistance, and permanence of the colors distributed by each manufacturer, even though printed charts don't reproduce the shades of color with the necessary precision.

Fig. 1. It is not necessary to buy the color charts, you can ask any specialized art supply store or manufacturer for them.

Fig. 2. To begin, it's important to limit yourself to a basic palette instead of wanting to include a lot of shades. Remember that it is not necessary to buy all the tones you are going to use since you can obtain them by mixing other colors.

The Mixing of Colors

When painting with acrylics, it is best not to mix different brands, that is, you should stick to one manufacturer's products. Otherwise, problems could arise when the paint sets after mixing it, since each manufacturer adds different types of agglutinants to his paints and offers a different quality of pigments.

It is also advisable not to combine paint excessively but instead to limit mixtures to two or three colors to avoid dirtying the tones. For this reason, it is important to practice mixing colors on a test paper, trying out various combinations and saving the best, making sure to write down how they were obtained (if you consider it necessary).

Above these lines you can see a mixture of various colors with variations in tonal density (fig. 1). There are two ways to lighten and darken opaque colors like these. The first is to do it by not using white or black (that is, mixing colors with lighter or darker colors). The second is to add white or black to the mixture, although this should be done with care since white can alter the character of certain colors, while the use of black in a mixture is not very common and, I would add, not recommendable.

As you practice mixing colors, you will see that some pigments are not opaque by nature, but sometimes transparent or translucent. If you use these pigments, you will have to mix them with a bit of white paint or another opaque color (fig. 4, next page).

On the other hand, sometimes colors from a tube, especially the darker colors, are difficult to tell apart when they are concentrated and you might find that when you want to use blue, you are using black instead (fig, 2). Be careful, for a mistake like that could ruin any mixture.

Fig. 1. The texture of some mixtures of dense acrylic colors can be mistaken for that of oil paints, which have a similar quality.

Fig. 2. It is necessary to put the colors on the palette in a certain order for, as you can see, it is difficult to tell some dark colors apart. In order to distinguish them, it may be necessary to spread some of the paint onto a white surface.

2

If you mix large quantities of paint it is best to use a palette knife. This does not mean that paintbrushes are no good, but if they become saturated with paint it will be difficult to clean them. When you use a smaller amount of paint in the mixture, you can use a paintbrush. But remember to wash it afterwards, or else, while you continue painting, place it in a jar full of water before the paint hardens.

Fig. 3. Looking at the tests above these lines, observe the plastic possibilities of acrylic paint mixtures.

Fig. 4. The opacity of some colors can be increased by adding a little white paint to the mixture, as is the case with yellow, one of the colors out of the range of acrylics that becomes more transparent when it dries.

Advantages and Disadvantages

As I have already explained, plastic or acrylic paint has considerable covering power and has one important advantage with respect to oil paint, which is that the colors dry more quickly and you can paint over them again in a very short time. Also, the high degree of dissolution of this type of paint makes it possible to apply it in a variety of ways, for example, with a paintbrush, spray can or airbrush. With the latter of these techniques, a granular surface *(gotelé)* common in industrial and artistic decorations can be achieved. The advantage acrylic paint has with respect to watercolors is that once it dries it is no longer soluble, so there is no limit to the number of washes that can be applied. Watercolors, on the contrary, are more soluble and if too many washes are applied, the colors lose their definition. Many artists choose acrylics because they enjoy applying layer upon layer of paint in a rapid

succession of layers without altering the previous layers.

Acrylics make it possible to paint in whatever consistency one desires: with impastos (fig. 1), glazes (fig. 2), sfumatos (fig. 3), collages, textures... This versatility is another of its principal virtues. We would like to point out its elasticity as well. While oil paints harden when they dry, acrylics become more flexible. As a result, an acrylic painting on canvas can be rolled up, stored and re-tensed without suffering any subsequent alterations on the pictorial surface.

However, the fact that it dries quickly cuts both ways, being at once its main advantage and its main disadvantage. For while it allows the artist to superimpose layers without having to wait for the previous layer to dry, at the same time it makes moving the paint across the surface of the canvas and mixing paints more difficult. With this

1

2

3

4

Fig. 1. When acrylic paint is applied thickly, its consistency and texture are similar to those of oil paint.
Fig. 2. This paint also offers the possibility of working with transparencies, that is to say, with semitransparent color washes that are superimposed one on top of the other, creating high quality chromatic effects.
Fig. 3. Sfumato is a combination of washes and the dry brush technique. It involves a succession of small superimposed strokes that create an effect of vibrant color.
Fig. 4. If you observe this fragment of a work done by Teresa Trol, you will see how the qualities of acrylics, dealt with in an opaque manner, resemble those of oil paint.

I mean that the paint cannot be extensively manipulated on the surface during a prolonged period of time, which forces the artist to work at a fast pace.

In any case, in order to solve this problem, manufacturers have recently added some ingredients to the paint known as retardants which prolong their drying time. It is worth remembering that under normal conditions all colors possess the same drying time.

Furthermore, it is advisable to close the tubes tightly when you finish painting, for otherwise the paint in the tubes could harden within a few hours. If there is paint incrusted in the opening or tip of the tube, the paint inside the tube will be blocked and it won't flow out. In order to avoid this it is advisable to keep acrylic paint tubes in a plastic container that closes hermetically. If despite these precautions the paint in the tip hardens, making it difficult to unscrew the cap, open the tubes while running hot water from the tap over them. It is said that acrylic paints, being synthetic substances, can adhere to all types of surfaces and are permanent. This is not true. They cannot adhere, for example, to oily surfaces and it is therefore not a good idea to use acrylic paint on top of a film of oil paint. The paint will end up cracking and flaking, coming off the surface.

As we already said in the previous chapter, it has been proven that acrylic paints darken a bit after they dry, especially if they have been diluted in water. However, the long-term effects are not yet known. The incorporation of plastic products as art material is so recent that that their aging process has not yet been studied satisfactorily, as has been the case with more traditional products. Therefore, it is yet too soon to see how this type of paint ages.

6

7

8

Fig. 6. Their quick drying speed, which is the best virtue of acrylics, is at the same time their greatest inconvenient. For this reason, it is necessary to close the tubes and jars of paint tightly when they are not in use. The best way to preserve them is by keeping them inside a plastic container that closes hermetically.

Fig. 7 & 8. Here are two more details taken from paintings done by Teresa Trol. In them, we can see the diversity of treatments that can be applied with acrylics, such as adding volume, working with sgraffito, piling on thick layers of paint with a brush, etc.

Mediums

Mediums are milky varnishes capable of giving paint a certain consistency, such as more volume, texture or transparency. Obviously, it is not necessary to mix paint with acrylic mediums. The paint can also be diluted in water, which is the best medium, and solvent in the case of acrylic paints. In this way a creamy, as well as a watery consistency similar to that of traditional watercolors can be achieved. The paints can also be used directly from the tube.

However, every day there are more and more additives that improve the control that artists have over this pictorial technique, such as retardants, which prolong the drying time and consistency modifiers, which change the viscosity of the paint. There are different compounds that can be added to paint in order to widen the range of effects. If you choose to explore the creative possibilities of acrylics, it is important to familiarize yourself with the appropriate medium to use and to discover how they work. Experimentation is recommendable. Here is a selection of the more important mediums:

Brilliant medium: Mixing this product with the paint gives it a shiny finish. If it is applied diluted it increases the transparency of the colors, which makes it appropriate for painting with glazes.

Glossy medium: Gives the pictorial surface a soft shine, so that the dull colors stick out more. However, it has the inconvenient that if too many layers are applied the colors may become cloudy.

Mat medium: Since it contains a wax or silica emulsion, it reduces the reflection of the pictorial surface considerably, and as with the previous medium, it in-

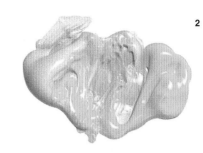

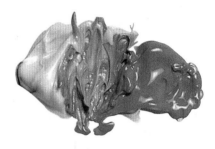

Fig. 1. Mediums are additive substances that give a certain consistency to acrylic paint. They are usually mixed with the paint beforehand without altering its color. When the mediums dry they become transparent.

Fig. 2. The most commonly used medium is water, which is the universal medium. With it you can thin down the colors until they attain a quality resembling that of watercolors.

Fig. 3. Thickening medium is used to give the paint more volume, when painting with a palette knife or adding relief to the texture of the pictorial surface. It comes in one pound packages and can be purchased in any fine arts store.

Fig. 4. Latex is a milky substance that is also used as a thickening medium. Once it has dried, it adds shine to the surface of the painting.

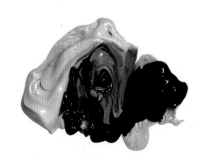

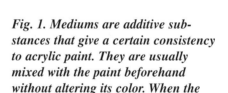

1

2

creases the transparency of the paint. Its adhesive properties make it appropriate for use in collages.

Gel: It's a thickening medium that is mixed with paint to increase its density and consistency. It's ideal for working with a palette knife and for producing effects of textured brushstrokes or impastos.

Mat gel: It's similar to gel, but is matter in appearance when it dries.

Dense gel: It's a kind of gel that has a denser composition, so of the three it is probably the best for working with impasto techniques.

Opaque gel: Opaque gel is also a paint thickener. Just one warning: This medium should make up no more than 50 % of the mixture. Otherwise the colors could be altered.

Retardant medium: It is very useful when working on wet, since this medium delays the drying of the paint for several hours. The thicker the paint the longer it takes to dry.

Latex: This synthetic product with a milky appearance is obtained from rubber trees. Today, however, it is manufactured synthetically. Sometimes this glue is used as an agglutinant or to increase the fluidity of the paint.

Iridescent medium: This medium is made out of diluted particles that when mixed with paint produce a range of metallic colors. Once the paint has dried, its appearance becomes more nacreous, the colors reflect more light and are more intense and shiny.

Polymer varnish: This is a protective plastic varnish made specifically for acrylic paint. It protects the pictorial surface from ultraviolet light and harsh atmospheric conditions.

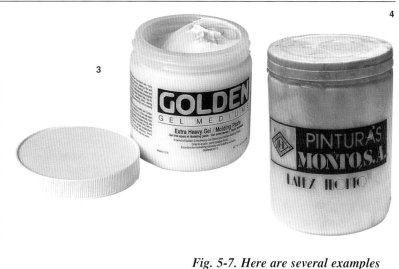

Fig. 5-7. Here are several examples of mediums used with acrylic paint, taken from various works by Teresa Trol. In the first image we see a pictorial surface in which the colors have been treated with brilliant medium (fig. 5). In the second example, a beautiful marshy landscape, it was necessary to add a retardant in order to keep the pictorial layer from drying before the sgraffito could be carried out (fig. 6). And finally, latex is very useful when mixed with sawdust or marble powder, since it gives the work very interesting textures (fig. 7).

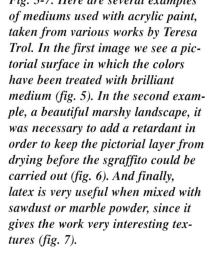

Materials

Tools used in acrylic painting are not essentially different from those used in oil painting: paintbrushes, palettes, palette knives, glass jars... If you want to use brushes or palette knives that you had previously used with oil paints, you must clean them carefully before using them with acrylics in order to eliminate any trace of oil or turpentine.

It is advisable to use hog bristle, bull-hair or better yet synthetic (nylon fiber) brushes, since natural bristles absorb acrylic paint and lose their flexibility, (and sable brushes wear down very quickly). Nylon brushes are easy to clean and are made to endure the wear and tear that comes from working with acrylics. They come in different thicknesses that go from 0 to 24 increasing in even numbers. They come in three shapes of bristles: round, flat and filbert (known also as cat's tongue).

To begin with, two or three round brushes, one big flat brush and one small flat one will be enough. You will see that working with acrylics it is necessary to constantly wash the brushes. It is therefore advisable to always have abundant water on hand.

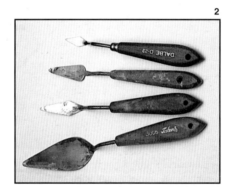

Fig. 1. If we are going to leave the brushes for a long period of time, it is best to use a tray like this one so that the bristles don't lose their shape.

Fig. 2. It is necessary to have a small assortment of palette knives in different shapes and sizes, which are very useful when working with impastos and when mixing large quantities of paint on the palette.

Fig. 3. The same brushes that are used for painting with oil paints can be used with acrylics. However, those that have harder bristles, like hog bristles or artificial bristles, are more effective.

This is important because, as you already know, the paint dries rapidly and can get stuck on the brushes. Once the paint has dried it will be very difficult to remove it. In order to keep the paintbrushes wet it is necessary to have jars with abundant water on hand. However, do not leave the brushes in the water for too long, since the bristles will lose their shape if they rest on the bottom of the jar. The best way to preserve your brushes is by placing them on a tray with the bristles immersed in water and the handles leaning on the edge of the tray. If you should forget to take these precautions and the paint dries on the brushes there is a special cleaning agent that gets them back into good condition, or you could immerse them in denaturalized alcohol for at least 12 hours and then remove the paint by rubbing the bristles with your fingers, but it is best not to take unnecessary risks. You will need a couple of palette knives at least to modify recently painted shapes and colors by scraping them and also to clean your palette. Palette knives used for painting are different from those used to mix colors in that their handles are bent at an angle and their blades are extremely flexible. They can be found in a large variety of shapes and sizes from small triangular or pear-shaped ones to large straight ones. Your painting set should also include pencils and charcoal for the sketches and sponges to absorb excess paint or to obtain certain textures. We will cover the topic of palettes and supports in the following chapters, since due to the singularity of the medium, these materials require special attention.

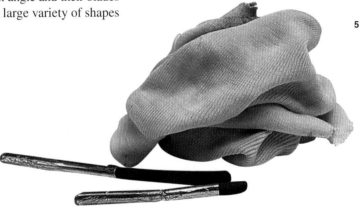

Fig. 4. Masking tape is very useful in acrylic painting, both to preserve the areas that you do not want to cover in paint and to fix the paper to the wooden support.

Fig. 5. Since the drawing is an essential guide for all painting, it is always advisable to have some charcoal and a rag at hand to do the preliminary sketch.

Fig. 6. Masking tape also provides a white frame for your painting, at the same time as it embellishes it. If you prefer, instead of using charcoal you can use pastels for the preliminary sketch, since it's a technique that's highly compatible with acrylic painting.

Palettes

Acrylic palettes come in different shapes and sizes, although if you prefer you can also make your own homemade palette as suitable as those sold in art supply stores. The secret of a good palette lies in the material it's made of. Being smooth, cardboard or plastic palettes are more suitable for acrylics than the wooden ones, which are used for oil painting. It is difficult to remove acrylic paint from wood since it penetrates through its pores and adheres to it.

The palette should be quite big so that there is room on it to mix colors. There are two types of palettes designed especially for painting with acrylics: There is the plastic palette with hollows for the colors in which the paint can be diluted by adding as much water as necessary and thereby keeping the colors from mixing. The other type of palette is the Staywet palette, which is especially designed for outdoor painting, where the drying of the paint can be an especially serious problem. The paint remains wet and malleable while you're working and if the plastic cover is used when you finish your painting session, the paints can be used again several days later since they won't have dried. However, this type of palette has one important disadvantage, namely that the space provided for mixing colors is rather limited. Staywet palettes are usually made of plastic or polystyrene which is highly stain-resistant. If you do not have a professional palette, you can mix paints on a home-made one such as a sheet of glass from which the dried paint can be easily removed.

Fig. 1. Palettes for acrylics should be made of plastic and have hollows or compartments that keep the paint from mixing. They can be found in various sizes and their price is very reasonable.

Fig. 2. If you need to mix large quantities of paint, it is best to use plastic plates. You will need at least two, one for mixing warm colors and another for the range of cold colors.

Fig. 3. Ceramic is perhaps the best material for an acrylics palette. However, nowadays they are almost no longer made and very difficult to find.

If you work on a small scale or you use acrylics as if they were watercolors you may find a plastic or ceramic palette like the ones used for watercolors useful, or even an old ceramic, metal or plastic plate (ceramic is probably the most pleasing surface for mixing paints). If you are working with large quantities of paint you will need a palette with deep hollows or else you may want to work with plastic plates.

It is advisable not to put too much paint on the palette and to screw on the top of the tube at once. The best way to keep the palette wet while you're working is by spraying it with water vapor regularly or by covering it with transparent plastic film. In this way you will keep the paint from drying while you take a short break.

Some final advice: whatever palette you choose always put the colors in a specific order (it doesn't matter which order as long as it's logical and you can remember it). Otherwise, you run the risk of making mistakes when mixing colors.

Fig. 4. The Staywet palette can be purchased or made at home. All you need is a plastic tray and a piece of clear plastic film that covers it completely. Inside, the colors will remain wet for hours.

Fig. 5. If you go out-of-doors to paint it would be a good idea to take a spray can with you to keep the paint moist, thereby keeping it from drying in the sun.

Supports for Acrylic

You can paint with acrylic paint on just about any type of material: cloth, cardboard, wood, Bristol board and even metallic surfaces like copper or zinc, although in these cases it is necessary to sandpaper the surface before painting on it. If you want to paint with paints that have been diluted in abundant water, watercolor paper is your best choice, and perhaps fine or medium-grained paper is the most recommendable. For this type of painting Bristol board is an excellent and cheap support. Hard cardboard is suitable for those artists who work with a series of very thin applications of color. On the other hand, if you are going to work with paint that has a creamier, thicker and denser consistency, you can use wood, canvas or a cloth-covered panel as a support.

If you are going to use cloth or canvas, be careful not to buy supports that are prepared especially for oil painting since acrylics will not adhere to a surface that contains oil or wax. Nowadays canvases with a dispersive surface suitable for acrylics can be bought in

place of those with an oily surface, which repels acrylic paint. The canvas can be primed once or twice. The latter has a denser surface and is more expensive, but not as flexible as the former. Whatever the support you choose may be, if you want you can prime it with an additional layer of acrylic medium which maintains the natural color of the cloth or you can cover it with a layer of acrylic plaster. The priming not only seals and protects the support, but it also creates a base that quickly accepts the application of paint. In order to carry out this operation, all you have to do is spread a thick layer onto the surface of the support and let it dry for a few minutes before starting to paint. Use a wide brush or a roller and spread the material quickly. Nowadays many artists prefer to prime their support themselves in order to adapt it to their own needs and in this way they can choose the base and save money.

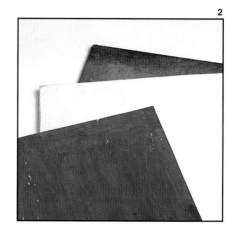

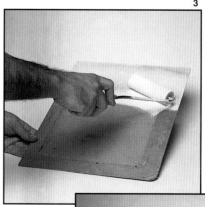

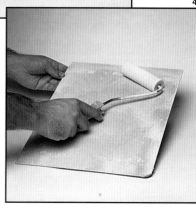

Fig. 1. For painting with acrylics any type of paper will do, from the rigid, glossy paper used for watercolors to mass-produced porous paper.

Fig. 2. In addition to paper, acrylic paint tolerates any type of rigid support. Above these lines you have some examples: varnish-covered Bristol board, a rigid piece of cardboard and a wooden panel.

Fig. 3 & 4. If the support is too porous you may choose to cover it with a layer of whiting and latex, which should be applied with a wide brush or roller. This should suffice to cover the pores of the wood.

Colored Backgrounds

Canvases sold for acrylic painting are normally white, but it is sometimes useful to apply a background color before starting to paint. The use of tonal papers or background colors is ideal for painting with acrylics due to the opacity of this type of paint. Many artists prefer to paint on a colored background since a white sheet of paper can be inhibiting or can even cause them to make a mistake as a result of what is known as simultaneous contrasts, since most colors look darker on a white surface than surrounded by other colors. Tonal backgrounds make it possible to judge relative light and darkness from the first applications of color. By using them it is easier for the artist to find suitable colors and tones and will make it possible to paint both dark and light colors with the same ease. Moreover, the possibility of seeing the color of the paper through small fragments of uncovered background color makes it possible to use the background color as a harmonious and unifying element since the repetition of the same colors in two or more different areas is a way of relating different elements. For this reason it is best to make the background a neutral color, like gray, ochre or a bluish hue.

The color should be subtle and discreet in order not to modify the superimposed colors excessively. Avoid using the same background colors all the time and learn to decide which is the most suitable for each painting. This choice will depend on the predominant color of the painting, although a background color related to the colors present in the model can also be used.

White bases are especially suitable for working with glazes since the light is reflected through the applied colors and gives the painting a luminous quality. This is the only case in which I would not advise you to use a background color.

If the paper which will be used as a support is very absorbent, it is also best to cover it with a background base in order to seal the pores and reduce its power of absorption. The background is easily tinted. Apply acrylic paint that has been diluted over the entire surface. In a few minutes the layer of color will be dry and ready for painting.

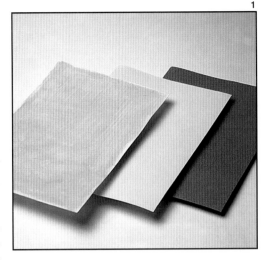

Fig. 1. Colored paper or Bristol board can also be used as a support. Another possibility is to use paper that has been tinted with a wash which will act as base or background color.

Fig. 2. Colored backgrounds should be prepared before starting to paint but after having studied the model. The background should always be chosen in relation to the theme.

Fig. 3. Here is one of the papers prepared by the artist Miguel Olivares for his works. Choosing a colored background gives the painting more coherence and chromatic harmony.

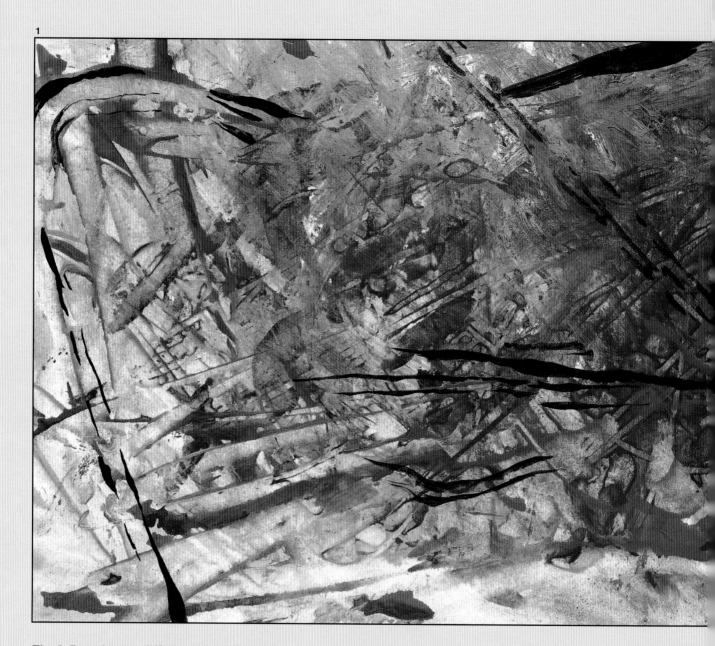

Fig. 1. By trying out different colors and through constant experimentation you will be able to master the different techniques of painting with acrylics. Here you have a small abstract composition made with this end in mind, that is, to experiment with textures, strokes, effects and possible concordance between colors.

ACRYLIC TECHNIQUES

The purpose of this section is to give you some advice about how to use acrylic paints so as to make the most of them. In the following chapters you will learn how to go about using these colors, what their possibilities are, and how to experiment with them. Some of the techniques put forward are traditional ones taken from oil painting (most of the techniques used in oil painting can also be used with acrylics) or watercolor, while others are specific to acrylic painting. He who masters these techniques will find a new dimension in his ability to communicate with others. Therefore, it is time to see how far this medium can take you. I advise you to read this section and try out the techniques to be found there before starting to paint, especially if you have never worked with this procedure before.

Washing Techniques

The plastic paint emulsion is perfectly soluble in water, which makes it possible to apply it in very thin almost transparent layers (similar to watercolors). This creates delicate washes and glazes, through which the white surface of the paper or canvas is reflected, thus increasing the luminosity of the painting. The difference between washes done with acrylics and those done with watercolors consists mainly in the fact that with acrylics you can work both with glazes and with opaque colors. Another difference is that, as opposed to watercolors, acrylic glazes do not dissolve if once they have dried, water is once again applied. In other words, acrylics are insoluble and permanent. In painting with watercolors applying washes is a slow process, since each layer must dry completely before the next one can be applied. On the other hand, acrylic washes sometimes dry within as little as fifteen minutes. For this reason, this technique is one of the most often used in the type of painting described in this book. It must be noted that just as with watercolors, acrylic washes must be applied quickly and confidently, without going back to make corrections.

Washes done with acrylic paints do not seem as delicate and light as those done with watercolors, but in compensation, they offer clear and intense colors. Very rich and intense tones can be obtained with the technique of superimposed glazes, since with each application of color, the previous layer is modified. This technique can also be used as a method for mixing colors. For example, if a bluish glaze is applied on top of a reddish wash, or vice versa, the result will be violet, though it will be much brighter and more vibrant than if it had been mixed on the artist's palette. Acrylic washes make it possible to obtain subtle mixtures and hazy colors.

This technique can also be combined with others. For example, a wash can be applied on top of a layer of thick paint. The new layer will be concentrated in the grooves and relief of the pictorial surface, thereby producing a curious effect of broken texture.

Usually, glazes are made by diluting the paint with water. However, the colors will be brighter if they are diluted with a mixture of water and brilliant medium or a medium that increases the fluidity of the paint. This will

1A

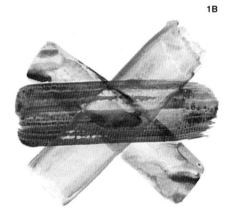

1B

1C

2

Fig. 1A, B & C. Glazes make it possible to modify the initial color as new washes are added. In this way, if we apply a layer of blue on top of a pink wash the result will be a violet color.
Fig. 2. The technique of working with semitransparent color glazes gives the paintings a certain refinement, as is the case with this **Still life** *by Carlant (artist's private collection).*

give the painting the exact volume desired and in this way it will spread more easily over the pictorial surface. All kinds of paper that are normally used for painting with watercolors can be used when painting with glazes. Glazes can also be applied directly to a canvas without priming it first or to other surfaces that have been covered with a plaster base.

Fig. 3 & 4. When painting with glazes it is important to experiment with the superposition of colors and the best way to do this is by applying a colored wash over strips of different tonalities.

Fig. 5 & 6. Painting with velatura, or the glazing technique, involves building up the painting, going from less to more, that is to say, starting with highly diluted washes that will become more intense as the work advances, and leaving the details and touches of more intense color for the end. We could compare it to the way in which an image appears progressively when a photograph is being developed. See how it is done in these two still lifes by Teresa Trol (artist's private collection).

Dry Brush Technique and Sfumato

This technique consists in painting with large amounts of paint and hardly any water, so that when the brush is rubbed against the paper the texture of the paper shows through. The dry brush technique provides a broken granular stroke that covers only part of the surface onto which it's applied. This is because the paint, being scarce, adheres only to the most elevated part of the paper's grain or the canvas's woven texture and therefore small flecks of the background color or previous layer show through. This technique is used especially with textured or tinted surfaces for in this way more daring results and broken color effects are achieved.

The strokes must be applied rapidly and confidently, since if you work with too much precision or too slowly the desired effect will be lost. It is important to get the right amount of paint on the brush. Otherwise, the surface will be covered with too much paint and the effect will be ruined.

The result of a dry brushstroke makes the painting more expressive, and it is suitable for suggesting textures like, for example, the bark of a tree, sand on a beach, reflections on the water, the

1A

1B

1C

1D

2

Fig. 1A, B, C & D. These sequences show the different possibilities of using the dry brush technique in painting. The dry brushstroke is granular and broken, thereby bringing out the rough nature of the paper. Fig. 2. See how the dry brush technique is used in this work, **View from the Besalú bridge,** *by Óscar Sanchís (artist's private collection) to produce an effect of broken color in the sky and on the structure of the bridge. Fig. 3. The sfumato technique consists in applying a succession of small, dry brushstrokes that when superimposed on the background color create interesting gradations and chromatic effects that give the work an impression of optical vibrancy.*

fur of an animal, the rocks on a cliff or blades of grass.
If the paint that is applied is diluted, a soft brush should be used. If, on the other hand, the paint is thick, it is better to use a synthetic or hog bristle brush. In both cases it is best to use a flat brush.

A technique related to the dry brush technique is that of sfumato. It is normally done with thick, rather than diluted, paint, although diluted paint can also be used. It consists in applying an uneven layer of paint on top of an existing color. The paint is usually applied with a soft rubbing movement using a hard brush, a rag or even the fingers. In this way the colors are blended into a coarse shape and the strokes are visible. This pictorial technique is taken from oil painting, although it is much more suitable for acrylics due to short time needed for the layers of paint to dry. This technique can be combined with the dry brush technique, since the two are closely related. Remember that in both techniques it is important to avoid covering the previous base completely.

3

4

Fig. 4. Although he worked with oil paints and not with acrylics, the work of the Catalan modernist painter Isidre Nonell must be mentioned in connection with this technique. In his work, **Reclined figure,** *he fills the surface of the painting with spasmodic superimposed brushstrokes that create a sfumato effect. In other words, there is no definition or lines outlining the figure portrayed in the painting. Everything is based on gradations and the blending of colors.*

Impasto

Impasto is the name given to paint which is applied in thick layers, so that the marks of the paintbrush or palette knife are easily recognizable. If colors are used just as they come out of the tube, their consistency, being relatively thick, will favor the development of this technique due to the special characteristics of one of the polymers used in the composition of acrylic paint.

The texture of acrylic impasto is very similar to that of oil paint, the only difference being, as I have already pointed out in previous chapters, the drying time, which in the case of acrylic paint can be even less than 24 hours. Even when applied in thick layers, acrylic paint remains flexible and does not crack. But remember that it must have a malleable consistency, yet be sufficiently thick so as to conserve the impressions and brushstroke marks made by the paintbrush or the palette knife.

As is the case with oil paints, acrylic impasto also allows the use of palette knives, not only to mix paints on the palette, but also to spread paint onto the surface of the painting. Impasto can be applied directly from the tube, either using a brush or pressed out of the tube directly onto the surface. But the effect obtained with a palette knife is very different from that obtained with the other methods that have been mentioned, since this tool flattens the paint against the surface leaving a series of smooth plateaus with a slight relief, thereby creating a complex and highly interesting surface. The palette knife is a very flexible tool that allows the artist not only to flatten the paint against the surface, but also to make incisions using the sgraffito technique, to speckle the surface with dots or to leave a prominent relief where the application of paint ends.

If you have chosen to cover the entire surface of the painting with impasto, there is a special relief paste that increases the volume of the paint it is mixed with, hardly changing its color. Some pastes imitate the texture of stucco, sand, or combined fibers. They can be mixed with colors or left to dry before reapplying another thin layer of paint on top.

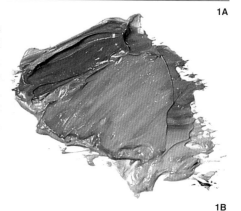

1A

1B

1C

1D

2

Fig. 1A-1D. Impasto consists in applying paint thickly onto the pictorial surface and can be done in various ways and with various instruments, such as a scraper (fig. 1A), a flat brush (fig. 1B), a flat palette knife (fig. 1C) and using the tip of the palette knife to speckle the surface with dots (fig. 1D).

Fig. 2. Palette knives are ideal tools for working with impasto, for they make it possible to lay large amounts of paint on the canvas.

Impasto, when applied to a landscape, tends to make the distant objects appear closer, so if you want to maintain the depth of the painting, save impasto for the foreground or for the center of interest, combining it with glazes for the more distant objects. Remember that once the impasto has dried, it is also possible to apply glazes onto the surfaces which are in relief.

Fig. 3. However, any instrument will do for painting with impasto. See, for example, how in this color test the fingertips have been used.

Fig. 4-6. The application of impasto provides numerous pictorial possibilities, such as the relief and guided marks obtained in the hat of the woman in the painting There is **Always a piece that doesn't fit,** *by Teresa Trol (artist's private collection, fig. 4); the rigorous speckling of the surface of the cloak of the woman in the painting* **My spiritual princess,** *also by Teresa Trol (artist's private collection, fig. 5); and giving strength and expressiveness to the colors in* **A cuban beach,** *by Bibiana Crespo (artist's private collection, fig. 6).*

Spattering or Spraying

This technique consists in spattering paint onto the surface of the support. It is an effective way of suggesting granular textures and making the colors more vivid. It is applied with washes and drops that enhance the atmospheric effect of the painting. Experiment with this technique by first immersing an old toothbrush in watered down paint and then passing your finger over its bristles. You will see how the paint spurts out in a drizzle of small drops that sprinkle the surface of the paper. Remember that in order for this technique to be successful, the paint must be wet, but not too runny. It is possible to cover a large surface with a great number of spattered drops in very little time and without the danger of the colors mixing thanks to the quick drying time of acrylic paint.
This technique is normally used to enhance the effect of dispersed color in motifs like the following: a wave breaking against the rocks of a cliff, the chromatic variety of dense vegetation, a heavy fall rain, the texture of sand on a beach bathed in sunlight, etc.
Spraying can also be done with other types of brushes and using other methods, so that different effects are obtained than with a toothbrush. For example, by using a brush with short bristles, a finer pulverization can be achieved. A large brush can also be dipped in paint and hit against the palm of the hand or against another brush in order to spray larger areas. In order to obtain big pearl-shaped drops instead of dots, spatter the paint while holding the brush at an angle. By varying the distance between the brush and the surface of the painting, you can increase or decrease the density of the drops.

Fig. 1. Here are different experiments with the spraying technique, in which different colors are blended. Spraying gives the work an unusual dynamism, making the pictorial surface vibrate. Try to experiment yourself with different combinations on a test paper.

Fig. 2. The tools necessary for spraying are short bristle brushes and a toothbrush. The toothbrush is the most suitable, since its bristles can be scraped better than those of other types of brushes.

On the other hand, if what you want is to spray an extensive surface with fine, uniform spots, use a pulverizer for plants or spray can like the ones used for fixatives. Don't forget that in all these methods it is necessary for the support to be lying flat on top of a table to keep the paint from running across the surface forming blotches.

Spraying can be used to animate or add interest, that is to say, variety, to a wide area bathed in a plain color that would otherwise be too monotonous. Whatever the method you decide to use, remember that when you spray paint it can get onto clothes, the floor, and other parts of the painting you do not wish to cover. Therefore, it is advisable to cover areas to be kept free of paint with cardboard or paper, the floor with newspapers and clothes with a smock. Spraying is a rather unpredictable technique so it is best for you to try it out first on a test paper before using it on your painting.

Fig. 3-5. In these sequences you can see three ways to practice spraying. With a toothbrush, the position of the bristles make it possible to control the direction of the spraying, producing small, abundant drops of color (fig. 3). A brush with short bristles is not quite as convenient and produces larger, more intense drops than a toothbrush (fig. 4). If you want to spray a very large surface, the best thing to do is to take two large flat brushes and hit them against each other (fig. 5). It will even be possible for you to guide the drops with this system. If you place the support at an angle, the drops will have an elongated form.

Fig. 6. An example of the spraying technique can be found in this **Irish landscape,** *by Óscar Sanchís (artist's private collection). As you can see, the spattering technique gives the landscape a pronounced atmospheric effect.*

Extruded Paint

1

As you have been able to see so far, the versatility of acrylic paint makes it possible to experiment with a wide variety of techniques without having to stick to the conventional use of a paint-brush. This chapter will deal with yet another technique, known as extrusion, that is, pressing paint out through a funnel or sleeve or directly from the tube through a nozzle. This method produces lines of paint, which is intense and has some relief. The technique is similar to that used by potters to obtain shapes with enamel or liquid clay. They normally use a pear-shaped through which they extrude the paint onto the decorated plate or jug.

It is necessary to prepare the paint sleeve beforehand. In order to do this, take a piece of glossy paper, if it's waxed paper so much the better, and form a cone or sleeve with it, similar to the one used by pastry chefs to decorate cakes with whipping cream, although it needn't be as big. Once you have made the cone, fill it with paint. Then squeeze the top so that the paint moves down and is pressed against the inside of the cone. Close the top by folding it several times and make a small cut or incision in the tip of the cone so that paint can come out. The next step is the actual painting. In order to do it, you can squeeze the cone with your fingers and guide the tip of the cone along the lines of the drawing or design you wish to paint.

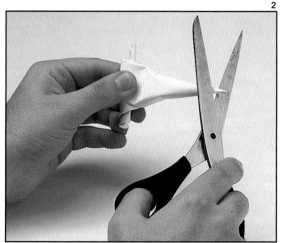

Fig. 1. To extrude the paint it is first necessary to make a sleeve or funnel. To do this all you have to do is roll a piece of paper into the shape of a cone.
Fig. 2. Fill the interior of the cone with paint and close the top by folding the paper several times.
Fig. 3. Finally, use a pair of scissors to make an incision in the tip of the cone to allow the paint to be pressed out, forming streaks on the surface.

There is also the option of applying paint directly from the tube. Although it is not necessarily a bad idea, the lines or streaks that can be obtained in this way are often too thick. Therefore, if you can't put a nozzle on the tube I would suggest making your own cone or else buying jars of acrylic paint that come with a nozzle. Painting with the extrusion technique is not as easy as it looks and it requires some experience, since it is necessary to control the amount of paint that comes out of the sleeve. For this reason, it is a good idea to experiment with the thickness of the line on a piece of test paper before applying the paint to the surface of your painting.

Extrusion is a fairly limited technique and can not be adapted to all styles of painting. It works best with certain themes like cubist, modernist and semiabstract compositions. The streaks or lines in relief that can be obtained with this method would seem out of place in a realistic or valuist painting.

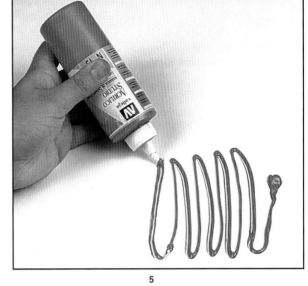

Fig. 4. It is best not to press the paint directly out of the tube onto the surface. However, there are some jars of acrylic paint, like the one in the picture, that make it possible to measure out the desired amount of paint and carry out the extrusion technique.

Fig. 5. Here is an example. Bibiana Crespo will paint a small composition using the extrusion technique. First, she prepares the background with blue and red washes.

Fig. 6. Once the previous dye has dried, she takes a tube of paint with an incorporated nozzle and extrudes the paint onto the surface, thereby creating a decorative jug with oriental influences.

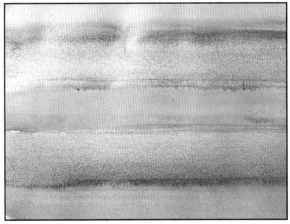

Fig. 7. The artist takes another color and paints another jug. The result is a firm line with a bit of relief that makes the outline of the jug stand out in relation to the rest of the composition.

Reserving White Spaces with Acrylics

Although acrylics are a medium used quickly and spontaneously, sometimes the composition must be planned meticulously. Straight lines or right angles are very easy to obtain by reserving white spaces with masking tape or stencils. Acrylic paints are especially suitable for this technique, because of their fast drying time, and also because acrylic colors can be used to create well-defined edges, which are highly suitable for abstract paintings or geometrical compositions.

Painting a perfectly clean contour with a brush requires a great deal of care and a steady hand. It is almost impossible to keep your hand from shaking and thereby obtaining a somewhat crooked line. Therefore, it is best to use a protective tape to create a mask or reserved space, instead of trusting too much in a steady hand and precise brushstrokes.

Do it in the following way: first of all, make sure the surface to be painted is sufficiently smooth so that the masking tape will stick to it without any problems. Then, use a pencil to draw a very light line, limiting off an area, and place the protective tape on that line, making sure that the edges stick to the paper. Paint the uncovered areas with fluid colors, extending the paint all the way up to the tape or even over it. Then, when the paint has dried, remove the tape with utmost care. You will see that the result is an even-colored line with well-defined margins.

You can carry out this operation as many times as you like, as long as the surface on which you are painting is dry.

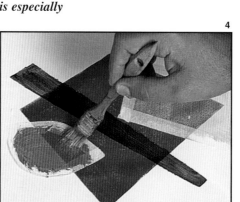

Fig. 1. In order to paint, reserving white spaces, you must first of all limit off the areas you wish to paint with masking tape. Then paint the interior, trying to stay inside the area set off by the tape.

Fig. 2. Once the first wash has dried, we can repeat the same operation, using different colors this time.

Fig. 3. As you can see, well-defined and clearly set-off edges can be obtained with this technique. For this reason, it is especially suitable for painting geometric compositions like this one.

Fig. 4. Finally, we will draw two more figures with masking tape, once again filling their interiors with yellow and orange. The paint should not be too diluted but have a certain consistency.

Fig. 5. Here is the result of the experiment: these well-defined silhouetted shapes.

If you like, you can lay on other colors. To do this, stick the masking tape on top of an acrylic wash that has dried, using it to create whatever shape you like. Paint in the area you have set off with diluted acrylic medium. Then apply a different color onto the same area, trying to avoid ruining the edges of the tape. A few minutes later, remove the tape carefully, so as not to damage the paint, and you will see how the superposition of different colored washes has created a curious effect. You can lay on as many layers of paint as you like, as long as the pictorial surface is dry before you do so. As you can see, this technique is very appropriate for producing abstract compositions, although it is sometimes also used for figurative painting, especially when you are painting an urban landscape and want to keep the outlines of the buildings or the lines of the streets leading off into the distance, clean and precise.

It is also possible to use wax to reserve white spaces. This technique is based on the principle that oil and water don't mix but are incompatible. Just as when you reserve white spaces with masking tape or using stencils, wax keeps the paint from getting on certain areas of the composition, although the effects obtained with wax are more pictorial. The method is extremely easy: First draw on the support using wax colors or pastels. Dilute some acrylic paint in a great deal of water and spread it softly over the area you have previously drawn on using a big brush with soft bristles. It is important for the paint to be extremely diluted because if it is too opaque, it could cover the wax completely and ruin the effect. Soon after applying the wash, you will see how the wax colors repel the paint which slides over the waxed areas, leaving areas of slightly mottled color. In order not to damage the surface of the paper, you should choose resistant paper when working with this method.

Fig. 6. The shapes can be as complex as you like, as long as you can cut out their profile with masking tape.

7

Fig. 7. You can also reserve white spaces with wax colors or oily pastels. Since wax colors are an oil-based medium and acrylics are water-based, both materials repel each other due to their incompatibility, thereby forming paint-free spaces. This can be done not only with white wax colors, but it is also possible to try to integrate other wax colors into the composition.

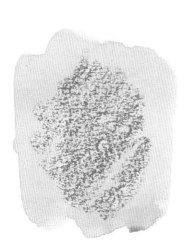

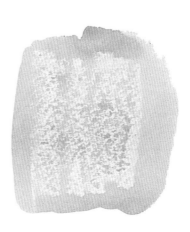

Textures

Acrylics can be used with any type of texture, be it by using paint to work with impasto or mixing it with other materials (such as sand, marble powder, sawdust or mediums) that give the paint more relief and consistency. There is a type of modeling paste made from marble powder that can be bought in glass jars or cans and can be used to give acrylic paint more density. This substance, which is similar to putty, is used to build up textures and relief effects before starting to paint. The previous texture gives better results if afterwards paint is applied in the form of glazes. That way the relief produced by the paste is enhanced by the diluted paint that sets itself in the grooves. Modeling paste can be mixed with paint, but the resulting mixture is so thick that it cannot be easily manipulated. When working with paste, try to apply it in layers that are 1/4 inch thick at the most and let it dry before adding the next layer. If the layers you apply are too thick, the outside film will dry faster than the inside and the surface will appear cracked.

Just as with latex, modeling paste is ideal for collages in relief, since it is capable of holding relatively heavy objects without them coming off. In addition to the different preparations and pictorial procedures, acrylic paint can be scraped and different tools can be used to make impressions in the paint, which makes it possible to obtain very interesting textures.

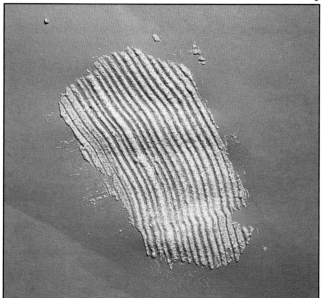

Fig. 1. Marble powder, sawdust and sand are some of the mediums that can be mixed with acrylic paint to give the work a textured surface.

*Fig. 2. Here is the painting, **Russia**, by Teresa Trol (artist's private collection), in which marble powder was used. Notice how the upper part of the painting has small rifts and ripples that give relief to the pictorial surface.*

Fig. 3. The pictorial surface can be modified by using different tools on it, for example, by scratching it with the teeth of a comb.

For example, different effects can be obtained by applying the paste with a palette knife, combing the paint with a comb which can produce either straight or wavy lines, spattering the paint on with a rag, etc. It is also possible to give the surface of the painting a certain relief by pressing down on the pictorial layer with objects while it is still moist. In general, when using these methods it is best to try to be creative rather than try to imitate reality since they are more suitable for creating abstract or decorative paintings than for figurative compositions. Finally, a couple of hints. First of all, when working with textures, a rigid support should be used or you will run the risk of having the paint crack. And secondly, when mixing colors with modeling paste or marble powder, remember that the resulting mixture will lighten the color of the painting.

Fig. 4-9. Here is a wide assortment of textures. As you can see, any object can be stuck on the pictorial surface to surprise the spectator with new effects: twigs and branches (fig. 4), leaves (fig. 5), fibers (fig. 6), and sand (fig. 7). Once you have prepared the texture, you can apply the paint so that the model can be identified (fig. 8 & 9).

Stenciling

This technique can be adapted to many mediums, but it is especially suitable for acrylic paint. It is normally used to decorate furniture or walls, but it offers interesting possibilities used with this type of painting, especially in paintings that are made up of flat forms and geometrical figures. Let's see what it consists in: A design is cut into a piece of paper, Bristol board or acetate. It is held down with masking tape and patches of paint are applied onto the surface of the painting through the spaces in the stencil. White spaces can be reserved using any type of material (wood, sheets of aluminum, canvas, plastic, etc.) but stencils are normally made of thin, rigid cardboard since it's the cheapest material to use. The most important thing to take into account is that the cardboard should not have too thick a texture. Otherwise, the masking tape couldn't keep the stencil in close enough contact with the surface and the paint would seep underneath.

In order to carry out this technique, stencils can be made in diverse ways. The only limit to their complexity is your patience. Making them is as easy as drawing the shape you need onto a piece of Bristol board and cutting it out with a cutting blade or a pair of scissors. Then place the stencil on the surface of the painting and apply the paint from the cut-out edges towards the center Make sure the stencils don't move while you're working, by fixing them into place with all the masking tape you need. The paint should be fluid, neither too watery (in which case the color would seep under the edge of the stencil) nor too thick. Before applying the paint, you should squeeze the water out of the brush until it's almost completely dry. When you have finished the operation, remove the stencil from the canvas in order to make sure that the painted area is clean and well-defined.

When working with thick layers of paint, the stencil should be removed carefully before the paint starts to form a plastic coating, that is to say, before it has dried, since otherwise it will stick to the edges. The stencil can be used as often as you like and in whatever position you choose. Try using it with different shapes and colors. It is also possible to put two or more stencils on top of each other and paint around them.

Stenciling can be effectively combined with collage techniques.

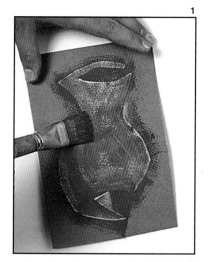

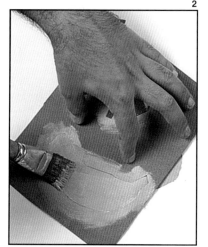

Fig. 1. Stenciling consists in applying paint through a hole cut into a Bristol board, acetate or wood.

Fig. 2. After cutting out each of the shapes you are going to use, apply paint in the open spaces, creating clear and well-defined shapes.

Fig. 4. You can also find stencils with floral forms or other ornamental motifs in stores.

Fig. 3. This it the final result: a combination of monochrome washes with cut-out shapes that are reminiscent of collages made with colored papers.

Scraping

There are many different ways of applying paint with acrylics, and the scraping technique which we will look at now, is very satisfying for the beginning painter since it offers very interesting results. This simple method can be carried out with a flat palette knife, a metal or plastic scraper or if neither of these tools are at hand, with a used credit card. This technique is related to the method of painting with a palette knife but the resulting layers are flatter, resembling soft opaque glazes. It is ideal for producing compositions with broken colors in which wide areas are covered with semitransparent paint, which is scraped onto the pictorial surface, coarsely superimposed onto previous glazes. The colors, being superimposed, enhance the pictorial effect and the texture of the surface of the painting and bring about a not very precise work with few details (filigrees can not be produced with this technique) but a high chromatic quality.

Painting using the scraping technique does not involve applying color in a uniform manner. On the contrary, variety can be given to a composition by contrasting areas of thinly-spread paint with others that have a lot of texture and abundant pictorial matter. If you want to include more graphic variety as well, you can use scrapers for plaster, which have a serrated edge.

Fig. 1. To practice this technique, you will need small pieces of acetate, a plastic scraper or if none is available, you can also use a credit card.

Fig. 2. Now let's see how this procedure should be carried out. To begin, take a wide plastic scraper and spread paint onto the more important parts of the composition, scratching the surface of the support.

Fig. 3. In a few minutes, the main

traits of the model have been resolved. Scraping does not give uniform washes, but rather continuous glazes where different colors mix and are blended at the same time.

Fig. 4. Here is the result. However small the cards or scrapers we use may be, we will never be able to achieve a detailed finish. For this reason, the scraping technique produces compositions that have few lines but are rich in color.

Collage

Collage is a method that consists in cutting and pasting paper or other objects onto the surface of a painting in order to create a design. Acrylic is a material that can be combined very well with the technique of collage, since both the paint and the mediums have a high adhesive capacity and are able to keep relatively heavy objects stuck to the surface of the painting As a result, objects such as wooden blocks, stones, straw, coins, colored paper, tissue paper, aluminum foil or magazine cut-outs can be incrusted into a thick layer of fresh acrylic paint or modeling paste. However, it is preferable to use latex to make a collage since it is a derivative with an adhesive power superior to that of acrylic and therefore more effective for this technique.

This section deals with two-dimensional collage and the juxtaposition of

colored paper more than the assembly of objects on the canvas. Most artists normally use the layer technique, which consists in superimposing successive layers of colored paper and then covering them with paint and sometimes with more medium as well. If you want to create additional textures, you can stick glossy paper that has a neutral PH onto the surface so as to obtain soft wrinkles and very interesting effects. Once you have prepared the surface in this way, cover the paper with tenuous washes to bring out the texture the wrinkled paper gives.

Since collage is an experimental technique, there are no rules about how to proceed. However, if you decide to try it out in its three-dimensional form, use a rigid support such as a wooden board. If, on the contrary, you want to stick to producing flat collages, a medium thick paper will do.

Fig.1. **Dublin Castle,** *by Gabriel Martín (artist's private collection). Collage and acrylic paint on paper.*
Fig. 2. **Palamós,** *by Gabriel Martín (artist's private collection). Collage and acrylic paint on paper.*
Fig. 3. **Landscape,** *by Teresa Trol (artist's private collection). Collage made from magazine cut-outs.*
Fig. 4. **Bouquet of flowers,** *by Teresa Trol (artist's private collection). Collage made from magazine cut-outs and felt-tip pen.*

Sgraffito

Sgraffito is a technique that makes it possible to achieve new effects and textures. It is not really a way of painting, but a way of manipulating and altering the pictorial layer after having applied the paint. It consists in scratching or scraping the moist surface of the paint with an object in order to allow the white color of the surface or the color that there is underneath to show through.

Sgraffito is more difficult to do with acrylics than with oil paints since the paint has to stay moist long enough for the sgraffito to be carried out and acrylics often dry too quickly. For this reason, if you want to include sgraffito in your paintings, it is advisable to work with layers of denser paint or mix the paint with a retardant medium that prolongs the drying time. Do not, under any circumstances, try doing sgraffito on a layer of dry paint, for you would ruin the pictorial surface and maybe even scratch or perforate the support, depending of whether you're working on paper or canvas.

Different effects can be created depending on the instrument you use to scratch the paint (a comb, an ice pick, the back of a paintbrush, a coin). It's a rather effective procedure for achieving detail and texture, like, for example, the bark of a tree, the woven surface of a wicker basket, someone's hair, ropes or electrical wires.

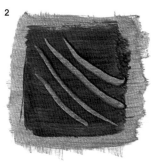

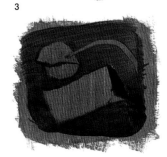

Fig. 1-4. Here you have different experiments probing the possibilities of sgraffito. By opening blank spaces on the pictorial surface while it's still moist, the color underneath shows through.

Fig. 5. Look at the sgraffito done on the facade of this **House at Plovdiv,** *by Óscar Sanchís (artist's private collection).*

Fig. 6. Sgraffito is used to make the painting **The wheat field** *by Teresa Trol (artist's private collection) more expressive.*

Fig. 7. There are special brushes with a rubber tip that are ideal for carrying out sgraffito techniques and eliminating all traces of paint from the pictorial surface.

Mixed Techniques: Oil and Acrylic

Mixing oil and acrylic is commonly called mixed technique, although there are many other combinations with acrylics (acrylics can also be used with colored pencils, pastels or watercolors). These two materials have become habitual companions and are especially suitable for combining transparencies with opaque paint, thanks to the extraordinary versatility and quick drying time of acrylic paint. Artists usually combine these two procedures in order to broaden their range of expressiveness, exploiting the differences between the two materials or blending them into a homogenous whole. Acrylics are used for pre-painting, that is, to tint large areas of color in the form of washes or to paint using a glazing technique, while oil paint is ideal for impasto and to give volume to the pictorial surface. However, these two procedures must be handled with care, since oil and water are incompatible and an incorrect use could lead to a premature deterioration of the painting.

The best way to start is with layers of acrylics. This will save a lot of time, since the first applications of paint will dry much more quickly than if they had been done with oil paints.

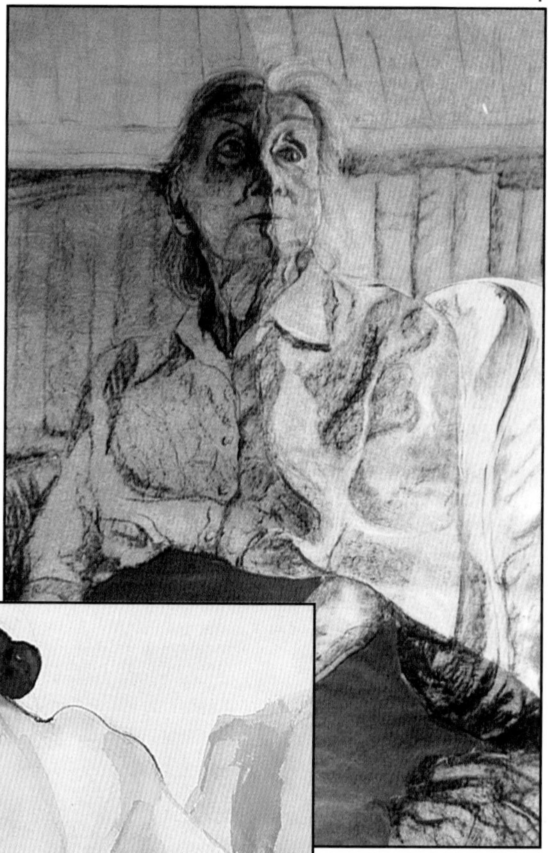

Fig. 2. **Lying female figure,** *by Bibiana Crespo. (Artist's private collection). Mixed technique (acrylics and watercolor).*

Fig. 1. **Grandma,** *by Teresa Trol. (Artist's private collection). Mixed technique (drawing and acrylics).*

Fig. 3. **The riverbank,** *by Ester Llaudet. (Artist's private collection). Mixed technique (acrylics and oil paints).*

Therefore, this should always be the order of application, oil on top of acrylic and not vice versa, since, as you know, acrylic paint does not adhere properly if it is applied on top of a layer of oil paint and it will eventually crack (even if the layer of oil paint is dry). At first it might seem that if we use thick layers of acrylic everything will go well, but do not be deceived, it is improbable that the painting will survive the passage of time.

If you want to achieve a strong contrast between materials, use acrylic paint in one area of the painting and oil paint in another. This technique is used habitually by some artists who deliberately juxtapose areas of color with monochrome areas in order to make an impact with the unexpected.

As you can see, there are but a few rules to using this mixed technique and there is no established method of working. Experience will be your best teacher.

Fig. 4. **Hibernia,** *by Gabriel Martín. (Private collection). Mixed technique (collage, oil paint and acrylics).*
Fig. 5. **Dublin,** *by Gabriel Martín. (Private collection). Mixed technique (collage, oil paint and acrylics).*
Fig. 6. **Landscape,** *by Ester Llaudet. (Artist's private collection). Mixed technique (acrylics and ink).*

Themes for Painting with Acrylics

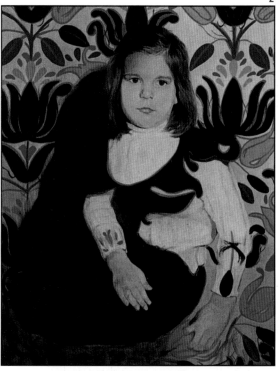

The motifs that are presented on these two pages are appropriate for painting with acrylics, although the truth is that acrylics are suitable for such a wide range of different techniques that they're appropriate for presenting just about any motif. But the intensity of the color that is achieved with this material makes the themes I will now mention especially attractive.

Still lifes are good motifs to begin with, since they allow us to place whatever objects we like and combine them in such a way as to achieve an interesting combination of shapes and colors, as well as working at our own pace and experimenting with different techniques and concepts.

In a landscape painting, just like with a still life, acrylics make it possible both to portray the subject in a strictly naturalistic way or in a colorist and imaginative fashion. The main disadvantage of this genre comes when working out-of-doors, since the paint dries very quickly. Urban landscapes, on the other hand, give the artist the opportunity to explore the interactions between the geometric shapes of a big city, such as the bold vertical and diagonal lines of the streets and avenues (which can be obtained using stencils or by reserving white spaces). All of this can be combined with other man-made elements such as fountains, vehicles and kiosks, and natural themes like parks and gardens.

Interiors also provide a great many possibilities with regard to compositions such as painting objects that contrast with the landscape which can be seen through an open window. This requires a careful control of tonality, color and the qualities and textures of the materials which are included in the interior.

Fig. 1-4. Here is a small selection of themes painted by professional artists. They include an interior landscape, **Boudoir** *by Teresa Trol, (artist's private collection, fig. 1), a portrait,* **Metamorphosis by nature***, also by Teresa Trol (artist's private collection, fig. 2) and a couple of landscapes,* **Romantic garden I** *and* **Romantic garden II***, by Grau Carod (artist's private collection, fig. 3 & 4).*

5

The human figure is another challenge for the artist and because it is so demanding and involves such a high degree of difficulty, acrylics are ideal for the first experiments. Their opacity and speed make it possible for the artist to control his mistakes and his lack of proportion by simply covering the previous design with a new layer of paint. Animals are also a suitable theme. The texture of their fur or feathers is one of their more interesting characteristics and acrylic paints are highly appropriate for representing a wide range of effects of this sort.

There are undoubtedly more themes to paint. It all depends on the interest they awaken in you. Therefore, I suggest you look around and analyze the world that surrounds you. Study the relations between things, how they emit color or how an object projects its shadow onto other objects. If you do this, you will soon discover interesting things to paint in your surroundings. When you examine nature closely, it is easy to find an appropriate subject matter.

6

7

8

Fig. 5-8. Perhaps these photographs could help you find similar motifs to paint. Works of art can come out of apparently small and unimportant things such as an urban landscape from the metropolitan area of London (fig. 5), a group of children swimming in a pool (fig. 6), some Mediterranean boats on the Catalan coast (fig. 7), and a romantic landscape with the charming castle of Carcasonne (fig. 8).

PRACTICAL EXERCISES

After having observed the possibilities of the various techniques, remember that the real potential of any material can only be discovered by experimenting with it. Therefore, I encourage you to practice by doing each of the following exercises, which are based on the work done by professional artists. Observing the work of other artists is an essential part of the learning process.

All the step-by-step exercises that are presented here are analyzed closely and the images are accompanied by captions and tips. The result is a practical section, which together with the first, more theoretical, section of the book, form a complete guide of the expressive qualities and versatility of acrylics. If you like, you can also use the outline-guides at the end of the book, which are designed to make the exercises easier for inexperienced painters.

View of a Town with Acrylics

We will begin with a very easy exercise. In consists in painting the view of a town with acrylics, first using glazes and then adding detail to the houses with a small brush in more intense, contrasting colors. This first exercise is going to be carried out by the Aragonese painter and engraver, Teresa Trol, who is an expert in acrylics, having painted numerous works using this medium throughout her career.

The model is an aerial view of Begur, a village on the Catalan coast (fig. 0). The first step is making a draft, although you should limit yourself to drawing the motif in just a few lines. Do not try for a finished drawing, but make the sketch as simple as possible. Use charcoal for this first step (fig. 1).

Once you have made a draft of the composition, wipe the surface with a rag in order to remove any remaining charcoal. You will see that after rubbing it out, you will still be able to make out the outlines of the drawing on the paper although these will be fainter. Take a medium-size paintbrush and apply soft washes of cadmium green for the vegetation and chrome oxide green on the roofs of some houses (fig. 2). Now, with a little ochre, burnt sienna and raw umber and using semi-transparent washes, paint the roofs of the nearest houses. At this point, only the most important traits of the painting will be outlined, the paint being applied as diluted as possible. The base of the areas which are to remain light in the finished painting, must remain white (fig. 3). The basic shapes of the composition have been set using washes and now it is time to continue working with a small brush adding contrast between light and dark tones to the painting to indicate the shape and tone of the houses and the vegetation in the foreground. Now paint the pronounced outlines and the textures and relief of the roofs and the facades of the houses.

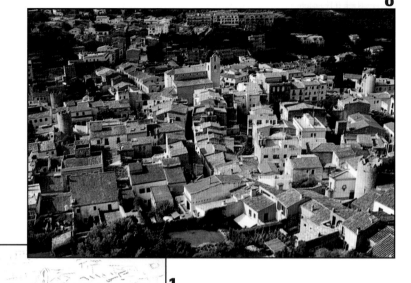

Fig. 0. The model is an aerial view of Begur, a village on the Costa Brava.

Fig. 1. The composition has been sketched with charcoal, combining thin lines with more intense ones.

Fig. 2. A general transparent wash is gently applied, which will act as a base on which we will begin applying more paint.

Fig. 3. At this point, the outlines of some of the houses have been sketched in using glazes.

4

As you can see, the new paint that is added easily covers what has already been painted (fig. 4).

Little by little the image of the village takes shape. Continue building it up. Take the dark alley that leads to the church as a point of reference. Starting there, work on each of the houses along the way individually. Start with the foreground, drawing parallel lines that simulate the placement of the roof tiles. Intensify the vegetation in the foreground with sap green and paint the openings, that is, the doors and windows, of the group of houses, black. You need to move upwards, over the surface of the paper, until you get to the church (fig. 5). Do not forget to decrease the intensity of the colors as the brush moves

5

upwards or, in other words, as you move further into the background and away from the spectator. At this point, finish outlining the houses more precisely, using a thin brush, and then try to accent the contrast between the lighter areas (roofs of the houses) and darker ones (openings and narrow streets).

Towards the end, the composition already has a powerful sense of space, which comes not only from the typical style of the houses, but also from the colors and light effects (fig. 6). To finish, apply an ultramarine blue wash to the background to give the painting more depth and to make the outline of the church tower and the roofs of the

6

village houses stand out. Use the same shade of ultramarine blue that you used for the vegetation in the background on the facades and roofs of the houses in order to achieve a greater unity of color in the painting. Shadows contain a great deal of blue. Make it visible. And here is the result (fig. 7): the view of a town built up using a combination of lines and glazes.

Fig. 4. In the foreground, the more intense lines, which have been made with a small brush, complement the previous washes.
Fig. 5. Once again using the small brush, the artist adds detail to the textures of the roofs, marks the openings of the houses and paints in the location of the dark alleys.
Fig. 6. As we move up the painting, the houses should not be as well-defined as those in the foreground. This will make them appear to be further away.
Fig. 7. The finished work is a good example of how washes can be combined with a meticulous and detailed finish.

TIPS

—Beginning painters tend to avoid landscapes with an excessive agglomeration of houses. However, this exercise shows that it can be a stimulating theme with considerable possibilities.

—Do not leave small brushes, especially the one used in this exercise, in a jar with water for too long, since the bristles tend to lose their shape as a result of their contact with the bottom of the jar.

7

Painting a Landscape with the Pointillist Technique

Since acrylic paint is suitable for different types of chromatic representations, there are hardly any themes that cannot be painted or pictorial techniques that cannot be developed with acrylics. For this exercise we are going to use the technique of pointillism, also known as divisionism, in order to test the chromatic generosity of acrylics, which is superior to that of any other known pictorial medium. Moreover, it is a technique that produces a vigorous effect that is easy to control and very pleasing. For this reason, it shouldn't pose too many problems. In order to do this exercise, we are accompanied by the artist Grau Carod.

Before we begin, it is important to choose a model that is of interest to us and that will allow us to develop the technique of painting by means of dots. For example, we can choose a landscape like this one, on the Catalan mountain of Montserrat, in which it is possible to portray color in different ways (fig. 0). It is always easy to achieve attractive results for the vegetation with this technique, since its texture is similar to the effects created by painting with dots. Sketch the composition onto the cardboard in a few lines. Remember that almost all the drawing will eventually be covered up (fig. 1).

Now take a small brush and start applying small touches of opaque color onto the surface of the painting: cobalt blue on the faraway hillsides, ochre on the middle ground and yellow and red on the foreground (fig. 2). In order to make the dots, it is best to hold the brush in a vertical position. Otherwise, the dots will come out elongated or deformed.

As you can see, the painting is filled with dots that begin to cover the white surface of the paper. The painting should be painted all at once, that is, the entire landscape should be painted at the same time instead of painting each part separately.

At this point, the different objects can be identified more

easily. You can obtain lighter secondary colors, like the green used for the hillsides in the middle ground , by mixing yellow and blue dots. In this way, the colors are mixed as they are viewed by the spectator and the result is much more effectist than if they had been mixed on the palette (fig. 3).

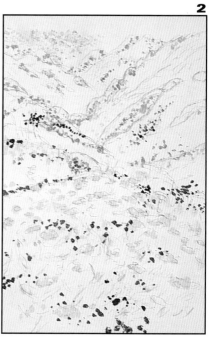

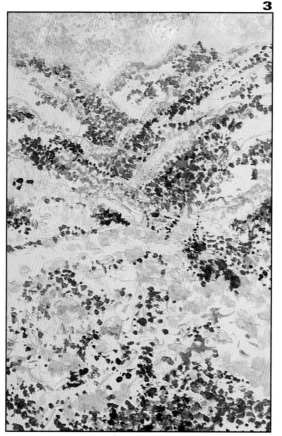

Fig. 0. The artist has chosen this theme because it is simple and perfectly suitable for painting by means of dots.
Fig. 1. The initial step is to make a minimal draft in pencil before applying the first colors.
Fig. 2. At first, the painting seems imprecise, because the dots that cover the surface have yet to give it meaning.
Fig. 3. A few minutes later, the painting already has the following appearance. Through the juxtaposition of dots, it possible to make out interesting color plays that the artist will complete little by little.

54

You can give shape to the light and shade by varying the size of the dots, placing them closer together or further apart and of course, by using different colored dots. The important thing at this stage is to finish establishing the character and the atmosphere of the painting. This can be done by adjusting the tones and the chromatic relations. At this point, the painting as a whole, seen from a certain distance, transmits the intense chromatic sparkling of the mountain landscape (fig. 4). If you look closely, you will see how blue is the only color that reverberates, that is, it is repeated over the entire surface of the painting. This expansion is interesting as it helps to give the painting chromatic harmony. You should do the same.

Continue giving the pointillist surface more density, but remember that it is not necessary to cover the white of the paper completely. Let the white filter through by leaving small spaces free of dots. This will give certain areas of the painting, such as the sky, more luminosity (fig. 5).

Exchange your brush for a thicker one and build up the foreground with red, yellow and orange dots, in other words, with warm colors. Warm colors are used here because they bring the pictorial ground closer, while the cold colors of the background make it seem further away. Notice how, by changing the size of the brush, the dots at the bottom of the painting are larger and more vigorous (fig. 6). The only thing left to do now is take a final look at the painting in its entirety and if the result is satisfactory enough, consider the exercise completed.

TIPS

—Always bear in mind that the only important thing is the way in which each individual sees the theme, and that is how he or she should represent it. To what extent that vision of the theme coincides with nature, is not important.

—The ideal instrument for this technique could be a brush that has lost its tip.

—What counts in art is knowing how to express oneself, since art is about expressing feelings and ideas, and not merely copying what we have before us.

Fig. 4. As you can see, the harmonization of the colors and the size of the dots can be controlled better with this technique than by spraying paint on.

Fig. 5. The surface of the paper is almost completely covered, and an optical mixture of colors has been achieved which gives the composition meaning and depth.

Fig. 6. With a painting like this one, it is possible to experiment with colors without being limited to the more or less realistic reproduction of the model.

55

Painting a Still Life with Stencils

Stenciling is interesting, fun and very easy. And to prove it we have prepared the following exercise. The plastic artist and engraver Bibiana Crespo will paint a creative composition for you using the stenciling technique. Since this method of using stencils is not suitable for achieving realistic resolutions, the painting must be interpreted in a freer, more abstract way.

To begin, choose several objects that have bright and contrasting colors and place them in front of a white wall on top of a solid-colored piece of cloth, which in this case is blue (fig. 0). The blue cloth provides a tonal contrast with the white wall and between the two they create a backdrop against which the smaller shapes can be organized so as to create the maximum chromatic impact.

Before you begin to apply the paint, you should discover the usefulness of limiting the palette. Choose a few key colors, suitable for the work at hand, which can be mixed. I advise you to choose ultramarine blue, cadmium red, lemon yellow, ochre, cobalt blue and carmine.

First cut out stencils in several geometric shapes that are related to the shapes suggested by the model. Lay them on the surface and start daubing on different colored paints (fig. 1).

Little by little you will see how the composition starts to come to life and these stenciled on shapes begin to relate to each other. At this stage, we can already identify part of the jug and some of the fruits (fig. 2).

0

1

2

4

3

Fig. 0. The colors of this still life are deliberately chosen for their contrast and impact.
Fig. 1. Fix the stencil firmly onto the surface and paint on top of the cut-out shape.
Fig. 2. Remove the stencil from the canvas to check to make sure that the painted area is clean and well-defined.
Fig. 3. Make sure that the stencils don't move as you paint. It should be enough to hold them down with your free hand.
Fig. 4. Using almost exclusively paint of a medium consistency, we have already sketched the main shapes of the composition.

The artist has now applied the first washes onto the blue cloth. Notice how the artist has used masking tape to reserve white spaces in the lower right-hand corner of the painting.

The stencils can be re-used, that is, they have more than one use as the same model can be used in different areas of the painting (fig. 3). If the shapes are superimposed, be careful not to ruin the previous color.

Mark the contrast between the light and shaded areas of the painting from the beginning (fig. 4). You will see how the light comes from above and from the right in such a way that the upper right-hand side of all the objects will be a bit lighter. Continue darkening the cloth with diluted and transparent ultramarine blue. Little by little increase the color in the shaded areas. Use the paint as it comes out of the tube for the fruits to give them the maximum impact and brightness.

Since the background is a large plain area, paint some abstract motifs with a stencil and light washes to make this area more interesting, but without overdoing it (fig. 5). Notice the effect caused by the reserved white spaces in the lower right-hand corner. Add color to the large areas in the background that surround the objects. With a somewhat smaller brush add the ornamental decoration to the jug. This gives the painting as a whole some graphic variety (fig. 6). The intention is not to give the painting a detailed finish, but rather to continue using large areas of color. Leave some small areas in the background white and keep the colors as simple and clear as you can. Intensify the color of the fruits progressively and add new areas of shade using the stencils (fig. 7).

When you are about to finish the painting, it is important to take a break and have a good look at the entire painting to determine whether there are parts that don't work well. It may be necessary to adjust the painting as the artist has done by outlining some parts of the composition with a reed and some Chinese ink (fig. 8).

5

6

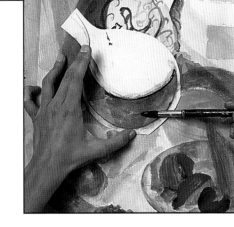

7

8

Fig. 5. Notice how the lighter touches of yellow are used to give shape to the illuminated areas on the pottery and group of fruits.

Fig. 6. The cloth should not appear to be lying flat on the table, but should act as a solid backdrop that helps to make the objects in the painting look like voluminous objects in real space.

Fig. 7. Continue working with stencils, using a different stencil with a different color than the ones used until now.

Fig. 8. The work done by Bibiana Crespo combines the stenciling technique with a fresh, childlike and vital style, creating a painting that is closer to fauvism than to realism.

TIPS

—Try not to work too much with one color on top of another, in order to keep the colors from smudging.

—As you paint, keep the colors as pure and bright as possible, using them directly out of the tube if necessary.

Painting a Still Life with the Dry Brush Technique

Now paint a still life, a good theme for a beginner to start practicing the painting on dry technique, since the objects that will be used as models are usually familiar objects that can be found on hand, and for this reason their basic structure is well known to the artist. Óscar Sanchís is the artist chosen to carry out the following exercise, which he will do using the dry brush technique that has already been explained in the first part of this book. This time I advise you to use outline-guide number 1 and practice the exercise following these instructions.

Before you begin, lets look at the model, a simple still life composed of a jug, a ceramic bowl with some fruit, a few objects with different textures, the tones of which contrast with the red background (fig. 0).

The paper chosen by the artist has a granular texture and it's ochre in color. This textured paper will enhance the effect of the brushstrokes applied with the dry brush technique, while the colored background will give the painting as a whole a certain sense of harmony.

Start by drawing a simple sketch of the model onto the cardboard with a hog bristle brush and a little cobalt blue and violet. It is only necessary to indicate with a minimum amount of precision the sizes and shapes of the objects and their relation to each other (fig. 1). The second stage of the painting consists in painting, or rather, outlining the red of the background with a wide brush, leaving the ochre of the paper visible. To do this, mix some cadmium red and pale pink (fig. 2).

We have begun with the background, because it is the largest individual area, but once you've given it a general exposure, move on quickly to the remaining areas of the painting

From now on you should work with a big, flat brush with hard bristles. Using a little orange and cadmium yellow paint the group of fruits, and with terra sienna mark the shaded areas of the jug and the fruit in the foreground (fig. 3). In this first stage, it is important to try to relate the tones and the colors as closely as possible, although they will change as the painting progresses.

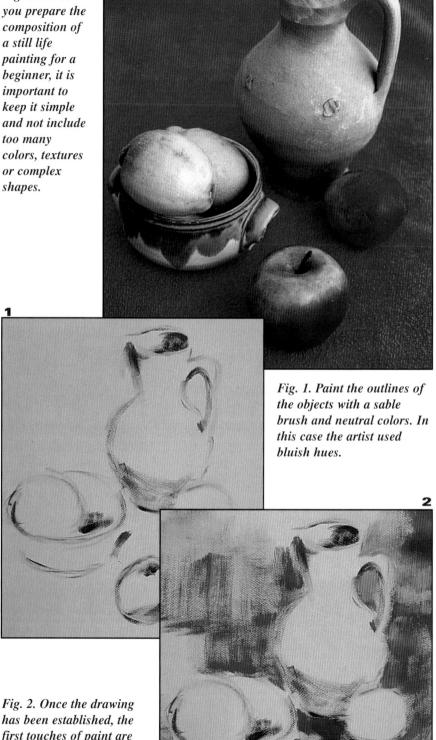

Fig. 0. When you prepare the composition of a still life painting for a beginner, it is important to keep it simple and not include too many colors, textures or complex shapes.

Fig. 1. Paint the outlines of the objects with a sable brush and neutral colors. In this case the artist used bluish hues.

Fig. 2. Once the drawing has been established, the first touches of paint are applied with a wide brush.

Use big brushes so that the surface has a feeling of freedom. In this way you will also avoid stubbornly wanting to prematurely paint small details. Use ultramarine violet to paint the darker areas of the background, and with a little cadmium green, paint the single apple in the foreground (fig. 4).

Now paint the ceramic bowl with short thick juxtaposed strokes of ultramarine blue (for the darker parts) and cobalt blue and a little white (for the lighter ones). Build up the painting as a whole. By this I mean that if you are painting part of the bowl or a reflection on the fruit, look, compare and make a decision about the tone and the color of the adjacent area, which might be a different fruit, the jug or the background. In this way you will build up the entire painting little by little without having to paint the objects separately (fig. 5).

The texture of the jug is finished off carefully with a fan brush and successive applications of color. Since acrylic dries so rapidly, the layers of paint can be laid on without waiting.

Take the wide brush again and intensify the red background with a medium shade of cadmium red and a little raw umber leaving the left side of the composition darker (fig. 6). The dry brush technique can be limited to just one

Fig. 3. The paint is applied on the paper using the dry brush technique, that is, dipping the brush in paint that has hardly been diluted in water.
Fig. 4. Although the painting is being built up with touches of color, the artist must pay careful attention to the tonal relations.
Fig. 5. Here is the first chromatic appraisal of the composition. From this stage on, we will work with a medium-size brush in order to give more detail to the shapes and create more precise effects.

area of the painting. However, in this case the artist wants the texture of the surface to be uniform and therefore, uses this technique for the background, the foreground and the fruits. You should do the same (fig. 7).

In order to carry out the last stage, before you finish it is worth observing the shapes and the small chromatic changes within each object more closely, paying special attention to the reflection of the colors on the surrounding colors. Use thick impasto strokes on the fruit in the bowl, to make their surfaces seem to reflect the light, while reinforcing the dark areas with an intense blue. See, for example, the background on the left side of the painting, that has been made darker to intensify the play between light and shade in the painting (fig. 8).

A simple still life like this one is an excellent way for the painter beginning to work with acrylics to get to know and experiment with this medium and practice the dry brush technique. It is also a very useful

6

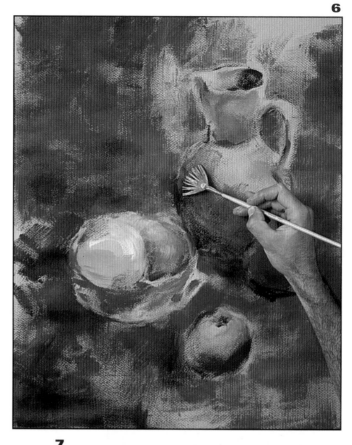

Fig. 6. The chromatic variations of the jug have been achieved by concentrating and superimposing brown and blue brushstrokes.

7

8

Fig. 7. Different colors and brushstrokes are used in different areas of the painting. Variations between diluted and concentrated paint are used to achieve a greater contrast.

Fig. 8. Creamy, concentrated paint is used for the reflections on the fruit in the bowl.

9

Fig. 9. The painting is nearly finished, but the bottom part of the composition has too much power. For this reason, the artist has decided to apply additional pink glazes to soften and unify the colors in the foreground.

theme for suggesting textures, in addition to allowing the artist to obtain subtle but vivid interactions between colors. By working inside, you won't have any of the typical problems encountered when working out-of-doors, such as changes in light or the too rapid drying of paints. Surely you became worried when you saw that, as you continued painting, the initial part of the drawing was lost or distorted by the paint. This is not a reason to worry, it is normal in a work like this one. All it means is that when you approach the final part of the process, you will need to reestablish the drawing in those areas where you consider it necessary. We don't need to worry about the fact that the colors are laid over each other,

either. Nor, as has been stated on several occasions, should each object be painted separately. But we should avoid adding the light effects before it's time, for they should be saved until the end. Otherwise, the touches of light could give the sensation of being part of the surface of the painting instead of something inherent to the objects. In other words, it could appear that they have no relation to the painting as a whole. You should try to see the touches of light as gaps that are clear of color, instead of considering them white reflections. Keep in mind that in order to carry out this painting the artist has not used one bit of white (fig. 9).

Painting with the Washing Technique

If in the previous exercise we practiced the dry brush technique, in this exercise we will work with washes and glazes. Josep Antoni Domingo, an expert in the art of painting with acrylics, will be our guide in this step-by-step exercise. The technique of velatura, or painting with glazes, is done quite similarly with acrylics as it is with watercolors, although the colors are a bit more opaque and when they dry they appear a bit shinier. Let's begin. To do this exercise with acrylics you will need several flat hog bristle brushes and a round sable brush for the details. In addition to this, you will need a palette with hollows, to put the paint in.

The model for this exercise is this beautiful view of Toulouse seen from the Saint Michel bridge. We have a contrasting foreground, rich in gradations of blue and green, and further in the distance we can make out a bridge and the outlines of the buildings of this old city in the south of France (fig. 0).

After fixing the paper onto the rigid support, use a soft brush on watercolor paper, starting with light washes of cadmium green and cerulean blue. As you can see in the image (fig. 1), the artist has avoided doing a preparatory sketch in pencil and tackles the theme directly with the confidence that comes from years of experience. However, if you do not feel sufficiently confident to do without a preliminary sketch, do not hesitate to do one or use outline-guide number 2.

Now paint the water of the river using horizontal strokes of cerulean blue (mixed with a bit of gray) (fig. 2). Start from above and move down the surface of the paper. When you get to the bottom of the sheet, you will find that an excess of paint has accumulated there. Get rid of it with a rinsed paintbrush or with a sponge. If you do not do this, the paint will dry forming pools of paint which will ruin the washes. Remember that once they have dried, acrylics cannot be

Fig. 0. This step-by step exercise is based on the splendid view from the Saint Michel bridge across the Garonne river as it flows through the city of Toulouse (France).
Fig. 1. The artist starts by suggesting, with light washes, the location of the trees and the bridge, obtaining a very soft and gentle effect.
Fig. 2. Working initially with only two colors, the artist establishes the outline of the composition and marks the tonal key.

modified as is the case with water-colors.

Now work on the arches of the bridge that appears at the top of the image using a little Venetian red (if you don't have this color you can use sienna instead) and Prussian blue so that the painting as a whole acquires a certain violet-like tendency, due to the cold colors adopted by the bodies as they withdraw into the background (fig. 3). This is an optical illusion caused by the water vapor and the dust particles in the air, that make the distant shapes and colors grayer.

Now apply some paint in a more concentrated form mixed with a little mat medium. Spread the greenish wash over the surface of the water to simulate the reflection of the vegetation. It is worthwhile to remember that the reflections are almost always darker than that which is reflected, in this case the branches of the trees (fig. 4).

Continue darkening the foliage of the vegetation by laying on new shades (ochre, terre-verte, and sap green). In this manner, the strokes of sap green will blend with the previous applications of yellow and cadmium green giving the impression of a delicate shade in the leaves (fig. 5). With a small brush dipped in burnt sienna and red, draw the thin branches of the vegetation that invades the central part of the composition. A succession of washes should also be applied to the sky, so that it becomes progressively darker as the colors of the painting are intensified.

4

Work on the foreground first, that is to say, on the vegetation. The paint should be applied smoothly onto the paper with a round sable brush, following the method used in modeling and allowing the previous washes of brighter colors to filter through. Acrylic paint possesses more of a physical presence than watercolor and for this reason the objects appear to be brought closer.

3

5

Fig. 4. The artist applies one color on top of the other, using the paint as if it were watercolor.

Fig. 5. The subtlety of the superimposed second tonal appraisal makes the color underneath the glaze shine through, giving the painting a brilliant effect.

Fig. 3. The water has been painted with horizontal strokes, using the technique known as wet on wet.

This allows us not only to portray detail and give it texture but also to stress space (fig. 6). In this way, the deep blue of the foreground brings the area forward in space. Continue working on the texture and shape of the big branch that crosses the center of the painting (fig. 7). Darken the blue of the sky with highly-diluted washes so that

it has a clear tonal gradation. Continue by beginning to build up the shapes of the buildings in the background, which still appear a bit faded. This task will be completed in the next stage, we'll leave it for the final finish. Finally apply a yellowish wash onto the water in the lower part of the painting in order to reproduce the reflection of the

vegetation on the crystalline surface of the calm waters of the river. It is interesting to note that some colors, like yellow, appear more solid when they are used on top of darker colors (fig. 8). To finish the painting, darken the blue of the lower area, add more details to the vegetation in the foreground and also to the buildings in the distance. In order to do this, use a small sable brush. Also add some shades of green to the water, add detail to the reflections and add textural effects to the foliage of the vegetation and the bark of the branches of the trees (fig. 9). The effect produced by the technique of velatura, or adding successive layers of glazes to a painting, is very peculiar. The colors are perceived as filtering through other colors and the effect is one of subtle and luminous mixtures. This can be seen especially in the leaves of the trees and the shadows that they project onto the surface of the water. Surely you have worried too much about finding the definitive colors for your painting on your palette, when this operation should have been carried out on the surface of the painting which is where the colors should be mixed and modified through this technique of superposing washes.

6 **7**

8

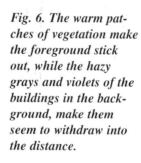

Fig. 6. The warm patches of vegetation make the foreground stick out, while the hazy grays and violets of the buildings in the background, make them seem to withdraw into the distance.

Fig. 7. The brush gives the water a sensation of calm movement, which is evoked by the light and reflections which are constantly moving.

Fig. 8. The rippling on the surface of the water is just enough to tone down the reflections of the trees, which have been painted with horizontal brushstrokes in order to contrast with the more energetic strokes used on the leaves.

TIPS

—The use of mat medium for paintings done with the glazes is quite common, since it makes the paint become more transparent.
—For extensive washes, palettes with individual ceramic or porcelain cavities are very useful.
—Acrylics can also be used together with watercolors, and perhaps this is one of the most satisfying ways of working with them, since it makes it possible to make the most of both.

9

Velatura makes it possible, also, to paint over and unify some areas without having to repaint them entirely. You may also have had problems in detailing the reflections on the water. The water, just like the sky, is an tricky theme, the effects of which are rather transitory and therefore difficult to capture without losing the sensation of movement. My advice would be to try to freeze the instant, making a couple of strokes with moderation in order to achieve a sensation of movement and fluidity.

Fig. 9. In the finished work, you will notice that the colors have a shine that can only be obtained in this way. Green painted on top of an area of more solid greens and blues will be richer and more intense. If, on the other hand, it is painted on top of a luminous yellow it will be more defined and clearer.

Painting a Seascape with Spattered Paint

0

As we have said before, spattering, or spraying, is an excellent way of suggesting certain textures although it is also used to give livelihood to a painting with too many plain colored areas. So let's experiment with this technique and see how this curious method of applying paint can develop out of a seascape done in the technique of painting on wet. To carry out this exercise we have with us once again Óscar Sanchís.

The model is the view of some rocky cliffs of the Catalan coast. Those in the foreground have very definite shapes and colors, while in the background there are several planes of vegetation and rocky formations (fig. 0). To begin, sketch the main lines of the composition lightly with a number 2 pencil on a tensed sheet of paper. This will allow you to modify the drawing with an eraser without any difficulties (fig. 1). If you want to do this exercise, you have a similar drawing in outline-guide number 3. Take a used toothbrush and start to spatter different areas of the surface with orange and blue paint. By using this tool you will achieve a rather controlled spraying made up of numerous small drops of paint (fig. 2A). The way to carry out the spraying is as follows: First wet the toothbrush in paint until the bristles are well-covered. Then shake it carefully trying to get rid of any excess water. Next, hold it over the surface of the painting rubbing the bristles with your thumb, which will produce a spraying effect. The paint should be moist but not too watery. If you are going to work on large surfaces, you can also fill a bottle with paint and spray it on using a spraying device, or you could recycle a plastic spray bottle like those used for cleaning windows (fig. 2B).

1

2B

2A

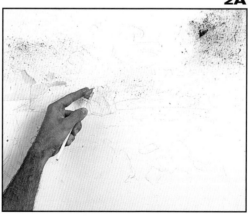

Fig. 0. We are going to paint this beautiful summer print of a rocky cove on the Costa Brava.
Fig. 1. The draft of the rocks in this seascape has been done in quite a bit of detail. You should also pay special attention to the shapes of the boats.
Fig. 2A. Instead of starting by applying washes, the first appraisal should be carried out by spraying on different colors.
Fig. 2B. In case you want to spray large surfaces, it's best to use a pulverizer like the kind we use to clean the house.

Then cover the bushes in the foreground with a semi-transparent yellowish wash and do the same for the water using ultramarine blue. Notice how the bluish wash brings out the outline of the vegetation in the foreground. This is known as contrasting complementary colors (fig. 3). The different applications of spattered paint (done with burnt umber, orange, green and ochre) should be applied freely, without worrying too much about coherence, covering the foreground and effectively transmitting the disorganized disposition of the leaves on the nearby bushes. The lighter tones of the rocks are painted with a mixture of ochre, cadmium orange and yellow (fig. 4). The first glazes should be very transparent. The colors will be intensified as the work progresses.

When these light colors have dried, tones of medium intensity, such as burnt sienna and burnt umber, are added and new applications of spattered paint (done with black, brown, green and gray) are applied onto the vegetation that covers the tops of the rocky cliffs as well as the foreground (fig. 5). Pay close attention to this spraying and you will see that this time the spattering is more violent and the dots are bigger. To achieve the rough textures of the rocks on the right you can use a small round brush.

Notice how both the trees and the rocks have been simplified and treated as large areas of color. The pictorial structure of the cliffs is almost abstract, but it retains sufficient detail for us to be able to identify the relief. The best way to achieve effects like those in the painting is to work on wet.

Spray the vegetation in the lower part of the image again using new colors (burnt umber, burnt sienna and violet). Since the bushes are closer we suggest using a bristle brush to spatter on the paint.

3

4

5

Fig. 3. The method the artist uses consists in spraying the basic areas with paint and then completing the process of building up the shapes with washes and using the wet on wet technique.

Fig. 4. The chromatic dynamism that the work will have can already be made out at this stage and the perfect communion between spraying and washes can also be seen.

Fig. 5. In order to paint the cliffs, the artist has concentrated his attention on the structure of the angular shapes that can be made out in the play between light and shadow.

67

In this way the drops will be coarser and larger, which will make the work more expressive (fig. 6). With a small brush add more spots to the vegetation, since the trees have noticeable and varied textures which provide us with a fascinating wealth of detail and shades of color. When you are about to finish the painting, it's a good idea to move a few steps back to decide what still needs to be done to unify the composition. It is important to vary the consistency of the paint and create attractive textures. To give life to the work, paint in some details with thick colors that will contrast with the diluted and faded tones of the washes. The spots where the white of the paper shows through correspond to the boats, which will be defined later (fig. 7).

As a finishing touch the vegetation on the tops of the cliffs in the background should be sprayed again using various colors (like violet, Hooker green, yellow, manganese blue and pink). And the dots are then redirected with a small brush. Finish by giving depth to the painting by contrasting and outlining the foreground. A few touches of more intense color on the water should be enough (fig. 8). At this stage, the sea has, in addition to different textures (areas treated with extensive washes, with spattered paint, with dense colors, etc.) an amalgam of colors (ochre, emerald green, ultramarine blue, indigo, sienna and pink) which defy the erroneous idea that many artists have of a smooth solid-colored surface with hardly any variations. With a small brush very carefully paint in the detail of the boats.

6

Fig. 6. Observe the variety of strokes and colors that have been used to define the copse at the top of the cliffs.

7

Fig. 7. Now, the saturated blue of the water contrasts with the brown colors of the cliffs and the adjacent vegetation, constituting the center of interest of this attractive seascape.

8

Fig. 8. The artist has enhanced the sensation of light in the foreground, increasing the contrast between the vegetation and the water.

As you will surely have noticed, the spraying technique is rather haphazard (which might have caused you some problems) since it's not possible to control exactly where the drops of paint will fall. However, it is a technique which offers a surprising finish and texture and is therefore worth mastering. Your colors might have gotten mixed as you sprayed them onto the paper, that is, some dots of different colors may have blended to form bigger dots. If this happened it's because, first of all, you were working with excessively thin paint, and in the second place, because you should have waited for one color to dry before spraying on another color on top of the first. In this way, the dots will follow each other creating glazes and the effect that will be produced will be similar to that produced in divisionism or pointillism.

When we find ourselves faced with a landscape as rich in motifs as this one, it is easy to be seduced by detail. You should avoid this. In order to do so, I advise you to deliberately use big brushes so as not to paint in an excessively detailed fashion. You will find this tactic useful when you want to give a painting a free and audacious air. A common mistake is to go over the painting too much, for thereby you lose the sense of fluidity.

You will also notice that this painting has a logical movement, that is to say, the rocks repeat a series of angular shapes, the water contains reflections and should be dealt with in horizontal strokes, whereas the strokes used on the vegetation should be made with scribbling movements. Try to make your strokes into the shape of these movements in order to keep it from looking static.

Fig. 9. Here is the elaborate texture of the finished work. Since acrylics dry quickly, it is possible to create a surface with a large amount of spattered paint in very little time, without running the risk of the colors mixing.

Painting a Landscape with a Palette Knife

Acrylics are a very flexible procedure which can be used in light washes, in a way similar to watercolors, or in impastos applied with a palette knife, as in the procedures reminiscent of the traditional techniques of oil painting. In order to do this exercise, we are going to use the second of the methods described.

Painting with a palette knife is an impasto technique. In this step-by-step exercise we count with the collaboration of Josep Antoni Domingo, who has already worked with us on previous exercises. In order to do this exercise, you will need two or three palette knives of different shapes and sizes, as well as outline-guide number 4. This technique requires patience and a steady hand. The method is laborious, so it is best not to begin with an excessively large painting. A 12 inch wide panel will do.

You can see the model in figure 0. It is a view of Uçhisar, a small village of the Capadocia, in the heart of Turkey, in the hours just before sunset.

The less experienced painter would have to do a preliminary drawing as a guide for the first applications of paint. But Josep Antoni Domingo goes directly to the building up of the main shapes using soft color washes. Try to place the fundamental shapes of the landscape as well, by making a first appraisal with hardly perceptible washes. This will allow you to make modifications if you make a mistake. (fig. 1).

When the initial pre-painting has dried, continue, still working with the brush, using thicker and more opaque paint to intensify the colors of the composition. Use ochre for the blades of grass in the foreground, emerald green, English red and ultramarine blue and violet in the middle ground and burnt umber, emerald green and cadmium green for the objects in the distance. Keep the colors as clean and pure as they are in the image, letting each area of color be clearly distinguishable on the canvas, and trying to keep them from mixing with the previous ones. Paint the sky with broad brushstrokes of cobalt blue, using a somewhat darker shade in the upper part of the canvas (fig. 2).

Fig. 0. The model for this exercise is a rural view of a village in central Turkey. It has pronounced contrasts of light and shade due to the fact that the sun is about to set.

Fig. 1. Without making a preliminary drawing, the artist starts outlining large areas with highly diluted paint that will act as a base for the successive layers.

Fig. 2. More tones have been added here, establishing a more specific color key.

3

Add a little emerald green to the sky, thereby suggesting the relief of the clouds that although inexistent in the model, the artist has considered would give the blue of the sky more variety. By pressing down lightly on the palette knife as you use it to move the paint across the paper, small irregular scratch marks will be produced that give the landscape a much richer texture (fig. 3).

Continue working on the painting with a small hog bristle brush, adding various shades to the background: emerald green and Hooker green for the vegetation, and bluish hues for the group of mountains on the right. Complete the shape of the houses using the palette knife to add new applications of paint that complement the initial shades (fig. 4) Before applying a second appraisal, let the previous layer dry slightly. The artist spreads the paint onto the surface with a triangular palette knife, using the paint as it comes out of the tube, thereby making the red of the roof of the mosque more intense, adding new shades to the intense blue that shapes the ravine on the left, projecting the violet shadows of the houses and applying new touches to the vegetation in the fields in the background (fig. 5). You should do the same.

The artist's palette knife flattens the paint against the surface of the support and leaves behind it a series of thin impastos with a slight relief where the application of color comes to an end. In this way, the color of the grass in the foreground is given even more life, by applying a thicker and creamier yellow which can be obtained by mixing ochre, white and a little bit of burnt umber.

Normally impasto is saved for the details

4

Fig. 3. Mix a certain amount of thick paint, load the palette knife and spread the paint onto the surface of the paper.

Fig. 4. Consider the possibility of bringing out the color of the sky with the help of the palette knife. All you have to do is comb the paint in order to flatten it and obtain a richer and more textured effect.

Fig. 5. In this illustration you can see the effects obtained though successive mixtures of paint.

5

in the foreground, but in this case the distant fields have not been outlined in order to bring out the group of houses that are lit up by the setting sun, houses whose shadows are usually represented with a group of scarce thick solid-colored spots applied with a small palette knife (fig. 6).

Go back to the foreground in order to add new shades, this time using brown that has been toned down with white for the blades of grass in order to reinforce the linear element. Do this with the tip of the triangular palette knife (triangular palette knives are able to achieve effects of surprising precision) Continue building up the details of the vegetation in the background using different greens and browns. Touch up some of the details like the openings of the houses, the chimneys and the fine strokes that run vertically up and down the minaret, which have been done using the edge of a palette knife loaded with paint and pressing down onto the surface (fig. 7). As a colophon the artist added some strokes of paint applied with a small round brush to finish off the definition of some textures and some details that could not be done with the palette knife.

Here is the finished work (fig. 8) Surely it is not what you expected. You may have imagined that paintings done with a palette knife produced vibrant works, with little definition and

6

TIPS

—If you have problems with the drying process, either because the impasto you have applied is too thick or because the atmospheric conditions you are painting in are excessively humid, it would be convenient to dispose of a hair drier.

—A palette knife with an undulated blade is ideal for achieving different effects. Use the tip of the blade to add details or to dot the surface with incisions. Use the flat part of the blade to modify large areas and the edge to make lines.

—If you have overdone it with the impasto technique, you can eliminate some of the excessively thick layers of paint by using the flat part of the palette knife to scrape it off.

7

Fig. 6. The intense violet color of the shadows provides a sense of balance with the blues of the ravine and the warmer colors of the facades of the houses which are illuminated by the sunlight.

Fig. 7. The richness of the colors has been obtained by spreading one layer of paint after another, dark on light or vice versa.

coarse impastos. But well-defined compositions like this one can also be achieved.

You may have let yourself be dominated too much by a desire to be effectist and that consequently your work has turned out excessively textured. You should learn to combine areas of flat color with denser impastos. Otherwise your work will appear too packed. As you can see in the painting done by Josep Antoni Domingo, the impastos have hardly any relief. If, on the contrary, the impastos have dried too quickly and this has made the posterior superposition of new colors difficult, what you have to do is add retardant medium to the mixture. In that way, the drying time will be lengthened and the paint that is applied will be able to be manipulated again on the support, even a couple of hours after being applied. It is not necessary to work quickly. What matters is the result.

Surely painting with a palette knife must have seemed more complicated than painting with a brush, at least at first. Don't worry. After this exercise work on it until you have acquired the necessary practice.

Fig. 8. The use of a palette knife for painting is usually associated with thick impastos, but the truth is that it can also be used to produce works like this one, full of delicate effects and detail.

Painting with Acrylic and *Collage*

In this step-by-step exercise we are going to combine two of the most flexible and expressive procedures: collage and acrylic paint. We are not going to be working with colored papers, but with textures, for paper that is crumpled up and stuck onto the surface can create a pictorial base with surprising relief effects. It will be up to you to decide how to make the most of it. For this exercise you will need two sheets of tissue paper or Japanese paper (fig. 0A). Óscar Sanchís is the artist we have chosen to paint the theme that you can see in the adjoining photograph. It's a view of the banks of the Nile River with the Pantheon of Aga Kan standing out above it (fig. 0B). The support we are going to use is watercolor paper of medium grain, onto which the artist will stick, for example, tissue paper

using a little white glue.
The texture will form the relief of the dry and arid hills which stand out over the banks of the river. Start cutting out a piece of tissue paper and crumpling it up until you have formed a small ball. Unfold it and glue it onto the support, pressing firmly with your fingers so that it sticks well. Here the artist has used latex to fix the material to the paper. However, if you like you can also use a medium, due to its adhesive power (fig. 1).
In this way the upper half of the paper will be covered with a texture full of creases and wrinkles which will be used as the background, to give the representation of the sand hills that surround the banks of the river more richness. As soon as you can see that

the glue has dried, take a flat hog bristle brush and paint the sky, forming a slight tonal gradation. Add white, violet and pink to the ultramarine of the sky, more as you move down towards the line where the hills begin (fig. 2).
As you can see, all the colors are diluted. However, they have a clear sfumato effect, which is normally used to make big flat areas more interesting like the sand or the sky, as well as making the surface more shiny. Do the same and blend the colors together by softly rubbing the different shades of ochre in the contours of the hills to make them appear to join the sky.

Fig. 0A. Tissue paper, if it is wrinkled before you stick it on, is very appropriate for bringing out textures using the collage technique.

Fig. 0B. Before you begin, you should choose a model that has certain textural characteristics which make it appropriate to be represented using the collage technique, such as this view of the Nile.

Fig. 1. In this exercise, the artist has started by gluing a big piece of wrinkled tissue paper onto the pictorial support.

Fig. 2. Once the basic structure has been situated, that is, by putting the paper in its place, the artist begins to paint the sky.

3

In this way you will achieve a better integration of the different planes (fig. 3).

At this point, the background has already been sketched. The sfumato effect of these first washes makes the tones more subdued in some parts of the composition, making some areas look softer and also giving them more light and freshness. With a little bit of cobalt yellow and a wide brush. Project some vertical lines onto the water. These will aid us in reproducing the reflections of the banks on the surface of the river (fig. 4). Once you have defined the colors and big shapes, continue working on the painting with more fluid and intense paint. Liven up the middle ground with loose touches of dark green (sap green, olive green and ochre), representing the clear line of the vegetation. In order to depict the foliage of the trees your strokes should be irregular, as if you were scribbling (fig. 5).

Now move on to the lower part of the image. Deal with the reflections on the water by projecting spots vertically from the bank, using brownish tones instead of green. When the water is spotted cover it with superimposed thick layers of light blue paint, moving the brush from left to right and vice versa, so that the new horizontal strokes of the water mix with the colors of the previous wash. As a result, the shapes will be attenuated, loose their definition and become more abstract. The reflections should be clearer and more intense the closer you move towards the shore (fig. 6).

The reason why the surface of the water has been dealt with in this way should be clear, namely, to give it a sensation of movement, a special vibration, in order to give a composition that is apparently calm and static a sense of rhythm.

Using thicker gray paint and a little carmine toned down with ochre, continue modeling the relief of the hills so that, in the areas where the paper is crumpled or wrinkled, the paint only sticks to the salient parts, creating a curious effect.

4

5

6

Fig. 3. Paint the sky and the outline of the hills trying for a sfumato effect, in order to obtain a speckled and broken color, with pink spots that are applied on top of the previous blue ones.

Fig. 4. At this point, the applications of acrylic paint give the work a sense of depth and connect the different planes of the composition.

Fig. 5. As you can see, the vegetation is painted in an intense shade of green, while the sky has a clear sfumato effect.

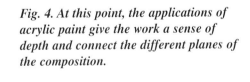

Fig. 6. The branches of the trees are depicted by means of rough strokes and nervous sgraffito.

7

Take a small brush and start giving volume to the white building located near the bank of the river and the pantheon that can be seen on top of the hill. At first work with merely two shades: white and ochre for the illuminated parts of the house and the pantheon respectively and a violet-gray for the darker facades (fig. 7).

The detail in figure 8 shows the variety of color and textural effects that can be obtained by gluing wrinkled tissue paper onto the surface of the support. Superimposing color washes onto the wrinkles in the paper brings about fantastic organic

8

forms that enrich the textural variety of the work, creating effects that are related to the aridity of the landscape.

Now it's time to add the finishing touches, adding some final details. In order to do this, you will have to use a small flat brush and with a bit thicker paint detail the architectural characteristics of the pantheon. Also paint the openings in the building on the left, near the shore, and define the sail boat on the right (fig. 9).

What makes a collage really good is not the quality of the materials but the way in which they have been used and wor-

Fig. 7. Now is the moment to sketch the buildings using scarcely two shades, these corresponding to light and shadow.

Fig. 8. By simply passing a brush with undiluted paint over the wrinkles and folds in the paper, more details and textures can be added to the hillsides.

Fig. 9. Use a smaller brush for the small details on the buildings and the boat on the right.

TIPS

—Acrylic paint is highly adhesive and this property makes it especially suitable to be used together with collage techniques.

—It is also possible to combine collage with a paste that makes it possible to create textures with thick impastos, onto which effects can be created in relief.

—One very important point that should be kept in mind when using paper as the main material is whether you are going to cut or tear it, since the contrast between the edge of cut and torn paper can be very effective (torn paper is usually more expressive and suggestive).

ked on with a certain base. A material as simple as crumpled tissue paper can produce a tremendously gratifying experience for the artist.

Your work may not have the textural effects that we indicate here. This could be because you have watered it down too much, or because you have applied too many or too thick layers of impasto. If the former is the case, the cause is that you have worked with paint that has been excessively thinned down in water. Dry brush strokes provide better results than glazes when applied on a textured surface like the one in this work, for the paint is deposited in the folds and wrinkles that the paper forms. The biggest difficulty you

may have encountered is the painting of the reflections on the water. It's a question of interpretation. However, here are some tips: do not try to reproduce the shape of the reflected body, for it should appear blurred, like a hazy spot and, if necessary, a bit deformed by the rippled surface on which it is reflected. The reflected colors should be a bit dimmer than the original ones. The direction of the strokes should also be kept in mind. They should integrate with each other in a harmonious fashion, without too much detail and without trying to paint a specific shape, simply as a set of spots that form an abstract composition (fig. 10).

Fig. 10. The art of collage is extremely flexible and can be oriented in many different directions. Therefore, it would be a good idea for you to continue experimenting and composing works like this one.

Painting a Sunset with Impasto

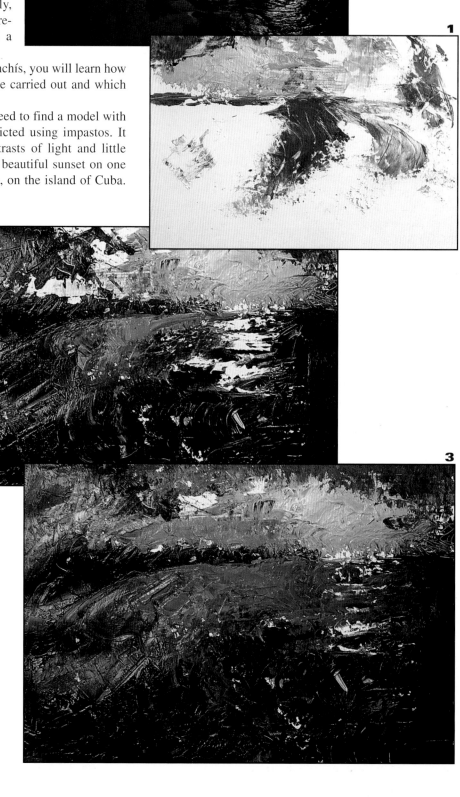

One of the most attractive aspects of painting is the possibility of giving volume to the surface of a work. This characteristic was not sufficiently exploited by the old masters, who tried to obtain a smooth uniform finish by combining glazes and scraped on paint, saving impasto for touches of light. But with the arrival of acrylic and mediums capable of giving paint more volume, a new field of possibilities has been opened. Currently, impasto is used quite assiduously to create works with vigorous colors and a strong expressionist effect.

Once again, with the help of Óscar Sanchís, you will learn how a work of these characteristics is to be carried out and which problems this may entail.

Before you begin painting, you will need to find a model with characteristics suitable for being depicted using impastos. It must be textured, contain sharp contrasts of light and little detail. We have found all of this in a beautiful sunset on one of the many beaches of Guardalavaca, on the island of Cuba. (fig. 0)

The artist has not made a preliminary drawing, but has started to paint right away using the palette knife to lay on the paint as it comes out of the tube, because he wanted the painting to develop out of its own momentum (fig. 1). After a few minutes of work, you will quickly see that it is the vertical chromatic emphasis brought about by the sun and its reflections on the water

Fig. 0. The model is a beautiful sunset on the beaches of Guardalavaca (Cuba).

Fig. 1. Here are the first patches of color. The surface of the paper has been worked on with scarcely three or four shades which are mixed directly on the support.

Fig. 2. Once the main outline has been made, the artist can proceed to identify the shapes.

Fig. 3. Make your impastos more dynamic by scraping the palette knife over the surface of the paper to give more vitality to your compositions.

4

Fig. 4. In some areas the fingers have been used to model the thick edges of the paint and achieve subtle tonal gradations.

which should be the prevailing aspect of the composition. Use the following colors for the first stages of the process: flesh color, ultramarine blue, cadmium red, cadmium yellow and ochre. Now is the moment to add thickening medium to the color mixtures. When mixing paint with relief paste, this increases the volume without changing the color and it can be applied directly onto the support (fig. 2).

The large masses of color, as you can see, have been painted very rapidly so that the artist can go back over some specific aspects without becoming too obsessed with the details or interfering with the basic design. Some of the shapes and local colors of the photograph on the previous page can begin to be discerned. Try to get to the same stage, by copying the process followed by the artist (fig. 3). Add a bigger and bigger proportion of modeling paste, as your work progresses.

Little by little, the violet hues become more prevalent in the sky (which is covered in a shade of violet toned down with white), on the coastline and the sea (here the violet hues have a certain indigo tendency) and in the lower area where the reflections are found (in these there is a larger proportion of cadmium red). The water of the bay, on the other hand, has been obtained by scraping on successive layers of ultramarine blue, cobalt blue and gray with a round-tipped palette knife. The paint can be manipulated in different ways. It is even possible to apply or remove it with the fingers. In figure 4 you can see how the artist uses his hand as a work instrument in order to finish off some details. Highly textured landscapes with expressive and extraordinarily subtle colors can be created in this way. At this stage, the strokes of the impasto, which imitate those of the landscape, stick out for their precision and the marks of the palette knife and the fingers emulate the marks of the terrain (fig. 5). Notice how, on the one hand, the sparkling of the light on the surface of the water acquires more volume and relief than any other part of the painting.

The artist continues to work with the paints. Here he is using a rounded palette knife to scrape on some layers of color before painting the outline of

the tree on the left. You should do the same. You need to work the impasto with your wrist, molding and guiding the paint so that the texture of the work forms the shapes of the landscape. As you can see, this technique owes a great deal to the art of sculpture (fig. 6).

Now work on the darker areas of the painting, which need to be given a little more life and some more

Fig. 5. A few minutes later, it becomes obvious that the powerful reflections of the sun on the surface of the water will become the focal point of this composition.

5

6

Fig. 6. The movement of the water of the sea and the rocking of the branches of the trees are depicted using the palette knife to scrape on the paint.

light. To this effect, apply light colors inside the darker ones, especially on the waves of the sea that break against the shore. Use a small triangular palette knife for this task. The effect of the sea foam and the touches of light on the waves have been done by scraping the palette knife against the still moist paint in order to get a bit of white (fig. 8).

7

Using the same palette knife and a violet-like color tending towards black, draw the branches of the tree on the right. Saturate the rest of the surface of the water with small black spots, in such a way that they mix with the other colors. Now look at the contrast between the different textures of the surface of the sea, with thick curls of paint in some places and the effects of graffito on the branches of the tree on the left. Impasto does not consist merely in accumulating paint, it also involves distributing and guiding it as if we were working with low relief (fig. 7). Add some more touches of light gray in the area where the waves break against the sand, and darken the central area even more, so that the sparkling reflection of the sun on the turbulent surface of the sea appears more luminous by contrast. Some of the areas of the painting are now already finished. The large quantity of paint that has been accumulated produces a disconcerting effect, giving a basically flat surface a three dimensional quality. Seen from a certain distance, the intense chromatic sparkling creates a radiant and vivacious seascape and an optic mixture of colors that surprises the spectator with its chromatic spectacularity.

This work painted by Óscar Sanchís shows how the palette knife and the impasto technique should be used as an expressive medium. Looking at the finished work, you can see how the

TIPS

—It is advisable to mix colors before adding modeling paste.

—When the paint has dried, the colors stick out less than when it was moist. This is because the paste is white, but when it dries it becomes transparent.

—Hold the palette knife at different angles, vary the amount of pressure exerted on the blade and use different parts of it to obtain different types of lines and effects.

8

9

Fig. 7. Try to include as many textures as possible in your painting, but do it following a selective criterion so that they will enhance the beauty of the painting as a whole.

Fig. 8. One of the characteristics of this painting is precisely the variety of textures that are produced with the palette knife.

Fig. 9. As you can see, the definition of the light and dark areas contributes to the attractiveness of the painting just as much as the textures.

Fig. 10. After the intense work with mixtures and impastos, here is the finished work. The scratching done with the palette knife and the relief of the pictorial layer contribute even more to the expressiveness of this work.

physical presence of the thick paint brings it forward in space, bringing it closer (speaking in terms of perspective) to the spectator, while the relief and the chromatic combinations make the painting more tangible and more expressionistic. Comparing the painting to the natural model shows that, despite the free treatment it was given, the painting is very true to the theme. Try to avoid being one of those painters who works slowly and hesitantly. This could cause you problems, not only because of the drying time but also in terms of the concept of the work. Do not be afraid to work rapidly

on the support. Establish the main traits of the composition and the relationships between colors immediately. Painting with impasto should be bold and spontaneous, not slow and stiff. The sensation of movement transmitted by the painting depends on the energy and impact of the strokes. One thick stroke on its own tends to transmit stasis but a series of free and fluid impastos will give life to the movement of the trees or the backward and forward motion of the waves. Do not try to produce a photographic copy. This is impossible when working with impasto since impasto does not allow

detail. Let your hand follow the contours of the landscape instinctively, so that the movements of the palette knife transmit the effect of fluidity of the water, the direction of the branches and the movement of the waves. Obviously, you will not obtain a "finished" image, but you will learn a lot about how landscapes using impasto work. Finally, I would advise you not to be misled. Although paintings with a lot of impasto give the impression of more freedom and improvisation, the truth is that they require a careful planning.

View of a Lake with the Scraping Technique

Now practice using the scraping technique. As has already been explained before, scraping consists in rubbing paint onto the surface of the work with a palette knife or plastic card, so that it is extended forming a smooth layer. The thickness of the layer depends on how much pressure is exerted. In this way, semi-transparent layers can be obtained as well as textured opaque impastos.

Grau Carod will carry out this step-by-step exercise and I would ask you to follow its development closely. The exercise that we propose is to paint a beautiful illustration of the Austrian lake known as the Attersee, a surface that reflects the light of the sky with pale blue or silver sparkles. The forms of the landscape and the movement of the water are rendered not only through the scraping movements, but also through the motifs that will be taken into consideration (fig. 0).

The support for this work will be a piece of Bristol board fixed with masking tape onto a panel that is resting on a table. When working in the scraping technique never use coarse-grained paper or other types of paper with an excessively wrinkled or engraved surface.

Mix the colors on the palette with a palette knife. When the paint has a semi-thick consistency move the paint over the

surface with a plastic card to form a thin layer. It is not necessary to draw anything before you begin. A preliminary painting done in relatively flat colors serves as a draft or base, situating the forms that make up the model (fig. 1).

After a few minutes, the base of the composition will be fixed. The surface of the lake appears cerulean blue, the middle ground has been done in ochre and terre-verte, the mountain on the right with cadmium green and emerald green and the one on the left with violet (cerulean blue and carmine, fig. 2). The violet color of the mountain can be explained by the law of contrast and atmosphere according to which bodies tend to present a gray or violet hue as they get further away from the spectator. In this first appraisal the colors have not been applied in a flat way but present an effect of broken color which makes it possible for the white of the paper to filter through.

Fig. 0. The model is a panoramic view of the waters of lake Attersee, near Salzburg, in Austria.
Fig. 1. When opaque techniques and less delicate treatments are used, it is not necessary to make a preliminary sketch. You can tackle the theme directly with paints.
Fig. 2. These are the basic colors: cerulean blue for the water and the sky, emerald green and violet for the mountains in the distance.

Although the consistency of the paint is that of paint as it comes out of the tube, the layer of paint is spread so thin that the color underneath shows through, creating an effect very similar to that of velatura. Continue applying new colors, one layer after another. Dip the card in a more intense shade of blue and work both on the middle ground and on the foreground, that is, on the surface of the water. Press down moving the card from top to bottom until you have achieved a veil of color simulating the reflections (fig. 3). Notice how the green of the vegetation is repeated as a reflection on the surface of the lake. Continue livening up the surface of the lake with new impastos of color, and I use the term impasto because each time you go through this process you should press down less on the palette knife and apply the paint more thickly. If you compare the resolution of the middle ground with that of the sky or the mountains in the distance, you will notice how the thin glazes of color contrast with the light impastos and bold contours (fig. 4).

Until now the artist has worked with a card that was about 3 1/2 inches wide. As the work progresses, smaller and smaller cards will be needed which will allow us to make the forms more explicit, enriching the planes by scraping the surface with somewhat more precision. Most of the scraping movements will be done from top to bottom so the lines will have a horizontal tendency. We will correct this tendency by changing the position of the panel in order to direct and control the application of the scraping, that is, we will turn the panel in order to adjust the stroke to the shapes found in nature (fig. 5).

Fig. 3. Here you have an example of the superimposition of color that can be obtained with a plastic card. In a way they have a certain likeliness with small impastos.

Fig. 4. Whatever the consistency of the paint may be, try to get the scraping movement to mirror the movement of the surface of the lake from the very beginning, in order to keep the painting from having a static appearance.

Fig. 5. The application of paint gives rise to a texture, obtained through a series of small scraping movements or veiled impastos that give the surface of the painting a vibrant and effectist appearance.

With a little ochre, yellow and cadmium red, suggest the rocky formations of the mountain on the left and also add more volume to the vegetation on this mountain, once again with ochre, terre-verte and chrome oxide green. Move down the surface of the painting. Add scraped on layers of titan white in the central area of the lake, in order to define the direct reflections of the sun. Finally work, once again with the wide card, on the foreground. Superimpose new impastos in more intense cerulean blue mixed with a dash of white. The foreground is always important in a landscape, be it natural or urban, since it has to lead the specta-tor's gaze towards the interior of the work and awaken an inte-rest for the colors, forms or textures (fig. 6).

The rock formations and the vegetation on the opposite shore of the lake have been defined by using thicker layers. In this way, the hill in the background already has, as you can see in figure 7, an extraordinary chromatic vividness. The scraping technique provides a mixture, or better yet blending, of colors reminiscent of the sfumato technique, although the resolution is in this case coarser and less pure.

At this stage, it is time to apply some final effects: intensify the shadow that the raft projects, darken the vegetation on the mountains even more, go over the reflections near the opposite shore and add some precise linear effects. In order to achieve them, it is necessary to move the plastic card longitudinally over the picto-rial surface (fig. 8).

Fig. 6. The artist applies one scraped on layer of paint on top of another, using the paint as if he were working with impasto.

Fig. 7. In this detail, you can see how the mountains on the oppo-site shore of the lake are built up.

Fig. 8. The directional scraping movements create an immense sense of movement.

8

TIPS

—When you paint the water, you will see that there is a logic to its movements, which are repeated. The waves of the sea curl, the waves of a stream flow around a central point and the surface of a lake always presents the same type of ripples.

—You can also work with a scrap-er. However, being more rigid, the applications it produces are thicker and more irregular.

—If you want to work with the scraping technique on wet, you can use a retardant, which will make it possible to manipulate the paint for a much longer period of time.

The finished work shows a rich variety of effects which are impossible to obtain with any other instrument of the pictorial tradition. The practice of scraping may seem a bit archaic since it does not allow the artist to produce lots of filigrees, that is, depict details, but, despite these hindrances, the final result obtained with the technique is surprising and effectist and has a great textural richness. Although there are no well-defined elements and the landscape has not been given the precision that is usually associated with drawings and paintings, the work transmits the strength and character of the place (fig. 9). One common mistake is to work the paint too much, thereby losing the sensation of fluidity that it should render. When painting a work with such textural richness, you must consider leaving some rest areas, that is, areas that are not as overloaded, with less pictorial information, so that the spectator can find a place to rest his eyes when looking at the work. Otherwise the painting will seem too saturated with elements. This function is fulfilled perfectly by the sky. If you look at it closely you will see that it is composed of subdued layers of scraped on paint, done in just one color in the manner of tonal gradations. Another common mistake is to lay on too much paint. We mustn't forget that we are scraping or moving the paint over the surface of the painting and not laying on paint (although in some areas of the painting this could be the case). To scrape on paint it is necessary to press down with the palette knife or plastic card so that the edge scratches the surface depositing the paint in the form of a thin semitransparent film.

Fig. 9. In the finished painting we can see an animated combination of shapes and textures. The scraping technique gives the image a wonderful pictorial quality.

Painting with Acrylics and Marble Powder

In the following step-by-step exercise, with the help of the artist Carlant, we will explain how to obtain interesting textures by mixing acrylic paint with marble powder. If you want to paint with marble powder you can chose one of two methods: the first is to apply a putty made of marble powder and latex to model and give volume to the pictorial surface before applying paint. A second possibility would be to add volume while you're working, by adding small quantities of marble powder to the paint mixtures thereby giving the paint the rough aspect that characterizes this technique. The artist has chosen the second of these options and is going to work painting directly with the palette knife instead of applying successive layers of paint with a brush in the traditional manner.

Carlant has decided to take as the model for his seascape, this corner of the Costa Brava, which is very suitable for achieving interesting textural effects thanks to the mobility of the surface of the water and the relief of the rocks (fig. 0).

Before you begin prepare the following colors on your palette: burnt sienna, ultramarine blue, ochre, permanent violet, cadmium red and raw umber. This limited palette will be enough to obtain all the shades needed for this painting.

The first step consists in drawing the model in pencil without paying too much attention to detail, since due to the fact that we will be working with opaque colors, the drawing will be covered by the pictorial matter (fig. 1). The preliminary sketch can be found in outline-guide number 5. I invite you to practice this exercise following the indications below.

First paint the background or areas of flat color. For the cape in the distance and the sea water, use a gray-violet base, the luminosity of which will be fundamental in creating the illusion of the light and the sun in this painting as will be seen further on. Paint using the base of the flat palette knife, extending the paint in a thick layer. In this way you will create a uniformly colored surface that will reflect the maximum amount of light possible (fig. 2A).

0

1

2A

2B

Fig. 0. We are going to paint a sunny corner of the Costa Brava. Clearly contrasting areas of light and shade can be seen on the rock formations.

Fig. 1. The draft provides the opportunity to appreciate how the main elements of the composition work, and to make sure that the painting is correctly balanced.

Fig. 2A. The drying properties of acrylics make it possible for the artist to build the background up rapidly, and apply new impastos after just a few minutes.

Fig. 2B. As you can see, the palette used by the artist is composed of burnt sienna, ultramarine blue, ochre, permanent violet, cadmium red and raw umber. In the center, which is white, you can see the marble powder.

3

The sky has been painted with even color. The sea, on the contrary, displays a tonal gradation that goes from the lighter areas at the top to the more intense shades of blue as you get closer to the foreground. Applying the paint with a palette knife may be slower and more complicated than using a brush, so you need to be patient and work on it until you have acquired the sufficient practice (fig. 3).

From here on, work on the painting using thick, opaque strokes. In order to represent the perpetual movement of the surface of the water and the waves, apply touches of different juxtaposed colors onto the water (cobalt blue, pinks, violet-like colors, greenish-yellows etc.). One color can be applied on top of another to obtain a greater relief or to enrich its tonality. To carry out this task, you should use a small palette knife (fig. 4).

To create small spots of color, hold the handle and press the metallic part down with your forefinger. This will make it easier to work in the smaller and more delicate areas. Also apply thick touches of paint onto the rocks. The best way to render the sea foam is by allowing the white of the support to show through on the edges of the rocky beach (fig. 5). The cape or headland that appears in the distance has been painted in grayish colors to emphasize the distance effect.

The artist continues moving down the painting, using the alla prima technique, that is, finishing off the areas of the painting as he covers them without going back over them. You should do the same. In order to capture the brightness and the quality of the light of the landscape use light colors with a pastel tendency for the sea and somewhat more intense colors on the rocks. In accordance with the laws of atmosphere in landscape, the color of the sea is lighter and has less contrast in the background than in the foreground. This effect also brings out the sunlight on the surface of the water (fig. 6).When painting the

4

5

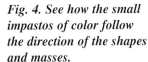

Fig. 3. Until now, the artist has worked applying solid-colored layers of paint onto large areas.

Fig. 4. See how the small impastos of color follow the direction of the shapes and masses.

Fig. 5. The treatment of the surface of the water gives the painting as a whole an agitated and mobile appearance.

6

Fig. 6. With an energetic movement of the corner of the sheet of paper, you can achieve a rough and speckled texture just like the artist.

rocks, you should keep in mind that the water, in contact with the rocks, creates a dark band at their base. In addition, to represent the relief of the rock formations it will be necessary to contrast the tones (fig. 7), highlighting the unevenness and cracks on their surface, through dramatic light and shade effects, without forgetting the use of chiaroscuro, the contrast between the lighter and darker areas. Finally cover the stony cove in the foreground with flat thick layers of violet-gray paint (fig. 8).

The painting is almost finished now and creates an illusion of reflected light through numerous brushstrokes and touches of juxtaposed colors. The colors are optically mixed when they are observed from a certain distance, and in this way they appear more intense. It is now time to add some finishing touches, resolving some details. Use the tip of your palette knife energetically to obtain graffito effects on the pictorial surface layer. Observe how once the surface has dried, it is very easy to paint on it with a brush. Take a small one and add detail to the group of grasses that appear at the bottom of the image. A more contrasting foreground helps to project the space of the work towards the back, producing more of an effect of distance and depth (fig. 9).

Seen from a certain distance, the intense chromatic sparkling of Carlant's landscape creates a radiant and

Fig. 7. To give the rocks more volume, you must work on the different planes separately and highlight the contrast between light and shade as much as possible.

Fig. 8. At this stage, the impastos have an extraordinary chromatic variety, even though only a limited range of colors has been used.

Fig. 9. Small sgraffito are carried out by scratching the pictorial surface with the tip of a palette knife while it's still moist.

TIPS

—Be generous with the marble powder and apply enough of it so as to fill in the texture.

—It is better to use hog bristle brushes for this technique since they are the most resistant. Marble powder easily erodes the tips of brushes.

—If you want to practice the sgraffito technique or modify the pictorial surface you will have to work quickly, since once the paste with marble powder has dried, it will not be possible to modify the layer of paint.

dynamic seascape, a flickering painting that depicts the luminous effects that are found on the surface of the water and in the shadows and natural semitones of the rock formations. The artist has worked on this painting one area at a time. This might have caused you some problems. Since the artist had a very clear idea of what the finished work would look like as he applied each thick layer of paint, he could predict with reasonable certainty how each brushstroke would affect the entire painting. For this reason I would advise you to close your eyes and try to imagine what the work you are about to paint will look like before you begin. Thinking about the painting before doing the actual painting is a very good exercise. As you can see, the painting has a harmonious range of

blues and browns. Therefore, you should not make the mistake of using too many colors, for you can obtain many shades and varieties by mixing a limited range of colors. You will see how the colors tend to whiten when they are mixed with marble powder. Do not worry. Instead of fighting against this effect, try to make the most of it. Accept the fact that you are working with slightly pastel shades. If you have tried to add too much detail to an area of the painting, you will have noticed how this is a difficult task since marble powder is a very coarse material and not very suitable for this type of work since it does not allow a detailed rendering with lots of filigrees.

Fig. 10. Not a single fragment of this painting is flat. All the tones and colors have been built up through an intricate network of small strokes reminiscent of the impressionists.

Female Portrait

We are going to paint the portrait of a young girl with acrylic paint. We will once again be joined by the artist Josep Antoni Domingo, who will paint this portrait using soft, thin glazes, carefully superimposed to make out the forms of the face and the qualities of the skin of the model.

Before starting to paint, the artist should think about how to place the model, both in terms of the illumination and of the general structure of the forms. This is the result. The face of a young girl, in a three quarter profile, is seen in diffused light, without too many contrasts that highlight the factions, although this will favor the toning down of colors and shapes (fig. 0).

To paint this figure, start by drawing the contours of the head with a pencil. Then do a first rendering of the facial features, so that the sketch resembles the person it is meant to portray (fig. 1). You can see an outline of this portrait in outline-guide number 6.

Start painting the hair with flat and very diluted paint (remember that you will have the chance to add more details later on). Work on the background, applying a mixture of chrome oxide green, permanent green and white, making sure that you extend it all the way to the border of the silhouette (fig. 2).

Continue working on the whole figure, dividing the skin tones into areas of light and shadow. At this stage, keep the tones separate. Add touches of light, by painting areas with soft yellowish washes, while applying sienna washes in the darker areas. Paint the tones and colors of the face and figure, making the whole painting come into harmony with the background (fig. 3). Now continue with an appraisal of the rest of the skin areas, like the shoulder and the hand. The facial factions have become more rounded as a result of the artist's gradual modeling of the skin tones, which he has done by using subtle gradations to blend the different areas of color on the face. You should do the same. Then paint the mouth, without using too intense or pure a shade of pink. The lips should be related to the rest of the facial tones and be integrated into the whole of the composition.

Fig. 0. The model the artist has chosen for this exercise is a portrait of a young girl in a three quarter profile.

Fig. 1. The constant observation of the face of the model, accompanied by hours of study and practice, will make it possible for you to capture the predominant features in a preliminary sketch.

Fig. 2. Paint the hair and apply the background color carefully, until you have finished outlining the left side of the figure.

Fig. 3. Start with the skin tones. Do not mix the colors on the surface but blend the edges of the different colored areas carefully.

4

With a little burnt umber and a small brush, place the eyes, at first painting only the line of the eyelids, the eyelashes and a circle for the pupils. This painting is now at an intermediate stage of definition. Although they will still be modified somewhat, the colors and the tones already form a satisfactory base for the building up of details (fig. 4).

Once the basic tones of the skin have been applied, the moment to think about

5

Fig. 4. Think of the face as a series of planes and simple forms and do not try for a photographic reproduction of the model.

Fig. 5. After the first washes, the most important thing to do is check the location of the features over and over again.

Fig. 6. Once he has gotten the painting to resemble the model and has gotten the qualities of the skin right, the artist has to decide what degree of detail and definition his work should have.

6

details has come. This means paying close attention to each of the facial elements (eyes, nose, mouth) and trying to detail them, or adjust their shapes to that of the model. Each area is painted with glazes, so that the image appears little by little as the colors and the features are intensified. Try to get the right tone for the skin using titan white, ochre, Venetian red, cadmium red, raw umber, permanent green and cobalt yellow. Highlight the shadows around the eyelids and do the same with the chin and the nose. Work on the hair using successive washes of burnt sienna and a little ultramarine blue. Continue elaborating these features with even more intense strokes wherever you want to give a sensation of depth (behind the ear, the hairline, on the neck etc.) and leave the areas that have touches of light lighter (fig. 5).

With a small brush paint the teeth. The white should be the same color as the paper. Now work on the shadows on the face and hands, being careful to maintain a tonal balance between the face and the rest of the head (fig. 6).

Mark the darker areas of the cheek and the shadows on the neck adding a touch of permanent green to the skin color.

Try to paint with exactitude but using more fluid strokes for the areas around the hair, in order to maintain the character and shape of loose hair. Use a pure magenta to paint the strap of the shirt (fig. 7).

As you can see, the artist has used a simple chromatic range: the creamy warm colors of the skin contrast with the green of the background and the magenta of the shirt strap. Add some finishing touches to the skin tones, reiterating the background color in the skin areas. Be careful not to flatten the face and maintain the tonal contrast between the touches of light and shadow (fig. 8).

The finished painting reflects the subtle use of washes and shows the good results obtained with acrylic paint. The inexperienced artist may feel the temptation to draw with the brush instead of painting. Do not make the mistake of painting what you think should be there instead of what is really there. Study the face of the model meticulously and then go about coloring it. If you find this difficult, reduce the motif to simple planes and treat the facial features as if they were abstract objects.

If you work with thin layers of color instead of thick ones, the danger of covering the pictorial surface too quickly will be reduced, since thin layers can be modified and corrected more easily than thick ones. Be careful with the eyes, which are a trap for inexperienced painters. The natural tendency is to make them too big, due to the great importance they have on the face.

TIPS

—Your palette should contain a range of skin tones going from light ones to very dark ones.

—The color of skin is not pink, as some artists believe. Skin tones vary greatly and can include shades of blue, violet, pink, salmon, ochre, brown, yellow... It all depends on the illumination as well as the race and age of the person who is being painted.

—Take frequent breaks while painting in order to move away from your work to judge how the painting is going, especially in regards to the characterization of the model.

Fig. 7. Fairly diluted paint has been used. The colors of the skin have been built up with a series of superimposed transparent color glazes.

Fig. 8. This detail clearly shows the method in which the artist works by superimposing glazes.

On the other hand, it is common that when you paint a portrait for the first time, the eyes are too elaborate and have too fixed a gaze, giving them as unnatural feel. The key to doing a good portrait is to make as exact a preliminary sketch as possible. If the features are not correctly placed from the beginning, there is little possibility of getting them right later. The artist will find him or herself, again and again, applying layer after layer of paint in order to correct the original painting.

Fig. 9. With a rather limited range of colors and based on a structure of modeled tonal surfaces, this beautiful image has been achieved, a figure portrayed in a rather realistic fashion.

Glossary

A

Alla Prima. A technique of direct painting which can be summarized as painting in only one session, quickly and without going back over the painting.

B

Blending. A procedure which consists in blending or smoothing the outlines or areas of contact between two colors so that they form a light gradation.

C

Chromatic harmonization. The connection that is established between the different colors within a painting.

Base. A prepared surface on which painting is done.

Chiaroscuro. Rembrandt is the great master of chiaroscuro. In his work the forms and colors of areas which are covered in the most intense shadows are still visible. In his books on the teaching of drawing and painting, JM Parramón has always defined this as "the art of painting light in shade".

Color (local). A body's own color, when this is not altered by shadows and reflections.

Color (tonal). The color produced by the shadow of bodies.

Composition. This describes the disposition of different elements which make up a work in the most harmonious and balanced way possible. Composing involves choosing the best conditions, in terms of harmony and balance, for a drawing or painting.

Contrast. Opposition between two different chromatic sensations.

Covering power. The power of a color with respect to its capacity to predominate over other colors in a mixture or glaze.

Cutter. A sharp knife for cutting paper, consisting of a blade in a plastic sleeve.

D

Direct painting. A painting technique called *alla prima* in Italian, *au premier coup* in French and *a la primera* in Spanish (see *alla prima*).

Draft. This is the name given to the preliminary stage of the drawing or painting process, from which a later work can then be derived. The draft allows many studies to be carried out before the artist develops his idea and decides how he is going to develop and work with it.

G

Gradation. Gradual decrease in tonal value, that is, the process of transition between an intense tone and a soft one so that there is no sudden change.

I

Impasto. A technique which consists in applying thick layers of paint with the aim of creating a textured surface.

Imprint. In sculpture, drawing and painting these words designate the way in which a work of art is carried out. For example, it may be done nervously, brusquely, delicately, slowly, quickly... In short, the imprint specifically defines the artist's personal style.

Induction of complements. This concerns the phenomenon derived from simultaneous contrasts where the following norm proven: "When modifying a certain color it will be sufficient to merely change the background which surrounds it."

M

Medium. This is the liquid which pigments are suspended in, for example, linseed oil used in oil paintings or acrylic resin used in acrylic paintings.

Modeling. Despite being associated with sculpture, this term can also be applied to drawing and painting where it refers to shading done by applying different tones in order to create the illusion of three dimensional space.

O

Opacity. The capacity of a wash to cover a previous layer of paint. Opacity varies from one pigment to another.

P

Palette, acrylic. Surface with hollows generally made of plastic, on which colors are mixed.

Palette knife. A small spatula which is used to mix colors, although it can also be used to spread paint onto the surface of the painting.

Priming. The first layer of pigment that the surface of the support is covered with in order to prepare it for the application of other colors.

R

Retardant. Substance which is added to acrylic paint in order to lengthen its drying time.

S

Saturation. Chromatic intensity, in other words, the intensity of color that a surface can reflect.

Sfumato. The subtle and minute gradation of tone and color used to blur or veil the contours of a form in painting.

Sgraffito. A technique of ornamentation in which a surface layer of paint is incised to reveal a ground of contrasting color.

Sketch. A preliminary drawing which tries to express the basic structure of bodies through simple geometric forms (cubes, rectangles, prisms...) called boxes, by analogy.

Stencil. A cut-out shape that is placed on a surface in order to create clean set-off images.

Surface. The material used for painting or drawing on, such as a wooden board, a canvas or a sheet of paper.

T

Techniques, mixed. This term refers to the use of different pictorial procedures in the same painting or for working on a combination of surfaces.

Texture. Tactile and visual quality presented by the surface of a drawing or painting. This can be smooth, granular, rough, cracked, etc. In all cases it refers to both visible and tactile qualities.

Tone. This term has a musical origin, but when applied to painting it refers to the vigor and relief of all the different parts of the work with respect to color and light.

Transparency. The way of applying paint in such a way that the light or color from a previous layer is allowed to filter through.

V

Value. Degree of light or darkness that a color can have.

Velatura. A layer of transparent color (glaze) superimposed on another color which intensifies or modifies it.

Volume. The three dimensional effect of a model in the two-dimensional space of a painting.

W

Washing. A style of drawing-painting which has been used since the Renaissance. It consists in a painting done in just one color, generally sepia, diluted in water. It can also be done in aniline, watercolors or Chinese ink.

Wet, painting on. A technique which consists in painting on an area or layer which has recently been moistened with water or which has been painted on and is still wet. The artist controls the level of moisture on the paper according to the effect he or she wants to create.

Acknowledgements

The author of this book would like to thank the following people and companies for their collaboration in the publication of this volume in the series *Techniques & Exercises*.

To Gabriel Martín Roig for his collaboration with the texts and in the general coordination of this book. To Antonio Oromí for his photographic work. To Vicennç Piera, of the company Piera, for his advice and orientation regarding materials and tools used for drawing and painting. To Manel Úbeda, of the company Novasis, for his help in the editing and production of the photocompositions and photomechanics. To Olga Bernad and Ani Amor for having lent us some of the photographs that have been used as models for painting. And a very special thanks to the artists: Carlant, Bibiana Crespo, Josep Antoni Domingo, Grau Carod, Ester Llaudet, Miguel Olivares, Óscar Sanchís and Teresa Trol.